AF683688

IMF-Supported Programs

Recent Staff Research

Edited by Ashoka Mody and Alessandro Rebucci

effectiveness

design

implementation

International Monetary Fund

© 2006 International Monetary Fund

Production: IMF Multimedia Services Division
Interior Design: Alicia Etchebarne-Bourdin
Cover Design: Martine Rossignol-Winner

Cataloging-in-Publication Data

[IMF-supported programs: recent staff research/edited by Ashoka Mody and Alessandro Rebucci]—Washington, D.C.: International Monetary Fund, 2006]

p. cm.

Includes bibliographical references
ISBN 1-58906-361-9

1. International Monetary Fund—Research. I. Mody, Ashoka. II. Rebucci, Alessandro. III. International Monetary Fund.
HG3881.5.I58I5 2006

The following symbols have been used throughout this paper:

. . . to indicate that data are not available;

— to indicate that the figure is zero or less than half the final digit shown, or that the item does not exist;

– between years or months (e.g., 1997–98 or January–June) to indicate the years or months covered, including the beginning and ending years or months;

/ between years (e.g., 1997/98) to indicate a fiscal (financial) year.

"n.a." means not applicable.

"Billion" means a thousand million.

Minor discrepancies between constituent figures and totals are due to rounding.

The views expressed in this publication are those of the authors and do not necessarily represent the views of the International Monetary Fund. The term "country," as used in this publication, does not in all cases refer to a territorial entity that is a state as understood by international law and practice; the term also covers some territorial entities that are not states, but for which statistical data are maintained and provided internationally on a separate and independent basis.

Price: US$37.50

Please send orders to:
International Monetary Fund, Publication Services
700 19th Street, N.W., Washington, DC 20431, U.S.A.
Tel.: (202) 623-7430 Telefax: (202) 623-7201
E-mail: publications@imf.org
Internet: http://www.imf.org

recycled paper

Contents

Foreword

A long tradition of research has sought to evaluate the effectiveness of IMF-supported programs. The IMF itself has devoted much institutional energy to assessing its performance, both to learn from the past and to deal with new challenges. In doing so, the staff of the IMF has contributed significantly to analyzing the IMF's ability to achieve its stated goals of fostering external viability and growth. IMF staff members have had the advantage of access to program details often not as easily available to external researchers. Staff contributions have also included methodological advances. Importantly, in conducting this research, we have not shied away from unpleasant conclusions.

This volume includes recent research that moves decisively beyond the typical characterization of programs. Though researchers have sometimes made the basic distinctions between the different types of IMF program—Stand-By Arrangements, and arrangements under the Extended Fund Facility and the Poverty Reduction and Growth Facility (as well as their predecessor facilities)—the nuances of programs are more extensive. In particular, the circumstances under which the program is designed, the limitations in program implementation, and the specific national and international economic conditions when the program is in effect all influence the ultimate outcome. The key achievement of the research reported here is to deal with this complexity while also providing simple insights. Of course, all research is work in progress, and these insights need to be verified by further work, but they do offer useful working hypotheses for our operations.

Looking ahead, I see two obvious areas for further work. First, as the essays in this volume demonstrate, the IMF's advice and financing are conditioned by a variety of political economy considerations. International political economy has a bearing on program selection, conditionality, and implementation. Similarly, domestic political economy shapes attitudes toward the IMF and, hence, the ability of the authorities to enter into constructive IMF-supported programs. A richer political economy analysis could make for more effective engagement.

Second, the IMF's governance structure also has implications for program design and implementation, and, hence, for the IMF's economic effectiveness. Though, once again, the task is a difficult one, careful analysis could provide useful input to the ongoing debates.

Raghuram G. Rajan
Economic Counsellor and Director, Research Department
International Monetary Fund

Contributors[1]

George Anayiotos	Senior Economist, Finance Department
Ruben Atoyan	Economist, Western Hemisphere Department
Emanuele Baldacci	Lead Researcher, Italian Statistical Office (ISTAT)
Reza Baqir	Resident Representative, Philippines
Roberto Benelli	Economist, Western Hemisphere Department
Michael Bordo	Professor of Economics, Rutgers University
James M. Boughton	IMF Historian
Aleš Bulíř	Senior Economist, Policy Development and Review Department
Chuling Chen	Analyst, Modeling and Research Department, (U.S.) Federal Home Loan Mortgage Corporation
Benedict Clements	Advisor, Western Hemisphere Department
Patrick Conway	Professor of Economics, University of North Carolina at Chapel Hill
Carlo Cottarelli	Deputy Director, Policy Development and Review Department
Atish Ghosh	Division Chief, Policy Development and Review Department
Curzio Giannini[2]	Deputy Head, International Relations Department, Banca d'Italia
Sanjeev Gupta	Assistant Director, African Department
Anna Ivanova	Economist, Fiscal Affairs Department
Olivier Jeanne	Deputy Division Chief, Research Department
Mohsin S. Khan	Director, Middle East and Central Asia Department

[1] All contributors are staff members of the International Monetary Fund unless otherwise indicated.
[2] Deceased.

Timothy Lane	Assistant Director, Western Hemisphere Department
Wolfgang Mayer	Professor of Economics, University of Cincinnati
Ashoka Mody	Assistant Director, European Department
Soojin Moon	Candidate Member, American Institute of Certified Public Accountants (AICPA)
Alex Mourmouras	Deputy Division Chief, IMF Institute
Carlos Mulas-Granados	Vice-Chairman, Prime Minister's Economic Bureau (Madrid)
Saleh M. Nsouli	Director, IMF Offices in Europe
Nienke Oomes	Economist, European Department
Rodney Ramcharan	Economist, Research Department
Alessandro Rebucci	Economist, Research Department
Ratna Sahay	Assistant Director, Western Hemisphere Department
Marcelo Selowsky	Assistant Director, Independent Evaluation Office
Sunil Sharma	Director, IMF-Singapore Regional Training Institute
Alun Thomas	Senior Economist, Policy Development and Review Department
Tsidi Tsikata	Deputy Division Chief, African Department
Juan Zalduendo	Senior Economist, Policy Development and Review Department
Jeromin Zettelmeyer	Assistant to the Director, Western Hemisphere Department

Overview

Ashoka Mody and Alessandro Rebucci[1]

IMF lending programs, though varying in objectives and duration, are often associated with a sharp and sustained redirection of the course of economic policy. An IMF-supported program is typically initiated when a country faces the need for external adjustment. The IMF provides financing and the country puts in place a program of policies to redress actual or potential external imbalances; also, where appropriate, economic reforms to raise long-term growth are introduced or accelerated. Continued lending is predicated on progress in implementing the program, which in turn is assessed on the basis of preset conditions (performance criteria) to be met by specified dates in the context of periodic reviews.

Does the policy redirection supported by IMF lending achieve its goals? The effectiveness of program lending in achieving its goals has long been the subject of research. The evaluation is amenable to analyses that assess the variations in economic indicators before and after the start of a program.[2] And although even sophisticated before-and-after analyses have their pitfalls, researchers have continued to exercise their ingenuity to identify, or isolate, the effects of an IMF program.[3]

The IMF's own staff has been active in—and, often, at the forefront of—assessing the effectiveness of program lending. This book describes the recent evolution of staff research on program lending, highlighting both methodological contributions and substantive findings. In the mid- and late 1980s, the overarching question posed was whether an IMF-supported program helped improve macroeconomic performance—as measured by growth, inflation, and current account outcomes—with the latter a proxy for the extent and speed of economic adjustment. (Haque and Khan (1998) summarize this research.) Recent IMF research has focused on more nuanced questions and made more pointed inquiries into the factors contributing to program success.

An advance in the research—and an organizing device for this book as well as a distinguishing feature of many of its chapters—has been to recognize that program effectiveness needs to be linked to the quality of program design and implementation, as well as to the degree of a country's external vulnerability. Analyses of effects before and after the adoption of a program implicitly assume either that the quality of policy design and the implementation of those policies do not vary across programs or that they do not matter. Since they obviously do matter, the links among design, implementation, and effectiveness are increasingly being explored. These links

[1] The authors are grateful to Timothy Lane, Anne Krueger, and Raghuram Rajan for their valuable comments in the preparation of this overview and to Paul Gleason for overseeing the copyediting and production of this publication.

[2] In contrast, the effects of surveillance (the analysis of economic conditions, policies, and prospects in member countries and the global economy) are felt in a diffuse manner, contemporaneous with many other economic developments, over an extended period and are thus not easy to identify. See IMF (2005).

[3] The appropriate techniques have, not surprisingly, remained controversial. A program must be judged against a benchmark, or the outcome that would have occurred if the program had not been put in place. This counterfactual experiment is not observable. Moreover, the benchmark evolves with the changing world economy and the country's economic conditions.

are complex, and, hence, researchers have focused on various elements of a large set of possibilities, guided, in part, by their inherent interest in the links but also constrained by their limited ability to quantify measures of design and implementation and, hence, subject them to statistical analysis. At the same time, interest has persisted in carrying out direct examinations of program effectiveness without focusing on design and/or implementation but with a clearer recognition that country conditions influence both the incentives for policy reform and the confidence of international capital markets that is necessary to reinforce domestic reform efforts.

Thus, the questions motivating recent research are framed as follows:

- How—and how much—does success depend upon the design of the program?
- To the extent that differences in program outcomes reflect differences in the quality of their actual implementation, why does implementation vary and how is it related, in particular, to program "ownership," or the commitment by country authorities to the policy reform package?
- Do differing economic conditions, such as the levels of external debt and reserves, influence the willingness and ability of countries, private markets, and the IMF to coordinate to achieve success?
- If a program brings an improvement in a country's economy, does that reflect the IMF's policy advice, its lending, its monitoring of the country's policies, or its "seal of approval" effect?

Though the questions are posed in these ambitious terms, the answers are necessarily more piecemeal and reflect, among other limitations, the particular ways in which the terms "design," "implementation," and "country conditions" are operationalized. The quality of design, sometimes construed as the composition of the policy advice (e.g., relative emphasis on fiscal or monetary discipline), is often inferred by comparing actual outcomes with those projected at the inception of the program. But the interpretation of these comparisons is not always straightforward. Similarly, assessments of implementation rely on such measures as the adherence of a program to its original conditions or its timetable or to the drawing down of the originally anticipated loan amount. The implicit assumption is that if the periodic reviews were delayed, the program was canceled, or a smaller-than-anticipated amount was borrowed, the program was not fully implemented. This may sometimes be true, but failure to meet conditions on the agreed schedule may also reflect corrections made as new information becomes available; and failing to draw the full amount may also reflect an improved economy with scaled-back requirements for external financing. Moreover, carrying out prescribed actions during the course of the program may be of little use if these actions are discontinued or reversed as soon as the program is over, necessitating the nontrivial task of assessing the sustainability of the policies put in place through the program. Finally, it is not straightforward to parsimoniously define the international and country context within which a program is formulated and implemented. Yet recent theoretical advances and empirical research suggest that such a context is relevant for program success. For example, applying theories proposing that success is most likely to be achieved when a country is in the "intermediate" state of external vulnerability—neither safe from a crisis nor imminently facing one—entails making judgments about, for example, levels of debt and reserves.

The rest of this overview reports on the contributions to this book, discussing them in the context of the broader questions they raise and pointing to the scope for further research. The next section discusses program design. This is followed by a section reviewing research on the determinants and the value of program implementation, also raising the issue of whether and how implementation is influenced by the nature of IMF governance. Next, the discussion of program effectiveness focuses—in line with recent research—on the IMF's role in capital account crises and in "catalyzing" private capital flows. A final section summarizes key findings and possible research directions.

Program Design

A challenge for good design—and a recurring theme in this research—is the need to adapt design to changing global and country economic conditions while preserving uniformity of treatment (as emphasized, in particular, by Boughton in Chapter 8). To this end, an eclectic approach to program design has evolved. Ghosh and others (Chapter 1) state that "a variety of different analytical tools are used to analyze and predict developments in particular sectors while the financial programming framework is used to ensure that projections for different sectors are consistent with key balance-sheet identities." They further note that although the IMF has maintained the overarching objective of "achieving (or maintaining) external viability," the variation in program objectives has resulted in different types of programs:

- classic stabilization and adjustment programs (whose primary objective is to correct a current account imbalance and restore official reserves to a safe level);
- capital account crisis programs (whose primary objective is to restore confidence in international capital markets to staunch a sudden loss of private external financing); and
- reform programs (whose priority is to support structural reforms designed to contribute to economic growth and stability over the long term to, for instance, meet the early needs of former transition economies and, more recently, of low-income developing countries).

Are IMF-supported programs well designed? The answer to this question depends on the definition of "well designed." One measure of good design is the realism of—or, at least, the absence of systematic bias in—macroeconomic projections and performance targets subject to conditionality (Baqir, Ramcharan, and Sahay, Chapter 2). Although such a representation of good design has some validity, it needs to be interpreted with caution. First, if outcomes fall short of projections, it could be that ambitious goals were set to achieve the best possible outcomes; more cautious goals may well be met, or even exceeded, but may be insufficient to achieve a sustainable transition to a higher growth path. Second, the evidence is that the goals are more overoptimistic as the horizon gets longer; however, the early stage, when a program has to be jump-started, may be the most important. An alternative approach to assessing program design is by examining the composition of policy adjustment. Baqir, Ramcharan, and Sahay (Chapter 2) and Gupta and others (Chapter 5) examine, respectively, the relative importance and the composition of fiscal measures. Given the range of policy measures undertaken, composition can be assessed in many ways, and in future research the choices made could be guided by appropriate theoretical considerations.

Divergence in program projections and outcomes is particularly evident for medium-to-long-run growth projections. Consistent with the analysis of Musso and Phillips (2002), Ghosh and others (Chapter 1) do not find a significant bias in short-run growth projections. Beyond a horizon of about one year, however, the overprediction of growth increases as the horizon lengthens, and this is so regardless of the type of program. Baqir, Ramcharan, and Sahay (Chapter 2) also conclude that overprediction of growth remains even when account is taken of performance benchmarks (or, in their terminology, "intermediate targets") that are not met.

In other words, the overprediction is not just a reflection of proposed ambitious measures that are eventually not realized. They conclude that, therefore, the bias in predictions reflects either unwarranted optimism or an inadequate analytical framework. They reach similar conclusions about inflation. There is no consensus on the sources of these biases or on their implications, though.

Any bias in current account projections appears to depend on the type of program. Ghosh and others (Chapter 1) find that classic IMF stabilization and adjustment programs and capital account crisis programs systematically tend to underpredict external adjustment. This occurs, in part, because growth—and, hence, imports—do not pick up as rapidly as expected, leading to a greater-than-expected improvement in the trade balance. In contrast, reform programs tend to overpredict external adjustment—leading to a greater-than-projected buildup of external debt—particularly for low-income countries.

The differences between projections and outcomes appear to have different causes. These may include insufficient information on the economic conditions prevailing at the time of program design, shortcomings in the framework applied for program projections, and the need for projections that are acceptable to both the authorities and the IMF's Executive Board. Formally, in fact, program projections are proposed by the authorities under programs formulated by them. Chapter 4 by Atoyan and others, which focuses on fiscal and external projections, concludes that inaccuracies in the preliminary statistical information base are the most serious source of projection errors. The authors note, however, that this is a common source of projection errors in policymaking that has been well documented in, for example, the formulation of U.S. monetary policy decisions. They further point to a "learning process" that takes place as new data become available and the size of the divergence declines. In contrast, in Chapter 3, Benelli suggests that the limited pool of IMF lending resources may induce a bias toward excessive optimism in the balance of payments projections of programs; although this does not explain why countries undertaking Stand-By Arrangements tend, on the contrary, to underestimate the balance of payments adjustment, it points to the possibility that, in practice, balance of payments projections are tailored to the financing provided rather than vice versa.

The contribution of the alleged analytical inconsistency to projection errors is, as yet, speculative. Although the underlying frameworks for program design meet the discipline of accounting identities, Baqir, Ramcharan, and Sahay (Chapter 2) conjecture that the design may not always be theoretically consistent. Behavioral or analytical inconsistency could arise because the toolkits currently used in program design—financial programming, the balance-sheet approach, vulnerability assessments, and debt-sustainability analyses—are not model-based, mutually consistent theoretical frameworks. In the face of a theoretical inconsistency, it would not be surprising to see policy outturns deviating from targets. Moreover, because inconsistently designed programs are likely to be more difficult to implement, they may also be less effective. Atoyan and others (Chapter 4) find that the projected timing and speed of adjustment in fiscal and external balances differs from those actually achieved and attribute this to inadequacies in the theoretical underpinnings, a plausible but not established conclusion. Thus, a fruitful area for future research would be to establish the extent to which behavioral consistency is lacking and assess how that affects program implementation and, ultimately, effectiveness.

Research could aid in the further integration of analytical frameworks, adapted to differing country circumstances. In Chapter 1, for instance, Ghosh and others note that the financial-programming framework is not easily adapted to designing reform programs or programs in capital-account-driven crises, because it takes growth and foreign financing as exogenous. Batista and Zalduendo (2004) argue that adopting an empirical, cross-country growth framework of reference may enhance the accuracy of growth projections under reform programs. Some progress along these lines has been achieved on both capital account issues and official financing with the development of debt-sustainability analysis and a balance-sheet approach to vulnerability, but there is scope for further advance in this direction. For instance, policy packages supported by reform programs and the associated conditionality now take into account the need to avoid buildups of external debt and debt-service obligations beyond specific thresholds in low-income countries. For capital account crisis programs, the typical policy package takes into account the linkages among different sectors of the economy in terms of both flows and stock positions, thus providing a more adequate cushion against relative price changes that may occur during adjustment to the crisis. Boughton (Chapter 8) also highlights, in the context of financial crises, the importance to program design of international investor psychology and domestic structural conditions.

In contrast to the comparison of projections and outcomes, the research on the composition of policy adjustment is more limited but points to the value of fiscal adjustment. In Chapter 2, Baqir, Ramcharan, and Sahay compare program objectives and performance targets with actual outcomes in a large set of recent programs. They conclude that, relative to the targets set, more ambitious fiscal contractions are associated with better growth performance while more ambitious monetary contractions are associated with worse outcomes. Chapter 5 by Gupta and others finds not only that strong fiscal consolidations (in absolute terms) are associated with higher economic growth in both the short and long terms but also that the composition of fiscal adjustment matters: fiscal adjustments achieved by curtailing current expenditures are, in general, more sustained and more conducive to growth. When public investment is also protected, the positive effect of fiscal adjustment on growth is further accentuated. Furthermore, Chapter 14 by Bulíř and Moon makes the point that the quality of fiscal adjustment is better under IMF programs (than in countries where there is no program) in the sense that it is directed more toward expenditure reductions than increases in revenue.

Program Implementation

Recent research on program implementation has focused on domestic political economy constraints. As noted, in empirical analyses, implementation has been measured in terms of program interruptions and completions. This, of course, is not necessarily the same thing as implementation of a policy package. Within the limits of the measures used, however, both the determinants of implementation and its influence on program outcomes have been examined. The findings suggest that a stronger political and institutional environment is conducive to better program implementation. Compared with programs that falter, better-implemented programs lead, in turn, to superior macroeconomic outcomes.

The implementation of IMF-supported programs depends to a significant extent on the domestic political and institutional environment. In Chapter 10, Ivanova and others quantify the factors that determine successful implementation of IMF-supported programs. They find that program implementation is weakened by strong special interests in the parliament, lack of political cohesion, political instability, ethno-linguistic divisions, and inefficient bureaucracies. In contrast, they find that IMF effort—proxied by the number of IMF staff members involved and the design of conditionality—does not significantly affect the probability of successful implementation of IMF-supported programs. Despite the authors' efforts to disentangle the direction of causation, the possibility remains that dealing with more difficult cases requires more staff and management resources.

Implementation has real consequences: the closer a program's implementation is to specifications originally agreed with the IMF's Executive Board, the more effective it appears to be. Chapter 9 by Nsouli, Atoyan, and Mourmouras finds that better program implementation is associated with better macroeconomic outcomes, including lower inflation, a stronger external position, and faster economic growth (though the results on growth are not statistically significant). Using a somewhat different approach (comparing program and non-program periods for the same country rather than comparing across countries), Chapter 15 by Chen and Thomas arrives at similar conclusions. It finds that program interruptions are associated subsequently with higher inflation, higher budget deficits, and lower growth than periods without a program. Completed programs are, instead, associated with marginally increased growth three years after the termination of the program.

The extent to which program conditions are implemented depends on the extent of domestic "ownership"—but this may itself depend on the content and form of conditionality. In Chapter 7, Khan and Sharma concede that ownership is an elusive concept but argue that it may be enhanced by giving the authorities greater flexibility in deciding *how* to achieve agreed outcomes. To this end, they favor "outcomes-based" conditionality, which involves "conditioning disbursements on the achievement of results rather than on the implementation of policies expected to eventually attain program objectives." They note that much of program conditionality is already outcomes-based—particularly with regard to macroeconomic conditions such as a floor on net international reserves. They suggest other possible outcomes that could form the basis for conditionality: the trade balance, the current account, investment, and growth.

Although outcomes-based conditionality has attractive features, it is not straightforward to operationalize. Country authorities are not in full control of outcomes. Thus, despite their best efforts, outcomes may diverge from those intended because of unforeseen developments. In contrast, the authorities have greater control over policies. Khan and Sharma note that policy- and outcomes-based conditionality will likely be combined in practice, with the precise combination reflecting "country circumstances" and "preferences." A variation of outcomes-based conditionality is the targeting of financial assistance to countries "that are likely to make the best use of it," as discussed in Chapter 11 by Jeanne and Zettelmeyer. These authors argue for ex ante conditionality, established before a country faces a crisis, rather than the ex post conditionality that currently follows a crisis in the context of an IMF-supported program. Ex ante conditionality specifies policy and outcome benchmarks that a country should meet to be eligible for financial support in the event of a liquidity crisis. As with outcomes-based conditionality, specification of ex ante conditionality has remained controversial. Experimenting with alternative forms of conditionality may be desirable, however, to improve its effectiveness. (In Chapter 14, for instance, Bulíř and Moon suggest that structural conditionality has not had a significant influence on the achievement of fiscal targets.)

The governance constraints faced by the IMF may hamper program design and implementation. In Chapter 6, Cottarelli argues that designing appropriate governance structures for an institution such as the IMF is difficult, because of underlying trade-offs between legitimacy and effectiveness. Attempts to enhance the IMF's legitimacy by placing constraints on its decision-making process may reduce the organization's operational flexibility and, hence, lower its effectiveness. He illustrates these trade-offs in three contexts. First, increased control of the IMF's functioning by national political authorities may restrict the possible range of technical decisions. Echoing the suggestions reported earlier for changes to the IMF's own approach to conditionality, he proposes that the IMF itself be monitored ex post—that is, on the basis of outcomes and results—rather than subjected to efforts to influence its technical processes. Second, Cottarelli is concerned that the legitimate need for transparency may conflict with the IMF's operational goals. Third, and finally, while recognizing that uniformity of treatment across countries grants legitimacy to IMF programs, he cautions that it may create inefficiencies in their technical design and processing. In particular, he argues that too much emphasis has been given to *formalistic* procedural uniformity of treatment rather than to establishing "substantive evenhandedness."

Further research, with a greater empirical bent, on the implications of the IMF's governance structure is needed. Is the distribution of power among different members of the Executive Board only an issue of member equality and representation, or does it also affect the overall institution's effectiveness? Do the governance structure of the IMF and domestic political economy interact? Does the governance structure exacerbate the political economy constraints that country authorities face by influencing their behavior in program negotiation and implementation?

Program Effectiveness

Pioneering research done at the IMF on program effectiveness examined the macroeconomic consequences of IMF-supported programs. These early efforts asked the overarching question whether an IMF-supported program helped improve macroeconomic performance as measured by growth, inflation, and current account outcomes. Despite the difficulties posed by the presence of "treatment effects" and the lack of differentiation across programs, this early literature reached three conclusions that have proved durable. (See Haque and Khan (1998) for a survey.) First, and not surprisingly, an IMF program helps to improve the country's external balance. Second, inflation falls following the start of a program, but the effect is not statistically significant. Third, growth falls initially, but recovers in the medium term, though possibly not to its pre-program level, under classical and capital account crisis programs. Dicks-Mireaux, Mecagni, and Schadler (2000) find, though, that the growth effects have been stronger in low-income countries. Academics have largely continued to view IMF programs as zero-one events and pursued the analysis of their impact on overall economic performance. Examples of more recent academic research in this vein include Przeworski and Vreeland (2000), Hutchinson (2001), and Barro and Lee (2002).

Recent IMF research has tended to identify conditions under which IMF programs may succeed and to infer from those findings the features of the IMF that contribute to success. Research by the IMF's staff has moved beyond the earlier literature in two important respects. First, researchers have sought to examine the conditions under which IMF programs are effective. In other words, rather than treating IMF programs as undifferentiated (and represented, therefore, in empirical work as a single dummy variable for the presence or absence of an IMF program), a greater effort has been made to identify the influence of initial country conditions. In this spirit, greater effort has also been made to distinguish different types of programs and, as noted above, to assess the costs of inadequate program implementation. Second, these differentiations have allowed a more forceful examination of the IMF's comparative advantages and, therefore, of its informational and lending roles.

In turn, the conditions for IMF effectiveness have been sought in the context of capital account crises and catalysis of capital flows. Outcomes under programs supporting adjustment to capital account crises have been mixed. The usual experience has been that the relatively large shock faced by the country is reflected, during the first year of the program, in a continuing decline in output, employment, and consumption, but this is followed by a sharp, positive reversal in confidence and private capital flows (see Chapter 1 by Ghosh and others). Jeanne and Zettelmeyer conclude, in Chapter 10, that official lending in the context of the 1990s financial crises did not create moral hazard at the expense of global taxpayers. Rather, domestic taxpayers, who ultimately had to repay the IMF and other official creditors, bore the costs of the crises. To limit the risk of governments borrowing irresponsibly from international markets—and placing themselves subsequently in the position of requiring official financing—Jeanne and Zettelmeyer suggest that the appropriate response is not to raise the interest rates charged by the IMF, but rather to condition large-scale crisis lending on sound pre-crisis policies and institutions.

IMF research has also focused on a more medium-term response of capital flows to IMF-supported programs, in addition to the implications for financing at times of capital account crises. In Chapter 12, Cottarelli and Giannini find that the *aggregate* evidence on the response of capital flows to IMF-supported programs, which is often referred to as the catalytic effect of IMF financing, is weak. They argue that the absence of such an effect is all the more remarkable, since empirical studies often fail to control for actual policy change, thereby biasing their results in favor of such an effect. This is one area, however, in which country differentiation turns out to be crucial.

The evidence suggests IMF-supported programs are most catalytic when the initial conditions are not too negative or the external financing need is only potential and not actual. Bordo and others (Chapter 13) reach this conclusion (as does an earlier study by Mody and Saravia (2003)). They investigate the IMF's role in maintaining emerging market economies' access to international capital markets and find that both macroeconomic aggregates and capital flows improve following the adoption of an IMF-supported program, although they may initially deteriorate somewhat. They also find that IMF programs are most successful in improving capital flows to countries in a state of vulnerability—as distinct from extreme distress. In such countries, IMF programs are also associated with improvements in external fundamentals. Consistent with these findings, the catalytic effect of IMF lending also appears salient in the context of precautionary programs—that is, those undertaken for crisis prevention.

IMF research has also identified specific features of IMF-supported programs that may make a catalytic effect possible. Building on the extensive taxonomy proposed by Cottarelli and Giannini, Chapter 13 by Bordo and others concludes that it is implausible to assert that the IMF's signaling role (the IMF's conferring of its "seal of approval" on a country's reform policies) is crucial to the catalytic process, since that assumes the IMF has information that others do not. Instead, they suggest, the IMF's monitoring role allows countries on the reform path to signal commitment. They also find only ambiguous support for the hypothesis that more lending is more catalytic.

Looking ahead, assessing program effectiveness remains a challenge, but progress is possible. The challenge arises from the absence of counterfactual experiments, pervasive endogeneity issues, measurement errors in the data, and potential omitted-variable biases. Establishing causal links between IMF programs and outcomes requires considerable finesse. The creative use of alternative data sources and methodologies may help overcome some of the methodological difficulties. Case studies, nonparametric and Bayesian estimation methods (such as those used in Rossi and Rebucci (2005)), and simulations of alternative program scenarios could be attempted. A data-collection effort to extend the sample of programs analyzed by IMF researchers to include programs approved in the 1970s and 1980s would be very valuable. Finally, the data used by the IMF staff's research are generally not publicly available, limiting their use by the academic community. Finding ways to provide access to program data without violating country confidentiality could enhance the credibility of the IMF staff's analyses and encourage further research in this area. Perhaps more importantly, there is scope for further investigating program modalities and the channels through which they succeed or fail. This would help in the design of more effective programs in the future. Joint analysis of program design, implementation, and effectiveness, in particular, is likely to be a promising direction for future research in light of linkages highlighted by the research reviewed in this book.

Conclusions

The contribution of recent IMF research has been the more precise identification of the conditions necessary for the success of IMF programs. The research has moved fruitfully from the question "Do programs work or not?" to "Under what conditions do programs work?" The challenge has been to give structure to this more nuanced question. The contributions to this book point to features of program design, the quality of program implementation, and the country conditions likely to contribute to program success. Much remains to be done, however. Not least is the challenge to further characterize the relevant design, implementation, and country conditions in the context of different types of programs and countries.

On program design, the research both points to specific recommendations and calls for future research. Among the specific recommendations, the value of fiscal adjustment is underscored, as is the effort to increase the accuracy of program projections. In turn, the quality of program projection is identified with more accurate and comprehensive information, especially on initial conditions. Authors call for more refined theoretical analytical frameworks to deal, for example, with capital account crises and the determinants of long-term growth.

Variations in program-implementation experiences tend to reflect differences in domestic institutions and political constraints. These findings are consistent with the call for greater country ownership of IMF-supported programs. Future research could usefully analyze more carefully the determinants and impact of program conditionality. The IMF's governance structure—in the specific sense of how operational control is exercised by national authorities, the degree of transparency, and the manner in which uniformity of treatment across member countries is achieved—may also be an important influence on program design and implementation.

Recent research on program effectiveness has focused on the IMF's role in the context of capital account crises and in catalyzing capital flows, distinguishing among different country economic conditions in evaluating success. In the resolution of capital account crises, the finding is that private creditors and the IMF were largely repaid; hence, to protect domestic taxpayers who bore much of the costs of the crises, the suggestion is that IMF lending be conditioned on the quality of precrisis policies and institutions. In helping countries maintain medium-term access to international capital markets, the IMF may be most effective when a member country is vulnerable to, but not yet in, a crisis. The research points to the value of a country committing itself to an altered policy course and using IMF monitoring as a signal of its commitment to reform. Further research will benefit from a more precise characterization and analysis of the varieties of IMF programs. New empirical approaches that enhance analysts' ability to attribute specific outcomes to IMF programs would also be useful.

References

Barro, Robert J., and Jong-Wha Lee, 2002, "IMF Programs: Who Is Chosen and What Are the Effects?" NBER Working Paper No. 8951 (Cambridge, Massachusetts: National Bureau of Economic Research).

Batista, Catia, and Juan Zalduendo, 2004, "Can the IMF's Medium-Term Growth Projections Be Improved?" IMF Working Paper 04/203 (Washington: International Monetary Fund).

Dicks-Mireaux, Louis, Mauro Mecagni, and Susan Schadler, 2000, "Evaluating the Effect of IMF Lending to Low-Income Countries," *Journal of Development Economics*, Vol. 61, No. 2, pp. 495–526.

Haque, Nadeem Ul, and Mohsin S. Khan, 1998, "Do IMF-Supported Programs Work? A Survey of the Cross-Country Empirical Evidence," IMF Working Paper 98/169 (Washington: International Monetary Fund).

Hutchison, Michael M., 2001, "A Cure Worse than the Disease? Currency Crises and the Output Costs of IMF-Supported Stabilization Programs," NBER Working Paper No. 8305 (Cambridge, Massachusetts: National Bureau of Economic Research).

International Monetary Fund (IMF), 2005, "The IMF's Multilateral Surveillance: Draft Issues Paper for an Evaluation by the Independent Evaluation Office," available on the Web at *http://www.imf.org/external/np/ieo/index.htm*.

Mody, Ashoka, and Diego Saravia, 2003 "Catalyzing Capital Flows: Do IMF Programs Work as Commitment Devices?" IMF Working Paper 03/10 (Washington: International Monetary Fund). Forthcoming in *Economic Journal*.

Musso, Alberto, and Steven Phillips, 2002, "Comparing Projections and Outcomes of IMF-Supported Programs," *Staff Papers*, International Monetary Fund, Vol. 49, No. 1, pp. 22–48.

Przeworski, Adam, and James Raymond Vreeland, 2000, "The Effect of IMF Programs on Economic Growth," *Journal of Development Economics*, Vol. 62, No. 2, pp. 385–421.

Rossi, Marco, and Alessandro Rebucci, 2005, "Measuring Disinflation Credibility Under IMF-Supported Programs: A Bayesian Approach with an Application to Turkey" (unpublished manuscript; Washington: International Monetary Fund). An earlier version of this paper was issued as IMF Working Paper 04/208.

Part I. Design

CHAPTER

1 Program Objectives and Program Success

Atish Ghosh, Timothy Lane, Alun Thomas, and Juan Zalduendo[1]

This paper examines how IMF-supported programs have evolved over the past decade, and to what extent national authorities have been successful in achieving their program goals.[2]

Introduction

Are IMF-supported programs a success or a failure? This is a key question in evaluating the role of the IMF, and a large body of literature has set about answering it.[3] Yet defining success, let alone measuring it, is far from straightforward. In part, this is because the circumstances facing member countries have evolved over time, as has the nature of problems that national authorities expect to address with IMF support. These changing circumstances have been accompanied by a broad range of facilities for IMF financing, which are often associated with different objectives: in addition to the Stand-By Arrangement, introduced in 1952 to address short-term balance of payments needs, financing is provided through the Extended Fund Facility (EFF), established in 1974 to address longer-term payments imbalances rooted in structural problems, and the Poverty Reduction and Growth Facility (PRGF), introduced in 1999, with its explicit eponymous goals.[4]

The paper is structured as follows. The second section presents the classic type of IMF-supported program and discusses how IMF-supported programs have evolved from that classic type. The third section examines experience under IMF-supported programs, including external adjustment and macroeconomic performance. The fourth section studies performance, while the fifth section draws some conclusions.

Types of IMF-Supported Programs

A useful starting point in discussing program design is the *classic type* of IMF-supported program. In this type of program, a country turns to the IMF for financing because it faces a loss of international reserves stemming from an external current account imbalance, often in the context of poor macroeconomic performance—such as high inflation or low growth. In this setting, the primary objective is to correct the current account imbalance and restore reserves to a safe level. The IMF provides temporary financing while this process is taking place, both to ease the adjustment burden and minimize the output loss, even though some temporary contraction in economic activity is unavoidable.[5] Indeed, growth typically dips during the program period owing to restrictive monetary and fiscal policies intended to bring aggregate demand into alignment with national income and the drying up of external financing that leads to lower investment. As confidence is restored, capital flows resume and economic activity picks up, enabling the country to finance its now sustainable deficits.

Although this classic adjustment paradigm remains surprisingly relevant, the past decade has also seen an important evolution in the kinds of circumstances in which the IMF has been providing financing. These newer programs can be classified into two broad categories. The first are the so-called *capital account crisis* programs, where the salient initial condition is a sudden loss of private external financing, which is in the nature of a stock adjustment—in fact, there need not be a sizable initial current account imbalance when these crises emerge—with pervasive consequences for economic performance.[6] Typically, this loss of financing puts

[1] This paper draws on analytical work undertaken as part of the 2004 Program Design project, which served as background material for the review of the 2002 IMF Conditionality Guidelines.

[2] The IMF-supported programs examined cover the period 1995–2000. Although this period includes only the early years of the PRGF, during the latter years of ESAF arrangements, these had already been redirected toward growth and poverty-reduction objectives.

[3] This literature has been reviewed by Haque and Khan (1998); some recent contributions include Barro and Lee (2002); Dicks-Mireaux, Mecagni, and Schadler (2000); and Przeworski and Vreeland (2000).

[4] The PRGF replaced the Enhanced Structural Adjustment Facility (ESAF) and the Structural Adjustment Facility (SAF), which were designed to support structural reforms in low-income countries.

[5] The IMF also requires that the resources it provides be used in a manner consistent with IMF purposes, which precludes the imposition of trade and payments restrictions for balance of payments purposes during the program period.

[6] See Ghosh and others (2002).

the exchange rate under pressure, leading to the abandonment of the initial exchange rate peg regime (which characterizes these countries) and to a large currency depreciation. In the presence of currency mismatches in domestic public and private sector balance sheets, the depreciation leads to a sharp contraction in economic activity, which brings about a large current account adjustment despite the fact that the initial current imbalances were small. In fact, the policy package in these programs is not intended to bring about current account adjustment, as this is already being forced by the markets. Instead, the proximate objective is to restore confidence with a view to attenuating the loss of financing.

The second group can broadly be characterized as *reform programs*, in which the country's main priority is to undertake a set of structural reforms designed to contribute to economic growth and stability over the longer term. Again, there need not be an external imbalance in the first place, but maintaining a sustainable external position is a constraint on policy choice.

Within the broad category of reform programs, one can identify some important and diverse groupings. Many *transition economies* fit the description (whether or not they have access to private financial markets): beyond their initial stabilization phase, their main priorities are undertaking structural reforms aimed at transition to the market economy, maintaining macroeconomic stability, and keeping a viable external position while they are doing so.

IMF-supported programs in *low-income countries* also have the broad features of reform programs and, though they differ from transition economies in many respects, share a common logic of program design: while the need to maintain external viability is generally an important constraint, the primary objective is not short-run adjustment of the current account but rather structural transformation of the economy to create a sound basis for growth. Low-income countries also have some important distinctive characteristics—in particular, the very long-term nature of the reform agenda and the prospect that they will be supported by concessional lending and grant aid over the foreseeable future.

A final type of program that fits the reform profile deals with *non-crisis emerging market countries*. These countries do not face acute balance of payments pressure, in part because they continue to enjoy access to private financial markets, but they seek support from the IMF to help maintain stability while they are undertaking other policy initiatives designed for longer-term growth and stability—which may include disinflation and various aspects of structural reform.

In sum, these programs are designed primarily to support sound policies and enhance the credibility of the authorities' policy programs, rather than to close an immediate balance of payments gap. In several emerging market countries, the purpose of such programs is to elicit lower inflationary expectations and interest rates to put domestic debt dynamics on a more sustainable footing, while maintaining access to external markets.

While the differing nature of these programs imply different objectives, all IMF-supported programs share the goal of achieving (or maintaining) external viability for at least two reasons. First, a loss of external viability would eventually force an abrupt adjustment, in turn jeopardizing any other program goals. Second, both economic logic and the IMF's Article of Agreements dictate that IMF resources be used to meet a country's balance of payments needs. Since the use of IMF resources adds to the country's external obligations, which will subsequently need to be repaid, IMF support essentially involves shifting the time profile of the country's external adjustment to minimize the associated economic and social disruption, including by allowing time for the adjustment to come through a supply response rather than demand management alone.

As IMF-supported programs have been designed to respond to different initial conditions than originally envisaged, with a different set of objectives in mind, the analytical framework used to design them has also evolved. In the past, the connections between policies and objectives were often analyzed on the basis of projections using the financial programming framework based on the monetary approach to the balance of payments—a special case of the Mundell-Fleming model.[7] In recent years, this framework has given way to a more eclectic approach, in which a variety of analytical tools are used to analyze and predict developments in particular sectors while the financial programming framework is used to ensure that projections for different sectors are consistent with key balance-sheet identities.

This eclectic approach has been viable in most cases, given that projections are often revised after a quarter or two and over that period are typically reasonably accurate (Table 1, Figure 1, and Figure 2). The IMF's analytical approach has been less successful in capital account crises—since neither IMF staff nor anyone else have been able to construct an accurate short-run model of the rapid and often massive stock adjustments that take place in a crisis setting. The balance-sheet approach has been developed to analyze these adjustments and to inform a sharper assessment of crisis vulnerability; this

[7] Specifically, the financial programming model assumes that real economic activity is determined on the supply side and where money demand and capital flows are interest inelastic. These assumptions are not unrealistic for many countries with limited capital mobility, repressed financial mobility, and constrained supply sides—which characterized many countries with IMF-supported programs in the past—but have become less relevant, particularly for emerging market countries. See IMF, Research Department (1987) on theoretical aspects of program design and Polak (1991).

Table 1
Statistical Characteristics of Program Projection Errors[1]

		Period t		Period $t+1$		Average Period $t+1:t+3$	
	Number of Observations	Mean error	RMSE	Mean error	RMSE	Mean error	RMSE
				Real GDP Growth			
PRGF-supported programs	56	−0.4	2.2	−1.2***	3.1	−1.3***	2.8
GRA-supported programs							
Transition countries[2]	27	0.1	3.7	−0.7	4.4	−0.5	2.9
Non-transition countries[2]	35	−0.3	2.7	−0.7	4.4	−2.4***	4.3
CACs[3]	9	−9.3***	10.7	−0.9	5.0	−0.4	2.3
				Current Account Balance			
PRGF-supported programs	48	−1.5**	4.9	−1.9***	4.8	−2.2***	4.1
GRA-supported programs							
Transition countries[2]	24	0.4	2.5	−0.4	2.3	−0.8	2.6
Non-transition countries[2]	28	2.4***	4.6	2.7***	5.2	1.6***	3.2
CACs[3]	8	5.6**	7.2	6.5**	8.7	...	...

Sources: IMF, Monitoring of Fund Arrangements (MONA) and World Economic Outlook (WEO) databases; and IMF staff estimates.

Notes: *** significant at 1 percent level; ** significant at 5 percent level; and * significant at 10 percent level. PRGF denotes the Poverty Reduction and Growth Facility. RMSE denotes root-mean-squared error. GRA denotes the IMF's General Resources Account.

[1] Data have been transformed so that they map into the interval (−100, 100). Errors are defined as actual minus projections. Table was constructed using a dataset of countries with available information for years t, $t+1$, $t+2$, and $t+3$.

[2] Excludes capital account crises.

[3] CAC stands for capital account crisis.

approach needs to be developed further to provide a clearer basis for the policy response in a crisis. A second area in which more work is clearly needed is the analysis of long-term growth and debt dynamics: while the IMF's debt-sustainability template provides a basis for prudent assessments of the debt dynamics, it has to contend with a continuing tendency toward over-optimism in medium-term growth projections. Deriving realistic growth projections poses a significant challenge, especially given that growth remains far from well understood by the economics profession at large.[8] These analytical issues should be borne in mind in considering the experience with IMF-supported programs in the remainder of the paper.[9]

What Happens in IMF-Supported Programs?

With these basic types in mind, we may now consider the macroeconomic outcomes of IMF-supported programs in the 1990s. Here we are simply trying to characterize what happened during the course of the programs and thereafter—rather than trying to establish what would have happened in the IMF's absence.[10]

We may first examine the experience of Stand-By Arrangements. Programs supported by these arrangements look, on average, surprisingly close to the classic type (Figure 3). At the outset of a typical program, the country faces substantial external imbalances, and these imbalances are reduced during the course of the program. Monetary and fiscal policies are tightened to help promote the external adjustment. Economic activity dips below trend during the program and subsequently recovers.

Programs adopted in the context of capital account crises display similar but more extreme patterns (Figure 4). In these cases, large current account adjustment takes place in the face of capital outflows. This adjustment is associated with a major slump in economic activity, followed by a sharp recovery. The major difference between capital account crisis programs and the classic adjustment paradigm lies in the orientation of policies: in capital

[8] See, for instance, Easterly (2001).

[9] A fuller discussion of the analytical frameworks for program design is presented in the set of papers on "The Design of IMF-Supported Programs," which is available on the IMF website (*http://www.imf.org/external/np/pdr/2004/eng/design.htm*).

[10] In contrast, the existing literature on the macroeconomic outcomes of IMF-supported programs typically seeks to distinguish the role of the IMF from some counterfactual—but, on the other hand, does not focus on the fact that different types of programs may have different objectives.

Figure 1

Growth and Current Account Balances: Projections and Actuals

(x-axis projections; y-axis actuals; GRA programs only)

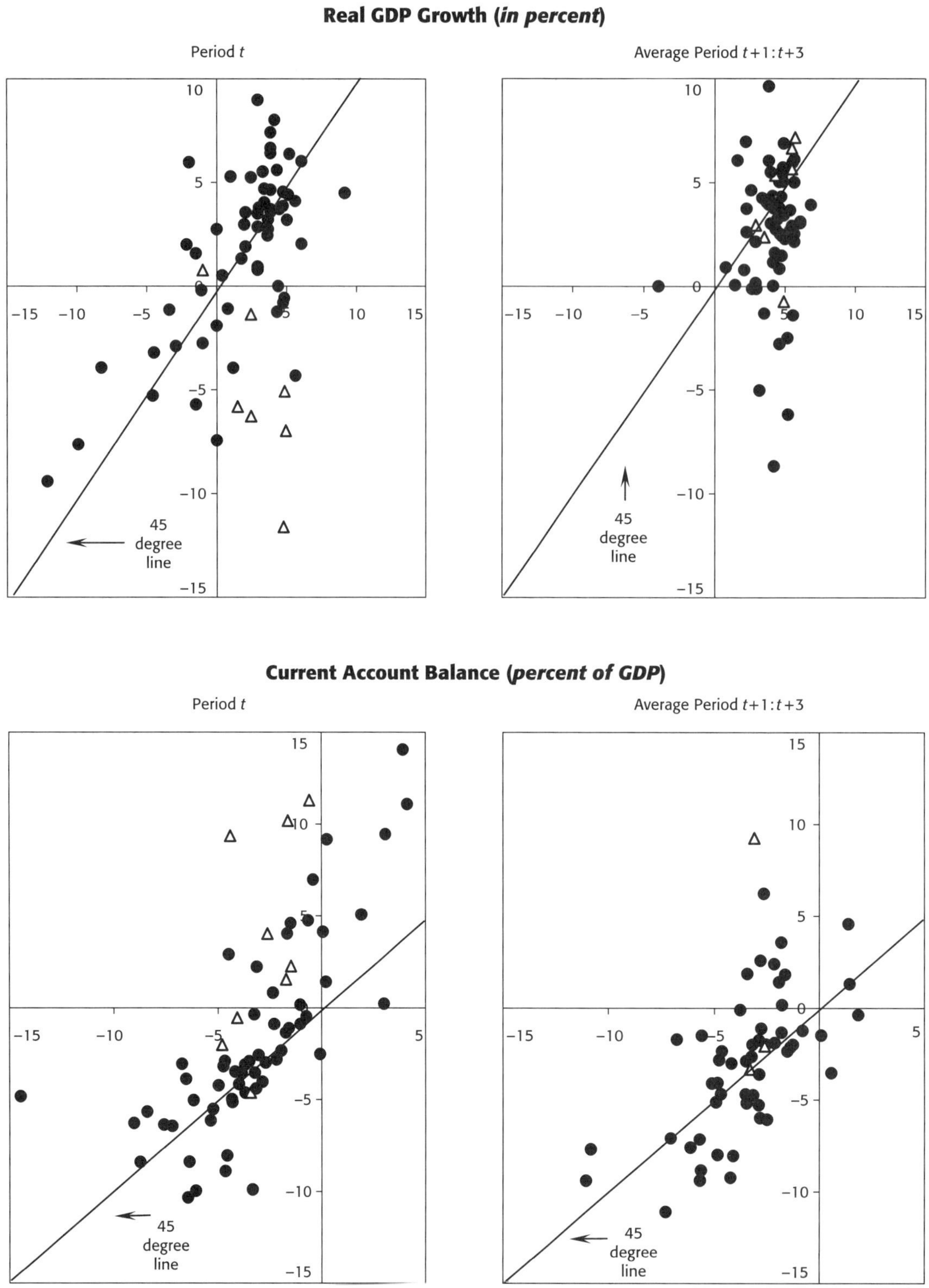

Sources: IMF, World Economic Outlook (WEO) and Monitoring of Fund Arrangements (MONA) databases; and IMF staff estimates.

Notes: Data were mapped into the interval (–100, 100). GRA denotes the IMF's General Resources Account. Capital account crisis countries are depicted by triangles.

Figure 2
Growth and Current Account Balances: Projections and Actuals
(x-axis projections; y-axis actuals; PRGF programs only)

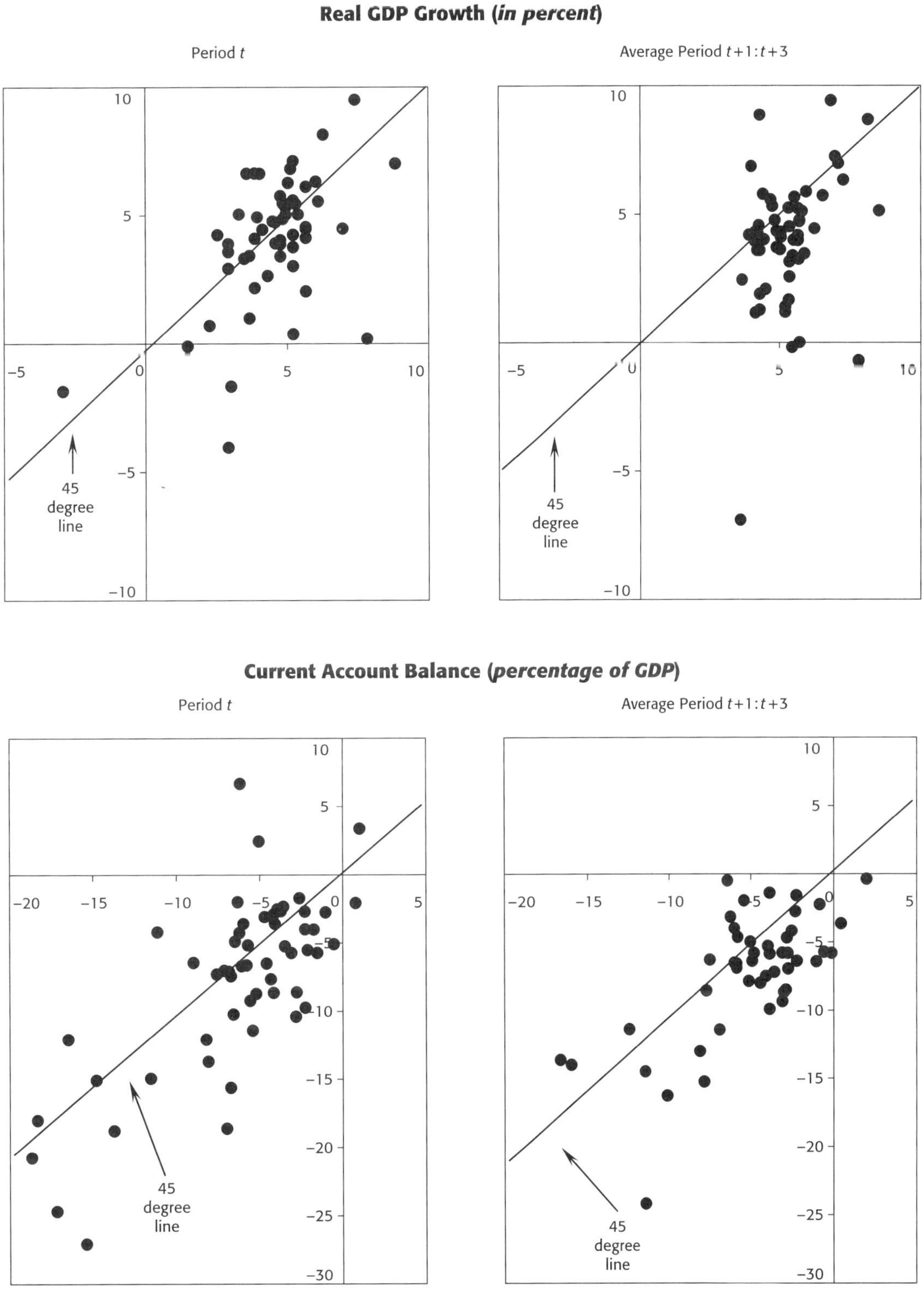

Sources: IMF, World Economic Outlook (WEO) and Monitoring of Fund Arrangements (MONA) databases; and IMF staff estimates.
Notes: Data were mapped into the interval (−100, 100). PRGF denotes the Poverty Reduction and Growth Facility.

Figure 3
Macroeconomic Performance Under GRA-Supported Programs, 1995–2003
(Excluding transition economies)

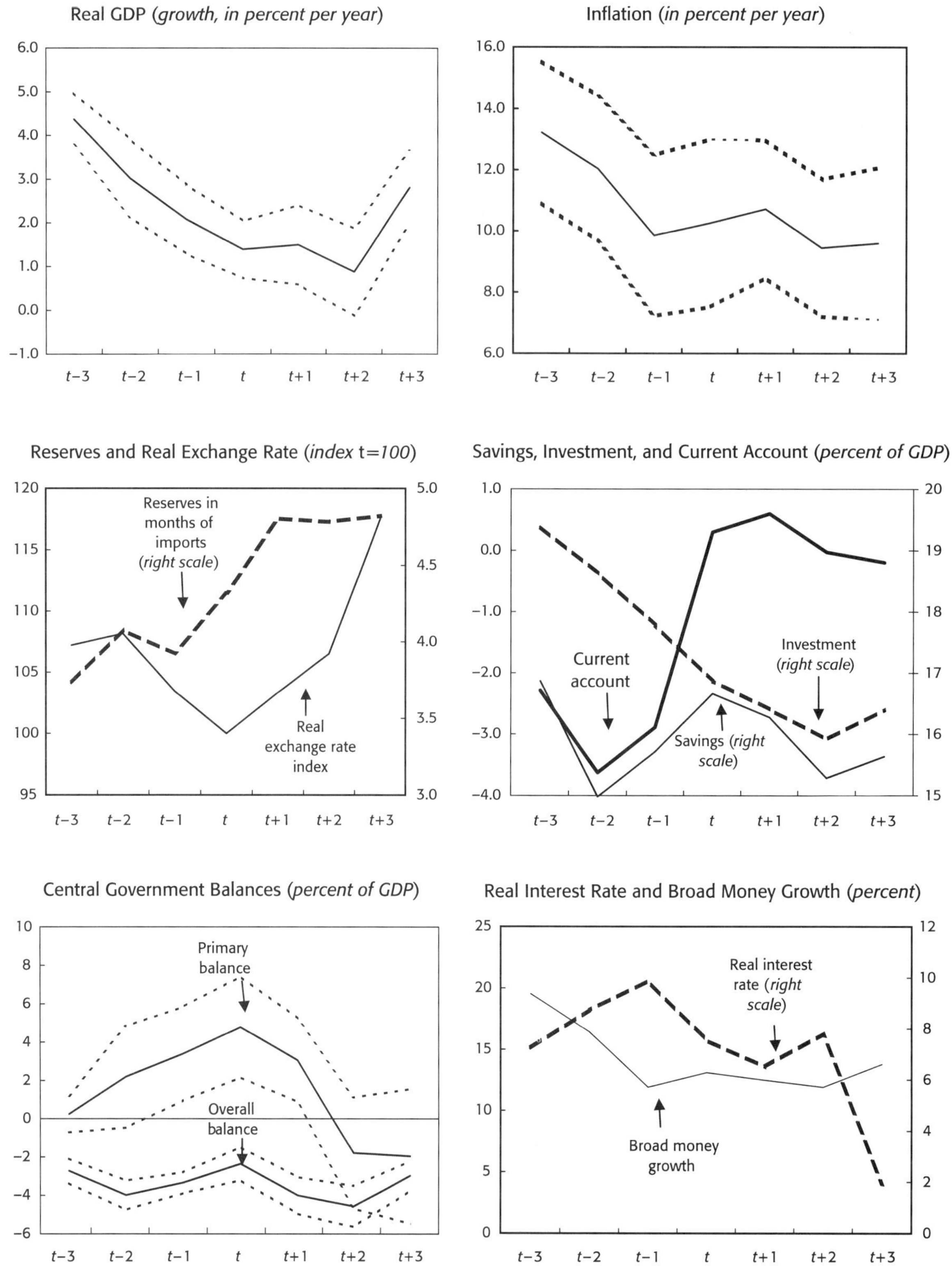

Sources: IMF, World Economic Outlook (WEO) database; and IMF staff estimates.

Notes: GRA denotes the IMF's General Resources Account. Standard error bands for real GDP growth, inflation, and government balances are shown by the dotted lines.

Figure 4

Macroeconomic Performance Under Capital Account Crisis Countries, 1995–2003[1]

(Excluding transition economies)

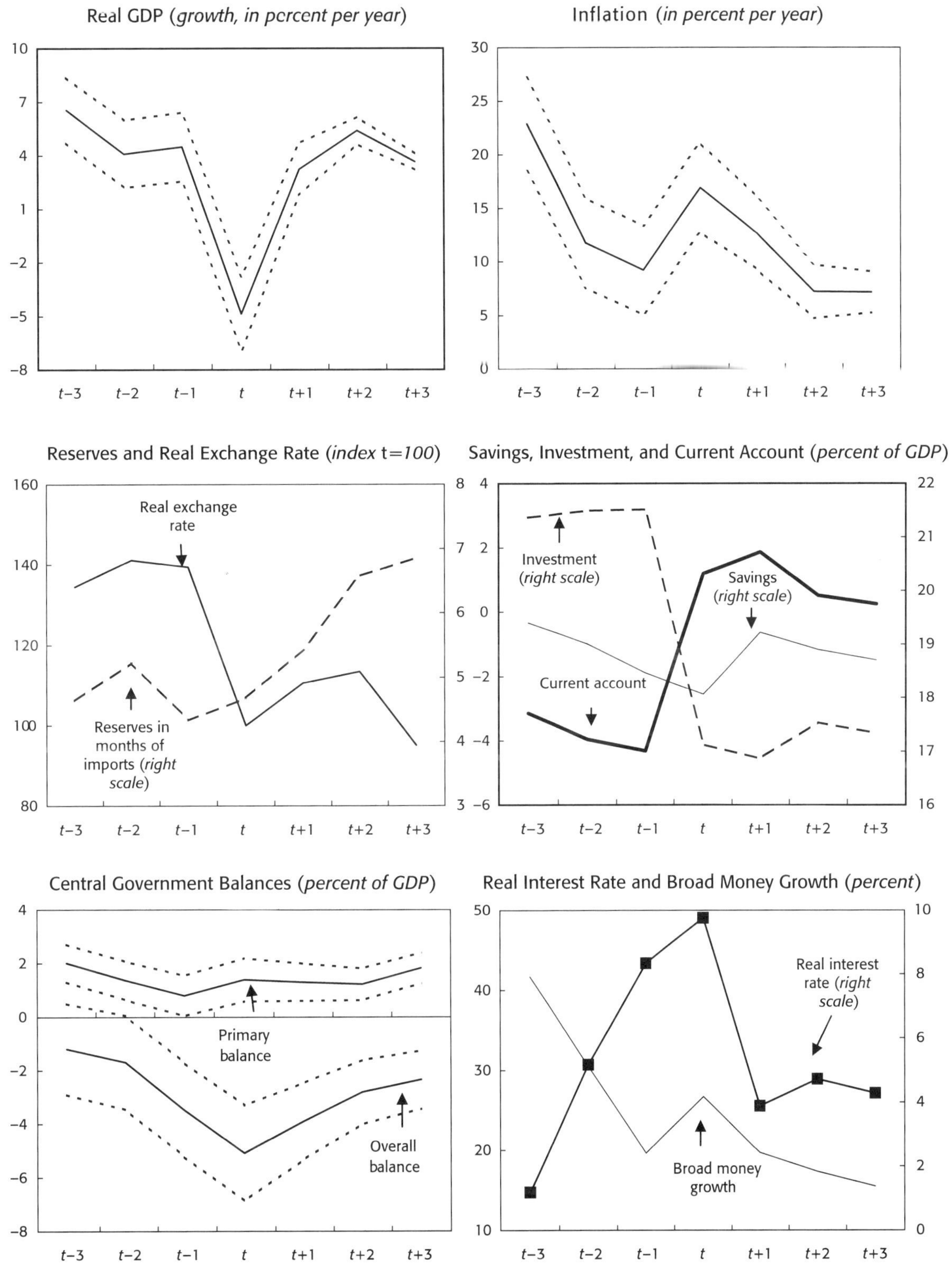

Sources: IMF, World Economic Outlook (WEO) database; and IMF staff estimates.

[1] Standard error bands for real GDP growth, inflation, and government balances are shown by the dotted lines.

account crises, fiscal policy is loosened to support economic activity (except, of course, in those crises that are driven by public sector imbalances), since the external adjustment is being forced on the country through capital outflows anyway. Monetary policy is tightened, although this is done mainly to attract capital rather than to foster adjustment through demand restraint.

Macroeconomic developments in low-income country programs supported by IMF concessional facilities display quite a different pattern (Figure 5). In those cases, while external deficits were quite large, little current account adjustment took place. However, in this set of programs, growth increased during the course of the program. On the negative side, these countries tended to experience an increase in external debt, corresponding to the continuing exacerbation of low-income countries' debt problems during this period.

Performance

External Adjustment

How well did programs succeed? Since IMF financial support is intended to bring about orderly external adjustment, and a failure to maintain external viability is likely to jeopardize any other program goals, a good starting point is the record on external adjustment. But even here, establishing what should constitute a "successful" program is not straightforward, since it is not only the overall amount but also the means and the time path of external adjustment that are important.

The importance of the time path of adjustment can be illustrated with reference to two extreme cases: Argentina (1995) and the Republic of Korea (1997). In the aftermath of the "tequila" crisis, in 1995 Argentina faced large bank deposit withdrawals, putting severe pressure on the balance of payments and calling into question the viability of the currency board arrangement. In the event, the authorities were able to stabilize capital outflows, a devaluation was avoided, and the government was even tapping the capital markets by year's end. The program was thus very successful in dealing with the immediate balance of payments problem. Yet, in retrospect, it is also clear that the failure to tackle the underlying weaknesses of the public finances resulted in a mounting public and external debt problem, culminating in the 2002 crisis.[11] In contrast, Korea's 1997 program met with very little initial success in stemming capital outflows or preventing a collapse of the exchange rate and of economic activity. Over the longer term, however, by enhancing the credibility of policies and instituting structural reforms, the IMF-supported program succeeded in restoring confidence and bringing about a return of private capital together with a replenishment of foreign exchange reserves. Neither extreme is optimal: Korea achieved a sharp reduction in its external debt, but at a cost of a wrenching external adjustment and contraction of output. In Argentina, the impact of adjustment was avoided in the short run—but at the cost of a highly disruptive crisis in the longer run.

This suggests that any measure of successful external adjustment must weigh the benefits of attenuating adjustment in the short run against the longer-run considerations of maintaining external viability. Medium-term debt sustainability provides one such measure. The basic principle is that if a country is solvent, it should be able to obtain financing rather than having to adjust its current account in response to a temporary shock. Therefore, unless the country is constrained in the financing it is able to obtain, the current account balance should adjust by as much as is required to maintain solvency—except inasmuch as it has a high level of external debt or low level of reserves, in which case a larger surplus (or smaller deficit) would be appropriate to reduce vulnerability to future balance of payments problems.

Programmed and actual current account balances (relative to the debt-stabilizing balance) for middle-income countries (those supported by Stand-By and Extended Arrangements) are plotted against the initial external debt ratio in Figure 6. Three points are apparent. First, consistent with reducing vulnerability, there is indeed a positive relationship between the initial level of external debt and the targeted improvement in the current account balance (relative to the debt-stabilizing balance). Second, actual adjustment was generally greater than the programmed adjustment—on average by about 1 percent of GDP. Third, in a large number of cases, adjustment was greater than would be required to stabilize the debt ratio. While it is difficult to establish exact thresholds at which debt should be considered high, most studies suggest a range of about 40–60 percent of GDP for developing and emerging market countries (Figure 6). Segmenting the figure according to whether the country undertook more adjustment than necessary to stabilize the debt ratio and whether the initial debt ratio exceeded 40–60 percent of GDP shows that in about one-quarter of the cases, the current account balance was higher than necessary to stabilize the debt ratio even though debt was below 40 percent of GDP (in the second section in Figure 6). In a further 21 percent of cases—including some notable capital account crises such as Korea (1997) and Mexico (1995)—current account balances exceeded the debt-stabilizing balance although the initial debt ratio was within the 40–60 percent of GDP range (in the second section in Figure 6). Finally, in about

[11] Daseking and others (2005).

Figure 5

Macroeconomic Performance Under Enhanced Structural Adjustment and Poverty Reduction and Growth Facility Programs, 1995–2003[1]

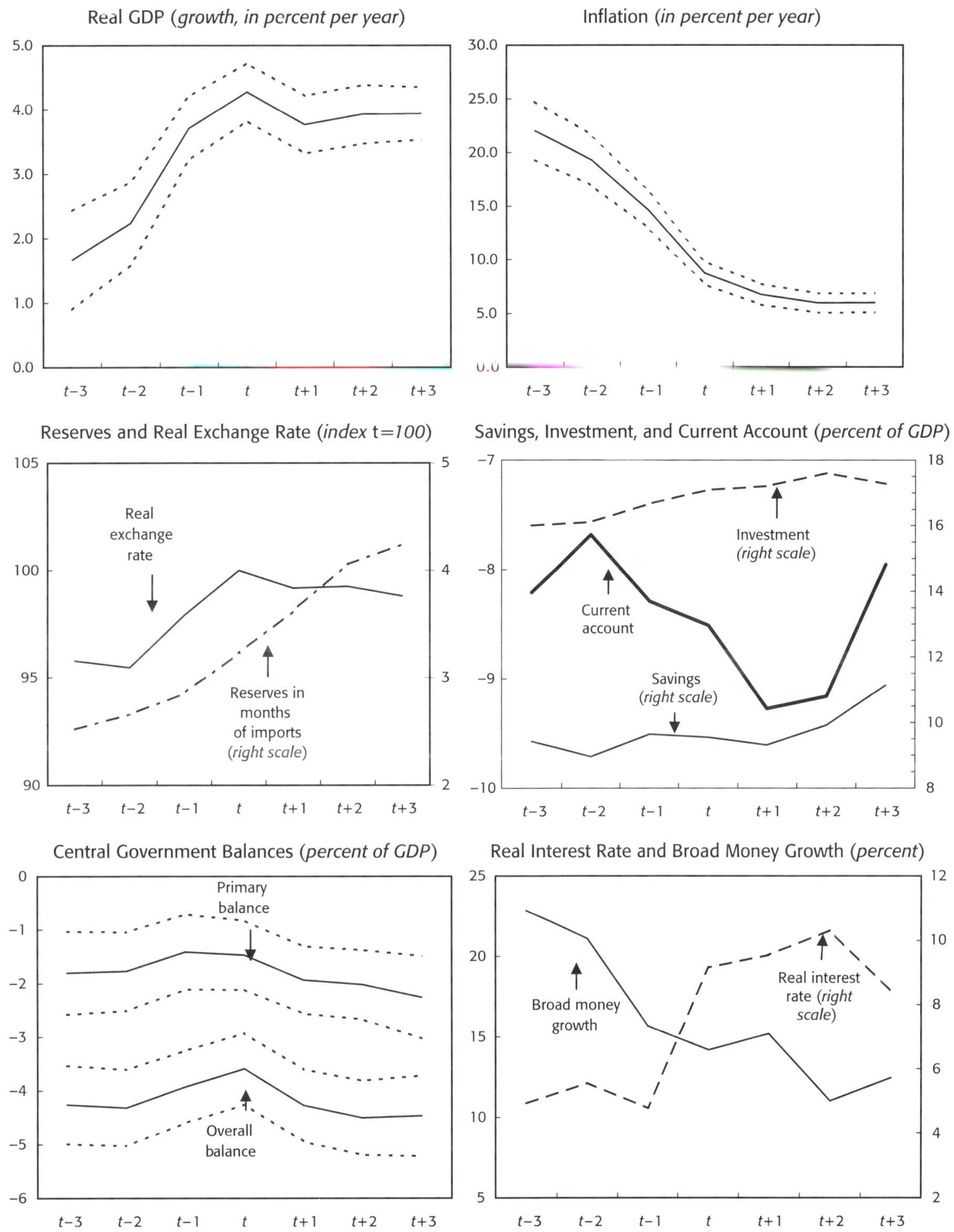

Sources: IMF, World Economic Outlook (WEO) database; and IMF staff estimates.

[1] Standard error bands for real GDP growth, inflation, and government balances are shown by the dotted lines.

Figure 6

Projected, Actual, and Debt-Stabilizing Current Account Balances in GRA-Supported Programs

(In percent of GDP)

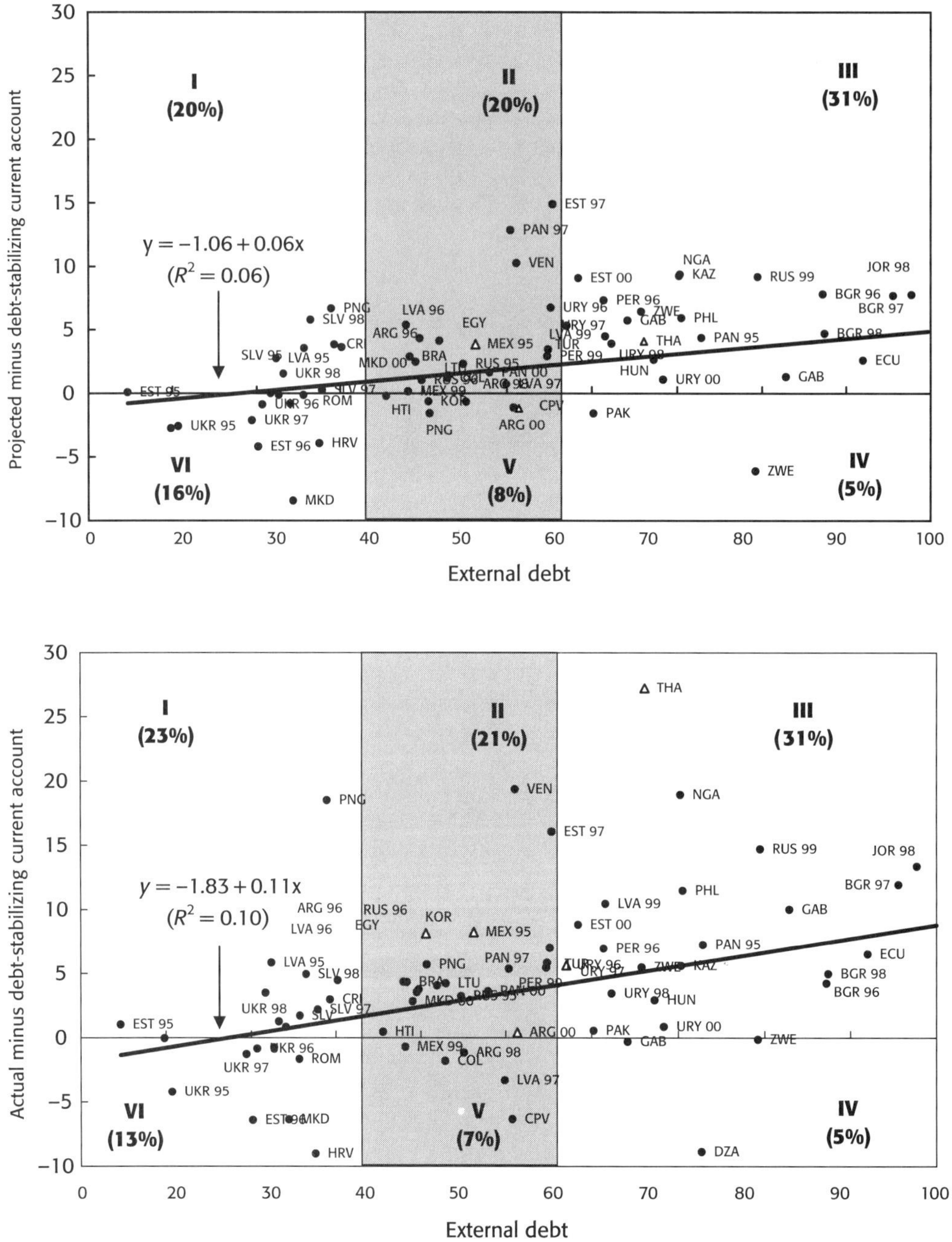

Sources: International Monetary Fund, Monitoring of Fund Arrangements (MONA) and World Economic Outlook (WEO) databases; and IMF staff estimates.

Notes: Country abbreviations are based on three-letter country codes used in IMF automated database systems. GRA denotes the IMF's General Resources Account. Capital account crisis countries are depicted by triangles.

30 percent of cases, current account balances exceeded the debt-stabilizing balance—but the country was starting from a high initial level of indebtedness.

To some extent, countries may have run larger current account balances than necessary to stabilize the debt ratio in order to build up reserves to reduce vulnerability to future crises. While this is part of the explanation, it does not account for it fully, since the excess current account balance (for countries in the first section) was, on average, almost 3 percent of GDP—against a programmed increase in reserves of 1½ percent of GDP. For countries in the second section, the difference is even more dramatic—8.7 percent of GDP against a programmed increase in reserves of 1½ percent of GDP, although a number of these countries are oil exporters that enjoyed a positive terms of trade boost from higher oil prices. As such, capital outflows are likely to have forced some of these countries to adjust their current account balances by more than would be indicated by considerations of debt sustainability.

IMF-supported programs in low-income countries present a sharply contrasting picture of external adjustment. First, the positive relationship between programmed current account adjustment and the country's initial external debt characteristic of the middle-income countries is not evident for the low-income countries—indeed, the relationship is slightly negative (Figure 7). Second, actual current account adjustment typically fell short of even this planned adjustment—often because of delays in disbursements of external grants. Facing such a delay, however, not only did these countries not adjust their current account deficits but, on average, they borrowed *more* than the corresponding shortfall. While these results may be consistent with the primary purposes of these programs to promote growth and reduce poverty, they also imply a growing debt burden in the absence of debt relief—corresponding to the persistent debt problems of low-income countries.

Macroeconomic Performance

Beyond external adjustment, national authorities often have a number of other objectives in their economic programs for which they are seeking IMF

Table 2

Macroeconomic Performance of Countries with IMF-Supported Programs[1]

	Number of Observations	Three Years Before Program	Program Period[2]	Three Years After Program
		PRGF-Eligible Countries[3]		
Inflation[3]				
1980–91	169	68	26	73
1992–2002	62	28	16**	8*
Real GDP growth[3]				
1980–91	169	2.1	2.6	2.4
1992–2002	62	2.4	4.1*	3.4**
Standard deviation of growth				
1980–91	169	3.9	3.4	3.2
1992–2002	62	3.0	3.0	2.4
		Non-PRGF-Eligible Countries[2]		
Inflation[3]				
1980–91	104	42	72	55
1992–2002	51	80	39	27**
Real GDP growth[3]				
1980–91	104	2.7	2.0	3.1
1992–2002	51	3.6	2.7	3.4
Standard deviation of growth				
1980–91	104	3.7	n.a.	3.5
1992–2002	51	3.0	n.a.	3.0

Sources: IMF, Monitoring of Fund Arrangements (MONA) and World Economic Outlook (WEO) databases; and IMF staff estimates.

[1] Average annual growth rates over 3-year periods unless otherwise specified.

[2] PRGF-eligible countries: program period is three years and includes the year in which the program begins. Non-PRGF-eligible countries: program period is one year–the year the program begins.

[3] Statistical significance of the average rate relative to the pre-program average rate; * at 1 percent; ** at 10 percent; n.a. stands for "not applicable." PRGF denotes Poverty Reduction and Growth Facility.

Figure 7
Projected, Actual, and Debt-Stabilizing Current Account Balances in Poverty Reduction and Growth Facility (PRGF)-Supported Programs

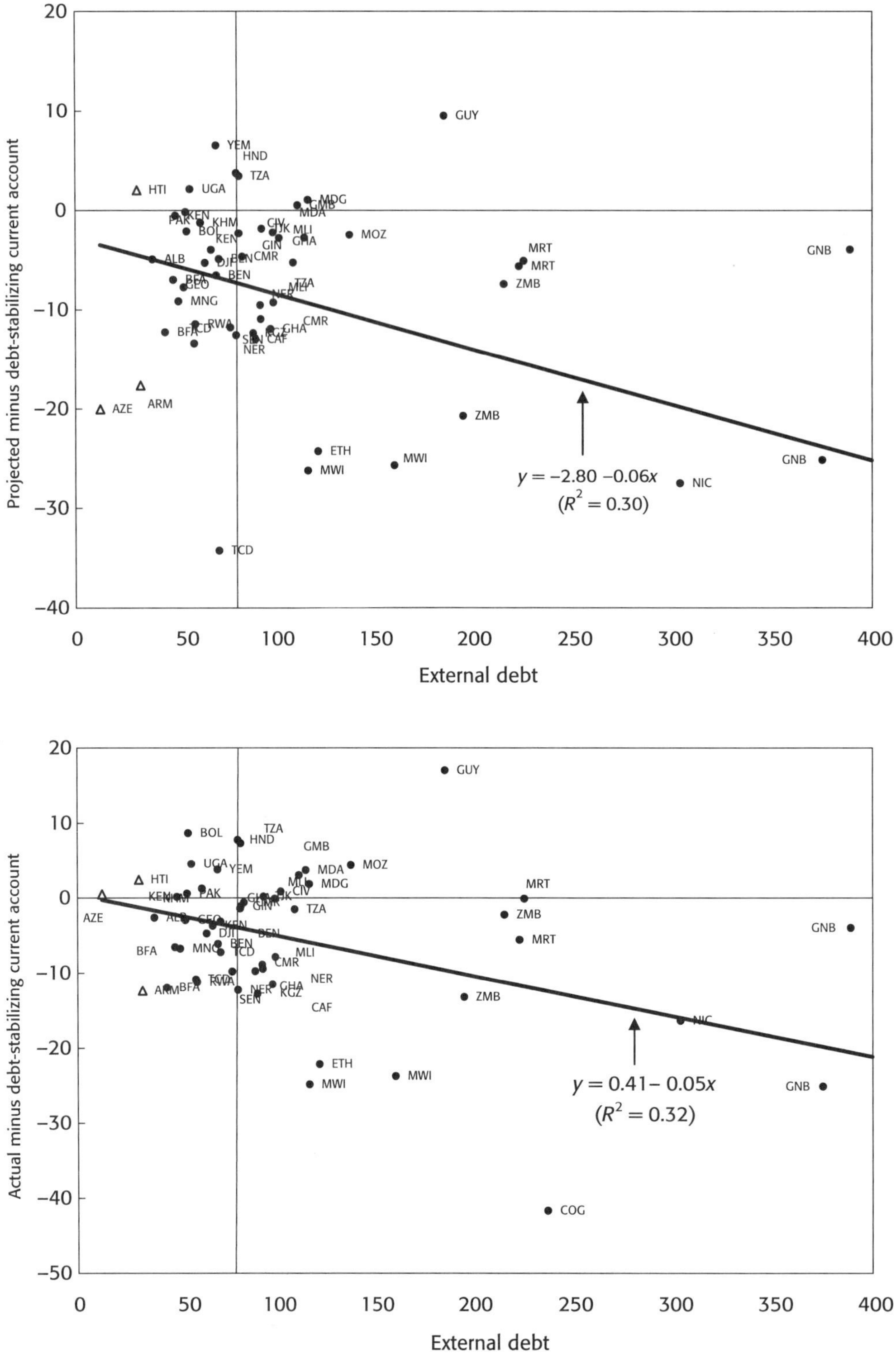

Sources: IMF, Monitoring of Fund Arrangements (MONA) and World Economic Outlook (WEO) databases; and IMF staff estimates.

Notes: Country abbreviations are based on three-letter country codes used in IMF automated database systems. Non-HIPCs (highly indebted poor countries) are depicted by triangles.

Table 3

Explaining Growth in PRGF Countries

(1992–2002, average annual growth rates)

	Coefficient Estimates	Three Years Preceding Program	Three-Year Program	Three Years Following Program
Real GDP per capita growth		–0.56	1.34	0.68
Change in per capita growth		1.90		–0.66
Contributing factors				
G-7 real GDP growth	0.6828***	0.50		0.10
Initial conditions				
Of which				
Initial income level	–0.0595***	–0.27		–0.37
Fertility rates	–0.0090	0.25		0.24
Macro policies				
Of which				
Inflation	–0.0376***	0.02		0.22
Fiscal balance	0.1360***	0.29		–0.01
Structural reforms	0.0285**	0.08		0.01
Shocks (internal and external)				
Of which				
Domestic shocks	–0.0409***	0.50		–0.06
Terms of trade	0.0247	0.08		–0.02
Constant	0.0052*	0.52		0.52
Unexplained		–0.08		–1.29
Number of observations	162	46		46
Number of countries	46	31		31
R-squared adj.	0.23			
F-statistic	26.21***			
Standard error of regression	0.039			

Sources: IMF, Monitoring of Fund Arrangements (MONA) and World Economic Outlook (WEO) databases; and IMF staff estimates.

Notes: Asterisks indicate statistically significant coefficient estimates; *** at 1 percent, ** at 5 percent, and* at 10 percent. PRGF denotes Poverty Reduction and Growth Facility. G7 denotes the Group of Seven.

support. These typically include lowering inflation and achieving macroeconomic stability, raising growth, and promoting poverty reduction. Without attributing outcomes to the IMF's support, Table 2 reports macroeconomic performance under countries' programs. Among the middle-income countries, during the 1990s, annual inflation fell from an average of 80 percent to less than 30 percent for the three years following the program. This contrasts with the experience of the 1980s, when inflation actually rose during the program period—and remained higher in the years following the program than it had been previously. Consistent with the classic adjustment paradigm, growth recovers to its pre-program rates, but there is not a marked improvement in the growth performance of the country.

Among low-income countries, in contrast, not only did inflation come down significantly, growth improved as well. Indeed, during the program period, annual growth was about 1½ percentage points higher, and in the three years following the program, about 1 percentage point per year higher, than the pre-program rate. Applying standard cross-country growth regressions suggests that the coincidence of better inflation performance and higher growth is not coincidental—improved growth in low-income countries can be explained by better macroeconomic policies (as captured by inflation and smaller fiscal deficits) as well as a more benign external and domestic environment (Table 3). At the same time, inasmuch as external resource flows have helped these countries contain their deficits (after grants) and foreign borrowing has limited their recourse to inflationary finance, it remains an open question whether this improved performance can be maintained without an unsustainable buildup of debt or greater grant financing.

Conclusions

This paper contrasts the classic framework of program design and the growing diversity of country circumstances and program objectives for which IMF-supported programs are now being designed. In view of this diversity, the concept of a financial program has changed. In the classic type of program, IMF financing enables a country to undertake needed external adjustment in a more gradual and orderly manner than would be possible in the absence of such support. The program achieves the country's objectives and safeguards IMF resources by ensuring that the financial flows implied by the policies envisaged will enable the country to repay the IMF on the arranged schedule.

Although this classic adjustment paradigm remains—perhaps surprisingly—relevant, the past couple of decades have also seen the emergence of programs with different characteristics. Foremost among these are capital account crises, where capital outflows force external adjustment on the country, and IMF-supported programs in low-income countries, where promoting growth and reducing poverty are the key objectives.

These differing objectives and characteristics of IMF-supported programs are reflected in outcomes. Defining program success requires a metric for judging the appropriate degree of adjustment; medium-term debt sustainability may provide such a metric. Among middle-income countries, especially but not exclusively in capital account crises, capital outflows (or, more generally, a lack of sufficient external financing) sometimes forced larger external adjustments than should be required for debt sustainability considerations. This experience raises important questions of whether larger official financing packages or action to "bail in" private creditors, or both, could result in better outcomes.

In low-income countries, the experience was quite different: adjustment typically fell short both of the programmed current account adjustment and the adjustment required to stabilize external debt ratios. In large part, this reflects the goals of these programs—promoting growth and reducing poverty. However, to the extent that the growth came at the price of mounting debt, it nevertheless raises questions about the longer-term viability of this approach. This experience argues for an increase in the grant element of external financing for low-income countries.

References

Barro, Robert, and Jong-Wha Lee, 2002, "IMF Programs: Who Is Chosen and What Are the Effects?" NBER Working Paper No. 8951 (Cambridge, Massachusetts: National Bureau of Economic Research).

Daseking, Christina, Atish Ghosh, Timothy Lane, and Alun Thomas, 2005, *Lessons from the Crisis in Argentina*, IMF Occasional Paper No. 236 (Washington: International Monetary Fund).

Dicks-Mireaux, Louis, Mauro Mecagni, and Susan Schadler, 2000, "Evaluating the Effect of IMF Lending to Low-Income Countries," *Journal of Development Economics*, Vol. 61 (April), pp. 495–526.

Easterly, William, 2001, *The Elusive Quest for Growth: Economic Adventures and Misadventures in the Tropics* (Cambridge, Massachusetts: MIT Press).

Ghosh, A., T. Lane, M. Schulze-Ghattas, A. Bulíř, J. Hamann, and A. Mourmouras, 2002, *IMF-Supported Programs in Capital Account Crises*, IMF Occasional Paper No. 210 (Washington: International Monetary Fund).

Haque, Nadeem Ul, and Mohsin S. Khan, 1998, "Do IMF-Supported Programs Work—A Survey of the Cross-Country Empirical Evidence," IMF Working Paper 98/169 (Washington: International Monetary Fund).

International Monetary Fund, Research Department, 1987, *Theoretical Aspects of the Design of Fund-Supported Adjustment Programs: A Study*, IMF Occasional Paper No. 55 (Washington: International Monetary Fund).

International Monetary Fund, 2004a, "The Design of Fund-Supported Programs—Overview" (unpublished; Washington: International Monetary Fund).

______, 2004b, "Fund-Supported Programs—Objectives and Outcomes" (unpublished; Washington: International Monetary Fund).

______, 2004c, "Policy Formulation, Analytical Frameworks, and Program Design" (unpublished; Washington: International Monetary Fund).

______, 2004d, "Macroeconomic and Structural Policies in Fund-Supported Programs—Review of Experience" (unpublished; Washington: International Monetary Fund).

Polak, Jacques, 1991, "Changing Nature of IMF Conditionality," OECD Technical Paper No. 41 (Paris: Organization for Economic Cooperation and Development), pp. 7–82.

Przeworski, J.A., and J. Vreeland, 2000, "The Effect of IMF Programs on Economic Growth," *Journal of Development Economics*, Vol. 62, pp. 215–76.

CHAPTER

2 IMF Programs and Growth: Is Optimism Defensible?

Reza Baqir, Rodney Ramcharan, and Ratna Sahay[1]

IMF-supported programs focus on key objectives (such as growth, inflation, and the external current account) and on intermediate policy targets (such as monetary and fiscal policies) needed to achieve these objectives. In this paper, we use a new, large dataset, with information on 94 programs between 1989 and 2002, to compare programmed objectives and policy targets to actual outcomes. We report two broad sets of results. First, we find that outcomes typically fell short of expectations on growth and inflation but were broadly in line with the programmed external current account objectives. Similarly, programmed intermediate policy targets were generally more ambitious than the policy outcomes. Second, and focusing on growth, we examine the relationship between objectives and policy targets, and find differences in the way ambitious monetary and fiscal targets affected the achievement of the growth objective. On the one hand, more ambitious fiscal targets, even when they were missed, led to better growth performance. On the other hand, more ambitious monetary targets tended to be associated with lower growth performance.

Introduction

IMF-supported programs are often described by those on the left as creating hardships on the population because they are said to be "too tight" (Stiglitz, 2002). Those on the right frequently disparage the objectives that were set in the programs but were not achieved. These criticisms refer to the intermediate targets set in IMF-supported programs in the areas of monetary and fiscal policy, as well as to the macroeconomic outcomes—such as inflation, employment, and growth. Are both groups correct? Is there any validity to these criticisms? Or, are the benchmarks by which IMF programs judged simply misplaced?

Defenders of IMF-supported programs would argue that the programmed objectives and targets should not be viewed as forecasts. The objectives are set high so that countries can aspire to achieve them. Similarly, targets are set tight to ensure that policy slippages are kept to a minimum. If targets are missed either because of negative exogenous shocks or because the programs were set too tight, mechanisms in IMF policies and procedures exist to provide waivers for missing these targets. As a matter of fact, ample evidence exists on the waivers given in IMF-supported programs to ensure that IMF loan disbursements are not interrupted unless a major policy slippage occurs. This raises the question of whether tight policy targets and ambitious objectives are deliberate. Also, if they are deliberate, do they help countries achieve better outcomes than they could otherwise?

In an earlier paper based on a much smaller sample size (Baqir, Ramcharan, and Sahay, 2003), we found that (a) IMF-supported programs were, indeed, optimistic—in particular, programmed objectives on inflation and growth were often not fully achieved; and (b) meeting the fiscal target was associated with meeting the growth target. Given the small sample of 29 countries in that paper, however, we were unable to report conclusive results and, in particular, to explore systematically the relationship between objectives and policy targets.

In this paper, we expand the dataset used in Baqir, Ramcharan, and Sahay (2003) to 94 countries and confirm our previous findings on the optimism on growth projections in IMF-supported programs. We then compare the programmed and actual values of intermediate policy targets and objectives separately, and uncover systematic patterns. We also explore the relationship between the intermediate policy targets and the objectives to understand why there are persistent shortfalls in achieving some objectives. On the latter, we focus on a recurrent finding in reviews of IMF-supported programs—the relatively poor performance on meeting the growth objective—by looking at the main intermediate policy targets in monetary and fiscal policy to explore these questions.

This paper is organized as follows. The next section discusses the IMF's financial programming

[1] The paper was presented at the IMF's Annual Research Conference held in Washington on November 4–5, 2004, the proceedings of which are to be published in *IMF Staff Papers*. The authors are grateful to the conference discussant, Michael Clemens, for his comments; Russell Kincaid, Alessandro Rebucci, and Carlos Végh for helpful discussions; Manzoor Gill for excellent research assistance; and Maansi Sahay Seth for her editorial suggestions.

framework. The third section describes the data. The fourth section systematically compares programmed objectives and policies with their actual outcomes. We examine the frequency with which program objectives are met simultaneously. We also look at the extent of adjustments that are programmed in different types of IMF-supported programs (Stand-By Arrangements and arrangements under the Poverty Reduction and Growth Facility) to see whether the adjustments differ across these groups. In the fifth section, we examine the relationship between objectives and fiscal and monetary policy targets, respectively. The sixth section concludes the paper.

The IMF's Financial Programming Framework

The relationship between intermediate policy targets (such as the fiscal balance and monetary aggregates) and macroeconomic outcomes (such as inflation and growth) in IMF-supported programs is derived from the monetary approach to the balance of payments. In turn, this approach produces a framework known as financial programming, which uses a series of macroeconomic accounting identities to link economic growth, inflation, the money supply, the external current account, the budget
18 deficit, and other macroeconomic variables.[2]

The intermediate policy targets derived within the financial programming framework, such as domestic credit and the fiscal balance, are designed to be consistent with the set of macroeconomic objectives—such as growth, current account adjustment, and inflation—chosen to help resolve the country's economic difficulties.[3] In other words, countries that meet the intermediate policy targets should conditionally expect to achieve the macroeconomic outcomes that underlie these targets.

To illustrate the financial programming approach, consider the classical money equation:

$$MV = PY$$

where M is money supply, V is velocity, P is the aggregate price level in the economy, and Y is the aggregate output. Typically, objectives are first established for inflation and growth, yielding P and Y. Next—and importantly—an assumption on velocity is made to arrive at the level of money supply consistent with program objectives. Money creation in excess of this amount would be inflationary. In practice, velocity is often chosen either by examining its historical pattern and making some assumption about how it is likely to be affected by particular factors in the near future and/or by estimating money demand functions. With money supply programmed, and given an external target on the net foreign assets of the country, the banking system's balance sheet yields the maximum tolerable level of net domestic assets:

$$\Delta NDA = \Delta M - \Delta NFA.$$

Given the balance of payments objective underlying the IMF-supported program, the assumption on velocity therefore directly affects the scope for credit creation in the economy. Programming higher velocity reflects an assumption that money demand will be low. In the event that money demand is higher than expected, tight money would drive up interest rates and constrain real activity in the economy, thereby affecting the growth outcome.

Net domestic assets can, in turn, be decomposed into net credit to the private sector (*CPS*), net credit to the government (*NCG*), and other items net (*OIN*):

$$\Delta CPS + \Delta NCG + \Delta OIN = \Delta M - \Delta NFA.$$

This equation gives the other set of relationships between fiscal policy and real activity. Once velocity has been set and the external objective chosen, a higher government deficit financed by the banking system would crowd out credit to the private sector. And to the extent that private sector credit facilitates investment, such crowding out would affect real output.[4] We use these relationships to examine, in the empirical section that follows, how assumptions on velocity and programmed fiscal adjustments affect growth outcomes.

Data

The data for this paper have been assembled from an internal IMF database on IMF-supported programs. In the sampling methodology, a unit of observation is defined as a program country-year: a calendar year in which disbursements were made to a particular country. Before disbursements are made, a document known as a staff report is issued and discussed at a meeting of the Executive Board, the body that decides IMF policy and approves IMF-supported programs. As their name suggests, staff reports contain the IMF staff's assessment of a country's economic situation and policies. They include the

[2] Underlying these identities are several behavioral relationships. Depending on data availability, IMF country desk economists estimate relationships—the typical ones include money demand functions, export and import functions, and investment and saving functions.

[3] Additional performance criteria are often set on structural reforms. These are not derived directly from the financial programming framework but are meant to be consistent with, and support, the policy targets.

[4] The trade-off with private sector credit would be correspondingly less if the deficit were financed from nonbank or external financing.

program's intermediate policy targets and their macroeconomic counterparts that are meant to correct the particular problem(s) that prompted the country to seek IMF assistance. After each such Executive Board meeting, the data in the staff report on the key macroeconomic indicators are recorded in the database.

Typically there are several Board meetings on a country's program in a given year. The staff report issued for each successive meeting contains an updated set of historical and programmed/projected data on key macroeconomic indicators. As such, there are several vintages of the programmed values for any variable of interest. We make use of the information in the evolving forecasts/programs by recording the programmed values for a variable x_t in years t, $t-1$, $t-2$, and $t-3$ from the most recent staff report in that particular year.

Data on outcomes are generally not released until after the end of the year. We therefore define the within-year horizon as the forecast made for x_t in year t. Similarly, a one-year horizon is defined as the value programmed for x_t in year $t-1$. For most empirical work, we focus on up to two-year horizons, since the number of observations declines sharply as the horizon length increases. We measure the actual as the most recent historical observation available on a particular variable for the entire set of staff reports for a country. For example, we record the actual fiscal balance for 1995 as that contained in a staff report dated 1998 if that particular report is the most recent available in the database for that country.

Conceivably, we could expand our data on actual outcomes by combining these data with other popular databases, such as the IMF's Government Finance Statistics (GFS) or International Financial Statistics (IFS). However, aside from growth and inflation, which are generally measured in the same way across databases, nearly all other variables of interest in the areas of monetary, fiscal, and external policies can potentially be measured in different ways across databases. This is particularly true for fiscal policy targets—indeed, staff report data on fiscal measures are often somewhat different from those reported in GFS. Hence, to avoid contaminating our data, we focus only on actual outcomes as recorded in the staff reports.

To facilitate our analysis by type of program, we divide all programs into three groups—the Stand-By Arrangements (SBAs), a subset of SBAs that we call "high-profile" SBAs, and arrangements under the Poverty Reduction and Growth Facility (PRGFs). Borrowings under the SBAs are typically for shorter periods and carry higher rates of charge than those under the PRGF. The high-profile SBAs are distinguished from other SBAs by the greater amounts of access they provide to the IMF's resources—they are also typically covered prominently by the media. We defined "large access" as all programs in the database with access exceeding two billion Special Drawing Rights (SDRs).[5] The list of large-access countries in our sample consists of Argentina, Brazil, Indonesia, the Republic of Korea, Mexico, the Russian Federation, Thailand, Turkey, and Uruguay.

The universe of our data consists of 94 countries for the years 1989–2002. The number of observations varies by country for each variable. Table 1 shows the distribution of available observations on actuals for key variables we use in the empirical work. On average, we have about 7–8 observations per country, which allows us to capture significant variation, both across countries and within countries, over time. We exploit both dimensions of this variation in the empirical work discussed later in this paper. The corresponding number of observations available for forecasts is considerably smaller. For example, a one-year growth forecast is available for 495 country-years, compared with 776 country-years for actuals.

Objectives and Targets: Programmed Versus Actual

To evaluate IMF-supported programs, it is of central interest to know whether both the objectives and the policy targets were met. If the objectives were not met (in either direction), it could suggest that programs were either not sufficiently ambitious or too ambitious. If the policy targets were not met (in either direction), it suggests either that policy efforts by the borrowing countries were insufficient or that the government exceeded its targets. If the policy targets were met but objectives were not (and vice versa), it may imply that the IMF program design was faulty or that the targets and objectives were inconsistent.[6]

Table 2 and Figures 1–3 summarize the programmed and actual outcomes for the main economic objectives in IMF-supported programs—the IMF's Articles of Agreement suggest that the most important goals include inflation, growth, and external current account balance (see Baqir, Ramcharan, and Sahay, 2003 for a detailed discussion). The tables compare the programmed outcomes with the actual ones. For each of the three objectives, the rows indicate values for all programs, PRGFs, SBAs, and high-profile SBAs.

[5] The SDR is an international reserve asset created by the IMF in 1969 to supplement the existing official reserves of member countries. SDRs are allocated to member countries in proportion to their IMF quotas. The SDR also serves as the unit of account of the IMF and some other international organizations. Its value is based on a basket of key international currencies. The SDR equaled roughly US$1.55 in December 2004.

[6] Of course, these inferences can be drawn only after taking into account exogenous shocks that could not have been anticipated when the program was designed and the targets and objectives were set. We assume that shocks are randomly distributed across the programs.

Table 1

Country List and Number of Observations for Key Variables

Country ID	Country Name	Number of Observations for Actuals on				
		Real GDP growth	Inflation	Current account balance	Fiscal balance	Broad money
ALB	Albania	10	9	10	10	10
ALG	Algeria	7	7	7	7	7
ARG	Argentina	12	12	5	12	8
ARM	Armenia	11	11	6	10	6
AZE	Azerbaijan	10	10	9	10	10
BEL	Belarus	3	3	3	3	3
BEN	Benin	13	13	9	13	13
BOL	Bolivia	9	9	9	9	0
BOS	Bosnia and Herzegovina	6	1	0	5	5
BRA	Brazil	6	6	1	6	2
BUL	Bulgaria	12	12	7	11	10
BUR	Burkina Faso	12	12	10	12	11
CAM	Cameroon	12	11	12	12	11
CAP	Cape Verde	5	3	4	3	3
CEN	Central African Republic	9	9	9	9	9
CHA	Chad	11	11	11	10	10
CMB	Cambodia	11	11	9	10	8
COL	Colombia	6	6	3	6	2
CON	Congo, Republic of	8	8	5	8	8
COS	Costa Rica	6	6	5	5	5
COT	Côte d'Ivoire	7	5	6	6	5
CRO	Croatia	10	10	4	9	7
CZE	Czech Republic	4	4	4	2	3
DJI	Djibouti	7	7	6	3	7
DOM	Dominican Republic	3	3	3	3	3
ECU	Ecuador	7	7	5	7	0
EGY	Egypt	7	7	7	7	7
ELS	El Salvador	8	8	8	8	8
EQU	Equatorial Guinea	3	3	3	3	3
EST	Estonia	10	10	8	9	9
ETH	Ethiopia	11	9	11	11	11
GAB	Gabon	9	9	9	9	8
GAM	Gambia, The	4	4	3	2	4
GEO	Georgia	10	7	5	10	9
GHA	Ghana	10	10	10	10	10
GUB	Guinea-Bissau	5	5	5	5	5
GUI	Guinea	8	8	5	8	8
GUY	Guyana	11	11	11	11	11
HAI	Haiti	4	4	4	4	4
HON	Honduras	11	11	11	11	11
HUN	Hungary	7	7	7	7	7
IND	Indonesia	7	7	4	7	2
JAM	Jamaica	7	7	7	7	7
JOR	Jordan	11	11	11	11	11
KAZ	Kazakhstan	8	8	4	8	7
KEN	Kenya	9	9	9	9	9
KOR	Korea, Republic of	6	6	6	6	4
KYR	Kyrgyz Republic	13	12	8	12	7

(Table continues on next page)

Table 1 *(concluded)*

Country List and Number of Observations for Key Variables

		Number of Observations for Actuals on				
Country ID	Country Name	Real GDP growth	Inflation	Current account balance	Fiscal balance	Broad money
LAO	Lao People's Democratic Rep.	11	11	10	11	8
LAT	Latvia	11	11	10	11	11
LES	Lesotho	9	7	7	9	8
LIT	Lithuania	12	12	3	11	9
MAC	Macedonia, FYR of	8	8	8	8	8
MAD	Madagascar	10	10	10	10	10
MAL	Mali	14	11	13	13	13
MAU	Mauritania	13	11	9	11	11
MEX	Mexico	8	8	8	8	8
MLW	Malawi	9	9	9	9	9
MOL	Moldova	10	10	7	10	8
MON	Mongolia	11	10	11	11	11
MOZ	Mozambique	9	9	9	8	8
NEP	Nepal	4	4	4	4	4
NGR	Nigeria	3	3	3	3	3
NIC	Nicaragua	8	8	6	7	7
NIG	Niger	12	12	11	10	11
PAK	Pakistan	13	10	11	12	12
PAN	Panama	8	8	8	8	8
PAP	Papua New Guinea	8	8	8	8	8
PER	Peru	10	10	6	10	9
PHI	Philippines	9	9	9	9	9
POL	Poland	5	5	5	5	5
ROM	Romania	10	10	8	10	8
RUS	Russian Federation	7	7	7	7	7
RWA	Rwanda	6	6	5	6	4
SAO	São Tomé and Príncipe	3	3	3	3	3
SEN	Senegal	11	11	11	11	11
SIE	Sierra Leone	6	6	6	6	6
SLO	Slovak Republic	5	5	4	4	4
SRI	Sri Lanka	4	4	4	4	4
TAJ	Tajikistan	6	6	6	6	4
TAN	Tanzania	8	8	6	7	5
THA	Thailand	6	6	6	3	5
TOG	Togo	6	6	6	6	6
TUR	Turkey	11	11	9	8	7
UGA	Uganda	9	9	9	9	9
UKR	Ukraine	9	9	7	8	7
URU	Uruguay	10	10	9	10	7
UZB	Uzbekistan	3	3	3	3	3
VEN	Venezuela, República Bolivariana de	3	3	3	3	3
VIE	Vietnam	10	10	7	10	9
YEM	Yemen	8	8	8	7	7
YUG	Yugoslavia	4	4	4	2	3
ZAM	Zambia	10	10	5	10	9
ZIM	Zimbabwe	10	10	10	10	8
Total		776	748	649	735	665
Average number of observations per country		8.3	8.0	6.9	7.8	7.1

Table 2
Objectives in IMF Programs: Program Versus Actual

	Program Horizon				Difference (*program* minus *actual*)		
	Two years	One year	Within-year	Actual	Two years	One year	Within-year
Real GDP growth (*in percent*)							
All program years	5.2	4.6	3.5	1.8	3.4	2.8	1.7
PRGFs	5.7	5.3	4.7	3.3	2.4	2.0	1.4
SBAs	4.5	3.8	2.0	0.3	4.2	3.5	1.7
High-profile SBAs	4.1	2.9	1.3	1.1	3.0	1.8	0.2
CPI inflation (*percent, end of period*)							
All program years	5.0	6.0	8.0	10.3	−5.3	−4.3	−2.3
PRGFs	4.3	5.0	7.0	8.4	−4.1	−3.4	−1.4
SBAs	6.0	7.0	9.1	13.2	−7.2	−6.2	−4.1
High-profile SBAs	6.0	6.3	6.6	8.9	−2.9	−2.6	−2.3
Current account balance (*percentage of GDP*)							
All program years	−8.6	−9.1	−9.4	−9.4	0.8	0.3	0.0
PRGFs	−11.4	−12.4	−13.2	−13.9	2.5	1.5	0.7
SBAs	−4.1	−4.7	−4.6	−4.5	0.4	−0.2	−0.1
High-profile SBAs	−2.1	−1.3	−1.3	−1.0	−1.1	−0.3	−0.3

Sources: IMF; Authors' calculations.

Notes: Table reports means by group except for inflation, for which medians due to outliers are reported. All observations are used for each sample. The same general pattern is preserved if sample size is kept constant across columns. The last three columns report the difference between the program columns and the actual columns. PRGFs denotes arrangements under the Poverty Reduction and Growth Facility. SBAs denotes Stand-By Arrangements.

Figure 1
Projection Errors, by Program Horizon: Growth
(Error=projected minus *actual, mean, and 95 percent confidence interval)*

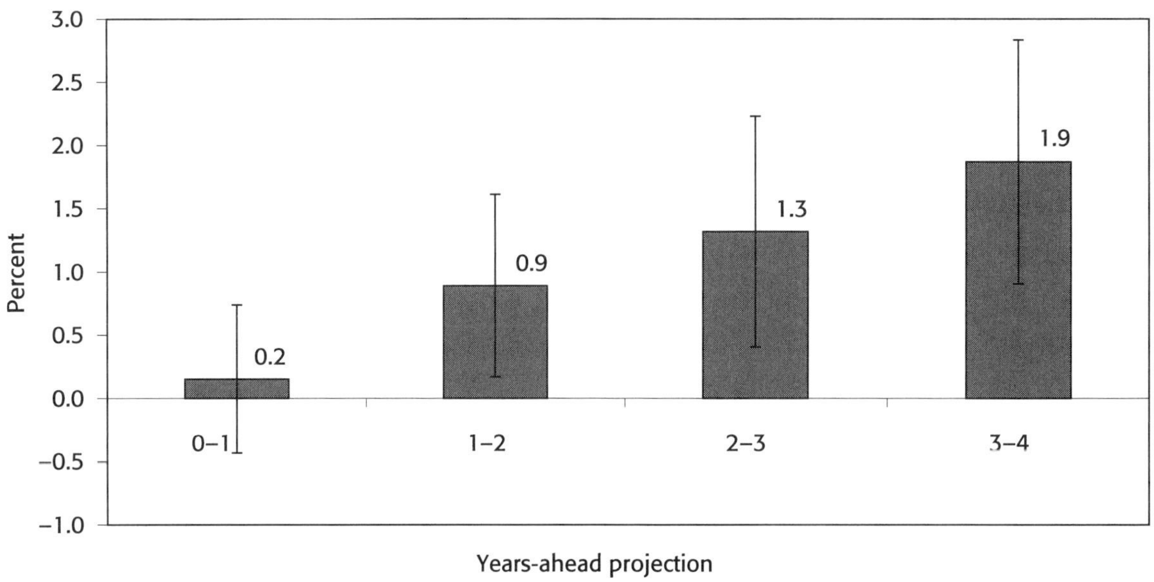

Figure 2
Projection Errors, by Program Horizon: Inflation
(Mean and 95 percent confidence interval)

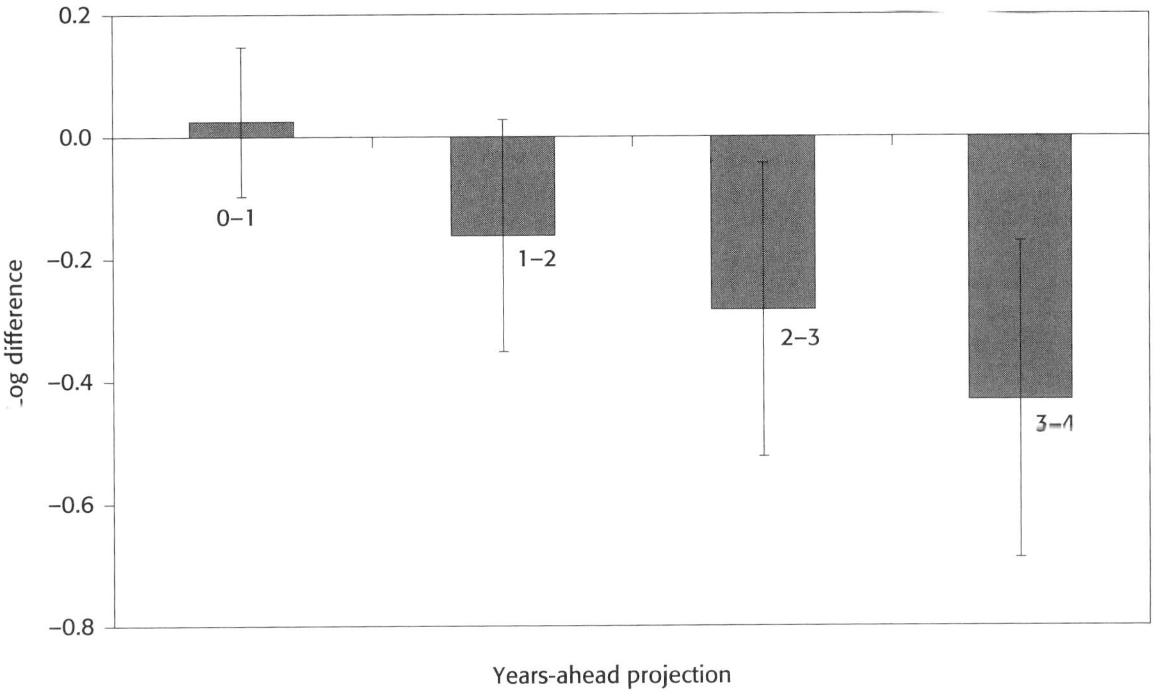

Figure 3
Projection Errors, by Program Horizon: Current Account
(Mean and 95 percent confidence interval, percentage of GDP)

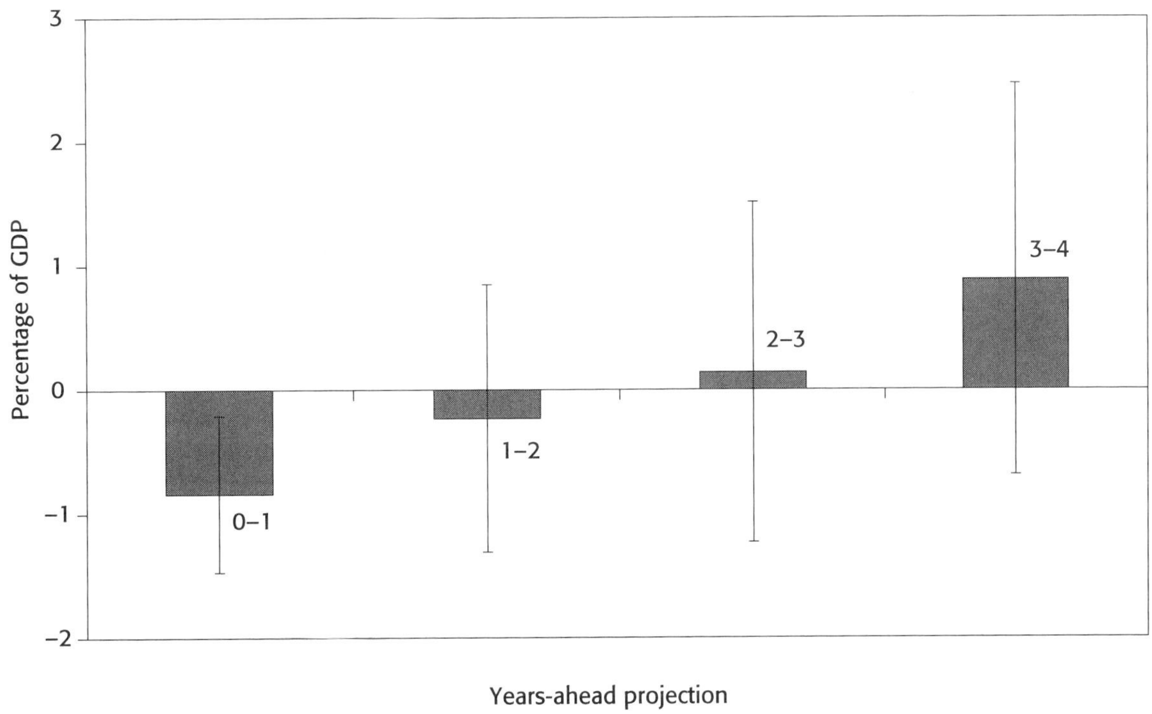

Objectives

Table 2 indicates that for all types and subsets of programs, programmed real GDP growth was consistently higher than actual outcomes. Moreover, programmed growth was progressively higher, the longer was the horizon of the forecasting period (Figure 1). When we compare the forecast errors in absolute terms, we see that the errors were higher in SBAs than in PRGF programs. It is notable, however, that the errors in the high-profile SBAs were lower than in the SBAs and even lower than those in the PRGF programs. This suggests that growth projections are more optimistic in SBAs than in PRGF programs, with one caveat: the projections in the high-profile SBAs were more realistic than in other SBAs and PRGFs, although the direction of the bias was the same in all types of program.

In the second set of rows in Table 2, the programmed and actual inflation rates are compared. As in our results on real GDP growth, programmed inflation is lower than the actual outcomes in all types of program. And as in our results on growth forecasts, the errors decrease as the horizon of the forecasting period becomes smaller (Figure 2). Comparing across programs, the inflation objectives are more optimistic in the SBAs than in the PRGFs. Within SBAs, the high-profile ones had more realistic programmed inflation, although differences between actuals and program objectives were less for the PRGFs. Again, the direction of the bias was the same across programs, which points to optimism toward achieving inflation objectives.

The results on the current account objectives are qualitatively different from those obtained on the growth and inflation objectives. Although the forecasting error falls with the length of the forecasting horizon, as in the previous cases, there is no bias, on average, in all programs. There are some differences across the types of program. In PRGF programs, on the one hand, the programmed current account balance is somewhat optimistic relative to the realized values; on the other hand, in the SBAs, the realized values were higher than the programmed ones. The high-profile SBAs performed best, since this group had the smallest bias compared with other SBAs and PRGFs.

We also explored the unconditional probability of meeting all three objectives at the same time (Figure 4). The figure shows that when all programs are considered, the probability of achieving all three objectives at the same time is about 10 percent. As is to be expected, this probability rises as the horizon of the forecast shortens, but only marginally. Figure 4 also indicates that the probability of meeting the current account objective is the highest, followed by the inflation and growth objectives, respectively. This should not be surprising, since the core function of IMF-supported programs is stabilization and restoration of balance of payments viability.

In summary, all three objectives—growth, inflation, and the current account—are unlikely to be met at the same time. Second, the inflation and growth objectives consistently reflect optimism in the formulation of IMF-supported programs, while the current account balance is met more frequently. Optimism about inflation and growth is highest in SBAs, followed by PRGFs and high-profile SBAs, respectively. Third, the extent to which the targets for the current account balance are exceeded is greatest in high-profile SBAs, followed by other SBAs and PRGFs, respectively. These results indicate that when they are judged by the values of the programmed objectives, the high-profile SBAs ap-

Figure 4

Unconditional Probability of Meeting Program Objectives

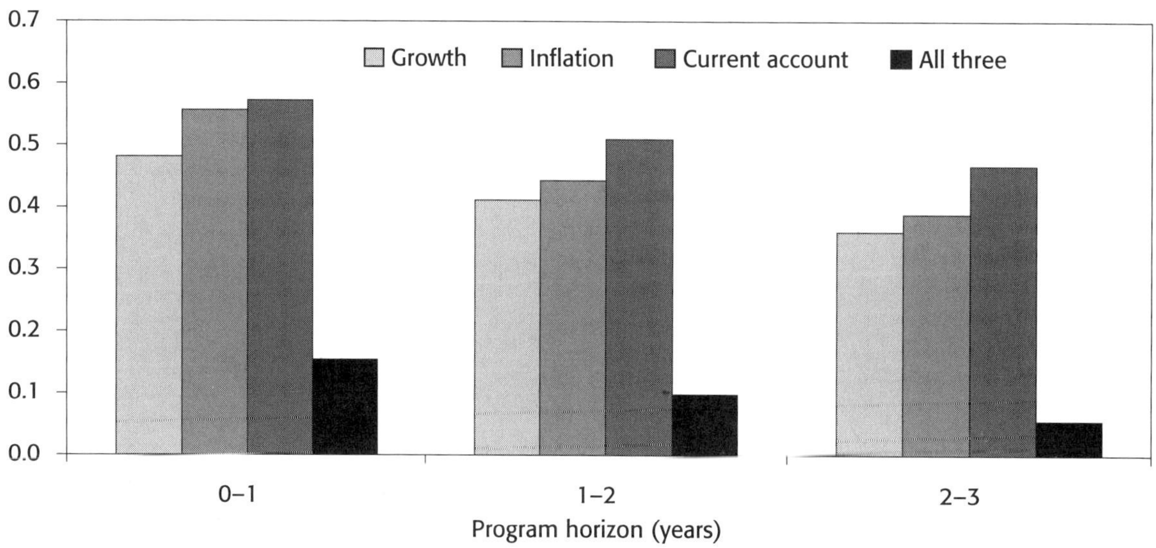

pear to have performed best, since either the bias is smaller than for other programs or the targets are exceeded. A question that arises is whether the IMF does a better job of designing programs in high-profile cases or simply sets them more realistically in such instances because, almost by definition, external scrutiny is greater.

Fiscal Policy Targets

Table 3 compares the fiscal policy targets set in programs with those realized. From top to bottom, the first two sets of rows relate to measures of fiscal balance, the next two to revenues, and the last two to expenditures.

The table indicates that both the fiscal-balance and primary-balance targets (shown in first two sets of rows) are missed consistently in all types of program; and, as expected, the forecast errors shrink as the forecast horizon declines. Three results are noteworthy. First, the targets in SBAs were missed by smaller margins than in PRGFs and in the one- and two-year horizons. Second, the targets in SBAs and PRGFs were missed by larger margins than in high-profile SBAs. Third, and finally, the bias in the overall fiscal balance is in the opposite direction in

Table 3

Fiscal Policy Targets in IMF Programs: Program Versus Actual

(Percentage of GDP)

	Program Horizon				Difference *(program* minus *actual)*		
	Two years	One year	Within-year	Actual	Two years	One year	Within-year
Fiscal balance, broadest coverage							
All program years	−2.5	−3.0	−3.5	−4.7	2.2	1.7	1.2
PRGFs	−3.1	−3.7	−4.3	−5.6	2.5	1.9	1.3
SBAs	−1.3	−2.0	−2.5	−3.8	2.5	1.8	1.3
High-profile SBAs	−1.9	−3.0	−3.8	−3.3	1.4	0.3	−0.5
Primary balance *(excluding grants)*							
All program years	−2.1	−2.5	−2.9	−3.8	1.7	1.3	0.9
PRGFs	−3.5	−4.2	−5.2	−6.1	2.6	1.9	0.9
SBAs	1.8	1.0	0.8	−0.7	2.5	1.7	1.5
High-profile SBAs	0.7	−0.4	0.0	−0.5	1.2	0.1	0.5
Revenues *(excluding grants)*							
All program years	20.1	20.6	21.0	21.4	−1.3	−0.8	−0.4
PRGFs	17.7	17.8	17.6	17.8	−0.1	0.0	−0.2
SBAs	26.7	26.7	27.1	27.3	−0.6	−0.6	−0.2
High-profile SBAs	22.6	21.5	20.4	21.7	0.9	−0.2	−1.3
Revenues *(including grants)*							
All program years	22.8	23.5	23.9	24.2	−1.4	−0.7	−0.3
PRGFs	20.7	21.2	21.3	21.3	−0.6	−0.1	0.0
SBAs	27.0	27.3	27.6	27.9	−0.9	−0.6	−0.3
High-profile SBAs	21.6	21.5	21.1	21.1	0.5	0.4	0.0
Total expenditures							
All program years	25.2	26.3	27.0	28.2	−3.0	−1.9	−1.2
PRGFs	23.8	24.4	24.7	25.9	−2.1	−1.5	−1.2
SBAs	28.2	29.3	30.1	31.3	−3.1	−2.0	−1.2
High-profile SBAs	23.2	24.3	24.1	23.4	−0.2	0.9	0.7
Primary expenditures							
All program years	22.8	23.5	23.9	25.3	−2.5	−1.8	−1.4
PRGFs	21.8	22.0	22.2	23.1	−1.3	−1.1	−0.9
SBAs	25.1	25.8	26.4	28.0	−2.9	−2.2	−1.6
High-profile SBAs	21.7	20.8	19.9	20.9	0.8	−0.1	−1.0

Sources: IMF; Authors' calculations.

Notes: Table entries report means by group. All available observations are used for each sample. The same general pattern is preserved if sample size is left constant across columns. PRGFs denotes arrangements under the Poverty Reduction and Growth Facility. SBAs denotes Stand-By Arrangements.

high-profile SBAs, compared with PRGFs and other SBAs for the within-year forecast horizon. That is to say, the actual outcomes on overall fiscal balance in high-profile SBAs were better than the ones programmed the previous year.

Regarding revenue targets and performance, the pattern is unexpected and striking. The actual revenue outcomes—whether measured with or without grants—are consistently better than the programmed targets for all programs and across almost all time horizons. This pattern is unexpected because we have seen that the growth outcomes were far worse than programmed, which should lead us to believe that the revenue performance would be worse than programmed. The second notable feature is that contrary to our expectations, errors in forecasting do not necessarily fall over time when revenues are measured without grants. It almost seems as if programs were made tighter over time when the targets came close to being reached early in their implementation.

The pattern of expenditure (programmed and actual values) is similar to that of the fiscal balance. Actual expenditures were higher than the programmed ones across all types of program. Also, as expected, forecast errors generally became smaller with the shortening of the forecast horizon. The only puzzling result is for high-profile SBAs: the programmed total expenditures were higher than the actuals, though this result did not hold when primary expenditures were considered. It appears that the interest costs were overestimated for the high-profile SBAs—the interest rate spreads turned out to be smaller than expected, perhaps owing to better performance, as we saw earlier, or to the credibility of the IMF programs themselves that IMF staff members did not fully take into account when the programs were designed.

In summary, the fiscal targets appear to have been met more often in the high-profile SBA programs, although, in general, more fiscal targets were achieved in PRGFs than in SBAs. Although it is generally true that the forecasting errors improved as the horizon shortened, this result did not necessarily hold for revenue projections, which did not change very much with the forecast horizon.

Monetary Policy Targets

Table 4 compares the programmed monetary policy targets with the actual outcomes under IMF-supported programs. To analyze adjustments under programs and to facilitate comparisons across countries, we look at the first differences (rather than the actual levels) of broad money, net domestic assets, and net foreign assets. In addition, the absolute values of velocity are compared across program types.

Several broad patterns emerge in comparing the programmed and actual values of the monetary policy targets. First, targets for broad money and domestic asset growth were generally missed in all types of program. Second, targets for foreign assets were met with greater precision, which is consistent with our earlier finding that external current account objectives are generally met in IMF-supported programs. Third, the errors in forecasting monetary targets were similar across PRGFs and SBAs, but higher for high-profile SBAs.

Interpreting the results on the income velocity of money is not a trivial task. We find that programmed velocity, relative to the realized values, is highest for PRGFs, followed by all SBAs and high-profile SBAs, respectively. In fact, for the high-profile SBAs, the forecasting error (programmed *minus* actual value) was negative. One interpretation of this result is that IMF-supported programs underestimated the pickup in the demand for money in PRGFs and most SBAs but overestimated the increase in the demand for money in the high-profile SBAs. Another interpretation is that the monetary programs were looser for the high-profile SBAs, compared with the other two types of program.

Were Objectives Less Optimistic and Fiscal Targets Less Tight for High-Profile SBAs?

One stylized fact that emerges from the previous subsections is that fiscal outcomes were closer to targets in high-profile SBAs than in other types of program. This could indicate that either program targets were not ambitious—so that it was easier to attain them—or that programs were designed better, so that outcomes were close to expectations. In this subsection, we examine evidence for the first of these two possible interpretations. Table 5 shows programmed fiscal adjustment by type of program and by type of the fiscal measure. Here, instead of comparing actuals to program values, as we did before, we summarize programmed fiscal *effort* (measured as the fiscal measure programmed for next year *minus* this year's actual outcome). The results are striking and systematic: first, the adjustment planned in all SBAs is always more than in high-profile SBAs. The adjustments programmed for high-profile SBAs, however, are not only always less than for other SBAs but also less than for the PRGFs. In fact, virtually all fiscal targets are relaxed in the within-year horizon in the high-profile SBAs.

Program Objectives and Intermediate Policies

IMF-supported programs are designed to set policies that are consistent with achieving certain objectives. As part of this exercise, the IMF's staff produces a "program scenario," which quantifies the objectives (growth, inflation, and others) and the intermediate policies (fiscal balance, monetary expansion, and others) consistent with these objectives. Our approach to examining the link between intermediate policy targets and objectives is to ask

Table 4
Monetary Policy Targets in IMF Programs: Program Versus Actual
(Percentage of GDP)

	Program Horizon				Difference *(program minus actual)*		
	Two years	One year	Within-year	Actual	Two years	One year	Within-year
Broad money							
All program years	22.7	23.4	23.5	25.9	−3.2	−2.5	−2.4
PRGFs	20.1	20.2	19.6	21.9	−1.8	−1.7	−2.3
SBAs	38.4	37.4	32.1	34.3	4.1	3.1	−2.2
High-profile SBAs	41.0	54.5	40.3	36.1	4.9	18.4	4.2
Increase in broad money							
All program years	3.3	3.7	3.6	5.9	−2.6	−2.2	−2.3
PRGFs	2.8	2.7	2.6	4.0	−1.2	−1.3	−1.4
SBAs	6.1	7.2	6.7	8.2	−2.1	−1.0	−1.5
High-profile SBAs	6.3	7.3	6.8	9.9	−3.6	−2.6	−3.1
Increase in net domestic assets							
All program years	1.9	2.1	2.1	2.9	−1.0	−0.8	−0.8
PRGFs	1.4	1.4	1.3	1.6	−0.2	−0.2	−0.3
SBAs	3.3	4.2	3.7	4.8	−1.5	−0.6	−1.1
High-profile SBAs	3.8	5.8	5.4	7.7	−3.9	−1.9	−2.3
Increase in net foreign assets							
All program years	1.4	1.7	1.8	1.9	−0.5	−0.2	−0.1
PRGFs	1.3	1.4	1.6	1.9	−0.6	−0.5	−0.3
SBAs	1.7	2.2	2.0	1.9	−0.2	0.3	0.1
High-profile SBAs	1.2	1.3	0.9	0.5	0.7	0.8	0.4
Velocity							
All program years	4.4	4.3	4.3	3.9	0.5	0.4	0.4
PRGFs	5.0	5.0	5.1	4.6	0.4	0.4	0.5
SBAs	2.6	2.7	3.1	2.9	−0.3	−0.2	0.2
High-profile SBAs	2.8	1.8	2.5	2.8	0.0	−1.0	−0.3

Sources: IMF; authors' calculations.

Notes: Table reports medians by group. The median is a better indicator of the central tendency for monetary variables owing to several outliers in the monetary series. All observations are used for each sample. The same general pattern is preserved if sample size is kept constant across columns. The last three columns report the difference between the program columns and the actual columns. PRGFs denotes arrangements under the Poverty Reduction and Growth Facility. SBAs denotes Stand-By Arrangements.

Table 5
Programmed Fiscal Adjustments, by Program Type
(Percentage of GDP)

	Programmed Change in Fiscal Measure			
			SBAs	
	All	PRGFs	All	High-profile
Fiscal balance, broadest coverage	0.54	0.55	0.53	−0.84
Primary fiscal balance excluding grants, broadest coverage	0.55	0.41	0.80	0.46
Revenue	0.53	0.67	0.33	0.02
Revenue excluding grants	0.36	0.36	0.36	−0.95
Expenditure	0.10	0.29	−0.19	−0.18
Primary expenditure	0.07	0.27	−0.21	−1.06

Notes: Table entries report the fiscal measure programmed for one year ahead *less* this year's actual. PRGFs denotes arrangements under the Poverty Reduction and Growth Facility. SBAs denotes Stand-By Arrangements.

whether achieving the intermediate policy targets helps to achieve program objectives. To address this question, we focus on the deviation of the outcomes from the programmed values (which we will refer to as "projection errors" for lack of a better term).[7] For example, the question posed is "does growth fall further short of its programmed value when the growth-consistent policy falls further short of its programmed value?" If there is no such relationship, or the relationship is in the opposite direction, it would cast serious doubt on the validity of the framework underlying program design. Conversely, the empirical relationship may turn out to be in the expected direction yet growth outcomes may still fall systematically short of programmed values even after controlling for the extent to which policy targets are achieved. That would suggest that there are other elements missing in the programming framework and/or that the optimism in setting growth targets is greater than could be justified by policy shortfalls.

We examine the relationship between the growth objective and two types of macro policies: fiscal and monetary.

Fiscal Policy

We start our investigation by recapitulating the statistics presented earlier on the systematic shortfall in growth outcomes compared with the programmed values. The equation shown in Table 6's second column regresses the projection error in growth on a constant, reflecting the normal approach to examining the extent of bias in a projection. Projection errors are defined as programmed values *minus* actual values. Such errors can be presented at different time horizons. For the sake of brevity, we present the results with the one-year horizon.[8] Thus, the figure in the first column indicates that, on average, actual growth is about 0.9 percentage points less than what was programmed a year earlier.[9]

In the second specification, we regress the projection error in growth on the projection error in the overall fiscal balance:[10]

$$e_{t-s}(g_{it}) = \alpha + \beta \cdot e_{t-s}(f_{it}) + \varepsilon_{it} \qquad (1)$$

where, for any variable x (g and f are growth and the fiscal balance, respectively) for country i, $e_{t-s}(x_t)$ denotes the projection error based on a projection made s periods ahead and defined as $e_{t-s}(x_t) \equiv {}_{t-s}x_t - x_t$. In our notation, ${}_{t-s}x_t$ denotes the s-period-ahead forecast, and x_t simply denotes the outcome for x in period t.

There are two points worth noting in the regression results. First, the coefficient of the projection

[7] As discussed previously, it is not quite right to think of the program numbers as projections in the sense that this term is generally used. Program numbers are best understood as the IMF staff's projections of outcomes conditional on the member country's achieving certain policy targets and adequate implementation of other elements of the program.

[8] While a within-year horizon may be too short for a meaningful test of program design, a two-year horizon may be too long, in that ensuing events can seriously weaken the assumptions on which targets were based. Thus, in general, we focus on the one-year horizon, although we conducted robustness checks for other lengths of horizon. The results for different horizon lengths were generally consistent.

[9] The slight variations from the summary statistics presented earlier were due to small differences in the sample sizes.

[10] We use the broadest available measure of the fiscal balance throughout.

Table 6

Regressions for Projection Errors in Growth and Fiscal Targets

	Dependent Variable					
	Proj. error in growth	Proj. error in growth	Proj. error in growth	Actual growth	Programmed growth	Proj. error in growth
Fiscal measure = Broad fiscal balance						
Country fixed effects	No	No	Yes	Yes	Yes	Yes
Constant	0.890***	0.736***	−4.717	4.995	2.734	−2.538
	(0.000)	(0.002)	(0.233)	(0.268)	(0.242)	(0.519)
Proj. error in fiscal measure		0.251***	0.471***			
		(0.000)	(0.000)			
Actual fiscal measure				0.559***		−0.512***
				(0.000)		(0.000)
Programmed fiscal measure					0.106**	0.431***
					(0.018)	(0.000)
Wald test (p-value)						0.59
No. of observations	313	287	287	735	445	287
R-squared	0.000	0.057	0.309	0.398	0.417	0.310
Fiscal measure = Broad primary fiscal balance, excluding grants						
Country fixed effects	No	No	Yes	Yes	Yes	Yes
Constant	0.890***	0.599**	4.439	−10.465**	7.892***	2.849
	(0.000)	(0.023)	(0.207)	(0.045)	(0.006)	(0.458)
Proj. error in fiscal measure		0.298***	0.276***			
		(0.000)	(0.009)			
Actual fiscal measure				0.502***		−0.345***
				(0.000)		(0.007)
Programmed fiscal measure					0.112**	0.210*
					(0.023)	(0.090)
Wald test (p-value)						0.33
No. of observations	313	207	207	584	361	207
R-squared	0.000	0.061	0.430	0.453	0.444	0.434

Notes: Projection error is defined as the programmed value *minus* the realized value. This table presents results for programmed values at the one-year horizon (see text). "Growth" refers to growth of real GDP in percentage points. Fiscal measures are in percentage of GDP. Parentheses report p-values for the estimated coefficients. An asterisk (*) denotes significance at 10 percent, ** at 5 percent, and *** at 1 percent. The Wald test corresponds to the null hypothesis that the sum of the coefficients on the actual and programmed fiscal measure in the last specification equals zero.

error on the fiscal balance is consistent with the financial programming framework. That framework implies that with other factors remaining the same, a smaller fiscal deficit creates more room for private sector credit while respecting overall conditions for money growth. To the extent that private sector credit is conducive to financing investment and growth, this is expected to allow a greater expansion of output. The coefficient suggests that a 1 percentage point improvement in the extent to which the fiscal target is met is associated with a ¼ of 1 percentage point improvement in the extent to which the growth target is met.

The second notable point is that the growth objective is not met, on average, even after controlling for the extent to which the intermediate policy target is met. This is indicated by the continued statistically significant coefficient on the constant term—the conventional measure of bias. When the programmed fiscal balance is exactly equal to the actual fiscal balance, actual growth performance remains systematically less than programmed, though the magnitude of the shortfall is somewhat less than the unconditional bias when we do not control for the extent to which policy targets are met. Systematically being optimistic in setting growth objectives can have serious consequences for other aspects of program design, particularly for debt dynamics (Helbling, Mody, and Sahay, 2003). Taken together, these two points suggest that although programs get the direction of the framework right, their growth assumptions are more optimistic than can be justified.

In the third data column of Table 6, we allow for country-specific heterogeneity by including a complete set of country fixed effects in the equation. The coefficient on the projection error on the fiscal balance strengthens, suggesting that programs usefully use country-specific information in program design. In terms of bias, in this specification there is one estimated constant per country. The joint test for all country-specific constants being equal to zero is not rejected, suggesting that one constant could have been estimated.[11]

A potential issue of interpretation in the previous specification is that a relationship estimated in the form of projection errors may be suppressing useful information in the respective relationships between actual growth and actual fiscal balance, and between programmed growth and programmed fiscal balance. The next two specifications in Table 6 essentially unravel this relationship. We first regress actual growth on actual fiscal balance and then do the same for the programmed values:

$$\begin{aligned} g_{it} &= \alpha_{1i} + \beta_1 \cdot f_{it} + \varepsilon_{1it} \\ {}_{t-s}g_{it} &= \alpha_{2i} + \beta_2 \cdot {}_{t-s}f_{it} + \varepsilon_{2it} \end{aligned} \qquad (2)$$

In each case, we get a significant relationship, although the magnitude is somewhat stronger for the relationship estimated in actuals. We formally test for whether actuals and programmed values can be pooled in the next column, where we regress the projection error in growth on both the actual and programmed levels of the fiscal balance:

$$\begin{aligned} ({}_{t-s}g_{it} - g_{it}) = (\alpha_{1i} - \alpha_{2i}) + \beta_2 \cdot {}_{t-s}f_{it} \\ - \beta_1 \cdot f_{it} + (\varepsilon_{2it} - \varepsilon_{1it}). \end{aligned} \qquad (3)$$

If $\beta_1 = \beta_2 = \beta$ and the errors are uncorrelated, we would simply get (1).[12] Table 6 shows the proximity between the estimated coefficients on β_1 and β_2. A Wald test for $\beta_1 = \beta_2$ is not rejected, vindicating our original approach.

The measure of fiscal balance we have used so far is the overall balance. There are two potential problems with it. First, to the extent that some revenue consists of fully funded grants—for instance, from official donors—an expansion of the deficit may not crowd out private sector credit and may not adversely affect growth. Hence, a more appropriate measure of fiscal balance in the context of the program framework may be one that excludes grants. Second, it may be more appropriate to look at the primary fiscal balance to more appropriately measure fiscal effort by a country. The bottom panel of Table 6 repeats the above set of specifications for the primary fiscal balance excluding grants. We get the same pattern, with very similarly sized estimated coefficients, and again the Wald test is not rejected.[13]

Implicit in the preceding discussion is the assumption that an improvement in the fiscal balance leads to an improvement in growth. In reality, growth outcomes may well affect the realized fiscal balance. In particular, such endogeneity could arise in two forms. First, buoyancy in revenues may yield procyclical movements in the revenue-to-GDP ratio. Second, government spending may react to external shocks to stabilize output. Externally driven slowdowns in growth may cause the government to increase public outlays. Similarly, in good times, the government may let the private sector take the lead and roll back its own spending. We address each of these potential problems in turn.

As a first step toward reducing potential bias in the previously estimated equations, we start by first differencing our data. Hence, we look at how the change in growth is correlated with the change in the fiscal balance. Although this automatically gets rid of country fixed effects, it allows us to additionally control for country-specific trends. Some countries may be on a "good path" with rising growth and fiscal balances. Using first differences and a complete set of country fixed effects allows us to control for such differences among countries. The first two rows of Table 7 show that the previously estimated relationships in levels survive when estimated in first differences, with and without country fixed effects. For example, an improvement of 1 percent of GDP in the fiscal balance is associated with an 0.5 percentage point increase in growth. The next two rows of Table 7 show that this relationship is not validated from the revenue side. There is no relationship between changes in the revenue ratio (including or excluding grants) and changes in growth. Thus, buoyancy is probably not contaminating our results. The last two rows show that the relationship between the fiscal balance and growth emanates from the expenditure side. A 1 percentage point *increase* in expenditure is associated with about an 0.3 percentage point reduction in growth.

To test whether expenditure, and hence our fiscal-balance measures, may be reacting to output shocks owing to countercyclical fiscal policy, we present results from instrumental variable regressions in Table 8.[14] In this specification, we identify the actual change in the fiscal balance by using the *programmed* change in the fiscal balance and export growth. Since adjustment programmed one year in

[11] The test may be compromised owing to the limited number of observations per country, however; in this specification, there are, on average, only 3–4 observations for *each* country. Since time-invariant, country-specific heterogeneity can be an important source of bias—which could contaminate our results—we include a complete set of fixed effects in all subsequent specifications.

[12] We address issues of endogeneity later in this subsection.

[13] We repeated these regressions for all possible permutations of the fiscal measures along the following dimensions: level of coverage (central government versus broadest available), treatment of grants (excluded from versus included in revenues), and interest expenditure (excluded from versus included in fiscal balance). We found the same general pattern of results reported previously.

[14] Kaminsky, Reinhart, and Végh (2004) find that fiscal policy is, in fact, procyclical for non-industrial countries.

Table 7

Regressions for Growth and Fiscal Targets, First Differences

	Dependent Variable = First Difference of Growth Rate											
	(1)	(2)	(3)	(4)	(5)	(6)	(7)	(8)	(9)	(10)	(11)	(12)
Country fixed effects	No	Yes	No	Yes	No	Yes	No	Yes	No	Yes	No	Yes
Fiscal balance, broadest coverage *(first difference)*	0.526*** (0.000)	0.532*** (0.000)										
Primary fiscal balance excluding grants, broadest coverage *(first difference)*			0.451*** (0.000)	0.458*** (0.000)								
Revenue *(first difference)*					0.046 (0.658)	0.047 (0.700)						
Revenue, excluding grants *(first difference)*							0.103 (0.425)	0.106 (0.499)				
Expenditure *(first difference)*									−0.319*** (0.000)	-0.312*** (0.000)		
Primary expenditure *(first difference)*											[illegible] (0.000)	[illegible] (0.002)
Constant	0.217 (0.425)	0.713 (0.916)	0.180 (0.534)	1.758 (0.786)	0.485 (0.108)	-0.328 (0.960)	0.383 (0.232)	2.306 (0.720)	0.451 (0.121)	1.343 (0.832)	0.488 (0.106)	1.157 (0.855)
No. of observations	609	609	459	459	407	407	349	349	414	414	385	385
R-squared	0.086	0.201	0.088	0.166	0.000	0.066	0.002	0.091	0.047	0.118	0.038	0.126

Notes: The table reports results from regressions of the change in the growth rate on the change in the fiscal measure listed in the first column. "Growth" refers to growth of real GDP in percentage points. Fiscal measures are in percent of GDP. Parentheses report *p*-values for the estimated coefficients. An asterisk (*) denotes significance at 10 percent, ** at 5 percent, and *** at 1 percent.

Table 8

Instrumental Variable Regressions for Growth and Fiscal Targets, First Differences

	Dependent Variable = First Difference of Growth Rate			
	(1)	(2)	(3)	(4)
Country fixed effects	No	Yes	No	Yes
Fiscal balance, broadest coverage *(first difference)*	1.274*** (0.000)	1.188*** (0.000)		
Primary fiscal balance excluding grants, broadest coverage *(first difference)*			0.399*** (0.008)	0.418** (0.016)
Constant	0.261 (0.541)	2.345 (0.723)	0.735* (0.072)	2.440 (0.688)
Test of overidentifying restrictions (*p-value*)				
Sargan test	0.40	0.28	0.62	0.39
Basmann's test	0.40	0.20	0.62	0.48
No. of observations	268	268	199	199
R-squared		0.141	0.060	0.272

Notes: The table reports the results from instrumental variable regressions of the change in the growth rate on the change in the fiscal balance measure. The change in the fiscal balance is instrumented with the change in the fiscal balance programmed 1–2 years ago and with export growth. The test of overidentifying restrictions is the test of the joint hypothesis that the instruments are valid and correctly excluded from the estimated equation. A rejection of the test casts doubt on the validity of the instruments. "Growth" refers to growth of real GDP in percentage points. Fiscal measures are in percentage of GDP. Parentheses report *p*-values for the estimated coefficients. An asterisk (*) denotes significance at 10 percent, ** at 5 percent, and *** at 1 percent.

Table 9
Regressions for Growth and Velocity

	Dependent Variable = Programmed *Less* Actual GDP Growth					
	(1)	(2)	(3)	(4)	(5)	(6)
Country fixed effects	No	No	Yes	Yes		
Programmed velocity *less* actual velocity		0.398** (0.014)	0.635*** (0.003)			0.643*** (0.002)
Lagged programmed velocity *less* actual velocity				0.438* (0.061)		
Programmed velocity					0.645*** (0.003)	
Actual velocity					−0.603** (0.013)	
Fiscal balance projection error (*broadest available measure*)						0.144*** (0.010)
Constant	0.138 (0.333)	0.185 (0.168)	1.033 (0.648)	4.770** (0.023)	−2.072 (0.413)	−1.498 (0.510)
No. of observations	332	279	279	176	279	275
R-squared	0.000	0.021	0.259	0.294	0.259	0.287

Notes: Projection error is defined as the programmed value *minus* the realized value. The table presents results for programmed values at the within-year horizon (see text). "Growth" refers to growth of real GDP in percentage points. Fiscal balance is in percent of GDP. Parentheses report *p*-values for the estimated coefficients. An asterisk (*) denotes significance at 10 percent, ** at 5 percent, and *** at 1 percent.

advance is predetermined relative to the actual realization of the shock in period *t*, we think it is a good instrument for identifying the exogenous variation in the actual change in the fiscal balance. In addition, export growth may capture external shocks to which fiscal policy may react. We run this specification both with and without country fixed effects. In each case, we find that the improvement in the fiscal balance, as identified, likely increases growth. We also test whether we should instead have these variables directly in the regression as right-hand-side variables by running a test of overidentifying restrictions. In each case, the test is not rejected, corroborating our approach.

Monetary Policy

We now turn to examining the relationship between growth and monetary policy in the context of IMF-supported programs. The approach we follow is similar to the one we followed for fiscal policy. The key relationship examined is between growth and velocity. An assumption on velocity is one of the first and integral assumptions made as part of program design. After the growth and inflation objectives have been set, an implicit assumption regarding money demand is made by projecting a specific velocity. Alternatively, a money demand function is estimated and an estimate for velocity is then derived. Setting the amount of monetary expansion under the program is key, since it establishes the overall "tightness" of the program. As discussed in the previous section on financial programming, after the monetary growth and the net foreign asset (NFA) targets have been set, the maximum tolerable expansion in net domestic assets is determined as a residual. Programming higher velocity would systematically lead to tighter monetary objectives, which, in turn, with other things held constant, would constrain total credit to the economy and, hence, output.[15]

Table 9 shows the results of the specifications we ran. One problem we encountered was the significant large volatility in the monetary aggregates typically observed in the early years in the transition countries, when many systemic changes and structural transformations took place. Under such circumstances, money demand was virtually impossible to predict. To be on the safe side, we therefore excluded all transition countries from the regressions

[15] As an alternative, one could also focus on the projection errors in net domestic assets. We found considerable instability in the measures of net domestic assets in our database, however. In part this is due to cases of very high inflation in the sample during which the relationships among monetary aggregates become particularly unstable.

in this subsection. Since this exclusion reduces our sample size, we use the within-year horizons in this section to maximize available observations. The first column regresses the projection error in growth on a constant. The second regression adds the projection error in velocity:

$$e_{t-s}(g_{it}) = \alpha + \beta \cdot e_{t-s}(v_{it}) + \varepsilon_{it} \qquad (4)$$

where v denotes velocity. The positive estimated coefficient suggests that programming higher velocity drives actual growth performance below the programmed value. The next specification adds a complete set of country fixed effects. Controlling for country-specific heterogeneity strengthens the relationship between the projection errors in velocity and growth. To reduce the scope for contemporaneous correlation between velocity and growth, the next specification lags the projection error in velocity. Although the number of observations drops, the coefficient is still significant at 10 percent. The next specification removes constraints on the coefficients on actual and programmed velocity and shows that the two coefficients are close in magnitude and opposite in sign, as hypothesized. A Wald test for $\beta_1 = \beta_2$ is not rejected, indicating that the regression could be run in terms of projection errors.

The last specification in Table 9 regresses the projection error in growth on both the projection error in velocity and the projection error in the broad fiscal balance. These results suggest that even after controlling for the projection error in the fiscal balance, higher-than-actual programmed velocity depresses growth; and conversely, even after controlling for the tightness of the monetary program, a higher fiscal surplus is associated with greater growth.

Conclusion

In this paper, we have attempted to analyze several aspects of IMF program design. We have documented systematically the relationship between programmed values and outcomes for key program objectives and the intermediate policies designed to achieve them. We find that IMF-supported programs achieve the objectives set for external current account adjustment more frequently than those set for inflation and growth. All three objectives are met simultaneously in about 10 percent of the programs. Likewise, the programmed values on intermediate policy targets on the fiscal and monetary variables were generally more ambitious than those actually achieved in the programs.

Second, we have explored the relationship between errors in growth objectives, on the one hand, and errors in fiscal and monetary policy targets, on the other hand. The evidence suggests that an improvement in the fiscal balance is associated with better growth outcomes, and that programming more ambitious fiscal targets helps to achieve higher growth. Fiscal targets are more often missed than met, however. Recognizing the difficulty in meeting fiscal targets, programs may tend to overcompensate by being tougher on the monetary policy side. Programming tight velocity may protect the country against missing the fiscal objective but does so at the cost of dampening growth.[16]

Third, we find systematic biases in growth and inflation projections even after controlling for policy implementation.[17] To the extent that ambitious objectives are used to spur authorities into action, this may not, in itself, be a problem. To the extent that the bias is more than what could be justified on grounds of inadequate policy implementation, however, there is cause for concern. One example of the costs of getting growth projections wrong is in the context of debt dynamics where IMF-supported programs may predict much lower debt-to-GDP ratios than are actually achieved.

One question we were not able to address is whether, in a constrained world where fiscal targets are likely to be missed, overcompensating by having tighter monetary programs is the best strategy for designing programs to achieve more ambitious objectives. Although a tighter monetary program is likely to entail output costs, it may be necessary to promote fiscal discipline, ensure inflation stability, and restore external current account balance (two other key objectives that we do not explore in greater depth in this paper).

Returning to the broader questions that we began with in this paper, we note that it is indeed the case that IMF-supported programs are ambitious with respect to their objectives and intermediate policy targets. In that sense, both those on the right and those on the left are correct: most program objectives are rarely fully achieved, and fiscal and monetary policy targets are ambitious. On the more interesting question of whether such ambition is defensible, this paper has attempted to substantiate that it is justifiable for the fiscal targets, because it helps achieve higher growth objectives than would otherwise be possible. There is also evidence, however, that growth objectives are ambitious to an extent that exceeds what can be explained by the need to ensure consistency with ambitious intermediate policy targets. The latter can, and have tended to, have unwarranted side effects: when growth is programmed too high, IMF-supported programs end up projecting lower debt-to-GDP ratios than those actually realized.

[16] Tighter monetary programs may be designed to bring down inflation, which may necessarily entail output costs. In this paper, we do not explore the relationship between intermediate policy targets and the inflation objective.

[17] Our results contrast with those of Musso and Phillips (2002), which does not find statistical bias in growth projections under IMF-supported programs. We note, however, that their sample, consisting of 54 countries, was much smaller than ours.

Bibliography

Bagci, P., and W. Perraudin, 1997, "Do IMF Programs Work?" Global Economic Institutions Working Paper.

Baqir, R., R. Ramcharan, and R. Sahay, 2003, "IMF Program Design" (unpublished: Washington: International Monetary Fund).

Barro, Robert J., and Jong-Wha Lee, 2002, "IMF Programs: Who Is Chosen and What Are the Effects?" NBER Working Paper No. 8951 (Cambridge, Massachusetts: National Bureau of Economic Research), pp. 1–37.

Bird, Graham, 2002, "The Credibility and Signaling of IMF Programs," *Journal of Policy Modelling*, Vol. 24, pp. 799–811.

Bulíř, A., and S. Moon, 2004, "Is Fiscal Adjustment More Durable When the IMF Is Involved?" *Comparative Economic Studies*, Vol. 46, pp. 373–99. This paper also appears, in somewhat different form, as Chapter 14 in this volume.

Conway, P., 1994, "IMF Lending Programs: Participation and Impact," *Journal of Development Economics*, Vol. 45 (December), pp. 365–91.

Dicks-Mireaux, Louis, Mauro Mecagni, and Susan Schadler, 2000, "Evaluating the Effect of IMF Lending to Low Income Countries," *Journal of Development Economics*, Vol. 61 (April), pp. 495–525.

Ghosh, A., T. Lane, M. Schulze-Ghattas, A. Bulíř, J. Hamann, and A. Mourmouras, 2002, *IMF-Supported Programs in Capital Account Crises*, IMF Occasional Paper No. 210 (Washington: International Monetary Fund).

Goldstein, Morris, and P. Montiel, 1996, "Evaluating Fund Stabilization Programs with Multicountry Data: Some Methodological Pitfalls," *Staff Papers*, International Monetary Fund, Vol. 33 (June), pp. 304–44.

Haque, Nadeem Ul, and Mohsin S. Khan, 1998, "Do IMF-Supported Programs Work? A Survey of Cross-Country Empirical Evidence," IMF Working Paper 98/169 (Washington: International Monetary Fund).

Helbling, Thomas, Ashoka Mody, and Ratna Sahay, 2004, "Debt Accumulation in the CIS-7 Countries: Bad Luck, Bad Policies, or Bad Advice?" in *The Low-Income Countries of the Commonwealth of Independent States: Progress and Challenges in Transition*, ed. by Clinton R. Shiells and Sarosh Sattar (Washington: International Monetary Fund and World Bank).

Kaminsky, Graciela L., Carmen M. Reinhart, and Carlos A. Végh, 2004, "When It Rains, It Pours: Procyclical Capital Flows and Macroeconomic Policies," in *NBER Macroeconomic Annual*, ed. by Kenneth Rogoff and Mark Gertler (Cambridge, Massachusetts: National Bureau of Economic Research).

Khan, Mohsin S., 1990, " The Macroeconomic Effects of IMF-Supported Adjustment Programs," *Staff Papers*, International Monetary Fund, Vol. 37 (June), pp. 195–231.

———, and M. Knight, 1981, "Stabilization Programs in Developing Countries: A Formal Framework," *Staff Papers*, International Monetary Fund, Vol. 28 (March), pp. 1–53.

———, 1985, *IMF-Supported Programs and Economic Growth*, IMF Occasional Paper No. 41 (Washington: International Monetary Fund).

Killick, T., M. Malik, and M. Manuel, 1995, "What Can We Know About the Effects of IMF Programmes?" *World Economy*, Vol. 15 (September), pp. 575–97.

Mussa, Michael, and Miguel Savastano, 1999, "The IMF Approach to Economic Stabilization," IMF Working Paper 99/104 (Washington: International Monetary Fund).

Musso, Alberto, and Steven Phillips, 2002, "Comparing Projections and Outcomes of IMF-Supported Programs." *Staff Papers*, International Monetary Fund, Vol. 49, No. 1, pp. 22–48.

Przeworski, Adam, and J.R. Vreeland, 2000, "The Effect of IMF Programs on Economic Growth," *Journal of Development Economics*, Vol. 62, pp. 385–421.

Reichmann, T., and R. Stillson, 1978, "Experience with Programs of Balance Payments Adjustment: Stand-By Arrangements in the Higher Credit Tranches, 1963–1972," *Staff Papers*, International Monetary Fund, Vol. 25 (June), pp. 119–39.

Santaella, J., 1995, "Four Decades of Fund Arrangements: Macroeconomics Stylized Facts Before the Adjustment Programs," IMF Working Paper 95/74 (Washington: International Monetary Fund).

Stiglitz, J., 2002, *Globalization and Its Discontents* (New York: Norton).

CHAPTER

3 Do IMF-Supported Programs Boost Private Capital Inflows? The Role of Program Size and Policy Adjustment

Roberto Benelli[1]

I analyze empirically whether program size (the size of financial assistance) and policy adjustment matter for the success of IMF-supported programs. I define a program as successful in boosting private capital flows if the initial program projections for net private capital flows are met or exceeded. I find that success is negatively associated with the size of financial assistance, especially in countries with market access, and that projection biases arising from binding constraints on the amount of IMF lending may account for this association. Moreover, policy adjustment seems to have a causal positive effect on the likelihood of program success.

Introduction

What determines the success of IMF-supported programs? A simple approach is to ask whether the financing that a country can raise from private sources meets or exceeds the target set by the program. Among the many criteria, this one is particularly relevant, because restoring capital market access is necessary for program viability when programs can provide only a fraction of a country's overall external financing need and, as a result, have to rely on private sources to help cover the remainder. Therefore, in this paper, I will define a program to be successful if net private capital flows do not fall short of their projections.

The purpose of this study is to analyze what determines program success. At a stylized level, a program consists of financial assistance—whose magnitude is often referred to as the "size of the program"—and policy adjustment; thus, it is worth asking whether these two components contribute to success. Theory does not permit one to make clear predictions on whether larger programs are more likely to succeed. On the one hand, a larger financial commitment may, for example, improve the IMF's incentives for better monitoring and program design, thereby generating a positive response from private investors (see Rodrik, 1996). On the other hand, IMF programs may encourage capital outflows by providing much-needed foreign currency reserves. Likewise, how policy adjustment affects capital flows is unclear in principle. Tight macroeconomic policies are usually considered desirable to restore investor confidence and encourage the return of private capital. However, critics of IMF programs during the Asian crisis in 1997 have seriously questioned that view (see Furman and Stiglitz, 1998).

Besides being straightforward, this approach has four advantages. First, by using program projections for net private capital flows as a benchmark for actual flows, I avoid the problem of defining a "counterfactual" scenario (what would have happened without a program) against which to define program success. Since programs contain projections for capital flows, each program itself provides the relevant benchmark for actual flows, and no counterfactual needs to be constructed.

Second, this approach allows me to deal directly with the implications of the requirement, mandated by the IMF's Articles of Agreement, that financial assistance be provided only in the presence of a proven balance of payments need. As a result of this requirement, programs typically aim at improving the current account balance; in fact, one of the most robust and less controversial findings in the literature on the effects of IMF programs is that the current account balance improves under IMF programs (see Haque and Khan, 1998). In turn, improving the current account tends to lower the country's demand for external sources of finance. Thus, one has to be careful not to confuse the reduction in net capital inflows caused by the external adjustment with the failure to generate private flows. Comparing net capital flows against a program-dependent benchmark eliminates any potential confusion.[2]

[1] I am very grateful to Eduardo Borenzstein, Peter Clark, Carlo Cottarelli, Olivier Jeanne, Gian Maria Milesi-Ferretti, Ashoka Mody, Alex Mourmouras, Alessandro Prati, Rodney Ramcharan, Roberto Rigobon, Jeronimo Zettelmeyer, and especially Paolo Mauro and Alessandro Rebucci for helpful discussions and comments. Any errors that remain are mine.

[2] The current account could improve more than projected because of an unpredictable exogenous shock such as, for example, an improvement in terms of trade, thus reducing the need for capital flows. Although in this case my approach signals a "failure," there will be no consequence for the unbiasedness of the econometric estimates of the effect of programs. This is discussed in more detail in the next section.

Third, this approach allows me to measure the strength (or weakness) of the "catalytic" effects of IMF lending. Although programs, particularly during the capital account crises of the 1990s, may have been designed to catalyze private capitals—that is, spur private capital inflows—the empirical evidence of catalytic effects is weak (see Cottarelli and Giannini, 2002). A direct way to assess catalytic effects is to ask whether the programs generate the net capital flows that have been projected by the IMF at the stage of program design. In this light, a shortfall in actual flows relative to these projections shows that the factors that should have generated catalytic effects have not played the expected role.

Fourth, this approach allows me to estimate how policy adjustment affects program success by isolating the *causal* effect of policy adjustment from its *endogenous response* to external shocks. The endogeneity problem arises because, for example, tight monetary and fiscal policies may not be sustainable if an exogenously determined, unexpected worsening in capital inflows causes a deep recession. Addressing this endogeneity problem requires valid instruments for the policy adjustment that takes place under the program. I use the *projected* policy adjustment—the change in inflation and the change in fiscal balance—as an instrument for the *actual* policy adjustment. The projected policy adjustment should meet the two requirements of a valid instrument: the projections should be correlated with what actually happened and not be correlated with the capital account shocks that occur during the program.[3]

The quality of the macroeconomic data for the sample considered here is not always high. This implies that clear and robust empirical regularities are unlikely to emerge and that all results have to be interpreted with caution. Nevertheless, the empirical evidence presented in this paper seems to provide a consistent picture of the effects of IMF programs. The first main finding is that program success does not seem to be a purely a random event; in particular, success is negatively associated with the size of financial assistance, especially in countries with access to private capital markets. Although this finding could mean that larger programs cause capital outflows, this causal interpretation is somewhat ambiguous, because I find some evidence that biases in projections for net private capital flows may account for the negative association between success and program size. These biases might be caused by the fact that the IMF's limited resources constrain the amount that can be lent in a program, especially when this amount is large (in relative terms). When these constraints are binding or close to being binding, the IMF's staff is more likely to feel pressure to generate relatively more optimistic projections to cover any residual financing gap that cannot be covered by additional program lending. Since this optimism is likely to be larger in larger programs, it could explain why shortfalls in net private capital flows are more likely to occur in larger programs.

The second main finding is that policy adjustment, especially in monetary policy, contributes to program success. Although it is not possible to estimate the causal effect precisely, it is, as expected, considerably smaller than the ordinary-least-squares (OLS) estimate—that is, the estimate that is computed without correcting for policy endogeneity. This finding therefore suggests that, in countries with market access, exogenous capital account shocks are very important determinants of what policy adjustment the domestic authorities can undertake.

The remainder of this section reviews some related literature. The following section presents the main data sources and the empirical framework used in the paper. The third section, "Are the Shortfalls in Net Private Capital Flows Random Errors?" provides some basic stylized facts about the paper's main object of interest—the shortfalls in net private capital flows—and a simple test of projection efficiency. The fourth and fifth sections—"Does Program Size Matter?" and "How Do Capital Flows Respond to Policy Adjustment?" respectively—study whether financial assistance and policy adjustment matter for program success. The sixth, and final, section provides conclusions.

The empirical literature on the effects of IMF programs is large and growing; here I will review only a few papers on the effects of programs on capital flows.[4] Several papers have studied the catalytic effects of IMF programs—that is, the validity of the hypothesis that a program can restore the confidence of international investors and thus spur private capital inflows. After thoroughly reviewing the literature, Cottarelli and Giannini (2002) and Bird and Rowlands (2002a and 2002b) conclude that the evidence of catalytic effects is weak. Ghosh and others (2002) reach similar conclusions in the context of the capital account crises that occurred during the 1990s.

Most of the literature does not take into account the potential bias that can result from the fact that adjusting the current account tends to lower the demand for net private capital inflows. For example,

[3] One problem with this empirical strategy is that the instrumental variable estimate of the causal effect of policy adjustment is inconsistent if the program projections are biased. However, the magnitude of this bias can be quantified and turns out to be fairly small.

[4] A recent example of the more general literature on the effects of IMF programs is Barro and Lee (2002). See Haque and Khan (1998) and Krueger (1998) for surveys of earlier studies on the effects of IMF programs, and Ramcharan (2003) for a recent survey. There is also an abundant literature on the moral hazard implications of IMF programs; see Dell'Ariccia, Schnabel, and Zettelmeyer (2002) and the references therein.

Rodrik (1996) studies the effect of past net bilateral and multilateral transfers on net private capital flows by regressing the latter on the former and finds that the effect of IMF lending is either not significantly different from zero or negative; Bird and Rowlands (1997) reach similar conclusions using an analogous approach. Mody and Saravia (2003) look at *gross* capital inflows (specifically, new bond issues) to avoid confusing the program-induced external adjustment with the lack of catalytic effects, because, if programs have a positive effect on investor confidence, one should observe more issues at better terms. It is not entirely clear, however, how a change in the *net* demand for external funds translates into a change in *gross* flows. Similar conceptual difficulties affect those papers that focus on specific asset classes or investment decisions, such as debt restructuring (Marchesi, 2003) or foreign direct investment (Edwards, 2000); moreover, it is difficult to gauge the macroeconomic relevance of findings based on individual asset classes.[5] Since program projections for net private capital flows have, in principle, to take the current account adjustment into account, my definition of program success is not subject to this problem.

Little empirical research has been devoted to the effect of program size. An exception is the paper by Mody and Saravia (2003), which finds that larger programs help raise the probability of issuing new bonds at a lower spread. My paper sheds light on the effect of size by studying whether size has a systematic relationship with the shortfall in net private capital flows.

Most of the literature does not take into account the fact that policy adjustment is endogenous—in spite of playing a central role in the programs, policy adjustment is often not taken into account at all. One approach that does attempt to control for macroeconomic policies is the Generalized Evaluation Estimator (GEE) discussed in Haque and Khan (1998) and recently applied by, among others, Dicks-Mireaux, Mecagni, and Schadler (2000) and Bulíř and Moon (2003). This approach attempts to estimate the economic policies that would have been in place in the absence of the program; these policy counterfactuals are then introduced as a control variable in the equation for the variable of interest, such as GDP growth. Because it uses policy *counterfactuals* rather than the *actual* policies followed under the program, the GEE approach does not have much to say about the effect of actual adjustment—in contrast to this paper. The approach of this paper is close to the one followed by Musso and Phillips (2001), which analyzes the effect of actual program implementation on programs' projection errors. However, these authors do not consider the fact that program implementation is likely to be endogenous. To control for policy endogeneity, I use the projected adjustment as an instrument for actual adjustment; a similar approach has been used by Berg and others (1999).[6]

Empirical Framework

In this section, I present the main source of the data used in the paper and then discuss the empirical framework that underpins the analysis of the following sections.

Data Sources

The main source is the Monitoring of IMF Arrangements (MONA) database, maintained by the IMF's Policy Development and Review Department. I study the Stand-By Arrangements and extended arrangements that have been included in MONA from its inception in 1992 through 2001. These are the arrangements used by the IMF for its ordinary, nonconcessional lending activity; in the following, I refer to them as "programs." The sample contains 136 programs, including 105 Stand-By Arrangements and 31 extended arrangements.[7]

I construct a residual measure of *net private capital flows* by subtracting from the overall balance the current account balance, official transfers, and official multilateral and bilateral borrowing. This measure of net private capital flows corresponds to the sum of the financial account balance and net errors and omissions in the Fifth Edition of the *Balance of Payments Manual* (IMF, 1993).[8] Using the information available at the start and conclusion of the program (or last available review), I construct measures of the initial program projections for and actual realizations of net private capital flows as percentages of gross domestic product, also provided by MONA.

The timing is delicate. For example, I could compare the projections and the realizations during the calendar year the program is approved, which I refer to as year T. However, this comparison would confuse the preprogram developments with the response to the program. Therefore I choose to compare the

[5] This bias is likely to be less severe in those papers that analyze how interest rate spreads respond to programs, such as Eichengreen and Mody (2001) and Mody and Saravia (2003).

[6] Finally, there are a few related studies on the consequences of tight monetary policy during the Asian crisis (see, for example, Basurto and Ghosh, 2000) or more generally on the effect of monetary policy on speculative attacks (see, for example, Kraay, 2003).

[7] MONA includes only three programs started in 1992. The actual number of programs used in the empirical analysis below will vary depending on data availability.

[8] My definition of net private capital flows corresponds to the sum of the financial account and net errors and omissions except for any transfer and borrowing from multilateral and bilateral entities that may be included in the financial account. This definition implicitly assumes that net errors and omissions are financial account transactions.

projections and outcomes in year $T+1$,[9] ignoring the very short-term response of net private capital flows.

The basic unit of observation is an individual program. Treating each program as a distinct episode raises thorny conceptual difficulties. First of all, any country may have multiple programs over the sample period. Furthermore, many substantial changes—for example, in program length or size—can intervene during a program.

Finally, I use the IMF's World Economic Outlook (WEO) database for series on purchasing-power-parity (PPP)-adjusted gross domestic product and the stock of external liabilities.

Why Use the Shortfalls in Net Private Capital Flows?

Suppose that the net private capital flows (denoted by k) to a country over a certain period following the adoption of a program are governed by the following equation:

$$k = \alpha + k_0 + \beta P + \varepsilon, \quad (1)$$

where α is a constant term; k_0 is a term that captures the effect on capital flows of initial conditions; P is a vector of program variables, e.g., policy adjustment and size of financial assistance; ε is an unobserved shock; and β is a vector of coefficients on program variables. In this framework, the signs and magnitudes of the coefficients in β determine whether and to what extent program variables help generate capital flows. Besides program variables, net private capital inflows respond to exogenous shocks, captured by the term ε. Examples of exogenous shocks are changes in the terms of trade, unexpected rises in export production, or changes in interest rates in advanced countries. As these shocks are, by definition, uncorrelated with the right-hand-side variables in the regression, there will be no bias in the estimated coefficients.

Many problems in empirically evaluating the effects of IMF programs stem from the fact that the econometrician cannot observe precisely the program's initial conditions, i.e., the term k_0 in equation (1). For example, countries are likely to start programs when they face serious economic difficulties, i.e., when k_0 is "unusually" low. Since the program characteristics, such as the size of financial assistance and policy adjustment, are likely to be negatively correlated with k_0—because the larger the initial economic difficulties, the larger the financial assistance and policy adjustment—ignoring k_0 when estimating equation (1) produces inconsistent estimates of β.

[9] Because of data constraints—my dataset is annual—I cannot control for the exact timing of program approval.

The approach based on explicitly modeling the selection of countries into programs (see, e.g., Edwards, 2000; and Przeworski and Vreeland, 2002) aims at inserting an omitted variable into an outcome equation such as (1). Intuitively, this approach compares program countries with countries without programs to estimate the probability of starting a program. This information is then used to construct a variable (the inverse Mill's ratio), which plays the role of k_0 in equation (1), that corrects for the omitted variable bias owing to self-selection. Having corrected for the self-selection problem, the econometrician can consistently estimate β and thus infer the effects of program variables on private capital flows.

In addition to the self-selection problem, k_0 is also related to the size of external adjustment that the country is to undertake under the program. For example, suppose that the program requires that a country considerably reduce its current account deficit. This adjustment would also reduce the demand for net private capital flows, in turn implying a smaller value for k_0. Since the magnitude of the expected external adjustment is likely to be positively correlated with program variables, the omission of k_0 would bias the estimate of β.

Rather than constructing k_0, I use the projections for net private capital flows made by the IMF at the beginning of the program. Using projections to control for the initial conditions has two main advantages. First, I avoid the complications of explicitly modeling the selection into IMF programs. Second, I indirectly take into account the size and nature of the shocks that lead to the program; since these shocks should in principle be taken into account by IMF staff "on the ground" when formulating their projections, they are included in the estimated equation. The main assumption underlying this approach is that the projections are formulated within a uniform and consistent framework across programs.[10]

Finally, to highlight that the shortfall in net private capital flows relative to their projections is my measure of program success, I rearrange equation (1) to work with the shortfall $k-k_0$ as my dependent variable.

Are the Shortfalls in Net Private Capital Flows Random Errors?

This section documents some basic facts about the projections for net private capital flows and their

[10] It is also worth noting that the exchange rate regime does not affect the notion of program success. The exchange rate regime is likely to affect what happens when actual flows differ from their projections but not whether a country receives as much capital as projected at the start of the program. For example, if net private capital flows exceed their projections, foreign reserve accumulation will occur in a fixed exchange rate regime and the exchange rate will appreciate in a pure float.

Figure 1

Distribution of Shortfalls in Year *T*+1 for All Programs

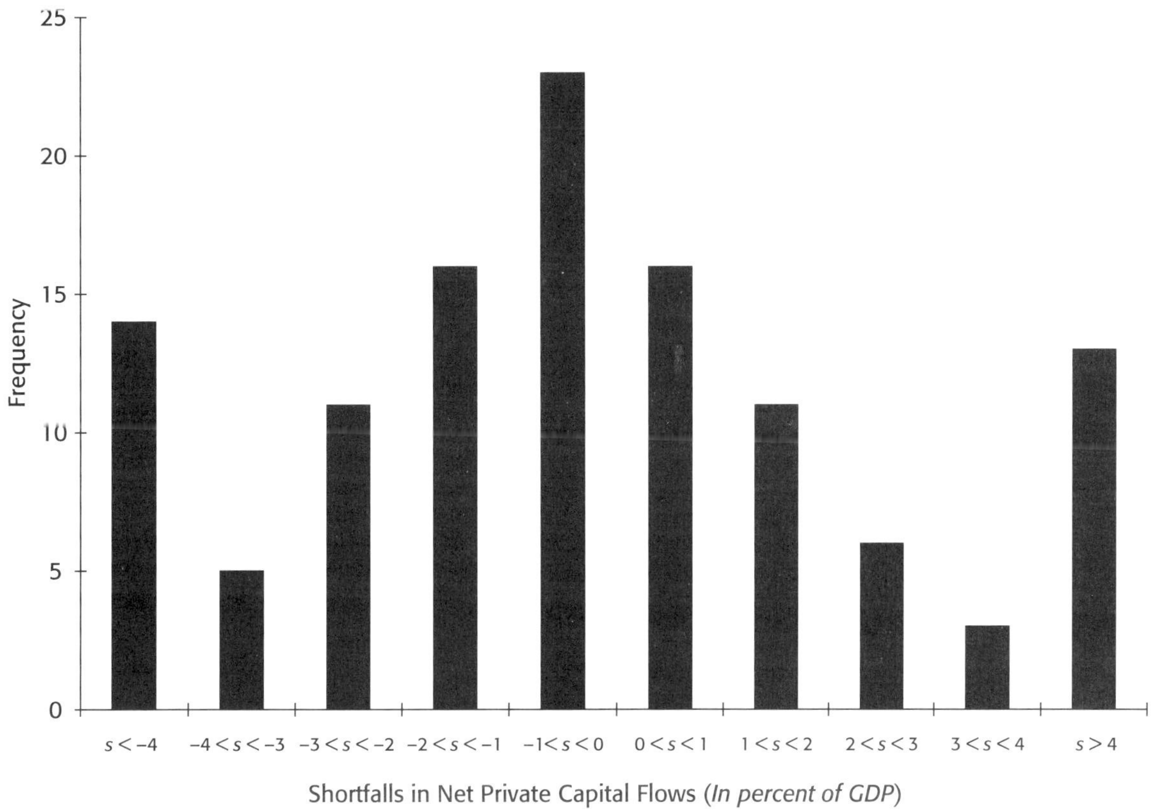

shortfalls and then provides a simple test of projection efficiency.

Some Summary Statistics

Figure 1 plots the distribution of the main object of interest, the shortfall in net private capital flows in year $T+1$ of the program, defined throughout the paper as the difference between projected and actual net private capital flows in percent of GDP. Although the distribution of the shortfalls appears to be fairly symmetric, it is centered below zero, i.e., the projections tend to be above the outcomes. The figure also shows outliers, large positive and large negative shortfalls corresponding to big failures and successes, respectively.

An important characteristic is whether a program is precautionary—that is, whether the domestic authorities state their intention not to draw the resources available under the program. There is empirical evidence that precautionary programs may be particularly suitable for conveying positive signals to private investors (see Mody and Saravia, 2003). To minimize the likelihood that the precautionary nature of a program is endogenous, my definition of "precautionary" includes only those programs that are precautionary on approval and not those that "turn precautionary" at a later stage.[11] This is because turning a program into a precautionary one is unlikely to be an exogenous policy decision. For example, unexpected large capital inflows owing to exogenous external reasons could ease the external financial constraint faced by a country, allowing it to turn its program into a precautionary one.

I identify the following stylized facts from Panel A of Table 1:

- Precautionary programs project larger net private capital inflows than do nonprecautionary programs, in terms of both mean and median. This is likely to depend on the fact that precautionary programs start in more tranquil times.
- In spite of being higher, the projections in precautionary programs tend to be "conservative"—that is, both the mean and median shortfall are negative—the mean shortfall is close to being statistically negative at the 10

[11] Two types of programs are precautionary on approval. The first type consists of those programs that are explicitly negotiated as such. The second type consists of a smaller subset of programs that are approved as nonprecautionary programs but in which the domestic authorities choose not to make the first drawing. I do not consider those programs (13 in the sample) that start as nonprecautionary but turn precautionary at a later stage.

Table 1

Summary Statistics of Projections and Shortfalls in Net Private Capital Flows, by Type of Program and External Source of Financing

	Nonprecautionary Programs							Precautionary Programs						
	Projected NKF[1]		Shortfalls in NKF[1]					Projected NKF[1]		Shortfalls in NKF[1]				
	Mean	Median	Mean	Median	S.D.	Mean=0[2]	N	Mean	Median	Mean	Median	S.D.	Mean=0[2]	N
A: All	−0.42	0.04	0.02	−0.17	5.82	0.48	84	3.09	2.44	−1.11	−0.59	5.57	0.12	35
B: Source of external finance[3]														
Private	−0.76	1.57	0.69	−0.18	4.79	0.28	16	2.9	2.32	0.51	0.61	1.1	0.11	8
Diversified	−2.9	−1.41	4.45	0.65	11.42	0.15	8	2.54	2.21	2.58	0.23	6.1	0.17	6
Public	−2.91	−2.16	0.51	0	4.98	0.31	23	−1.02	−0.32	−5.17	−0.69	9.14	0.07	8
C: Market access[4]														
Yes	−1.04	0.07	1.47	0	6.58	0.1	33	2.79	2.32	1.19	0.49	3.82	0.11	16
No	0.05	0.04	−0.92	−0.49	5.12	0.1	51	3.35	2.74	−3.06	−1.21	6.14	0.02	19

[1] NKF denotes net private capital flows. S.D. denotes standard deviation. N denotes number of programs.

[2] *P*-value for the test of the hypothesis that the mean shortfalls is zero against the alternative hypothesis that the mean is positive (if mean shortfall is positive) or negative (if mean shortfall is negative).

Classification

[3] The main source of external financing is from IMF, *World Economic Outlook*, various issues. (See text for discussion.)

[4] Market access is a dummy variable that takes the value one if the country's main source of external financing is not official (for the developing, nontransition economies) or if the country is included in the JP Morgan's EMBI Global Plus Index (for the transition economies).

percent confidence level. By contrast, the nonprecautionary programs tend to be "right," i.e., both the mean and median shortfalls are close to zero.

- Nonprecautionary programs tend to be more heterogeneous than precautionary programs, both in terms of initial projections and subsequent shortfalls.

Does a country's access to private capital markets affect how capital flows respond to a program? I measure a country's market access using the IMF's WEO classification of developing, nontransition countries by main source of external financing. This classification defines three groups of countries depending on the main source of external financing: countries relying on official financing, on private financing, and on diversified financing.[12] I interpret this classification as a measure of capital account openness because countries with more open capital accounts are more likely to borrow from private sources.[13]

Panel B shows that relying on private sources of external financing does not necessarily lead to larger shortfalls; instead, it is the countries with diversified financing that tend to have the largest shortfalls. Although, as expected, the projected net private capital flows are larger in countries with private financing (in terms of both mean and median), the shortfalls tend to be larger in countries with diversified financing; only for precautionary programs are the median (but not the mean) shortfalls larger in countries with private financing. The average shortfalls are not, however, significantly different from zero, possibly because of the very small number of observations in each subgroup.

To include transition economies, I construct a new dummy variable for market access by taking into account whether a transition economy is included in the JP Morgan Emerging Markets Bond Index (EMBI) Global. Specifically, the dummy variable takes the value of 1 if a transition economy is included in this index and if a nontransition economy (classified by WEO) relies on private or diversified financing.[14] Panel C shows that the shortfalls tend to be larger in those countries with market access (in terms of both mean and median).

A Simple Test of Projection Efficiency

Comparing projections of private capital flows with actual flows is interesting per se because of its implications for projection efficiency. Although statistical tests of the efficiency of forecasts are common in

[12] A net debtor country is allocated to either of the first two subgroups if official sources (including official grants) or private sources (including direct and portfolio investment) account for at least two-thirds of its total external financing in the four years before the country is classified. Countries that do not meet these two criteria are classified as relying on diversified financing.

[13] This notion is somewhat similar to other de facto capital account openness measures that are based on the actual behavior of capital flows; see Edison and others (2002) for a survey.

[14] According to this criterion, 33 nonprecautionary programs (39 percent of the total) and 16 precautionary programs (45 percent of the total) take place in countries with market access.

Figure 2

Projected and Actual Net Private Capital Flows for All Programs

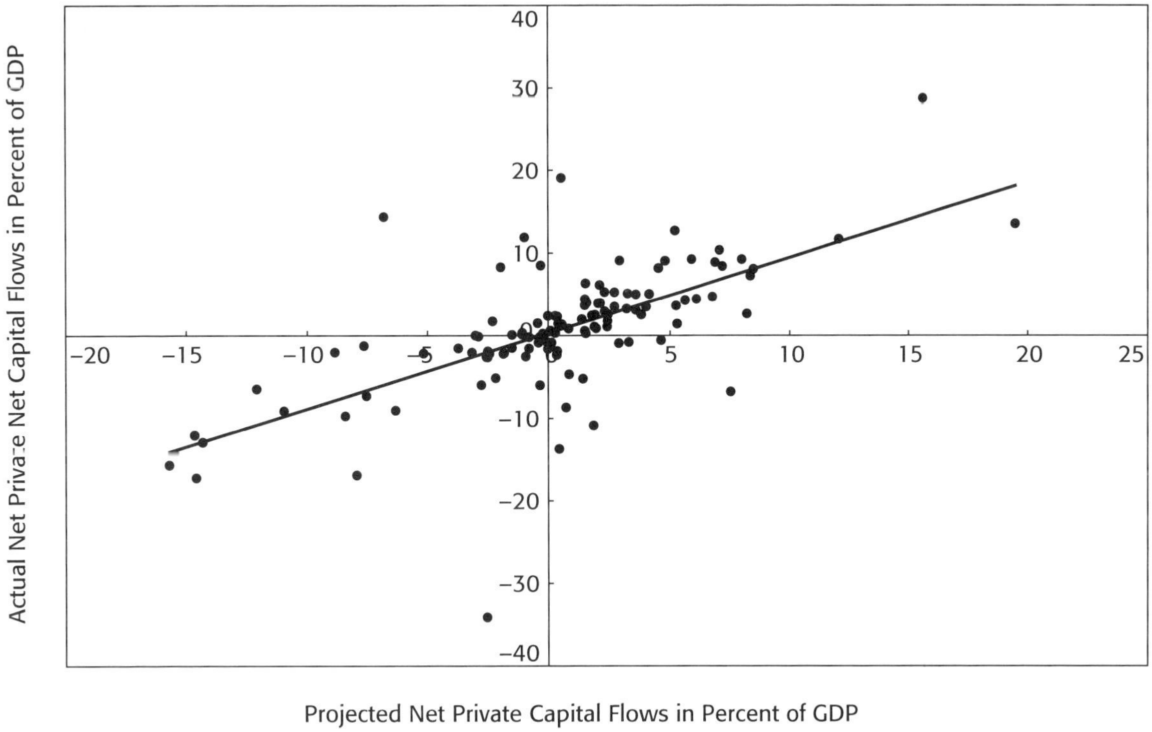

a variety of contexts,[15] they may not be appropriate in the context of programs. Their main limitation is that they assume that the projections are *unconditional* optimal forecasts (in a statistical sense) of the variable being projected. Yet, program projections are conditional on the implementation of the policy adjustment negotiated between the domestic authorities and the IMF; moreover, they may themselves result from negotiations (see Musso and Phillips, 2001; and Mussa and Savastano, 1999).

Figure 2 plots actual net private capital flows in percentage of GDP against their projections; the figure confirms the large variation in projections and outcomes pointed out above. However, no major bias is apparent, since actual flows are roughly distributed along the 45-degree line. (The slope of the least-square line is 0.91, with an intercept of 0.28.)

A formal test of projection efficiency can be based on the intuitive idea that projections should be "right on average." In other words, if projections rely on all the available information, it should not be possible to predict systematically the projection error. For example, if the projections were on average optimistic, lowering them would eliminate the error. This implies that the projection error should not be correlated with the projection itself. In the regression of actual net private capital flows on projections,

$$k = \alpha + \beta \bar{k} + u, \tag{2}$$

efficiency requires that the intercept be 0 and the slope 1. In column 1 of Table 2, based on the sample of all programs, the projections for net private capital flows meet the minimal efficiency requirement (this is also documented by Musso and Phillips, 2001): the slope of the equation is very close to 1. Although the intercept is positive, it is not statistically significant at the usual confidence levels; the joint hypothesis that the constant is 0 and the slope is 1 cannot be rejected at the usual confidence levels.

Columns 2 and 3 carry out the test separately for precautionary and nonprecautionary programs. In column 2, the test of efficiency does not reject the hypothesis that projections are efficient for nonprecautionary programs. On the other hand, column 3 shows that projections do not meet the efficiency requirement for precautionary programs: the slope coefficient is well below 1 (and not statistically significant from 0) and the constant is very large and statistically significant from 0 at the 10 percent significance level; the test statistic of the null joint

[15] See Loungani (2000) and Zitzewitz (2001) for applications to consensus forecasts and equity earning forecasts, respectively. Musso and Phillips (2001) reviews various concepts of forecast efficiency.

Table 2
Test of Projection Efficiency

	(1) All	(2) Nonprecautionary	(3) Precautionary
	Dependent variable: NKF in year $T+1$		
Projection	0.918***	0.972***	0.312
	(0.103)	(0.113)	(0.376)
Constant	0.280	−0.032	3.180*
	(0.536)	(0.641)	(1.614)
R-squared	0.428	0.470	0.048
F-test for unbiased projection[1]	0.44	0.03	1.97
Probability > *F*	0.644	0.970	0.155
Number of observations	119	84	35

Notes: Robust standard errors appear in parentheses. NKF stands for net private capital flows. An asterisk (*) denotes significance at 10 percent, (**) at 5 percent, and (***) at 1 percent.
[1] Test of the joint hypothesis that slope is 1 and constant is 0.

hypothesis that the slope is 1 and the constant is 0 is close to the rejection region. (The *p*-value is 0.155.) However, this result may be driven by three observations corresponding to two large negative shortfalls and one large shortfall: if these observations were dropped, projections would pass the efficiency test.

For future reference, it is worth noting that the small slope coefficient found for precautionary programs implies that the shortfalls tend to grow with the magnitude of the projections; this observation will be useful below to interpret the findings on program access.[16]

These tests, together with the summary statistics previously shown, suggest that the shortfalls in net private capital flows may not be truly random errors. In particular, it is worth asking whether program variables can explain them, in the following sense:

- Are the shortfalls systematically associated with program size? This question is addressed in the fourth section.
- Can macroeconomic adjustment explain the shortfalls? Does the association between shortfalls and policy adjustment, if present, arise from the causal effect of policy adjustment on capital flows or is it due to reverse causation from capital flows to policy adjustment? This issue is studied in the fifth section.

Does Program Size Matter?

At a theoretical level, it is unclear whether program size affects private capital flows. On the one hand, larger programs could help attract private investors because, for example, larger programs could induce better program design and policy monitoring by improving IMF incentives (Rodrik, 1996) or because they could signal IMF confidence in a country's policies.[17] Moreover, by providing foreign currency reserves that can be used to fend off a speculative attack, a larger IMF program could lower both capital outflows and the likelihood of crises (see Morris and Shin, 1998; and Corsetti, Guimarães, and Roubini, 2003). The effect of program size could be nonlinear because programs may need to be as large as the country's external liabilities to restore investor confidence (see Chang and Velasco, 2000)[18] or because the government's optimal adjustment effort could vary in a nonmonotonic fashion with program characteristics (see Morris and Shin, 2003; and Corsetti, Guimarães, and Roubini, 2003). On the other hand, larger programs could simply facilitate the flight of domestic and foreign investors by providing much-needed foreign currency resources. This paper addresses this ambiguity by studying the association between shortfalls in net private capital flows and program size.

A country quota, the country share in the IMF capital, constrains the amount a country can borrow under a program—program "access" in the IMF terminology. Currently, annual and cumulative limits constrain access to 100 percent and 300 percent of quota, respectively. However, the IMF's Executive Board can waive these access limits in case of exceptional circumstances; starting from the end of 1997,

[16] The large point estimate of the constant implies that precautionary programs with low projections for net private capital inflows tend to exhibit large negative shortfalls.

[17] Cottarelli and Giannini (2002) review the channels through which adopting an IMF program could affect the response of international investors.

[18] Partial bailouts may be ineffective, or even precipitate crises (see Zettelmeyer, 2000).

Table 3
Summary Statistics of Program Access

	Nonprecautionary Programs			Precautionary Programs		
	Access (*percent of quota*)	Access (*percent of GDP*)[1]	Access (*percent of external debt*)[2]	Access (*percent of quota*)	Access (*percent of GDP*)[1]	Access (*percent of external debt*)[2]
Mean	59.8	0.46	5.89	40.03	0.33	2.40
Median	43.3	0.40	2.17	27.7	0.27	1.43
Standard deviation	79.84	0.29	9.86	48.94	0.20	3.24
Minimum	11.1	0.10	0.39	15.6	0.12	0.53
Maximum	646.2	1.95	58.67	320	1.07	15.73
Number of observations	97	95	94	39	39	3

[1] Average of purchasing-power-parity (PPP)-adjusted GDP in years $T-3$ through T.
[2] Total external debt, excluding programs with average initial access exceeding 100 percent of external debt.

exceptional access has been granted using a dedicated lending facility, the Supplemental Reserve Facility.[19]

The first data issue is to measure access itself. I measure program access as the *original program access per program year*—that is, access approved at the start of the program divided by the original program maturity (in years). This definition has two advantages. First, it ensures that access is comparable to the variable of interest, shortfalls in net private capital flows in year $T+1$. Second, it ensures that I do not treat programs with longer maturity as larger programs. This definition also implies that I do not take into account that access can change during the program—in fact, augmentations of program access are frequent, although reductions are less frequent. Since I do not include augmentations or reductions as part of program access, I minimize the likelihood that my measure of access is endogenous.[20]

The second data issue arises because, to carry out a cross-program analysis, I need to scale program access. Quotas, the official IMF scaling factor for program access, may not reflect accurately the "true" country size, implying that access as a percentage of quota may not accurately reflect program size.[21] Therefore I consider other scaling factors for program access. The first plausible alternative is to use a country's GDP. In particular, I use the average PPP-adjusted GDP between year $T-3$ and year T to prevent nominal exchange rate movements and output collapses before the program from affecting my measure of program size—although I find similar results if I use GDP in U.S. dollars at market exchange rates. I also scale access by the stock of external liabilities at the end of year $T-1$ because some of the theoretical papers discussed above predict that the stock of external liabilities is the relevant measure to gauge program size.

Although quotas may not accurately reflect program size, they may still matter as a scaling factor because they determine how the IMF operates as a multilateral policy institution. On the one hand, a large program in percentage of quota may signal IMF confidence in a country's economic policies. On the other hand, large access in percentage of quota may signal that the lending constraints are binding or close to being binding. In practice, these lending constraints are likely to be smaller than the official annual and cumulative access limits mentioned.

Table 3 shows that, uniformly across the three scaling factors, precautionary programs tend to grant lower access (in terms of mean and median) and to be more homogeneous (as measured by the standard deviation) than nonprecautionary programs.[22] Furthermore, mean access is larger than median access across the three scaling factors, reflecting the presence of a few very large access programs. A recent, thorough review of access in IMF programs is provided by IMF (2003a, 2003b).

[19] See the IMF (2003a, 2003b) review on access limits. The purpose of the Supplemental Reserve Facility is to lend to countries that face capital account pressures owing to financial contagion.

[20] This problem arises if, as plausible, changes in access take place in response to how private capital flows react to program characteristics. A similar problem would arise if actual disbursements or outstanding credit were used (as done by Barro and Lee, 2002).

[21] For example, although the programs in the Republic of Korea (1997), Brazil (1998), Thailand (1997), and Indonesia (1997 and 1998) stand out as large programs in terms of percentage of quota, they are comparable to many other programs in percentage of GDP.

[22] Table 3 excludes two nonprecautionary programs in transition economies for which access in percentage of external debt exceeds 100 percent owing to the very low initial external debt. Including them causes the standard deviation of access in percentage of external debt to jump to over 80 (from below 10) and the mean to jump to about 15 (from about 5).

Table 4

Shortfalls and Program Access

	(1)	(2)	(3)	(4)	(5)	(6)	(7)	(8)	(9)	(10)	(11)	(12)
	Nonprecautionary Programs							Precautionary Programs				
	Dependent variable: Shortfall in NKF in year $T+1$											
Access *(percent of quota)*	0.017** (0.008)			0.019** (0.009)	0.019 (0.018)	0.073* (0.042)	−0.013 (0.028)	0.143** (0.067)			−0.016 (0.090)	0.006 (0.088)
Access *(percent of average PPP-adjusted GDP)*		2.391 (1.566)							1.721 (3.517)			
Access *(percent of external debt)*			−0.023 (0.041)							−0.116 (0.108)		
Access *(percent of quota × projected NKF)*				−0.001 (0.002)							0.021* (0.012)	
Exceptional access					22.469** (10.082)							
Access *(percent of quota × exceptional access)*					−0.049* (0.026)							
Squared access *(percent of quota)*						−0.001*** 0.000						
Access *(percent of quota × market access)*							0.029 (0.022)					0.111* (0.058)
Constant	−1.034 (0.630)	−0.990 (0.908)	0.269 (0.753)	−1.148* (0.670)	−1.478 (1.063)	−3.346** (1.623)	−0.244 (0.825)	−5.656** (2.210)	−1.642 (1.556)	−0.842 (1.130)	−2.884* (1.678)	−3.177* (1.877)
R-squared	0.065	0.016	0.001	0.071	0.289	0.137	0.08	0.151	0.002	0.005	0.301	0.225
Number of observations	84	81	83	84	84	84	84	35	35	35	35	35

Notes: Robust standard errors appear in parentheses. NKF denotes net capital flows. PPP denotes purchasing power parity. An asterisk (*) denotes significance at 10 percent, (**) at 5 percent, and (***) at 1 percent. Column 4 is based on a sample that excludes programs with access exceeding 100 percent of external debt.

The main finding from the regression analysis in Table 4 is that program access is positively and significantly associated with the shortfalls in net private capital flows only when it is scaled by quotas. The coefficient on access in percentage of quota is positive and significant for both nonprecautionary and precautionary programs (see columns 1 and 8, respectively). By contrast, the other two measures of program access—access in percentage of PPP-adjusted average GDP and access in percentage of external debt—are not statistically significant; for both types of programs, access in percentage of PPP-adjusted GDP is positively associated with the shortfalls (columns 2 and 9) while access in percentage of external debt is negatively associated with them (columns 4 and 10). It is also worth pointing out that the coefficient on access in percentage of quota is an order of magnitude larger for precautionary programs; it is also quantitatively nonnegligible: an increase in access of 10 percentage points of quota is associated with a *larger* shortfall of about 1.5 percent of GDP.[23]

Why is access in percentage of quota significantly associated with the shortfalls in private flows while the other access measures are not? An explanation

[23] If I drop the three outliers that imply that the projections in precautionary programs are not efficient (see the third section, "Are the Shortfalls in Net Private Capital Flows Random Errors?"), the coefficient on access in percentage of quota is only three times as large for precautionary programs.

could be that the positive association between shortfalls and access in percentage of quotas is due to institutional constraints on IMF lending. If lending constraints—expressed in percentage of quotas—limit the amount that can be lent in a program, IMF staff may be forced to generate optimistic projections for private capital inflows to "close" the financing gap that would otherwise occur. Since the pressure to generate more optimistic projections is likely to be stronger when access is large relative to quota, larger programs are likely to be associated with larger projection biases (in the direction of optimism) and therefore with larger shortfalls.

As regards precautionary programs, projection biases may play a role to generate the positive association between shortfalls and program access. Column 11 provides some evidence on this by introducing an interaction term between program access and projections for net private capital flows. I would expect that, if optimistic projections substitute for program access at higher levels of access, the positive association between shortfalls and program access should become stronger as the projections increase (because, at higher access, projections need to be more optimistic). The interaction term turns out to be positive and statistically significant and roughly accounts for the magnitude of the coefficient on access in column 8,[24] while the coefficient on access becomes statistically insignificant. As regards nonprecautionary programs, the interaction term is fairly small and statistically insignificant (see column 4), implying that the association between program access and shortfalls may be genuinely structural, i.e., that larger programs could *cause* larger shortfalls.

Do exceptional access programs account for the positive association between access and shortfalls?[25] Column 5 introduces a dummy variable for exceptional access and an interaction term between this dummy and program access. Interestingly, the coefficient on access in percentage of quota remains very close to the estimate in column 1, but is not significant at the usual confidence levels. The dummy variable for exceptional access is large and statistically significant (at the 5 percent level)—not a surprising finding given that IMF programs during the capital account crises of the 1990s witnessed very large and unexpected net capital outflows (see Ghosh and others, 2002)—and the interaction term is negative and statistically significant (at the 5 percent level). Thus, within the exceptional access programs, larger programs were associated with smaller shortfalls. Although the very small number of cases does not allow general conclusions on the systematic effect of exceptional access, the largest programs do not seem to account for the positive association between program access and shortfalls documented earlier. Column 6 bolsters this conclusion: the quadratic term does not pick up any important nonlinearities.

Does access to private capital markets matter for the association between program access and shortfalls in net private capital flows? Columns 7 and 12 introduce an interaction term between program access and the market access dummy described in the previous section. Relative to columns 1 and 8, where the coefficient on program access does not vary with market access, the coefficient on access is smaller and statistically insignificant for both nonprecautionary (column 7) and precautionary programs (column 12). Instead, program access has a large coefficient when interacted with the market access dummy:[26] the interaction term accounts entirely for the effect of program access. In other words, the positive association between shortfalls and program access is present only in countries with market access.[27]

Why does program access matter only in countries with market access? An explanation could be that restricting the sample to countries with market access simply "cleans" the data by removing countries that rely mainly on official financing and thus do not provide information on how private capital flows respond to programs. Yet, countries without market access may still have significant interactions with private capital markets. For example, capital flight can take place even in countries that officially have low access to private capital markets. This finding could then mean that market access boosts the capital outflows financed by IMF-provided foreign currency reserves. This conclusion is not completely uncontroversial, since projection biases might be more likely in countries with market access because, in these countries, the constraints on IMF lending might be more likely to bind. Overall,

[24] The marginal effect of access is 0.034 when evaluated at the median program access, climbing to 0.112 when evaluated at the median *plus* one standard deviation of access. However, this result is not robust to outliers: the interaction term is negative but statistically insignificant if outliers are dropped.

[25] There are six nonprecautionary programs in the sample that granted "exceptional access" on approval: Mexico in 1995; the Republic of Korea, Thailand, and Indonesia in 1997; and Brazil in 1998 and in 2001. Cases in which exceptional access was granted by augmenting existing programs are not considered here.

[26] The interaction term is significant at the 10 percent level only for the precautionary programs, and is very close to being significant at the 10 percent level for the nonprecautionary programs.

[27] Shortfalls and program access are positively associated only in countries with market access especially when I measure access in percentage of external debt: the coefficient on access in percentage of external debt estimated on countries with market access is positive, large, and statistically significant, and is even larger when I exclude exceptional access cases (the R-squared coefficient climbs to over 40 percent). There is virtually no association between shortfalls and program access in the sample of countries without market access. These estimates are available from the author upon request.

however, it seems difficult to explain the positive association between shortfalls and program access entirely as a consequence of projection biases,[28] i.e., this association provides some evidence that market access tends to lower the likelihood of success.

I can summarize the findings on program access as follows:

- I have found some evidence of a positive association between shortfalls in net private capital flows and program access.
- This evidence is consistent with the hypothesis that larger programs cause private capital outflows. However, the causal interpretation of this association is ambiguous because of potential projection biases. In particular, I have found some evidence that lending constraints may force IMF staff to produce more optimistic projections at higher levels of access, which, in turn, implies that larger shortfalls are more likely at higher levels of access.
- Exceptional access cases or failure to account for nonlinearities do not seem to account for these findings. Moreover, this association is stronger in countries with market access, i.e., market access seems to lower the probability of success (but the effect of market access is likely to be nonmonotonic).

How Do Capital Flows Respond to Policy Adjustment?

How private capital flows respond to policy adjustment has received considerable attention. In this section, I assume that domestic authorities can influence capital flows by adjusting their macroeconomic policies—I do not consider here the other major dimension of policy adjustment in programs, structural adjustment. The econometric problem in estimating the causal effect of policy adjustment is that policy adjustment is endogenous, i.e., it is likely to depend on the developments in the balance of payments, and hence on capital flows. For example, tight monetary and fiscal policies may not be sustainable if a negative capital account shock causes a deep recession. The following simple system describes the feedback between policy adjustment and shortfalls in net private capital flows:

$$\bar{k}-k=\beta p+\varepsilon \tag{3}$$

$$p=\bar{p}+\eta+\lambda\varepsilon, \tag{4}$$

with $E(\varepsilon)=E(\eta)=E(\varepsilon\eta)=0$. Since my purpose is to identify the portion of the shortfalls in net private capital flows owing to policy adjustment, equation (3) decomposes the shortfall in net private capital flows ($\bar{k}-k$) as a sum of the effect of actual policy adjustment (p) and an exogenous shock (ε). This shock is shorthand for all the factors that affect capital flows for reasons beyond the authorities' control, e.g., interest rates in industrialized countries or terms of trade changes; for simplicity, I call it a capital account shock. In equation (4), actual policy adjustment is the sum of the initial projection ($\bar{p}$); an exogenous policy shock (η), e.g., a shock to the preferences of the domestic authorities; and a term capturing the feedback of capital account shocks on policy adjustment ($\lambda\varepsilon$). For example, if $\lambda<0$, then a shock $\varepsilon>0$ raises the shortfall and simultaneously reduces policy adjustment. Whenever $\lambda\neq 0$, the OLS estimate of the policy parameter β is inconsistent because policy adjustment is endogenous.

The main identifying assumption in equation (3) is that the projected policy adjustment $\bar{p}$ does not appear on the right-hand side. This exclusion restriction is based on the assumption that the IMF's staff takes into account all the relevant information on what is known to affect capital flows when it formulates its projection $\bar{k}$, including, in principle, the relationship between the projected policy adjustment $\bar{p}$ and the projected capital flows $\bar{k}$.[29] Under this exclusion restriction and assuming that the shocks ε and η are orthogonal to the projection $\bar{p}$, the projection $\bar{p}$ is an instrument for the actual policy adjustment p in equation (3). However, this instrument may be invalid if the projections $\bar{p}$ and $\bar{k}$ have a common bias, e.g., owing to optimism in the projections; I discuss this possibility at the end of the section.

Focusing on the relationship between policy adjustment and shortfalls in net private capital flows only, as in equation (3), is not necessarily restrictive. This is because the shortfalls are defined relative to the initial projections for private capital flows; these should, in principle, take into account the economic conditions that led to the program. For brevity, in what follows I focus on nonprecautionary programs.

Measuring Policy Adjustment

The first empirical problem is to measure policy adjustment in a way that is comparable across countries.

[28] In particular, it is hard to believe that the statistically and quantitatively strong positive association between shortfalls and program access in percentage of external debt in countries with market access (see previous footnote), in which access in percentage of external debt accounts for up to 40 percent of the variation in shortfalls, is purely due to projection biases.

[29] Working with an equation in terms of shortfalls such as (3) rather than with an equation that includes the projected flows as a right-hand-side determinant for actual flows is not restrictive because the coefficient on projected flows turns out to be very close to one.

Measuring the stance of economic policies is a well-known problem in the literature on cross-country growth regressions, where the economic policy stance is studied as a possible determinant of economic growth (see, e.g., Fischer, 1993), and in the literature on the effects of monetary policy on speculative attacks, where the stance of monetary policy affects the likelihood of a currency attack (see, e.g., Kraay, 2003).

To measure the monetary policy stance, I would ideally use a policy instrument that is directly controlled by the monetary authorities, e.g., the discount rate charged by the central bank on the liquidity provided to the commercial banks. A simple alternative is to measure the monetary policy stance with a policy outcome, e.g., inflation. The main problem with using inflation is that it can be seen as a more general indicator of macroeconomic policy (see Fischer, 1993).

I use inflation to measure monetary policy. Since programs typically require an adjustment in economic policy, I focus on the *change* in the end-of-period inflation rate between years T and $T+1$, even though some policy adjustment may start before the program is formally approved as "prior actions" (see Knight and Santaella, 1997; and Mussa and Savastano, 1999). Given the lags in monetary policy, the inflation rate in year T is unlikely to fully reflect the program-induced adjustment in monetary policy, especially for the programs approved in the later months of the year. However, the inflation rate in year $T+1$ should reflect the policy adjustment owing to the program, and, as a result, the change in inflation between years T and $T+1$ should capture the monetary policy adjustment.

I use two alternative proxies for adjustment in fiscal policy: the change in overall balance and in primary balance between year T and year $T+1$. The overall fiscal balance captures the weight of the public sector in the economy and, in particular, the demand for foreign capital originating from the public sector. However, using the overall balance has the shortcoming that interest payments are likely to depend on the supply of capital flows, implying that the overall balance may be endogenous. The primary balance does not suffer from this shortcoming; moreover, it may better capture the policy effort of domestic authorities. I use both measures of fiscal adjustment in this paper.

Interpreting the association between shortfalls in net capital flows and fiscal adjustment is somewhat problematic because, holding private savings constant, fiscal consolidation raises national savings and correspondingly lowers the need for external financing. If the shortfall rises more than one for one with the improvement in fiscal balance, fiscal adjustment has "perverse" effects on capital flows because the shortfall exceeds the reduction in the demand for external financing owing to the fiscal adjustment. By contrast, if the increase in the shortfall is less than one for one, fiscal adjustment has catalytic effects.[30]

Association Between Policy Adjustment and Capital Flows

When I do not take into account that policy adjustment is endogenous, I find a positive association between the shortfalls in net private capital flows and the change in inflation, i.e., a tightening in monetary policy is associated with a lower shortfall. Column 1 of Table 5 shows that this association is statistically significant at the 5 percent confidence level but quantitatively very small: reducing inflation by 10 percentage points is associated with a smaller shortfall of only 0.02 percent of GDP.

To assess whether large changes in inflation account for this association, I estimate it by allowing the coefficient on inflation change to vary with the magnitude of inflation change. There are reasons to expect that large inflation changes may be neutral because high inflation economies tend to develop sophisticated indexation practices; in the context of economic growth, for example, Fischer (1993) finds no relationship between inflation and growth when inflation is high. Column 2 estimates a piecewise linear function with breaks at –70 and 70.[31] I find that the coefficient on intermediate inflation changes is 0.083, which is larger than the coefficients on large inflation increases and decreases, with both coefficients very close to zero. Although statistically insignificant, the coefficient on intermediate inflation change is economically meaningful: reducing inflation by 10 percentage points is associated with a smaller shortfall of almost 1 percent of GDP. Column 3 shows a similar point estimate when I restrict the sample to programs with intermediate inflation changes.

If restoring investor confidence is critical for how capital flows respond to a program, as is often argued in the literature on catalytic effects of IMF programs, I would expect that the association between shortfalls and policy adjustment is stronger in countries with market access. Column 4 shows that this association is quantitatively stronger for these countries: the point estimate (with a p-value of 0.12) implies that reducing inflation by 10 percentage points is associated with a smaller shortfall of about 1.6 percent of GDP. To gauge its order of magnitude, it is worth recalling that average annual access for nonprecautionary programs is 1.6 percent of GDP. Thus, the reduction in the shortfall owing to a 10 percentage point fall in inflation is as large as average program access!

[30] This problem seems less severe with regard to monetary adjustment because, in contrast to fiscal policy, this effect does not arise directly from the balance of payments identity.

[31] I found virtually identical estimates using higher thresholds but no statistically significant results using smaller thresholds.

Table 5

Association Between Shortfalls and Policy Adjustment for Nonprecautionary Programs

	(1)	(2)	(3)	(4)	(5)	(6)	(7)	(8)
	Adjustment in Inflation				Adjustment in Fiscal Balance			
	All	All	Excluding large inflation changes[1]	Excluding large inflation changes— market access	All	All	Market access	Market access
	Dependent variable: Shortfall in NKF in year $T+1$							
Inflation change[1]	0.002**		0.091	0.159				
	(0.001)		(0.084)	(0.101)				
Moderate inflation change[2]		0.083						
		(0.085)						
Large inflation decrease[2]		0.002**						
		(0.001)						
Large inflation increase[2]		−0.001						
		(0.002)						
Overall adjustment					−0.357		−0.927	
					(0.408)		(0.760)	
Primary adjustment						−0.206		−1.032
						(0.343)		(0.894)
Constant	0.144	0.915	1.277	3.089*	0.329	0.178	1.446	0.806
	(0.678)	(0.219)	(1.363)	(1.661)	(0.767)	(0.733)	(1.049)	(0.888)
R-squared	0.01	0.067	0.078	0.284	0.031	0.011	0.167	0.139
Number of observations	83	83	73	29	82	78	33	30

Notes: NKF denotes net capital flows. An asterisk (*) denotes significance at 10 percent, (**) at 5 percent, and (***) at 1 percent.

[1] Large inflation changes are changes in inflation between years T and $T+1$ above 70 percentage points in absolute value.

[2] Moderate inflation changes, large inflation decreases, and large inflation increases are changes in inflation between −70 and +70 percentage points, below −70 percentage points, and above +70 percentage points, respectively.

Concerning fiscal policy, the association between fiscal adjustment and shortfalls in net private capital flows is negative for both measures of fiscal adjustment, indicating that a larger fiscal adjustment is associated with a smaller shortfall, but statistically insignificant and quantitatively small (see columns 5 and 6 of Table 5). The point estimates imply that a fiscal adjustment of 1 percent of GDP is associated with a lower shortfall of between 0.2 and 0.4 percent of GDP. This association is statistically and quantitatively stronger in countries with market access: in columns 7 and 8, the coefficients on overall and primary adjustment are much larger (in absolute value) and close to being significant (their p-values are about 0.2); the R-squared coefficients are also larger. These estimates imply that improving fiscal balance by 1 percent of GDP is associated with a smaller shortfall of about 1 percent of GDP.

Causal Effect of Policy Adjustment

Although the previous findings show that policy adjustment is associated with lower shortfalls in net private capital flows, it is not clear which way the causation runs, i.e., the association between policy adjustment and shortfalls could be the effect of exogenous capital account shocks on policy adjustment. To control for policy endogeneity, I instrument for the actual policy adjustment using the projected adjustment.

Starting from monetary policy, in equation (3) I instrument the actual inflation change using the projected inflation change. Table 6 reports the two-stage least-square (2SLS) estimates of equation (3). The bottom panel of Table 6 reports the first-stage regressions of actual inflation change on its projection. In the countries with market access (column 2), the projections are statistically significant at the 1 percent level in predicting actual inflation changes and explain a large portion of its variation. The projections are less accurate in the broader subsample that includes the countries without market access (column 1). Overall, there seems to be a sufficiently strong association between projections and actual inflation changes, as shown by the large R-squared coefficients. I discuss at the end of the section whether the second requirement of a valid instrument—that it be uncorrelated with the error term in equation (3)—is likely to be met.

Turning to the two-stage least-square estimates in the top panel, the Hausman test points out a statistically significant difference between the OLS and

Table 6
Causal Effect of Policy Adjustment for Nonprecautionary Programs

	(1)	(2)	(3)	(4)	(5)	(6)
	Adjustment in Inflation		Adjustment in Fiscal Balance			
	All	Market access	All	All	Market access	Market access
	Two-stage least squares Dependent variable: Shortfall in NKF in year $T+1$					
Inflation change[1]	0.030	0.048				
	(0.041)	(0.041)				
Overall adjustment			1.002		0.619	
			(0.792)		(1.706)	
Primary balance				0.686		1.778
				(0.431)		(1.714)
Constant	0.846	2.357	−0.120	0.119	1.918	3.309
	(1.097)	(1.563)	(0.970)	(0.951)	(1.500)	(2.970)
Hausman test statistic (H)[2]	1.09	5.00**	4.00**	11.65***	1.03	3.69*
Probability>H	0.300	0.025	0.045	0.001	0.311	0.055
Number of observations	66	27	68	59	28	22
	First-stage regression Dependent variable: Actual policy adjustment					
Projected inflation change	0.507***	0.915***				
	(0.089)	(0.142)				
Projected overall adjustment			0.684***		0.676	
			(0.189)		(0.532)	
Projected primary adjustment				0.867***		0.767*
				(0.182)		(0.411)
Constant	−3.109	3.406	−0.125	−0.156	−0.667	−1.098*
	(2.284)	(3.393)	(0.365)	(0.377)	(0.722)	(0.549)
R-squared	0.334	0.624	0.166	0.285	0.058	0.149
Number of observations	66	27	68	59	28	22

Notes: Robust standard errors in parentheses. An asterisk (*) denotes significance at 10 percent, (**) at 5 percent, and (***) at 1 percent.
[1] Excluding large inflation changes (larger than 70 percentage points in absolute value).
[2] Hausman test for adjustment in inflation is not based on robust covariance matrix, because when the robust covariance matrix is used, the finite-sample covariance matrix of the estimators' difference is not positive definite.

2SLS estimates for only countries with market access, providing evidence that reverse causality is potentially important, at least in countries with market access. As expected, the 2SLS estimates of the effect of inflation change are smaller than the previous OLS estimates because the latter pick up the effect of exogenous capital account shocks on policy adjustment as well. In column 1, based on all programs, the causal effect of inflation change is quantitatively small and not statistically significant. In countries with market access (column 2), the point estimate is larger, 0.048 (with a p-value of 0.26), but only one-third of the OLS estimate. Although reverse causality explains a large portion of the association between inflation changes and shortfalls, the causal effect of policy adjustment is not quantitatively irrelevant: reducing inflation by 10 percentage points lowers the shortfall by about 0.5 percent of GDP.

Turning to fiscal adjustment, the first-stage regressions show that the association between actual fiscal adjustment and its projection is not as strong as for monetary adjustment. In three out of four cases shown in Table 6, the Hausman test rejects the null hypothesis that the OLS estimates are not statistically different from the 2SLS estimates, indicating that the endogeneity bias in the OLS estimates is potentially important. This result is not surprising given that all the 2SLS point estimates of the coefficient on fiscal adjustment in the top panel of Table 6 have a different sign relative to the OLS estimates in Table 5. However, these estimates are not significant at the usual confidence levels—but in column 2 the estimate is close to being significant at the 10 percent level, and the p-value is 0.11. Only for primary adjustment in countries with market access (column 4) is the coefficient larger than 1, which, according to the previous interpretation, indicates "perverse" effects of fiscal adjustment.

To summarize, on the one hand, the association between shortfalls in net private capital flows and inflation change is not merely the result of reverse causation from capital flows to policy adjustment—it supports the hypothesis that, in countries with market access, tight monetary policy helps stimulate private capital inflows (as claimed by Rogoff, 2003). On the other hand, there is no evidence that fiscal adjustment has either systematic catalytic or perverse effects. The negative association between fiscal adjustment and shortfalls in net private capital flows found in Table 5 thus appears to be due to the reverse causation of capital account shocks on policy adjustment. Given the poor statistical precision of the estimates, though, caution should be used in interpreting these findings.[32]

Concluding Remarks

In this paper, I have defined a program to be successful if the program projections for net private capital flows are met or exceeded. Starting from the premise that a program consists of financial assistance and policy adjustment, I have focused on the size of financial assistance (the "program size") and policy adjustment as determinants of program success. This approach has several advantages: it avoids the thorny issue of defining counterfactual scenarios; it allows me to control for the fact that programs differ in the mix of policy adjustment and financing they prescribe; and it allows me to estimate the causal effect of policy adjustment. Although data quality hampers the statistical precision of some of the findings, the empirical evidence seems to depict a consistent picture of the effects of IMF programs on private capital flows.

The first main finding is that program success is not purely a random event. In particular, success is negatively associated with the size of financial assistance, especially in those countries with access to private capital markets. This empirical association is difficult to interpret unambiguously: it could mean that larger programs facilitate capital outflows, but it could also mean that the IMF often hits a binding lending constraint on the size of its lending. In fact, I have found some evidence that the negative association between success and program size could arise from projection biases. These biases, in turn, seem to arise from the fact that the pressure on the IMF's staff to generate optimistic projections in response to binding lending constraints is likely to be stronger in larger programs.

The second main finding is that policy adjustment—more in monetary policy than in fiscal policy—seems to contribute to program success, especially in countries with market access. Although the causal effect of policy adjustment is not estimated precisely, the estimates are smaller when controlling for policy endogeneity. This suggests that exogenous capital account shocks are important determinants of what policy adjustment the domestic authorities undertake, especially in countries with market access.

[32] Estimating the causal effects of policy adjustment relies on the assumption that the projected policy adjustment is a valid instrument for the actual adjustment. In an appendix of the IMF Working Paper version of this chapter (Benelli, 2003), I show that this problem is not likely to be quantitatively important.

References

Barro, Robert J., and Jong-Wha Lee, 2002, "IMF Programs: Who Is Chosen and What Are the Effects?" NBER Working Paper No. 8951 (Cambridge, Massachusetts: National Bureau of Economic Research).

Basurto, Gabriela, and Atish R. Ghosh, 2000, "The Interest Rate-Exchange Rate Nexus in the Asian Crisis Countries," IMF Working Paper 00/19 (Washington: International Monetary Fund).

Benelli, Roberto, 2003, "Do IMF-Supported Programs Boost Private Capital Inflows? The Role of Program Size and Policy Adjustment," IMF Working Paper 03/231 (Washington: International Monetary Fund).

Berg, Andrew, Eduardo Borensztein, Ratna Sahay, and Jeromin Zettelmeyer, 1999, "The Evolution of Output in Transition Economies: Explaining the Differences," IMF Working Paper 99/73 (Washington: International Monetary Fund).

Bird, Graham, and Dane Rowlands, 1997, "The Catalytic Effects of Lending by the International Financial Institutions," *World Economy*, Vol. 20, No. 2, pp. 955–75.

———, 2002a, "IMF Lending: How Is It Affected by Economic, Political and Institutional Factors?" *Policy Reform*, Vol. 4, pp. 243–70.

———, 2002b, "Do IMF Programmes Have a Catalytic Effect on Other International Capital Flows?" *Oxford Development Studies*, Vol. 30, No. 3, pp. 229–49.

Bulíř, Aleš, and Soojin Moon, 2003, "Do IMF-Supported Programs Help Make Fiscal Adjustment More Durable?" IMF Working Paper 03/38 (Washington: International Monetary Fund). This paper also appears, in somewhat different form, as Chapter 14 in this volume.

Chang, Roberto, and Andrés Velasco, 2000, "Liquidity Crises in Emerging Markets: Theory and Policy," *NBER Macroeconomics Annual 1999*, ed. by Ben S. Bernanke and Julio Rotemberg (Cambridge, Massachusetts: MIT Press).

Corsetti, Giancarlo, Bernardo Guimarães, and Nouriel Roubini, 2003, "The Trade-Off Between an International Lender of Last Resort to Deal with Liquidity Crises and Moral Hazard Distortions: A Model of the IMF's Catalytic Finance Effect," NBER Working Paper No. 10125 (Cambridge, Massachusetts: National Bureau of Economic Research).

Cottarelli, Carlo, and Curzio Giannini, 2002, "Bedfellows, Hostages, or Perfect Strangers? Global Capital Markets and the Catalytic Effect of IMF Crisis Lending," IMF Working Paper 02/193 (Washington:

International Monetary Fund). This paper also appears, in somewhat different form, as Chapter 12 in this volume.

Dell'Ariccia, Giovanni, Isabel Schnabel, and Jeromin Zettelmeyer, 2002, "Moral Hazard and International Crisis Lending: A Test," IMF Working Paper 02/181 (Washington: International Monetary Fund).

Dicks-Mireaux, Louis, Mauro Mecagni, and Susan Schadler, 2000, "Evaluating the Effect of IMF Lending to Low-Income Countries," *Journal of Development Economics*, Vol. 61 (April), pp. 495–525.

Edison, Hali, Michael Klein, Luca A. Ricci, and Torsten M. Sløk, 2002, "Capital Account Liberalization and Economic Performance: Survey and Synthesis," IMF Working Paper 02/120 (Washington: International Monetary Fund).

Edwards, Martin S., 2000, "Reevaluating the Catalytic Effects of IMF Programs," paper presented at the Annual Meeting of the American Political Science Association, Washington, September.

Eichengreen, Barry, and Ashoka Mody, 2001, "Bail Ins, Bailouts, and Borrowing Costs," *Staff Papers*, International Monetary Fund, Vol. 47, Special Issue, pp. 155–87.

Fischer, Stanley, 1993, "The Role of Macroeconomic Factors in Growth," *Journal of Monetary Economics*, Vol. 32, pp. 485–512.

Furman, Jason, and Joseph E. Stiglitz, 1998, "Economic Crises: Evidence and Insight from East Asia," *Brookings Papers on Economic Activity: 2*, Brookings Institution, pp. 1–135.

Ghosh, Atish, Timothy Lane, Marianne Schulze-Ghattas, Aleš Bulíř, Javier Hamann, and Alex Mourmouras, 2002, *IMF-Supported Programs in Capital Account Crises*, IMF Occasional Paper No. 210 (Washington: International Monetary Fund).

Haque, Nadeem Ul, and Mohsin S. Khan, 1998, "Do IMF-Supported Programs Work? A Survey of the Cross-Country Empirical Evidence," IMF Working Paper 98/169 (Washington: International Monetary Fund).

International Monetary Fund (IMF), 1993, *Balance of Payments Manual*, Fifth Edition (Washington: International Monetary Fund).

———, 2003a, "Review of Access Policy Under the Credit Tranches and the Extended Fund Facility," available on the Web at *http://www.imf.org/external/np/tre/access/2003/011403a.htm*.

———, 2003b, "Access Policy in Capital Account Crises—Modifications to the Supplemental Reserve Facility (SRF) and Follow-Up Issues Related to Exceptional Access Policy," available on the Web at *http://www.imf.org/external/np/tre/access/2003/pdf/011403.pdf*.

Knight, Malcolm, and Julio A. Santaella, 1997, "Economic Determinants of IMF Financial Arrangements," *Journal of Development Economics*, Vol. 54, pp. 405–36.

Kraay, Aart, 2003, "Do High Interest Rates Defend Currencies During Speculative Attacks?" *Journal of International Economics*, Vol. 59, pp. 297–321.

Krueger, Anne O., 1998, "Whither the World Bank and the IMF?" *Journal of Economic Literature*, Vol. 36 (December), pp. 1983–2020.

Loungani, Prakash, 2000, "How Accurate Are Private Sector Forecasts—Cross-Country Evidence from Consensus Forecasts of Output Growth," IMF Working Paper 00/77 (Washington: International Monetary Fund).

Marchesi, Silvia, 2003, "Adoption of an IMF Programme and Debt Rescheduling: An Empirical Analysis," *Journal of Development Economics*, Vol. 70, pp. 403–23.

Mody, Ashoka, and Diego Saravia, 2003, "Catalyzing Capital Flows: Do IMF Programs Work as Commitment Devices?" IMF Working Paper 03/100 (Washington: International Monetary Fund).

Morris, Stephen, and Hyun Song Shin, 1998, "Unique Equilibrium in a Model of Self-Fulfilling Currency Attacks," *American Economic Review*, Vol. 88, No. 3, pp. 587–97.

———, 2003, "Catalytic Finance: When Does It Work?" (unpublished; New Haven, Connecticut: Yale University).

Mussa, Michael, and Miguel Savastano, 1999, "The IMF Approach to Economic Stabilization," IMF Working Paper 99/104 (Washington: International Monetary Fund).

Musso, Alberto, and Steven Phillips, 2001, "Comparing Projections and Outcomes of IMF-Supported Programs," IMF Working Paper 01/45 (Washington: International Monetary Fund).

Przeworski, Adam, and James Raymond Vreeland, 2002, "The Effect of IMF Programs on Economic Growth," *Journal of Development Economics*, Vol. 62, No. 2, pp. 385–421.

Ramcharan, Rodney, 2003, "Assessing IMF Program Effectiveness" *IMF Research Bulletin*, Vol. 4 (June).

Rodrik, Dani, 1996, "Why Is There Multilateral Lending?" in *Annual World Bank Conference on Development Economics 1995*, ed. by M. Bruno and B. Pleskovic (Washington: World Bank).

Rogoff, Kenneth, 2003, "The IMF Strikes Back," *Foreign Policy*, Vol. 134 (January/February).

Zettelmeyer, Jeromin, 2000, "Can Official Crisis Lending Be Counterproductive in the Short Run?" *Economic Notes*, Vol. 29, No. 1, pp. 13–29.

Zitzewitz, Eric, 2001, "Measuring Herding and Exaggeration by Equity Analysts and Other Opinion Sellers" (unpublished; Palo Alto, California: Stanford University).

CHAPTER

4 Macroeconomic Adjustment in IMF-Supported Programs: Projections and Reality[1]

Ruben Atoyan, Patrick Conway, Marcelo Selowsky, and Tsidi Tsikata

This paper examines the accuracy of IMF projections in 175 programs approved in the period 1993–2001, focusing specifically on ratios of the fiscal surplus to GDP and external current account surplus to GDP. Four potential reasons for the divergence of projections from actual values are identified: (a) mismeasured data on initial conditions; (b) differences between the "model" underlying the IMF projections and the "model" suggested by the data on outturns; (c) differences between reforms and measures underlying the projections and those actually undertaken; and (d) random errors in the actual data. Our analysis suggests that while all are important, incomplete information on initial conditions is the largest contributor to projection inaccuracy. We also investigate the role of revisions over time in projection error, and find that they improve projections for fiscal account data, while the current account continues to indicate a great deal of variability in the revision process.

Introduction

In this paper, we examine the accuracy of IMF projections associated with 175 IMF-supported programs approved in the period 1993–2001. For each program, the IMF staff prepares a projection of the country's future performance. This projection is based on the country's initial situation and upon the predicted impact of reforms agreed on in the context of the IMF program.[2] We focus on the projections of macroeconomic aggregates—specifically, on the ratios of fiscal surplus to GDP and of current account surplus to GDP—during the years immediately following the approval of the IMF program. We will compare these projections to the actual data for the same years.

Our comparison is statistical. We begin with descriptive statistics for the two macroeconomic aggregates, and demonstrate that the projection deviates substantially from the observed value. We then use a simple vector autoregressive model of the determination of these two aggregates to decompose the deviation into components. We find that the "model" revealed by IMF staff's projections differs significantly from the model evident in historical data. We also find, however, that a substantial amount of the deviation in projections from historical values is due to the incomplete information on which the IMF staff bases projections. We provide a complete decomposition of these effects. We also investigate the degree to which revisions to the projection eliminate these deviations owing to incomplete information. We find that revisions tend to approximate more closely the historical data, but that substantial differences remain between the revised projections and the historical data.

The data we analyze come from two distinct sources. The projections (also called "envisaged" outcomes) are drawn from the Monitoring of IMF Arrangements (MONA) database.[3] The data on historical outcomes are drawn from the World Economic Outlook (WEO) database of the IMF

---

[1] A version of this paper was presented at the Conference on the Role of the World Bank and the IMF in the Global Economy, held at Yale University during April 25–27, 2003. An abbreviated version is to be published by Routledge in a volume of conference proceedings.

[2] We will hold to a specific definition of "projections" in this paper. We do not consider projections to be identical to "forecasts." We define a forecast to be the best prediction possible of what is to occur at a given time in the future. A projection in this context is a prediction based on the participating country undertaking and completing all structural and policy reforms agreed to in the letter of intent approved between the participating government and the IMF. The two could diverge if the best prediction includes only partial implementation of policy and structural reform.

[3] When an IMF program is approved, the IMF staff uses the best statistics available at that time for current and past macroeconomic data to create projections for the evolution of those variables over the following years. These projections represent the "original program" projections for that IMF program. Program performance is reviewed periodically over time, and at each review the IMF staff creates a new set of projections for the macroeconomic data reflecting the best available information of that time. We will use the "first review" projections for each program in a later section.

as reported in June 2002. Given the difference in sources, some data manipulation is necessary to ensure comparability.[4] The data are redefined in each case to be relative to the initial program year: it is denoted the "year T" of the program.[5] We will examine four projection "horizons" in this study. For each projection horizon, we will compare the IMF staff projection with the historical outcome. The year prior to "year T" is denoted $T-1$. The horizon-T data will be projections of macroeconomic outcomes in period T based on information available in $T-1$: in other words, a one-year-ahead projection. The horizon-$T+1$ data are projections of macroeconomic outcomes in period $T+1$ based on information available in $T-1$, and are as such two-year-ahead projections. The horizon-$T+2$ and horizon-$T+3$ projections are defined analogously. The number of observations available differs for each projection horizon owing to (a) missing projection data, or (b) projection horizons that extend beyond the end of the available historical data. The numbers of observations available for comparisons are as follows for horizons T through $T+3$, respectively: 175, 147, 115, and 79.

We will focus on two macroeconomic aggregates. The historical fiscal surplus as a share of GDP for country j in year t will be denoted y_{jt}. The historical current account surplus as a share of GDP will be denoted c_{jt}. The projections of these two variables will be denoted $\hat{y}_{jt}$ and $\hat{c}_{jt}$, respectively. Other variables will be introduced as necessary and defined at that time. It will be useful for exposition to describe projections of these ratios as the change observed in the ratio between period $T-1$ (just before the program began) and the end of the time horizon. We use the notation $\Delta\hat{y}_{jk}$ and $\Delta\hat{c}_{jk}$ to represent the change in the projection ratio between period $T-1$ and the end of horizon k: for example, $\Delta\hat{c}_{jT}=\hat{c}_{jT}-\hat{c}_{jT-1}$. Historical data from the WEO are differenced analogously.

Each program is treated as an independent observation in what follows. However, it is important to note that the database includes multiple programs for many participating countries. These programs may overlap for a given country, in the sense that the initial year (year T) for one program may coincide with a projection year (e.g., year $T+2$) for a previous program in that country.

[4] For example, the projections are reported on an annual basis but the year is not invariably a calendar year. For some programs, the fiscal year was used as the basis of data collection and for projections. In those instances, the historical data are converted into fiscal-year equivalents through weighted-average conversion of the calendar-year data.

[5] The "year T" of each program is defined by IMF staff to be that fiscal year (as defined by the country) in which the program is approved. Programs are typically not approved at the beginning of year T, but rather at some point within the year.

Figure 1a

Mean Historical and Projected Changes in Fiscal Ratios

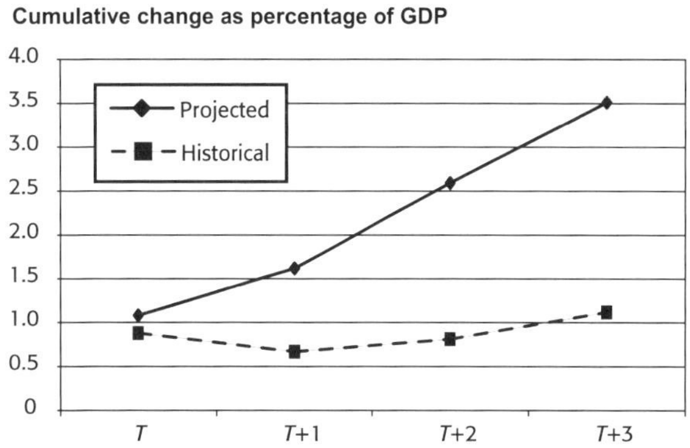

What Does the Record Show?

For an initial pass, we compare the historical outcomes for the countries participating in IMF-supported programs with the outcomes projected by IMF staff when the programs were originally approved.[6] When we compare the mean of $\Delta\hat{y}_{jk}$ and $\Delta\hat{c}_{jk}$ for various projection horizons k with the mean of the actual Δy_{jk} and Δc_{jk}, we find that projections differ substantially from those actually observed. Figure 1a illustrates the pattern of mean changes in projected and historical fiscal ratios.[7] The two mean changes are nearly coincident for horizon T, while for longer horizons the historical and envisaged changes diverge sharply. The mean projected change in the fiscal ratio rises with the length of the horizon; at horizon $T+3$, the projected change in the fiscal ratio is 3.5 percentage points. The change actually observed over those time horizons was quite different: 0.68 percentage point for horizon $T+1$ and up to 1.12 percentage points for horizon $T+3$.

Figure 1b illustrates the pattern for changes in projected and actual current account ratios. The mean projected change in the current account ratio is negative for horizon T and horizon $T+1$. The change becomes positive and grows for longer projection horizons. The historical change in the current account ratio for participating countries followed a different dynamic: improvement for horizon T, followed by deterioration in longer horizons. Negative changes in mean current account ratio continued three and four years after adoption of the IMF program.

[6] In this section, we use the projections from the "original program."

[7] The data on which Figures 1 and 2 are based are reported in Table 1.

Figure 1b

Mean Historical and Projected Changes in Current Account Ratio

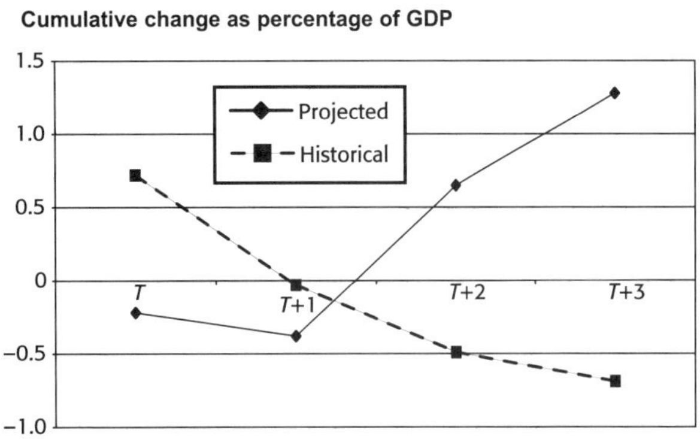

While these mean differences are suggestive, they cover up the great variability in projections and realizations for both ratios. Figures 2a through 2h illustrate the historical and envisaged changes in each variable for each projection horizon. The diagonal line indicates values at which projected change is just equal to historical change. The dispersion in values around the diagonal lines is quite striking.[8] For both fiscal and current account ratios, there is evidence of projected changes exceeding historical changes. This is especially striking for the fiscal ratios over time, as the proportion of observations to the right of the diagonal line rises with the projection horizon. There is also evidence of historical values more extreme than projected, especially for the changes in the current account ratio.

The correlations between projected and historical changes of the two ratios over the various time horizons are as follows:

Horizons	T	$T+1$	$T+2$	$T+3$
Fiscal ratio (Δy_{jk}, $\Delta \hat{y}_{jk}$)	0.61	0.56	0.31	0.56
Current account ratio (Δc_{jk}, $\Delta \hat{c}_{jk}$)	0.54	0.38	0.32	0.38

There is a good, though not perfect, correlation between projected and historical changes for horizon T. For longer projection horizons the correlation is lower. The horizon $T+2$ correlations exhibit the lowest values, with horizon $T+3$ correlations rising again to equal those of horizon $T+1$.

[8] Table 1 reports the standard deviations of the projected and actual changes in the database; these are in all cases and for all projection horizons at least as large as the mean values.

It is not surprising that the projections are inexact at any projection horizon. Nor is it surprising that the shortest horizon exhibits the closest fit to the actual, since longer-horizon projections required predictions on intermediate-year outcomes that almost surely will be inexact. It will be useful, however, to decompose the projection error into parts—can we learn from the record to identify the source of the projected imprecision?

Decomposing Projection Error

Begin with g_T, a macroeconomic variable observed at time T. Define s_T as the vector of policy forcing variables observed at time T. Denote the projection of Δg_T to be

$$\Delta \hat{g}_T = f(X_{T-1}, \Delta \hat{s}_T), \tag{1}$$

with X_{T-1} a matrix representing that information available to the forecaster at time $T-1$ and $\hat{s}_T$ the matrix of projected policy outcomes consistent with the government's letter of intent.[9] The actual evolution of the variable g_T can be represented by the expression

$$\Delta g_T = \phi(\zeta_{T-1}, \Delta s_T), \tag{2}$$

with ζ_{T-1} the matrix of forcing variables at time $T-1$ (including a random error in time T), s_T the matrix of observed policy outcomes, and ϕ the true reduced-form model. Projection error can then be represented by the difference $(\Delta \hat{g}_T - \Delta g_T)$.[10]

$$(\Delta \hat{g}_T - \Delta g_T) = \phi(\zeta_{T-1}, \Delta s_T) - f(X_{T-1}, \Delta s_T). \tag{3}$$

There are four potential sources for this projection error. First, the projection model $f(.)$ may not be identical with the true model $\phi(.)$. Second, the historical policy adjustment (Δs_T) may differ from the projected policy adjustment $(\Delta \hat{s}_T)$. Third, the information set X_{T-1} available for the projections may not include the same information as the forcing vector ζ_{T-1} for the true process. Finally, there is random error in realizations of the macroeconomic variable.

Consider a simple example. There is a single projection of change in a variable g_T. The forcing matrix is simply the lagged variables g_{T-1} and g_{T-2}.[11] The policy matrix is represented by the single instrument s_T.

[9] By contrast, we consider the forecast of Δg_T to be defined as $\Delta g^e{}_T = f(X_{T-1}; \Delta s^e{}_T)$, with $\Delta s^e{}_T$ representing the forecaster's best prediction as of period $T-1$ of the policy vector to be observed in period T.

[10] Hendry (1997) provides an excellent summary of the possible sources of projection (in his case forecasting) error when the projection model is potentially different from the actual model. This example can be thought of as a special case of his formulation.

[11] g_{T-2} enters the expression through the term Δg_{T-1}.

Figures 2a–2h

Fiscal Ratios and Current Account Ratios

Figure 2a. Fiscal Ratios in Horizon *T*

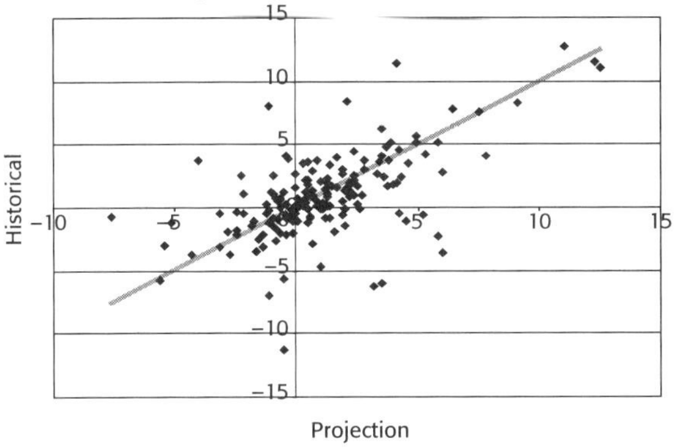

Figure 2b. Current Account Ratios in Horizon *T*

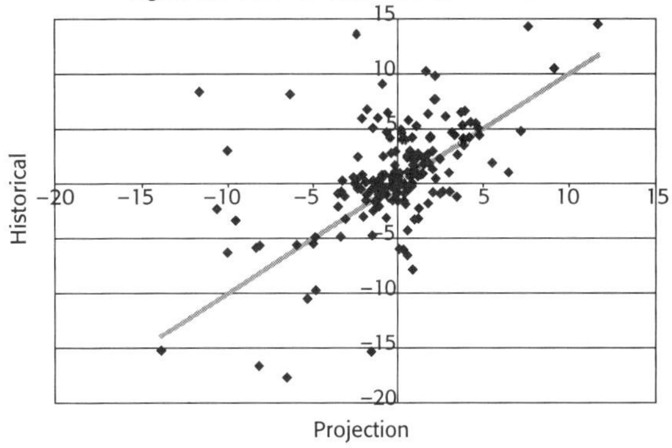

Figure 2c. Fiscal Ratios in Horizon *T*+1

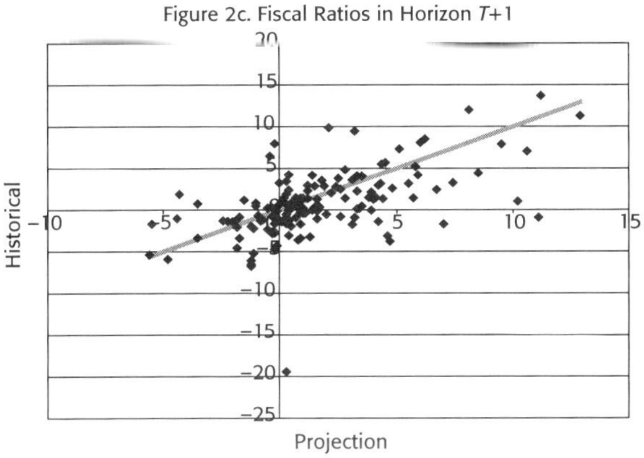

Figure 2d. Current Account Ratios in Horizon *T*+1

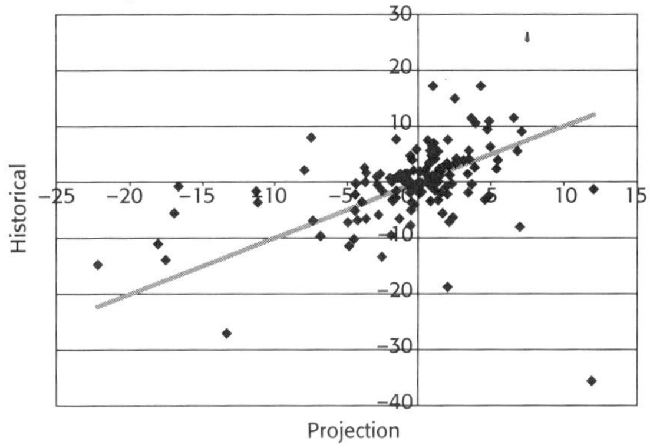

Figure 2e. Fiscal Ratios in Horizon *T*+2

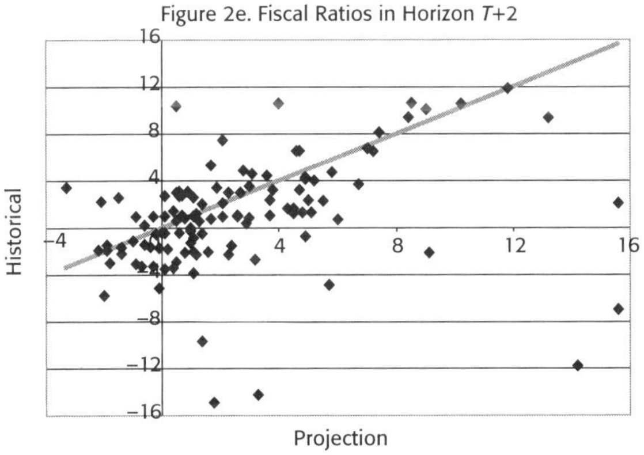

Figure 2f. Current Account Ratios in Horizon *T*+2

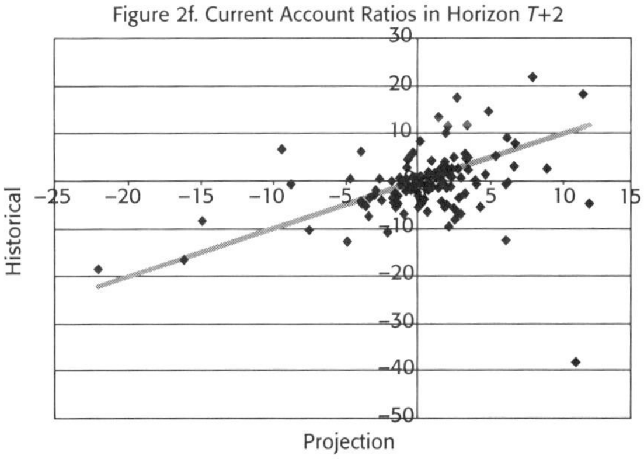

Figure 2g. Fiscal Ratios in Horizon *T*+3

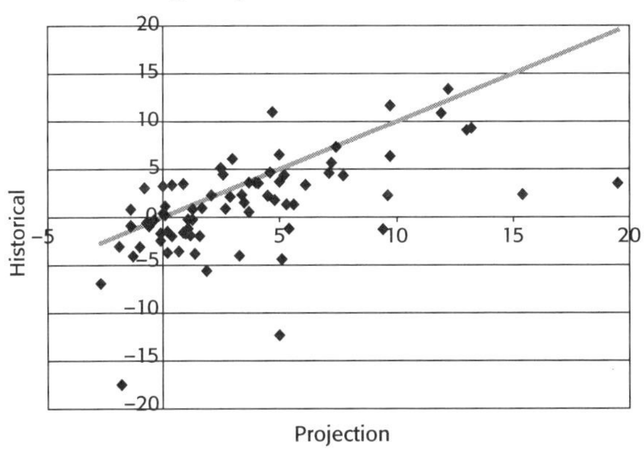

Figure 2h. Current Account Ratios in horizon *T*+3

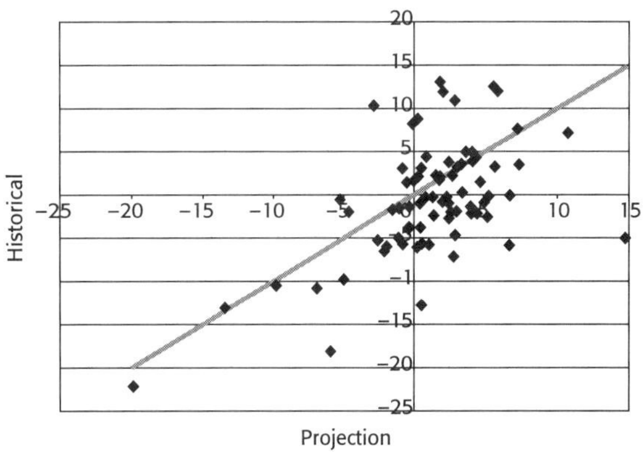

Table 1
Projecting the Change in Macroeconomic Aggregates

Horizon T

Variable	N	Mean	Std dev	Sum	Minimum	Maximum
		Simple Statistics				
$\Delta\hat{y}_{jT}$	175	1.08651	2.88011	190.14000	−7.60000	12.50000
Δy_{jT}	175	0.87778	3.25935	153.61161	−11.33896	12.72751
$\Delta\hat{c}_{jT}$	175	−0.22187	3.47920	−38.82699	−13.89236	11.66200
Δc_{jT}	175	0.72340	4.77454	126.59449	−17.68986	14.49604

Correlations:		$\Delta\hat{y}_{jT}$	Δy_{jT}	$\Delta\hat{c}_{jT}$	Δc_{jT}
	$\Delta\hat{y}_{jT}$	1.00000			
	Δy_{jT}	**0.60489**	1.00000		
	$\Delta\hat{c}_{jT}$	0.24256	0.12334	1.00000	
	Δc_{jT}	0.19968	0.30303	**0.53486**	1.00000

Horizon $T+1$

Variable	N	Mean	Std dev	Sum	Minimum	Maximum
		Simple Statistics				
$\Delta\hat{y}_{jT+1}$	147	1.62408	3.22486	238.74000	−5.60000	12.90000
Δy_{jT+1}	147	0.67722	3.93298	99.55073	−19.42935	13.69233
$\Delta\hat{c}_{jT+1}$	147	−0.37867	4.98040	−55.66390	−22.23187	12.01531
Δc_{jT+1}	147	−0.03233	7.07135	−4.75294	−35.61176	25.90529

Correlations:		$\Delta\hat{y}_{jT+1}$	Δy_{jT+1}	$\Delta\hat{c}_{jT+1}$	Δc_{jT+1}
	$\Delta\hat{y}_{jT+1}$	1.00000			
	Δy_{jT+1}	**0.56182**	1.00000		
	$\Delta\hat{c}_{jT+1}$	0.13572	−0.02165	1.00000	
	Δc_{jT+1}	0.12453	0.04358	**0.38254**	1.00000

(Continued on next page)

Table 1 (*concluded*)

Horizon $T+2$

Variable	N	Simple Statistics				
		Mean	Std dev	Sum	Minimum	Maximum
$\Delta \hat{y}_{jT+2}$	115	2.59478	3.67922	298.40000	−3.30000	15.60000
Δy_{jT+2}	115	0.81807	4.85553	94.07814	−16.72117	11.88877
$\Delta \hat{c}_{jT+2}$	115	0.64742	4.64897	74.45280	−22.04280	11.68855
Δc_{jT+2}	115	−0.49056	7.32857	−56.41476	−38.14743	21.78397

Correlations:		$\Delta \hat{y}_{jT+2}$	Δy_{jT+2}	$\Delta \hat{c}_{jT+2}$	Δc_{jT+2}
	$\Delta \hat{y}_{jT+2}$	1.00000			
	Δy_{jT+2}	**0.31046**	1.00000		
	$\Delta \hat{c}_{jT+2}$	0.11603	−0.21840	1.00000	
	Δc_{jT+2}	−0.03683	−0.11606	**0.32365**	1.00000

Horizon $T+3$

Variable	N	Simple Statistics				
		Mean	Std dev	Sum	Minimum	Maximum
$\Delta \hat{y}_{jT+3}$	79	3.51000	4.27596	277.29000	−2.70000	19.50000
Δy_{jT+3}	79	1.11918	4.85320	88.41557	−17.48994	13.35470
$\Delta \hat{c}_{jT+3}$	79	1.28198	4.91608	101.27681	−19.89594	14.73079
Δc_{jT+3}	79	−1.37587	12.09842	−108.69398	−81.569321	21.75981

Correlations:		$\Delta \hat{y}_{jT+3}$	Δy_{jT+3}	$\Delta \hat{c}_{jT+3}$	Δc_{jT+3}
	$\Delta \hat{y}_{jT+3}$	1.00000			
	Δy_{jT+3}	**0.55890**	1.00000		
	$\Delta \hat{c}_{jT+3}$	0.14194	−0.12499	1.00000	
	Δc_{jT+3}	−0.02829	0.01113	**0.38530**	1.00000

Notes: Std dev denotes standard deviation. N denotes the number of observations.

Equations (1) and (2) can then be rewritten in the following form:

$$\Delta \hat{g}_T = a_1 \Delta \hat{g}_{T-1} + a_2(g_{T-1} + \eta_{T-1}) + b_1 \Delta \tag{1e}$$

$$\Delta g_T = \alpha_1 \Delta g_{T-1} + \alpha_2 g_{T-1} + \beta_1 \Delta s_T + \varepsilon_T. \tag{2e}$$

The coefficients (α_1, α_2, β_1) represent the true model while (a_1, a_2, b_1) are coefficients from the model used for projections. In the projection rule, the forecaster perceives $\hat{g}_{T-1} = (g_{T-1} + \eta_{T-1})$ with η_{T-1} a random error. This imprecision may occur because the information set available to the forecaster is less precise than the set available after later revisions. The variable ε_T represents the stochastic nature of realizations of the actual variable.

$$\begin{aligned}(\Delta \hat{g}_T - \Delta g_T) = {} & [(a_1 - \alpha_1)\Delta g_{T-1} \\ & + (a_2 - \alpha_2) g_{T-1} + (b_1 - \beta_1)\Delta s_T] \\ & + b_1(\Delta \hat{s}_T - \Delta s_T) + [a_2 \eta_{T-1} \\ & + a_1(\Delta \hat{g}_{T-1} - \Delta g_{T-1})] + e_T\end{aligned} \tag{3e}$$

The projection error thus illustrates the four components mentioned previously. First, there is the possibility that the forecaster's model differs from that evident in the historical data; this will lead to the deviations summarized within the first set of square brackets. Second, there could be a divergence between the projected policy adjustment and the actual policy adjustment. Third, there is the potential that projection error is due to mismeasurement of initial conditions or to past errors in forecasts of variable growth. Fourth, the error may simply be due to the stochastic nature of the variable being projected.

In the sections that follow, we decompose theprojection error into these four parts for the fiscal balance/GDP ratio and the current account balance/GDP ratio in countries with IMF-supported programs. First, we create a reduced-form model that represents well the evolution of the actual data. We estimate the model implicit in the projected data, and compare the coefficients from this projection model with those from the actual data. Second, we examine the envisaged and historical data for evidence that revisions in the data led to the discrepancies. Third, we perform a decomposition exercise to determine the percentages of deviations of projection from historical values that can be attributed to differences in models, differences in initial conditions, differences in policy response, or simply random variation in the historical data.

Fiscal and Current Accounts

We begin with the macro identity

$$y_{jt} = c_{jt} - p_{jt} \tag{4}$$

holding for all countries j and time periods t. y_{jt} is the fiscal surplus as a share of GDP, c_{jt} is the current account surplus as a share of GDP, and p_{jt} is private savings as a share of GDP.

We posit as well that there is a "normal" level of private saving specific to each country and to each time period. This normal level p^n_{jt} can be represented by a country-specific component, a component that is common to all countries for a given time period, and a positive relationship between foreign saving opportunities and private saving.

$$p^n_{jt} = \alpha_j + \beta_t + \delta c_{jt}. \tag{5}$$

Combining (4) and (5), and defining $e_{jt} = (p_{jt} - p^n_{jt})$ as the excess private saving in any period yields

$$y_{jt} = -\alpha_j - \beta_t + (1 - \delta) c_{jt} - e_{jt}. \tag{6}$$

The variables y_{jt} and c_{jt} can be represented by a vector autoregression. With appropriate substitution, this vector autoregression can be rewritten in error-correction form as[12]

$$\begin{aligned}\Delta y_{jt} = {} & a_o - a_{12}\Delta y_{jt-1} - b_{12}\Delta c_{jt-1} \\ & + (a_{11} + a_{12} - 1) y_{jt-1} \\ & + (b_{11} + b_{12}) c_{jt-1} + \varepsilon_{yjt}\end{aligned} \tag{7a}$$

$$\begin{aligned}\Delta c_{jt} = {} & b_o - a_{22}\Delta y_{jt-1} - b_{22}\Delta c_{jt-1} \\ & + (a_{21} + a_{22}) y_{jt-1} \\ & + (b_{12} + b_{22} - 1) c_{jt-1} + \varepsilon_c.\end{aligned} \tag{7b}$$

There is, in general, no way to assign contemporaneous causality in (7a) and (7b). If it were possible to assert that the current account ratio is exogenously

[12] We will refer to the "error-correction form" as one that includes both lagged differences and lagged levels of the two variables as explanatory variables for the current differenced variables. This can be derived from a general AR specification of the two variables; the AR(2) specification is used here for ease of illustration. The form presented in the text can be derived from the following AR(2) set of equations:

$$y_{jt} = a_o + a_{11} y_{jt-1} + a_{12} y_{jt-2} + b_{11} c_{jt-1} + b_{12} c_{jt-2} + \varepsilon_{yjt}$$

$$c_{jt} = b_o + a_{21} y_{jt-1} + a_{22} y_{jt-2} + b_{21} c_{jt-1} + b_{22} c_{jt-2} + \varepsilon_c.$$

Specification tests are used to choose the lag length appropriate to the empirical work. In a world in which y_{jt} and c_{jt} are nonstationary but are cointegrated on a country-by-country basis, further simplification is possible. If y_{jt} and c_{jt} are nonstationary in the current dataset, equation (6) represents a cointegrating relationship. The "error-correction" variable e_{jt} can then be inserted in the equations (7) in place of the terms in y_{jt-1} and c_{jt-1} and will have the coefficient associated with y_{jt-1} in (7). It is impossible to verify a nonstationary relationship in this dataset, given that we have only scattered observations from each country's time series. We do investigate that possibility in the second and fourth columns of Tables 2 and 3, with support for that interpretation of the error-correction term in the Δy_{jt} equation. Hamilton (1994, Ch. 19) provides a clear derivation of this error-correction form from the underlying autoregression.

determined, for example, then the contemporaneous change Δc_{jt} could be a separate regressor in the Δy_{jt} equation to account for that contemporaneous correlation.

The econometric effects modeled here can be divided into three groups. The first group, represented by the terms in Δc_{jt-1} and Δy_{jt-1}, capture the autoregressive structure of the system. The second group, represented by the terms in y_{jt-1} and c_{jt-1}, capture the adjustment of these variables in response to deviations from the "normal" relationship described in (6). The third group represents random errors. Although the direction of contemporaneous causality cannot be verified, there is a version of dynamic causality that can be checked. The coefficients of y_{jt-1} and c_{jt-1} represent the degree to which the current account and fiscal ratios respond to deviations from the norm.

The system of equations in (7) will hold for all t, and thus should be in evidence at time T when the IMF-supported program is introduced. The system has excluded policy interventions from the derivation for simplicity, but it is straightforward, though messy, to introduce them. One way to do so will be through definition of a policy response function, by which Δs_{jT} is itself a function of c_{jT-1} and y_{jT-1}. The second will be to incorporate the policy variables as exogenous forcing variables. The approach we use will incorporate parts of each.

Estimation Using Historical Data

The results of the coefficient estimates from equations (7) for all programs in the sample at horizon T using historical data are summarized in Table 2a. Specification testing revealed that lagged first-difference terms with lag length greater than two did not contribute significantly to the regression.[13] The contemporaneous causality imposed on the model is that changes in the fiscal account are caused by changes in the current account, and not vice versa.[14] The error-correction term (e_{jT-1}) was derived from the regression in levels (i.e., not first differenced) reported in Annex I.

For the ratio of fiscal balance to GDP, the estimation results suggest the following insights (see the first two columns of Table 2a):

- There is significant positive contemporaneous correlation between the two variables, and the normalization chosen here assigns causation to Δc_{jT}. For a 1 percent increase in the current account ratio, there is a 0.28 percent increase in the fiscal ratio.
- The current first-difference responds positively and significantly to shocks in the own ratio in previous periods. For a unit shock to Δy_{jT-1}, there are other things equal a 0.25 increase in Δy_{jT}. For a unit shock to Δy_{jT-2}, the transmitted shock is positive and significant at 0.16. Past positive current account shocks have small negative effects on Δy_{jT} with the two-period lagged effect significant at the 90 percent level of confidence.
- The coefficient on y_{jT-1} is significantly different from 0, but not from –1. It implies that for an average country, a deviation from its "normal" fiscal account ratio will lead to an adjustment in the next period that erases 82 percent of that deviation.

For the ratio of current account to GDP, the estimation explains a lower percentage of the variation (as indicated by the R^2 statistic of 0.56). The second set of columns reports coefficients and standard errors for that specification, and indicates the following:

- The lagged first-difference terms have no significant effect on the current first difference.
- The coefficient on c_{jT-1} of –0.40 is significantly different from both 0 and –1. It indicates that 40 percent of any deviations of the current account ratio from its normal value is made up in the following period.

The last four columns of Table 2a report the results of error-correction regressions in which y_{jT-1} and c_{jT-1} are replaced by e_{jT-1} from equation (6), as implied by a cointegrating relationship between the two variables. As is evident in comparing the first set and third set of results, the cointegrating relationship captures nearly all of the explanatory power in the Δy_{jT} regression. The cointegrating relationship is less effective in the Δc_{jT} equation, however, as indicated by the R^2 statistic.[15]

These results are specific to the data for horizon T. Results for horizon $T+1$ are presented in Table 2b. The construction of these data differs somewhat, in that the endogenous variable is a two-period forecast; we chose to use two-period lags on the right-hand side of the equation for comparability. For horizon $T+1$, the contemporaneous effect of the current account ratio on the fiscal ratio is halved—

[13] Statistical confidence in this paper will be measured at the 90 percent, 95 percent, and 99 percent levels. In the text, statistical significance will indicate a degree of confidence greater than 95 percent unless otherwise indicated.

[14] This assumption will be justified, for example, if the participating country is constrained in its international borrowing, so that the ratio of current account surplus to GDP is set by foreign lenders.

[15] While imposition of the cointegration condition through the error-correction variable is effective for the fiscal ratio, our comparison of projections with historical data will be based on the system without this condition imposed. As Clements and Hendry (1995) demonstrate, the imposition of the cointegration condition in estimation when cointegration exists improves forecast accuracy, most notably for small (i.e., N = 50) samples. For larger samples, the improvements in forecast accuracy are small.

Table 2a

Regression Results, Historical Current and Fiscal Account Ratios, Horizon T

	Δy_{jT}		Δc_{jT}		Δy_{jT}		Δc_{jT}	
	Coefficient	S.E.	Coefficient	S.E.	Coefficient	S.E.	Coefficient	S.E.
Δc_{jT}	0.28**	(0.06)			0.25**	(0.05)		
Δy_{jT-1}	0.25**	(0.10)	–0.08	(0.19)	0.23**	(0.10)	–0.04	(0.20)
Δc_{jT-1}	–0.05	(0.05)	–0.04	(0.10)	–0.02	(0.05)	–0.23**	(0.09)
Δy_{jT-2}	0.16**	(0.08)	–0.01	(0.16)	0.14*	(0.08)	0.13	(0.16)
Δc_{jT-2}	–0.07*	(0.04)	–0.02	(0.08)	–0.05	(0.04)	–0.17**	(0.07)
y_{jT-1}	–0.82**	(0.11)	–0.09	(0.21)				
c_{jT-1}	0.16**	(0.07)	–0.40**	(0.12)				
e_{jT-1}					–0.81**	(0.11)	–0.17	(0.22)
N	176		176		176		176	
R^2	0.78		0.56		0.78		0.50	

Notes: Full sample, Horizon T. Standard errors (S.E.) appear in parentheses.
* Indicates significance at the 90 percent level of confidence.
** Indicates significance at the 95 percent confidence level.
A complete set of time and country dummies was included in the regressions, but their coefficients have been suppressed for brevity.

Table 2b

Regression Results, Historical Current and Fiscal Account Ratios, Horizon $T+1$

	Δy_{jT+1}		Δc_{jT+1}		Δy_{jT+1}		Δc_{jT+1}	
	Coefficient	S.E.	Coefficient	S.E.	Coefficient	S.E.	Coefficient	S.E.
Δc_{jT+1}	0.14**	(0.06)			0.12**	(0.05)		
Δy_{jT-1}	0.09	(0.11)	–0.15	(0.24)	0.08	(0.10)	0.01	(0.26)
Δc_{jT-1}	–0.04	(0.07)	–0.12	(0.16)	–0.01	(0.06)	–0.55***	(0.12)
y_{jT-1}	–1.13***	(0.17)	0.47	(0.37)				
c_{jT-1}	0.23**	(0.10)	–0.83***	(0.21)				
e_{jT-1}					–1.10***	(0.16)	0.27	(0.41)
N	147		147		147		147	
R^2	0.83		0.72		0.83		0.65	

Notes: Variable definition (this table only for all variables g_j):

$\Delta g_{jT+1} = g_{jT+1} - g_{jT-1}$

$\Delta g_{jT-1} = g_{jT-1} - g_{jT-3}$

Full sample, Horizon $T+1$. Standard errors (S.E.) appear in parentheses.
** Indicates significance at the 95 percent confidence level.
*** Indicates significance at the 99 percent confidence level.
A complete set of time and country dummies was included in the regressions, but their coefficients have been suppressed for brevity.

this is perhaps due to the doubling of the length of the time horizon. The autoregressive structure of the fiscal ratio, significant in horizon T, is no longer significant for horizon $T+1$. By contrast, the lagged "level" effects have larger coefficients. This effect in the current account ratio equation is significantly larger, as well, with the coefficient (0.833) more than double the comparable term for horizon T (–0.40).

Estimation Using Projected Data

If we interpret the estimated model of the preceding section to be the "true" model (2), we posit that the model used in forming projections for IMF programs should have a similar form. We can use similar econometric techniques to those of the previous section to derive the economic model implied by

Table 3a

Regression Results, Envisaged Current and Fiscal Account Ratios, Horizon T

	$\Delta\hat{y}_{jT}$		$\Delta\hat{c}_{jT}$		$\Delta\hat{y}_{jT}$		$\Delta\hat{c}_{jT}$	
	Coefficient	S.E.	Coefficient	S.E.	Coefficient	S.E.	Coefficient	S.E.
$\Delta\hat{c}_{jT}$	0.15*	(0.09)			0.20**	(0.08)		
$\Delta\hat{y}_{jT-1}$	−0.15*	(0.09)	−0.15	(0.12)	−0.14	(0.09)	−0.15	(0.13)
$\Delta\hat{c}_{jT-1}$	−0.09	(0.06)	−0.0004	(0.08)	−0.09	(0.06)	−0.06	(0.09)
$\Delta\hat{y}_{jT-2}$	−0.03	(0.08)	0.16*	(0.10)	−0.05	(0.08)	0.11	(0.11)
$\Delta\hat{c}_{jT-2}$	−0.06	(0.04)	0.04	(0.06)	−0.08*	(0.04)	−0.04	(0.06)
$\hat{y}_{jT-1}$	−0.44**	(0.09)	−0.02	(0.11)				
$\hat{c}_{jT-1}$	0.08	(0.07)	−0.33**	(0.08)				
em_{jT-1}					−0.44**	(0.09)	−0.04	(0.12)
N	165		165		165		165	
R^2	0.85		0.76		0.05		0.69	

Notes: Full sample, Horizon T. Standard errors (S.E.) appear in parentheses.
* Indicates significance at the 90 percent confidence level.
** Indicates significance at the 95 percent confidence level.
A complete set of time and country dummies was included in the regressions, but their coefficients have been suppressed for brevity.

the projections. We report the results of this estimation exercise in Table 3a for projection horizon T.

The results from estimating the projection model for the fiscal ratio suggest the following (see the first set of columns in Table 3a):

- There is significant contemporaneous correlation between the projected fiscal and current account ratios. For a 1 percentage point increase in the current account ratio, there is evidence of a 0.15 percentage point increase in the fiscal ratio. This is roughly half of the response found in the actual data. By implication, the IMF staff model will project a 0.85 percentage point increase in the ratio of private net savings to GDP in response to such a current account shock, while the historical data indicate a 0.72 percentage point increase in the private saving ratio in response to such a shock.
- A 1 percentage point increase in last period's fiscal ratio will trigger an 0.15 percentage point decrease in this period's ratio. This suggests that the projection is relying on fiscal policy correction to overcome any inertia in fiscal stance over time and to offset past excesses with current austerity.[16] This response also is less than was observed in the historical data.
- There is evidence of an error-correction effect in the data. The coefficients on the lagged ratios have the correct signs, and that associated with $\hat{y}_{jT-1}$ is significantly different from zero. The coefficient −0.44 indicates that the projection is designed to make up 44 percent of any deviation of fiscal ratio from the country's "normal" ratio within a single year. This adjustment is also roughly half of the adjustment observed in the historical data.

The results from estimating the projection model for the current account ratio are reported in the second set of columns in Table 3a:

- There is no significant evidence of an autoregressive structure in $\Delta\hat{c}_{jt}$, just as was true in the historical analysis.
- Past shocks to the fiscal ratio have a significant lagged effect on the current account ratio, a feature unobserved in the actual data.
- There is a significant error-correction effect as evidenced by the coefficient on $\Delta\hat{c}_{jt-1}$. The coefficient −0.33 indicates that the projection is constructed to make up about ⅓ of any deviation of the current account ratio from its normal value within a single year. The coefficient on $\hat{y}_{jT-1}$ is insignificantly different from zero. These features are quite similar to those observed in the historical data.

When the envisaged data are examined with the cointegrating relationship imposed, the evidence is once again stronger for the fiscal ratio. In that regression (reported in the third set of columns), the cointegrating variable (em_{jT-1}) has explanatory

[16] We would observe this negative coefficient, for example, if we had a model that required the government to balance its budget over each two-year period. There could be excess spending in odd years, but it would be offset by spending cuts in even years.

Table 3b

Regression Results, Envisaged Current and Fiscal Account Ratios, Horizon T+1

	$\Delta\hat{y}_{jT+1}$		$\Delta\hat{c}_{jT+1}$		$\Delta\hat{y}_{jT+1}$		$\Delta\hat{c}_{jT+1}$	
	Coefficient	S.E.	Coefficient	S.E.	Coefficient	S.E.	Coefficient	S.E.
$\Delta\hat{c}_{jT+1}$	0.158*	(0.08)			0.179**	(0.08)		
$\Delta\hat{y}_{jT-1}$	−0.175*	(0.10)	0.020	(0.16)	−0.165*	(0.09)	0.104	(0.16)
$\Delta\hat{c}_{jT-1}$	0.049	(0.08)	−0.208*	(0.12)	0.034	(0.07)	−0.364***	(0.12)
$\hat{y}_{jT-1}$	−0.462***	(0.11)	−0.029	(0.18)				
$\hat{c}_{jT-1}$	0.048	(0.09)	−0.370***	(0.14)				
em_{jT-1}					−0.474***	(0.11)	−0.128	(0.19)
N	129		129		129		129	
R^2	0.86		0.72		0.86		0.68	

Notes: Variable definitions (this table only for all variables $\hat{g}_j$):

$\Delta\hat{g}_{jT+1} = \hat{g}_{jT+1} - \hat{g}_{jT-1}$

$\Delta\hat{g}_{jT-1} = \hat{g}_{jT-1} - \hat{g}_{jT-3}$

Full sample, Horizon T+1. Standard errors (S.E.) appear in parentheses.
* Indicates significance at the 90 percent confidence level.
** Indicates significance at the 95 percent confidence level.
*** Indicates significance at the 99 percent confidence level.
A complete set of time and country dummies was included in the regressions, but their coefficients have been suppressed for brevity.

power nearly equal to the lagged $\hat{c}_{jT-1}$ and $\hat{y}_{jT-1}$ reported in the first set of columns. In the equation for the current account ratio, the results are much weaker.

For time horizon T+1 (Table 3b), the projection "model" is quite similar to that of horizon T. The contemporaneous and lagged "level" effects are almost identical for the fiscal ratio, as is the lagged "level" effect for the current account ratio. The autoregressive terms differ somewhat, but the differences are not statistically significant. The similarity of error-correction effects is quite striking, as it suggests that the projected adjustment from imbalance occurs totally in horizon T—there is no further adjustment in horizon T+1. This is quite different from the historical record, where adjustment continues in fairly equal increments from horizon T to horizon T+1.

Divergence Between Projected and Actual Policy

We note from the preceding discussion that there is substantial evidence of difference between the coefficients in Tables 2a and 3a, and between Tables 2b and 3b. We interpret these differences as evidence that the "model" used in IMF projections and the "model" generating the historical data are significantly different. However, as the earlier discussion demonstrated, model differences are only one source of projection errors. In this subsection, we use the framework of equation (3e) to decompose the observed projection error for horizon T into components.

As the earlier discussion indicated, the projection error can conceptually be decomposed into four parts: differences in models, differences in policy response, mismeasurement of initial conditions at time of projection, and random errors.[17] Projection error is measured directly as the projection of the variable for horizon T *minus* the realization of the variable. Errors in initial conditions are measured as the difference between projected and historical observations of the level of the variable in period T–1. Two policy variables are considered indicators of the importance of policy reform conditions in the error: the difference between projected and historical depreciation of the real exchange rate ($\Delta\hat{e}_{jT}-\Delta e_{jT}$), and the difference between projected and historical change in government consumption expenditures as a share of GDP ($\Delta\hat{w}_{jT}-\Delta w_{jT}$).[18] We hypothesize

[17] For now we treat each program as if it were approved at the beginning of year T, so that the projected effects of the program on macroeconomic adjustment have a full year to take hold. In fact, programs are approved at different times within year T. Thus, the timing of approval within the year may explain part of the projection error. We explore this in Annex II.

[18] The variable for government consumption expenditures is available in consistent format in both historical and envisaged data. The variable on real depreciation is constructed in both cases as nominal depreciation *minus* CPI inflation for the horizon in question. These variables are explicit in the historical data. In the envisaged data, the nominal exchange rate is derived as the ratio between GDP in home currency and GDP in U.S. dollars.

that the former should have a significant effect on the current account, while the latter should be a significant component of the fiscal surplus.

Estimation of (3e) using the error-correction framework presented in equations (8) is complicated by the simultaneity of the macroeconomic balances and the policy variables over which conditions are defined. As (3e) indicates, $(\Delta\hat{e}_{jT}-\Delta e_{jT})$, $(\Delta\hat{w}_{jT}-\Delta w_{jT})$, Δe_{jT} and Δw_{jT} will all be included as regressors in the estimation framework, but all of these are potentially simultaneously determined with the macro balances. We address this by estimating the equations with both ordinary least squares (OLS) and two-stage least squares (2SLS), with the 2SLS results presumed to be free of simultaneity bias.[19] For each equation, as implied by (6), year-specific dummy variables are included to control for year-to-year differences in capital availability on world markets, we also include significant country-specific dummy variables to control for abnormally large cross-country differences in macro balances. Those results are reported in Table 4. The top panel reports the results of regressions in the current account ratio and the fiscal ratio. There are two columns: the first with OLS estimates, on a slightly larger sample, and the second with 2SLS estimates on a consistent-size sample of 162 observations across all variables. The bottom panel reports the regressions that served as the "first stage" of the 2SLS. The first column reports OLS results over the largest sample for which data were available for that regression, while the second column reports OLS results over the consistent 2SLS sample of 162 observations.

We interpret the results as follows. Take as example the coefficient on c_{jT-1} in the two regressions. Given our derivation in equation (3e), this coefficient should represent the difference between the projection coefficient and the actual coefficient. When we compare the results of Tables 2 and 3, we find this to be the case. Consider the 2SLS results. In the fiscal ratio regression of Table 4, the coefficient of –0.11 is quite similar to the difference (0.08–0.16) of the coefficients reported in Tables 2 and 3. For the current account ratio, the coefficient of 0.04 is also very similar to the difference (–0.33–(–0.40)) of the coefficients reported in Tables 2a and 3a. A positive coefficient in this regression indicates that the projection incorporated a more positive response to that variable than was found in the actual data.

We separate the discussion into the various types of errors.

Differences in modeling. If the projections used a different model from that evident in the actual data, we expect to find significant coefficients on the variables c_{jT-1}, y_{jT-1}, Δc_{jT-1}, Δy_{jT-1}, Δe_{jT}, and Δw_{jT} in the top panel. Our discussion of Tables 2a and 3a indicated that we anticipated greater evidence of differing models in the fiscal projections than in the current account projections. This point is partially supported by results reported in Table 4. Consider the OLS results. In the fiscal ratio estimation, there are significant coefficients on c_{jT-1} (–0.11), Δe_{jT} (0.01), Δy_{jT-1} (–0.08), and Δw_{jT} (0.10). If we consider the last case for illustration: a positive Δw_{jT} should reduce the fiscal balance. The coefficient (0.10) indicates that the IMF projections incorporated less pass-through of increased government expenditures into the reduced fiscal ratio than was actually observed, leaving a positive projection error. However, the 2SLS results suggest that differences in modeling are less apparent than is suggested by the OLS estimates, since only the coefficient on c_{jT-1} (–0.10) remains significantly different from zero.

For the current account ratio, there is no significant evidence of differences in modeling. All coefficients on these variables are both small and insignificantly different from zero.

Mismeasurement of initial conditions. Another source of projection error will be the difference between the initial conditions known to IMF staff and the actual initial conditions available in historical data. For these differences to be a significant source of projection error, the coefficients on the variables $(\hat{c}_{jT-1}-c_{jT-1})$ and $(\hat{y}_{jT-1}-y_{jT-1})$ must be significantly different from zero.

In the fiscal ratio regression, the difference in initial fiscal ratios $(\hat{y}_{jT-1}-y_{jT-1})$ is a significant contributor to projection error. The 2SLS coefficient (–0.30) indicates that when IMF staff had access to artificially high estimates of the previous period's fiscal ratio, they adjusted downward the projected necessary policy adjustment necessary. This response was a rational one, given the error-correction nature of the fiscal ratio, but was based on an incorrect starting point.

In the current account ratio regressions, the differences in initial conditions are the only significant determinants of projection error. With coefficients (–0.31) for $(c_{jT-1}-c_{jT-1})$ and (–0.25) of $(\hat{y}_{jT-1}-y_{jT-1})$ in the 2SLS version, the regressions suggest that the projections were in error largely because of incomplete information about the true value of the current account ratio in the preceding period.

Differences in policy response. If the projections included a policy response at variance with that actually observed, the coefficients on $(\Delta\hat{w}_{jT}-\Delta w_{jT})$ and $(\Delta\hat{e}_{jT}-\Delta e_{jT})$ will be significant in the two regressions. In both the 2SLS and OLS results, there is little evidence of this. In the fiscal 2SLS regression, there is a significant coefficient (–0.47) on $(\Delta\hat{w}_{jT}-\Delta w_{jT})$. This indicates that when the IMF projected smaller expenditure increases than actually occurred, the projection error on the fiscal ratio was, on average, positive—as expected.

[19] Both sets of results are reported because the systems approach to estimation reduces the number of observations usable in estimation. The OLS results thus provide a more comprehensive analysis, although one potentially tainted by simultaneity bias.

Table 4
Estimation of Projection Error Equations

	$\Delta\hat{c}_{jT}-\Delta c_{jT}$	
	OLS	2SLS
c_{jT-1}	0.01	0.04
$\hat{c}_{jT-1}-c_{jT-1}$	−0.41**	−0.31**
y_{jT-1}	−0.10	−0.02
$\hat{y}_{jT-1}-y_{jT-1}$	−0.19	−0.25*
Δe_{jT}	−0.0003	−0.002
$\Delta\hat{e}_{jT}-\Delta e_{jT}$	−0.005	−0.001
N	172	162
R^2	0.59	0.59

	$\Delta\hat{y}_{jT}-\Delta y_{T}$	
	OLS	2SLS
c_{jT-1}	−0.11**	−0.10**
$\hat{c}_{jT-1}-c_{jT-1}$	−0.06	−0.07
y_{jT-1}	0.01	0.04
$\hat{y}_{jT-1}-y_{jT-1}$	−0.34**	−0.30**
Δe_{jT}	0.01**	0.01
$\Delta\hat{e}_{jT}-\Delta e_{jT}$	0.007	0.009
Δw_{jT}	0.10**	0.02
$\Delta\hat{w}_{jT}-\Delta w_{jT}$	−0.47**	−0.47**
Δc_{jT-1}	0.03	0.03
Δy_{jT-1}	−0.08*	−0.08
N	167	162
R^2	0.74	0.71

	$\Delta\hat{e}_{jT}-\Delta e_{jT}$	
	OLS	OLS
$\Delta\hat{e}_{jT-1}-\Delta e_{jT-1}$	0.14**	−0.03
Δe_{jT-1}	−0.03**	−0.05**
N	166	162
R^2	0.68	0.68

	$\Delta\hat{w}_{jT}-\Delta w_{jT}$	
	OLS	OLS
$\hat{w}_{jT-1}-w_{jT-1}$	−0.02	−0.03
w_{jT-1}	0.15**	0.14**
Δw_{jT-1}	−0.06	−0.06
$\hat{w}_{jT-1}-\Delta w_{jT-1}$	−0.28**	−0.23**
N	166	162
R^2	0.52	0.53

	Δe_{jT}	
	OLS	OLS
Δe_{jT-1}	0.01**	0.03**
c_{jT-1}	−0.10	0.04
y_{jT-1}	0.37	0.28
N	174	162
R^2	0.65	0.74

	Δw_{jT}	
	OLS	OLS
w_{jT-1}	−0.39**	−0.38**
Δw_{jT-1}	−0.13**	−0.16**
y_{jT-1}	0.27**	0.29**
N	173	162
R^2	0.61	0.60

Notes: The two-stage-least-squares (2SLS) procedure used the estimating equations in the two lower panels for Δe_T, $\Delta\hat{e}_T-\Delta e_T$, Δw_T, and $\Delta\hat{w}_T-\Delta w_T$, and estimated those equations simultaneously with the two reported in the upper panel. The equations in the two lower panels are all ordinary least squares (OLS), since they did not include endogenous regressors. The coefficients differ because of the number of observations included: those with 165 were estimated in the simultaneous equation system, while those with other numbers of observations were estimated as single equations.

* Indicates significance at the 90 percent confidence level.

** Indicates significance at the 95 percent confidence level.

Standard errors and other regression statistics are available from the authors on request.

The regressions in the bottom panel hold some clues as to why the projections differed from historical values. As is evident in the $(\Delta\hat{w}_{jT}-\Delta w_{jT})$ regression, previous forecast errors were significant determinants of this policy projection error, as was a bias toward more positive projections as the previous period's fiscal ratio rose. The policy projection errors in the real exchange rate depreciation $(\Delta\hat{e}_{jT}-\Delta e_{jT})$ had no significant contribution to either regression in either specification.

Random errors. As the R^2 statistics indicate for the two regressions, the preceding three sources of projection error explain only 59 percent (for the current account ratio) and 71 percent (for the fiscal ratio) of total projection error. The remainder should be considered random shocks.

An Empirical Decomposition of Projection Error

In previous subsections, we identified several potential sources of projection errors. The magnitude and significance of the regression coefficients reported in Table 4 shed some light on the relative importance of each of the sources. To investigate this issue in more detail and to get a better insight into the relative contributions of each of the sources to the resulting projection errors, we implement the following exercise. Setting variables used in the 2SLS regressions of Table 4 to their mean values and using estimated coefficients, we compute the contribution of each of the model variables to the projection errors for current account and fiscal balance ratios, $(\Delta\hat{c}_{jT}-\Delta c_{jT})$ and $(\Delta\hat{y}_{jT}-\Delta y_{jT})$, respectively. Using means of projection errors as anchors, we can draw some conclusions about the relative contributions of differences in modeling, differences in initial conditions, and differences in policy response to the projection errors. Tables 5a and 5b summarize the results of the described experiment for current account and fiscal balance projection errors, respectively.

In the case of current account ratios, the most significant source of projection error comes from the measurement of the initial conditions. This component is responsible for 44.55 percent of the total projection error, while differences in modeling and differences in policy response generate forecast errors with magnitudes of only 16.63 percent and 0.85 percent, respectively. The positive signs of percentage contributions of all three sources suggest that these sources of errors tend to bias the current account mean projection error toward negative values.

However, when the components of the forecasting error for fiscal-balance ratios are considered, the two major sources of the errors are differences in modeling (166.17 percent) and mismeasurement of initial conditions (–52.78 percent). It appears that the model used in projections tends to make the projection error more positive while the measurement error in the initial conditions pulls the projection error in the negative direction, as occurred in the case of the current account projection errors. Differences in policy response are responsible for approximately 16 percent of the total mean projection error.

Projection errors of both variables are greatly influenced by the year- and country-specific factors captured by the corresponding dummy variables.

It is evident, in examining the data, that there is substantial mismeasurement in the fiscal and current account ratios when the initial values in the two databases are compared. Simple statistics for the actual and projection ratios are as follows (based on 175 observations):

Horizons	Mean	Standard Deviation	Minimum	Maximum
c_{jT-1}	–6.24	7.89	–39.82	11.08
$\hat{c}_{jT-1}$	–5.09	5.99	–39.92	10.41
y_{jT-1}	–4.36	4.11	–20.48	5.61
$\hat{y}_{jT-1}$	–4.22	4.42	–22.60	4.00

The difference in mean between historical and projected data for the current account ratio is quite striking. The value of $\hat{c}_{jT-1}$ should be known (i.e., historical) at the time of the projection. Differences of this magnitude are an indication that there has been substantial revision in the macroeconomic aggregates over time.[20] The difference in mean for the fiscal ratio is not so pronounced. The standard deviations are large, and these differ substantially between actual and projection databases. There is more variability in the actual current account ratios than in those projected; by contrast, there is more variability in the projected fiscal ratios than there is in the actual ratios.

Figures 3 and 4 present the scatter-plots of actual and projected ratios. The 45 degree line represents those combinations for which projected coincides with actual. As the figures show, there is tremendous measurement error even in these initial conditions. There is also a strong positive correlation of projection with actual: for $(c_{T-1}, \hat{c}_{T-1})$ it is 0.84, while for $(y_{T-1}, \hat{y}_{T-1})$ it is 0.86. There is not the perfect match that would exist in theory, but the match is quite strong.

Examining the Role of Revisions

New information is made available to IMF staff on a continuous basis throughout the duration of the IMF program. The staff periodically revisits its initial projections in the context of a program review, and updates them to reflect the information more recently received. We should then observe that the IMF projections converge to the actual performance as revisions are made over the duration of a multiperiod IMF program: imprecision in initial conditions will be eliminated, projected policy reform can be revised in light of observed behavior, and inaccuracy in the forecasting model can be reduced. Moreover, one can expect that for multiperiod programs, the IMF staff's major efforts in the design of the original programs would be concentrated on the improvement of short-horizon projections while less emphasis is placed on long-horizon projections since initial projections can be fine-tuned in the context of later reviews.

Assuming that the new information is efficiently incorporated, we expect to observe that the IMF projections converge to the historical performance as revisions are considered. Therefore, any assessment of the quality of the IMF projections will be incomplete without examining the evolution of projections. We address this issue by comparing the projections of the original programs (OPs) with

[20] We have been careful in constructing the dataset, but we must admit as well the possibility that the definition of current account used in the historical data may differ in some instances from the definition used in the envisaged data. While we see no reason for this difference to be systematic, it may well represent some of the observed difference in mean values.

Table 5a

Forecast Error Components: Current Account Ratios

Variable	Coeff.	Mean	Effect	Percent Effect	Total Percent Effect by Type
c_{jT-1}	0.04	−6.64	−0.25	25.46	
y_{jT-1}	−0.02	−4.39	0.08	−8.23	Differences in modeling: 16.63 percent
Δe_{jT}	0.00	−3.14	0.01	−0.60	
$(\hat{c}_{jT-1} - c_{jT-1})$	−0.31	1.26	−0.40	40.38	Mismeasurement of initial conditions: 44.55 percent
$(\hat{y}_{jT-1} - y_{jT-1})$	−0.25	0.16	−0.04	4.17	
$(\Delta\hat{e}_{jT} - \Delta e_{jT})$	0.00	8.46	−0.01	0.85	Differences in policy response: 0.85 percent
$t93$	0.97	0.10	0.10	−10.43	
$t94$	0.37	0.15	0.06	−5.78	
$t95$	1.14	0.14	0.16	−16.54	
$t96$	1.99	0.11	0.22	−22.60	
$t97$	1.84	0.11	0.20	−20.83	Year-specific: −125.53 percent
$t98$	3.35	0.10	0.35	−35.93	
$t99$	1.31	0.11	0.15	−14.90	
$t00$	0.50	0.10	0.05	−5.37	
$t01$	−1.21	0.06	−0.07	6.85	
Country dummies					Country-specific: 163.50 percent
$\Delta c_{jT} - \Delta c_{jT}$		**−0.98**			
Total:			**−0.98**	**100**	**100 percent**
Number of observations			**162**		

Table 5b

Forecast Error Components: Fiscal Balance Ratios

Variable	Coeff.	Mean	Effect	Percent Effect	Total Percent Effect by Type
c_{jT-1}	−0.10	−6.64	0.68	265.67	
Δc_{jT-1}	0.03	−0.57	−0.01	−5.63	
y_{jT-1}	0.04	−4.39	−0.19	−74.68	Differences in modeling: 166.17 percent
Δy_{jT-1}	−0.08	0.10	−0.01	−3.03	
Δe_{jT}	0.01	−3.14	−0.04	−14.43	
Δw_{jT}	0.02	−0.28	0.00	−1.73	
$(\hat{c}_{jT-1} - c_{jT-1})$	−0.07	1.26	−0.09	−33.98	Mismeasurement of initial conditions: −52.78 percent
$(\hat{y}_{jT-1} - y_{jT-1})$	−0.30	0.16	−0.05	−18.80	
$\Delta\hat{e}_{jT} - \Delta e_{jT}$	0.01	8.46	0.07	28.22	Differences in policy response: 15.99 percent
$\Delta\hat{w}_{jT} - \Delta w_{jT}$	−0.47	0.07	−0.03	−12.24	
$t93$	−0.12	0.10	−0.01	−4.77	
$t94$	0.42	0.15	0.06	25.34	
$t95$	1.19	0.14	0.17	66.65	
$t96$	−0.11	0.11	−0.01	−4.96	Year-specific variables: 182.08 percent
$t97$	0.08	0.11	0.01	3.38	
$t98$	0.35	0.10	0.04	14.53	
$t99$	1.30	0.11	0.14	56.64	
$t00$	0.42	0.10	0.04	17.40	
$t01$	0.36	0.06	0.02	7.87	
Country dummies	−1.36	0.01	−0.02	−6.60	Country-specific variables: −211.46 percent
$\Delta\hat{y}_{jT} - \Delta y_{T}$		**0.25**			
Total:			**0.25**	**100**	**100 percent**
Number of observations:			**162**		

Figure 3
Initial Conditions for Fiscal Account Ratio

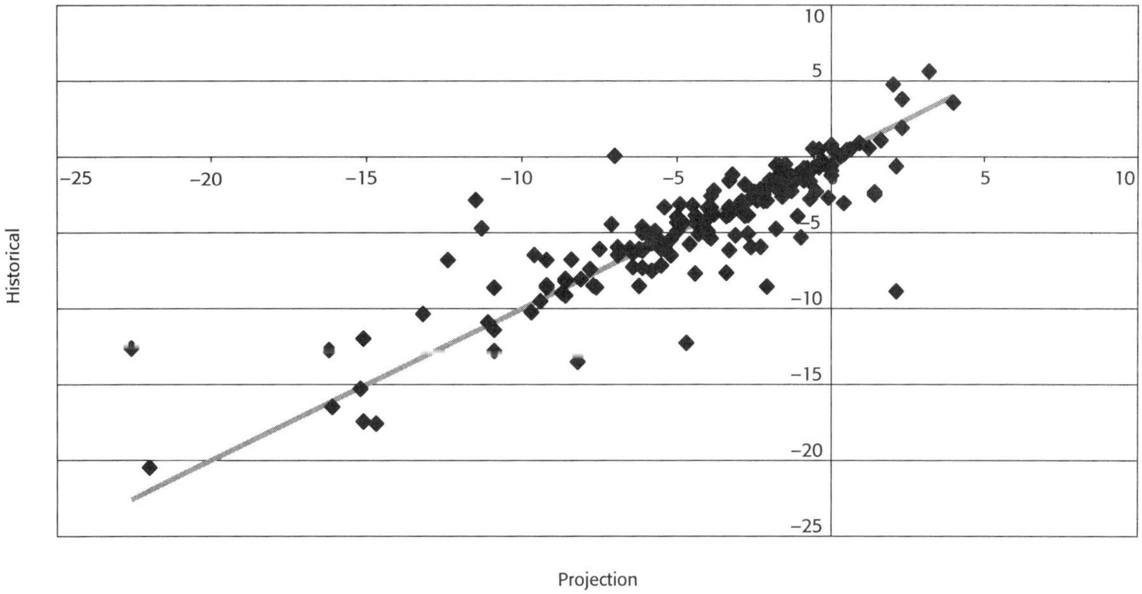

Figure 4
Initial Conditions for Current Account Ratio

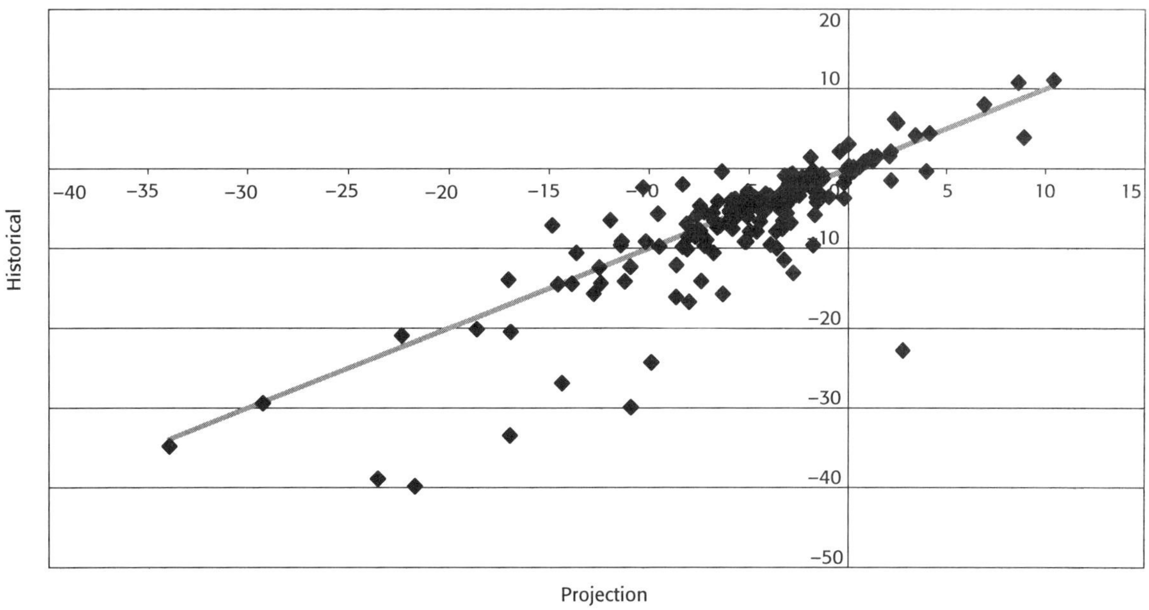

Figure 5a
Means of Projected and Historical Changes in Fiscal Ratios

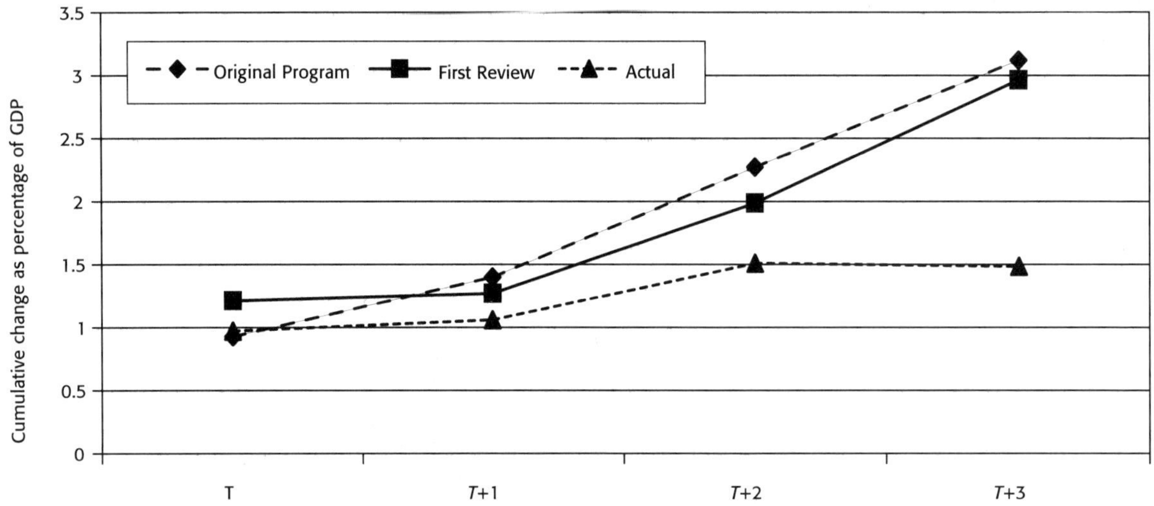

Figure 5b
Means of Projected and Historical Changes in Current Account Ratios

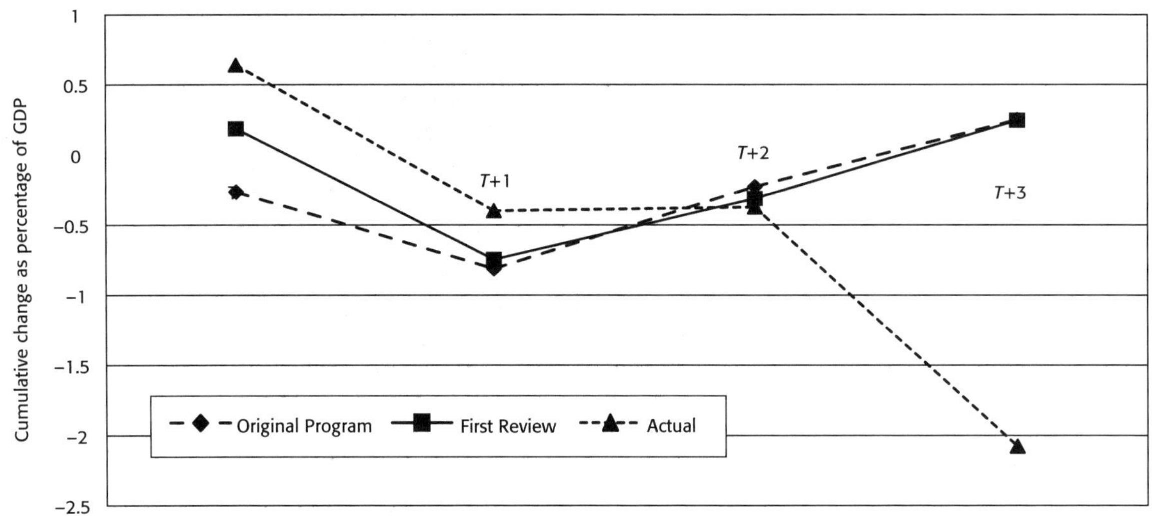

those reported in the first reviews (FRs), which take place during the first program year.[21] Some basic qualitative information on the evolution of the outcome projections can be illustrated by Figures 5a and 5b, where we compare historical and envisaged mean changes in the fiscal and current account ratios. These plots are based on the data summarized in Table 6.[22] An obvious observation is that for the vast majority of projection horizons, the first-review projections, $\Delta\hat{y}^{FR}_{jk}$ and $\Delta\hat{c}^{FR}_{jk}$, are closer to the actual outcomes, Δy_{jk} and Δc_{jk}, than the original program projections, $\Delta\hat{y}^{OP}_{jk}$ and $\Delta\hat{c}^{OP}_{jk}$. The only exception is the change in the fiscal ratio for the horizon *T*.

[21] Actual timing and number of reviews vary from program to program. In general, Stand-By Arrangements and extended arrangements (SBAs and EFFs) have more frequent reviews than arrangements under the structural adjustment facilities (SAF, ESAF, and PRGF). Further, the completion of reviews is often held up by difficulties in complying with conditionality. For these reasons, we plan in future research to address the relationship between review timing and projection error.

[22] Figures 5a and 5b include similar information to that of Figures 1a and 1b. They differ, however, in the number of observations used in creating the mean values. For example, Figure 1a uses 175 observations for horizon *T* to calculate the mean historical and envisaged change in the fiscal ratio, while Figure 5a uses 120 observations for which both original program and first review observations of fiscal ratio are available.

Table 6

Projecting the Change in Macroeconomic Aggregates (Original Program (OP) Versus First Review (FR))

Variable	N	Mean	Std Dev	Sum	Minimum	Maximum
			Horizon T			
$\Delta\hat{c}^{FR}_{jT}$	120	0.18624	3.67482	22.34863	−11.25961	14.09314
$\Delta\hat{c}^{OP}_{jT}$	120	−0.26392	3.25906	−31.66988	−13.89236	9.14219
Δc_{jT}	120	0.64113	4.33661	76.93582	−16.63708	14.29500
$\Delta\hat{y}^{FR}_{jT}$	120	1.21250	2.68248	145.50000	−5.50000	9.40000
$\Delta\hat{y}^{OP}_{jT}$	120	0.92700	2.82961	111.24000	−7.60000	11.00000
Δy_{jt}	120	0.97491	2.95418	116.98875	−6.27027	12.72751
			Horizon T+1			
$\Delta\hat{c}^{FR}_{jT+1}$	95	−0.74583	5.81160	−70.85403	−26.17494	11.90127
$\Delta\hat{c}^{OP}_{jT+1}$	95	−0.81342	5.31906	−77.27510	22.23187	11.90477
Δc_{jT+1}	95	−0.39908	7.35763	−37.91262	−35.61176	17.19095
$\Delta\hat{y}^{FR}_{jT+1}$	95	1.27189	3.35196	120.83000	−5.60000	13.30000
$\Delta\hat{y}^{OP}_{jT+1}$	95	1.40253	3.18396	133.24000	−5.60000	12.90000
Δy_{jT+1}	95	1.05813	3.75009	100.52207	−6.76704	13.69233
			Horizon T+2			
$\Delta\hat{c}^{FR}_{jT+2}$	74	−0.31151	5.18034	−23.05211	−17.31635	11.10499
$\Delta\hat{c}^{OP}_{jT+2}$	74	−0.22570	4.91495	−16.70172	−22.04280	10.81110
Δc_{jT+2}	74	−0.37456	8.12439	−27.71773	−38.14743	21.78397
$\Delta\hat{y}^{FR}_{jT+2}$	74	1.98784	3.49077	147.10000	−4.70000	13.50000
$\Delta\hat{y}^{OP}_{jT+2}$	74	2.27838	3.15904	168.60000	−3.30000	13.20000
Δy_{jT+2}	74	1.51000	4.07910	111.73996	−14.88070	11.88877
			Horizon T+3			
$\Delta\hat{c}^{FR}_{jT+3}$	50	0.24462	5.16137	12.23123	−14.73737	12.91443
$\Delta\hat{c}^{OP}_{jT+3}$	50	0.24960	4.89254	12.48019	−19.89594	7.35647
Δc_{jT+3}	50	−2.07739	14.24848	−103.86963	−81.56932	21.40533
$\Delta\hat{y}^{FR}_{jT+3}$	50	2.96400	4.02060	148.20000	−3.90000	13.10000
$\Delta\hat{y}^{OP}_{jT+3}$	50	3.11580	3.52157	155.79000	−1.90000	13.00000
Δy_{jT+3}	50	1.48644	4.21497	74.32213	−12.33862	11.64537

Notes: N denotes number of observations; Std Dev denotes standard deviation.

Assessment of only mean changes might be misleading, since, as we showed in the previous sections, there is a great deal of variability in envisaged and historical data. Some additional insights on the evolution of the projections can be obtained by examining developments in correlations between envisaged and actual changes. Table 7 reports those correlations for fiscal and current account ratios for both first reviews and original programs. As we found in the regressions of the previous section, envisaged changes in fiscal ratios exhibit higher correlation with the actual changes than do comparable changes in envisaged and actual current account ratios. This observation is true for projections drawn from the original program as well as those from the first reviews. Inaccuracy of the current account projections seems to worsen significantly with the length of the projection horizon. Also, there is a strong pattern showing that the projection performance of the first reviews, measured by the correlation coefficient, improves relative to the projections of the original programs for all variables and all projection horizons. The gain in forecasting power is particularly noticeable over short horizons—and

Table 7

Correlations Between Projected and Actual Outcomes for Changes in Macroeconomic Aggregates (Original Program (OP) Versus First Review (FR))

Horizons	T	$T+1$	$T+2$	$T+3$
Fiscal ratio (Δy_{jk}, $\Delta \hat{y}_{jk}^{FR}$)	0.69635	0.76157	0.70624	0.60535
Fiscal ratio (Δy_{jk}, $\Delta \hat{y}_{jk}^{OP}$)	0.60742	0.69037	0.65761	0.57322
Correlation improvement ($\rho_y^{FR} - \rho_y^{OP}$)	0.08893	0.0712	0.04863	0.03213
Current account ratio (Δc_{jk}, $\Delta \hat{c}_{jk}^{FR}$)	0.69175	0.46345	0.33955	0.35714
Current account ratio (Δc_{jk}, $\Delta \hat{c}_{jk}^{OP}$)	0.50390	0.34193	0.30747	0.35449
Correlation improvement ($\rho_c^{FR} - \rho_c^{OP}$)	0.18785	0.12152	0.03208	0.00265

decreases as the length of the projection horizon extends.

Bias, Efficiency, and Accuracy of Revisions

Musso and Phillips (2001) suggested an interesting approach to evaluating projections. They analyze projections on the basis of three major characteristics: bias, efficiency, and accuracy. In this paper, we follow their approach and document some of the facts along these three dimensions to compare the relative performance of the projections of the original programs and their first revisions.

Bias. By bias, we refer to the divergence of the distribution of projection errors from the zero-mean normal distribution. Table 8 presents statistics characterizing the distribution of $(\Delta\hat{c}_T - \Delta c_T)$ and $(\Delta\hat{y}_T - \Delta y_T)$ for the original programs as well as for their first revisions.[23] Several observations can be made from the information presented in Table 8:

- The null hypothesis of the true mean of the distribution being zero is rejected more frequently for the original program projection errors than for those from the first reviews. It is especially noticeable for the fiscal balance ratios.
- Standard deviations are considerably smaller for the first-review projection errors than those for the original programs. The difference is greater for short horizons and becomes very small or even reverses for longer horizons.
- For the horizon T, positive skew of the distribution of the projection errors for both variables suggests that projection errors are more likely to be far above the mean than they are to be far below the mean. This result can be observed for both groups of projections. However, for longer horizons, the skew tends to be negative, reflecting the opposite trend.
- For both variables and for most of the horizon lengths, the distribution of errors has more mass in the tails than a Gaussian distribution with the same variance. The only exceptions are projection error distributions for horizon T changes in the current account (FR), and horizon $T+1$ changes in the fiscal balance (both OP and FR).
- For the OP projection errors, most of the tests find statistically significant evidence that the distributions exhibit lack of normality. The only exception is the $T+1$ horizon for fiscal balances. For the FR projection errors, the results are mixed. Some of the goodness-of-fit tests for normal distribution cannot reject the null hypothesis of normality.[24]

Efficiency. We test the efficiency of the FR and OP projections by regressing the value of the historical change on a constant term and the value of projected change as illustrated in equations (8a) and (8b) for macroeconomic variable g_T, with v_T and u_T as random errors. We perform the estimation for changes in variables as well as for the levels.

$$\Delta g_T = c_0 + c_1 \Delta\hat{g}_T + v_T \quad (8a)$$

$$g_T = d_0 + d_1 \hat{g}_T + u_T. \quad (8b)$$

This type of efficiency test is referred to as the weak criterion since it uses a limited information set (Musso and Phillips, 2001). We would conclude that the projection was an efficient estimate of the historical datum if the intercept were insignificantly different from zero and the slope were insignificantly different from unity. Tables 9 and 10 report results of the estimation in changes and in levels, respectively.

There is a striking relationship between historical and projected changes found in the data: in each case, for the original program (except horizon $T+3$ changes in current account ratios), the hypothesis of weak efficiency is strongly rejected by the data. The

[23] Projection errors are calculated as the differences between envisaged values and actual realizations.

[24] We used Kolmogorov-Smirnov, Cramer-von Mises, Anderson-Darling, and chi-square tests to check normality. The results are reported in Table AIII.3.

Table 8

Program Projection Errors

Horizon		*T*	*T*+1	*T*+2	*T*+3
		Projection Errors in Changes of Fiscal Balance Ratios to GDP			
Mean	OP	0.048	−0.492**	−1.334*	−1.809*
	FR	−0.238	−0.252	−0.543	−1.478*
Median	OP	−0.014	−0.492	−0.786	−1.541
	FR	−0.232	−0.341	−0.548	−1.728
Standard deviation	OP	2.565	2.852	4.070	3.673
	FR	2.211	2.471	2.952	3.663
Skewness	OP	0.028	−0.009	−2.406	−1.582
	FR	0.827	0.312	−1.731	−1.591
Kurtosis	OP	4.32	1.636	10.100	4.747
	FR	6.142	1.057	9.812	6.467
Normality test	OP	Rejected	Mixed (3/4)	Rejected	Rejected
	FR	Rejected	Mixed (3/4)	Mixed (1/4)	Mixed (2/4)
		Projection Errors in Changes of Current Account Ratios to GDP			
Mean	OP	0.905*	0.258	−0.595	−2.176
	FR	0.455	0.262	−0.222	−2.220
Median	OP	0.583	0.669	−0.614	−0.666
	FR	0.281	0.410	−0.228	−0.994
Standard deviation	OP	3.897	7.260	7.766	12.492
	FR	3.204	6.824	7.832	12.726
Skewness	OP	1.222	−2.630	−2.555	−4.612
	FR	0.241	−3.405	−3.072	−4.702
Kurtosis	OP	5.442	17.961	17.032	29.405
	FR	1.825	24.079	18.618	29.359
Normality test	OP	Rejected	Rejected	Rejected	Rejected
	FR	Rejected	Mixed (1/4)	Rejected	Rejected

Notes: * Significantly different from zero at the 90 percent confidence level (based on student's *t*-test).
** Significantly different from zero at the 95 percent confidence level (based on student's *t*-test).
Mixed (*X*/4): *X* out of four tests cannot reject normality of the error terms at the 95 percent confidence level.
OP denotes original program; FR denotes first review.

Table 9
Test of "Weak" Efficiency (in changes)

	Original Program			First Review		
	Coeff.	S.E.	*t*–statistic	Coeff.	S.E.	*t*–statistic
Fiscal balance ratios						
			Horizon: *T*			
Intercept (H_0: Intercept=0)	0.387*	0.227	1.709	0.045	0.214	0.210
Slope (H_0: Slope =1)	0.634***	0.076	–4.792	0.767***	0.073	–3.192
R^2		**0.369**			**0.485**	
			Horizon: *T*+1			
Intercept (H_0: Intercept=0)	–0.084	0.296	–0.284	–0.056	0.265	–0.211
Slope (H_0: Slope =1)	0.731***	0.082	–3.281	0.848**	0.075	–2.027
R^2		**0.439**			**0.577**	
			Horizon: *T*+2			
Intercept (H_0: Intercept=0)	–0.168	0.498	–0.337	–0.182	0.379	–0.480
Slope (H_0: Slope =1)	0.542***	0.114	–4.018	0.814**	0.096	–1.938
R^2		**0.211**			**0.492**	
			Horizon: *T*+3			
Intercept (H_0: Intercept=0)	–0.804	0.613	–1.312	–0.395	0.598	–0.661
Slope (H_0: Slope =1)	0.704**	0.12	–2.467	0.635***	0.12	–3.042
R^2		**0.377**			**0.366**	
Current account ratios						
			Horizon: *T*			
Intercept (H_0: Intercept=0)	0.818**	0.345	2.371	0.489*	0.288	1.698
Slope (H_0: Slope =1)	0.671***	0.106	–3.104	0.816**	0.079	–2.329
R^2		**0.254**			**0.479**	
			Horizon: *T*+1			
Intercept (H_0: Intercept=0)	–0.096	0.671	–0.143	–0.006	0.650	–0.009
Slope (H_0: Slope =1)	0.467***	0.130	–4.100	0.583***	0.113	–3.690
R^2		**0.114**			**0.215**	
			Horizon: *T*+2			
Intercept (H_0: Intercept=0)	–0.568	0.803	–0.707	–0.365	0.850	–0.429
Slope (H_0: Slope =1)	0.507***	0.169	–2.917	0.550***	0.169	–2.663
R^2		**0.097**			**0.120**	
			Horizon: *T*+3			
Intercept (H_0: Intercept=0)	–2.183	1.649	–1.324	–2.221	1.734	–1.281
Slope (H_0: Slope =1)	1.016	0.353	0.045	1.004	0.350	0.011
R^2		**0.127**			**0.134**	

Notes: * The null hypothesis (H_0) can be rejected at the 90 percent confidence level.
** The null hypothesis can be rejected at the 95 percent confidence level.
*** The null hypothesis can be rejected at the 99 percent confidence level.
Coeff. denotes coefficient; S.E. denotes standard error.

Table 10
Test of "Weak" Efficiency (in levels)

	Original Program			First Review		
	Coeff.	S.E.	*t*-statistic	Coeff.	S.E.	*t*-statistic
Fiscal balance ratios						
			Year: *T*			
Intercept (H_0: Intercept=0)	−1.870***	0.345	−5.420	−1.483***	0.297	−4.993
Slope (H_0: Slope =1)	0.493***	0.076	−6.671	0.685***	0.071	−4.437
R^2		**0.263**			**0.437**	
Current account ratios						
			Year: *T*			
Intercept (H_0: Intercept=0)	−1.529**	0.694	−2.203	−1.121**	0.529	−2.119
Slope (H_0: Slope =1)	0.706***	0.101	−2.911	0.912	0.081	−1.086
R^2		**0.289**			**0.512**	

Notes: ** The null hypothesis (H_0) can be rejected at the 95 percent confidence level.
*** The null hypothesis can be rejected at the 99 percent confidence level.
Coeff. denotes coefficient; S.E. denotes standard error.

rejection is in all cases based on an estimate of c_1 or d_1 that is significantly less than unity. When the FR results are examined, weak efficiency is once again rejected. However, when compared with the OP results, the coefficient estimates of c_1 and d_1 are closer to the hypothesized value of unity.[25]

Accuracy. We test relative accuracy of the OP and FR projections by comparing them with a random-walk benchmark projection. That is, we investigate whether the IMF projections of the year-T values of the variables do better than if the projections were simply set equal to the T–1 values. We draw our conclusions from Theil's U statistic and report results in Table 11.[26] Larger values of the U statistic indicate a poor projection performance. The benchmark random-walk projections for OP are based on the T–1 value of the variable as it is documented in OP, while the benchmark random-walk projection for FR uses the initial conditions from the revised data of FR.

For the fiscal balance, both OP and FR projections perform better than the random walk. However, only the FR projection outperforms the random walk for the current account; the OP projection for this variable is slightly worse than that of its random-walk counterpart. Overall, the FR projections exhibit lower values of the U statistic, reflecting their more accurate projections.[27]

An Empirical Decomposition

The preceding results suggest that the IMF staff modifies its projections to incorporate new information, and that the revised projections have better forecasting power when compared with the projections of the original programs. It is possible to decompose the difference in the OP and FR projections using a methodology similar to that of equation (3e) and Table 4. The details of this analysis are reported in Annexes I–III. The salient findings for our purpose are as follows:

- There is a substantial difference in initial conditions used in the two projections, and these differences contribute significantly to the improvement of FR over OP.
- There is also evidence that the model used in the FR projections differs significantly from that used in the OP projections.

[25] There is a difficulty in this type of estimation that is not addressed by Musso and Phillips (2001). Since the right-hand-side variable is only an estimate of the true OP projection, the regression may be characterized by error-in-variables. This will cause the slope coefficient to be biased downward. We investigated this possibility using an instrumental-variable technique. The resulting slope coefficients were, in most cases, closer to unity and insignificantly different from unity for the fiscal ratio, thus exhibiting weak efficiency. They were farther from unity for the current account ratio, thus sustaining the conclusion of inefficiency for that variable.

[26] The Theil's U Statistic:

$$U = \sqrt{\frac{1/N\sum_{jt}(g_{jt} - \hat{g}_{jt})^2}{1/N\sum_{jt} g_{jt}^2}}.$$

[27] The pattern of errors in OP and FR projections are similar to those observed by Howrey (1984) in his study of inventory investment. He found in that case that there was evidence of substantial revision to initial data in inventory investment over the period 1954–80. He also found, however, that knowledge of the revision reduced only marginally the variance of projection error.

Table 11
Test of Accuracy (in levels)

Projection Model	Number of Observations	Theil's *U* Statistic: Fiscal balance ratios	Theil's *U* Statistic: Current account ratios
Original program	121	0.695	0.696
Benchmark for OP (random walk)	121	0.788	0.639
First review	120	0.571	0.568
Benchmark for FR (random walk)	120	0.760	0.635

Notes: OP denotes original program; FR denotes first review.

There is evidently "learning by doing" in these projections at the modeling stage as well as at the stage of data collection.

Conclusions

Envisaged and historical observations on the fiscal and current account ratios in countries participating in 175 IMF programs between 1993 and 2001 deviated strongly from one another. Our statistical analysis suggests that the causes can be separated into four components.

First, the IMF staff was apparently working with quite different information about the initial conditions of the program countries than is currently accepted as historical. This difference leads to substantial divergence even if the IMF staff used the model revealed by the historical data. This result is consistent with the conclusions of Orphanides (2001); and Callan, Ghysels, and Swanson (2002) on the making of U.S. monetary policy.

Second, the IMF staff did appear to have a different model in mind when making its projections. Its model was characterized by gradual fiscal account adjustment, both in response to contemporaneous current account shocks and to long-run imbalances, while the model revealed by historical data was characterized by more rapid adjustment to both types of imbalances. Further, its envisaged response was concentrated in horizon T, while the historical response to shocks was roughly equally proportioned across horizons T and $T+1$.

Third, there is a difference between projected and historical implementation of policy adjustment. Given the level of aggregation of the policy variables investigated (total government consumption expenditures, real exchange rate depreciation) we cannot conclude that the difference is due to a failure to meet the conditions of the program; the differences could also be due to shocks that worsened the performance of these aggregates even when conditions were fulfilled. This is a question that can, and should, be investigated further.

Fourth, there is ample evidence that, like other macroeconomic projections, IMF projections are quite inaccurate. The evidence on "accuracy" reported here is instructive—while the projections outperform a random walk most of the time, they are not much better. The Meese and Rogoff (1983) results remind us of the difficulty in projecting exchange rates in time series. The project described here indicates the inaccuracy of simple models in a panel (i.e., time-series and cross-section of countries) format.

Our results on revisions indicate that the IMF staff learns from past projection errors—and from new information. However, even that learning leaves large gaps to fill. The largest margin for improvement may well be in "just-in-time" data collection, so that the errors owing to incomplete information, especially from initial conditions, can be eliminated.

Annex I. Creating the Error-Correction Residuals

In the following tables (AI.1–AI.3), we use the IMF's World Economic Outlook (WEO) dataset covering those programs with time horizon T. There are 175 observations in general, although somewhat more when considered in levels.

Creating the error correction residual e_{jt}

Dependent variable: y_{jt} (WEO)

Table AI.1

Analysis of Variance

Source	DF	Sum of Squares	Mean Square	*F* Value	*Pr* > *F*
Model	86	5,518.14566	64.16448	6.58	<.0001
Error	96	935.61705	9.74601		
Uncorrected total	182	6,453.76271			

Root MSE	3.12186	*R*–square	0.8550
Dependent mean	−4.33059	Adjusted *R*–square	0.7252
Coefficient of variance	−72.08859		

Parameter Estimates

Variable	DF	Parameter Estimate	Standard Error	*t* Value	*Pr* > |*t*|
C_{jt}	1	0.09996	0.06203	1.61	0.1103
*t*93	1	−7.41751	1.72365	−4.30	<.0001
*t*94	1	−4.83851	1.91288	−2.53	0.0131
*t*95	1	−6.31586	1.84898	−3.42	0.0009
*t*96	1	−5.37486	1.92894	−2.79	0.0064
*t*97	1	−3.98082	1.88383	−2.11	0.0372
*t*98	1	−3.63622	1.95216	−1.86	0.0656
*t*99	1	−4.64533	1.95383	−2.38	0.0194
*t*00	1	−5.26644	1.97374	−2.67	0.0090
*t*01	1	−5.92937	1.83106	−3.24	0.0017

Notes: DF denotes degrees of freedom; MSE denotes mean square error.

This is the formulation used to create the error correction variable ($e_{T-1} = y_t -$ predicted value) for WEO data. A complete set of country dummies was used as well, but is suppressed here.

The following regression results report the coefficients used in creating the error-correction variable for envisaged data:

Table AI.2

Analysis of Variance

Dependent variable: y_{jt} (envisaged)

Source	DF	Sum of Squares	Mean Square	*F* Value	*Pr* > *F*
Model	95	6,449.94187	67.89412	5.29	<0.0001
Error	97	1,244.26623	12.82749		
Uncorrected total	192	7,694.20810			

Root MSE	3.58155	*R*–square	0.8383
Dependent mean	−4.47401	Adj. *R*–square	0.6799
Coefficient of variation	−80.05230		

Notes: DF denotes degrees of freedom; MSE denotes mean square error.

Table AI.3
Parameter Estimates

Variable	DF	Parameter Estimate	Standard Error	*t* Value	*Pr* > |*t*|
C_{jt}	1	0.31664	0.07861	4.03	0.0001
*t*93	1	−6.84332	1.81926	−3.76	0.0003
*t*94	1	−4.68806	1.95701	−2.40	0.0185
*t*95	1	−5.69861	1.90593	−2.99	0.0035
*t*96	1	−3.85602	1.93132	−2.00	0.0487
*t*97	1	−3.34252	1.93759	−1.73	0.0877
*t*98	1	−2.74118	1.85499	−1.48	0.1427
*t*99	1	−4.38718	2.07410	−2.12	0.0370
*t*00	1	−3.95966	2.08914	−1.90	0.0610
*t*01	1	−5.05367	2.00406	−2.52	0.0133

Notes: DF denotes degrees of freedom. A complete set of country dummies was used as well, but it has been suppressed here for brevity.

Annex II. Does the Timing of Approval of IMF-Supported Programs Matter to These Results?

76

Projection errors, especially for the initial program year (year *T*), may reasonably be hypothesized to depend on the point in time during the year when a program was approved. We investigated this hypothesis in two ways. First, we calculated Pearson correlations of the approval month with the size of the projection error for horizons *T* and *T*+1 (Table AII.1). Second, we regressed the projection error on dummy variables indicating the quarter of year *T* in which approval occurred (Table AII.2).

The Pearson correlations provide no evidence of a significant approval-time effect in either variable. For the fiscal ratio, there is no evidence of a significant approval-time effect for either OP or FR projection errors. For the current account ratio, a number of coefficients are positive and significant. However, they do not grow uniformly over the sample; the largest deviations from the mean occur for programs approved in the second and third quarters of "year *T*."

We did the same exercise for the deviation in initial conditions (Table AII.3); in that case, the hypothesis is that programs approved later in year *T* will have more accurate information on the initial conditions, so that deviations will be lessened. There is no evidence of a significant effect in the Pearson correlations. There is some evidence of this in the regression results, however (Table AII.4). For both OP and FR versions of the fiscal ratio and the OP version of the current account ratio, the deviation in initial conditions is significantly larger, on average, for programs approved in the first quarter of year *T* than for those approved later in year *T*. There is thus a downward bias in the fiscal ratios used as initial conditions in projections created in the first quarter of year *T* relative to the historical data, most likely because the IMF staff did not have access to the later revisions when creating its projections.

Table AII.1
Pearson Correlations for Projection Errors

	Fiscal Balance: Original Program (approval month in *T*)	Fiscal Balance: First Review (approval month in *T*)	Current Account: Original Program (approval month in *T*)	Current Account: First Review (approval month in *T*)
Horizon *T*	0.01905	−0.02677	0.00687	0.06711
	0.8364	0.7716	0.9406	0.4665
	120	120	120	120
Horizon *T*+1	−0.05439	−0.15750	0.14289	0.14916
	0.5853	0.1234	0.1499	0.1406
	103	97	103	99

Notes: Each cell in this table includes three statistics: the top entry is the Pearson correlation coefficient; the middle entry is Prob>|r| under the null hypothesis of zero correlation; and the bottom entry is the is the number of observations.

Table AII.2

Regressions on Quarterly Dummies (Horizon *T*) for Projection Errors

	Fiscal balance (OP)	Fiscal balance (FR)	Current account (OP)	Current account (FR)
Quarter 1	0.06	−0.11	0.44	−0.15
	(0.46)	(0.40)	(0.69)	(0.57)
Quarter 2	−0.27	−0.47	1.08*	0.94*
	(0.39)	(0.34)	(0.60)	(0.49)
Quarter 3	0.26	−0.16	1.76**	0.26
	(0.51)	(0.44)	(0.77)	(0.63)
Quarter 4	0.44	−0.04	0.13	0.63
	(0.59)	(0.51)	(0.90)	(0.74)
R^2	0.01	0.02	0.07	0.04
Number of observations	120	120	120	120

Notes: OP denotes original program; FR denotes first review. Standard errors appear in parentheses.
* Indicates significance at the 90 percent confidence level.
** Indicates significance at the 95 percent confidence level.

Table AII.3

Pearson Correlations for Discrepancies in Initial Conditions

(Actual – Projection)

	Fiscal Balance: Original Program (approval month in *T*)	Fiscal Balance: First Review (approval month in *T*)	Current Account: Original Program (approval month in *T*)	Current Account: First Review (approval month in *T*)
All horizons	0.13744	0.10628	0.09385	−0.11611
	0.1328	0.2440	0.3076	0.2028
	121	122	120	122

Notes: Each cell in this table includes three statistics: the top entry is the Pearson correlation coefficient; the middle entry is Prob>|r| under the null hypothesis of zero correlation; and the bottom entry is the is the number of observations.

Table AII.4

Regressions on Quarterly Dummies for Discrepancies in Initial Conditions

	Fiscal Balance (OP)	Fiscal Balance (FR)	Current Account (OP)	Current Account (FR)
Quarter 1	−0.80**	−0.73**	−1.75**	1.56
	(0.39)	(0.35)	(0.73)	(1.11)
Quarter 2	−0.37	−0.40	−0.95	−0.82
	(0.34)	(0.31)	(0.63)	(0.96)
Quarter 3	0.27	0.05	−0.75	0.62
	(0.44)	(0.39)	(0.82)	(1.23)
Quarter 4	−0.18	−0.21	−0.34	−2.17
	(0.51)	(0.46)	(0.95)	(1.44)
R^2	0.05	0.05	0.07	0.04
Number of observations	120	120	120	120

Notes: OP denotes original program; FR denotes first review. Standard errors appear in parentheses.
** Indicates significance at the 95 percent confidence level.

Table AII.5

Regressions on Quarterly Dummies (Horizon *T*) for Differences in Initial Conditions Between First Review (FR) and Original Program (OP)

	Fiscal Balance (FR – OP)	Current Account (FR – OP)
Quarter 1	−0.072	−0.176
	(0.171)	(0.367)
Quarter 2	0.023	0.074
	(0.148)	(0.317)
Quarter 3	0.215	0.323
	(0.190)	(0.408)
Quarter 4	0.032	0.904*
	(0.222)	(0.477)
R^2	0.013	0.039
Number of observations	120	120

Notes: * Indicates significance at the 90 percent confidence level. Standard errors appear in parentheses.

If there is a value to this information, it should also be evident in the initial conditions as reported in FR relative to OP for each program. In Table AII.5, we compare the initial conditions, with deviations measured as FR values *minus* OP values. A similar regression on approval times within year T yields little evidence of a systematic bias, with only the current account ratio showing any deviation of significance. The estimated coefficients are suggestive, though, rising from negative values for Q1 approval to ever-increasing values for subsequent quarters.

Annex III. What New Information Do Revisions Incorporate?

The results in the text suggest that IMF staff modifies its projections to incorporate new information and that the revised projections have better forecasting power relative to the original program. However, it is not yet clear whether this is a reflection of adjusting projections for new values of the initial conditions that contain less measurement error, or a sign of using new information to modify the entire scope of the model used in projection. We choose to address this issue by estimating regressions of the following general form:

$$\Delta\hat{g}_{jT}^{OP} = a_1\Delta\hat{g}_{jT-1}^{OP} + a_2\hat{g}_{jT-1}^{OP} + b_1\Delta\hat{s}_{jT}^{OP} + v_{jT}^{OP} \quad \text{(A3a)}$$

$$\Delta\hat{g}_{jT}^{FR} = \tilde{a}_1\Delta\hat{g}_{jT-1}^{FR} + \tilde{a}_2\hat{g}_{jT-1}^{FR} + \tilde{b}_1\Delta\hat{s}_{jT}^{FR} + v_{jT}^{FR} \quad \text{(A3b)}$$

The form is the same as that advanced in the previous section. The difference in projections can be stated in somewhat different form in equation (A3c). When we subtract (A3a) from (A3b), we note four different reasons why the two projections will not be the same: an updating of information on past events (within the first set of square brackets in (A3c)), increased information on policy implementation, a change in the "model" used in projection (within the second set of square brackets in (A3c)), and projection errors.

$$\begin{aligned}\Delta\hat{g}_{jT}^{FR} &= \Delta\hat{g}_{jT}^{OP} \\ &+\left[\tilde{a}_1(\Delta\hat{g}_{jT-1}^{FR} - \Delta\hat{g}_{jT-1}^{OP}) + \tilde{a}_2(\hat{g}_{jT-1}^{FR} - \hat{g}_{jT-1}^{OP})\right] \\ &+\tilde{b}_1(\Delta\hat{s}_{jT}^{FR} - \Delta\hat{s}_{jT}^{OP}) \\ &+\left[\begin{matrix}(\tilde{a}_1 - a_1)\Delta\hat{g}_{jT-1}^{OP} + (\tilde{a}_2 - a_2)\hat{g}_{jT-1}^{OP} \\ +(\tilde{b}_1 - b_1)\Delta\hat{s}_{jT}^{OP}\end{matrix}\right] \\ &+(v_{jT}^{FR} - v_{jT}^{OP}). \end{aligned} \quad \text{(A3c)}$$

Here, we regress projected changes in the macroeconomic variable as projected in the first review of the program ($\Delta\hat{g}_{jT}^{FR}$) on the projected change of the variable as it was originally planned at the outset of the program ($\Delta\hat{g}_{jT}^{OP}$) and on the terms reflecting improvement of the information on the initial conditions ($\Delta\hat{g}_{jT-1}^{FR} - \Delta\hat{g}_{jT-1}^{OP}$) and ($\hat{g}_{jT-1}^{FR} - \hat{g}_{jT-1}^{OP}$). We also incorporate a term representing differences in projected changes in the policy variable, ($\Delta\hat{s}_{jT}^{FR} - \Delta\hat{s}_{jT}^{OP}$), to capture changes in the implementation of conditions associated with the programs. Finally, all the terms within the second set of square brackets are included to study whether the forecasting model has changed.

We predict that the value of the coefficient on $\Delta\hat{g}_{jT}^{OP}$ will be unity, as would be the case, for example, if the first review simply caused a mean-preserving contraction in the distribution of random errors. Values of $\tilde{a}_1$ and $\tilde{a}_2$ differing significantly from zero will indicate that the revision observed in FR reflects the improved information about the initial conditions governing the economic success of the program. Figure AIII.1 illustrates the interpretation of this model. With $\tilde{a}_1$ and $\tilde{a}_2$ significantly different from zero and the coefficient on $\Delta\hat{g}_{jT}^{OP}$ being unity, the revision should trigger the "old model, new initial conditions" scenario pictured there. However, if the new information available during implementation of the program called for correction of the entire

Figure A.III.1
Incorporation of New Information in Projections

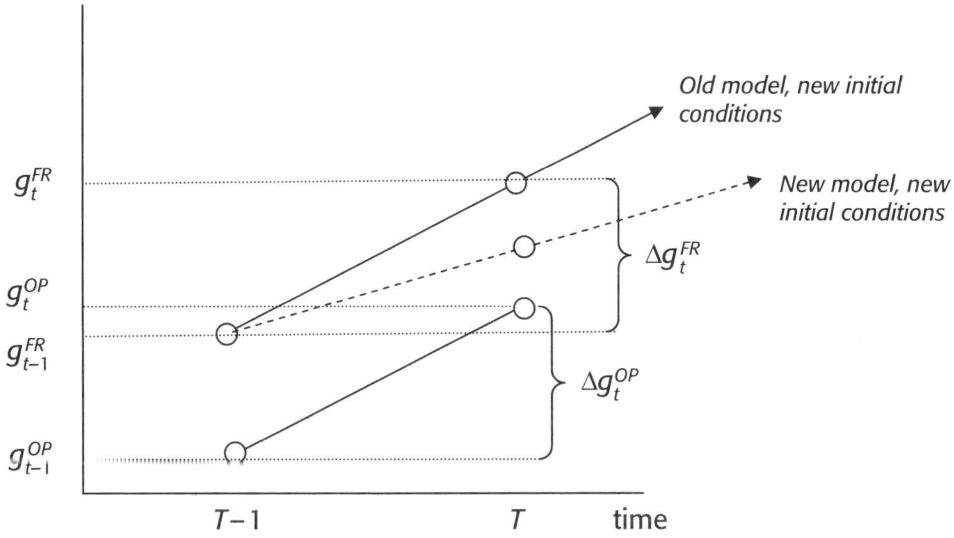

projection model, the coefficients on $\Delta\hat{g}_{jT-1}^{OP}$, $\hat{g}_{jT-1}^{OP}$, and $\Delta\hat{s}_{jT}^{OP}$ would be significantly different from zero and the estimates would follow the "new model, new initial conditions" scenario in Figure AIII.1.

Table AIII.1 summarizes the results of the model estimation for the ratio of fiscal balances to GDP for all programs in the sample at horizon T. Changes in fiscal ratios as they are projected in the first reviews of the programs are regressed not only on terms representing the error-correction structure of fiscal ratios but also on the similar terms corresponding to the current account ratios. A complete set of time and country dummy variables was also included in the regressions. The following insights can be obtained from the first column of Table AIII.1:

- The value of the coefficient on $\Delta\hat{y}_{jT}^{OP}$ is 0.986, which is not statistically different from unity. This could be interpreted as if the correction of the projection reported in the first review of the program is just a modification of the projection owing to the more accurate initial conditions. The updated information set available at the moment of revision is incorporated into the same projection model that was used to create OP projections. This result is consistent with the fact that none of the terms included to capture projection model modification is significantly different from zero.
- The coefficient on $(\Delta\hat{y}_{jT-1}^{FR} - \Delta\hat{y}_{jT-1}^{OP})$ is negative and significant. One of the potential explanations of this fact can be outlined as follows. Suppose that reduction of the measurement error results in an improvement in the fiscal balance in the years preceding the program relative to what it had been originally thought to be when the program was designed. That would mean that $(\Delta\hat{y}_{jT-1}^{FR} - \Delta\hat{y}_{jT-1}^{OP})$ is a positive number. Given our finding, this would result in a reduction of the projected change in the fiscal ratio projected in the first review of the program. Moreover, the value of the coefficient, –0.973, is not significantly different from –1, which suggests that this is a one-to-one relationship. This finding makes intuitive economic sense, because if the government's budget deficit is not as bad as was originally thought, the required correction of the fiscal balance is also less demanding.
- Specification testing reveals that changes in lagged first-difference terms with lag length greater than 1 do not contribute significantly to the regression. At the same time, none of the current account ratio terms is significantly different from 0, which suggests that improvement in the data quality of the current account has little effect on the projections of the fiscal ratios.
- The coefficient on the difference in the policy variable, $(\Delta\hat{s}_{jT}^{FR} - \Delta\hat{s}_{jT}^{OP})$, is negative and significant, implying that differences in policy between OP and FR are also responsible for the amendments of the original projections. Moreover, the negative sign of this coefficient suggests that a greater observed real depreciation results in less positive forecasts of changes in fiscal balance ratios.[28]
- Finally, testing jointly that both lagged level terms are not significantly different from zero

[28] Although it would be more reasonable to use total government expenditure as a policy variable in the regression for fiscal balances, the number of observations available for the first reviews limits the use of this variable as a proxy for a policy variable.

Table AIII.1
Regression Results, Fiscal Account Ratios (first review versus original program)

	$\Delta\hat{y}^{FR}_{jl}$		$\Delta\hat{y}^{FR}_{jT}$	
	Coefficient	Standard error	Coefficient	Standard error
$\Delta\hat{y}^{OP}_{jT}$	0.986***	0.141	0.970***	0.130
$(\Delta\hat{c}^{FR}_{jT} - \Delta\hat{c}^{OP}_{jT})$	0.040	0.137	0.047	0.124
$(\Delta\hat{y}^{FR}_{jT-1} - \Delta\hat{y}^{OP}_{jT-1})$	−0.973***	0.357	−0.756***	0.271
$(\Delta\hat{c}^{FR}_{jT-1} - \Delta\hat{c}^{OP}_{jT-1})$	0.314	0.237	0.210	0.224
$(\Delta\hat{y}^{FR}_{jT-2} - \Delta\hat{y}^{OP}_{jT-2})$	−0.350	0.406	−0.203	0.316
$(\Delta\hat{c}^{FR}_{jT-2} - \Delta\hat{c}^{OP}_{jT-2})$	−0.246	0.221	−0.206	0.192
$(\hat{y}^{FR}_{jT-1} - \hat{y}^{OP}_{jT-1})$	0.211	0.553		
$(\hat{c}^{FR}_{jT-1} - \hat{c}^{OP}_{jT-1})$	−0.308	0.209		
$\Delta\hat{y}^{OP}_{jT-1}$	0.075	0.087	0.035	0.076
$\hat{y}^{OP}_{jT-1}$	−0.043	0.133	−0.066	0.114
$\hat{e}^{OP}_{jT}$	−0.009	0.008	−0.012*	0.007
$(\Delta\hat{e}^{FR}_{jT} - \Delta\hat{e}^{OP}_{jT})$	−0.045***	0.016	−0.041***	0.016
Number of observations	91		91	
R^2	0.988		0.986	
Adjusted R^2	0.926		0.925	

Notes: Full sample, Horizon *T*.
* Significantly different from zero at the 90 percent confidence level.
*** Significantly different from zero at the 99 percent confidence level.
A complete set of time and country dummies was included in the regressions, but their coefficients have been suppressed for brevity.

allows us to conclude that revisions to initial conditions do not contribute systematically to the changes observed in FR relative to OP.

The second column in Table AIII.2 reports results of the estimation of a similar model when the lagged level terms are excluded from the regression.

- The coefficient on $\Delta\hat{y}^{OP}_{jT}$ is still insignificantly different from unity and the hypothesis that the IMF staff does not modify the projection model as the new information arrives is strongly supported by the data.
- At the same time, the coefficient on $\Delta\hat{e}^{OP}_{jT}$ is significantly different from zero at the 90 percent confidence level, providing some support for the hypothesis that the scope of the projecting model was amended.
- The coefficient on $(\Delta\hat{y}^{FR}_{jT-1} - \Delta\hat{y}^{OP}_{jT-1})$ is still negative, although much smaller in absolute value.
- The policy variable coefficient is still significantly different from zero.

Similarly, Table AIII.2 presents outcomes of the model estimation for the current account ratios for all programs in the sample at horizon *T*. Once again, we regress changes in current account ratios from the first reviews of the programs on terms representing the error-correction structure of current account ratios and on the similar terms corresponding to the fiscal ratios, as well as on the policy variable and the set of time and country dummies. The first column of the table represents the case in which the error-correction terms are included in the regression:

- The value of the coefficient on the originally projected change in the current account, $\Delta\hat{c}^{OP}_{jT}$, is 0.411 and the null hypothesis of the true value of this coefficient being unity is rejected at the 99 percent confidence level. Unlike our

Table AIII.2

Regression Results, Current Account Ratios (first review versus original program)

	$\Delta\hat{c}^{FR}_{jT}$		$\Delta\hat{c}^{FR}_{jT}$	
	Coefficient	Standard error	Coefficient	Standard error
$\Delta\hat{c}^{OP}_{jT}$	0.411*,+++	0.234	0.439***,+++	0.207
$(\Delta\hat{y}^{FR}_{jT-1} - \Delta\hat{y}^{OP}_{jT-1})$	−0.194	1.037	−0.211	0.666
$(\Delta\hat{c}^{FR}_{jT-1} - \Delta\hat{c}^{OP}_{jT-1})$	−0.297	0.691	−0.171	0.547
$(\Delta\hat{y}^{FR}_{jT-2} - \Delta\hat{y}^{OP}_{jT-2})$	−1.099	0.939	−1.279*	0.728
$(\Delta\hat{c}^{FR}_{jT-2} - \Delta\hat{c}^{OP}_{jT-2})$	0.037	0.474	0.084	0.428
$(\hat{y}^{FR}_{jT-1} - \hat{y}^{OP}_{jT-1})$	0.185	1.250		
$(\hat{c}^{FR}_{jT-1} - \hat{c}^{OP}_{jT-1})$	0.178	0.586		
$\Delta\hat{c}^{OP}_{jT-1}$	−0.085	0.201	−0.066	0.180
$\hat{c}^{OP}_{jT-1}$	−0.366***	0.142	−0.382***	0.126
$\hat{e}^{OP}_{jT}$	0.013	0.012	0.013	0.011
$(\Delta\hat{e}^{FR}_{jT} - \Delta\hat{e}^{OP}_{jT})$	−0.018	0.043	−0.025	0.036
Number of observations	91		91	
R^2	0.939		0.938	
Adjusted R^2	0.651		0.688	

Notes: Full sample, Horizon *T*.
* Significantly different from zero at the 90 percent confidence level.
*** Significantly different from zero at the 99 percent confidence level.
+++ Significantly different from unity at the 99 percent confidence level.
A complete set of time and country dummies was included in the regressions, but their coefficients have been suppressed for brevity.

result for the case of fiscal ratio projections, the projected change in the current account ratio in the revision of the program appears to be derived under a different model relative to the change in the current account projected at the beginning of the program.

- Modification of the projection model is also strongly supported by the fact that the coefficient on $\Delta\hat{c}^{OP}_{jT-1}$ is significant at the 99 percent confidence level.

Excluding the lagged level terms from the regression gives us a slightly better understanding of the relationship between the considered variables.

- The coefficient on the originally projected change in the current account, $\Delta\hat{c}^{OP}_{jT}$, is still significantly different from unity at the 99 percent confidence level and takes the value of 0.439. Thus, we still find strong support for distinguishing between the original program and first-review projection models.
- However, one of the terms representing changes in the initial conditions for fiscal ratio, $(\Delta\hat{y}^{FR}_{jT-2}-\Delta\hat{y}^{OP}_{jT-2})$, is significantly different from zero at the 90 percent confidence level, with a coefficient value of −1.279. This suggests that the projection of the current account ratio is significantly affected by the changes in the initial conditions of the fiscal balance ratios. Moreover, the sign of the estimated coefficients indicates that an improvement in the initial conditions of the fiscal balance relative to what it was originally assumed to be when the program was designed induces a reduction in the projected change in the current account for some given values of the other variables. This result is supported by our previous finding that the coefficient on $(\Delta\hat{y}^{FR}_{jT-1}-\Delta\hat{y}^{OP}_{jT-1})$ in the regression of fiscal balances reported in Table AIII.1 is negative. To illustrate this, suppose that reduction of the measurement error results in the improvement of the fiscal balance initial conditions relative to what it had been originally thought to be

Figure A.III.2
Distribution of Differences in *T*–1 Levels Between FR and OP for Fiscal Ratios

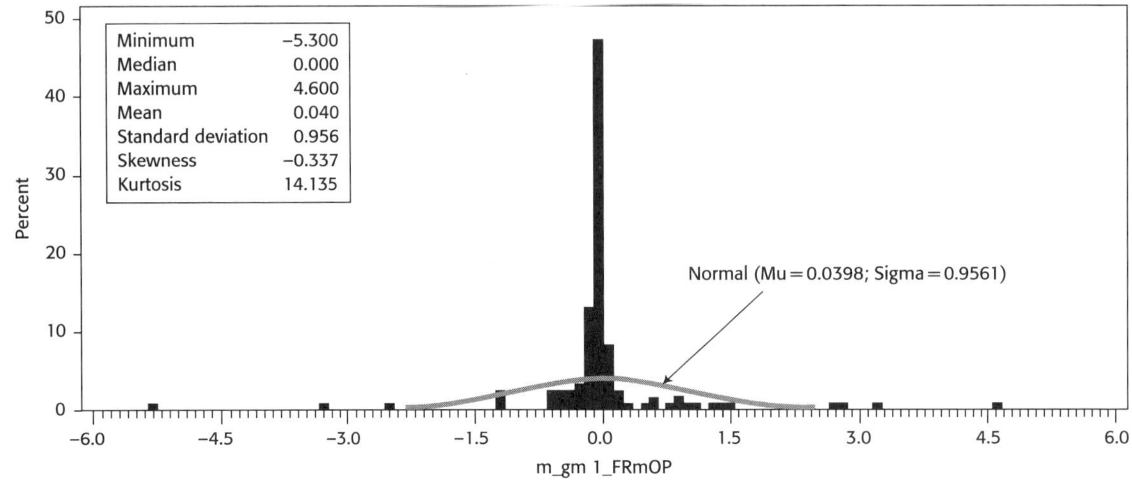

Notes: FR denotes first review; OP denotes original program.

Figure A.III.3
Distribution of Differences in *T*–1 Levels Between FR and OP for Current Account Ratio

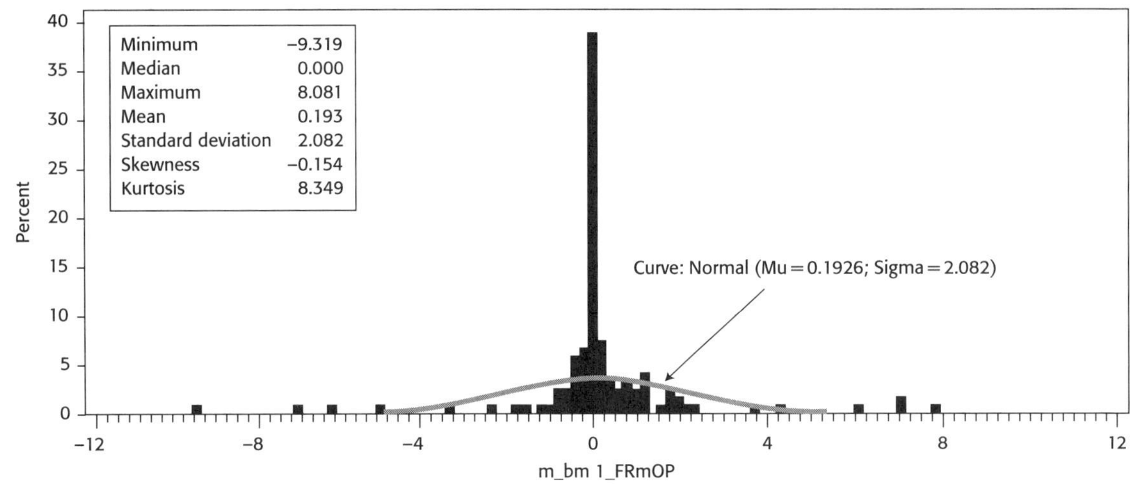

Notes: FR denotes first review; OP denotes original program.

when the program was designed, implying that $(\Delta\hat{y}^{FR}_{jT-1}-\Delta\hat{y}^{OP}_{jT-1})$ is positive. Since the coefficient on this term is negative, this would result in the reduction of the projected change in the fiscal ratio projected in the first review of the program, $\Delta\hat{y}^{FR}_{jT}$. Then the macro identity written in the first-difference form, $\Delta\hat{y}^{FR}_{jT}=\Delta\hat{c}^{FR}_{jT}-\Delta\hat{p}^{FR}_{jT}$, suggests that for any given value of private saving, $\Delta\hat{p}^{FR}_{jT}$, the projected change in the current account, $\Delta\hat{c}^{FR}_{jT}$, also reduces. This decrease in the current account ratio as a result of improvement in the initial conditions for fiscal ratios is captured in our model by the negative sign of the coefficient on the corresponding terms.

Our analysis shows that the correction in the initial conditions has a strong influence on the magnitude of the projections for both fiscal and current account ratios. Therefore, it appears to be logical to look at the magnitude of those corrections and their distribution. Figures AIII.2 and AIII.3 illustrate the distribution of the corrections in the levels of fiscal balance ratio to GDP and the distribution of the corrections in the levels of current account ratio to GDP, respectively, for the year *T*–1. These corrections are large, varying between –5.3 percent and 4.6 percent of GDP for fiscal ratios and between –9.3 percent and 8.1 percent of GDP for current account ratios. The mass of the distributions is

Table AIII.3
Goodness-of-Fit Tests for Normal Distribution for Corrections in Initial Conditions

Variable	Test	Statistic	P Value (H_0: normal)
$(y^{FR}_{jt-1} - y^{OP}_{jt-1})$	Kolmogorov-Smirnov	0.3179	< 0.010
	Cramer-von Mises	3.9281	< 0.005
	Anderson-Darling	18.6995	< 0.005
	chi-square	17,877.8796	< 0.001
$(c^{FR}_{jt-1} - c^{OP}_{jt-1})$	Kolmogorov-Smirnov	0.24224	< 0.010
	Cramer-von Mises	2.73701	< 0.005
	Anderson-Darling	13.70785	< 0.005
	chi-square	9,843.90054	< 0.001

Note: H_0 denotes the null hypothesis.

concentrated around 0. The negative skew in both cases shows that the corrections of the initial conditions are more likely to be far below the mean than they are to be far above the mean. Also, both distributions have kurtosis that exceeds 3, which implies that they have more mass in the tails than a Gaussian distribution with the same variance. Table AIII.3 reports results of the goodness-of-fit tests for the normal distribution. All of the tests strongly reject the null hypothesis of the initial condition corrections having a Gaussian distribution.

References

Callan, Myles, Eric Ghysels, and Norman R. Swanson, 2002, "Monetary Policy Rules with Model and Data Uncertainty," *Southern Economic Journal*, Vol. 69, pp. 239–65.

Clements, Michael P., and David Hendry, 1995, "Forecasting in Cointegrated Systems," *Journal of Applied Econometrics*, Vol. 10, pp. 127–46.

Hamilton, James, 1994, *Time Series Analysis* (Princeton, New Jersey: Princeton University Press).

Hendry, David, 1997, "The Econometrics of Macroeconomic Forecasting," *Economic Journal*, Vol. 107, pp. 1330–57.

Howrey, E.P., 1984, "Data Revision, Reconstruction and Prediction: An Application to Inventory Investment," *Review of Economics and Statistics*, Vol. 66, No. 3, pp. 386–93.

Meese, Richard, and Kenneth Rogoff, 1983, "Empirical Exchange Rate Models of the Seventies: Do They Fit Out of Sample?" *Journal of International Economics*, Vol. 14, pp. 3–24.

Musso, Alberto, and Steven Phillips, 2001, "Comparing Projections and Outcomes of IMF-Supported Programs," IMF Working Paper 01/45 (Washington: International Monetary Fund).

Orphanides, Athanasios, 2001, "Monetary Policy Rules, Macroeconomic Stability and Inflation: A View from the Trenches," Working Paper (Washington: Board of Governors of the Federal Reserve System).

CHAPTER

5 Fiscal Policy, Expenditure Composition, and Growth in Low-Income Countries

Sanjeev Gupta, Benedict Clements, Emanuele Baldacci, and Carlos Mulas-Granados[1]

This paper assesses the effects of fiscal consolidation and expenditure composition on economic growth in a sample of 39 low-income countries during the 1990s. The paper finds that strong budgetary positions are generally associated with higher economic growth in both the short and long terms. The composition of public outlays also matters: countries where spending is concentrated on wages tend to have lower growth, while those that allocate higher shares to capital and nonwage goods and services enjoy faster output expansion. Finally, initial fiscal conditions also have a bearing on the nexus between fiscal deficits and growth.

Introduction

A large body of empirical research supports the notion that healthy budgetary balances are, over the long run, good for growth (Easterly, Rodriguez, and Schmidt-Hebbel, 1994). The effect of fiscal consolidation on growth in the short run, however, remains open to question, as a number of studies—largely for industrial countries—have drawn the conclusion that under some circumstances, fiscal contractions can stimulate growth.[2] A central theme in these works is that the composition of fiscal adjustment plays a key role in determining whether fiscal contractions lead to higher growth and are also sustainable over time. These studies show that improving fiscal positions through the rationalization of the government wage bill and public transfers, rather than increasing revenues and cutting public investment, can foster higher growth, even in the short run.

The purpose of this paper is to assess whether fiscal consolidation and improvements in the composition of public expenditure have positive repercussions for growth in low-income countries. While some aspects of this issue have been assessed in other studies,[3] an in-depth econometric evaluation—drawing on a wide sample of low-income countries—has yet to be undertaken. For example, in the group of 36 different empirical studies that Kneller, Bleaney, and Gemmell (1998) identify as the core of the empirical research on the effects of fiscal policy on growth, only three studies (including Landau, 1986; and Easterly, Rodriguez, and Schmidt-Hebbel, 1994) were based on developing countries, and none of those was based on low-income countries alone.

A number of important related issues have not yet been fully examined in the literature. None of these studies, for example, have addressed whether deficits that are financed from abroad have a different impact on growth than those financed from domestic sources. In addition, the important issue of whether the macroeconomic effects of fiscal policy differ in low-deficit countries—as opposed to those that have yet to achieve a modicum of macroeconomic stability—has yet to be assessed for a wide sample of countries.[4]

This paper attempts to fill some of these gaps and aims to provide some empirical evidence of the effects of fiscal adjustment and expenditure composition on economic growth. More specifically, the paper addresses the following two questions:

- What is the impact of the fiscal stance, expenditure composition, and the nature of budget financing on economic growth in low-income countries?
- Are these effects independent of initial fiscal conditions?

This paper does not restrict its analysis to episodes of fiscal adjustment, as has been done in studies for

[1] The authors wish to thank Shamit Chakravarti and Erwin Tiongson for their help in preparing this paper. Emanuele Baldacci was an economist, and Carlos Mulas-Granados was a summer intern, in the IMF's Fiscal Affairs Department when this paper was prepared. This article was previously published in the April 2005 issue of the *Journal of International Money and Finance* and appears here with permission of Elsevier, the journal's publisher.

[2] See, for example, McDermott and Wescott (1996); Alesina and Perotti (1996); Alesina, Perotti, and Tavares (1998); Alesina and Ardagna (1998); Buti and Sapir (1998); Alesina and others (1999); and Von Hagen and Strauch (2001).

[3] See Mackenzie, Orsmond, and Gerson (1997); Abed and others (1998); and Kneller, Bleaney, and Gemmell (1999).

[4] See Adam and Bevan (2000) for a study based on 17 low-income countries.

industrial countries. Instead, it assesses the effects of both fiscal expansions and fiscal consolidations on growth in 39 low-income countries with IMF-supported programs in the 1990s.[5] These programs, on average, have targeted relatively small reductions in budget deficits.[6] Furthermore, the elimination of budget imbalances has not been the sole aim of these IMF-supported programs, which also sought, among other things, to improve the composition of public expenditure and revenues. As such, an exclusive focus on episodes of fiscal adjustment—defined as periods of sharp deficit reduction—would be of only limited interest in examining the impact of fiscal policy on growth in low-income countries.

The results of this study confirm that there is a strong link between public expenditure reform and growth, as fiscal adjustments achieved through curtailing current expenditures are, in general, more conducive to growth. Fiscal consolidations tend to have the most positive effects on growth when they lead to a reduction in the government's domestic borrowing requirement. When public investment is also protected, the positive effect of fiscal adjustment on growth is further accentuated. The fiscal consolidation-growth nexus is also influenced by a country's initial fiscal conditions—in particular, whether the country has reached a certain degree of macroeconomic stability or not.

The rest of this paper is structured as follows: the second section surveys the literature on the effects of fiscal policy and budget composition on economic growth; the third section describes the data used in the empirical subsection; and the fourth section presents some baseline econometric results of the effects of fiscal policy and expenditure composition on economic growth. Particular attention is given to examining the robustness of the results and whether results differ for low-deficit ("post-stabilization") countries. The fifth section concludes the paper and elaborates on some policy implications of the results.

Literature Review

The effects of fiscal policy on economic growth have been the subject of long debate. With respect to short-term effects, a large body of empirical research, primarily for industrial countries, has been devoted to understanding under which conditions fiscal multipliers can be small (and even negative) (Alesina and Perotti, 1996; Alesina and Ardagna, 1998; and Perotti, 1999). Perotti (1999), for example, shows that consolidations tend to be expansionary when debt is high or growing rapidly, while Alesina and Perotti (1995) and Alesina and Ardagna (1998) find that in addition to the size and persistence of the fiscal impulse, budget composition matters in explaining different private sector responses to fiscal policy (and hence the effect on growth). Fiscal adjustments that rely primarily on cuts in transfers and the wage bill tend to last longer and can be expansionary, while those that rely primarily on tax increases and cuts in public investment tend to be contractionary and unsustainable (Von Hagen and Strauch, 2001).

The potential effects of fiscal policy on long-term growth has also generated substantial attention (Tanzi and Zee, 1996). Most recently, the burgeoning work in the field of endogenous growth suggests that fiscal policy can either promote or retard economic growth, as investment in physical and human capital—both of which can be affected by taxation and government expenditures—can affect steady-state growth rates (Chamley, 1986; Barro, 1990 and 1991; Barro and Sala-ì-Martin, 1995; and Mendoza, Milesi-Ferretti, and Asea, 1997).

In both strands of the literature, the effect of fiscal policy on growth can be nonlinear. This may occur, for example, because the private sector's response to fiscal policy may be nonlinear, implying a complex relationship between the size and composition of public spending and revenues and growth. Giavazzi, Jappelli, and Pagano (2000), for example, find that in industrial and developing countries, the nonlinear effects of fiscal policy on national savings tend to be associated with large and persistent increases in the primary deficit.

There are good reasons to believe that for some (but not all) low-income countries, fiscal contractions may also be expansionary. As in the industrial countries, expansionary contractions are more likely to be observed in countries that have not yet achieved a degree of macroeconomic stability.[7] For these countries, the overriding imperative of reining in inflation and achieving low budget deficits are such that increases in public spending—even if potentially productive—may not have a salutary effect on growth. By contrast, countries in a "post-stabilization" phase can exercise more choice over expenditure priorities, including by allocating resources to important structural reforms, such as the decompression of the civil service payscale. In these

[5] This includes countries that have obtained concessional loans from the IMF since 1999 under the Poverty Reduction and Growth Facility (PRGF), which replaced the Enhanced Structural Adjustment Facility (ESAF). One of the basic tenets of the PRGF is that a stable macroeconomic position is critical for promoting growth and reducing poverty. For further information on the characteristics of the PRGF, see *http://www.imf.org/external/np/exr/facts/prgf.htm*.

[6] For example, for ESAF-supported programs over the 1986–95 period, the deficit was targeted, on average, to decrease by about 1 percentage point of GDP relative to the preprogram year (Abed and others, 1998).

[7] For an empirical analysis of the impact of initial conditions on the effectiveness of fiscal policy during recessions in industrial and middle-income countries, see Baldacci and others (2001).

Table 1
Descriptive Statistics
(as percentages of GDP, unless otherwise specified)

Variable	Observations	Mean	Standard Deviation
Budget balance	429	−6.30	7.9
Tax revenue	425	15.00	7.5
Nontax revenue	423	2.50	2.2
Grants	426	4.20	4.6
Current spending	425	19.70	9.5
Capital spending	425	9.00	7.2
Domestic financing	372	1.70	4.9
External financing	372	4.60	6.1
Per capita real GDP growth	429	−0.50	8.3
Change in:			
Budget balance	390	0.40	5.8
Tax revenue	386	0.02	3.2
Nontax revenue	384	−0.06	1.2
Grants	386	0.03	2.6
Current spending	386	−0.50	4.8
Capital spending	386	0.05	3.4
Domestic financing	333	−0.20	4.8
External financing	333	−0.10	5.2
Per capita GDP growth	390	0.50	10.1

Source: Authors' calculations.
Note: Sample averages using data from 1990 until 2000.

countries, higher public spending—even if it results in higher deficits—could expand, rather than contract, economic activity. In sum, the relationship between the fiscal policy stance and growth will differ across countries, depending on their initial fiscal conditions. This also has important implications for the econometric specifications used to link fiscal policy and growth (see the subsequent discussion).

Another important issue to be considered in the analysis is the nexus between the composition of fiscal deficit financing and growth. Many studies have found that fiscal consolidations can have an indirect impact on private investment (and thus growth) by affecting the level of aggregate demand and monetary variables. Deficits largely financed by domestic sources may also lead to inflationary pressures. High levels of inflation have been found to reduce growth and can lead to macroeconomic and financial instability (Fischer, 1983; Sarel, 1996; and Khan and Senhadji, 2001).

In sum, the theoretical framework underlying the empirical analysis carried out in this paper assumes that fiscal policy can affect the steady-state and short-run growth rate through its effects on private sector behavior and on human and physical capital formation. It also acknowledges that initial and accompanying macroeconomic and fiscal conditions are important.

Statistical Data and Descriptive Analysis

Data

In this paper, three aspects of a country's fiscal policy are examined in relation to their impact on growth: the fiscal policy stance, as measured by the level and changes in the general government budgetary balance; the financing of budgetary deficits; and expenditure composition. Data for these variables were constructed on the basis of the IMF's World Economic Outlook (WEO) database, as well as a database for 39 IMF member countries supported by Enhanced Structural Adjustment Facility (ESAF) and Poverty Reduction and Growth Facility (PRGF) arrangements during the period 1990–2000.[8]

The fiscal policy stance is measured by the general government budget balance on a cash basis.

[8] The countries are Albania, Armenia, Benin, Bolivia, Burkina Faso, Cambodia, Cameroon, the Central African Republic, Chad, Djibouti, Ethiopia, The Gambia, Ghana, Georgia, Guinea, Guinea-Bissau, Guyana, Honduras, Kenya, the Kyrgyz Republic, the Lao People's Democratic Republic, Lesotho, the former Yugoslav Republic of Macedonia, Madagascar, Malawi, Mali, Mauritania, Moldova, Mozambique, Nicaragua, Niger, Rwanda, São Tomé and Príncipe, Senegal, Tajikistan, Tanzania, Vietnam, the Republic of Yemen, and Zambia.

Table 2
Bivariate Correlations
(variables expressed as percentages of GDP, unless otherwise specified)

Variables	Per Capita Real GDP Growth	Number of Observations
Budget balance	0.23***	429
Tax revenue	−0.03	425
Nontax revenue	0.03	423
Grants	0.05	425
Current spending	−0.24***	425
Capital spending	0.16***	425
Domestic financing	−0.25***	372
External financing	−0.07	372
Change in:		
Budget balance	0.20***	390
Tax revenue	0.09**	386
Nontax revenue	0.08*	386
Grants	0.11**	384
Current spending	−0.16***	386
Capital spending	0.12***	386
Domestic financing	−0.16***	333
External financing	−0.01	333

Source: Authors' calculations.
Notes: Bilateral correlations using annual data from 1990 through 2000.
* significant at 10 percent; ** significant at 5 percent; *** significant at 1 percent.

This is defined as total revenues and grants *minus* total expenditures and net lending.[9] A positive change in the budget balance can be interpreted as a consolidation, and a negative change as an expansion. As reported in Table 1, the average budget deficit for the sample is 6.3 percent of GDP. Deficits were generally reduced during the period, with an average annual improvement of approximately ½ of one percentage point of GDP.

The deficit can be financed from either domestic or external sources. Domestic financing includes both bank and nonbank financing, with the latter measure including privatization receipts. For the countries included in the sample, external financing predominated, while domestic financing averaged less than 2 percent of GDP.

Fiscal deficits are also used to identify "post-stabilization" countries, which are defined as those that had an average budget deficit (after grants) below 2.5 percent of GDP during the 1990–2000 period.[10] Based on this criterion, only seven countries can be considered post-stabilizers (Benin, The Gambia, Lesotho, the former Yugoslav Republic of Macedonia, Mauritania, Senegal, and Tanzania).

Macroeconomic indicators have also been extracted from the WEO database. Following earlier studies, growth is measured on a real per capita basis.[11] Other variables used in the regression analysis to control for initial and accompanying conditions include the labor force (as a percentage of the total population), terms of trade, and private investment. These variables are used to control for the effects of private sector and external sector activity on growth. We also control for the level of initial primary and secondary enrollment as indicators of human capital endowment in each country. Data are taken from World Development Indicators of the World Bank.

Fiscal Policy and Growth: Bivariate Analysis

Simple correlations reported in Table 2 show a significant association between fiscal adjustment, expenditure composition, and growth consistent with previous findings in the literature on industrial countries. For example, stronger budget balances are

[9] The difference between revenues and expenditures can be different from the cash deficit for countries that measure expenditures on a commitment basis.

[10] This roughly corresponds to the low-deficit country group identified in the ESAF review (Abed and others, 1998).

[11] Growth of per capita GDP is used most frequently in the empirical literature assessing the effects of fiscal policy on growth, as this controls for differences among countries in the population growth rate. See, for example, Aschauer (1989); Barro (1990, 1991); Easterly and Rebelo (1993); Devarajan, Swaroop, and Zou (1996); Easterly, Loayza, and Montiel (1997); and Kneller, Bleaney, and Gemmell (1999, 2000).

strongly and positively associated with per capita growth. The composition of public expenditure also matters for growth; higher capital outlays are associated with more buoyant growth, while higher current expenditures and domestic financing of the deficit are associated with less favorable economic performance.

These results hold for the short-run correlations as well. Annual changes in the budget balance are positively correlated with changes in per capita growth. Correlation coefficients[12] are also significant for the various measures of public expenditure (including capital outlays) and for domestic financing.

These preliminary findings are consistent with the empirical results obtained by Easterly and Rebelo (1993) and Kneller, Bleaney, and Gemmell (1999, 2000), who found that balanced budgets and investment in transport and communications are consistently correlated with growth in a sample of low-income countries.

Econometric Analysis

The Econometric Models

The relationship between expenditure composition, fiscal adjustment, and growth can be estimated by regressing the annual rate of real per capita GDP growth on a set of regressors, including fiscal variables and other control variables. Three specifications of the relationship are used here. In Model A, fiscal variables are measured as a share of GDP, without a variable included on the fiscal balance; this allows us to capture the effects of particular expenditure items (e.g., wages) not only on the composition of expenditure but also on the deficit. In Model B, we measure fiscal variables in relation to total expenditures or total revenues, so as to assess directly the impact of expenditure or revenue composition on growth, while at the same time including a variable for the budget balance. In Model C, we address how the nature of the deficit financing affects growth by substituting the budget balance variable with variables for domestic and external financing of the deficit.

Each of the three models is formulated as follows:

Budget components (revenue and expenditure) measured as a share of GDP (Model A):

$$g_{i,t} = \alpha + \sum_{l=1}^{k} \beta_l Y_{ilt} + \sum_{h=1}^{q} \beta_h XGDP_{iht} + u_{it} \qquad (1)$$

where g_{it} is the growth rate of real per capita GDP; Y_{ilt} is a vector of nonfiscal independent variables (initial level of GDP per capita, private investment ratio, terms of trade, labor force, initial level of primary and secondary enrollment rates); and $XGDP_{iht}$ is a vector of independent fiscal variables aimed at capturing the effect of the composition of the budget. These variables are measured in percentage of GDP and include public sector wages and salaries, expenditures on other goods and services, transfers and subsidies, interest payments on government debt, capital expenditures, tax revenues, nontax revenues, and grants. In order to avoid perfect collinearity among regressors, the budget balance is not included.[13,14]

Fiscal balance as share of GDP and expenditure composition by economic category (Model B):

$$g_{i,t} = \alpha + \sum_{l=1}^{k} \beta_l Y_{ilt} + \sum_{h=1}^{q} \beta_h XBALEXP_{ihl} + u_{it} \qquad (2)$$

where $g_{i,t}$ and Y_{ilt} are defined as before and $XBALEXP_{iht}$ is a vector of independent fiscal variables aimed at capturing the effect of the budget balance and the composition of expenditures. The budget balance is measured as a percentage of GDP, while all expenditure items are measured as shares of total public expenditures. The expenditure categories include public wages and salaries, public transfers and subsidies, interest payments on government debt, public expenditures on other goods and services, and public capital expenditures.

Source of deficit financing expressed as a share of GDP and expenditure composition by economic category (Model C):

$$g_{i,t} = \alpha + \sum_{l=1}^{k} \beta_l Y_{ilt} + \sum_{h=1}^{q} \beta_h XFINEXP_{iht} + u_{it} \qquad (3)$$

where $g_{i,t}$ and Y_{ilt} are defined as before and $XFINEXP_{iht}$ is a vector of independent fiscal variables aimed at capturing the effect of the deficit financing (both domestic and external financing as percentages of GDP), and the composition of expenditures as shares of total public expenditures. This specification is the same as the previous one,

[12] Correlation coefficients are calculated using the Spearman rank correlation formula to avoid the effect of outliers.

[13] Theoretical models have generally incorporated the government budget constraint, which implies that a change in revenues or spending of a given magnitude has to be matched by offsetting changes elsewhere. This has not, however, been the approach taken in the empirical literature. In many cases, applied studies estimate the effect of selected expenditures and revenues on growth, which implicitly assumes that the effect of the excluded items on growth is neutral. We avoid this by including all budget items in the specification. In this respect, we follow Kneller, Bleaney, and Gemmell (1999), who emphasize the need to include all fiscal policy variables in the equations to avoid omitted variables bias.

[14] For example, adjustment based on selective increases in import tariff rates would most likely have a more adverse effect on growth than would raising revenues from a broad-based value-added tax (VAT).

but it replaces the budget balance with its financing sources (expressed as ratios to GDP).

The baseline regressions use a fixed-effects estimator. The results are then tested for robustness by running a Generalized Method of Moments (GMM) estimator to address potential problems with endogeneity and serial correlation arising from the dynamic specification mentioned previously. A pooled mean-group (PMG) estimator is also used to capture the effects of both short-run and long-run dynamics and to relax the assumption of homogeneity of short-run coefficients. The relative merits of these methods are discussed in the respective subsections.

Baseline Regressions

The models above are estimated in levels and in first differences (changes) in order to capture both long- and short-run effects of fiscal policy on growth. An alternative formulation of this model, involving a nested specification in which both short-run and long-run effects are estimated simultaneously, is found in Bassanini, Scarpetta, and Hemmings (2001). This model could not be fully estimated in the present context owing to the relatively short length of our sample. The results from a revised version of the Bassanini, Scarpetta, and Hemmings model are discussed in the next subsection.

An important problem that is encountered in panel data estimation is the presence of unobserved country-specific effects (Easterly, Loayza, and Montiel, 1997).[15] Excluding unobservable country-specific effects could lead to serious biases in the econometric estimates, notably when these effects are correlated with the other covariates. To address this, we used a least-squares-dummy-variable (LSDV) estimator that allows the intercept in the regression to be country-specific for the estimation of Models A, B, and C.[16]

Results from the baseline regressions (see Table 3) are consistent with the empirical literature and show that, on average, fiscal adjustments have not been harmful for growth—in the long as well as the short term. According to these results, a 1 percent improvement in the fiscal balance has a positive and significant impact in the long term on the rate of GDP growth, raising it by ½ of one percentage point (Model B). An even larger coefficient is estimated for the short-term effect of a change in the fiscal balance on growth. The composition of deficit financing also matters. Domestic financing of the budget tends to be more harmful for growth than external financing (Model C): in the long term, an increase in domestic financing by 1 percent reduces the per capita growth rate by ¼ of a percentage point. The estimated coefficient for the short-term relationship is even larger.

Expenditure composition is also critical for growth. In Model A, a one percentage point of GDP increase in spending on wages and salaries reduces growth by ½ of a percentage point, while a one percentage point increase in the ratio of capital outlays to GDP increases growth by more than ½ of a percentage point. Expenditures on other goods and services are also found to increase the growth rate, but only in the short term. Interest payments have a statistically insignificant impact on growth. Finally, in the models that assess the impact of expenditure composition directly (Models B and C), the coefficients for spending on wages are significant, but only in the long run. The share of capital expenditures in total outlays is positively related to growth under all model specifications, except for the long-run coefficients estimated in Model C. The results suggest that a 1 percent increase in the allocation of public spending to capital outlays can raise the growth rate by 0.1 percentage point of GDP in the long term and by almost 0.25 percentage point of GDP in the short term. The share of public outlays devoted to the interest bill is also negatively correlated with growth. A 1 percent increase in the ratio of interest to total public spending tends to reduce growth by ¼ of one percentage point in the long run and by more than ⅓ of one percentage point in the short run.

Sensitivity Analysis

In order to assess the sensitivity of the econometric results presented above, this subsection reports the main results of the robustness analysis.

Reverse causality is not found to affect significantly the parameter estimates. A common issue in the literature on fiscal policy and growth is the likely presence of endogeneity or reverse causality. It could be the case that economic growth itself influences fiscal variables. For example, when economic growth slows down, the ratio of government spending to GDP is likely to increase if the nominal level of expenditure is fixed, or if the revenue effort is sensitive to cyclical developments. Moreover, some degree of reverse causality could also be present in the relationship between growth and investment.[17]

[15] Unobservable time-specific effects are less common. In fact, following Greene (2000), when such effects do exist, it would be more efficient to include an explicit linear or nonlinear time trend in the equation.

[16] Test for serial correlation for the three models revealed no first-order autocorrelation for the residuals.

The number of countries included in the regression varies according to the specification. On average, about 28 countries are included.

[17] A related issue is whether the model fully captures the effect of the budget balance on growth, as the inclusion of private investment (as an independent variable) de facto blocks the indirect effects of the budget deficit on growth via its effects on private investment. Estimates that omit private investment from the specification, however, do not lead to significantly different results, including for the fiscal balance. This assessment should be viewed as preliminary, however, given the need to assess the deficit-investment relationship in a model especially specified for that purpose.

Table 3

Budget Composition and Growth in Low-Income Countries: Fixed Effects

	Model A. Budget Composition *(as percentage of GDP)*		Model B. Budget Balance and Composition of Expenditures		Model C: Budget Financing and Composition of Expenditures	
	Real per capita GDP growth	Change in real per capita GDP growth	Real per capita GDP growth	Change in real per capita GDP growth	Real per capita GDP growth	Change in real per capita GDP growth
Initial GDP per capita level[1]	0.205 (0.92)	0.203 (0.10)	−0.816 (−0.39)	0.475 (0.23)	−0.314 (−0.14)	0.332 (0.16)
Labor force	0.837*** (2.88)	2.894*** (5.24)	0.618** (2.21)	2.799*** (4.68)	0.687** (2.33)	2.329*** (3.85)
Terms of trade	−0.003 (−0.52)	0.001 (0.18)	−0.005 (−0.90)	−0.362 (−0.04)	−0.005 (−1.01)	−0.005 (−0.55)
Private investment	0.267* (1.77)	0.279 (1.44)	0.396*** (2.75)	0.582*** (2.81)	0.391** (2.28)	0.75*** (3.27)
Initial primary enrollment	−0.136 (−0.99)	−0.006 (−0.05)	−0.159 (−1.21)	−0.016 (−0.11)	−0.211 (−1.54)	−0.031 (−0.21)
Initial secondary enrollment	0.057 (0.51)	−0.048 (−.037)	0.162 (1.51)	−0.051 (−0.36)	0.150 (1.33)	−0.034 (−0.25)
Budget balance *(as percentage of GDP)*			0.458*** (4.22)	0.551*** (3.39)		
Domestic financing *(as percentage of GDP)*					−0.797*** (−5.08)	−1.336*** (−5.94)
External financing *(as percentage of GDP)*					−0.383*** (−2.93)	−0.595*** (−3.22)
Wages and salaries *(as percentage of GDP)*	−0.525* (−1.78)	−0.396 (−0.87)				
Wages and salaries *(as percentage of total expenditure)*			−0.213** (−2.23)	−0.229 (−1.53)	−0.250** (−2.38)	−0.235 (−1.51)
Transfers and subsidies *(as percentage of GDP)*	0.110 (0.42)	−0.424 (−1.08)				
Transfers and subsidies *(as percentage of total expenditure)*			0.054 (0.49)	0.033 (0.19)	−0.047 (−0.37)	−0.008 (−0.05)

(Table continues on next page)

Table 3 *(concluded)*

	Model A. Budget Composition *(as percentage of GDP)*		Model B. Budget Balance and Composition of Expenditures		Model C: Budget Financing and Composition of Expenditures	
	Real per capita GDP growth	Change in real per capita GDP growth	Real per capita GDP growth	Change in real per capita GDP growth	Real per capita GDP growth	Change in real per capita GDP growth
Interest payments *(as percentage of GDP)*	−0.293 (−0.90)	−0.367 (−0.73)				
Interest payments *(as percentage of total expenditure)*			−0.118 (−1.11)	−0.370*** (2.20)	−0.227* (−1.92)	−0.415*** (−2.35)
Other goods and services *(as percentage of GDP)*	0.420 (1.36)	1.722*** (3.96)				
Other goods and services *(as percentage of total expenditure)*			0.015 (0.16)	0.068 (0.45)	0.043 (0.44)	0.175 (1.10)
Capital expenditure *(as percentage of GDP)*	0.567*** (2.96)	0.874*** (3.52)				
Capital expenditure *(as percentage of total expenditure)*			0.154* (1.96)	0.282** (2.25)	0.072 (0.82)	0.237* (1.81)
Tax revenue *(as percentage of GDP)*	−0.056 (−0.29)	0.053 (0.17)				
Nontax revenue *(as percentage of GDP)*	0.095 (0.81)	1.49*** (2.63)				
Grants *(as percentage of GDP)*	0.079 (0.33)	0.209 (0.71)				
Number of observations	249	220	250	221	225	197
Adjusted R-squared	0.10	0.33	0.16	0.21	0.17	0.31
F test	1.77	3.86	2.41	2.62	2.30	3.50
Probability	0.00	0.00	0.00	0.00	0.00	0.00

Notes: *t*-statistics appear in parentheses; * denotes significance at 10 percent, ** significance at 5 percent, and *** significance at 1 percent..
[1] Multiplied by 100.

Table 4

Fiscal Policy, Budget Composition, and Growth in Low-Income Countries: Controlling for Reverse Causality, 1990–2000

	Model A. Budget Composition *(as percentage of GDP)*				Model B. Budget Balance and Composition of Expenditures				Model C: Budget Financing and Composition of Expenditures			
	Real per capita growth (GMM-IVREG)	Real per capita growth (GMM-ABond)	Change growth (GMM-IVREG)	Change growth (GMM-ABond)	Real per capita growth (GMM-IVREG)	Real per capita growth (GMM-ABond)	Change growth (GMM-IVREG)	Change growth (GMM-ABond)	Real per capita growth (GMM-IVREG)	Real per capita growth (GMM-ABond)	Change growth (GMM-IVREG)	Change growth (GMM-ABond)
Per capita growth (*t*–l)		−0.109** (−2.05)		−0.329*** (−9.24)		−0.265*** (−21.78)		−0.371*** (16.38)		−0.229*** (−6.18)		−0.424*** (−16.21)
Initial GDP per capita level[1]	0.396* (1.96)		0.039 (0.31)		−0.041 (−0.22)		0.033 (0.34)		−0.061 (−0.32)		−0.006 (−0.06)	
Labor force	0.847* (1.74)	1.784*** (9.60)	2.89*** (3.12)	2.669*** (11.30)	0.75 (1.60)	0.936*** (4.32)	2.120** (2.03)	2.18** (16.72)	0.802* (1.74)	1.149*** (5.38)	1.76** (2.05)	1.69*** (5.90)
Terms of trade	−0.003 (1.34)	0.003*** (3.66)	0.001 (0.42)	0.004 (1.47)	−0.005*** (−2.94)	−0.002*** (−2.64)	−0.001 (−0.29)	0.003 (1.01)	−0.005*** (−3.18)	−0.004*** (−3.38)	−0.004 (−0.73)	−0.001 (−0.62)
Private investment	0.266* (1.69)	0.106 (1.49)	0.279* (1.69)	0.167 (1.30)	0.383*** (2.84)	0.393*** (5.28)	0.466** (2.29)	0.642*** (5.97)	0.356** (2.36)	0.760*** (3.90)	0.602** (2.26)	0.533*** (3.14)
Initial primary enrollment	−0.797 (−1.80)		−0.068 (−0.89)		−0.546 (−1.27)		0.006 (0.09)		−0.519 (−1.24)		0.072 (0.67)	
Initial secondary enrollment	0.346 (1.45)		−0.021 (−0.23)		0.352 (1.58)		−0.052 (−0.77)		0.335 (1.51)		−0.072 (−0.87)	
Budget balance *(as percentage of GDP)*					0.435*** (4.24)	0.536*** (9.59)	0.462*** (2.21)	0.662*** (17.35)				
Domestic financing *(as percentage of GDP)*									−0.606*** (−3.06)	−0.929*** (−6.80)	−0.977*** (2.73)	−0.991*** (−6.79)
External financing *(as percentage of GDP)*									−0.415*** (−3.54)	−0.459*** (−7.07)	−0.511** (−2.57)	−0.605*** (−8.86)
Wages and salaries *(as percentage of GDP)*	−0.521 (−0.86)	−0.385* (−1.89)	−0.396 (−0.58)	−0.511* (−1.92)								
Wages and salaries *(as percentage of total expenditure)*					−0.214* (−1.85)	−0.350*** (−7.09)	−0.244* (−1.76)	−0.263*** (−6.26)	−0.220* (−1.65)	−0.280*** (−3.58)	−0.255* (1.83)	−0.344*** (−3.14)
Transfers and subsidies *(as percentage of GDP)*	0.109 (0.46)	−0.059 (−0.50)	−0.424 (−0.58)	−0.528***								
Transfers and subsidies *(as percentage of total expenditure)*					0.081 (0.92)	−0.004 (−0.09)	−0.001 (0.00)	−0.005 (−0.09)	0.039 (0.40)	−0.018 (−0.19)	−0.070 (−0.21)	0.230*** (3.00)

(Table continues on next page)

Table 4 *(concluded)*

	Model A. Budget Composition (*as percentage of GDP*)				Model B. Budget Balance and Composition of Expenditures				Model C: Budget Financing and Composition of Expenditures			
	Real per capita growth (GMM-IVREG)	Real per capita growth (GMM-ABond)	Change growth (GMM-IVREG)	Change growth (GMM-ABond)	Real per capita growth (GMM-IVREG)	Real per capita growth (GMM-ABond)	Change growth (GMM-IVREG)	Change growth (GMM-ABond)	Real per capita growth (GMM-IVREG)	Real per capita growth (GMM-ABond)	Change growth (GMM-IVREG)	Change growth (GMM-ABond)
Interest payments (*as percentage of GDP*)	−0.298 (−0.74)	−0.188 (−1.63)	−0.367 (−0.87)	0.005 (0.03)								
Interest payments (*as percentage of total expenditure*)					−0.139 (−1.09)	−0.248*** (−4.42)	−0.303 (−1.59)	−0.379*** (−6.12)	−0.218 (−1.47)	−0.194** (−2.08)	−0.314* (−1.67)	−0.412*** (−5.16)
Other goods and services (*as percentage of GDP*)	0.400 (0.95)	1.417*** (6.26)	1.72*** (3.05)	0.932*** (4.12)								
Other goods and services (*as percentage of total expenditure*)					−0.002 (−0.03)	0.129** (2.28)	0.048 (0.40)	0.035 (0.87)	0.003 (0.05)	0.149** (2.44)	0.109 (0.89)	0.064 (0.77)
Capital expenditure (*as percentage of GDP*)	0.552 (1.57)	0.710*** (7.10)	0.874** (2.41)	0.735*** (5.48)								
Capital expenditure (*as percentage of total expenditure*)					0.116 (1.35)	0.185*** (5.03)	0.194 (1.38)	0.358*** (10.35)	0.071 (0.69)	0.180*** (3.69)	0.145 (1.00)	0.293*** (4.44)
Tax revenue (*as percentage of GDP*)	−0.043 (−0.18)	0.067 (1.04)	0.053 (0.20)	0.059 (0.31)								
Nontax revenue (*as percentage of GDP*)	0.104 (0.27)	1.518*** (5.01)	1.49** (2.35)	1.44*** (3.88)								
Grants (*as percentage of GDP*)	0.090 (0.25)	0.185 (0.97)	0.209 (0.61)	0.328*** (5.10)								
Number of observations	249	201	220	172	250	201	221	172	225	179	197	151
Regression tests–Wald χ^2 (12)	–	3,644.13	–	18,158.87	–	26,400.36	–	18,255.53	–	7,060.64	–	108,082.74

Notes: Absolute value of *t* and *z* statistics appear in parentheses; * denotes significance at 10 percent, ** significance at 5 percent, and *** significance at 1 percent. Model A: Hansen-*J* Test: (GMM 0-levels) = 0.01; (GMM 0-changes) = 0.00; serial of over 2: (GMM-ABond-levels) = 0.41; (GMM-ABond-changes) = 0.25. Model B: Hansen-*J* Test: (GMM 0-levels) = 0.62; (GMM 0-changes) = 1.32; serial of over 2: (GMM-ABond-levels) = 0.08; (GMM-ABond-changes) = 0.21. Model C: Hansen-*J* Test: (GMM 0-levels) = 1.04; (GMM 0-changes) = 2.32; serial of over 2: (GMM-ABond-levels) = 0.12; (GMM-ABond-changes) = 0.10.

[1] Multiplied by 100.

If economic growth is a determinant of any of the right-hand-side variables in our model, estimation techniques that do not take into account this endogeneity will yield biased and inconsistent parameter estimates. To address this concern, we estimate the previous models using a GMM estimator,[18] instrumenting for the investment rate, fiscal balance ratio, and the shares of government spending and revenues to GDP. We use as instruments the lagged values of these variables, the other exogenous variables in the model, and a set of instruments not included in the model.[19] Results are presented in Table 4 and broadly confirm the findings of the previous subsection. Accounting for the endogeneity of fiscal balances leads to the same positive effect of fiscal consolidation on growth as in the baseline regressions. A difference in the results, however, is that the coefficient for the share of wages and salaries becomes insignificant in Model A, although it remains significant and negatively correlated with growth in the remaining specifications. The short-run effect of capital outlays on growth is not affected by the use of the GMM estimator; however, the long-run coefficient turns insignificant. The specification in the preceding regression does not allow for any dynamics between the dependent and independent variables. Growth relationships are dynamic, however, as growth in a given period is not unconnected with past growth trends. If the true model is not static, parameter estimates based on a static fixed-effects estimator are biased and inconsistent, even when the error terms are not serially correlated. Thus, we estimated Models A, B, and C using unobserved country-specific effects and allowed for the lagged growth rate to be included among the determinants of economic growth. These models can be estimated using the GMM estimator proposed by Arellano and Bond (1991). The GMM estimate also controls for endogeneity by using the lagged values of the levels of the endogenous and the predetermined variables as instruments. Both the validity of the instruments and the presence of serial correlation in the residual, which would eliminate the consistency of the estimator, can be tested once the equation is estimated.

Introducing a dynamic specification does not lead to significantly different results from the baseline, while it improves the results compared with the static GMM estimator. GMM estimates of the dynamic model with country-specific effects are reported in Table 4. The results are, in general, consistent with the static fixed-effects estimates presented in the previous subsection. The effect of fiscal consolidation on growth is larger and more significant than under the GMM and LSDV estimates of the static model. The contributions of capital outlays and government spending on wages are still correctly signed and statistically significant, and in most cases larger in size than in the baseline and GMM regressions. The negative effect on growth of an increase in domestic financing is larger, while the effect of external financing of the deficit is broadly unchanged. The coefficient of the lagged dependent variable is negative and significant, as expected,[20] for all models. Finally, both the Sargan test for the validity of instruments and the test for the serial correlation of residuals confirm that GMM provides consistent estimates of the parameters.

A variety of other estimators were utilized to test the robustness of the results, including the generalized-least-squares (GLS) estimate of the random effect model. The results confirm the main findings of the previous subsection.[21] Results are also consistent with these estimates when we use a robust technique to control for the possible presence of outliers in the data. The method is based on an iterative algorithm that first runs ordinary-least-squares (OLS) estimates and calculates[22] Cook's *D* statistics for the residuals, eliminating those observations for which $D>1$. The second step of the algorithm is to run a regression on the new dataset, and calculate case weights based on the inverse of the residual.[23] The results show that the effect of outliers in our data is not substantial.[24]

A further robustness test was carried out by replicating a modified version of the model used by Bassanini, Scarpetta, and Hemmings (2001). This specification tries to capture the effect of the simultaneous inclusion of both short-run and long-run effects of fiscal variables in the growth equation using the PMG estimator. We were not able to fully replicate the nested specification used by Bassanini, Scarpetta, and Hemmings, given the short time

[18] The GMM estimator used here deals with a heteroskedastic error process. This estimator is more efficient than the traditional instrumental variables estimator.

[19] The instruments include total revenue, current government spending, and total government spending, all as ratios to GDP. All instruments were found to be valid according to the Hansen-Sargan test.

[20] A negative coefficient for the lagged growth rate can be interpreted as the tendency of the annual growth rate to converge toward an average long-run trend. Countries would still tend toward different, specific growth rates as a result of the error-component structure in the equation.

[21] These and other results not reported in the paper are available from the authors upon request.

[22] Although most results are consistent with the baseline regression for Models A and B, in the case of Model C the coefficient of the level of domestic financing is not statistically significant. For the majority of the short-run coefficients, the variables are significant and correctly signed.

[23] For a full description of this procedure, see Hamilton (1991).

[24] Although most results are consistent with the baseline regression for Models A and B, in the case of Model C, the coefficient of the level of domestic financing is not statistically significant. For the majority of the short-run coefficients, the variables are significant and correctly signed.

Table 5

Budget Composition and Growth in Low-Income Countries: Nested Models with Fixed Effects[1]

(Dependent variable: real per capita GDP growth)

	Model A. Budget Composition *(percent of GDP)*	Model B. Budget Balance and Composition of Expenditures	Model C: Budget Financing and Composition of Expenditures
Initial GDP per capita level[2]	0.003 (1.07)	−0.001 (−0.38)	−0.001 (−0.43)
Labor force	0.510* (1.77)	0.443 (1.48)	0.413 (1.06)
Terms of trade	−0.006 (−1.00)	−0.006 (−0.93)	−0.007 (−0.92)
Private investment	−0.026 (−0.15)	0.343* (1.91)	0.452* (1.80)
Initial primary enrollment	−0.139 (−0.36)	−0.130 (−0.91)	−0.139 (−0.67)
Initial secondary enrollment	0.020 (0.10)	0.133 (1.19)	0.135 (0.94)
Budget balance *(percent of GDP)*		0.348** (2.54)	
Domestic financing *(percent of GDP)*			−0.521* (−1.79)
External financing *(percent of GDP)*			−0.378 (−1.63)
Wages and salaries *(percent of GDP)*	−0.833*** (−2.82)		
Wages and salaries *(percent of total expenditure)*		−0.196* (−1.79)	−0.145 (−0.96)
Transfers and subsidies *(percent of GDP)*	0.287 (0.76)		
Transfers and subsidies *(percent of total expenditure)*		0.063 (0.50)	0.084 (0.50)
Interest payments *(percent of GDP)*	−0.023 (−0.07)		
Interest payments *(percent of total expenditure)*		−0.159 (−1.33)	−0.138 (−0.83)
Other goods and services *(percent of GDP)*	0.424 (1.28)		
Other goods and services *(percent of total expenditure)*		0.032 (0.27)	−0.016 (−0.10)
Capital expenditure *(percent of GDP)*	0.214 (1.05)		
Capital expenditure *(percent of total expenditure)*		0.172* (1.96)	0.213* (1.71)
Tax revenue *(percent of GDP)*	−0.300 (−1.31)		
Nontax revenue *(percent of GDP)*	−0.049 (−0.12)		
Grants *(percent of GDP)*	0.041 (0.15)		
Number of observations	229	230	201
Adjusted *R*-squared	0.68	0.30	0.17
F test	3.07	2.53	1.47
Probability	0.00	0.00	0.02

Notes: *t*-statistics appear in parentheses. * significant at 10 percent; ** significant at 5 percent; and *** significant at 1 percent.

[1] The regressions includes the following variables, denoted in changes, and their interaction with country dummies: total expenditure and total revenue (Model A); deficit (Model B); and domestic and external financing (Model C).

[2] Multiplied by 100.

dimension of our sample. Instead, we included the most important fiscal variables in first differences[25] in the level specification of the three models, and allowed their coefficients to be country-specific to account for differentiated short-term responses of growth to fiscal policy. We estimated this model using a fixed-effects estimator. The results confirm the stability of the fiscal coefficients estimated in the baseline regressions (Table 5). The negative effect of fiscal deficits on growth is confirmed by these estimates. In Model B, the long-run coefficient of the fiscal balance is significantly and positively signed, but smaller than the corresponding coefficient in the baseline regression. Similar significant and consistently signed coefficients are found for the share of wages in total government spending and the ratio of capital to total public outlays. Results for Model A show a much larger and significant negative effect of the wage bill on growth. The ratio of capital spending to GDP, however, becomes insignificant in this specification. Model C also confirms the main findings of the baseline model. In this model, however, domestic financing is found to be detrimental to growth but external financing does not significantly affect growth.

Finally, results do not change much when the possible effects of the business cycle and time trends are removed from the data. The possible effects of the business cycle are partially eliminated by smoothing the data using a three-year moving-average filter. Once again, the results are not sensitive to this transformation of the original data. The reason why business cycle effects may be weaker in low-income countries than in the industrial countries is the absence of automatic stabilizers. This feature makes it highly unlikely that business cycles affect tax collection or public expenditures, and thus the overall budget balance. Moreover, in our sample, we do not find sufficient evidence that unobservable time effects are a serious problem, as evidenced by the results for regressions that include time dummies to control for nonlinear time trends in the data.

Nonlinear Effects of Fiscal Policy on Growth: Pre- and Post-Stabilization Countries

The results in the previous section suggest that fiscal consolidation is not harmful for growth in low-income countries. Quality fiscal adjustments based on the reallocation of public expenditure to more productive uses, and the reduction of the budget deficit, were found to be conducive to higher growth. Of interest is whether these results hold for all countries in the sample, in particular for countries that have already achieved a modicum of macroeconomic stability (i.e., "post-stabilization" countries (Adam and Bevan, 2001)).

With the purpose of assessing the effect of initial fiscal conditions on the fiscal-policy-growth nexus, we split the sample into post- and pre-stabilization countries. A post-stabilization country is defined as a country that maintained an average fiscal deficit (after grants) below 2.5 percent of GDP during the period 1990–2000.[26]

Results for post-stabilization countries point to the positive effects of capital outlays and selected current expenditures on growth. Econometric results for the two subgroups are reported in Table 6 using LSDV.[27] Interestingly, the results suggest that for countries with low budget deficits, additional fiscal consolidation may not yield higher growth. Even more important, domestic financing is not harmful for growth in the short run and less harmful than external financing in the long run in these countries, unlike the case of countries that have not yet achieved stabilization. The results should be interpreted with caution, though, in view of the small sample size for post-stabilization countries and the poor performance of some of these models in terms of *F* tests. Nevertheless, the results support the notion that the relationship between budget deficits and growth in these countries differs from that for the sample as a whole. Results for pre-stabilization countries are fully consistent with the "expansionary contractions" thesis.

Conclusions and Policy Implications

The empirical evidence provided in this study suggests that in low-income countries fiscal consolidations were not harmful for long- or short-term growth during the period 1990–2000. This paper sought to shed light on the relationship between fiscal adjustment, expenditure composition, and economic growth in low-income countries. Consistent with the previous findings in the literature on industrial countries, the results point to a significant

[25] In Model A, we use the first difference of total government spending and total revenues as a share of GDP. In Models B and C, we use the fiscal balance and domestic and external deficit financing, respectively.

[26] The criterion used to group the countries in the sample is similar to the one used in a study of ESAF-supported programs for 1986–95 (see Abed and others, 1998), where "low initial deficit" countries were defined as those with initial deficits (before grants) of 5 percent, with grants of approximately 2½ percent of GDP. Post-stabilization countries included in the regressions are The Gambia, Lesotho, the former Yugoslav Republic of Macedonia, Mauritania, Senegal, and Tanzania. Benin is the seventh post-stabilization country but is excluded because data on the other control variables are unavailable.

We also applied the same threshold to the 1996–2000 averages in order to test the robustness of our results to alternative definitions of "post-stabilization." The results confirm the findings of this subsection.

[27] Results for Model A are reported in Table 6. Results for Models A–C were also replicated using the LSDV estimator, which confirmed these findings. These results are not included in the paper for the sake of brevity but are available from the authors upon request.

Table 6

Fiscal Policy, Budget Composition, and Growth in Low-Income Countries (Pre- and Post-Stabilization Countries): Fixed Effects, 1990–2000

	Model A. Budget Composition				Model B. Budget Balance and Composition of Expenditures				Model C: Budget Financing and Composition of Expenditures			
	Real per capita GDP growth		Change in per capita GDP growth		Real per capita GDP growth		Change in per capita GDP growth		Real per capita GDP growth		Change in per capita GDP growth	
	Pre-stabilization countries	Post-stabilization countries	Pre-stabilization countries	Post-stabilization countries	Pre-stabilization countries	Post-stabilization countries	Pre-stabilization countries	Post-stabilization countries	Pre-stabilization countries	Post-stabilization countries	Pre-stabilization countries	Post-stabilization countries
Initial GDP per capita level[1]	1.466 (1.55)	−1.423 (−0.41)	−0.018 (−0.02)	−0.012 (−0.05)	1.010 (1.21)	−3.402 (−1.18)	0.290 (0.31)	−1.4[illegible]3 (−0.6[illegible])	0.013 (1.51)	−9.726 (−2.75)	0.422 (0.48)	−0.132 (−0.55)
Labor force	0.833** (2.62)	0.967 (0.63)	2.792*** (4.73)	0.218 (0.11)	0.571* (1.87)	1.68 (1.29)	2.56*** (4.03)	0.6[illegible]5 (0.2[illegible])	0.601* (1.91)	4.591*** (2.83)	2.10*** (3.32)	4.50 (1.52)
Terms of trade	−0.004 (−0.63)	−0.004 (−0.09)	0.002 (0.23)	0.045 (0.73)	−0.006 (−1.00)	0.033 (0.86)	−0.001 (−0.09)	0.[illegible]0 (0.[illegible]0)	−0.007 (−1.13)	0.030 (0.79)	−0.006 (−0.65)	0.043 (0.70)
Private investment	0.600*** (2.83)	−0.207* (−2.01)	0.518** (2.01)	−0.285** (−2.34)	0.650*** (3.29)	−0.192* (−1.91)	0.990*** (3.71)	−0.[illegible]67*** (−2.[illegible]1)	0.695*** (2.95)	−0.114 (−0.96)	1.22*** (4.12)	−0.346** (−2.48)
Initial primary enrollment	0.052 (0.40)	−0.179 (−0.31)	−0.009 (−0.10)	−0.015 (−0.30)	−0.010 (−0.09)	−0.55 (−1.12)	0.0197 (0.21)	−0.[illegible]31 (−0.[illegible]9)	0.018 (0.15)	−1.638** (−2.73)	−0.003 (−0.04)	−0.055 (−1.03)
Initial secondary enrollment	−0.469 (−1.57)	1.463 (0.44)	−0.045 (−0.16)	0.050 (0.23)	−0.273 (−1.03)	3.21 (1.18)	−0.151 (−0.48)	0.[illegible]57 (0.[illegible]9)	−0.527 (−1.54)	9.154** (2.72)	−0.116 (−0.36)	0.153 (0.69)
Budget balance *(percentage of GDP)*					0.563*** (4.16)	0.118 (1.41)	0.804*** (4.11)	−0.[illegible]43 (−0.[illegible]6)				
Domestic financing *(percentage of GDP)*									−1.09*** (−5.36)	−0.206* (−1.98)	−1.57*** (−6.21)	0.141 (0.75)
External financing *(percentage of GDP)*									−0.44*** (−2.81)	−0.364*** (−3.02)	−0.723*** (−3.31)	−0.108 (−0.70)
Wages and salaries *(percentage of GDP)*	−0.305 (−0.86)	−0.768* (−1.91)	−0.896* (−1.74)	−6.01 (−0.82)								
Wages and salaries *(percentage of total expenditure)*					−0.233* (−1.97)	0.019 (0.25)	−0.300* (−1.68)	−0.[illegible]064 (−0.[illegible]52)	−0.246* (−1.98)	0.033 (0.28)	−0.283 (−1.58)	0.002 (0.02)
Transfers and subsidies *(percentage of GDP)*	−0.039 (−0.11)	0.411 (1.28)	−0.985** (−2.08)	0.862** (2.37)								
Transfers and subsidies *(percentage of total expenditure)*					−0.010 (−0.08)	0.338*** (3.36)	−0.110 (−0.53)	[illegible].306** ([illegible].11)	−0.159 (−1.06)	0.527*** (4.45)	−0.188 (−0.84)	0.429** (2.76)

(Table continues on next page)

Table 6 *(concluded)*

	Model A. Budget Composition				Model B. Budget Balance and Composition of Expenditures				Model C: Budget Financing and Composition of Expenditures			
	Real per capita GDP growth		Change per capita GDP growth		Real per capita GDP growth		Change per capita GDP growth		Real per capita GDP growth		Change per capita GDP growth	
	Pre-stabilization countries	Post-stabilization countries	Pre-stabilization countries	Post-stabilization countries	Pre-stabilization countries	Post-stabilization countries	Pre-stabilization countries	Post-stabilization countries	Pre-stabilization countries	Post-stabilization countries	Pre-stabilization countries	Post-stabilization countries
Interest payments *(percentage of GDP)*	−0.538	−0.756	−0.526	0.755								
	(−1.44)	(−1.02)	(−0.97)	(0.74)								
Interest payments *(percentage of total expenditure)*					−0.150	0.290*	−0.403**	0.444*	−0.260**	0.277	−0.454**	0.313
					(−1.25)	(1.79)	(−2.20)	(1.72)	(−2.00)	(1.61)	(−2.41)	(1.07)
Other goods and services *(percentage of GDP)*	0.667	0.655**	1.932***	0.711*								
	(1.63)	(2.33)	(3.59)	(2.01)								
Other goods and services *(percentage of total expenditure)*					0.037	0.142*	0.041	0.197*	0.090	0.060	0.135	0.125
					(0.31)	(1.80)	(0.22)	(1.87)	(0.73)	(0.67)	(0.72)	(1.06)
Capital expenditure *(percentage of GDP)*	0.682***	−0.037	1.327***	−0.032								
	(3.00)	(−0.18)	(4.32)	(−0.18)								
Capital expenditure *(percentage of total expenditure)*					0.148	0.139*	0.327**	0.171*	0.044	0.248***	0.221	0.260**
					(1.56)	(1.98)	(2.21)	(1.86)	(0.44)	(3.15)	(1.48)	(2.65)
Tax revenue *(percentage of GDP)*	−0.057	−0.099	0.238	−0.312								
	(−0.21)	(−0.48)	(0.60)	(−1.45)								
Nontax revenue *(percentage of GDP)*	−0.387	0.524**	1.306*	0.479								
	(−0.58)	(2.08)	(1.85)	(1.16)								
Grants *(percentage of GDP)*	−0.100	0.487	−0.099	0.554								
	(−0.35)	(0.85)	(−0.31)	(0.94)								
Number of observations	200	49	177	43	201	49	178	43	184	41	161	36
Adjusted *R*-squared	0.13	0.16	0.39	0.14	0.20	0.33	0.28	0.13	0.22	0.51	0.38	0.30
F test	1.97	1.59	4.64	1.45	2.71	2.74	3.37	1.48	2.69	4.08	4.29	2.07
Probability	0.00	0.12	0.00	0.19	0.00	0.00	0.00	0.18	0.00	0.00	0.00	0.06

Notes: The *t*-statistics appear in parentheses.; * denotes significance at 10 percent, ** significance at 5 percent, and *** significance at 1 percent.

[1] Multiplied by 100.

relationship between fiscal adjustment and per capita growth. A reduction of 1 percentage point in the ratio of the fiscal deficit to GDP leads to an average increase in per capita growth of ½ of a percentage point both in the long term and in the short term. This implies that a reduction in the average deficit in low-income countries from about 4 percent of GDP to 2 percent of GDP could boost per capita growth by about 1–2 percentage points a year.

Tilting the overall composition of public expenditure toward more productive uses is particularly important for boosting growth. Fiscal consolidations achieved through cutting selected current expenditures tend to trigger higher growth rates than adjustments based on revenue increases and cuts in more productive spending—a result consistent with the findings for industrial countries. According to the results of our analysis, protecting capital expenditures during a fiscal adjustment leads to higher growth. Reductions in the public sector wage bill are not harmful for growth for the sample as a whole.

The composition of deficit financing is also a key factor affecting growth in low-income countries. Fiscal consolidations, especially those leading to a sizable reduction in domestic financing of the deficit are likely to trigger higher growth rates. The empirical estimates indicate that adjustments based on reducing domestic financing have about 1½ times the effect on growth as adjustments based on reductions in both domestic and external financing.

The effects of fiscal policy on growth tend to be nonlinear. The results above hold for countries that have not yet achieved stable macroeconomic conditions. In post-stabilization countries, fiscal adjustments no longer have a salutary effect on growth. In this context, an expansion of selected current expenditures for these countries is compatible with higher growth. The design of fiscal frameworks in PRGF-supported programs is consistent with these results, as post-stabilization countries target relatively larger increases in public spending and in the fiscal deficit (IMF, 2002).

Additional research is needed to disentangle the channels through which fiscal policy affects growth. Given the reduced-form model tested here, the paper has not examined the demand- and supply-side channels through which fiscal policy affects growth, nor the role of accompanying policies (such as monetary and external sector policies) that have been underscored in previous work in this field (Baldacci and others, 2001; and Thomas, 2001). Additional research is needed in this area.

References

Abed, George, and others, 1998, *Fiscal Reform in Low-Income Countries: Experience Under IMF-Supported Programs*, IMF Occasional Paper No. 160 (Washington: International Monetary Fund).

Adam, Christopher S., and David L. Bevan, 2000, "Fiscal Policy Design in Low-Income Countries," paper prepared for UNU/WIDER (United Nations University/World Institute for Development Economics Research) research project on "New Fiscal Policies for Poverty Reduction and Growth" (unpublished, November).

———, 2001, "Nonlinear Effects of Public Deficits on Growth," paper prepared for the Cornell/ISPE (International Seminar in Public Economics) Conference, New York, September.

Alesina, Alberto, and Silvia Ardagna, 1998, "Tales of Fiscal Adjustment," *Economic Policy: A European Forum*, No. 27, pp. 487–546.

———, Roberto Perotti, and Fabio Schiantarelli, 2002, "Fiscal Policy, Profits, and Investment," *American Economic Review*, Vol. 92, pp. 571–89.

Alesina, Alberto, and Roberto Perotti, 1995, "Fiscal Expansion and Fiscal Adjustments in OECD Countries," *Economic Policy*, Vol. 21, pp. 205–48.

———, 1996, "Fiscal Adjustments in OECD Countries: Composition and Macroeconomic Effects," IMF Working Paper 96/70 (Washington: International Monetary Fund).

———, and Jose Tavares, 1998, "The Political Economy of Fiscal Adjustments," *Brookings Papers on Economic Activity: 2*, Brookings Institution, pp. 192–248.

Arellano, Manuel, and Stephen Bond, 1991, "Some Tests of Specific Action for Panel Data: Monte Carlo Evidence and an Application to Employment Equations," *Review of Economic Studies*, Vol. 58, pp. 277–97.

Aschauer, David A., 1989, "Is Public Expenditure Productive?" *Journal of Monetary Economics*, Vol. 23, pp. 177–200.

Baldacci, Emanuele, Marco Cangiano, Selma Mahfouz, and Axel Schimmelpfennig, 2001, "The Effectiveness of Fiscal Policy in Stimulating Economic Activity: An Empirical Investigation," paper presented at the IMF Annual Research Conference (Washington: International Monetary Fund).

Barro, Robert J., 1990, "Government Spending in a Simple Model of Endogenous Growth," *Journal of Political Economy*, Vol. 98, No. 1, pp. 103–17.

———, 1991, "Economic Growth in a Cross Section of Countries," *Quarterly Journal of Economics*, Vol. 106, pp. 407–43.

———, and Xavier Sala-i-Martin, 1995, *Economic Growth* (New York: McGraw-Hill).

Bassanini, Andrea, Stefano Scarpetta, and Phillip Hemmings, 2001, "Economic Growth: The Role of Policies and Institutions. Panel Data Evidence from OECD Countries," Economics Department Working Papers, No. 283 (Paris: Organization for Economic Cooperation and Development).

Buti, Marco, and Andre Sapir, 1998, *Economic Policy in EMU* (Oxford, United Kingdom: Oxford University Press).

Chamley, C., 1986, "Optimal Taxation of Capital Income Equilibrium with Infinite Lives," *Econometrica*, Vol. 54, No. 3, pp. 607–22.

Chu, Ke-young, and others, 1995, *Unproductive Public Expenditure: A Pragmatic Approach to Policy Analysis*, IMF Pamphlet Series, No. 48 (Washington: International Monetary Fund).

Devarajan, Shantayanan, Vinaya Swaroop, and Heng-fu Zou, 1996, "The Composition of Public Expenditure and Economic Growth," *Journal of Monetary Economics*, Vol. 37, pp. 313–44.

Easterly, William, Norman Loayza, and Peter Montiel, 1997, "Has Latin America's Post-Reform Growth Been Disappointing?" *Journal of International Economics*, Vol. 43, pp. 287–311.

Easterly, William, and Sergio Rebelo, 1993, "Fiscal Policy and Economic Growth: An Empirical Investigation," NBER Working Paper No. 4499 (Cambridge, Massachusetts: National Bureau of Economic Research).

Easterly, William, Carlos A. Rodríguez, and Klaus Schmidt-Hebbel, 1994, *Public Sector Deficits and Macroeconomic Performance* (Washington: World Bank).

Fischer, Stanley, 1983, "Inflation and Growth," NBER Working Paper No. 1235 (Cambridge, Massachusetts: National Bureau of Economic Research).

Gerson, Philip, 1998, "The Impact of Fiscal Policy Variables on Output Growth," IMF Working Paper 98/1 (Washington: International Monetary Fund).

Giavazzi, Francesco, Tullio Jappelli, and Marco Pagano, 2000, "Searching for Nonlinear Effects of Fiscal Policy: Evidence from Industrial and Developing Countries," NBER Working Paper No. 7460 (Cambridge, Massachusetts: National Bureau of Economic Research).

Greene, William, 2000, *Econometric Analysis* (Upper Saddle River, New Jersey: Prentice Hall).

Hamilton, L.C., 1991, "How Robust Is Robust Regression?" *Stata Technical Bulletin*, Vol. 2, pp. 21–26.

International Monetary Fund, 2002, "Review of the Key Features of the Poverty Reduction and Growth Facility—Staff Analyses," available on the Web at *http://www.imf.org/external/np/prgf/2002/031502.htm*.

Ize, Alain, 1991, "Measurement of Fiscal Performance in IMF-Supported Programs: Some Methodological Issues," in *How to Measure the Fiscal Deficit*, ed. by Mario I. Blejer and Adrienne Cheasty (Washington: International Monetary Fund).

Jones, Larry E., Rodolfo E. Manuelli, and Peter E. Rossi, 1993, "On the Optimal Taxation of Capital Income," NBER Working Paper No. 4525 (Cambridge, Massachusetts: National Bureau of Economic Research).

Khan, Mohsin S., and Abdelhak S. Senhadji, 2001, "Threshold Effects in the Relationship Between Inflation and Growth," *Staff Papers*, International Monetary Fund, Vol. 48, No. 1, pp. 1–21.

King, Robert G., and Sergio Rebelo, 1990, "Public Policy and Economic Growth: Developing Neoclassical Implications," NBER Working Paper No. 3338 (Cambridge, Massachusetts: National Bureau of Economic Research).

Kneller, Richard, Michael Bleaney, and Norman Gemmell, 1998, "Growth, Public Policy and the Government Budget Constraint: Evidence from OECD Countries," University of Nottingham, Department of Economics Discussion Paper No. 98/14.

______, 1999, "Fiscal Policy and Growth: Evidence from OECD Countries," *Journal of Public Economics*, Vol. 74, pp. 171–90.

______, 2000, "Testing the Endogenous Growth Model: Public Expenditure, Taxation and Growth Over the Long Run," University of Nottingham, Department of Economics Discussion Paper No. 00/25.

Landau, Daniel, 1986, "Government and Economic Growth in the Less Developed Countries: An Empirical Study for 1960–80," *Economic Development and Cultural Change*, Vol. 35, pp. 35–75.

Mackenzie, George A., David Orsmond, and Philip Gerson, 1997, *The Composition of Fiscal Adjustment and Growth: Lessons from Fiscal Reforms in Eight Economies*, IMF Occasional Paper No. 149 (Washington: International Monetary Fund).

McDermott, C. John, and Robert F. Wescott, 1996, "An Empirical Analysis of Fiscal Adjustments," *Staff Papers*, International Monetary Fund, Vol. 43 (December), pp. 725–53.

Mendoza, E., Gian Maria Milesi-Ferretti, and P. Asea, 1997, "On The Ineffectiveness of Tax Policy in Altering Long-Run Growth: Harberger's Superneutrality Conjecture," *Journal of Public Economics*, Vol. 66, pp. 99–126.

Perotti, Roberto, 1999, "Fiscal Policy in Good Times and Bad," *Quarterly Journal of Economics*, Vol. 114, No. 4, pp. 1399–1436.

Sarel, Michael, 1996, "Nonlinear Effects of Inflation on Economic Growth," *Staff Papers*, International Monetary Fund, Vol. 43 (March), pp. 199–215.

Tanzi, Vito, and Howell H. Zee, 1996, "Fiscal Policy and Long-Run Growth," IMF Working Paper 96/119 (Washington: International Monetary Fund).

Thomas, Alun, 2001, "An Exploration of the Private Sector Response to Changes in Government Saving Across OECD Countries," IMF Working Paper 01/69 (Washington: International Monetary Fund).

Von Hagen, Jürgen, and Rolf Strauch, 2001, "Fiscal Consolidations: Quality, Economic Conditions, and Success," *Public Choice*, Vol. 109, pp. 327–46.

Part II. Implementation

CHAPTER

6 Efficiency and Legitimacy: Trade-Offs in IMF Governance

Carlo Cottarelli[1]

Designing appropriate governance structures for an international financial institution such as the IMF is difficult, because steps to enhance the legitimacy of such an institution through constraints on its decision-making process may affect its operational efficiency. Potential trade-offs between legitimacy and efficiency exist for any public institution but are arguably more severe for an international one, because delegating power to it is politically controversial and, thus, likely to imply tighter constraints. The paper also underscores that the trade-offs are not absolute, however: they depend on the specific ways in which legitimacy is pursued—that is, on the specific constraints that are set. Strategic reforms should, thus, aim at improving the terms of the trade-off by exploring steps that are Pareto-improving in the dimensions of legitimacy and efficiency.

Introduction

The ability of an international organization to achieve its goals ultimately rests on its legitimacy (Woods, 2000; and Van Houtven, 2002, p. 66). Legitimacy means that its actions must be seen as expressing an accepted source of power delegated to it by sovereign countries. An institution that is not regarded as legitimate will face key obstacles in achieving its goals and will likely be ineffective. However, establishing legitimacy typically requires the imposition of constraints on the operations of such international organization—rules, systems of checks and balances, transparency requirements—and these, in principle, may come into conflict with the efficient pursuit of the international institution's goals, or what will be called here its operational efficiency (the ability to achieve its goals without wasting resources). Governance structures aimed at enhancing the institution's legitimacy may reduce its operational efficiency, giving rise to the potential trade-offs between legitimacy and operational efficiency.

This paper is about these trade-offs as they apply to the governance of the IMF. It should be stressed from the outset that these trade-offs are common to any public or political institution, but they become more severe for an international institution because the delegation of power to an international institution remains a politically difficult act. This implies that the constraints set on international institutions to boost their legitimacy in the eyes of sovereign countries (and their national voters) may have to be stronger than those set on domestic institutions, thus potentially affecting more deeply their operational efficiency. This potentially low efficiency has implications for the achievement of the institution's stated goals. In principle, low efficiency can be offset by the adequate provision of resources, so as to at least preserve an institution's effectiveness. But releasing resources to an international institution is also a controversial action for sovereign states. International institutions may end up being subject to particularly tight resource constraints. Consequently, limited efficiency is likely to translate into limited effectiveness.

The paper discusses the legitimacy-efficiency trade-offs with respect to three dimensions:

- *Control of political power over the operational decisions of international "technocrats"* (second section). Close control by national political authorities is one way to enhance the legitimacy of an international institution, but it may lead to decisions that are suboptimal from a technical perspective. The paper argues that the political control over the IMF is pervasive at the formal level. In practice, owing to information-processing constraints, the control is less pervasive, although unevenly applied across countries. Yet, its costs in terms of efficiency are not trivial. Here the challenge is to find forms of control that reduce the disturbance to operational efficiency, based perhaps on more operational independence coupled with strong ex post accountability.
- *Transparency in IMF decision making* (third section). Transparency enhances legitimacy, and,

[1] I would like to thank Mark Allen, Jim Boughton, Michael Deppler, Enrica Detragiache, Atish Ghosh, Luc Hobloue, Jeroen Kremers, Kate Langdon, Alessandro Leipold, Ashoka Mody, Miria Pigato, Alessandro Rebucci, Abebe Selassie, and Ignazio Visco for their helpful comments; Jeff Frieden, Anne Krueger, and J.J. Polak for useful discussions on some of the topics covered in this paper; and Jolanta Stefanska and Michael Filippello for excellent research assistance.

in many respects, can also lead to increased effectiveness. However, it may also come into conflict with operational efficiency, given the confidential nature of the financial matters the IMF deals with. This section explores the various channels through which transparency may involve costs, a necessary step in the search for more effective forms of transparency.
- *Uniformity of treatment across countries* (fourth section). Uniformity of treatment also enhances legitimacy but may involve spending resources on activities that have low priority for the purpose of achieving the IMF's operational goals. Avoiding waste and arbitrary selection at the same time is a difficult task.

The resource-constraint issue, which, as noted, implies that low efficiency may impair effectiveness, is discussed in the fifth section. That section also illustrates how the particular nature of IMF work, as well as outdated work processes, may further constrain the efficient management of IMF resources. The sixth section concludes the paper.

Before proceeding with the paper, two points must be underlined. First, this paper is, by its nature, somewhat lopsided, as it focuses more on the need for efficiency than on the need for legitimacy. This aims at provoking the discussion on an issue—the search for efficiency—that is often disregarded. Moreover, the paper's focus on the existence of trade-offs between efficiency and legitimacy does not mean that the author believes those trade-offs are inevitable. Indeed, their extent depends on the specific ways through which legitimacy is pursued. The challenge is thus to find possible ways in which the terms of the trade-off could be improved. For example, as noted, forms of political monitoring that are focused on ex post accountability do not directly affect operational decisions, contrary to direct political control. Also, other steps advocated in the past to boost IMF legitimacy—such as more transparent procedures for the selection of IMF management or changes in the distribution of political control across various member countries—may achieve that goal with no undesired effects on efficiency.[2] Reforms should, thus, aim at improving the terms of the trade-off by exploring steps that are Pareto-improving in the legitimacy and efficiency dimensions. However, while examples of such steps are provided, a full discussion of possible lines of reform goes beyond the scope of this paper—whose goal is to highlight the existence of potential trade-offs, not to find solutions. More work, as well as expertise in areas such as delegation theory, is needed to address the difficult issues raised in this paper.

Second, assessing the magnitude of the trade-offs is admittedly a difficult and essentially judgmental task. But this does not justify neglecting their existence. Indeed, one should wonder to what extent some of the alleged mistakes in IMF work during the last few years were due to governance structures reflecting an inadequate appreciation of the trade-offs, rather than to specific errors in judgment.[3]

Appropriate Degree and Form of Political Control

Public opinion often perceives the IMF as a monolith, and little attention is paid to the various components of its governance structure. A bird's-eye view of the latter is therefore useful (see Van Houtven, 2002, Chapter 3 for a more detailed discussion).

IMF Governance Structure

The IMF governance structure involves four entities:

- *The direct representatives of countries' interests* (the "capitals," as they will be referred to hereinafter). Formally, the main bodies representing the capitals are the Board of Governors—which includes ministers of finance and central bank governors—and its International Monetary and Financial Committee (IMFC). These bodies provide the ultimate source of political oversight but meet infrequently (typically twice a year). Meetings of the IMFC are now routinely preceded by preparatory meetings at the Deputies' level.
- *The Board of Executive Directors* (EDs)—hereinafter referred to as "the Board"—where 24 EDs in Washington, D.C. represent the IMF's 184 member countries. The Board "exercises all the powers for conducting the IMF's business, except those that the Articles of Agreement—that is, the Fund's statute—have reserved for the Board of Governors" (Van Houtven, 2002, p. 14). The Board provides close political oversight over management (see next paragraph) and staff, meeting at IMF headquarters for at least three days a week. Thus, the "representatives" of

[2] See, for example, Akyüz (2002), Woods (2000), Buira (2003), Caliari and Schroeder (2003), and Passacantando (2004).

[3] For example, the report of the Independent Evaluation Office on Argentina (IMF, 2004) argues that the IMF supported weak policies in that country for too long, focused its fiscal analysis too narrowly, did not analyze sufficiently the long-term sustainability of the exchange rate regime, and did not enforce conditionality. While highlighting these shortcomings is important, it is equally important to understand the underlying causes of those shortcomings and, in the perspective of this paper, whether they could be explained by inadequate governance structures. For example, and bringing forward some of the issues raised later, did those errors reflect "clientelism" of IMF staff with respect to the authorities (see the relevant subsection), or implicit political pressures, or the inadequacy of the provision of human resources?

IMF shareholders follow the IMF's work, and approve its decisions, virtually on a daily basis. This is an unusual governance feature with respect to, say, a private corporation. Note also that the EDs, while to some extent independent,[4] generally operate, for key decisions, in concert with "the capitals."

- *The Managing Director*, appointed by the Board, is at the same time the IMF's Chief Executive Officer, head of the staff, and the Chairman of the Board. It is common to refer to the Managing Director, First Deputy Managing Director, and Deputy Managing Directors collectively as "management."
- *The staff*—currently some 2,700 international civil servants—represent the IMF's "technical" voice. They execute IMF policies in the same way that, for example, central bank employees execute monetary policy at the national level.

In addition to this formal structure, there are other forums in which IMF business is discussed, such as the G-7 (Group of Seven), G-20, and G-24 meetings.

This governance structure—particularly the role of the Board in making and monitoring IMF decisions—suggests a relatively limited degree of delegation from the political to the technical dimension. Things are more complex than they appear, though, and quite naturally differ across the range of activities performed by the IMF. To explore the actual allocation of decision-making power, it is useful to review how the relationship between various components of IMF governance—and, in particular, between what I will call the "political pole" (the Board and "the capitals") and the technical pole (management and staff)—has evolved over time.[5]

Some History

The issue of the appropriate degree of political oversight was hotly debated when the IMF was established. British and U.S. views diverged on this. The U.S. side, headed by Harry Dexter White, envisaged close political oversight, involving a Board working at the IMF headquarters. The British side, headed by John Maynard Keynes, was against close oversight, and the British "plea for independence" was clear from the very beginning. In the words of Robert Skidelsky (Keynes's biographer):

> The British wanted the two institutions [IMF and the World Bank] to be apolitical, deciding matters on technical grounds. To this end they wanted them located outside Washington; and wanted the Fund, in particular, to be under the unencumbered control of the Managing Director and his staff, with the twelve Executive Directors and their alternates representing their countries and regions on a part-time basis, and at part-time salaries. The Americans wanted the Fund and Bank to be located in Washington: they wanted the executive directors to be full time.... (Skidelsky, 2003, pp. 829–30).

The British view reflected a number of concerns: (a) political considerations might overrule technical considerations;[6] (b) insufficient delegation might prevent efficiency;[7] and (c) the IMF might be seen as operating more under rules than under discretion (Martin, 2002, p. 16). American views eventually prevailed, as close political oversight was seen as the needed counterpart for accepting the obligations of membership (Van Houtven, 2002, p. 65), and the IMF ended up with a Board of political appointees sitting in continuous session. Indeed, in the early days of the IMF's life, EDs had a direct role not only in vetting IMF decisions daily but also in running IMF business, including by actively negotiating with countries and heading field missions (Martin, 2002, p. 20). However, it soon became clear that this governance structure was de facto impracticable, owing primarily to informational constraints, as the membership and activities of the IMF increased: "Growth of membership and turnover on the Board meant that it did not build up the kind of institutional memory that the staff gained over time" (Martin, 2002, p. 23).[8]

Thus, as of the early 1950s, the role of management and staff gradually increased (Horsefield, 1969, p. 470–73; Gold, 1972, p. 172; and Strange, 1973, p. 279).[9] In the words of one of the U.S. EDs, "The result was a strong Management/staff and an

---

[4] An Executive Director cannot be legally dismissed until his or her term has expired. However, this formal independence does not apply to the "appointed EDs" (those representing the countries with the five largest quotas), who can be dismissed at any time and for any reason (see, for example, Kafka, 1996, p. 331).

[5] This split between political and technical poles is a simplification, as each component of each of the poles plays a specific role. Moreover, the role of management, as interface between staff and the Board, cannot be seen as fully technical. More generally, reflecting their personalities and backgrounds, some members of management may be closer to the political pole than others.

[6] The submission of the British delegation at the Atlantic City meeting of June 1944 that preceded the July 1944 Bretton Woods conference considered that, "so far as practicable, we want to aim at a governing structure doing a technical job and developing a sense of corporate responsibility to all the members, and not the need to guard the interests of particular countries" (quoted in Horsefield (1969), p. 86). See also Boughton (2001), p. 1032.

[7] At the Savannah conference of March 1946, which at that point had to give operational interpretation to the Articles of Agreement, the Canadian representatives argued that "the Board could not achieve the best results if it was engaged in a continuous study of figures and memoranda" (Horsefield, 1969, p. 132).

[8] See also Kafka (1996, p. 327).

[9] The Board's decisions of January 12, 1948 formalized and detailed the relationship among staff, management, and the Board, including assigning to the staff the task of conducting negotiations with country authorities. However, the Board's rein on the staff remained initially tight, as "the composition of each staff mission was subject to Board approval, and the Board outlined detailed instruction for them" (de Vries and Horsefield, 1969, p. 471).

Executive Board that acted largely on management recommendations" (Southard, 1979, p.7).

Between the early 1950s and the early 1990s the balance of power between the two poles went through various fluctuations, with no clear trend. Overall, while the Board never became a rubber stamp for management/staff decisions, it retained a more significant role in setting general policies and guidelines, rather than in decisions on specific countries (Boughton, 2001, p. 1031). The obvious exceptions were country cases with higher political value for the key shareholders—where the political role of the capitals over the Board was probably more important, however.

A more definite trend may have emerged since the mid-1990s, with a number of steps aimed at increasing the information available to the political pole and its capability of vetting, ex ante, the positions taken by the technocratic pole:

- More information has been required to be disclosed to the Board: for example, side letters[10] have been required to be disclosed to the Board since September 1999. Also, as of early 2003, all "comfort letters" and similar statements made by staff to other international financial institutions (IFIs), donors, and creditors on country developments must be transmitted to the Board.
- The technical pole's discretion in shaping program conditions and modalities has been constrained: conditionality has been streamlined, particularly as concerns structural measures. Moreover, prior actions—steps that staff requires to be taken by countries as a condition of presenting a program (or the review of a program) to the Board—have become formal conditions for the use of IMF resources. Finally, detailed provisions have been issued regarding the conditions under which large lending operations can be recommended by staff (the so-called exceptional access cases, for which early Board involvement is now also required).
- Requirements for ex ante scrutiny of programs by the Board have been tightened: as of mid-2003, before presenting a new program to the Board for countries with prolonged use of IMF resources (some 80 percent of program countries outstanding in mid-2004), an ex post assessment report justifying the need for a new program and outlining its main features needs to be discussed by the Board. Negotiations on a new program cannot be completed before such discussion has taken place.

Moreover, within the political pole, there seems to be a clear trend toward shifting control away from the Board and toward the capitals of the largest countries:

> The major industrial countries, the Group of Seven ... have exhibited a growing tendency in recent years to act as a self-appointed steering group or "Directoire" of the IMF. Recent reports of the finance ministers to the heads of state and government at the annual summit meetings have sometimes tended to deal with IMF matters in a manner that raises the question of whether they will leave the Executive Directors representing the Group of Seven countries with the necessary margin for discussion and room for give-and-take that is essential for consensus building (Van Houtven, 2002, pp. 30–31).[11]

There are four reasons for these trends: (1) the increasing size of IMF financial support in several headline cases during the 1990s called for closer political oversight over the use of "international taxpayers' money;" (2) the role played by the IMF as the number of programs increased raised the question of whether unelected technocrats had not acquired too much power; (3) the end-of-the-century crises raised questions on IMF effectiveness (delegating political power is always controversial, but more so if results are mixed); and (4) with the dramatic development in communication technologies, it has become easier for the capitals to exert their influence on the Board (Kenen and others, 2004, pp. 99–100).

Key Features of IMF Governance and Its Implications for Efficiency

The key features of the IMF governance structure can thus be summarized as follows.

- First, at the *formal level*, political control is pervasive, as most IMF actions have to be approved by the Board. This formal control has increased in recent years.
- Second, in *practice*, the ability of the political pole to exert its influence is limited by its constraints in processing information. The view that the Board does not have the resources to monitor staff effectively is indeed quite widespread (De Gregorio and others, 1999, pp. 21, 78–82; Harper, 1998, pp. 284–85; Caliari and Schroeder, 2004; and, perhaps more significantly, IMF, 1999, pp. 33–34). Thus, it remains to be seen whether the recent effort to

[10] Side letters are letters that program countries send to management on confidential aspects of program policies (e.g., in the exchange rate area).

[11] As these changes were implemented, more radical proposals to enhance political control were being discussed. See a description of the French reform proposal in De Gregorio and others (1999, p. 99) and of the Miyazawa proposal also in De Gregorio and others (1999, p. 95).

strengthen formal control over the technocratic pole will succeed in enhancing actual control.[12] The information processing constraints remain severe; in this respect, the ratio between professional staff working for the Board and regular professional staff has remained roughly constant over the last 10 years (at about 9½ percent).[13]

- Third, although there is no firm evidence of this, it stands to reason that, in the most relevant cases as well as in the setting of key policy guidelines, the balance of power is tilted toward the political pole.[14] Within the political pole, however, power rests primarily with the capitals of the larger shareholders. Even leaving aside arguments of political weight, larger countries (and, more generally, advanced countries) can devote more resources to monitoring the IMF, and can thus play a more significant role. And, as argued, the role of the "large" capitals has increased in recent years.

The preceding configuration raises issues of legitimacy and equality of treatment across countries.[15] Here, however, we focus on its implications for the IMF's efficiency.

The first implication relates to the risk that IMF decisions (in cases where the political stakes are high) reflect direct political pressures, originating typically in the capitals, rather than technical factors. How severe is this problem? Leo Van Houtven, former IMF Secretary, while noting that "it could not be expected that decisions would always be taken exclusively on technical grounds," eventually concludes that "the limited occurrence of political decisions in the IMF has been remarkable" (Van Houtven, 2002, pp. 43–44). Econometric work on whether IMF decisions reflect political factors yields mixed results.[16] Surveys do indicate that political pressures are not unusual, with 7 percent of mission chiefs reporting that technical judgment was overridden by political pressures "frequently" or "always," and 48 percent reporting that political pressures had been experienced "occasionally" or "sometimes" (IMF, 2002, p. 64). Moreover, various IMF watchers have reported several cases of direct political pressures.[17] Be this as it may, the frequency of cases of direct political interference is not all that matters: the perception that there have been cases of political interference affects the IMF's credibility, and hence its effectiveness, in all cases. Furthermore, the perception that the IMF is a "geopolitical slush fund" (Willett, 2004) and that the IMF serves "the ad hoc political purposes of broad foreign policy" (Calomiris, 2000, p. 86) remains quite widespread (see also Allegret and Dulbecco, 2004). The controversy surrounding IMF decisions taken in early 2003 to roll over the loans to Argentina is still fresh.[18]

A second, and perhaps more subtle, implication of the IMF's formal political dependence is the alleged "clientelism" of IMF staff vis-à-vis country authorities. Bordo and James (2000, p. 8) notes that "IMF staff reports on member countries are thought to be insufficiently critical because of the development of a sort of 'clientelism,' in which good relations with officials and ministers develop." The issue of "clientelism" is also raised in IMF (1999, p. 65): "A view that exists in the institution is that a report that is incisive but offends the authorities is damaging to a mission chief's career while one that is bland and later turns out to be lacking in some important respects will be overlooked."

While, again, the existence of clientelism should not be exaggerated, some aspects of IMF culture may encourage it. In particular, managers are assessed partly on the basis of their ability in keeping good relationships with country authorities. This may affect, in particular, surveillance cases, as this is where a harsh assessment given by staff may be more strongly objected to by country authorities (particularly in "calm waters," that is, when surveillance is potentially more effective in preventing future crises).

[12] Reversals did occur in the past. For example, some 20 years ago, the Board asked that at the end of a program, an assessment of its success or failure be included in the first staff report following the conclusion of the program. This initiative—similar to the new "ex post assessments" discussed above—eventually fell into disuse.

[13] Moreover it has been argued that, because of the increased speed at which decisions have to be taken in today's world of high capital mobility, the actual balance of control has shifted toward the staff (De Gregorio and others, 1999, p. 80), except with respect to large countries such as the United States (De Gregorio and others, 1999, p. 82), which can devote larger resources to staff monitoring.

[14] The difficulties faced by the IMF management's initiative to establish a new debt-restructuring mechanism for sovereign debt—in plain English, a mechanism to deal with the cases of country bankruptcies—show that when it comes to major policy issues, the technocratic pole has limited traction.

[15] For example, Van Houtven (2002) argues that the shift of power toward the capitals and away from the Board has reduced the role of developing countries: decisions at the Board are taken by consensus, thus partly enhancing the role of countries with limited formal voting rights.

[16] Bird (2003, pp. 248–52) lists a number of papers that do find econometric evidence of political factors in IMF decisions, including Stiles, 1991; Thacker, 1999; and Barro and Lee (2002). However, the evidence in Bird and Rowlands (2001) is more nuanced. After reviewing this literature, Bird (2003) concludes that the picture is not "completely clear."

[17] See lists in De Gregorio and others (1999) and Bordo and James (2000, pp. 39–40); see also Stiles (1990) and *Financial Times*, October 5, 2004, p. 4, "G7 Interfered in IMF Bid to Push Through Russia Reform."

[18] See, for example, the leader (editorial) in *Financial Times*, January 20, 2003, "The G7 Blinks: The IMF Has Been Forced to Take a Huge Gamble."

Does clientelism reflect the IMF's political governance structure? This is hard to prove. But it stands to reason that the voice of country authorities is amplified by the fact that the IMF is not formally independent from political forces, and that political representatives sit in Washington, D.C. in continuous sessions.[19]

The third implication relates to the ongoing shift in decision-making power from the Board to the capitals. As argued by Kenen and others (2004, pp. 99–101), this shift affects efficiency as decisions are taken by officials who have more limited knowledge of the IMF than do EDs and have only occasional or no contact with staff. Allegret and Dulbecco (2004, p. 10) take a similar view. This problem is particularly severe in areas where the political pole retains a higher degree of control, namely in setting policy guidelines.

The fourth implication relates to the role of the Board in the IMF's daily management. From a corporate governance perspective, it is unusual that shareholders' representatives participate in daily management activities. The rationale for more detached participation (focused, for example, on setting goals and monitoring results) rests on the information-processing constraints that are at the basis of any principal-agent relationship. Given the cost of evaluating information, it is more efficient for decisions at the daily level to be delegated to the management of a company or an institution. Moreover, a body representing shareholders must potentially be large. In the IMF's case, the large size of the Board also reflects its political nature and the related need to give voice, without excessive pooling, to all member countries.[20]

The report of the external evaluation of surveillance points candidly at the atypical role of the Board in terms of governance: "Everything we know about institutional governance indicates to us that a group of 24 is, to put it mildly, extremely large for useful exchanges of views, discussion, and group decision making" (IMF, 1999, p. 75).

Van Houtven (2002, p. 23) also notes that the "decision making and management of the IMF would be better served by a smaller Board." Kafka (1996, p. 333) expresses a similar view.[21]

What impact does the Board's atypical role have on efficiency? As discussed, many believe that the Board does not have enough resources to challenge the staff's views and that, in practice, in the majority of cases it performs only a formal role. However, this activity of formal control is quite time consuming—for the Board as well as the staff. It is time consuming for the Board because trying to absorb (and react to) all the information provided by staff is not easy; about two-thirds of the Board's time is spent on country matters rather than in setting policy guidelines or in monitoring their overall implementation. And for the staff, it is time consuming because it results in the production of activities that may be carried out largely as a formality. With the increased weight of the political pole in the last few years, the trend toward formal "micromanagement" has, if anything, increased, with the Board expressing views and imposing formal requirements on quite technical and detailed issues.[22]

Trade-Off and Right Balance

Political oversight is needed by domestic institutions and, to an even greater extent, by international organizations, because they must be seen by sovereign countries as exercising legitimate powers. Without legitimacy, the IMF ultimately would be ineffective.[23] Some forms of political control can hamper operational efficiency, however; hence a trade-off arises. The question is: what form and degree of delegation from the political pole to the technocratic pole—in other words, the degree of "slack" in the principal-agent relationship—are most appropriate for an institution such as the IMF? This issue has not been studied much. Models of delegation[24] have found limited application to the study of international organizations, possibly because of the

[19] There are provisions that, in principle, protect staff from political pressures, but their effective role is doubtful. In particular, Article XII, Section 4(c) of the Articles of Agreement includes a provision obliging countries to "respect the international character of … [the staff's] duty and … refrain from all attempts to influence any of the staff." But this article is not well known even to IMF staff, a sign that IMF culture does not emphasize it. In a sample of IMF economists I contacted, only 7 percent knew that such a provision existed.

[20] Indeed, the Board's political nature has also made it difficult for the Board to operate through committees: "The glaring absence of meaningful committee work speaks volumes for the constraints under which Directors apparently operate, de facto if not legally, as country and constituency representatives" (IMF, 1999, p. 75). This "size" issue is typical of international organizations. As noted by Lister (1984, p. 101), "a perennial problem of international organization has been to fashion an executive organ that is both small enough to deal expeditiously with the flow of regular business and yet representative enough to act authoritatively."

[21] As IMF Secretary, Leo Van Houtven was directly in charge of the relationships with the Board; Alexandre Kafka was an Executive Director for more than 30 years.

[22] Examples are the list of indicators staff should use to assess countries' vulnerabilities, templates for debt sustainability, the reporting of the effectiveness of IMF surveillance in specific countries, the reporting of relationships with the World Bank, the reporting of statistical issues, and the background papers prepared for Article IV consultations.

[23] Indeed, various authors have underscored that some form of political control can enhance the IMF's effectiveness. De Gregorio and others (1999, p. 93) argues that peer pressure can be an important tool in the IMF's hands. Cunliffe (quoted in De Gregorio and others, p. 125) argues that "granting independence to the IMF would result in the dissipation of support for the institution."

[24] See, for a recent survey, Bendor, Glazer, and Hammond (2001); and, regarding delegation from politicians to bureaucrats, Alesina and Tabellini (2004).

complexity of the issues involved—for example, those related to the existence of multiple "principals" (the country members), which have, in turn, various principals (each country's stakeholders).

I have argued in the preceding text that the current approach results in (a) political influences that are often not transparent and are exercised unevenly across countries; and (b) excessive resources being spent in pro forma activities, reducing at the same time the actual political oversight, the ability to set proper guidelines, and efficiency. Could a different approach work better? Various proposals have been put forward:

- *Giving the IMF more operational independence, while enhancing its ex post accountability*, as proposed, for example, by De Gregorio and others (1999), Bordo and James (2000), and Allegret and Dulbecco (2004). Note, however, that the proposal in De Gregorio and others (1999) and Allegret and Dulbecco (2004) to make the Board independent does not address one issue raised in this paper, namely the difficulty a large body, such as the Board, has in managing a financial institution on a daily basis. This issue could perhaps be better addressed by reviving the idea of a nonresident board, in charge of broad oversight, rather than of specific decisions, as advocated originally by Keynes and more recently by others.
- *Enhancing the protection of staff from explicit and implicit political pressure.* A critical step, recommended by the report of the External Evaluation of Surveillance, would be to alter the incentive structure by making it clear that management will back up staff members who give frank advice (IMF, 1999, p. 67).
- *Reassessing the role of the Board, with the aim of minimizing activities that result in merely formal control, while increasing its role vis-à-vis the capitals* (Van Houtven, 2002). One specific step proposed by Woods (2000) is to increase the amount of time the Board could spend on setting policy guidelines by considerably reducing its responsibilities for country decisions.

Appropriate Degree of Transparency

Transparency is key to the legitimacy of a public institution. Until recently (the mid-1990s), in determining the extent of IMF transparency, the balance between legitimacy and (at least what was perceived as) efficiency was biased toward the latter. It was assumed that the confidential nature of IMF business was incompatible with a high degree of operational disclosure. However, during the last few years, it has become clear that secrecy weakens IMF legitimacy. Moreover, it has been noted that transparency is also important for efficiency. First, it allows closer monitoring and accountability of IMF staff; and, hence, in a principal-agent perspective, it should boost efficiency. Second, transparency in the IMF's advice (e.g., the publication of IMF staff reports) magnifies the IMF voice; if markets listen to it, inappropriate policies are more directly penalized, enhancing the "peer pressure" mechanism on which IMF surveillance has traditionally relied. Indeed, the shift toward greater transparency has partly reflected the Fund's attempt to enhance its effectiveness in the aftermath of the Asian crisis.

While the benefits of transparency in terms of legitimacy and efficiency have been appropriately emphasized over the last few years, the debate has been somewhat one-sided. There are also potential tradeoffs between transparency and efficiency, and acknowledging them is a necessary step in establishing appropriate transparency policies. The reader will, I hope, forgive me if, to correct this one-sidedness, the rest of this section is somewhat biased in the opposite direction.

Some Definitions

When I use the term "transparency policies" (or, for simplicity's sake, "transparency"), I refer to policies that require the dissemination of documents to an audience that would not otherwise receive them. The following should be noted:

- I am referring to the dissemination of *documents*, as one cannot assume that the content of the document (that is, the *information*) is unaffected by the dissemination constraint.[25]
- Typically, IMF documents contain (a) information on a certain country or country group (e.g., data on reserves, the decision of a government to devalue, information on certain financial institutions, the government's intention to introduce a certain measure); (b) views of staff, or of other components of IMF governance, on a certain policy issue (e.g., whether exchange rate levels or regimes are appropriate, whether banking supervision is adequate, or whether political risks exist); and (c) assessments of IMF performance. In what follows, I will focus primarily on (a) and (b).[26]
- Discussions on transparency should always identify the original and new recipients of the documents. In what follows, I will focus on changes in transparency rules that broaden the

[25] Strictly speaking, using the term "transparency policies" as a synonym for publication requirements is not appropriate, since the latter does not necessarily involve a higher degree of dissemination of information. Nevertheless, I will follow the standard convention.

[26] What follows could, however, also be applied to assessments of IMF performance (self-assessments or assessments by outside experts). The latter, however, also bring to the fore some additional issues, including whether excessive emphasis on past "mistakes" may reduce the credibility of the IMF in the future.

dissemination of documents from the technocratic pole (and the country authorities of a specific country) to either the political pole or the general public.

Potential Drawbacks of Transparency

I will first consider the specific mechanisms through which transparency vis-à-vis the public at large can affect IMF efficiency. I will also initially (and perhaps unrealistically) assume that the dissemination requirement does not alter the information in the document to be published. In this context, transparency has three direct drawbacks:

- Transparency—for example, the publication of IMF views regarding the sustainability of an exchange rate regime under current policies—can cause a negative market reaction (say, a speculative attack) that could have been avoided through a change in policies (IMF, 1999, p. 75). The stress here is on the fact that the negative market reaction could have been avoided had country authorities been given sufficient time to react to the IMF's views. Supporters of full transparency often argue that if the IMF's views can trigger a crisis, they might as well be released, since the crisis will occur one way or another. This view misses the point that the IMF's confidential advice could, one would hope, lead to a policy change that would avoid the crisis. Moreover, a vulnerability assessment is always probabilistic in nature, but most readers will only consider the modal projection or outlook, which could precipitate a crisis.
- In countries with an IMF-supported program, transparency (in particular, the publication of letters of intent) may disrupt the conditionality process. A program, as well as its related conditionality (that is, the set of conditions that need to be met for the IMF to continue to support a program), is not carved in stone at its inception. Conditions are often modified as developments unfold (Mussa and Savastano, 1999). This process of program negotiation and renegotiation is more difficult to manage if markets are fully aware of the contents of letters of intent. For example, failure to take certain actions covered by conditionality may trigger a crisis even when the IMF would have been willing to waive them. Conversely, waiving conditions may be inappropriately seen as a watering down of a program. The key point is that the negotiation/conditionality process requires time, and transparency, in a world of high capital mobility, dramatically cuts the time available for this process to work effectively and for an optimal redesign of a program. Thus, in this context, conditionality may end up acting as a coordinating device for speculative attacks (creating a reverse catalytic effect).
- Transparency about a government's intention to implement a measure can prevent the implementation of that measure if public knowledge of the government's intention leads to a coalescence of vested interest against it.

In the preceding cases, the original information is provided to the public, so, at least, the expected benefits usually linked to transparency (a more informed public) can be reaped. But one cannot assume that the information in the documents to be published will not be affected by the publication requirement. First, given the costs arising if the original information is disseminated, country authorities may be unwilling to share all of the information they have with IMF staff. This would prevent the IMF from effectively performing its functions, as staff will not be in a position to provide adequate advice to country authorities (IMF, 1999, p. 75). And second, given the limited protection of staff vis-à-vis political pressures (see the second section), or because of the risk of causing a crisis, staff may be inclined to be less candid in documents that are going to be published. This implies that the correct information would not be provided to the public, giving rise to a pro-forma transparency.

Whether the above drawbacks apply also with respect to transparency vis-à-vis the Board depends on whether the information provided to the Board would or would not leak to the public. This is a controversial issue. IMF (1999, p. 78) concludes that "any such discussions [on confidential issues] could only be reported to the Board in a quite general way if their substance were expected to remain confidential." Van Houtven (2002, p. 19) also notes that "delicate issues may arise in cases when the need for disclosure of information to Executive Directors appears difficult to reconcile with the requirements of confidentiality of a member country." Martin (2002, p. 40) refers to the "occasional embarrassing leaks from the Executive Board," although leaks of sensitive material have been infrequent (and there also have been examples of leaks from staff). However, even without leaks, countries may be unwilling to share with other countries specific information. As noted by Martin (2002), "For any borrowing country, some states are likely to be political adversaries. They will then be reluctant to reveal sensitive information to the Board."

Transparency in IMF History

How have these considerations affected IMF work over the last sixty years? For many decades after the IMF was set up, the issue of transparency vis-à-vis the public was not regarded by IMF shareholders as critical. Transparency issues did feature prominently in the discussions leading to the establishment of the IMF, but only as far as they related to the information to be provided *to the Board*. Thus, at the Savannah conference of March 1946, Keynes took the view that no country would be willing to confide in the Managing Director if the Executive Directors were to be made acquainted with everything that was going on (Horsefield, 1969, p. 133).

In any event, as discussed above, the shift to the staff in early 1948 of the responsibility for dealing with country authorities created a barrier between the Board and member countries (Martin, 2002, p. 37). This situation prevailed during the following decades. The issue, however, resurfaced periodically, with the technocratic pole reiterating the following:

> The confidentiality of relations between member governments and the Fund management and staff, so fundamental to the successful operations of the Fund, could be impaired.... [W]ere a member government to believe that any information provided to the Fund would be made available to governments around the world, there would be a devastating effect on the future of the Fund. (de Vries, 1985, p. 994, referring to staff and management views in the late 1970s).

During the 1990s, however, the demand from the world public opinion for more transparency vis-à-vis the public mounted rapidly (see, for example, De Gregorio and others, 1999, pp. 84–85) and the technocratic pole, also in consideration of potential benefits in terms of effectiveness (see the previous discussion of this issue), came to accept the need for change (Van Houtven, 2002, p. 69). Thus, the IMF has started publishing a number of previously unpublished documents, including staff reports and letters of intent (IMF, 2003).

The pressure on the technocratic pole for more transparency vis-à-vis the Board has increased in parallel. As discussed in the previous section, this has, for example, involved the disclosure to the Board of all side letters, as well as more frequent and informal Board discussions of country developments.

Unresolved Issues

While the move toward transparency has merits, and is in any case unavoidable, it has been assumed that at least some of its potential drawbacks could be easily minimized through appropriate policies.[27] In particular, rules allow the deletion of "highly market-sensitive material" from published staff reports. However, the deletion policy may not be perceived as sufficient protection by the countries involved. First, the request for deletion needs to be approved by IMF management—consequently it is far from certain what would be regarded as "highly market-sensitive." Second, the flexibility in making changes, even for highly market-sensitive information, is limited.[28] And third, since the deletion policy covers only highly market-sensitive information, it does not address other concerns the authorities may have, including the risk that untimely publication of policy intentions would make the policy implementation more difficult.[29]

Thus, the majority of the Board has typically focused on the benefits from transparency rather than on the existence of trade-offs. For example, the following refers to a recent Board discussion:

> Directors considered that candor and transparency were essential dimensions of surveillance, and took note of efforts to improve information provided to the Executive Board and to boost publication of staff reports.... Some Directors noted, however, that there may be trade-offs between transparency and candor (IMF, 2003).[30]

I side with those who believe these trade-offs should be explored more extensively.[31] Ultimately, increased publication of IMF documents can enhance the IMF's efficiency: when the voice of the IMF is heard publicly, governments (particularly in democratic countries) may be more willing to act under pressure from public opinion and the markets. But acknowledging the existence of costs is an important step toward finding more efficient forms of transparency. In particular, the following questions seem to deserve further scrutiny:

[27] Others have assumed that transparency, even in delicate areas such as exchange rate assessment, cannot be a problem in any case. The recent report of the IMF's Independent Evaluation Office acknowledges the inherent sensitivity of exchange rate assessments for countries with pegged exchange rates, as such assessments could "alarm the markets" (IMF, 2004, paragraph 238), but concludes that the problem can be resolved by making such discussions "a routine exercise, something markets expect to occur as a matter of procedure." However, it is not clear why the fact that assessments of exchange rate regimes are routinely made would diminish the impact of an IMF statement that concluded that a certain regime is not sustainable.

[28] Deletions are possible, but modifications need to be limited to what is required to keep the text intelligible and grammatically correct. Moreover, deletions cannot be used to eliminate entire sections of a report or several paragraphs. Finally, the presumption is for a high degree of parsimony in distinguishing material that is clearly highly market sensitive from what is only politically sensitive.

[29] A side letter can be used to protect the confidentiality of measures whose early disclosure would make their implementation more difficult. But this approach can only be followed for program countries, and not for countries where the IMF is only engaged in surveillance.

[30] The reference to a trade-off between transparency and candor (rather than between transparency and effectiveness) should not mislead the reader. The issue is that as a result of requiring publication of staff reports, these may turn out to lack candor and thus to be ineffective.

[31] Mohammed (2000, p. 203) also points out the costs arising from excessive transparency. At the time of his writing. Mohammed was Advisor to the Chairman of the Group of Twenty-Four (G-24), the intergovernmental group of developing countries set up to concert their position on monetary and finance issues. He had earlier been Director of the IMF's External Relations Department. Kafka (1996, p. 335) also warns about the limits of transparency. Williamson (2000) actually blames the IMF for excessive transparency when it "forced Thailand to reveal in October 1997 that it had mortgaged all its reserves" (p. 336).

- How to make sure that, in spite of publication requirements, countries provide the necessary information. Self-assessments conducted by the IMF on the implementation of transparency policies are quite sanguine on the outcomes of the experiment. However, only time will tell how the provision of information to the IMF by member countries has been affected by publication requirements.
- How to make sure that the publication of internal IMF documents does not result in a pro forma transparency, where the most important information is actually not disclosed.
- To what extent it would be appropriate to delay the publication of some documents, in contrast to the current practice of virtually immediate publication.[32] This would still allow ex post accountability while reducing the risk of ex ante censorship.
- What the appropriate degree of transparency vis-à-vis the political pole (of the Board and the capitals) is. The extent to which the information acquired by the technocratic pole, and all views held by it, should be shared with the Board (and "the capitals") is not entirely clear at present.

Appropriate Degree of Uniformity of Treatment Across Countries

Evenhandedness in the treatment of country members is seen as a critical requirement for the IMF[33] as it seeks to enhance its legitimacy. And yet, economic conditions do differ across countries. Thus, it stands to reason that efficiency requires selectivity—applying certain procedures or approaches to only the countries that really need them. In theory, there is no contradiction between evenhandedness and selectivity. One can, for example, use some screening process that is applied to identify countries that, for example, require more in-depth work. What ultimately matters is that countries be assessed on objective grounds—a uniformity of treatment *in substance*. In practice, however, *formalistic* uniformity of treatment is much easier to establish than substantive evenhandedness. This may lead to a bias toward the application of the same formal procedures to all countries, with a consequent loss in terms of resources and, hence, efficiency.

While the need for selectivity in IMF surveillance work is, in principle, accepted, difficulties have arisen in practice. If anything, trends in recent years seem to have been toward less selective approaches—as advocated by some developing countries (see, for example, Mohammed, 2000, p. 203). The key surveillance process—the Article IV consultation—takes place annually for most countries, with fewer than one-tenth of the IMF membership on a 24-month cycle.[34] Even in the latter case, staff visits often take place in years without formal Article IV consultations. Various standard surveillance tools, many of which have been introduced in recent years to strengthen IMF surveillance (for example, those to assess public debt and external debt sustainability), have to be applied to all countries. Moreover, major new expansions in the IMF mandate—in particular the assessment of the application of standards and codes—have covered all countries.

This bias against selectivity emerged clearly during the Board discussion of the so-called vulnerability assessment exercise, one of the few examples of selective practices, that was introduced by IMF staff and management in 2001 to monitor more closely countries with higher vulnerabilities. The press information notice summarizing the Board discussion on this issue indicated the following:

> The periodic vulnerability assessment exercise ... provides a platform for an independent assessment by relevant functional departments of key issues in individual countries, offers an opportunity to exchange views on analyses of vulnerability across different regions, and provides inputs for bilateral surveillance activities and program design. Several Directors saw merit in applying this exercise to advanced economies and not just emerging market economies. Other Directors pointed out that developments in advanced economies were examined at high frequencies through other mechanisms (IMF, 2003).

More selectivity in IMF work has been advocated in several reform proposals in recent years, but the attention has not focused on selectivity in the country dimension. Following Feldstein (1998), the need for focusing the IMF on its core areas of (macroeconomic) responsibility has been widely accepted, at least in principle. Correspondingly, various authors have underscored the need to reduce the overlap, in terms of issues covered, in the mandates of the main international economic institutions (for a recent discussion, see Kenen and others, 2004, pp. 95–97).

While a pruning of IMF responsibilities is needed, one should not forget that a rigid breakdown of economic problems by their nature is not easy. In particular, macroeconomic issues and structural issues are often closely related, and excessively constraining the scope of the IMF's work would inevitably

---

[32] De Gregorio and others (1999, p. 88) notes that delaying the publication of documents would reduce the risk of negative market reactions.

[33] For example, the October 2004 IMFC communiqué noted that, "Effective and evenhanded IMF surveillance across the whole membership is central to promoting high and sustainable growth in member countries and to crisis prevention" (IMFC, 2004). In the IMF, the term "surveillance" refers to the monitoring of countries' economic developments and policies.

[34] Program countries are also on a 24-month cycle, but they are, of course, subject to much closer monitoring as part of the program discussions.

impair its effectiveness.[35] Combining selectivity in the issue dimension with selectivity in the country dimension—dealing with certain issues only in countries where those issues are macroeconomically relevant—could thus provide a more effective approach. The question is how to do this without impairing the principle of uniformity of treatment across countries.

In this respect, two avenues could be explored:

- At the "micro level," consideration should be given to broadening the use of screening processes to avoid applying essentially the same formal procedures to all countries.
- At the "macro level," the key issue is whether the responsibilities in terms of country coverage of the international economic organizations—which involves significant overlap between the Organization for Economic Cooperation and Development (OECD) and the IMF for industrial countries, and between the World Bank and the IMF for nonindustrial countries—should not be revised. Some have, for example, argued that the IMF should reduce its work on industrial countries (see, for example, Polak, 2004). A milder alternative would be to identify a "leading institution" in the relationship between the international community and each country. The issue is, once more, a difficult one, since it involves trade-offs. Leaving aside the question of legitimacy, it has been argued that the overlapping of responsibilities may foster healthy competition (Krueger, 1997, p. 23) and, possibly, accountability.

Resource Constraints, Efficiency, and Trade-Offs

Constraints on an institution's efficiency would not impair its effectiveness if an adequate amount of resources were made available. It is thus important to assess the tightness of the IMF's human-resource constraint.

Few IMF-watchers have addressed this issue.[36] This is surprising because the adequacy of human resources is critical to the effectiveness of any decision-making process. Bordo and James (2000, p. 6), in discussing the size of the IMF, does start by providing information on both human and financial resources, but it then tackles only the latter's adequacy. Vaubel (1994, pp. 53–54) points to the rapid increase of IMF staff since 1960 and wonders whether it represents "a textbook case of Parkinson's Law" and concludes—without reporting any supporting empirical evidence—that the increase was not explained by increased balance of payments imbalances worldwide but was more correlated with the increase in IMF quotas. However, other critics—perhaps most forcefully Jeffrey Sachs and the Meltzer Commission—have argued that the IMF is understaffed, given the number of program cases usually handled.[37] In the same vein, IMF (1999, p. 73) also pointed out the inadequacy of its own human resources, concluding that "there is no doubt that many Fund staff are chronically overworked."

Yet, a cursory look at the growth of IMF staff over the last thirty years suggests no dearth of resources. From 1970 to 2002, the number of staff increased in relation to the number of member countries, although much less markedly with respect to the number of IMF-supported programs (Table 1). However, this increase needs to be interpreted in light of rising IMF responsibilities (for example, during the 1990s in international standards and codes, anti-money laundering, financial sector analysis, governance, and provision of information related to transparency requirements) and the increased complexity of problems, particularly as a result of increased capital mobility.[38]

Moreover, the increase in IMF staff does not say much about the adequacy of its level. IMF teams seem small by many standards. A typical IMF "mission" team includes, besides the mission chief, four (rarely five) economists who usually have additional assignments to carry out when at headquarters. A resident representative assists the team in most program cases, and in key surveillance cases. Other staff are also involved in reviewing the work of mission teams on a part-time basis, with reviewers typically working on tens of countries at the same time.

Is this resource endowment sufficient? Consider the following:

- Economic policy teams in central banks and finance ministries of industrial countries typically

[35] For example, many of the turn-of-the-century emerging market crises deeply reflected underlying structural problems. This, of course, does not mean that the IMF should deal, *at the technical level*, with areas where it does not have enough expertise. But, the overall assessment policy design and, in the case of program countries, the negotiation process with country authorities can hardly be broken down without an effectiveness loss.

[36] At the Savannah conference of March 1946, when IMF goals had already been crystallized in the Articles of Agreement, the views on the appropriate size of the staff ranged widely from the 30 professionals proposed by the British delegation to the 300 proposed by the U.S. delegation (Skidelsky, 2003, p. 830). The width of this range, however, partly reflects the more rule-based approach the British side envisaged for the IMF (see the second section).

[37] "The Meltzer Commission noted that the IMF, with just one thousand or so professional staff, could not and should not try to run dozens of countries' economic programs" (Sachs, 2000). The Meltzer Commission—or, more properly, the International Financial Institution Advisory Commission—was established in November 1998 by the U.S. Congress to consider the future roles of seven international financial institutions, including the IMF.

[38] For example, the increase in resources used for surveillance during FY2001/2002 was devoted to new tasks in financial surveillance and standards and codes, and to multilateral surveillance, with no increases in the resources available for bilateral surveillance.

Table 1

Number of Fund Staff Relative to IMF Member Countries and Fund-Supported Programs

	Year			
Staff	1970	1980	1990	2002
All staff				
Per country	8.7	10.1	11.9	14.7
Per program	43.3	48.8	34.8	51.6
Professional staff and managers				
Per country	...	5.9	7.6	10.5
Per program	...	28.9	22.2	36.6

Note: Three dots (...) indicate that the data were not available.

include hundreds of economists.[39] IMF teams are expected to cooperate with country authorities, but, in practice, local economists may not have adequate skills, and may have different goals than the IMF staff's, making full cooperation difficult.

- Each of the four mission team economists is typically in charge of one sector (real, monetary, fiscal, and balance of payments). This means, for example, that the critical balance of payments sector is typically the responsibility of a single economist. Thus, a single person deals with monitoring and projecting trade flows, the service account, the capital account, external debt stocks, competitiveness, trade restrictions, issues related to external debt negotiations, and so on.
- The availability of human resources assigned to program countries rises only modestly with the size of the financial resources committed by the IMF, as the composition of country teams, particularly in area departments (that is, those more directly in charge of dealing with country authorities), is fairly similar across countries. The relation between the amount of human and financial resources assigned to a country is depicted in Figure 1, which reports on the vertical axis the log of the ratio between human resources (in staff-years) and the log of millions of Special Drawing Rights (SDRs) committed. The relationship is negative, since the amount of human resources does not rise proportionately with the size of lending. The implicit elasticity is quite low (0.11) for the whole IMF (top panel) and is particularly low for area departments (0.08)—indeed only one-half that of other departments (0.16). This means that as the size of a program increases, the amount of resources increases more slowly for the teams in charge of a more direct contact with the authorities, while a faster increase is observed for the staff in charge of review work and other noncore activities.
- Program work attracts more resources than surveillance work, but the increase is, again, relatively modest. An econometric estimate relating the human resources assigned to a certain country to measures of its size, a dummy for program countries, the amount of lending, and the country type (industrial or not) shows that, on average, the existence of a program increases the human-resource allocation by less than a third with respect to a surveillance-only relationship (Table 2). This is not much, taking into account the responsibilities that fall on the staff when they are engaged in program work.

The scarcity of the IMF's human resources is exacerbated by the high turnover across countries of IMF staff. Some 60 percent of the teams of nonprogram countries change with each mission. Perhaps more important, since mission teams often include economists assigned only temporarily to a country, the turnover of regular desk economists (on their main country assignment) is also high: based on a sample of area department economists, collected in May 2004, the median time that desk economists and mission chiefs had worked on their main assignments were 12 months and 13 months, respectively.

Whether high turnover is an inevitable feature of IMF work is controversial. Some IMF watchers see this as a requirement for an international organization, given that it allows staff to benefit from "cross-fertilization" of experiences (Feinberg and Gwin, 1989, p. 26; De Gregorio and others, 1999, p. 19). High turnover may also reduce the risk of clientelism. Others, however, have regarded this

[39] The Bank of England's staff in the Monetary Analysis and the Financial Stability Departments includes some 220 professionals. About 200 professionals work at the U.K. Treasury on macroeconomic, financial, and structural reform issues. The Research and Economics directorates of the European Central Bank (ECB) include some 180 professionals. The Monetary Affairs and the Research and Statistics Departments of the Board of Governors of the (U.S.) Federal Reserve System include some 160 professionals. The U.S. Treasury team working in the Domestic Finance and Economic Policy Departments includes some 140 professionals.

Figure 1
Allocation of IMF Financial and Human Resources Across Program Countries

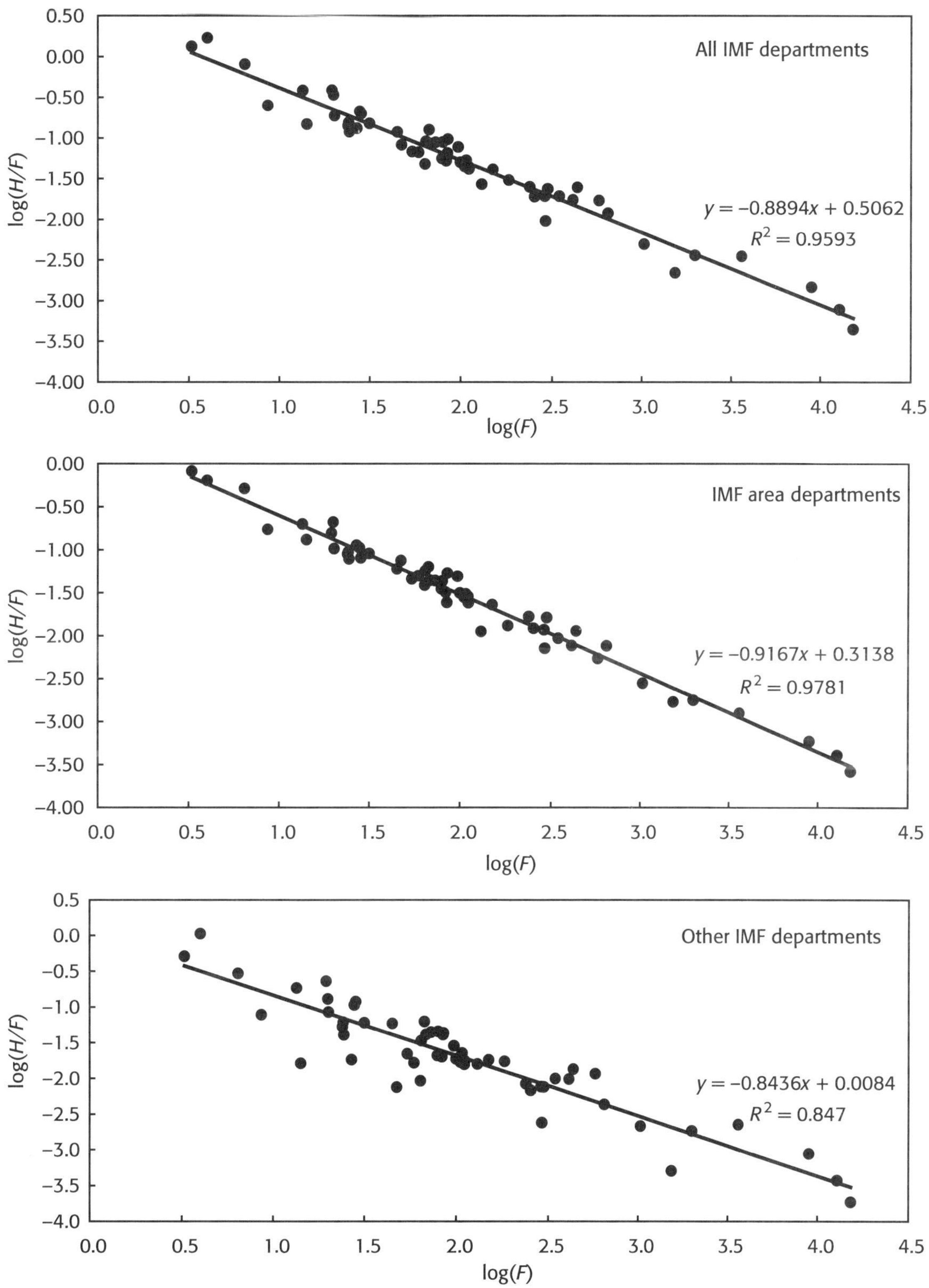

Notes: *H* denotes the amount of human resources, measured in staff-years, used in FY2003 and FY2004; *F* denotes the approved amount of lending for programs outstanding as of September 30, 2003, in millions of Special Drawing Rights (SDRs).

Table 2

Factors Affecting the Allocation of IMF Human Resources Across Countries: Regression Results Based on FY 2003/04

(Dependent variable: number of staff-years)

Regressors	Coefficient	*t*-Statistics
Constant	0.10	2.50
Log (per capita GDP)[1]	0.21	8.85
Log (SDR)[2]	–0.05	–1.03
Program dummy[3]	0.43	4.33
Industrial country dummy[4]	–0.30	–5.00

Notes: $R^2 = 0.50$; standard error = 0.24; and number of observations = 177.
[1] At purchasing-power-parity exchange rates.
[2] Amount of approved lending per program, in millions of Special Drawing Rights (SDRs).
[3] Equal to 1 for program countries.
[4] Equal to 1 for industrial countries.

turnover as excessive (IMF, 1999, pp. 31–32; IMF, 2002, pp. 88, 137), pointing out the lack of familiarity with country features that it generates. Other potential drawbacks are shortsightedness in work planning (and, thus, insufficient incentives to start work initiatives with longer-term yields) and reduced accountability, since successors have to deal with problems that were left unattended (IMF, 2002, p. 68). Be this as it may—and I believe turnover is excessive—to the extent that high turnover is regarded as necessary, it should be taken into account in assessing the adequacy of IMF resources.

Little work has been done by IMF staff to assess the adequacy of the *level* of human resources (while, of course, the effect on the existing resource endowment of *changes* in tasks assigned to the IMF is routinely assessed). One exception is Ivanova and others (2003), which tries to assess whether the probability of success of IMF programs depends on the size of staff teams. The results suggest that team size has little effect on program outcomes. This result—which is puzzling, short of concluding that economic science is so inconsequential that the work of economists does not have value added—can have two explanations: (a) assuming there is a minimum threshold for effectiveness, the size of staff teams may currently fall so short of that threshold that a marginal additional amount of resources does not help; and (b) the organization of staff teams is not adequately modified to accommodate increased availability of resources.[40]

[40] Anecdotal evidence suggests that the latter may be the case. For some time, the Russia desk benefited from a large increase in staff resources. The experiment ran into organizational difficulties, with many concluding that IMF teams larger than four or five economists are ineffective. However, the work organization of the Russian desk did not change as resources increased. This led to a duplication of functions (with, say, two economists covering, in competition, the same sector) and related coordination problems. Absorbing new resources typically requires a new work organization—for example, assigning senior economists the task of supervising more junior ones.

This discussion suggests at least the need for a comprehensive assessment of the adequacy of the IMF's human resources. It is critical to stress that the issue has to be addressed by taking a fresh look at the level of resources, not at increments. Of course, should resources be found insufficient, the conclusion should not necessarily be that they need to be increased. Possibly, tasks need to be streamlined (see the fourth section on selectivity) or efficiency needs to be improved (for example, by exploring ways to reduce excessive turnover).

Conclusions

This paper has highlighted a number of issues that should be explored further to support the ongoing effort to strengthen IMF governance with the goal of simultaneously enhancing its legitimacy and efficiency. It has underscored the existence of trade-offs that make this goal elusive: features of governance that could enhance the IMF's legitimacy may weaken its operational efficiency. But synergies—or, at least, Pareto improvements—are also possible, and some of them also have been highlighted.

For example, reforms aimed at a redistribution of political oversight among countries may enhance legitimacy without increasing the degree of involvement of political control over day-to-day operations. Strengthening the protection of staff against political influences would help increase candor in published IMF documents and, hence, lead to genuine, rather than pro forma, transparency. Ex post accountability can be a substitute for close ex ante monitoring by the political pole of the technocratic pole. Reduced direct political pressure would also be consistent with uniformity of treatment across countries and alleviate the risk that selectivity in processes will be perceived as reflecting political discrimination.

The intention of this paper was not to propose solutions, but to highlight issues. Considerably more work is needed before reaching conclusions. Topics that deserve further work include the following:

- How the political pole could monitor the technocratic pole without undue costs in terms of efficiency, and, in this respect, (a) the role that explicit political considerations should play in affecting IMF decisions; (b) the role of the Board in day-to-day management of the IMF; and (c) steps to avoid staff's potential "clientelism."
- How to reconcile transparency and confidentiality needs, and how to avoid forms of pro forma transparency that would damage both efficiency and accountability.
- The possibility of improving efficiency through more selectivity in the country dimension—more specifically, the scope for increased prescreening to identify countries to which more resource-intensive procedures should be applied, and for ways to reduce the overlapping of country responsibilities across international organizations.
- The adequacy of the amount and use of the IMF's human resources.

References

Akyüz, Yilmaz, 2002, "Towards Reform of the International Financial Architecture: Which Way Forward?" in *Reforming the Global Financial Architecture, Issues and Proposals*, ed. by Yilmaz Akyüz (Penang: United Nations).

Alesina, Alberto, and Guido Tabellini, 2004, "Bureaucrats or Politicians?" NBER Working Paper No. 10241 (Cambridge, Massachusetts: National Bureau of Economic Research).

Allegret, J.P.A., and P. Dulbecco, 2004, *Why International Institutions Need Governance? The Case of the IMF*, 21st Symposium on Banking and Monetary Economics, Nice, June 10–11.

Barro, Robert, and Jong-Wha Lee, 2002, "IMF Programs: Who Is Chosen and What Are the Effects?" NBER Working Paper No. 8951 (Cambridge, Massachusetts: National Bureau of Economic Research).

Bendor, J., A. Glazer, and T. Hammond, 2001, "Theories of Delegation," in *Annual Review of Political Science*, Vol. 4, pp. 235–69.

Bird, Graham, 2003, "Political Economy Influences Within the Life Cycle of IMF Programmes," in *The IMF and the Future, Issues and Options Facing the Fund* (New York: Routledge).

———, and D. Rowlands, 2001, "IMF Lending: How Is It Affected by Economic, Political and Institutional Factors," *Journal of Policy Reform*, No. 4.

Bordo, Michael D., and Harold James, 2000, "The International Monetary Fund: Its Present Role in Historical Perspective," NBER Working Paper No. 7724 (Cambridge, Massachusetts: National Bureau of Economic Research).

Boughton, James M., 2001, *Silent Revolution: The International Monetary Fund, 1979–89* (Washington: International Monetary Fund).

Buira, Ariel, 2003, "The Governance of the IMF in a Global Economy," in *Challenges to the World Bank and IMF, Developing Country Perspectives*, ed. by Ariel Buira (London: Wimbledon Publishing Company).

Caliari, Aldo, and Frank Schroeder, 2004, "Reform Proposals for the Governance Structures of the International Financial Institutions" (unpublished: New Rules for Global Finance).

Calomiris, Charles W., 2000, "When Will Economics Guide IMF and World Bank Reforms?" in *Cato Journal*, Vol. 20 (Spring/Summer), pp. 85–103.

De Gregorio, José, Barry Eichengreen, Takatoshi Ito, and Charles Wyplosz, 1999, "An Independent and Accountable IMF, Geneva Reports on the World Economy 1" (London: Center for Economic Policy Research).

de Vries, Margaret Garritsen, 1985, *The International Monetary Fund 1972–1978, Cooperation on Trial*, Vols. I and II: *Narrative and Analysis* (Washington: International Monetary Fund).

———, and J. Keith Horsefield, *The International Monetary Fund, 1945–1965: Twenty Years of International Monetary Cooperation* (Washington: International Monetary Fund).

Feinberg, Richard E., and Catherine Gwin, 1989, "Reforming the Fund," in *The International Monetary Fund in a Multipolar World: Pulling Together* (Washington: Overseas Development Council).

Feldstein, Martin, 1998, "Refocusing the IMF," *Foreign Affairs*, Vol. 77 (March/April), pp. 20–33.

Gold, Joseph, 1972, *Voting and Decisions in the International Monetary Fund* (Washington: International Monetary Fund).

Harper, Richard H.R., 1998, *Inside the IMF, An Ethnography of Documents, Technology and Organisational Action* (London: Academic Press).

Horsefield, J. Keith, 1969, *The International Monetary Fund 1945–1965, Twenty Years of International Monetary Cooperation*, Vol. I: *Chronicle* (Washington: International Monetary Fund).

International Monetary and Financial Committee (IMFC) of the Board of Governors of the International Monetary Fund, 2004, communiqué, October 2.

International Monetary Fund (IMF), 1999, *External Evaluation of IMF Surveillance, Report by a Group of Independent Experts* (Washington).

———, 2002, *Evaluation of Prolonged Use of IMF Resources*, Independent Evaluation Office (Washington).

———, 2003, *The Fund's Transparency Policy: Progress Report on Publication of Country Documents* (Washington).

———, 2004, *Evaluation of the Role of the Fund in Argentina, 1991–2001*, Independent Evaluation Office (Washington).

Ivanova, Anna, Wolfgang Mayer, Alex Mourmouras, and George Anayiotos, 2003, "What Determines the Implementation of IMF-Supported Programs?" IMF Working Paper 03/08 (Washington: International Monetary Fund). This paper also appears, in somewhat different form, as Chapter 10 in this volume.

Kafka, Alexandre, 1996, "Governance of the Fund," in *The International Monetary and Financial System: Developing-Country Perspectives*, ed. by G.K. Helleiner (New York: St. Martin's Press).

Kenen, Peter B., Jeffrey R. Shafer, Nigel L. Wicks, and Charles Wyplosz, 2004, *The International Economic and Financial Cooperation: New Issues, New Actors, New Responses* (London: Center for Economic Policy Research).

Krueger, Anne O., 1997, "Whither the World Bank and the IMF?" NBER Working Paper No. 6327 (Cambridge, Massachusetts: National Bureau of Economic Research).

Lister, Frederick K., 1984, *Decision-Making Strategies for International Organizations: The IMF Model*, Monograph Series in World Affairs, Vol. 20, Book 4 (Denver, Colorado: University of Denver, Graduate School of International Studies).

Martin, Lisa L., 2002, "Distribution, Information, and Delegation to International Organizations: The Case of IMF Conditionality" (unpublished; Cambridge, Massachusetts: Harvard University).

Mohammed, Aziz Ali, 2000, "The Future Role of the IMF: A Developing Country Point of View," in *Reforming the International Financial System, Crisis Prevention and Response*, ed. by Jan Joost Teunissen (The Hague: FONDAD).

Mussa, Michael, and Miguel Savastano, 1999, "The IMF Approach to Economic Stabilization," IMF Working Paper 99/104 (Washington: International Monetary Fund).

Passacantando, Franco, 2004, "*Democrazia e Governance internazionale: il caso delle istituzioni di Bretton Woods*" (upublished; Rome: Banca d'Italia).

Polak, J.J., 2004, "If the Bretton Woods Conference Were to Be Held Now, It Would Not Succeed," interview in *IMF Survey*, Vol. 33 (August 23).

Sachs, Jeffrey D., 2000, "Cutting the IMF and World Bank Down to Size," in *Project Syndicate*. Available on the Web at *http://www.project-syndicate.org/commentaries/commentary_text.php4?id=296&lang=1*.

Skidelsky, Robert, 2003, *John Maynard Keynes 1883–1946, Economist, Philosopher, Statesman* (London: Macmillan).

Southard, Frank A., 1979, *The Evolution of the International Monetary Fund* (Princeton, New Jersey: International Finance Section, Department of Economics, Princeton University).

Stiles, Kendall W., 1990, "IMF Conditionality: Coercion or Compromise?" in *World Development*, Vol. 18, No. 7, pp. 959–74.

———, 1991, *Negotiating Debt: The IMF Lending Process* (Boulder, Colorado: Westview Press).

Strange, Susan, 1973, "IMF: Monetary Managers," in *The Anatomy of Influence: Decisionmaking in International Organizations*, ed. by R.W. Cox and H.K. Jacobson (New Haven, Connecticut: Yale University Press).

Thacker, S., 1999, "The High Politics of IMF Lending," *World Politics*, No. 52, pp. 38–75.

Van Houtven, Leo, 2002, *Governance of the IMF, Decision Making, Institutional Oversight, Transparency, and Accountability*, IMF Pamphlet No. 53 (Washington: International Monetary Fund).

Vaubel, Roland, 1994, "The Political Economy of the IMF: A Public Choice Analysis," in *Perpetuating Poverty, The World Bank, the IMF, and the Developing World*, ed. by Doug Bandow and Ian Vásquez (Washington: Cato Institute).

Willett, Thomas D., 2004, "IMF: Governments Need to Be Persuaded to Mend Their Ways," letter to the *Financial Times* (April 27).

Williamson, John, 2000, "A Mixed Record for IMF Advice," in *Reforming the International Monetary and Financial System*, ed. by Peter B. Kenen and Alexander K. Swoboda (Washington: International Monetary Fund).

Woods, Ngaire, 2000, "The Challenge of Good Governance for the IMF and the World Bank Themselves," *World Development*, Vol. 28, No. 5, pp. 823–41.

CHAPTER

7 IMF Conditionality and Country Ownership of Adjustment Programs

Mohsin S. Khan and Sunil Sharma[1]

This article uses finance and agency theory to establish two key propositions about IMF conditionality and country ownership of IMF-supported adjustment programs—first, that the conditionality attached to these programs is justified and, second, that country ownership of these programs is crucial for their success. Because IMF conditionality and country ownership are both necessary, the challenge is designing conditionality that maximizes ownership while providing adequate safeguards for IMF lending. The article analyzes several recent proposals aimed at enhancing country ownership of policies contained in IMF-supported programs. These proposals include encouraging countries to design their own adjustment and reform programs, streamlining structural conditionality, introducing flexibility in the timing of structural policy measures (floating tranche conditionality), and applying conditionality to outcomes rather than policies (outcomes-based conditionality).

Introduction

International Monetary Fund (IMF) lending in support of adjustment programs is conditional on the borrowing countries adopting certain agreed policies. The conditions attached to these loans are commonly referred to as *IMF conditionality*. As the literature on the subject shows, discussions of the nature and merits of IMF conditionality have a long history (see, for example, Williamson, 1983; Polak, 1991; Guitián, 1995; James, 1996; and Boughton, 2001, Chapter 13). The issue has recently gained renewed attention, with questions raised about whether the conditions the IMF imposes on borrowing countries have been too intrusive and whether the design and implementation of IMF conditionality have undermined country ownership of adjustment programs aimed at correcting macroeconomic imbalances.

This viewpoint has gained considerable currency as a result of the capital account crises in Mexico, East Asia, the Russian Federation, and Brazil in the 1990s. But during such crises, which require rapid responses, there may not be enough time to secure full country support for all the policy actions needed. Moreover, in the midst of a serious currency and financial crisis, there may be greater agreement between the country authorities and the IMF on the immediate problems facing the country and the short-run measures needed to address them. Conditionality and ownership issues are probably less relevant for the recent capital account crisis cases and more relevant in standard IMF programs dealing with current account crises in low-income countries—and that is where most attention has been focused. The IMF itself has engaged in a comprehensive analysis of conditionality and ownership issues (see IMF, 2001a).

This chapter draws on finance and agency theory to establish two basic propositions about IMF conditionality and country ownership of adjustment programs. First, some form of conditionality exists in all borrower-lender relationships: key to the ability to borrow is the ability to pledge income back. The IMF must have assurances that it will be repaid, and this requires that it place conditions on its loans. The analysis here is designed to dispel the fairly widespread notion—articulated, for example, by Díaz Alejandro (1984)—that conditionality stems from a "patron-beneficiary" relationship between the IMF and borrowing countries. As he puts it, "This is the key justification for 'conditionality'; if you ask for a gift, you must listen to your patron" (Díaz Alejandro, 1984, p. 7). Finance considerations alone provide the justification for conditionality being a necessary part of IMF lending. Thus, the view expressed by Killick (1997) that IMF conditionality should be the exception rather than the rule is incorrect. Indeed, this article argues that it should be exactly the reverse.

Second, country ownership of programs is essential, because it aligns the incentives of the borrower and the lender. For the borrowing country, program ownership is critical because without a firm commitment from the government and other relevant constituencies, the difficult policy measures needed to correct economic problems are less likely to be implemented. For the IMF, country ownership increases the probability that programs will succeed

[1] The authors are grateful to Shanta Devarajan, Stanley Fischer, Morris Goldstein, Laurence Harris, Harold James, Vijay Kelkar, Peter Montiel, Jean Tirole, and several IMF colleagues for helpful discussions and comments. This article was previously published in the Fall 2003 issue of the *World Bank Research Observer*, and suggestions made by that journal's referees helped sharpen the analysis. This article appears here with the permission of Oxford University Press, the journal's publisher.

and consequently augments the protection of its resources provided by conditionality. Thus, the Poverty Reduction Strategy Papers (PRSPs), developed jointly by the IMF and the World Bank, put substantial emphasis on country ownership. In sum, both IMF conditionality and country ownership have a clear rationale—the challenge is reconciling the two. This chapter considers various recent proposals for achieving such a reconciliation.

IMF Lending and Conditionality

This section examines the main features of IMF lending by comparing them with private loan contracts. It then assesses the implementation and effectiveness of IMF conditionality.

Conditionality in Private Financial Contracts

Between every borrower and lender there is a fundamental asymmetry in information. Borrowers always know more about their abilities, opportunities, and intentions than do lenders. This information asymmetry gives rise to two incentive problems: adverse selection and moral hazard.

Adverse selection arises before a transaction occurs and stems from the fact that information deficiencies make it difficult for lenders to distinguish good risks from bad. The IMF faces a different selection problem than do private lenders in that only members experiencing distress approach it for financing, and all have a right to its resources. Moral hazard arises after a lender has given funds to a borrower.[2] Having obtained the funds, it may be in the borrower's interest to take risks that may raise returns—but also increase the likelihood of default. In the financial world, contract designs and collateral, transparency, and reporting requirements attempt to mitigate such moral hazard. Monitoring by shareholders, debt holders, market analysts, rating agencies, and independent company directors serves the same purpose. Such monitoring is costly to firms, but it is done to assure investors that their claims will be respected (Greenbaum and Thakor, 1995; and Mishkin, 1998).

Pledging collateral is expensive, but firms incur that cost to assure lenders that borrowed funds will be used for stated purposes and in ways that will not jeopardize their eventual repayment. Indeed, the very existence of financial markets depends on such assurance. To that end, corporate governance and institutions and practices of finance share the common rationale of increasing resources that can be pledged to outside debt and equity holders while maintaining appropriate incentives for managers and workers. Collateral is provided so that in the event of default, or if the borrower does not live up to the terms of the contract, the lender can recover its resources by taking control of the pledged assets and selling them.

In new or emerging firms with little physical or financial collateral, relinquishing control rights to venture capitalists provides the needed assurance that funds will be well spent, because the venture capitalists have considerable say in decision making. The allocation of control rights to investors should be designed to provide maximum assurance to investors without impairing the functioning of the firm and its ability to exploit commercial opportunities. Still, in many circumstances and for many firms—especially those in distress or those that have little reputational or financial capital—relinquishing such control rights may be costly and will almost certainly impose substantial limits on management discretion.

Generally, the imposition of such conditionality—the allocation of return streams, liquidity, and control rights—is made contingent on the evolution of the borrowing firm's balance sheet and follows a simple carrot-and-stick logic. Posting collateral that can be sold by the lender in case of default provides the borrower with an incentive to prevent default. Agency considerations dictate that the transfer of collateral rights to the lender be made contingent on default or on observable measures of financial and nonfinancial performance.

Such conditionality also serves another purpose when it comes to control rights. After an adverse shock, a borrowing firm is more likely to gamble for resurrection—that is, engage in riskier behavior—the greater is the deterioration of its financial health. Contingent transfer of control rights protects investors in that it prevents firms from undertaking excessively risky activities to repair balance sheets. Hence it serves two purposes. Ex ante, it provides incentives for preventing default. And ex post, it constrains firms' ability to take gambles.

Even if a firm does not engage in risky strategies when its performance deteriorates, the contingent transfer of control rights provides the lender with the option of reexamining the new situation. For example, in a new enterprise the venture capitalist obtains full control if the firm performs poorly—whereas if the firm is profitable, the venture capitalist may retain cash-flow rights but agree to cede control and liquidation rights to the entrepreneur (Kaplan and Stromberg, 2000).

IMF Conditionality

IMF lending and its associated conditionality follow broadly the same principles as private financial contracts, though several additional dimensions make IMF lending qualitatively different. The IMF is

[2] More formally, moral hazard can be defined as actions of economic agents maximizing their utility to the detriment of others in situations where they do not bear the full consequences of their actions owing to uncertainty, asymmetric information, and incomplete or restricted contracts (see Kotowitz, 1987; and Stiglitz, 2000).

mandated by its Articles of Agreement to extend temporary financial assistance to member countries facing balance of payments difficulties "under adequate safeguards" (Article I). Like any lender, the IMF thus needs assurances from its borrowers that the funds lent to them will be used for the purposes defined by the Articles of Agreement, and in a manner that does not jeopardize their contractual servicing and repayment. Therefore many of the finance propositions relevant to private financial institutions also apply to the IMF.

A key aspect of IMF lending is that countries in need of IMF loans generally do not possess internationally valuable collateral. If they did, they could use it to borrow from private lenders and would not require IMF resources. In a crisis situation, though, even if a country had internationally acceptable collateral, it still might not be able to use it to borrow from private capital markets. There is an important difference between national income and income that can be pledged to foreign lenders, including the IMF. Foreign loans can be used to produce both tradable and nontradable outputs, but foreigners typically have no demand for a country's nontradables. In the absence of collateral, private loan contracts typically would include various covenants, coupled with monitoring. Formally, a covenant is designed to protect the lender and prohibit the borrower from taking actions that could reduce the probability of repayment. Covenants can impose clear obligations on the borrower, impose limitations on or prohibit certain actions, and specify when a borrower is considered to be in default.

IMF conditionality can be viewed as a complex covenant written into the loan agreement. The policy prescriptions in IMF-supported programs essentially provide safeguards that the country will be able to rectify its macroeconomic and structural imbalances and will be in a position to service and repay the loan.[3] Thus the conditionality associated with IMF programs can be viewed as a substitute for collateral.

Conditionality attached to sovereign lending has a long history. For example, in 1818, Prussia, effectively bankrupted by the Napoleonic wars, approached Nathan Rothschild (of the House of Rothschild) for a loan and was asked to pledge "Prussian royal domains" as collateral (Ferguson, 1998).

For many analysts, the modern model for conditional lending to sovereign governments in the absence of collateral is the Turkish agreement of 1881—known as the Decree of Mouharrem—which was implemented after the Turkish government defaulted on its foreign debt in 1875. The decree created the Council of Ottoman Debt, comprising seven members that represented different groups of bondholders. A large portion of the Turkish government's revenue was placed under the council's direct control and used by it to service and repay the debt (Anderson, 1966).

The League of Nations also attached strict conditions to its adjustment programs (or "reconstruction schemes" as they were known) for six European countries in the 1920s. These conditions included maintenance of fiscal equilibrium and monetary discipline as well as currency reform. The League developed various means to enforce the programs and safeguard the interests of foreign creditors and bondholders, including appointing a commissioner to each country and an adviser to each central bank to administer and monitor the programs (Santaella, 1993; and James, 2001).

Agreeing to IMF conditionality is an imposition on a country even though the two may share the same objectives—external viability, price stability, sustained high growth, reduced systemic risk, and so on. To be sure, the covenant in the loan agreement required by the IMF is far more complex and has different characteristics than covenants in simpler private financial transactions. It also may not always be part of the explicit contract, but it is always part of the implicit one, regardless of the language used in the documentation. The challenge in designing IMF conditionality is to specify the optimal covenant—the best policy conditions given the circumstances of the country, the disbursement intervals for the loan, the type of monitoring involved, and so on—to achieve program objectives while providing sufficient safeguards to the IMF. Still, at a general level, IMF lending conforms to the principles governing private lending.

At the same time, IMF lending differs in significant ways. First, as noted, defining conditionality in IMF lending is much more complicated than in private financial transactions, where covenants may be quite straightforward. It basically involves assessing the macroeconomic imbalances or structural deficiencies that led to a country's macroeconomic problems, and then negotiating an agreement with country authorities that will address those issues.

Second, it is difficult, if not impossible to establish the "value" of IMF conditionality. The value of negotiated conditionality largely depends on the degree to which the authorities of the borrowing country adopt the program and are willing to expend effort and political credibility to implement it.

Third, unlike private lenders—for whom it may be sufficient to deal with a firm's management—the IMF faces what in agency theory is called "moral hazard in teams" (Holmström, 1982). This refers to situations in which a principal's payoff depends on the joint efforts of two (or more) agents. Typically, the detailed negotiations for an IMF-supported program are conducted with certain government representatives (central bank, finance ministry),

[3] Additional safeguards are provided by the fact that IMF claims are de facto senior to claims of other creditors, and that funds are disbursed in tranches, conditional on the implementation of satisfactory policies (which are monitored) to correct the imbalances.

while the success of the program depends on many other stakeholders in society—other ministries, trade unions, professional associations, civic groups, and nongovernmental organizations (NGOs).

Fourth, the IMF is by design a cooperative that makes loans to its sovereign members. In the event of default, there is no court to which it can appeal and no tangible collateral that can be used to cover lost resources. The enforcement mechanism for ensuring that borrowing countries live up to their obligations essentially amounts to a combination of moral suasion, maintenance of the borrower's reputation, peer pressure, and the threat of being shut out of international capital markets. Unlike private firms—where lending is generally subject to well-defined legal codes that can be enforced in courts and where shareholders or investors can change the management of a company or take it over—the IMF obviously cannot replace sovereign governments, and can only refuse to provide financing to a country in arrears.

Finally, relative to private lenders the IMF, given its mandate and cooperative structure, faces what in other contexts has been called the "Samaritan's dilemma" (Buchanan, 1975; and Lindbeck and Weibull, 1988). For example, to provide the right incentives ex ante a private lender may impose harsh conditions on a borrower in the event of poor performance, but ex post (that is, after poor performance) it may not want to impose those conditions for a number of reasons. For instance, selling certain assets (or liquidating the company) may be worth less than keeping the assets with the company (or maintaining the company as a going concern).

But the IMF faces a different incentive problem, because a borrowing country is always more valuable as a "going concern." Hence country authorities know that in the event of poor performance, at worst the program will be renegotiated (Drazen and Fischer, 1997). This creates the wrong incentives, ex ante. Countries know that, faced with poor performance and a weak economy, the IMF is unlikely to impose harsh conditionality ex post because it has to be concerned about the welfare of borrowing countries. And, being a cooperative institution, the IMF cannot simply walk away and "cut its losses." Thus ex ante penalties have limited credibility because they are unlikely to be enforced ex post. This is one reason it has been suggested that the IMF should lend only to prequalified countries with good policy environments. In other words, the IMF should lend only to countries that have good economic track records and that can provide good "collateral" (see Meltzer and others, 2000).

Implementation of IMF Conditionality

Conditionality is implemented through program design and monitoring that tracks whether agreed policies are implemented in a timely and effective manner. Program design begins with in-depth analysis of the sources of a country's macroeconomic imbalances. (See Mussa and Savastano, 1999 for a recent description of the IMF's approach to economic stabilization.) The next step is to agree with the authorities on policy objectives and on macroeconomic policies and structural reforms to achieve those objectives.

Monitoring takes various forms, depending on the borrowing country's circumstances and the IMF lending facility being used. It generally includes prior actions, performance criteria, macroeconomic and structural benchmarks, and reviews. Monitoring also prohibits actions inconsistent with the IMF's Articles of Agreement, such as the introduction of new foreign exchange restrictions. Releases of IMF financing are linked to compliance with monitoring arrangements.

Prior actions are required when upfront implementation is critical to program success or to allay doubts about the authorities' commitment. Examples of required actions include passing an agreed budget, realigning the exchange rate, adopting structural reforms, or enacting relevant laws. Such actions must be taken prior to the approval of a program by the IMF's Executive Board, which then triggers the first disbursement.

Performance criteria normally include quantitative targets for specified financial aggregates (such as bank credit, net international reserves, or fiscal balance) and often include structural measures (such as tariff reductions, tax system revisions, or privatization of public enterprises). Meeting these criteria triggers the release of subsequent tranches of committed IMF resources.

Macroeconomic and structural benchmarks set targets for macroeconomic variables and structural policies important for effective program implementation. They do not directly affect scheduled disbursements.

Finally, reviews are used to assess overall progress toward program objectives, identify any sources of slippage (resulting from lack of policy implementation, external shocks, or program design issues), and take corrective actions. Reviews are usually specified as performance criteria—precluding further disbursements if the review is not concluded by the scheduled review date.

A common question is whether IMF conditionality works. Meltzer and others (2000, p. 35) argue that "numerous studies on the effects of IMF lending have failed to find any significant link between IMF involvement and increases in growth or income." The IMF, not surprisingly, disagrees. The IMF's mandate is to provide short-term lending to support balance of payments adjustments, and it believes that its conditional lending has generally improved the external accounts of borrowing countries.

What is the evidence on the effectiveness of IMF conditionality? Specifically, have IMF-supported adjustment programs achieved their objectives of improving current account balances, increasing international reserves, lowering inflation, and raising growth? This is essentially an empirical question that requires evaluating the effects that past programs have had on the macroeconomic variables of interest. Such evaluations are conducted periodically by the IMF's Policy Development and Review Department and by its recently created Independent Evaluation Office, with the results reported to the Executive Board. In addition, a number of studies over the past twenty years, both inside and outside the IMF, have examined the question using a variety of empirical methods.

Almost all the empirical studies surveyed by Haque and Khan (2002) show that IMF-supported programs have improved current account balances and the overall balance of payments in borrowing countries. The results for inflation are less clear. Most of the studies indicate that while inflation usually falls, the decline is generally statistically insignificant. For growth, output is generally depressed in the short run—that is, during the stabilization phase—but increases as macroeconomic stability is established. Overall, the most recent empirical results in particular indicate that, on average, IMF-supported programs and the conditionality they incorporate have been reasonably effective in achieving their main macroeconomic objectives.

Country Ownership of Programs

The case for country ownership of IMF-supported adjustment programs has a strong theoretical foundation. In the context of agency theory, principal-agent problems arise in situations where one party (the principal) relies on the other (the agent) to achieve certain objectives. Owing to information asymmetries and lack of perfect monitoring technology, if the agent's actions and their results cannot be easily verified and monitored, the agent has greater scope for pursuing its own interests rather than those of the principal.

But principal-agent theory also says that an agent will do a better job for the principal if the two parties' objectives are closely aligned. Thus if the realization of conditions hinges on cooperation and implementation by the agent, agent ownership of the project is essential. As Tirole (2002) puts it, in this case ownership is not a goal but a necessity.

IMF lending can be cast in a principal-agent framework as well. In this case borrowing governments are the agents and the IMF—the delegated monitor of a revolving fund—is the principal. This principal-agent relationship is complex because of the nature of the task and the underlying loan contract, the mandate and structure of the principal, and the characteristics of the agents. And this complexity, combined with the difficulty of specifying all contingencies in the contract, makes country ownership of programs all the more critical for their success.

The problem is that country ownership of IMF-supported programs is an elusive concept. Implicitly, it refers to a situation in which the policy content of the program is similar to what the country would have chosen in the absence of IMF involvement—because the country shares with the IMF both the objectives of the program and an understanding of the appropriate economic model linking those objectives to economic policies. In such a situation, the country owns the program in the sense that it is committed to its spirit rather than to just complying with its letter. Thus the country will not deviate from its agreement with the IMF even if given the opportunity.

But because countries only borrow from the IMF when they face distress caused by macroeconomic or structural imbalances, sufficient safeguards are needed when providing access to IMF resources and to avoid moral hazard—requiring conditionality with some "bite." Hence full country ownership is unlikely, and the real challenge is maximizing ownership in the context of conditionality. As noted, program conditionality is likely to place substantive constraints on the authorities' actions and use of funds. In addition, given that programs generally involve economic and social trade-offs, perceptions may be created that conditionality does not take proper account of a country's circumstances, including its economic priorities, political conditions, culture, and traditions. And this can—and sometimes does—lead to differing views on objectives, program strategies, and the pace of reform.

Ownership matters because it directly affects program implementation.[4] Program agreements cannot envisage all the possible contingencies that could affect a program and specify in advance actions that the authorities should take in response. When a country owns a program, decisions on such actions are likely to be made quickly and in support of the program, making it more likely that the program will succeed. In addition, ownership makes it easier to generate domestic political support for the program because it will likely be seen at least partly as an indigenous product, rather than a foreign imposition.

Ownership also matters for the catalytic role that IMF lending can play in increasing a country's access to foreign lenders. International flows of private capital have become increasingly important in recent decades, and a critical issue for borrowing in

[4] There is no direct empirical evidence on the link between ownership and IMF-supported programs. But some evidence on the importance of ownership for project lending is provided by the World Bank. The Bank's Operations Evaluation Department rates government commitment to each project (measuring in a sense the degree of ownership) using a variety of objective and subjective indicators. The relationship between project outcomes and government commitment turns out to be strongly positive (and statistically significant).

international markets is lenders' ability to exercise control rights. Foreign investors also confront moral hazard in teams: the payoffs to investments depend on the behavior and efforts of private borrowers as well as of the government of the country where the private borrowers reside (Tirole, 2002).

Firms investing across borders design appropriate covenants to mitigate moral hazard among private borrowers. Control rights not vested with the investor, but that affect borrower behavior, are actually shared between the borrower and the government. Returns to a foreign investment depend on the environment created by government policies on domestic liquidity creation and management, tax and labor laws, and other institutional factors. And when differences arise between a lender and a borrower, or in times of distress, treatment of parties to a contract is crucially affected by public attitudes and policies toward law enforcement, bankruptcy, and corporate governance.

Government policies that reduce the amount of tradables or other internationally valuable collateral also hurt foreign investors. Such policies include taxing exports, failing to invest in infrastructure (which inhibits exports and tourism), depreciating the domestic currency when foreigners hold assets in that currency, depleting foreign exchange reserves, and creating incentives for currency and maturity mismatches that increase credit and default risks.

Whether such government moral hazard is important is an empirical issue and depends on the circumstances. The hazard may be limited because governments lose power and credibility after a crisis, and in such cases IMF conditionality associated with adjustment programs places constraints on the authorities' policy choices (De Gregorio and others, 1999). But it may be cause for concern: as in private firms, the threat of losing one's job after a crisis may prevent misbehavior—but it may also increase moral hazard by creating incentives to gamble for resurrection. Moreover, government actions that affect the mix of tradables and nontradables, and hence hurt foreign investors more than domestic ones, are less likely to generate adverse reactions from a country's population (Tirole, 2002).

Consequently, country ownership of policies that reduce moral hazard related to foreign investment is likely to be important for a country's access to international capital markets. Such policies provide assurance to foreign investors that the government will not devalue their claims and, in the event of poor performance or adverse shocks to borrowers, will not inhibit the transfer of control rights to creditors. Of course, governments cannot relinquish control rights as easily as firms, but that simply means that in their case the set of transferable rights will be more limited.

The feasibility of achieving a particular degree of ownership, and determining when it has been achieved, are problematic issues that vary by country. A complicating factor in assessing the degree of ownership is that most countries, especially democratic ones, have multiple stakeholders.

In pluralistic societies, does ownership refer to the views on program design and objectives held by the key ministers and central bank officials who negotiate the program with the IMF? Or does it refer to the views of the domestic bureaucracy that has to implement the program? Or to the views of the parliament that has to approve the necessary legislation? Or to the views of civil society at large? And if the views of civil society carry the most weight, how are its members to be assessed and made to influence program design and implementation in the face of competing interests? Thus ownership is intricately connected to trust in domestic institutions, effectiveness of political structures, and whether the government—negotiating on behalf of its citizens—has sufficient support to speak for a fair majority.

A widespread perception exists that program ownership by borrowing countries is insufficient. In recent years the number of program objectives has tended to increase because the IMF has taken on tasks that go beyond its traditional mandate of establishing macroeconomic and financial stability.[5] In many programs the number of structural objectives has been expanded to facilitate transitions to market economies, integrate domestic economies with the world economy, diversify production and exports, develop financial sectors, and promote high-quality growth. In the 1990s, these program goals were explicitly specified for transition economies and made prominent for sub-Saharan African countries. In addition, in the Mexican (1994–95) and East Asian (1997–98) crises, the key roles played by financial sector fragilities and corporate governance shortcomings expanded the list of goals. The problem is that country ownership is less likely when programs have too many objectives—because as the number of objectives increases, it becomes less likely that the authorities and the IMF will agree on the full range of objectives or on how they are to be attained.

Borrowing countries may be partly responsible for the lack of ownership. Some countries may be so eager for initial disbursements and for the catalytic role of IMF financing that they are willing to agree to programs without being convinced that the associated conditionality is appropriate. Such agreements have a greater chance of unraveling at critical decision points when it becomes clear that difficult policy measures are unlikely to be implemented. In private markets, if a lender has serious doubts about a borrower's intentions or is not provided sufficient

[5] Feldstein (1998), for example, argues that the IMF has been too intrusive in its interventions and should ask two questions of each conditionality measure. First, is the measure needed to restore access to international capital markets? Second, would the IMF ask the same measure of a major industrial country if the country had a program?

collateral, the optimal course of action is not to lend. Given the IMF's cooperative structure, and the Samaritan's dilemma it faces, it is much more problematic for the organization to refuse to lend to a member in need (see Drazen and Fischer, 1997).

New Initiatives to Foster Greater Ownership

A number of proposals have recently been made to enhance country ownership of IMF-supported programs. Four such initiatives are considered here: encouraging countries to design their own programs (specifically in the context of PRSPs), streamlining structural conditionality, introducing flexibility in the timing of structural policy measures (floating tranche conditionality), and applying conditionality to outcomes rather than policies (outcomes-based conditionality).[6] The IMF is already implementing some of these proposals (see IMF 2001a, 2001b, and 2001c).

Encouraging Countries to Design Their Own Programs

The IMF could require or encourage borrowing countries to produce "home-grown" programs. In some cases this may be seen as forcing ownership, but program designs can be worked out cooperatively between the country and the IMF. If countries lack the expertise and capacity to develop their own programs, the IMF could provide technical assistance and training or encourage the authorities to hire independent technical advisers.

While there are examples of home-grown programs, for several reasons this approach has generally not worked very well. First, countries often use overly optimistic assumptions when designing their programs. For example, countries may underestimate the extent of their difficulties and overestimate the potency of their policy instruments.

Second, if the process of formulating a program—with its associated domestic political compromises—hardens the authorities' negotiating position with the IMF, it will likely cause significant delays in program negotiation.

Third, countries may prefer to have the IMF prepare the program because they do not have, or choose not to have, domestic mechanisms for making decisions on difficult trade-offs. This may require the IMF to force issues requiring decisions.

And fourth, from a negotiating standpoint, countries may want to see the IMF's position before offering their own in a program document.

To increase program ownership by low-income countries, the IMF and the World Bank recently began encouraging the production of Poverty Reduction Strategy Papers.[7] The papers are intended to specify and detail a country's policies for reducing poverty (see Ames, Bhatt, and Plant, 2002). PRSPs have three key elements:

- they are prepared by country authorities in consultation with various levels of government, local communities, civil society groups, donors, and multilateral agencies;
- they diagnose the country's poverty situation, with the aim of identifying the main obstacles to raising incomes and welfare; and
- they set goals for poverty reduction, define the immediate and long-term policy actions needed to achieve those goals, and design a system for monitoring progress.

Recent experience with PRSPs suggests that they could foster program ownership in several ways. (For a comprehensive review of the PRSP approach and its early experiences, see IMF, 2002a and 2002b.) By creating a forum for dialogue—both within the government and among other stakeholders in society—the papers can identify the concerns and views of affected groups as well as policymakers. Thus, they should enable policymakers and donors to better understand the different facets of poverty and the main concerns of poor people. In this regard, the challenge for governments is to strengthen democratic institutions and provide a voice to all domestic constituencies. In many developing countries, it cannot be assumed that nongovernmental organizations and civil society groups have the capacity to adequately participate in such a dialogue and engage in policy design, monitoring, and implementation.

PRSPs should also lead to better, more systematic collection of data and more effective monitoring. As a result, they can be used to manage expectations and set realistic goals, evaluate the trade-offs and constraints involved, and develop priorities for policy action. Again, increased ownership will require ensuring that countries have the technical capacity to formulate and analyze different policy paths. In addition, the effectiveness of PRSPs will depend on how much they contribute to better governance and on how policy strategies deal with corruption.

By offering a coherent strategy for attacking poverty, PRSPs could enhance coordination of program and nonprogram aid from multiple donors and multilateral agencies. Bulíř and Hamann (2001) show that for many countries aid is highly volatile

[6] Other proposals not discussed here include preselecting countries eligible for IMF lending, developing policy options for country authorities to choose from, and investing time and effort in selling programs at home and abroad (see Khan and Sharma, 2001).

[7] Heavily indebted poor countries (HIPCs) seeking debt relief and countries eligible to borrow under the IMF's Poverty Reduction and Growth Facility are required to produce a PRSP and have it approved by the Executive Boards of the IMF and the World Bank before seeking new program support.

(more so than fiscal revenues), mildly procyclical, and not very predictable. As Svensson (2000) argues, when donors are unable to monitor reform efforts, aid disbursements are likely to be tied to economic performance—and hence procyclical.

Aid volatility and unpredictability can complicate expenditure management, especially for governments with deficient fiscal infrastructure, resulting in adjustments borne mostly by poorer and weaker segments of society. To the extent that PRSPs help coordinate donor efforts and reduce the cost of mobilizing and using aid, they could contribute to the success of IMF and World Bank programs—and thus enhance country ownership.

For the IMF and the World Bank, an important aspect of facilitating country production of poverty strategies will be coordinating advice and technical assistance to member countries. Such coordination will involve ensuring that the macroeconomic and financial conditionality attached to IMF lending is consistent with the sectoral and project-based conditionality (for structural and social policies) attached to World Bank lending. Such consistency will be achieved only if the IMF and the Bank agree on their respective conditionalities, and then use them in programs that respect—to the extent possible—the overall strategies articulated by member countries. A collaborative approach will enable countries to access and use effectively the IMF's Poverty Reduction and Growth Facility and the Bank's Poverty Reduction Support Credit Facility.

Streamlining Structural Conditionality

The past two decades have seen a major increase in structural conditions in IMF-supported programs (Goldstein, 2000; and IMF, 2001c). The expansion of structural conditionality would appear to limit the scope for domestic policy choices, reducing country ownership. But there is considerable validity for the expansion (IMF 2001a, 2001b, and 2001c). Still, many structural reforms are of a microeconomic nature and therefore likely to be more intrusive than macroeconomic policies. Country ownership of programs is essential for the design and implementation of these microeconomic measures because they have a different impact on various segments and vested interests in society.

It is widely felt that the IMF has gone too far with structural conditionality and overloaded programs with structural measures. Many structural reforms are not required to achieve macroeconomic stability. There is also no evidence that programs with more structural conditions have been more successful. In fact, programs with more structural conditions seem to have the same success rate as those with less (IMF, 2001c).

Increased structural conditions pose two main dangers. First, they may reduce country ownership of programs and consequently impair their effectiveness. Second, a failure to implement structural reforms not critical for macroeconomic stability may undermine confidence in the overall program—possibly triggering reactions in domestic and international capital markets that could make overall program objectives harder to achieve.

It would be difficult and undesirable to turn back the clock and eliminate all structural conditions from programs. But careful thought should be given to which structural reforms are essential to achieving a program's main objectives. These reforms will vary by country, but sharply pruning the list of structural conditions is possible without jeopardizing a program's success or the IMF's ability to be repaid. In other words, prioritizing or streamlining structural conditionality does not mean weakening overall conditionality.

The IMF has acknowledged that structural conditionality has expanded too much, and a major effort is under way to streamline it. IMF management recently defined broad principles for staff to use in determining the appropriate scope of structural conditionality in programs. In summary, the principles in the Interim Guidance Note on Streamlining Structural Conditionality (IMF, 2001b, Box 3) are as follows:

- Structural reforms critical to achieving a program's macroeconomic objectives generally must be covered by IMF conditionality.
- Structural reforms relevant—but not critical—to a program's macroeconomic objectives and within the IMF's core areas of responsibility may be subject to conditionality.
- For structural reforms relevant to a program's macroeconomic objectives but neither critical nor in the IMF's core areas of responsibility, conditionality generally should not apply.

These principles represent an important shift by the IMF from comprehensive to parsimonious structural conditionality. Experiences with programs negotiated since the issuance of these principles will show whether this intention is being achieved.

Adopting Floating Tranche Conditionality

Performance criteria and structural benchmarks in IMF-supported programs have specific dates attached to them. Countries often find that rigid timetables for major structural reforms constrain their choices and strain their implementation capacity.[8] Thus programs could be designed to allow for greater flexibility in the timing of structural reforms, increasing the scope for country ownership.

[8] In many cases, rigid program schedules have posed serious problems for borrowing countries. One example involves the passage of laws: some legislatures have been surprised to learn that a program has committed them not only to a specific legislative agenda but also to a set of deadlines under which the relevant legislative actions must be taken.

One way to achieve this goal is through floating tranche conditionality for structural reforms. Under this approach, IMF loan disbursements would not be tied to specific dates. Instead, disbursements would be made available upon completion of certain agreed reforms. This approach gives countries flexibility in the timing of program implementation.[9] It also allows for disbursements associated with the implementation of one part of a program to be unlinked from those associated with another part of a program.

The floating tranche approach could be used to divide conditionality into two parts. One part of IMF financing could be conditional on achieving the usual quantitative performance criteria under a predetermined schedule, while the other part could be dependent on implementing certain structural reforms at any time prior to the expiration of the program (provided that the macroeconomic program stays on track). In the floating tranche part, the country would have control over when it undertook reforms—and assurances that when it did, it would receive related funding. The IMF would be protected because it would disburse funds only when reforms were undertaken.

The segmentation of conditionality would require decisions on the proportion of IMF financing subject to standard fixed tranche conditionality and that subject to floating tranche conditionality. Such decisions would be based on judgments about the relative importance of a program's different parts in achieving its overall objectives.

Not all structural reforms would be subject to floating tranche conditionality, because some are essential to macroeconomic improvements. For example, an independent central bank could be considered necessary to promote monetary stability, and a proper tax collection system might be needed to achieve fiscal discipline. The timing of such reforms could not be left open. In other words, in deciding which reforms are subject to fixed or floating tranche conditionality, the interdependence between structural measures and macroeconomic management would have to be taken into account. Final decisions would be made on a case-by-case basis and would be the result of negotiations and agreements between the IMF and the country authorities.

There is experience with a form of floating tranche conditionality in the context of the Higher Impact Adjustment Lending (HIAL) initiative, which was introduced by the World Bank in sub-Saharan Africa in 1995. The tranching innovations under the initiative have two objectives: to give governments more freedom in the timing of agreed reforms, thereby increasing ownership, and to reduce pressure on the World Bank to disburse funds when conditions have not been met. These objectives are to be achieved through multiple but smaller tranches, increased disbursements after the implementation of reforms, and the introduction of independent floating tranche arrangements.

Prior to the HIAL initiative, adjustment loans typically were disbursed in two tranches. HIAL introduced floating tranches, with single tranche operations as an alternative in special circumstances. Floating tranches are usually targeted at policy reforms in certain sectors, and in some cases are in addition to regular tranches. Under HIAL, floating tranches have been applied to reforms involving the financial and banking sectors, the parastatal and public sectors, privatization, and civil service reform. A tranche is released only when the structural condition is met, regardless of when that happens. Of the 21 HIAL operations in 17 African countries during 1996–98, about two-thirds used the new tranching mechanisms.

In 1999, the World Bank's Operations Evaluation Department conducted an evaluation of these 21 operations (World Bank, 1999). The study found that the HIAL initiative was associated with positive policy outcomes in terms of fiscal adjustment and exchange and interest rate policies. Moreover, the countries involved did better than nonparticipating comparator countries in increasing growth, lowering inflation, improving current account balances, stabilizing foreign exchange reserves, and achieving more sustainable debt paths. Even though HIAL programs differ in other ways from other World Bank programs, and the evaluation did not take into account the role of exogenous factors, the results provide some support for the use of floating tranches.

Basing Conditionality on Outcomes, Not Policies

Outcomes-based conditionality involves conditioning disbursements on the achievement of results rather than on the implementation of policies expected to eventually attain program objectives. Changing from policy-based conditionality to outcomes-based conditionality—leaving the choice of policies to the country authorities—has been advocated by, among others, Díaz Alejandro (1984, p. 7):[10]

> I propose that the international community should return to the key rationale for conditionality, and negotiate with countries borrowing on concessional

[9] In principle, prior actions in IMF-supported programs can be thought of as a variant of floating tranche conditionality. A country agrees to undertake certain measures before the program (or program review) is discussed by the IMF's Executive Board. Thus the timing of the Board meeting and the disbursement of funds depend on the prior actions having been taken. Reviews can also be considered a form of floating tranche conditionality, since their completion (and accompanying disbursement) depends on agreed policy measures being taken.

[10] Spraos (1986) makes a similar point but on the grounds that the links between outcomes and policy variables are too tenuous to make policy-based conditionality especially meaningful.

terms only regarding the balance-of-payments targets, leaving to the countries the decision as to what policy instruments should be employed to achieve them.

Under the outcomes-based approach, IMF conditionality would focus on objectives rather than policy instruments and actions. Performance criteria for the disbursement of funds would be based on whether the targets for policy objectives were achieved by set dates. The policy objectives would be negotiated with the IMF, but the policy content of programs would largely be left up to country authorities.

This approach is not as radical as it might seem, because programs already define outcome variables as performance criteria. For example, IMF-supported programs include a floor on net international reserves as a performance criterion. Similarly, the adoption of an inflation-targeting framework has made inflation one of the key variables monitored in the IMF program for Brazil. Presumably, as more countries adopt the inflation-targeting approach to monetary policy, more programs will follow the Brazilian model. Other variables that could be subject to outcomes-based conditionality include the trade balance, the current account, investment, and growth.

In principle, there are two major benefits to this approach. First, the country authorities would be responsible for designing policies to achieve desired goals (as long as the policies are not prohibited by the IMF's Articles of Agreement). Hence the authorities would bear the risk of success or failure. This approach would enhance country ownership by requiring that the authorities and the IMF agree only on program objectives—and not necessarily on the mechanisms linking these objectives to specific policies.

Second, funds would be disbursed only on the attainment of certain goals, providing incentives for the country and the IMF to fashion appropriate policies. IMF resources would be safeguarded because disbursements would depend on countries achieving the desired results. If policies did not have the envisaged outcomes, the country and the IMF would have to rethink the economic strategy.

Implementing this approach would undoubtedly present a few challenges. First, outcomes-based conditionality could lead to the backloading of funds that may be needed earlier to fill a temporary liquidity gap or to finance structural reforms. It would also lead to greater uncertainty for the country authorities about the availability of funds, since the agreed policies might not lead to the anticipated results.

Second, there may be significant lags in the reporting of data on outcomes, particularly for the real sector and for trade accounts. In addition, data on outcomes may be subject to frequent revisions, making timely monitoring and disbursements problematic.

Third, program outcomes are influenced not just by policies under the control of country authorities but also by exogenous factors beyond their control. Though true in principle, however, it is not clear that exogenous shocks create serious problems for program projections. For example, a recent study of program projections by Musso and Phillips (2001) shows that projections for growth, inflation, and international reserves were accurate relative to simple random-walk projections. But projections for current and capital accounts did not outperform projections from the random-walk model.

The more difficult question in this regard is, if exogenous factors force a program to go off course, to what extent should the authorities bear the risk of failure? And should there be some assurance of IMF disbursement if it is judged that the authorities made a good effort to attain the goals? Thus, even outcomes-based conditionality will require sifting the evidence to determine whether outcome targets were missed because of exogenous factors or because the authorities genuinely came up short—and if it is the former, whether there would be a case for waivers as there is under policy-based conditionality.

Outcomes-based conditionality also raises the question of whether and when it would be feasible for the IMF to disburse funds based on promises to achieve certain goals if it had not had any influence on the policy measures to attain them. In the private sector such condition-free lending is made only to blue-chip clients or those with good collateral, high net worth, or both. Similarly, the IMF would likely provide such loans only to countries with strong records of economic performance and management, reputations for good governance, histories of paying debts as contracted, and to those facing situations that are not too dire.

Otherwise, giving borrowing countries complete freedom in their choice of policy actions would not provide adequate safeguards for IMF resources. Even for the best clients, contract and loan covenants are likely to provide complete freedom for policy choices only as long as the client's capacity to repay is not impaired by endogenous or exogenous factors. To protect its resources, the IMF, like other lenders, will specify contingencies in the loan contract if the borrower's health deteriorates—for whatever reason.

Two points can be made in response to the problems raised regarding outcomes-based conditionality. First, even under outcomes-based conditionality, funds will be disbursed in tranches. For example, a program to correct an imbalance in the balance of payments could take multiple steps to achieve its goal of attaining a comfortable level of international reserves. The first tranche could be disbursed based on a promise, but subsequent tranches would be released only after the country had achieved certain levels of international reserves. In fact, even the release of the first tranche could require some prior actions. Hence, by splitting monitoring and disbursement into smaller components, outcomes-based criteria can simultaneously provide sufficient safeguards and prevent excessive backloading of financing.

Second, like any creditor, the IMF would combine outcomes-based conditionality with a monitoring system so that if a borrower's position deteriorated sufficiently, the IMF would intervene to contain the damage, take prompt corrective action, and try to change the borrower's strategy. As noted earlier, there would likely be ex ante ownership but ex post conditionality. That is, a program might have little bite initially, but stricter constraints would be imposed if certain events occurred. And because all possible contingencies cannot be specified ex ante, the IMF would design outcomes-based programs with the option of intervening, should doing so be necessary to protect its resources.

Conclusion

This article has drawn on the well-established literature on agency theory and finance to argue that conditionality must apply to all IMF lending and that country ownership of IMF-supported programs is essential. Because ownership matters for the success of these programs, the IMF and country authorities share an incentive to create contracts that maximize ownership—subject to the safeguards that the IMF requires for its resources.

There is a widespread perception that countries often lack sufficient ownership of the programs they negotiate with the IMF. Here it is important to distinguish between countries in crisis and those with emerging imbalances. Crisis countries have less room for maneuver, and their problems require rapid responses. In such cases ownership may be less important—and, given the exceptional and extreme circumstances, agreements may be easier to reach. But in other countries the extra time spent on negotiations may be a necessary price to pay for better program outcomes. In fact, different IMF facilities could cater to countries in different circumstances, and the scope and types of conditionality could differ depending on the facility used.

Ownership can be enhanced by limiting the objectives of IMF-supported programs—which would also allow for more focused conditionality. If a program's objectives are to establish and maintain macroeconomic and financial stability, the range of structural measures required by IMF conditionality would be narrower. In its capacity as policy adviser, the IMF can advise on the merits of various structural reforms. But in the context of programs, it should include only conditions that directly support macroeconomic objectives. Encouraging the domestic formulation of programs, selling programs to multiple country stakeholders, discussing different policy options, and increasing information flows would all help increase country ownership of programs.

To date the design of conditionality has focused on policy actions rather than outcomes. This chapter has argued that there is merit in shifting the emphasis toward outcomes-based conditionality and exploring the use of floating tranches, especially for structural reforms. Outcomes-based conditionality would increase country ownership by giving the authorities greater discretion and flexibility in choosing the policy mix and the timing of structural measures. This increased leeway in program implementation would be tied to explicit acknowledgment of ownership, improvements in data and reporting (to facilitate monitoring by external observers), and acceptance of responsibility for program outcomes.

For the IMF, outcomes-based conditionality would have to be combined with an agreed monitoring system for programs and the establishment of rules for borrower behavior. Such rules would be applied uniformly and enforced through peer pressure and international norms—since the IMF has no recourse to legal action.

While a good case can be made for incorporating outcomes-based conditionality in IMF lending, this is not an either-or matter. Programs would presumably combine policy-based and outcomes-based conditionality. The balance would depend on the country's circumstances, preferences, and economic problems and on the accuracy with which different policy actions and outcomes can be monitored (Dixit, 2000; Drazen and Fischer, 1997). Programs with such a balance would align IMF conditionality more closely with country ownership—undoubtedly the shared goal of the IMF and its member countries.

References

Ames, Brian, Gita Bhatt, and Mark Plant, 2002, "Taking Stock of Poverty Reduction Efforts," *Finance & Development*, Vol. 39 (June), pp. 9–12.

Anderson, Matthew S., 1966, *The Eastern Question: 1774–1923* (New York: St. Martin's Press).

Boughton, James M. 2001, *Silent Revolution: The International Monetary Fund 1979–1989* (Washington: International Monetary Fund).

Buchanan, James M. 1975, "The Samaritan's Dilemma," in *Altruism, Morality and Economic Theory*, ed. by Edmund S. Phelps (New York: Sage Foundation).

Bulíř, Aleš, and Javier Hamann, 2001, "How Volatile and Unpredictable Are Aid Flows, and What Are the Policy Implications?" IMF Working Paper 01/167 (Washington: International Monetary Fund).

De Gregorio, José, Barry Eichengreen, Takatoshi Ito, and Charles Wyplosz, 1999, "An Independent and Accountable IMF," *Geneva Reports on the World Economy: 1* (Geneva: International Center for Monetary and Banking Studies).

Díaz Alejandro, Carlos F. 1984, "IMF Conditionality: What Kind?" *PIDE Tidings* (January–February), pp. 7–9.

Dixit, Avinash, 2000, "IMF Programs as Incentive Mechanisms" (Princeton, New Jersey: Princeton University).

Drazen, Allan, and Stanley Fischer, 1997, "Conditionality and Selectivity in Lending by International Financial Institutions" (Washington: International Monetary Fund).

Feldstein, Martin, 1998, "Refocusing the IMF," *Foreign Affairs* (March–April), pp. 20–33.

Ferguson, Niall, 1998, *The House of Rothschild: Money's Prophets 1798–1849* (New York: Viking).

Goldstein, Morris, 2000, "IMF Structural Conditionality: How Much Is Too Much?" (Washington: Institute for International Economics).

Greenbaum, Stuart I., and Anjan V. Thakor, 1995, *Contemporary Financial Intermediation* (Fort Worth, Texas: Dryden Press).

Guitián, Manuel, 1995, "Conditionality Past, Present, and Future," *Staff Papers*, International Monetary Fund, Vol. 42 (December), pp. 792–835.

Haque, Nadeem Ul, and Mohsin S. Khan, 2002, "Do IMF-Supported Programs Work? A Survey of the Cross-Country Empirical Evidence," in *Macroeconomic Management: Programs and Policies*, ed. by M.S. Khan, S.M. Nsouli, and C.H. Wong (Washington: International Monetary Fund).

Holmström, Bengt, 1982, "Moral Hazard in Teams," *Bell Journal of Economics*, Vol. 13, pp. 324–40.

International Monetary Fund (IMF), 2001a, "Conditionality in Fund-Supported Programs—Overview" (Washington: International Monetary Fund).

———, 2001b, "Conditionality in Fund-Supported Programs—Policy Issues" (Washington: International Monetary Fund).

———, 2001c, "Structural Conditionality in Fund-Supported Programs" (Washington: International Monetary Fund).

———, 2002a, "Review of the Poverty Reduction Strategy Paper Approach—Early Experience with Interim PRSPs and Full PRSPs" (Washington: International Monetary Fund).

———, 2002b, "Review of the Poverty Reduction Strategy Paper Approach—Main Findings and Issues for Discussion" (Washington: International Monetary Fund).

James, Harold, 1996, *International Monetary Cooperation Since Bretton Woods* (Washington: International Monetary Fund and New York: Oxford University Press).

———, 2001, *The End of Globalization: Lessons from the Great Depression* (Cambridge, Massachusetts: Harvard University Press).

Kaplan, Steven N., and Per Stromberg, 2000, "Financial Contracting Theory Meets the Real World: An Empirical Analysis of Venture Capital Contracts," NBER Working Paper No. 7660 (Cambridge, Massachusetts: National Bureau of Economic Research).

Khan, Mohsin S., and Sunil Sharma, 2001, "IMF Conditionality and Country Ownership of Programs," IMF Working Paper 01/142 (Washington: International Monetary Fund).

Killick, Tony, 1997, "Principals, Agents and the Failings of Conditionality," *Journal of International Development*, Vol. 9, pp. 483–95.

Kotowitz, Yehuda, 1987, "Moral Hazard," in *The New Palgrave: A Dictionary of Economics*, ed. by John Eatwell, Murray Milgate, and Peter Newman (New York: Norton).

Lindbeck, Assar, and Jorgen Weibull, 1988, "Altruism and Time Consistency: The Economics of Fait Accompli," *Journal of Political Economy*, Vol. 96, No. 6, pp. 1165–82.

Meltzer, A.H., C.F. Bergsten, C.W. Calomiris, T. Campbell, E.J. Feulner, W.L. Hoskins, R.L. Huber, M.H. Johnson, J.I. Levinson, J.D. Sachs, and E.E. Torres, 2000, *International Financial Institution Advisory Commission Report* (Washington: U.S. Congress).

Mishkin, Frederic, 1998, *The Economics of Money, Banking and Financial Markets* (New York: Addison-Wesley).

Mussa, Michael, and Miguel Savastano, 1999, "The IMF Approach to Economic Stabilization," IMF Working Paper 99/104 (Washington: International Monetary Fund).

Musso, Alberto, and Steven Phillips, 2001, "Comparing Projections and Outcomes of IMF-Supported Programs," IMF Working Paper 01/45 (Washington: International Monetary Fund).

Polak, Jacques J., 1991, "The Changing Nature of IMF Conditionality," *Essays in International Finance*, Vol. 184 (Princeton, New Jersey: International Finance Section, Princeton University).

Santaella, Julio A., 1993, "Stabilization Programs and External Enforcement," *Staff Papers*, International Monetary Fund, Vol. 40 (September), pp. 584–621.

Spraos, John, 1986, "IMF Conditionality: Ineffectual, Inefficient, Mistargeted," *Essays in International Finance*, Vol. 166 (Princeton, New Jersey: Princeton University).

Stiglitz, Joseph E., 2000, "The Contribution of the Economics of Information to Twentieth Century Economics," *Quarterly Journal of Economics*, Vol. 115, No. 4, pp. 1441–78.

Svensson, Jakob, 2000, "When Is Foreign Aid Policy Credible? Aid Dependence and Conditionality," *Journal of Development Economics*, Vol. 61, No. 1, pp. 61–84.

Tirole, Jean, 2002, *Financial Crises, Liquidity Provision and the International Monetary Financial System* (Princeton, New Jersey: Princeton University Press).

Williamson, John, ed., 1983, *Fund Conditionality* (Washington: Institute for International Economics).

World Bank, 1999, "High Impact Adjustment Lending (HIAL): Initial Evaluation," Operations Evaluation Department Report No. 19797 (Washington: World Bank).

CHAPTER

8 Different Strokes? Common and Uncommon Responses to Financial Crises

James M. Boughton

Much of the debate on the management of financial crises has focused on structural and psychological issues related to conditions that are supposed to be necessary to restore investor confidence. Nonetheless, the paramount requirement in the short term is for countries in crisis to adopt correct macroeconomic policies. An analysis of conventional macroeconomic models reveals that countries can afford to run expansionary policies to restore internal balance only if they can afford to ignore the requirements for external balance. This arithmetic does not depend on whether macroeconomic policies were inappropriate before the crisis hit.

Introduction

The recent proliferation of literature on international financial crises has demonstrated the variegation of causes leading countries to economic disaster. Once thought to be almost universally originating from fiscal and other macroeconomic policy errors, financial crises are now generally understood to emanate just as easily from external shocks or from internal structural imbalances. Less attention has been paid to the implications of this discovery for post-crisis economic and financial management. It has become fashionable to criticize the IMF for applying univariate solutions to multivariate problems, for being "an overbearing organization with a well-thumbed book of macroeconomic-policy nostrums,"[1] but that line of attack leads only to other questions. For example, if a country is initially in fiscal balance, does it follow that fiscal contraction is an inappropriate response to an external shock? More generally, does the uniqueness of each crisis and each country's circumstances imply that a unique response is required?

Most of the literature on this topic has focused on two issues. First, it has been argued that countries with a strong initial macroeconomic policy stance should be encouraged to use their room for maneuver to respond to a negative shock with expansionary, not contractionary, policy. Feldstein (1998), for example, has complained that the IMF mishandled the 1997 crisis in the Republic of Korea. The IMF, he suggested (p. 29), responded with its

> traditional ... prescription of budget deficit reduction ... and a tighter monetary policy..., which together depress growth and raise unemployment. But why should Korea be required to raise taxes and cut spending to lower its 1998 budget deficit when its national savings rate is already one of the highest in the world, when its 1998 budget deficit will rise temporarily because of the policy-induced recession, and when the combination of higher private savings and reduced business investment are already freeing up the resources needed to raise exports and shrink the current account deficit?

Similarly, Corden (2001) argued that the "first instinct of the IMF was for fiscal tightening. It ignored the good fiscal policies of the Asian governments. Obviously this was inappropriate and was proven to be so, given the deep slumps that developed" (p. 55). Corden acknowledged the "limits to fiscal expansion, set by the funds available to the IMF," but he concluded that the strategy should have been to run as expansionary a policy as possible.

A second criticism, derivative to the first, is that macroeconomic policies should be tailored to the need to restore market confidence. In Feldstein's view of the Korean crisis, "the primary need was to persuade foreign creditors to continue to lend by rolling over existing loans as they came due.... The key ... was to persuade lenders that Korea's lack of adequate foreign exchange reserves was a temporary shortage, not permanent insolvency" (1998, p. 31). Corden took a more nuanced view, noting the dependence of confidence on both long-term fiscal discipline and "the need for temporary fiscal expansion," with balance between these factors being case specific (2001, p. 48).[2]

[1] "Sick Patients, Warring Doctors," *Economist* (September 18–24, 1999), p. 81. The opposite criticism also surfaces with some frequency. For example, Minton-Beddoes (1995) accused the IMF of "ad hoc improvisations" in violation of its own rules and mandate, as a consequence of a "quest for relevance" (pp. 128–29).

[2] For earlier examples of similar criticisms of IMF crisis management, see Buiter (1990) and Killick (1995). Radelet and Sachs (1998) also focused on the desirability of aiming the crisis response at restoring market confidence.

The central role of investor psychology in financial crises is indisputable and may be illustrated by two examples. First, consider the infamous case of the closing of 16 Indonesian banks in 1997 (see Enoch, 2000). Faced with an incipient collapse of the banking system because of declining confidence in the banks' soundness, the government accepted IMF advice to close the weakest banks but resisted closing all of those identified as insolvent. The argument that the banks remaining open were sound enough to survive was partly financial and partly political, but it also reflected a psychological judgment that depositors would recognize and accept the systemic improvement and would leave their money in the open banks. The strategy failed disastrously, not because the financial analysis was wrong but because it misjudged the requirements for reinstating confidence. Instead of aborting the panic, it catalyzed it, as depositors feared that the 16 closings heralded a more general shutdown.

A second example may be drawn from the Mexican debt crisis of August 1982 (see Boughton, 2000 and 2001). Mexico's fiscal policy was unsustainably expansionary, but the newly elected government was promising to correct the situation when it took office in December. IMF staff urged the authorities to act earlier and more decisively, but as long as the major international bank creditors were prepared to maintain their exposure, there appeared to be no reason to panic. Why did the banks approve a large syndicated loan to Mexico at the end of July and then refuse to roll over other jumbo loans two weeks later? That catastrophic loss of confidence was not triggered by a spate of bad news in the first half of August, but by a reassessment of the bad news that had been accumulating for several years. Should the IMF have responded more forcefully and more publicly? To answer that question requires a complex judgment about market psychology and expectations.

Evaluating the policy implications of these psychological factors is not straightforward. Since the outcome depends on expectations that are extrinsic to the model, analysts are confronted with the possibility of multiple equilibria.[3] Nonetheless, countries hit by economic or financial crises must adjust macroeconomic policies, economists must advise them on how to do so, and the IMF must base its lending decisions on the soundness and appropriateness of those policies. What do conventional models tell us about how to make such judgments? Do they give wrong answers because they omit important economic relationships?

This paper will abstract both from second-guessing the "animal spirits" of investors and from analyzing the structural details of IMF-supported adjustment programs in order to look more closely at the underlying macroeconomics.[4] As noted above, a key proposition in much of the criticism of the IMF response to the Asian crisis is that if fiscal policy was acceptable before the crisis, it should follow that the traditional prescription of budget tightening is inappropriate and will only injure the economy. The difficulty with that argument is that macroeconomic theory does not generate an optimum fiscal policy. All that theory tells us is that governments must limit the growth of debt so as to satisfy the intertemporal budget constraint.

As long as current and future deficits are small enough to rule out a long-run Ponzi game, a wide range of fiscal policies might be implied by prevailing economic conditions. In practice, depending on circumstances, advocates of fiscal soundness have appealed for governments to adopt policy goals such as (a) balancing the budget over the business cycle, (b) placing a ceiling on the ratio of debt to output, or even (c) eliminating debt or a subset of it, at least in net terms. No generally accepted macroeconomic model supports any such objective as an optimizing strategy except under restrictive assumptions. Instead, welfare maximization places fiscal policy within a broader structure such as stabilizing output growth at a sustainable (noninflationary) rate or, more generally, optimizing a social welfare function. In any such model, shifts in exogenous conditions that affect national saving or investment rates might well require a shift in the level and timing of fiscal actions.[5]

One way to isolate the role of macroeconomics in the debate is to examine the macro models that are in use at the IMF to see if they rule out certain plausible outcomes or omit key relationships that would generate those outcomes. The next section of this paper summarizes the properties of three theoretical macro models that have been developed by IMF staff to analyze the linkages between aggregate demand and external payments positions. That review is followed by some general conclusions about the use of macroeconomic policies in response to financial crises.

Theoretical Macro Models at the IMF

Of the numerous IMF-developed policy analysis models, three are particularly apt for illustrating the nature of the recommended policy responses to

[3] A growing segment of the finance literature endogenizes expectations consistently with the predictions of the model so as to generate multiple equilibria intrinsically. For a survey, see Masson (2001). The basic point for the problem at hand is that expectations need not be irrational to generate multiple equilibria.

[4] For overviews on the actual practice of IMF financial programming, see Fischer (1997) and Mussa and Savastano (1999). For detailed inside analyses of the IMF's handling of the Asian crisis, see Lane and others (1999) and Boorman and others (2000).

[5] For an exposition, see Blanchard and Fischer (1989, especially pp. 126–35 and 583–91).

internal or external shocks: Jacques Polak's classic model of the monetary approach to the balance of payments, the "merged" model developed by Mohsin Kahn and others to endogenize economic growth, and the Mundell-Fleming model, which was modified recently by Timothy Lane and others to study the effects of capital flows in the context of the Asian crisis. A common feature of these three models, at least in their simplest form, is that they treat capital flows as exogenous and thus can be used to analyze small open economies that depend on externally rationed credit for financing the balance of payments. Although the IMF may provide credits to offset part of a capital outflow, and the IMF's involvement may induce other capital to flow back in, countries in financial crisis typically still face a lower net inflow than they did before.[6]

These models have not been used directly to generate performance criteria for IMF-supported adjustment programs. Rather, they have been used to generate key insights on how such programs are or should be designed—on the linkages between domestic credit creation and the balance of payments, between output growth and the current account, between capital flows and the growth-payments nexus, and so forth. The extent to which more modern macroeconomic concepts—notably intertemporal dynamics, time consistency, expectations theory, and the role of credibility—have been incorporated in empirical program design is difficult to determine.[7]

The Polak Model

The basis for financial programming and consequently for policy conditionality at the Fund is the "Polak model," which was first developed in the 1950s to link domestic credit creation to national income and international reserves. In its simplest guise, as exposited in Polak (1998), the model may be written as follows (with some modifications from Polak's notation):

$$\Delta L = k\Delta Y \qquad (1.1)$$

$$M = mY \qquad (1.2)$$

$$\Delta R = X - M + K \qquad (1.3)$$

$$\Delta L = \Delta R + \Delta D, \qquad (1.4)$$

where all variables are expressed as nominal values:

L = stock of money
Y = GNP
R = international reserves
M = imports
X = exports
K = capital inflow to nonbank sector
D = domestic credit of the banking system.

It is useful to think of this as a "fiscal" version of the model. For a country with primitive financial markets and given values of X and K, an increase in the fiscal deficit will be financed primarily by domestic credit expansion, D. Alternatively, equation (1.4) may be replaced by a slightly less aggregated financial sector:

$$\Delta L = q\Delta H \qquad (1.4')$$

$$\Delta H = \Delta R + \Delta D_c, \qquad (1.5)$$

where H = the monetary base, or "high-powered money," and D_c = domestic credit of the central bank. This "monetary" version is a little more transparent, since D_c is a directly observed policy instrument.

Obviously, a great deal of structure—fiscal policy, inflation, exchange rate adjustment, productivity shocks—must be added to this model before it can yield useful policy prescriptions. To that end, IMF staff have developed or adapted many country-specific models that build on the simplified framework and incorporate the policy instruments and other variables that are needed to explain each country's particular circumstances. D_c in this general model can be thought of as a metaphor for the full range of macroeconomic policy actions. Expansionary policy is represented by an increase in D_c, and policy "adjustment" is represented by a decrease. Similarly, R is a metaphor for external stability, which in a more complete model would be represented by a combination of reserve and exchange rate adjustment.

The policy implications of an exogenous shift in capital flows may be illustrated by solving the model for internal and external balance:

$$Y = \frac{1}{qm+k}\left[kY_{-1} + q(X + K + \Delta D_c)\right]$$

$$\Delta R = -\frac{qm}{qm+k}\Delta D_c - \frac{mk}{qm+k}Y_{-1} + \frac{k}{qm+k}(X+K).$$

Because of the simplicity of the model, not only do all fiscal and monetary policies have similar effects; so do all external shocks. A shift in capital

[6] This analysis does not examine the rationality of assuming that capital markets allocate credit to countries exogenously rather than on the basis of a market-clearing response to conditions in the country. For an analysis of the role of international capital markets in generating and spreading financial crises, see Calvo (2000 and 2004).

[7] Two key elements that are not explicit in the class of models reviewed here are the effects of forward-looking expectations and of the policymaker's credibility on the timing of policy responses; see Burnside, Eichenbaum, and Rebelo (2001); and Clarida, Gali, and Gertler (1999). Those factors are at least implicit in many IMF-supported adjustment programs, even if they are not introduced through a formal model; see the exchange between Sebastian Edwards and Morris Goldstein in Edwards (1989).

flows is perfectly substitutable for an export shock, regardless of whether X responds to a shift in foreign demand or to a supply shock in the export commodity or industry. In any event, the preferred policy response to such a shock depends critically on whether the goal is to restore internal or external balance. To stabilize domestic output in the face of an exogenous loss of capital inflows ($\Delta K < 0$), D_c must be increased commensurately. Conversely, to prevent the capital outflow from depleting net international reserves or forcing depreciation, D_c must be cut.

Much of the criticism and defense of the IMF involves a dialogue of the deaf. Critics such as Buiter, Corden, and Feldstein accuse the IMF of urging countries to tighten policies in circumstances when expansion would be needed to stabilize and restore output; the IMF defends its advice on the grounds that an initial contraction is needed to stabilize and restore reserves or, more generally, to stabilize the exchange rate. This debate, however, has nothing to do with the structure of the underlying macroeconomic model.

To reconcile these two positions requires (a) a recognition by the critics that external stability and international reserves are important—regardless of the exchange regime—and that reserves cannot be replenished purely through official financing without creating moral hazard problems,[8] and (b) a recognition by the IMF's defenders that output is important, not only for the obvious reasons but also
134 because a sharp drop in output can bring a loss of confidence that will aggravate the initial adverse shock. If an objective function that weighted output and reserve losses were added to the model, the sign on the reaction of D_c to K would become ambiguous.[9] For countries with very low initial levels of reserves, a perceived need for exchange rate stability to prevent disruption of production and trade, and poor access to new sources of external financing, the necessity of a cut in D_c remains clear. In other cases, viable policy options involve more flexibility.

The Merged Model

The Polak model alone does not provide guidance on the effects of adjustment programs on output. The potential rate of output growth is left unexplained, as is the division of nominal income growth into its real and inflationary components. In a series of papers written in the late 1980s, Mohsin Khan, Peter Montiel, and Nadeem Ul Haque attempted to endogenize real growth by merging the Polak model with the class of growth models used at the World Bank.[10] The following is a slightly simplified version of the model presented in Khan, Montiel, and Haque (1990). The full model includes the exchange rate, government consumption, and lump-sum taxes as policy instruments, in addition to domestic credit. It thus adds some of the structure that is needed for practical financial programming. In this modification, the exchange rate and government consumption are fixed, taxes are proportional to nominal income, all lagged and fixed exogenous variables are set equal to unity, and second-order terms are ignored.

$$\Delta L = k\Delta Y \tag{2.1}$$

$$\Delta M = m\Delta y + b\Delta P \tag{2.2}$$

$$\Delta R = X - M + K \tag{2.3}$$

$$\Delta L = \Delta R + \Delta D \tag{2.4}$$

$$\Delta Y = \Delta y + \Delta P \tag{2.5}$$

$$Y - T - C - I = \Delta L - K_p - \Delta D_p \tag{2.6}$$

$$G - T = K_g + \Delta D_g \tag{2.7}$$

$$\Delta X = -c\Delta P \tag{2.8}$$

$$\Delta y = \frac{I}{\rho(1 + \Delta P)} \tag{2.9}$$

$$C = (1 - s)(Y - T) \tag{2.10}$$

$$T = tY \tag{2.11}$$

$$K = K_p + K_g \tag{2.12}$$

$$D = D_p + D_g. \tag{2.13}$$

The new notation is mostly standard macroeconomic usage. D is debt to banks, and the subscripts p and g refer to the debt of the private and public sectors, respectively. K_p and K_g are capital flows to these two sectors. The coefficients b and c are responses of imports and exports to relative prices, and ρ is the incremental capital-output ratio (ICOR).

Although this model is much more detailed than the basic Polak model, the principal difference comes from the addition of equation (2.5), which

[8] Replacement of private with official capital bails out private investors, shifts the burden of risks, and poses new threats to other countries (potentially including those in remote parts of the world). Even if official capital could be mobilized in unlimited amounts for this purpose, the quality of the new equilibrium would be fundamentally different from the old. The solution to an exogenous capital outflow therefore must involve recreating the conditions—economic, political, and psychological—that induced capital into (or to stay in) the country before the crisis.

[9] Normally, output and reserves would both be lower in the new short-term equilibrium. The question is not whether the *economy* would have to adjust, but whether a contractionary policy action would be necessary to reach that point or whether policy could be eased somewhat to soften the blow from the capital outflow.

[10] For a similar but less detailed extension of the Polak model, see Chand (1989).

allows the domestic price level to absorb some of the shock that would otherwise fall on output, and equation (2.9), which allows investment to raise output via the capital stock. If the dynamics in this model were explicit, a sustained tightening of monetary policy would have less severe short-run effects but more severe long-term effects than in the basic model.

The merged model can readily be solved for three equations representing roughly the real, monetary, and external sectors. Following Khan, Montiel, and Haque (1990), these equations are labeled (BB) (for the real, or "[World] Bank," side), (MM), and (BP).

$$\rho\Delta y = K + \Delta D \qquad \text{(BB)}$$

$$k(\Delta y + \Delta P) = \Delta D + \Delta R \qquad \text{(MM)}$$

$$\Delta R + m\Delta y + b'\Delta P = K, \qquad \text{(BP)}$$

where $b' \equiv b + c$.[11]

As with the Polak model, this system may be solved for the requisite demand-management policy (ΔD) in response to an exogenous capital outflow ($-K$), first assuming that the goal is to prevent output from falling and then assuming that the goal is to prevent reserves from falling. The first case is quite straightforward. From (BB), with $\Delta y = 0$, $\Delta D = -K$. The central bank must raise domestic credit so as to compensate exactly for the outflow of foreign capital. Consequently, from the solution to (MM) and (BP), $\Delta R = K$. That is, reserves fall by the full amount of the outflow, and the current account is unaffected.

Stabilizing output is not feasible if reserves are insufficient to compensate for the outflow ($R_0 < -K$). Taking the alternative strategy of stabilizing reserves ($\Delta R = 0$), the solution is more complex.

$$\Delta D = \frac{k(\rho - m + b')}{mk + b'(\rho - k)}K \qquad (2.14)$$

$$\Delta y = \frac{(b' + k)}{mk + b'(\rho - k)}K. \qquad (2.15)$$

The signs on these expressions are ambiguous and depend particularly on the relative magnitudes of the ICOR (ρ) and the income elasticity of import demand (m). As a benchmark, consider the situation if the price elasticities of demand are identical for imports and exports ($bN = 0$). Then

$$\Delta D = \left(\frac{\rho}{m} - 1\right)K \qquad (2.14')$$

$$\Delta y = \frac{1}{m}K. \qquad (2.15')$$

In this situation, a capital outflow results unambiguously in a fall in output, but it does not necessarily follow that a contractionary demand management policy is needed to stabilize reserves. The capital outflow itself pulls output down and thus reduces demand for imports. If that effect is strong enough, reserves may be stabilized without any policy adjustment. If $bN > 0$, the need for adjustment may be further reduced.

The merged model, in this comparative-statics form, is a longer-term model. In the short run, the Polak model shows unambiguously that contraction is required to stabilize reserves. The implication of this extension is that additional temporary financing may be a sensible substitute for demand contraction as a means of stabilizing reserves until the adjustment process represented by equations (2.14) and (2.15) is completed. Nonetheless, even if reserves are stabilized temporarily through new financing with no change in macro policies, output (or at least income, via the real exchange rate) still must fall eventually in order to bring about the equilibrating drop in import demand.

The Modified Mundell-Fleming Model

Fund staff working on Asian economies in the aftermath of the 1997 crisis developed a variant of the Mundell-Fleming model to analyze the short- and medium-term effects of exogenous capital flows (Lane and others, 1999, Appendix 7.2). This model is also useful for explicitly endogenizing the domestic interest rate and the exchange rate. The structure of this model is such that an exogenous capital outflow leads to a depreciation that generates the current account surplus (or reduced deficit) needed to offset the outflow. In a fixed-exchange-rate system, a decline in output would normally be needed to generate that surplus, but here it will force enough currency depreciation to get the needed result. Output will actually rise as a corollary effect, unless the negative wealth effect of depreciation on consumer demand is sufficiently large.

The model is readily understood as a single reduced-form equation and an equilibrium condition:

$$Y = C(Y,E) + I(r) + G + X(Y,E) \qquad (3.1)$$
$$0 < C_Y < 1,\ C_E < 0,\ I_r < 0,\ X_Y < 0,\ X_E > 0$$

$$X = -K, \qquad (3.2)$$

where X = net exports (the current account balance) and E = the exchange rate (domestic-currency price

[11] The (BB) equation derived from the full model contains an additional RHS term, $+[s(1-t)+t-k]y$. The equation has been simplified here by assuming $k = t + s(1-t)$; that is, that saving is absorbed at the margin by money demand. This simplification masks the role of shifts in saving propensities or tax rates, but it does not affect the analytical results discussed subsequently. See Khan, Montiel, and Haque (1990, pp. 172–73).

of foreign exchange). Other variables are in conventional notation. Note that this, like the Polak model, is a fixed-price model. Because countries are assumed to have limited resources, international reserves are also fixed (compare equation (3.2) with equation (1.3) or (2.3)).

Now consider the model's comparative-statics multiplier effects. First, the fiscal multiplier, assuming that monetary policy controls r and that the latter is fixed, is

$$\frac{dY}{dG}\bigg|_{(dr=dK=0)} = \frac{1}{1-C_Y+\varepsilon}$$

$$\text{where} \quad \varepsilon = \frac{C_E X_Y}{X_E}.$$

In the conventional Mundell-Fleming model, $C_E = 0$, so $\varepsilon = 0$. Otherwise, $\varepsilon > 0$, and the fiscal multiplier is reduced but still positive. Qualitatively, this is a standard Keynesian effect.

Second, the effect of an exogenous capital outflow with fixed domestic policies but a flexible exchange rate is

$$\frac{dY}{dK}\bigg|_{(dr=dG=0)} = -\frac{1+C_E/X_E}{1-C_Y+\varepsilon}$$

$$0 < -\frac{dY}{dK} \le \frac{dY}{dG} \quad \text{if } |C_E| < X_E.$$

This result suggests that allowing the≡ capital outflow to generate depreciation while holding domestic interest rates and government spending fixed will lead perversely to an increase in output. In the special case where $C_E = 0$, a capital outflow has the same effect as an expansionary fiscal policy. Capital inflows thus have a Dutch-disease effect in this model: they cause the exchange rate to appreciate and weaken output. This effect is, of course, inconsistent with the conventional wisdom that developing countries need capital inflows to grow. As a corollary, if output was initially on target, the appropriate fiscal response to a capital outflow is to cut spending.

The difficulty here is in the assumption that the domestic interest rate (r) is determined solely by monetary policy. Capital inflows should be allowed to reduce the cost of financing investment and thereby to raise aggregate supply as well as demand. The simplest way to model this relationship is to let domestic investment be a positive function of capital inflows.[12] Then

$$Y = C(Y,E) + I(r,K) + G + X(Y,E) \quad I_k > 0 \qquad (3.1')$$

and

$$\frac{dY}{dK}\bigg|_{(dr=dG=0)} = -\frac{1+C_E/X_E - I_K}{1-C_Y+\varepsilon}$$

$$\frac{dY}{dK} > 0 \text{ if } |C_E X_E - I_K| > 1.$$

Now capital inflows raise output in two ways: via a wealth effect from currency appreciation and a financial effect on capital investment. If we assume that those two effects are large enough to make $dY/dK > 0$, while the wealth effect alone is not so large as to nullify the normal Keynesian fiscal effect, then we have the expected comparative static results. Third, using this expanded version, we can calculate the required fiscal response to an exogenous capital outflow, holding r constant and letting the exchange rate depreciate.

Let $\eta \equiv 1 + C_E/X_E - I_K$.

$$\text{Then} \quad \frac{dG}{dK}\bigg|_{dY=dr=0} = \eta.$$

If $\eta < 0$ (as needed to get $dY/dK > 0$), then $dG/dK < 0$. The appropriate response to an exogenous outflow is to raise government spending. That keeps output on target, while the exchange rate depreciates to generate the required strengthening of the current account. In terms of macroeconomics, this is the real core of the criticism of the IMF's handling of the Asian crisis. Rather than contracting domestic demand, a country facing a financial crisis can simply let the exchange rate absorb the brunt of the attack.

The obvious response to this criticism is that the required depreciation might be so large as to destabilize the economy, and it could trigger fears of a continuing depreciation spiral. Tightening monetary and fiscal policies may be a more measured and balanced response to an outflow. Which policy is preferable in a particular set of circumstances cannot be determined from macroeconomic theory, but insights could be gleaned from a more detailed empirical analysis of the country's productive structure (see Furman and Stiglitz, 1998). Some industries, some agricultural sectors, and some financial firms would gain from devaluation, and some would lose. Because both the balance of interests and investor expectations vary from case to case, so does the optimum exchange regime.

Fourth, consider the effect of a capital outflow when monetary policy keeps the exchange rate fixed rather than the interest rate. This regime may require allowing international reserves (R) to vary, as in the first two models reviewed above.

---

[12] An alternative approach is to assume that the negative wealth effect from depreciation exceeds the direct effect of depreciation on the current account ($|C_e| > X_e$). That would correct the sign on dY/dK, but it would also reduce the magnitudes of both dY/dG and dY/dK. If neither capital flows nor fiscal policy has a sizable effect on output, the realism and relevance of the model seem doubtful.

$$X = \Delta R - K. \tag{3.2'}$$

In the general case, where the goal is to stabilize output, the interest-rate response (with G fixed) is

$$\frac{dr}{dK} = -\frac{I_K}{I_r} > 0$$

and the reserve response is simply $dR = dK$. Thus, as in the earlier models, a capital outflow requires a cut in interest rates (or a rise in government spending), and reserves must be allowed to fall by the full amount of the exogenous outflow.

When output stabilization is not feasible and the goal must be to restore external balance, output must be allowed to fall:

$$\frac{dY}{dK} = \frac{1}{X_Y} > 0$$

In this case, however, the sign of the policy response is ambiguous:

$$\frac{dr}{dK} = \frac{(1 - C_Y - X_Y) + I_K X_Y}{-X_Y I_r} < 0$$

$$\text{unless } |I_K X_Y| \geq (1 - C_Y - X_Y).$$

A capital outflow will require a hike in interest rates to stabilize reserves unless the drag on investment reduces import demand by enough to offset the conventional multiplier effect. While this secondary effect might be quite strong in some cases, it is less likely that it would work quickly enough to prevent a temporary depletion of reserves. In any situation where the initial reserve stock is vulnerable to attack, the central bank is unlikely to have time to allow the adjustment of investment and import demands to bring about a new equilibrium.

Implications and Conclusions

What can one learn from macroeconomic theory about the appropriate and viable policy responses to a financial crisis? Several implications emerge from the above review.

First, the fundamental explanation for differences in view on this issue is found even in the simplest monetary model. If a country has enough resources to withstand the shock of a sudden capital outflow, it can afford the luxury of aiming to stabilize output in the face of the shock. The required resources might come from holding a large initial stock of foreign exchange reserves (as explicitly modeled here), from imposing controls or taxes on outflows, or from acquiring replacement financing from external sources or domestic saving. In any case, output stabilization will call for an expansionary monetary or fiscal policy under most circumstances. If the country lacks the necessary resources, contractionary adjustment policies will be required to stabilize external flows unless currency depreciation is a viable alternative. Whether depreciation would bring larger or smaller welfare losses than would a contraction of aggregate demand is a structural issue on which macro models offer little guidance.

Second, although the three models reviewed above differ substantially in their coverage of macroeconomic relationships, they all lead to similar conclusions about the need for conventional policy adjustment in cases where external balance is essential and the availability of financing is limited. Perverse situations could arise, as illustrated by the Dutch-disease implications of the modified Mundell-Fleming model. Those situations, however, appear to be inconsistent with prevailing conditions in most emerging markets. As long as capital inflows are growth stimulating, the withdrawal of such flows is likely to require a standard adjustment response.

Third, the argument that a country with a strong initial fiscal position need not tighten in response to a financial crisis is contradicted by these models. What matters for macroeconomic equilibrium is not the fiscal balance but the overall level of national saving. A withdrawal of foreign capital requires an offsetting increase in domestic capital to restore external balance, irrespective of the initial fiscal position. In the crisis in the Republic of Korea, the effect of the initial capital outflow on *net* saving was offset by a collapse of business investment, after which the IMF approved a softening of the fiscal requirements in the program. The problem was not an inadequate macroeconomic framework but a limited ability to predict the effects of fiscal tightening on investor confidence.

Fourth, the structure that is omitted from these models is primarily long term in nature. No role is given to shifts or differences in the distribution of wealth across production sectors or income groups. No allowance is made for deficiencies in the quality of governance or the sustainability of the natural environment or exhaustible resources. It is not hard to construct arguments for less orthodox approaches to adjustment in the presence of those types of structural problems. A country with a weak government, a poor political system, an inefficient economic structure, a high incidence of poverty, or a vulnerable physical environment may not be able to withstand the shock of a sharp economic downturn. Even if the downturn is a temporary by-product of policy corrections that are expected to bring long-term economic and social benefits, the government may not have enough credibility to convince potential creditors and donors to support it through the transition. Nonetheless, if the short-run requirements for stability are paramount in a crisis, heterodox solutions that require time to work will be of no practical value.

Beyond these specific observations, one may draw some more general conclusions that may help clarify the debate on policy responses.

First, at least two methods for examining the macroeconomic requirements for stability have validity and are useful under carefully specified circumstances: (a) find the required policy adjustment, taking the availability of financing as given; or (b) find the level of financing required to generate a desired outcome. The IMF uses primarily the former, while the World Bank and many outside observers focus more on the latter. The suggestion that financing is readily enough available to treat it as an endogenous equilibrating variable in the midst of a financial crisis is not obviously valid.

Second, the core of the debate over appropriate policy responses has less to do with macroeconomics than with investor psychology and national economic and political structure. To resolve such a debate requires better modeling of those processes and relationships. Would structural optimization provide an escape from the need to adjust macro policies, and escape from the trade-off between currency depreciation and financial collapse? What are the requirements for restoring investor confidence? What effects would sudden shifts in income distribution have on production and spending decisions? These and related structural questions cannot be answered satisfactorily by reference to the current generation of economic models.

Third, macroeconomic analysis does support the argument that responses to financial crises should be tailored to each country's circumstances, but not for the reasons most commonly advanced in the literature. What matters crucially in this context is not the initial fiscal position but the short-term constraints on external balance. If a country in crisis can afford to sacrifice reserve or exchange rate stability or can attract replacement financing quickly, it can—and must—expand domestic policies and forgo the more usual forms of adjustment.

References

Blanchard, Olivier Jean, and Stanley Fischer, 1989, *Lectures on Macroeconomics* (Cambridge, Massachusetts: MIT Press).

Boorman, Jack, Timothy Lane, Marianne Schulze-Ghattas, Aleš Bulíř, Atish R. Ghosh, Javier Hamann, Alex Mourmouras, and Steven Phillips, 2000, "Managing Financial Crises: The Experience in East Asia," *Carnegie-Rochester Conference Series on Public Policy*, Vol. 53 (December), pp. 1–67.

Boughton, James M., 2000, "From Suez to Tequila: The IMF as Crisis Manager," *Economic Journal*, Vol. 110 (January), pp. 273–91.

_______, 2001, *Silent Revolution: The International Monetary Fund, 1979–1989* (Washington: International Monetary Fund).

Buiter, Willem H., 1990, "Allocative and Stabilization Aspects of Budgetary and Financial Policy," in Willem H. Buiter, *Principles of Budgetary and Financial Policy* (Cambridge, Massachusetts: MIT Press).

Burnside, Craig, Martin Eichenbaum, and Sergio Rebelo, 2001, "Prospective Deficits and the Asian Currency Crisis," *Journal of Political Economy*, Vol. 109, No. 6, pp. 1155–97.

Calvo, Guillermo, 2000, "Capital Market Contagion and Recession: An Explanation of the Russian Virus," in *Wanted: World Financial Stability*, ed. by Eduardo Fernandez-Arias and Ricardo Hausmann (Washington: Inter-American Development Bank), pp. 49–52.

_______, 2004, "Contagion in Emerging Markets: When Wall Street Is a Carrier," in *Latin American Economic Crises: Trade and Labour*, ed. by Enrique Bour, Daniel Heymann, and Fernando Navajas (Houndsmills, Basingstoke, Hampshire, England and New York: Palgrave Macmillan), pp. 81–91.

Chand, Sheetal K., 1989, "Toward a Growth-Oriented Model of Financial Programming," *World Development*, Vol. 17 (April), pp. 473–90.

Clarida, Richard, Jordi Gali, and Mark Gertler, 1999, "The Science of Monetary Policy: A New Keynesian Perspective," *Journal of Economic Literature*, Vol. 37 (December), pp. 1661–1707.

Corden, W. Max, 2001, "The World Financial Crisis: Are the IMF Prescriptions Right?" in *The Political Economy of International Financial Crisis: Interest Groups, Ideologies, and Institutions*, ed. by Shale Horowitz and Uk Heo (Lanham, Maryland: Rowman and Littlefield), pp. 41–61.

Edwards, Sebastian, 1989, "The International Monetary Fund and the Developing Countries: A Critical Evaluation" (with comment by Morris Goldstein, and reply), in *IMF Policy Advice, Market Volatility, Commodity Price Rules, and Other Essays*, ed. by Karl Brunner and Allan H. Meltzer (Amsterdam: North-Holland), Carnegie-Rochester Conference Series on Public Policy, Vol. 31 (Autumn).

Enoch, Charles, 2000, "Interventions in Banks During Banking Crises—The Experience of Indonesia," IMF Policy Discussion Paper PDP/00/2 (Washington: International Monetary Fund), available on the Web at *http://www.imf.org/external/pubind.htm*.

Feldstein, Martin, 1998, "Refocusing the IMF," *Foreign Affairs*, Vol. 77 (March/April), pp. 20–33.

Fischer, Stanley, 1997, "Applied Economics in Action: IMF Programs," *American Economic Review*, Vol. 87 (May), pp. 23–27.

Furman, Jason, and Joseph E. Stiglitz, 1998, "Economic Crises: Evidence and Insights from East Asia," *Brookings Papers on Economic Activity: 2*, Brookings Institution, pp. 1–114.

Khan, Mohsin S., Peter Montiel, and Nadeem Ul Haque, 1990, "Adjustment with Growth: Relating the Analytical Approaches of the IMF and the World Bank," *Journal of Development Economics*, Vol. 32, pp. 155–79.

Killick, Tony, 1995, *IMF Programmes in Developing Countries: Design and Impact* (London and New York: Routledge).

Lane, Timothy, Atish R. Ghosh, Javier Hamann, Steven Phillips, Marianne Schulze-Ghattas, and Tsidi Tsikata, 1999, *IMF-Supported Programs in Indonesia, Korea, and Thailand*, IMF Occasional Paper No. 178 (Washington: International Monetary Fund).

Masson, Paul, 2001, "Multiple Equilibria, Contagion, and the Emerging Market Crises," in *Financial Crises in*

Emerging Markets, ed. by Reuven Glick, Ramon Moreno, and Mark M. Spiegel (Cambridge, United Kingdom: Cambridge University Press), pp. 73–98.

Minton-Beddoes, Zanny, 1995, "Why the IMF Needs Reform," *Foreign Affairs*, Vol. 74 (May/June), pp. 123–34.

Mussa, Michael, and Miguel Savastano, 1999, "The IMF Approach to Stabilization," in *NBER Macroeconomics Annual 1999*, ed. by Ben S. Bernanke and Julio J. Rotemberg (Cambridge, Massachusetts: National Bureau of Economic Research), pp. 79–122.

Polak, Jacques J., 1998, "The IMF Monetary Model at Forty," *Economic Modelling*, Vol. 15, pp. 395–410.

Radelet, Steven, and Jeffrey Sachs, 1998, "The East Asian Financial Crisis: Diagnosis, Remedies, Prospects," *Brookings Papers on Economic Activity: 1*, Brookings Institution, pp. 1–74.

CHAPTER

9 Institutions, Program Implementation, and Macroeconomic Performance

Saleh M. Nsouli, Ruben Atoyan, and Alex Mourmouras[1]

This paper assesses empirically the links among a country's institutions and political environment, its implementation of IMF-supported programs, and macroeconomic performance in a sample of 197 programs approved between 1992 and 2002. We find that a stronger institutional and political environment is associated with better macroeconomic outcomes, especially at longer time horizons. This direct beneficial impact of institutions on macroeconomic outcomes is in addition to their indirect impact through better program implementation. We also find that program implementation exerts an independent influence on macroeconomic outcomes, especially over shorter time horizons of up to two years. Better-implemented programs are associated with lower inflation and with initially weaker but ultimately stronger external and fiscal outcomes, but with a statistically insignificant impact on economic growth.

Introduction

The quality of a country's institutions—broadly defined to include the formal and informal rules of economic and political interactions—is a key determinant of sustainable economic progress. Weak institutions are behind many development failures (IMF, 2003; Rodrik, Subramanian, and Trebbi, 2002; and North, 1997). Many developing and transition economies participating in IMF-supported programs are bedeviled by corruption, weak and uneven enforcement of property rights, and other institutional failings. These institutional drawbacks have increasingly become the focus of concern for international financial and development institutions, which have made structural reform the subject of their conditionality.

Despite the significance of a country's institutions for its macroeconomic performance, the empirical literature on IMF-supported reforms lacks a systematic quantitative assessment of their importance. Most evaluations of IMF-supported programs simply ignore the effect on macroeconomic performance of variation in institutions, either across countries or over time within a country. These evaluations are also generally inconclusive. Although inflation, the balance of payments, and the public finances seem to improve in countries that adopt IMF-supported programs, the impact on economic growth is ambiguous.[2]

The quality of a country's institutions also shapes the extent to which it succeeds in implementing its IMF-supported programs. Program interruptions and the uneven record of implementation of some IMF-supported programs are rooted, at least in part, in weak institutions in the countries making use of IMF resources. Until recently, detailed data on program implementation were lacking. Most studies simply captured countries' decision to participate in IMF-supported programs and did not consider how variation in program performance affected macroeconomic outcomes. This is an important omission, because a large proportion of IMF-supported programs are known to suffer major interruptions (see Ivanova and others, 2003 and Mecagni, 1999). Recently, the literature has begun to investigate quantitatively the links between institutions, program implementation, and macroeconomic performance (Ivanova and others, 2003; Joyce, 2003; and Dreher, 2004).

This paper sets out to measure the effect of variation in institutional quality on the macroeconomic performance of countries implementing IMF-supported programs. Building on the recent literature, it develops a statistical framework to assess empirically the links among a country's institutions and political environment, its implementation of IMF-supported programs, and macroeconomic performance. We first update the results on program implementation reported in Ivanova and others, 2003 by adding the outcomes of 25 recent programs to the sample of that paper. The qualitative results regarding program implementation remain qualitatively

[1] We thank our colleagues at the IMF and the University of North Carolina at Chapel Hill for useful input when the project was under way. We are especially indebted to Alex Dreher, Shigeru Iwata, Timothy Lane, and Gene Leon for many helpful suggestions on an earlier draft. We alone are responsible for any remaining errors.

[2] This is understandable, given the econometric difficulties of constructing counterfactuals and the long and variable lags between progress in microeconomic and structural policies and improvements in economic performance. Haque and Khan (1998) discuss the problem of the counterfactual and the stylized facts of the macroeconomic impacts of IMF-supported programs.

similar: the rate of program interruption continues to be high, exceeding 40 percent. We then assess the effect of variation in institutions on program implementation and macroeconomic performance using four indicators of performance: inflation, economic growth, the balance of payments, and the fiscal balance. Our measures of program implementation come from the IMF's Monitoring of IMF Arrangements (MONA) database, which contains detailed information on a large number of IMF-supported programs approved since the early 1990s. Information on borrowing countries' institutions and domestic politics comes from the International Country Risk Guide (ICRG).

Our empirical framework is flexible, designed to take into account both the time-series properties of macroeconomic variables and the endogeneity of program implementation. In the data, inflation, growth, and most other macroeconomic indicators tend to be highly serially correlated and mean-reverting. We therefore examine the impact of institutions, politics, and program implementation, taking into account the autoregressive structure of the main macroeconomic and institutional variables, using a methodology suggested by the literature on the error correction mechanism. Instrumental variables are used to handle the endogeneity bias that exists because macroeconomic shocks also impact program performance.

Our findings are mixed. When the endogeneity of program implementation is properly accounted for, we find that institutions and program implementation both matter for macroeconomic performance. The response of macroeconomic variables to programs is often nonmonotonic, however. For example, although better-implemented programs are associated with lower inflation rates, the fiscal and external current account balances typically deteriorate for two years after program approval before they turn around. And, as in previous work, we could not detect statistically significant associations between program implementation and economic growth at any time during the three years following program approval.

The paper is structured as follows. The second section sets the stage for the empirical analysis. It describes the measures of program implementation and institutional development used and presents descriptive statistics. The third section describes the econometric methodology and main results. The fourth section provides a conclusion.

Measuring Program Implementation and Institutional Development

Overview

Disbursements of IMF loans are tied to prior actions by the recipient country, the observance of performance criteria, and the completion of program reviews—and thus to fulfillment of conditionality. Breaches of conditionality, if not followed by waivers because the breach was judged minor or temporary, or by required corrective action to keep the program on track, can lead to program interruptions. Following Ivanova and others (2003), we use two complementary measures of program implementation. The first measure captures the premature "cancellation" of an IMF-supported program. This index takes the form of a binary variable indicating whether a program experienced a major and irreversible interruption. An "irreversible" interruption occurs when either the last scheduled program review was not completed, or all scheduled reviews were completed but the subsequent annual arrangement was not approved. The second implementation measure is the ratio of disbursements to commitments. It is a continuous variable indicating the share of available IMF credit actually drawn. This measure contains information on actual program duration and the extent to which the IMF's financial commitments under the program were fulfilled.

A variety of indicators can be used to assess the institutional and political setting in countries participating in IMF-supported programs. Based on country and time coverage and the ability to capture various aspects of governance, we choose to focus on the ICRG political risk indicators, which allow us to ascertain the short- and medium-term impacts of the political and institutional environment on economic performance and program implementation. Somewhat arbitrarily, we divide the 12 ICRG components into two groups. The first group proxies for basic institutional quality, protection of property rights, and contract enforcement. It includes indices for the Investment Profile, Corruption in Government, Law and Order, and the Quality of the Bureaucracy. The second group serves as a proxy for political outcomes. It is captured by the following variables: Government Stability, Socioeconomic Conditions, Internal Conflict, External Conflict, Military in Politics, Religious Tensions, Ethnic Tensions, and Democratic Accountability. These variables provide useful information about the internal and external political factors influencing program implementation and economic performance.[3]

Descriptive Statistics

Table 1 updates the results on program implementation presented in Ivanova and others (2003). In our sample of 197 IMF programs approved between 1992 and 2002, 41 percent of all programs (including precautionary arrangements) experienced an irreversible interruption, compared with about 44 percent reported in Ivanova and others (2003).

[3] See the ICRG Guide to the Rating System for details (*http://www.prsonline.com*).

Table 1
Program Implementation by Type of Arrangement

	Including Precautionary Arrangements				Excluding Precautionary Arrangements			
	All	EFF	ESAF/ PRGF	SBA	All	EFF	ESAF/ PRGF	SBA
Programs having irreversible interruptions[1]	41.12	40.00	45.31	38.89	42.77	34.78	45.31	43.06
Number of observations	197	25	64	108	159	23	64	72
Quantitative implementation index[2]	79.18	87.21	77.09	78.52	79.36	86.95	77.09	78.85
Number of observations	182	24	62	96	151	23	62	66
Structural implementation index[3]	66.37	73.98	70.97	60.54	68.41	76.54	70.97	62.44
Number of observations	168	24	63	81	142	22	63	57
Overall implementation index[4]	74.29	83.27	72.91	72.81	74.81	83.71	72.91	73.45
Number of observations	166	23	62	81	141	22	62	57
Share of committed funds disbursed[1]	62.05	72.56	80.02	48.47	74.54	78.87	80.02	68.02
Number of observations	193	25	64	104	156	23	64	69

Source: IMF, Monitoring of IMF Arrangements (MONA) database.

Notes: This table updates Table 1 in Ivanova and others (2003). Multiyear arrangements are treated as one program. Each cell contains the average percentage value of the *implementation index* that is based on a sample of programs approved between 1992 and 2002. SBA stands for Stand-By Arrangement; EFF stands for Extended Fund Facility; ESAF stands for Enhanced Structural Adjustment Facility; and PRGF stands for Poverty Reduction and Growth Facility.

[1] The *irreversible interruption index* and the share of committed funds disbursed were computed as defined in the text.

[2] The *quantitative implementation index* for a given macro performance criterion is equal to 100 percent if macro performance criterion was met or met after modification; and it is equal to zero if macro performance criterion was not met, not met after modification, waived, or waived after modification. The *quantitative implementation index* for a program is then computed as the average of those indices across all macro performance criteria for this program.

[3] The *structural implementation index* for a given structural condition is equal to 100 percent if structural condition was met or met with a small delay for structural benchmarks; it is equal to 50 percent if the structural condition was partially met or delayed for performance criteria; and it is equal to zero if the structural condition was not met. The *structural implementation index* for a program is then computed as the average of those indices across all structural conditions for this program.

[4] The *overall implementation index* for a given program is the average of *quantitative* and *structural implementation* indices over all conditions in this program.

Countries with fewer program interruptions tend to have higher disbursement rates: the correlation coefficient between program interruptions and the disbursement share is –0.7. When precautionary arrangements are excluded, the average disbursement share is approximately 75 percent, compared with 71 percent in the sample examined by Ivanova and others (2003). The improvement in implementation reflects the fact that our sample contains more Stand-By Arrangements, which tend to have fewer interruptions than programs supported under the Extended Fund Facility and the Poverty Reduction and Growth Facility.

Improvements in the institutional climate, as reflected in higher ICRG indicators, are generally positively correlated with better program implementation, as measured by higher disbursement shares and fewer program interruptions. As in earlier studies (Dollar and Svensson, 2000; and Ivanova and others, 2003), greater government stability and a stronger investment profile in the year immediately preceding program approval are both associated with fewer interruptions (Table 2). On average, the risk of program interruption is much lower in environments in which governments are friendlier toward foreign investment and are better able to carry out their programs. Improvements in the investment profile over a horizon of two years after the beginning of a program lead to significantly fewer interruptions. Lower corruption (a higher ICRG score) and improvements in socioeconomic conditions in the year after program approval are also associated with better implementation of conditionality as measured by the quantitative implementation index.

The political and institutional climate in countries in which programs are interrupted varies systematically from that in countries in which programs are completed. Figure 1 plots the average change in each of the ICRG variables during the program relative to the last preprogram year, distinguishing between interrupted and uninterrupted programs. Program interruptions are associated with less progress in improving the investment climate and in improving the quality of the bureaucracy, and with intensified internal conflict. Successful program implementation is associated with greater initial influence of the military, followed by a significant reduction in subsequent years. Program interruptions tend to be accompanied by sharp

Table 2

Correlation of Program Implementation Indices with ICRG Risk Ratings at Different Horizons

	Panel A. Correlation with $T-1$ Risk Ratings		Panel B. Correlation with $T+1$ Risk Ratings		Panel C. Correlation with Change in Risk Ratings from $T-1$ to $T+1$	
	Irreversible interruption index	Disbursement share[1]	Irreversible interruption index	Disbursement share[1]	Irreversible interruption index	Disbursement share[1]
Bureaucracy quality	−0.026	−0.127	−0.016	−0.072	−0.026	0.042
Corruption	−0.090	0.027	−0.006	−0.028	0.119	−0.078
Democratic accountability	−0.045	−0.089	−0.038	−0.062	−0.014	−0.034
Ethnic tensions	−0.004	0.050	−0.024	0.101	0.008	0.038
External conflict	0.047	−0.183*	0.025	−0.032	−0.020	0.143
Government stability	−0.191**	−0.033	−0.067	0.011	0.076	0.008
Internal conflict	0.093	−0.160	0.025	0.006	−0.098	0.142
Investment profile	−0.199**	0.045	−0.274***	0.167*	−0.185**	0.058
Law and order	−0.025	−0.167*	0.034	−0.054	0.072	0.102
Military in politics	−0.065	−0.059	−0.019	−0.035	0.067	−0.047
Religious tensions	−0.090	0.028	−0.115	0.097	−0.068	0.102
Socioeconomic conditions	−0.032	0.162*	−0.124	0.187	−0.093	0.049

Notes: The symbols *, **, and *** denote significance at the 90, 95, and 99 percent confidence levels, respectively.

[1] Correlation coefficients with the share of committed funds disbursed are computed excluding precautionary arrangements.

Figure 1

Quality of Institutions in Interrupted and Completed Programs

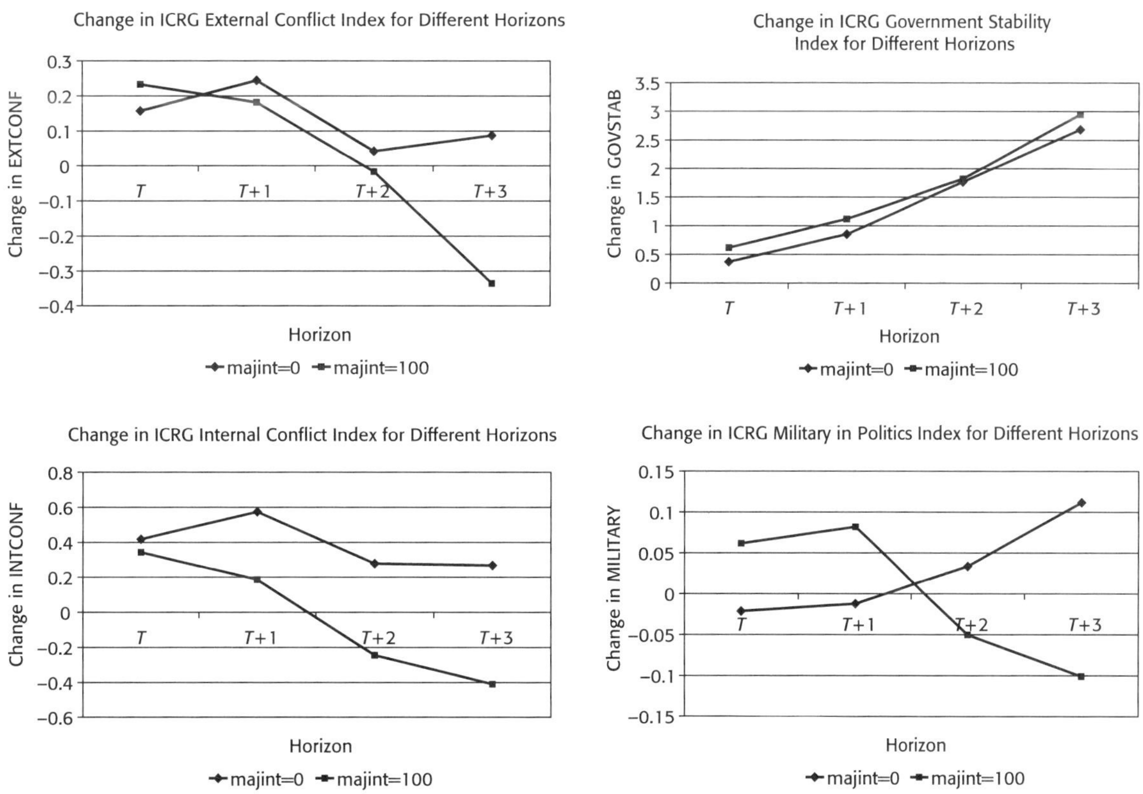

(Figure continues on next page)

Figure 1 (*concluded*)

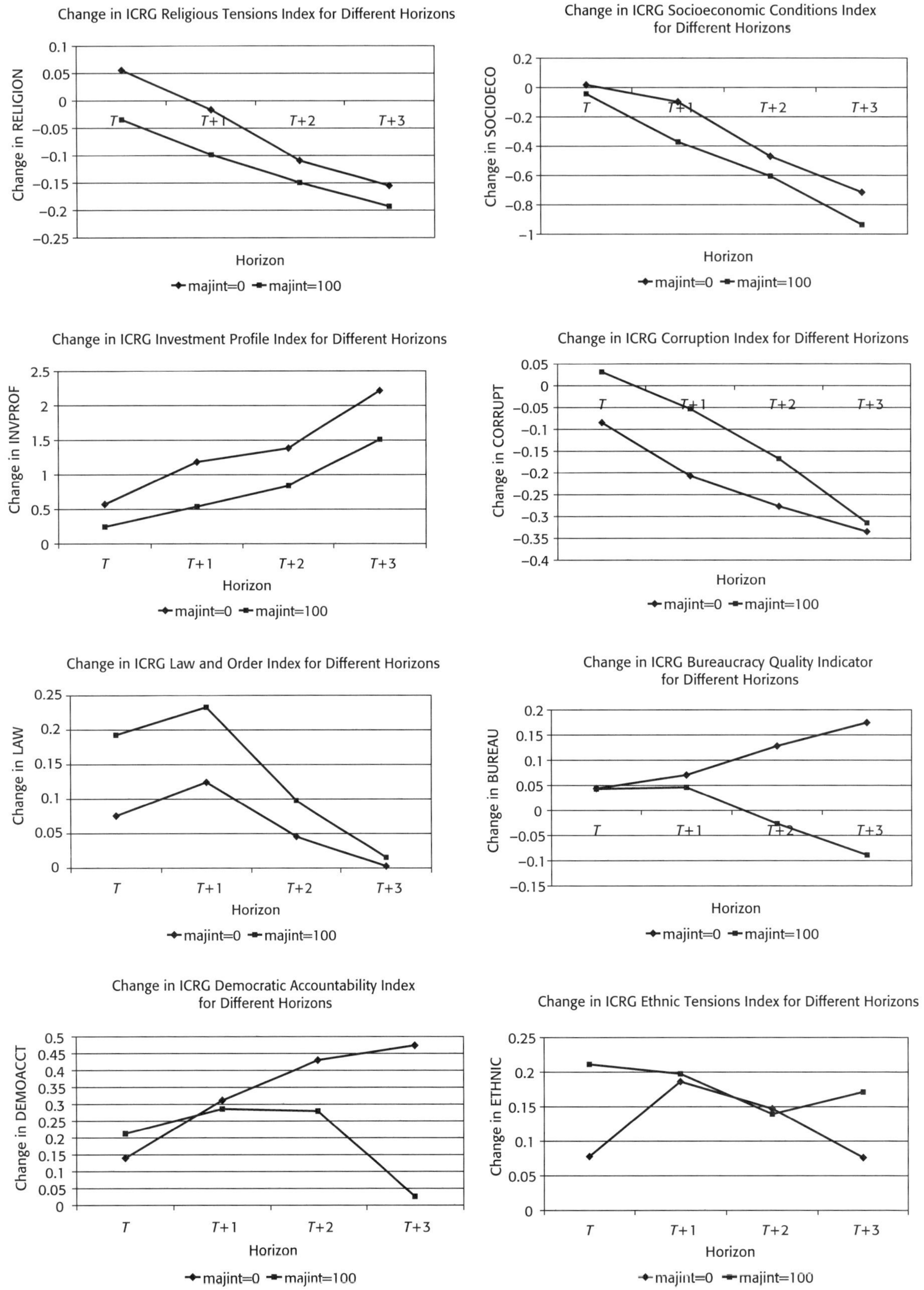

Figure 2
Macroeconomic Performance in Interrupted and Completed Programs

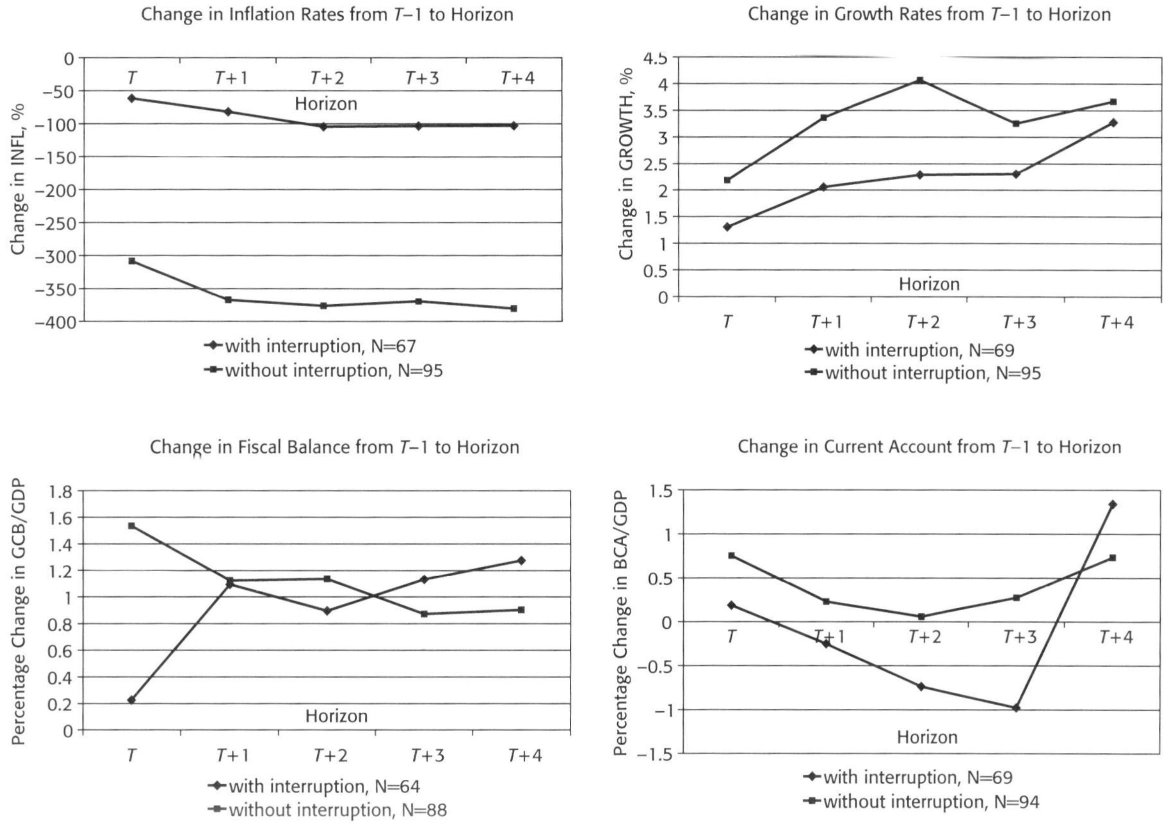

increases in the military's involvement in the third and fourth years after program approval.

Countries completing IMF programs appear to be more successful in reducing inflation than countries that experience program interruptions, as reflected in mean changes in macroeconomic outcomes between period $T-1$ and five different horizons (Figure 2). Uninterrupted programs are also associated with sharp improvements in fiscal balances in the first year of the program, followed by a gradual deterioration in subsequent years. On the other hand, countries whose programs are interrupted register very modest improvements in fiscal balances initially but then catch up with the others. The external current account balance improves in countries whose programs do not get interrupted. Interrupted programs are associated with slight improvements in the current account in the year immediately following program approval, followed by steady deterioration.

Correlation analysis and comparisons of macroeconomic performance in completed versus interrupted programs, although suggestive, mask a great deal of variability in the data. Each country starts from different initial economic, institutional, and political conditions. While they are engaged in IMF-supported programs, countries are subject to a variety of external and internal shocks that influence macroeconomic outcomes and program implementation. We now turn to a more rigorous econometric methodology to properly take into account this broad spectrum of country-specific effects.

Econometric Methodology and Results

Methodology

Most empirical research on the macroeconomic impacts of IMF-supported programs relies on panel data. Our framework, by contrast, relies on a pooled dataset in which each program is treated as an independent observation in the context of a statistical model that takes into account the short-run autoregressive, mean-reverting nature of macroeconomic variables. We assess the impact of program implementation on growth, inflation, and the fiscal and external balances once country-specific institutional and political effects are taken into account. Similar to the "before-and-after approach," our approach compares macroeconomic outcomes under the program with those in the last preprogram year for a sample of countries that chose to participate in such programs. We do not address issues related to sample selection bias, i.e., the systematic differences between countries that agree to participate in IMF-supported programs and those that do not. Our focus is on a narrower question. Given that certain countries do self-select into the "treatment" of IMF-supported programs, we ascertain the relative impacts of program implementation and institutions on macroeconomic outcomes.

Consider $M_{i,T}$, a macroeconomic variable observed at time T in country i. Since we consider macroeconomic development only in countries implementing IMF-supported programs, the index i is also a unique country-program identifier. Following Atoyan and others (2004), the evolution of $M_{i,T}$ can be represented by

$$\Delta M_{i,T} = f(X_{i,T-1}, IMPL_i, INST_{i,T-1}, \Delta INST_{i,T}), \quad (1)$$

where $X_{i,T-1}$ is a vector of noninstitutional forcing variables at time $T-1$ that also includes a random term in time T, $IMPL_i$ is the measure of program implementation in country i, $INST_{i,T-1}$ is a vector of domestic political and institutional initial conditions, $\Delta INST_{i,T}$ is a vector of contemporaneous changes in country i's political and institutional environment, and $f(.)$ is the reduced-form data-generating process.

Hypothesizing that macroeconomic variables are influenced by their own values in previous periods, because of institutional or psychological inertia, we assume that growth, inflation, and the current account and fiscal balances follow a finite-order autoregressive process. Assuming second-order autoregression, the reduced-form model can be conveniently written in the following form:

$$\begin{aligned}\Delta M_{i,T} = {} & \gamma_0 + \gamma_1 \Delta M_{i,T-1} + \gamma_2 M_{i,T-1} \\ & + \gamma_3 IMPL_i + \gamma_4 INST_{i,T-1} \\ & + \gamma_5 \Delta INST_{i,T} + \varepsilon^M_{i,T}, \end{aligned} \quad (2)$$

where $\varepsilon^M_{i,T}$ is a stochastic disturbance to M. Equation (2) is the "autoregressive and mean-reversion form," as it includes both lagged differences and the lagged level as the regressors for the current first-difference of the variable M. It captures the autoregressive structure of M via the first-difference term $\Delta M_{i,T-1}$. The adjustment of M in response to deviations from its "normal" historical value is captured via the mean-reversion term $M_{i,T-1}$. The coefficient γ_2 is a partial adjustment coefficient. It shows what percentage of the deviation from the long-run equilibrium will be covered each year following the deviation. Note that because $\gamma_2 = (\beta_1 + \beta_2 - 1)$ with β_1 and β_2 representing the autoregressive (AR) parameters in the underlying AR(2) process, small negative values of the coefficient are consistent with M being highly persistent.

Equation (2) holds for all T and i, including periods in which IMF-supported programs are in effect. As these programs are designed to improve macroeconomic performance, equation (2) incorporates their impacts into the model. Equation (2) also captures the impact of institutional and political conditions on the macroeconomy. In implementing equation (2), we treat institutional and political developments during the IMF-supported program as exogenous and mean-reverting. Including first differences and lagged levels of institutional variables in the regressions assumes that there are long-run levels of institutional development and that deviations from these levels are temporary.[4] This view of institutions is certainly valid in analyzing short-term programs such as Stand-By Arrangements. It is probably less appropriate for programs with greater structural orientations, such as those supported under the Extended Fund Facility and the Poverty Reduction and Growth Facility, which aim to improve the supply response of the economy. The nature of institutional change that takes place in the context of IMF-supported programs is ultimately an empirical question. In the event, there is little correlation in the data between program implementation and institutional development (see Table 2, Panel C).[5]

We estimate the following system of four equations, one for each macroeconomic outcome variable:

$$\begin{aligned}\Delta INFL_{i,T} = {} & \gamma^I_0 + \gamma^I_1 \Delta INFL_{i,T-1} + \gamma^I_2 INFL_{i,T-1} \\ & + \gamma^I_3 IMPL_i + \gamma^I_4 INST_{i,T-1} \\ & + \gamma^I_5 \Delta INST_{i,T} + \varepsilon^I_{i,T}\end{aligned}$$

$$\begin{aligned}\Delta GROWTH_{i,T} = {} & \gamma^G_0 + \gamma^G_1 \Delta GROWTH_{i,T-1} \\ & + \gamma^G_2 GROWTH_{i,T-1} + \gamma^G_3 IMPL_i \\ & + \gamma^G_4 INST_{i,T-1} + \gamma^G_5 \Delta INST_{i,T} + \varepsilon^G_{i,T}\end{aligned}$$

$$\begin{aligned}\Delta GCB_{i,T} = {} & \gamma^B_0 + \gamma^B_1 \Delta GCB_{i,T-1} + \gamma^B_2 GCB_{i,T-1} + \gamma^B_3 IMPL_i \\ & + \gamma^B_4 INST_{i,T-1} + \gamma^B_5 \Delta INST_{i,T} + \varepsilon^B_{i,T}\end{aligned}$$

$$\begin{aligned}\Delta BCA_{i,T} = {} & \gamma^C_0 + \gamma^C_1 \Delta BCA_{i,T-1} + \gamma^C_2 BCA_{i,T-1} + \gamma^C_3 IMPL_i \\ & + \gamma^C_4 INST_{i,T-1} + \gamma^C_5 \Delta INST_{i,T} + \varepsilon^C_{i,T}. \end{aligned} \quad (3)$$

Note that, in equations (3), monetary and fiscal policies are kept in the background. Program implementation serves as a proxy for the impact of macroeconomic policies on macroeconomic outcomes. As in Ivanova and others (2003) and Dollar and Svensson (2000), the probability of implementation of an

[4] Note that excluding contemporaneous changes in institutions from the model addresses a potential endogeneity problem that is present if the error term affecting macroeconomic variables also affects institutional developments during the program period.

[5] An alternative approach would be to run regressions with only first differences of institutional variables. The qualitative results remained unchanged when we reestimated our regressions in this manner. This makes us confident that our results are robust.

IMF-supported program is related to the underlying political and institutional factors in the borrowing country, to the IMF financial and human resource effort in the program, and to initial economic conditions in the country. Although the probability of program implementation is unobservable, it is related to the observable implementation index:

$$IMPL_i = \theta_0 + \theta_1 INST_{i,T-1} + \theta_2 INITIAL_i + \theta_3 FUND_i + \varepsilon_i^{IMPL}. \quad (4)$$

In equation (4), the θs are vectors of coefficients. $INITIAL_i$ is a vector of initial conditions represented by the preprogram values of real GDP per capita, inflation, the GDP growth rate, the current account balance, and the fiscal balance. $FUND_i$ is a vector of program-specific variables that are important in determining program outcomes. These variables are either directly under IMF control or provide information about the nature of the relationship between the country and the IMF. Our regression approach in equation (4) is similar to that used in Ivanova and others (2003).

Since we are interested in several potentially mean-reverting macroeconomic indicators, a vector error correction model (VECM) could be considered. In equation (2), M would then represent a 4×1 vector of variables (inflation, growth rate, fiscal balance, and current account balance). We pursued this approach by estimating the augmented version of the VECM and comparing results with the ones obtained from estimating equations (3). The results confirm the existence of a long-run relationship among some of the macroeconomic variables.[6] On the other hand, the marginal benefit of incorporating this information into our analysis, which focuses on the relative importance of program implementation and institutional factors for macroeconomic outcomes, seems small. If a VECM representation is adopted, the testing down approach on the institutional and political factors yields identical model specification to the one we already have. The estimated coefficients and their significance levels change only marginally relative to those obtained by considering only a variable's own autoregressive and mean-reversion terms. To simplify the presentation and economize on degrees of freedom, we do not present VECM results.[7] These are available on request from the authors.

The properties of the ordinary-least-squares (OLS) estimator in equations (3) depend on the stochastic properties of the explanatory variables, and in particular on whether or not they are distributed independently of the disturbance term. In addition, shocks to macroeconomic outcomes are likely to impact program implementation, implying that $Corr(IMPL_i, \varepsilon_{i,T}^{M}) \neq 0$. Consequently, the OLS estimator is likely to be biased.[8]

We employ two related instrumental variable (IV) techniques to correct for potential endogeneity bias. One is the two-stage-least-squares (2SLS) procedure, where we first regress the program implementation measure on the exogenous variables and a set of instruments that are correlated with the implementation measure but are not related to the error terms in equations (3). In the second stage, we estimate the system of equations (3) by OLS using the predicted values of the implementation measures instead of the actual ones.

In general, it is difficult to find instruments that are related to program implementation but do not systematically affect economic performance. The best candidates are variables that describe the nature of the relationship between member countries and the IMF: a country's quota in the IMF; the cumulative time spent in an IMF-supported program (number of months in program mode since 1980); the amount approved in relation to the country's IMF quota; and the dollar cost of the program starting six months before program approval.[9]

Our second IV procedure is 3SLS. This has the advantage of incorporating information from the cross-correlations of the error terms in equations (3) and producing sharper (more efficient) parameter estimates.[10] To arrive at 3SLS estimates, we use the 2SLS estimates to obtain an estimate of the contemporaneous variance-covariance matrix of the errors in equations (3). Applying the generalized-least-squares method to the transformed single-equation representation of the system yields 3SLS estimates, which are consistent and asymptotically more efficient than 2SLS estimates.

Model Specification

There is a broad consensus that domestic institutions and politics are key determinants of economic performance in countries borrowing from international

[6] The coefficient on the lagged fiscal balance term is significant in the inflation equation. The lagged first difference and the lagged level of inflation are significant in the growth equation. The lagged first difference and the lagged level of the fiscal balance significantly influence the evolution of the current account.

[7] We formally test a set of restrictions that turns the VECM into an autoregressive model. With an exception of the growth equation, we cannot reject the null hypothesis that the data-generating process was indeed just an autoregression (the p-values are 0.15, 0.02, 0.15, and 0.40 for inflation, growth, the fiscal balance, and the current account balance, respectively).

[8] The OLS estimator is still useful in model selection because it is less sensitive than the alternatives to the presence of multicollinearity, errors in variables, or misspecification, particularly in small samples. After relying on OLS to choose an appropriate model, we compare its predictions with those from the same model estimated by alternative means.

[9] An overidentifying restrictions test could not reject the null hypothesis of overidentified restrictions for either implementation measure.

[10] A shock that affects economic growth has informational content for inflation, the fiscal deficit, and the external current account.

financial institutions. There is less agreement on precisely which aspects of the institutional and political environment are especially important. Although all the ICRG indices could be included in the regression analysis, this would lead to collinearity problems and a loss of precision. On the other hand, omitting relevant institutional and political variables would lead to biased estimates.

This dilemma dictates a parsimonious approach to model specification. We use changes in macroeconomic variables over a one-year horizon following program approval as a testing horizon. This implicitly assumes that if a certain institution or political feature is important at high frequencies, it will also be influential over longer horizons. This strategy produces results that are robust with respect to the choice of program implementation measure.

Our model specification technology is described as a "testing down" approach. We start with an unrestricted model that includes all ICRG indices as regressors and then simplify it in light of sample evidence. Specifically, we estimate each of the equations in (3) separately while systematically dropping regressors with low t-statistics. The adjusted R^2 is used as an additional consideration in model selection.

Our results indicate that inflation in program countries is influenced considerably by such institutional factors as the prevalance of law and order, the quality of the bureaucracy, and the country's investment climate. On the political side, only variations in ethnic tension and internal conflict appear to matter for inflation. Economic growth is affected by the investment profile, government stability, and initial socioeconomic conditions.[11] Corruption in the political system, democratic accountability, ethnic tension, external conflict, and military involvement in politics are important for the evolution of fiscal balances. Finally, corruption, ethnic tension and external conflict, government stability, the investment climate, and military participation in the country's political life have significant impacts on the evolution of the current account.

Main Findings

What Determines Program Implementation?

Table 3 presents first-stage regressions of the implementation measures on initial economic conditions, ICRG indicators during the year preceding program approval, and our instruments. To obtain the predicted values used in the second-stage regressions, we employ the complete model (columns 1 and 3). However, to overcome the collinearity problem discussed above, the discussion in the rest of this subsection relies on estimates (columns 2 and 4 of Table 3) that drop some of the ICRG indices that appear to be insignificant.

When the share of committed funds disbursed is used as a measure of program implementation, none of the variables reflecting initial economic conditions is significantly different from zero. This could suggest that programs are tailored to participating countries' circumstances or that their outcomes are independent of initial economic conditions (see Ivanova and others, 2003).

Reduced ethnic tension and greater government stability before program approval improve program implementation. Coefficients on the ICRG ratings of ethnic tensions and government stability in the year preceding program approval are positive and significant. In addition to a larger proportion of funds being disbursed in countries where racial and ethnic tensions are less pronounced, better program implementation is positively correlated with the general public's perception of a government's ability to carry out its declared programs. Other factors remaining the same, a one-point increase in either rating raises disbursements by about 8 percent.

Reductions in internal conflict and improvements in law and order in the year before program approval are associated with lower disbursements. The coefficient on the initial level of the internal conflict index is negative and highly significant. The magnitude of the effect is rather large: a one-point increase in the rating would lower disbursements by just over 6 percent. The coefficient on the initial level of the law and order rating is also negative and significant. These results may reflect the IMF's financial involvement in countries where observance of the law is not very good initially, often because the countries are recovering from conflict.

There is some evidence that greater initial involvement by the military in politics is associated with lower disbursements of IMF financing. The coefficient on the corresponding ICRG index is positive and significant.

Countries with a history of IMF-supported programs seem to have higher disbursement shares. Every additional month spent in IMF-supported programs translates into 0.2 percent more funds disbursed. Taken literally, higher disbursement ratios could manifest better program design and implementation, and the length of IMF engagement simply reflects the long-term nature of the needs of these low- and middle-income countries. But the reasons for—and results of—prolonged financial association between member countries and the IMF are complex (see IMF, 2002 for a recent evaluation).

The size of programs, as measured by the amount of IMF financing committed in relation to a country's quota, appears to be important in determining program outcomes. Countries with larger programs tend to have higher disbursement shares. These

[11] Contemporaneous changes in socioeconomic conditions are excluded from the analysis. This avoids the problems associated with dependent variables appearing on the right-hand side of the equation.

Table 3
Determinants of Program Implementation: First-Stage Regressions

Dependent Variable	Disbursement Share[1,3,4]		Irreversible Interruption Index[2,3,4]	
Regression number	(1)	(2)	(3)	(4)
Intercept	0.680**	0.848***	−0.397	−0.085
Initial per capita real GDP	−0.012	−0.013	−0.066	−0.072
INFL (*T*−1)	0.0002	0.0002	0.002	0.002
GCB_Y (*T*−1)	0.116	0.209	−3.509	−3.230
BCA_Y (*T*−1)	0.091	0.049	−0.753	−1.198
GROWTH (*T*−1)	−0.002	−0.003	0.046	0.056*
Bureaucracy quality (*T*−1)	−0.017		−0.070	
Corruption (*T*−1)	0.006		0.322*	0.358**
Democratic accountability (*T*−1)	−0.019		−0.104	
Ethnic tensions (*T*−1)	0.073**	0.076**	0.097	
External conflict (*T*−1)	0.006		−0.034	
Government stability (*T*−1)	0.071*	0.078**	0.044	
Internal conflict (*T*−1)	−0.061**	−0.062***	−0.221*	−0.217**
Investment profile (*T*−1)	0.021		0.090	
Military in politics (*T*−1)	0.041	0.044*	0.101	
Religion tensions (*T*−1)	0.019		0.144	0.189
Socioeconomic (*T*−1)	−0.008		0.040	
Law and order (*T*−1)	−0.066	−0.069*	−0.092	
Fund effort per program year	0.041	0.043*	0.036	0.050
Fund quota (log)	−0.034	−0.046	0.095	0.052
Number of months spent in IMF programs	0.002**	0.002**	−0.002	−0.0003
Amount approved as a fraction of quota	0.024**	0.025**	0.088	0.094
Dummy for precautionary arrangement	−1.121***	−1.109***		
Observations	115	115	115	115
Log likelihood	−14.695	−15.676	−61.998	−63.251
Correlation coefficient/correctly predicted *(percent)*	0.807	0.803	75.66	75.66

Notes: The symbols *, **, and *** denote significance at the 90, 95, and 99 percent confidence levels, respectively.
[1] Results are obtained using the tobit model: $y=\max(X'\beta+\varepsilon,0)$.
[2] Results are obtained using the probit model. Parameter estimates are computed to reflect the probability of no irreversible interruption: $Pr(\text{Interruption}=0)=F(X'\beta)$, where F is normal cumulative distribution function.
[3] The chi-square statistics for the estimated parameters are available from the authors upon request.
[4] All regressions include year dummies.

packages are often provided in response to capital account emergencies. They require not only more financing but also greater front-loading of assistance than suggested by usual IMF phasing rules.

The IMF's effort at program design and implementation, as measured by staff hours and the dollar cost of staff resources, is only marginally important in raising a program's prospects of success. Although larger quotas have an ambiguous net effect on program implementation a priori (see Box 1), the coefficient on the country's IMF quota is negative, suggesting that the implementation of IMF-supported programs could be weaker in countries with larger IMF quotas.

Our findings are broadly similar when the interruption index is used as the measure of program implementation. Almost all the variables describing the initial economic conditions of participating countries have insignificant coefficients. The only exception is the lagged level of a country's growth rate, which has a marginally significant coefficient. This can be interpreted as evidence that countries that were growing relatively fast before program initiation are less likely to have an irreversible interruption of the program.

Reduced government corruption has a strikingly positive impact on the probability of successful program implementation. The coefficient on the preprogram level of corruption is positive and significant, and its magnitude is impressive. On average, a one-point improvement in the ICRG corruption index, all other determinants of program success

Box 1. List of Instrumental Variables

The outcomes of IMF-supported programs are endogenous. Instrumental variables (IVs) help us obtain unbiased estimates of the impact of IMF-supported programs on the economic performance of participating countries. The instruments must be correlated with program implementation (lack of program interruptions and the share of committed funds disbursed) and not be direct determinants of the economic policy outcomes (inflation, economic growth, fiscal balance, and current account). The following IVs are used in the analysis:

IMF quota (log). A country's quota determines the member's voting power in the IMF. Countries with larger quotas have more bargaining power and systemic importance in the world economy. Greater bargaining power could allow countries to extract more concessions from the IMF, leading to less conditionality and more lenient IMF treatment. The coefficient on the IMF quota in the implementation measure regressions would then be positive. On the other hand, the size of the quota also reflects a country's systemic importance in the world economy and its access to international capital markets. Governments of large countries might be less cooperative with IMF conditionality if the perceived political costs were too high. In that case, the parameter estimate could have a negative sign.

Number of months spent in IMF programs since 1980. This variable captures the extent of a country's financial involvement with the IMF. The length of the country's history under IMF-supported programs could lead, through learning-by-doing, to better program design and higher implementation rates as government officials and IMF staff gain more experience and knowledge of country-specific factors and IMF procedures.

Amount approved as a fraction of IMF quota. This variable is expected to capture the financial importance of a particular program. Large values would be positively correlated with the severity of crises and the willingness of the authorities to implement IMF-supported reforms.

IMF effort per program year, including six months prior to program approval. This is a direct measure of the dollar cost of IMF programs. It is computed from the IMF's Budget Reporting System data on hours spent by staff on program implementation and estimated average staff salaries by grade. More effort invested in program implementation is expected to be positively correlated with program implementation.

held constant, coincides with a 35.8 percent better chance of having no program interruption.

As in the regressions using the disbursement share as the measure of program implementation, the coefficient on the initial level of internal conflict is negative and significant, and for similar reasons. The coefficient on the preprogram level of political violence is negative: an improvement in this rating by one point is associated with a 21.7 percent higher chance of an irreversible interruption.

With the exception of the coefficient on the number of months spent in program mode, the variables characterizing the relationship between a country and the IMF enter the regression with the expected signs. However, none of the coefficients is significantly different from zero. As in Ivanova and others (2003), this result suggests that the implementation of IMF-supported programs is largely determined by the country's domestic political economy and institutions. Variables under IMF control have only a marginal impact on program outcomes.

What Determines Macroeconomic Outcomes?

This subsection summarizes the empirical links among macroeconomic performance, the institutional and political environment, and program implementation (Tables 4 through 11). In all the regressions in these tables, the dependent variable is the change in the macroeconomic outcome between period $T-1$ (the preprogram year) and the end of the first, second, or third years after program approval (T, $T+1$, or $T+2$). Each table reports OLS, 2SLS, and 3SLS estimates, using the disbursement share or lack of program interruptions as the measure of program performance. Unless otherwise noted, in what follows we will refer to results obtained using the 3SLS procedure and the disbursement share as the measure of program implementation.

Inflation

Inflation is highly persistent in program countries. The coefficients on lagged inflation are highly significant for all horizons (Tables 4 and 5). For the average program, about three quarters of any deviation from "normal" inflation after a program is approved is reversed within a year. Deviations of inflation from its long-run equilibrium are erased almost completely in three years.

In contrast to many other studies, which were unable to link IMF-supported programs with price stability, our findings represent reasonable evidence that better program implementation leads to lower inflation. After correcting for endogeneity bias, the coefficients on the disbursement share have a negative sign and decline in absolute value for each of the three years following program approval, although only the result for the first year is statistically

Table 4

Program Implementation, Institutions, and Inflation: Regressions Using the Share of Committed Funds Disbursed

Dependent Variable	ΔINFL (T−1 to horizon)								
Regression number	(1)	(2)	(3)	(4)	(5)	(6)	(7)	(8)	(9)
	OLS			2SLS			3SLS		
Horizon	*T*	*T*+1	*T*+2	*T*	*T*+1	*T*+2	*T*	*T*+1	*T*+2
Disbursement share	13.862	−55.659	2.778	−140.87	−90.624	−9.000	−150.828*	−103.740	−12.621
RGDPPC (*T*−1)	−8.361**	−6.406*	−0.277	−10.622***	−7.222*	−0.643	−10.602***	−7.013*	−0.474
ΔINFL (*T*−1)	−0.158	0.0003	−0.001	−0.214**	−0.002	−0.001	−0.180*	−0.004	−0.002
INFL (*T*−1)	−0.731***	−0.958***	−0.976***	−0.682***	−0.950***	−0.977***	−0.739***	−0.954***	−0.975***
Bureaucracy quality (*T*−1)	−26.488**	−12.571	−4.100	−27.744**	−13.581	−4.317*	−27.964**	−12.012	−5.537***
Change in bureaucracy quality (*T*−1 to horizon)	−46.700	−11.681	−2.909	−73.494*	−14.381	−4.211	−74.746**	−14.256	−3.954
Ethnic conflict (*T*−1)	−15.834	−5.164	−1.969	−6.632	−4.066	−1.299	−4.275	2.152	1.031
Change in ethnic conflict (*T*−1 to horizon)	−5.246	−12.083	−3.455	−11.568	−12.110	−4.060	−12.868	−12.904	−4.606*
Internal conflict (*T*−1)	13.151**	7.478	1.033	6.974	6.149	0.061	6.605	7.658	0.330
Change in internal conflict (*T*−1 to horizon)	17.336*	11.734	−0.425	23.794**	12.419	−0.154	24.206**	13.982*	−0.461
Investment profile (*T*−1)	−9.834	3.493	−0.809	−2.854	3.715	−0.110	−2.784	3.456	0.487
Change in investment profile (*T*−1 to horizon)	−17.426	−3.723	−1.623	−19.212	−7.275	−1.851	−19.558	−9.327	−1.566
Law and order (*T*−1)	12.738	5.862	5.700**	14.470	8.730	7.348***	12.342	5.639	6.603***
Change in law and order (*T*−1 to horizon)	−87.059***	−34.277	1.430	−86.529***	−30.469	2.516	−84.579***	−22.859	4.800*
Observations	123	122	116	115	115	109	115	115	109
R^2	0.586	0.596	0.982	0.626	0.592	0.983	0.625	0.590	0.983

Notes: OLS denotes ordinary least squares; 2SLS denotes two-stage least squares; and 3SLS denotes three-stage least squares. The symbols *, **, and *** denote significance at the 90, 95, and 99 percent confidence levels, respectively. Standard deviations and *t*-statistics for the estimated parameters are available from the authors upon request. All regressions include intercept, precautionary arrangement, and year dummies.

significant.[12] A similar pattern is observed when the lack of program interruptions is considered as the measure of program implementation. The absence of program interruptions is correlated with greater price stability in the year following program approval, followed by slightly higher inflation rates over longer horizons. However, these results are only marginally significant.

Better institutions also lead to lower inflation in countries implementing IMF-supported programs.[13] Inflation is lower, the better is the government bureaucracy at the start of the program and the more it improves subsequently. The importance of the quality of the bureaucracy index is highest in the first year of the program and declines afterward. Inflation is also lower, the more the legal system improves and the more the public observes the law. Interestingly, a higher degree of law and order before the start of the program and improvements in this regard during the program are associated with slightly higher inflation at horizon *T*+2.

The role of political factors in inflation performance in countries under IMF-supported programs is more difficult to interpret. Lower inflation is associated with increased political violence in the first two years of the program. Tight demand-side policies that succeed in reducing inflation could also trigger public protests against austerity, as has occasionally been the case in countries implementing IMF-supported programs.[14]

Recognizing that cross-country inflation regressions are dominated by outliers, we also examine whether ethnic tensions and internal conflicts are still the primary determinants of inflation when such observations are excluded from the sample. We

[12] The inflation dynamics reported here are similar to those in Conway (1994). Killick (1995) finds reduction in inflation to be significant. Barro and Lee (2002) reports coefficients on contemporaneous and lagged IMF loans that are similar in sign but insignificant.

[13] Our findings on the impact of institutions on macroeconomic performance in program countries are robust to the choice of implementation measure.

[14] This cannot be formally tested in our model, because we treat political variables as exogenous.

Table 5

Program Implementation, Institutions, and Inflation: Regressions Using Irreversible Interruption Index

Dependent Variable	ΔINFL (T–1 to horizon)								
Regression number	(1)	(2)	(3)	(4)	(5)	(6)	(7)	(8)	(9)
	OLS			2SLS			3SLS		
Horizon	*T*	*T*+1	*T*+2	*T*	*T*+1	*T*+2	*T*	*T*+1	*T*+2
Non–interruption dummy	1.364	–18.019	3.400	–38.409	28.532	16.575*	–32.152	29.726	13.730
RGDPPC (*T*–1)	–7.688**	–6.026*	–0.262	–10.512***	–6.447	–0.329	–10.182***	–6.241	–0.195
ΔINFL (*T*–1)	–0.165	–0.002	–0.001	–0.207*	–0.001	0.001	–0.172	–0.003	–0.001
INFL (*T*–1)	–0.724***	–0.957***	–0.977***	–0.706***	–0.986***	–0.991***	–0.769***	–0.992***	–0.984***
Bureaucracy quality (*T*–1)	–25.676**	–14.196	–4.103	–25.351*	–13.776	–4.125*	–25.928**	–12.195	–5.463**
Change in bureaucracy quality (*T*–1 to horizon)	–38.449	–13.225	–2.957	–63.094*	–13.866	–3.911	–66.295*	–14.974	–4.020
Ethnic conflict (*T*–1)	–12.467	–8.963	–1.694	–10.522	–11.185	–2.043	–7.869	–10.586	–2.102
Change in ethnic conflict (*T*–1 to horizon)	–5.445	–12.690	–3.344	–7.393	–10.723	–3.092	–8.472	–12.180	–3.885
Internal conflict (*T*–1)	12.615**	8.928	1.082	8.375	10.639	1.211	8.677	12.822	1.279
Change in internal conflict (*T*–1 to horizon)	17.151*	12.357*	–0.481	19.309*	12.131	–0.501	20.607**	14.480*	–0.637
Investment profile (*T*–1)	–8.569	1.037	–0.842	–4.825	–1.951	–1.231	–6.345	–2.885	–0.315
Change in investment profile (*T*–1 to horizon)	–16.780	–4.559	–1.737	–17.045	–7.490	–1.706	–18.050	–9.764	–1.355
Law and order (*T*–1)	11.033	8.005	2.480**	18.171	9.767	6.592**	15.386	6.772	6.285***
Change in law and order (*T*–1 to horizon)	–85.731***	–36.979	1.589	–83.905***	–34.745	2.187	–82.277***	–28.345	4.010
Observations	126	123	116	115	115	109	115	115	109
R^2	0.582	0.589	0.982	0.617	0.589	0.984	0.614	0.587	0.983

Notes: OLS denotes ordinary least squares; 2SLS denotes two-stage least squares; and 3SLS denotes three-stage least squares. The symbols *, **, and *** denote significance at the 90, 95, and 99 percent confidence levels, respectively. Standard deviations and *t*-statistics for the estimated parameters are available from the authors upon request. All regressions include intercept and year dummies.

reestimate the model on a sample that excludes all observations with annual change in inflation greater than 50 percent, which cuts the sample size by approximately 30 percent. The results are somewhat reassuring. In the inflation equation, ethnic tensions still play an important role in determining the evolution of inflation. Internal conflicts become insignificant but, by contrast, government stability turns out to be significant. This is not very surprising since the two indices are highly correlated in our sample.

Growth

Economic growth is highly serially correlated and mean-reverting during the course of IMF-supported programs (Tables 6 and 7). As in the case of inflation, deviations of the growth rate from long-run equilibrium are very short lived. Approximately 90 percent of any deviation in growth rates from the country's "normal" growth pattern is made up within three years. The largest adjustment, 83–84 percent, occurs within one year after the realization of the shock.

At first glance, better program implementation appears to be associated with more rapid economic growth, as suggested by positive and significant estimated coefficients in OLS regressions of the disbursement share. Unfortunately, this result is not robust—it appears to be driven by the endogeneity of program implementation. The corresponding 2SLS and 3SLS estimates are positive at all horizons, but the parameters are not significantly different from zero. In addition, the impact of program performance on economic growth is fragile to the choice of implementation measure. Although fewer program interruptions appear to be associated with higher growth rates, the OLS results are not significant, and the coefficients turn negative when IV techniques are used.

These mixed findings are consistent with those of the existing literature. Recovery of growth rates from the initial drop (a V-shaped response of output) was reported by Conway (1994). Khan (1990) and Przeworski and Vreeland (2000) find significantly

Table 6

Program Implementation, Institutions, and Growth: Regressions Using the Share of Committed Funds Disbursed

Dependent Variable	ΔGROWTH (T−1 to horizon)								
Regression number	(1)	(2)	(3)	(4)	(5)	(6)	(7)	(8)	(9)
	OLS			2SLS			3SLS		
Horizon	*T*	*T*+1	*T*+2	*T*	*T*+1	*T*+2	*T*	*T*+1	*T*+2
Disbursement share	2.814*	2.331*	1.412	2.607	0.484	2.921	2.579	0.639	2.309
RGDPPC (*T*−1)	0.209	0.169	0.551***	0.277*	0.077	0.515***	0.266*	0.072	0.534***
Δ*GROWTH* (*T*−1)	−0.205**	−0.203***	−0.017	−0.249***	−0.248***	−0.023	−0.210***	−0.212***	−0.033
GROWTH (*T*−1)	−0.850***	−0.785***	−0.946***	−0.829***	−0.758***	−0.931***	−0.840***	−0.753***	−0.896***
Government stability (*T*−1)	0.471	0.463	0.049	0.163	0.369	0.097	−0.025	0.299	−0.076
Change in government stability (*T*−1 to horizon)	1.185**	0.364	0.023	1.022*	0.330	0.062	1.117**	0.305	−0.250
Investment profile (*T*−1)	−0.578	0.216	0.634	−0.623	−0.049	0.463	−0.568	−0.042	0.462
Change in investment profile (*T*−1 to horizon)	0.963*	1.079***	0.841***	1.228**	0.764**	0.849**	1.029**	0.678**	0.857**
Socioeconomic (*T*−1)	−0.536	−0.607	−0.013	−0.525	−0.467	0.019	−0.420	−0.529	−0.036
Observations	125	124	118	115	115	109	115	115	109
R^2	0.687	0.744	0.660	0.704	0.744	0.641	0.701	0.743	0.638

Notes: OLS denotes ordinary least squares; 2SLS denotes two-stage least squares; and 3SLS denotes three-stage least squares. The symbols *, **, and *** denote significance at the 90, 95, and 99 percent confidence levels, respectively. Standard deviations and *t*-statistics for the estimated parameters are available from the authors upon request. All regressions include intercept, precautionary arrangement, and year dummies.

Table 7

Program Implementation, Institutions, and Growth: Regressions Using the Irreversible Interruption Index

Dependent Variable	ΔGROWTH (T−1 to horizon)								
Regression number	(1)	(2)	(3)	(4)	(5)	(6)	(7)	(8)	(9)
	OLS			2SLS			3SLS		
Horizon	*T*	*T*+1	*T*+2	*T*	*T*+1	*T*+2	*T*	*T*+1	*T*+2
Non-interruption dummy	0.555	0.825	0.195	−0.443	−0.388	−0.321	−0.544	−0.529	−0.268
RGDPPC (*T*−1)	0.144	0.177	0.566***	0.204	0.081	0.536***	0.190	0.070	0.525***
Δ*GROWTH* (*T*−1)	−0.199**	−0.208***	−0.039	−0.250***	−0.242***	−0.035	−0.211**	−0.208***	−0.050
GROWTH (*T*−1)	−0.857***	−0.789***	−0.931***	−0.829***	−0.757***	−0.920***	−0.842***	−0.759***	−0.898***
Government stability (*T*−1)	0.354	0.483	0.095	0.094	0.369	0.091	−0.103	0.300	−0.058
Change in government stability (*T*−1 to horizon)	0.894*	0.400	0.080	0.873	0.350	0.063	0.992*	0.326	−0.210
Investment profile (*T*−1)	−0.378	0.137	0.480	−0.335	−0.127	0.374	−0.306	−0.085	0.334
Change in investment profile (*T*−1 to horizon)	1.120**	1.013***	0.784***	1.372**	0.700**	0.736**	1.143**	0.620**	0.738**
Socioeconomic (*T*−1)	−0.398	−0.639*	−0.078	−0.481	−0.494	−0.049	−0.370	−0.543	−0.107
Observations	128	125	118	115	115	109	115	115	109
R^2	0.677	0.736	0.649	0.692	0.742	0.631	0.690	0.740	0.629

Notes: OLS denotes ordinary least squares; 2SLS denotes two-stage least squares; and 3SLS denotes three-stage least squares. The symbols *, **, and *** denote significance at the 90, 95, and 99 percent confidence levels, respectively. Standard deviations and *t*-statistics for the estimated parameters are available from the authors upon request. All regressions include intercept and year dummies.

Table 8

Program Implementation, Institutions, and Fiscal Balance (Ratio to GDP): Regressions Using the Share of Committed Funds Disbursed

Dependent Variable	ΔGCB_Y ($T-1$ to horizon)								
Regression number	(1)	(2)	(3)	(4)	(5)	(6)	(7)	(8)	(9)
	OLS			2SLS			3SLS		
Horizon	*T*	*T*+1	*T*+2	*T*	*T*+1	*T*+2	*T*	*T*+1	*T*+2
Disbursement share	0.024**	0.020**	0.013	−0.013	−0.039**	−0.021	−0.024	−0.038*	−0.019
RGDPPC (*T*−1)	0.002**	0.0003	−0.0006	0.002**	−0.001	−0.001	0.002*	−0.001	−0.001
Δ*GCB_Y* (*T*−1)	0.156*	−0.349***	−0.131	0.161**	−0.323***	−0.096	0.100	−0.321***	−0.059
GCB_Y (*T*−1)	−0.623***	−0.523***	−0.434***	−0.651***	−0.497***	−0.527***	−0.451***	−0.472***	−0.558***
Corruption (*T*−1)	−0.010***	−0.005	−0.006	−0.009**	−0.006	−0.006	−0.006*	−0.006*	−0.006
Change in corruption (*T*−1 to horizon)	−0.008	0.005	0.002	−0.008	0.003	0.003	−0.003	0.002	−0.001
Democratic accountability (*T*−1)	0.001	0.002	0.007	0.002	−0.003	−0.001	−0.002	−0.002	0.002
Change in democratic accountability (*T*−1 to horizon)	−0.008	−0.007*	0.0007	−0.009*	−0.008**	−0.004	−0.008*	−0.008**	0.0004
Ethnic conflict (*T*−1)	0.001	−0.005*	−0.004	0.001	−0.002	−0.001	0.001	−0.002	−0.002
Change in ethnic conflict (*T*−1 to horizon)	−0.015**	0.0006	−0.005	−0.016**	−0.003	−0.006	−0.015**	−0.004	−0.007
External conflict (*T*−1)	0.004*	0.005*	0.004	0.002	0.003	0.003	0.003	0.003	0.004
Change in external conflict (*T*−1 to horizon)	0.009***	0.004	0.005	0.006*	0.002	0.001	0.006**	0.003	0.003
Military in politics (*T*−1)	0.004**	0.003	0.002	0.003	0.005**	0.003	0.003	0.004*	0.003
Change in military in politics (*T*−1 to horizon)	0.006	0.0007	−0.005	0.008	−0.001	−0.006	0.001	−0.001	−0.005
Observations	119	118	112	115	115	109	115	115	109
R^2	0.510	0.603	0.392	0.505	0.639	0.456	0.472	0.637	0.443

Notes: OLS denotes ordinary least squares; 2SLS denotes two–stage least squares; and 3SLS denotes three-stage least squares. The symbols *, **, and *** denote significance at the 90, 95, and 99 percent confidence levels, respectively. Standard deviations and *t*-statistics for the estimated parameters are available from the authors upon request. All regressions include intercept, precautionary arrangement, and year dummies.

negative effects of IMF program participation on economic growth. At the same time, Killick (1995), Bagci and Perraudin (1997), and Dicks-Mireaux, Mecagni, and Schadler (2000) report positive and significant effects. One possibility is that the extent of program implementation does matter for economic growth, but that the leads are greater than three years and therefore we have been unable to capture them. Certainly the structural reforms of many programs in the 1990s took a long time to come to fruition. Many countries—including transition economies—began to experience faster growth only in the late 1990s; such a delayed response would not be captured in our methodology.

Not surprisingly, improvements in institutions during the course of program implementation are associated with better growth performance. This is most evident in the case of the investment profile, which measures the risk to foreign business operations in the country, including risk of repatriation of profits. A one-point increase in the ICRG Investment Profile rating is associated with roughly a 1 percent increase in the growth rate, and this result is robust to the length of the horizon and the choice of estimation technique. Improvements in the ability of the government to stay in office, which are influenced by the cohesion of the government and by the extent of the public's approval of its policies, appear to have a significant positive impact on growth, at least in the first year of a program. These findings are robust to the choice of implementation measure and to omitting outliers.[15]

Public Finances

The fiscal balance (in relation to GDP) is persistent and mean-reverting, but less so than inflation and growth. Improvements in the fiscal balance persist for two years but are then reversed (Tables 8 and 9). This pattern could be consistent with governments implementing IMF-supported reforms aiming to balance their budgets over a four-year horizon. The

[15] We define outliers as countries growing or shrinking by more than 10 percent a year.

Table 9
Program Implementation, Institutions, and Fiscal Balance (Ratio to GDP): Regressions Using the Irreversible Interruption Index

Dependent Variable	ΔGCB_Y (T–1 to horizon)								
Regression number	(1)	(2)	(3)	(4)	(5)	(6)	(7)	(8)	(9)
	OLS			2SLS			3SLS		
Horizon	*T*	*T*+1	*T*+2	*T*	*T*+1	*T*+2	*T*	*T*+1	*T*+2
Non-interruption dummy	0.016***	0.014**	0.008	–0.010	–0.023	–0.035*	–0.022	–0.020	–0.032*
RGDPPC (*T*–1)	0.002*	0.001	–0.001	0.002*	–0.001	–0.001	0.002	–0.001	–0.001
Δ*GCB_Y* (*T*–1)	0.190**	–0.354***	–0.141	0.168**	–0.308***	–0.089	0.099	–0.310***	–0.057
GCB_Y (*T*–1)	–0.576***	–0.534***	–0.433***	–0.632***	–0.508***	–0.522***	–0.436***	–0.484***	–0.558***
Corruption (*T*–1)	–0.012***	–0.007*	–0.007	–0.008*	–0.003	–0.002	–0.004	–0.004	–0.004
Change in corruption (*T*–1 to horizon)	–0.008	0.003	0.001	–0.007	0.003	0.004	–0.002	0.001	–0.0003
Democratic accountability (*T*–1)	0.002	0.003	0.007	0.002	–0.003	–0.002	–0.002	–0.002	0.002
Change in democratic accountability (*T*–1 to horizon)	–0.006	–0.008*	0.0002	–0.008	–0.008**	–0.003	–0.007*	–0.008**	0.00003
Ethnic conflict (*T*–1)	0.002	–0.004	–0.004	0.002	–0.003	–0.002	0.001	–0.003	–0.002
Change in ethnic conflict (*T*–1 to horizon)	–0.014**	0.001	–0.005	–0.016**	–0.004	–0.006	–0.015**	–0.004	–0.007
External conflict (*T*–1)	0.003*	0.005**	0.005	0.002	0.003	0.002	0.003	0.003	0.004
Change in external conflict (*T*–1 to horizon)	0.008***	0.005*	0.005	0.007**	0.002	0.001	0.007**	0.003	0.003
Military in politics (*T*–1)	0.005**	0.003	0.002	0.003	0.004**	0.003	0.004*	0.004*	0.002
Change in military in politics (*T*–1 to horizon)	0.008	0.003	–0.004	0.008	–0.002	–0.006	0.001	–0.001	–0.005
Number of observations	122	119	112	115	115	109	115	115	109
R^2	0.499	0.609	0.392	0.492	0.634	0.471	0.458	0.631	0.459

Notes: OLS denotes ordinary least squares; 2SLS denotes two-stage least squares; and 3SLS denotes three-stage least squares. The symbols *, **, and *** denote significance at the 90, 95, and 99 percent confidence levels, respectively. Standard deviations and *t*-statistics for the estimated parameters are available from the authors upon request. All regressions include intercept and year dummies.

mean-reversion term is highly significant. Approximately 45 percent of any deviation of the fiscal balance from its long-run average is offset within a year. The speed of adjustment is much slower than for inflation or growth.

As in the regressions explaining growth, program implementation appears to be associated with improvements in the public finances when simultaneity bias issues are ignored, but these results are reversed in the regressions using IV approaches. Regardless of the choice of implementation measure, the OLS estimates are positive and significant for the first two years, whereas the 2SLS and 3SLS estimates are negative. If anything, better program implementation seems to be associated with larger fiscal deficits: IV estimates of the coefficient on the disbursement share two years after program approval are significant.[16] The results are similar when the lack of program interruptions measure is considered. They suggest that fiscal deficits in countries with completed programs are about 3 percent larger than in countries whose programs were interrupted.

This finding and our similar finding for the current account balance (see the subsequent discussion) likely reflect the impact of additional financial resources flowing into countries that are successful in implementing IMF-supported reforms. Better program implementation makes more financing available to countries participating in IMF-supported programs, which allows more gradual adjustment and larger fiscal and external deficits.

The most important institutional factor influencing fiscal outcomes is the initial level of corruption, but its effect is anomalous. Lower corruption is associated with weaker fiscal outcomes over time. We do not have a good explanation for this result.

Several aspects of the political environment play an important role in determining fiscal outcomes in countries with IMF-supported programs. First, improvements in the government's responsiveness to its people are associated with larger deficits. This

[16] Schadler and others (1993) also find some evidence of negative effects of IMF lending on the fiscal balance. By contrast, Conway (1994) finds significant fiscal deficit reduction.

Table 10

Program Implementation, Institutions, and Current Account (Ratio to GDP): Regressions Using the Share of Committed Funds Disbursed

Dependent Variable	ΔBCA_Y ($T-1$ to horizon)								
Regression number	(1)	(2)	(3)	(4)	(5)	(6)	(7)	(8)	(9)
	OLS			2SLS			3SLS		
Horizon	*T*	*T*+1	*T*+2	*T*	*T*+1	*T*+2	*T*	*T*+1	*T*+2
Disbursement share	0.008	0.022	0.060***	−0.082**	−0.039	0.024	−0.080**	−0.038	0.020
RGDPPC (*T*−1)	−0.0008	−0.001	0.0006	−0.002	−0.003	−0.0001	−0.002	−0.003	−0.0001
ΔBCA_Y (*T*−1)	−0.145	−0.172*	−0.118	−0.215**	−0.195*	−0.155	−0.160*	−0.190*	−0.157
BCA_Y (*T*−1)	−0.157**	−0.217**	−0.371***	−0.149**	−0.125	−0.394***	−0.114*	−0.143*	−0.435***
Corruption (*T*−1)	−0.011	−0.005	−0.014*	−0.007	−0.002	−0.016**	−0.006	−0.002	−0.017**
Change in corruption (*T*−1 to horizon)	−0.002	−0.005	0.009	0.002	−0.001	−0.002	0.002	−0.003	−0.002
Ethnic conflict (*T*−1)	−0.008*	−0.008	−0.002	−0.006	−0.007	0.001	−0.006	−0.007	0.001
Change in ethnic conflict (*T*−1 to horizon)	−0.010	−0.002	−0.008	−0.016*	−0.016*	−0.006	−0.016*	−0.015	−0.006
External conflict (*T*−1)	0.003	0.0001	−0.0001	0.001	−0.003	−0.003	0.001	−0.002	−0.003
Change in external conflict (*T*−1 to Horizon)	0.008	−0.0008	−0.005	0.003	−0.002	−0.010**	0.004	−0.002	−0.012**
Government stability (*T*−1)	0.014***	0.013*	0.010	0.009*	0.010	0.002	0.008*	0.010	0.002
Change in government stability (*T*−1 to horizon)	−0.004	0.005	−0.002	−0.005	0.005	−0.007	−0.003	0.004	−0.007
Investment profile (*T*−1)	−0.014***	−0.013**	−0.009*	−0.009**	−0.010*	−0.006	−0.008**	−0.011**	−0.006**
Change in investment profile (*T*−1 to horizon)	−0.016***	−0.018***	−0.007*	−0.016***	−0.015***	−0.003	−0.019***	−0.016***	−0.003
Military in politics (*T*−1)	0.011***	0.012***	0.010**	0.007**	0.010**	0.008*	0.007**	0.010**	0.008*
Change in military in politics (*T*−1 to horizon)	0.004	0.003	−0.002	0.006	0.003	−0.001	0.005	0.004	−0.001
Number of observations	124	123	117	115	115	109	115	115	109
R^2	0.392	0.379	0.443	0.460	0.407	0.451	0.460	0.406	0.449

Notes: OLS denotes ordinary least squares; 2SLS denotes two-stage least squares; and 3SLS denotes three-stage least squares. The symbols *, **, and *** denote significance at the 90, 95, and 99 percent confidence levels, respectively. Standard deviations and *t*-statistics for the estimated parameters are available from the authors upon request. All regressions include intercept, precautionary arrangement, and year dummies.

could be evidence that democratic incumbents tend to postpone fiscal consolidation. Second, declines in ethnic tension are contemporaneously correlated with improved fiscal balances. This could reflect a country's return to normalcy, which is associated with improved revenue collection and lower military spending. Third, less military involvement in politics in the preprogram year, as well as declines in the risk of external conflict (ranging from trade restrictions to full-scale warfare) are positively and significantly associated with lower fiscal deficits.

Current Account

Shocks to the current account are longer lived and have larger permanent components than other macroeconomic outcomes (Tables 10 and 11). Only about 10 percent of any deviation from a country's "normal" ratio of the current account to GDP is made up for in one year.

Most studies find that participation in IMF-supported programs helps improve the current account. Our results on the impact of program implementation on the current account are more nuanced. Countries that do a better job at implementing programs experience a deterioration of the current account for about two years, but this is followed by a sharp improvement in the trade balance for the third year. Disbursement of 100 percent of committed funds is accompanied by an 8 percent deterioration of the current account in the first year (relative to the preprogram year), followed by a numerically noticeable but statistically insignificant 2 percent improvement in the third year. Our mixed results are similar to Barro and Lee's (2002). By contrast, Conway (1994) finds evidence of improvement in the current account in countries participating in IMF-supported programs, but it does not correct for the extent of program implementation.

The only institutional variables that matter for the current account are the initial investment

Table 11

Program Implementation, Institutions, and Current Account (Ratio to GDP): Regressions Using Irreversible Interruption Index

Dependent Variable	ΔBCA_Y (*T*−1 to horizon)								
Regression number	(1)	(2)	(3)	(4)	(5)	(6)	(7)	(8)	(9)
	OLS			2SLS			3SLS		
Horizon	*T*	*T*+1	*T*+2	*T*	*T*+1	*T*+2	*T*	*T*+1	*T*+2
Non-interruption dummy	0.002	0.010	0.024**	−0.037	−0.024	0.032	−0.032	−0.024	0.030
RGDPPC (*T*−1)	−0.001	−0.001	0.0008	−0.002	−0.003	0.001	−0.002	−0.003	0.001
ΔBCA_Y (*T*−1)	−0.133	−0.172*	−0.105	−0.235**	−0.197*	−0.180	−0.173*	−0.192*	−0.180*
BCA_Y (*T*−1)	−0.158**	−0.208**	−0.366***	−0.136**	−0.115	−0.365***	−0.105*	−0.135*	−0.399***
Corruption (*T*−1)	−0.012*	−0.007	−0.019**	−0.004	0.0004	−0.019**	−0.003	−0.0001	−0.020**
Change in corruption (*T*−1 to horizon)	0.0002	−0.005	0.007	0.0004	−0.0004	0.0001	−0.0005	−0.002	0.0002
Ethnic conflict (*T*−1)	0.006	−0.005	0.002	−0.006	−0.006	0.003	−0.006*	−0.006	0.003
Change in ethnic conflict (*T*−1 to horizon)	−0.011	−0.002	−0.007	−0.015	−0.016*	−0.004	−0.015	−0.014	−0.004
External conflict (*T*−1)	0.003	0.0003	0.0006	0.002	−0.002	−0.002	0.002	−0.002	−0.002
Change in external conflict (*T*−1 to horizon)	0.008*	0.0004	−0.003	0.005	−0.001	−0.009**	0.006	−0.001	−0.010**
Government stability (*T*−1)	0.013**	0.014**	0.010	0.009*	0.010	0.001	0.008*	0.010	0.001
Change in government stability (*T*−1 to horizon)	−0.003	0.006	−0.003	−0.006	0.005	−0.007	−0.003	0.005	−0.008
Investment profile (*T*−1)	−0.011***	−0.011**	−0.005	−0.009**	−0.008*	−0.005	−0.009***	−0.009*	−0.005
Change in investment profile (*T*−1 to horizon)	−0.016***	−0.018***	−0.006	−0.014***	−0.014***	−0.002	−0.019***	−0.015***	−0.002
Military in politics (*T*−1)	0.011***	0.012***	0.010**	0.006*	0.010**	0.008*	0.007**	0.010**	0.008**
Change in military in politics (*T*−1 to horizon)	0.004	0.005	0.0001	0.006	0.003	−0.001	0.006	0.004	−0.0003
Number of observations	127	124	117	115	115	109	115	115	109
R^2	0.385	0.368	0.416	0.443	0.395	0.448	0.430	0.393	0.447

Notes: OLS denotes ordinary least squares; 2SLS denotes two-stage least squares; and 3SLS denotes three-stage least squares. The symbols *, **, and *** denote significance at the 90, 95, and 99 percent confidence levels, respectively. Standard deviations and *t*-statistics for the estimated parameters are available from the authors upon request. All regressions include intercept and year dummies.

profile and its change during the program period. Both are highly significant and enter the regressions with negative signs. Not surprisingly, the better a government's attitude toward inward investment, the larger the current account deterioration during the period considered.

Of the political variables, the ones relevant for the evolution of the external current account are external conflict, government stability, and military involvement in politics. The coefficient on the change in the external conflict index is negative and highly significant for the *T*+2 horizon. Improvements in the index are associated with the elimination of embargoes and of trade restrictions and are correlated with a worsening of the current account. A one-point increase in this rating is correlated with a 1.2 percent deterioration of the current account over three years. Governments that are more stable in the preprogram year tend to have better current account performance. Similar positive effects on the current account appear to result from less military involvement in politics before the program initiation. These results are robust to the choice of program implementation measure.

Conclusion

This paper has examined the nexus among institutions, policy implementation, and economic performance in countries undertaking IMF-supported reforms. We employed a short-run statistical model that treats institutions and politics as exogenous and mean-reverting, that takes into account the autoregressive and mean-reverting nature of macroeconomic outcomes, and that corrects for the endogeneity of program implementation with respect to macroeconomic performance.

Our main findings are fourfold. First, the quality of institutions and the domestic political environment matter for macroeconomic outcomes in countries implementing IMF-supported programs, especially at longer horizons of up to three years. This direct beneficial impact of institutions on the macroeconomic variables is in addition to their indirect impact through better program implementation. As expected, improvements in the government bureaucracy and better enforcement of law and order are associated with lower inflation. However, declines in internal conflict are associated with higher inflation. Improvements in a program country's investment profile and in government stability lead to faster economic growth. Easing of external conflict and lower military involvement in politics before program approval are associated with stronger fiscal outcomes as military expenditure declines. On the other hand, reductions in ethnic tension and improvements in government accountability are associated with weaker fiscal outcomes, perhaps because programs may provide for higher targeted expenditure. Greater government stability and reductions in the military's involvement in politics before the program starts are associated with a strengthening of the external current account. However, lower ethnic tension and improvements in a program country's investment profile lead to a deterioration of the current account.

Second, the institutional and political environment is quantitatively important for the implementation of IMF-supported programs. Rates of disbursement of IMF loans are higher and program interruptions less frequent in countries where ethnic tensions are low, where governments are stable and less corrupt, and where the military is less involved in politics. In addition, more IMF loans are disbursed and fewer interruptions are experienced in countries in which internal conflict was intense and law enforcement weak before program approval. Arguably, this reflects the IMF's role, as lender and policy adviser, in facilitating the return to normalcy of countries experiencing natural or political shocks.

Third, program implementation varies systematically with the duration of a country's financial engagement with the IMF and the size of its quota. More funds are disbursed and fewer program interruptions are experienced in countries that have spent more time in previous IMF-supported programs. Implementation is also better for larger programs (as measured by the amount of program financing approved in relation to the country's IMF quota).

And fourth, after the impact of institutions on the macroeconomic situation is taken into account, the extent of program implementation exerts an independent influence on macroeconomic outcomes, especially over shorter horizons of up to two years. Better-implemented programs are associated with lower inflation, with initially weaker but ultimately stronger external and fiscal outcomes, and with a statistically insignificant impact on economic growth. These results are to be contrasted with those of studies that do not correct for program implementation; these studies conclude that program participation has ambiguous effects on inflation. Correcting for differences in implementation thus provides some evidence linking successful implementation of IMF-supported reforms to more progress in achieving price stability.

What, then, are the policy implications of this analysis for the IMF? The first issue is the lack of clear-cut results linking program implementation to the resumption of economic growth in countries implementing IMF-supported reforms. One possibility is that successful program implementation has favorable impacts on growth that are only felt beyond the three-year horizon captured in our model. The length of lags in the operation of IMF-supported structural reforms should be a topic of future research. Further, the lack of conclusive links between program implementation and growth suggests that it might be useful for the IMF to seek to identify structural reforms that could pay off quickly in terms of economic growth, both at the program design stage and at the implementation stage. At the program design stage, the IMF could monitor regularly published institutional and political indicators relevant to economic growth—such as the ICRG ratings of the level of ethnic tension, government accountability, and the investment climate. These indicators would also need to be carefully monitored during program implementation to ascertain whether IMF-supported reforms are on track toward meeting their growth objectives. Information on the determinants of the investment profile—viability of contracts, threat of expropriation, ease of profit repatriation, and payment delays—could provide high-frequency feedback concerning the extent to which programs are on track in implementing investment-friendly reforms.

Second, paying due attention to relevant political and institutional developments is critical to the successful design and implementation of IMF-supported programs. Quantitative information and analysis could be a useful complement to information from IMF missions and resident representatives in assessing rapidly changing political environments, indicating the potential for successful program implementation. A decline in political indicators below thresholds historically associated with inadequate program implementation could give the IMF an early warning signal, much as financial vulnerability indicators provide useful signals of impending financial crisis. The IMF has on occasion responded to heightened political uncertainty by requiring the major political forces in a country—the government and the main opposition parties in parliament—to endorse a program at an early stage. Systematizing these efforts, as the IMF has been doing by increasing the emphasis on ownership, could yield dividends in terms of improved program design, implementation, and macroeconomic performance. It would enable the IMF to avoid situations in which, having designed and implemented first-best programs that failed to fully take into account relevant political and institutional factors, one ends up in a third-best world when these "ideal" programs are not properly executed. In econometric terms, one would ideally want initial ($T-1$) institutional and political variables to enter implementation regressions (such as those in Table 3) with insignificant coefficients. That would provide evidence that IMF-supported programs are well tailored to the specifics of each country's politico-institutional climate and that the success or failure of a program is independent of initial political conditions. Unfortunately, we have such neutrality only for the initial economic conditions. More generally, it might be useful to consider incorporating quantitative political and institutional indicators and analysis in IMF surveillance work.

Third, we have treated institutions as exogenous and mean-reverting processes, yet institutional development is an important objective of IMF-supported programs with a structural orientation. It would be useful to assess systematically the impact of better implementation of IMF-supported programs on the dynamics of institutional and political factors. In such a model, the evolution of formal and informal institutions would be endogenous to the politico-economic process, including participation in IMF-supported programs. To the extent that IMF-supported programs promote welfare-improving institutional change, their beneficial effects are going to be larger than suggested by models, such as ours, that treat institutions as exogenous.

References

Atoyan, Ruben, Patrick Conway, Marcelo Selowsky, and Tsidi Tsikata, 2004, "Macroeconomic Adjustment in IMF-Supported Programs: Projections and Reality," IMF Independent Evaluation Office BP/04/2 (Washington: International Monetary Fund). This paper also appears, in somewhat different form, as Chapter 5 in this volume.

Bagci, Pinar, and William Perraudin, 1997, "The Impact of IMF Programmes," Working Paper No. 24 (London: Global Economic Institutions Research Program, Center for Economic Policy Research).

Barro, Robert, and J. Lee, 2002, "IMF Programs: Who Is Chosen and What Are the Effects?" NBER Working Paper No. 8951 (Cambridge, Massachusetts: National Bureau of Economic Research).

Conway, Patrick, 1994, "IMF Lending Programs: Participation and Impact," *Journal of Development Economics*, Vol. 45 (December), pp. 365–91.

Dicks-Mireaux, Louis, Mauro Mecagni, and Susan Schadler, 2000, "Evaluating the Effect of IMF Lending to Low-Income Countries," *Journal of Development Economics*, Vol. 61, pp. 495–526.

Dollar, David, and Jakob Svensson, 2000, "What Explains the Success or Failure of Bank-Supported Adjustment Programs?" *Economic Journal*, Vol. 110 (October), pp. 894–917.

Dreher, Axel, 2004, "IMF and Economic Growth: The Effects of Programs, Loans, and Compliance with Conditionality," Working Paper, University of Konstanz (July). Available on the Web at *http://econwpa.wustl.edu:8089/eps/if/papers/0404/0404004.pdf*.

Haque, Nadeem Ul, and Mohsin Khan, 1998, "Do IMF-Supported Programs Work? A Survey of the Cross-Country Empirical Evidence," IMF Working Paper 98/169 (Washington: International Monetary Fund).

International Country Risk Guide (ICRG), 2003, *Brief Guide to the Ratings System* (East Syracuse, New York: Political Risk Services Group, Inc.).

International Monetary Fund (IMF), 2002, *Evaluation of the Prolonged Use of IMF Resources* (2 vols.). (Washington: Independent Evaluation Office, International Monetary Fund).

______, 2003, "Growth and Institutions," Chapter III of *World Economic Outlook* (April) (Washington: International Monetary Fund).

Ivanova, Anna, Wolfgang Mayer, Alex Mourmouras, and George Anayiotos, 2003, "What Determines the Implementation of IMF-Supported Programs?" IMF Working Paper 03/08 (Washington: International Monetary Fund). This paper also appears, in somewhat different form, as Chapter 10 in this volume.

Joyce, Joseph, 2003, "Promises Made, Promises Broken: A Model of IMF Program Implementation," Working Paper No. 2003-03 (Wellesley, Massachusetts: Department of Economics, Wellesley College). Available on the Web at *http://www.wellesley.edu/Economics/joyce/PROM4.pdf*.

Khan, Mohsin, 1990, "The Macroeconomic Effects of Fund-Supported Adjustment Programs," *Staff Papers*, International Monetary Fund, Vol. 37 (June), pp. 195–231.

Killick, Tony, 1995, *IMF Programmes in Developing Countries: Design and Impact* (London: Routledge).

Mecagni, Mauro, 1999, "The Causes of Program Interruptions," in *Economic Adjustment and Reform in Low-Income Countries*, ed. by Hugh Bredenkamp and Susan Schadler (Washington: International Monetary Fund).

North, Douglass, 1997, "Introduction," in *The Frontiers of the New Institutional Economics*, ed. by John Drobak and John Nye (New York: Academic Press), pp. 3–13.

Przeworski, Adam, and James R. Vreeland, 2000, "The Effect of IMF Programs on Economic Growth," *Journal of Development Economics*, Vol. 62, pp. 385–421.

Rodrik, Dani, Arvind Subramanian, and Francesco Trebbi, 2002, "Institutions Rule: The Primacy of Institutions over Geography and Integration in Economic Development," NBER Working Paper No. 9305 (Cambridge, Massachusetts: National Bureau of Economic Research).

Schadler, Susan, Franek Rozwadowski, Siddharth Tiwari, and David Robinson, 1993, *Economic Adjustment in Low-Income Countries—Experience Under the Enhanced Structural Adjustment Facility*, IMF Occasional Paper No. 106 (Washington: International Monetary Fund).

CHAPTER

10 What Determines the Implementation of IMF-Supported Programs?

Anna Ivanova, Wolfgang Mayer, Alex Mourmouras, and George Anayiotos[1]

The paper provides a quantitative analysis of the factors that determine successful implementation of IMF-supported programs. To this end, we construct new measures of program implementation and compliance with conditionality for 170 IMF programs approved between 1992 and 1998. The main hypothesis tested is whether IMF effort and the design of conditionality significantly affect the probability of successful implementation of IMF-supported programs. We find that program implementation depends primarily on the borrower's domestic political economy. Strong special interests in the parliament, political instability, inefficient bureaucracies, lack of political cohesion, and ethno-linguistic divisions weaken program implementation. IMF effort, the design of conditionality, and initial and external conditions do not materially influence program prospects.

Introduction

At the heart of the International Monetary Fund's operations are conditional lending programs that give borrowing countries breathing space while they correct their macroeconomic and structural imbalances. These programs provide mutual assurances. On the one hand, member countries are assured that they will continue receiving IMF financing if they meet the specified conditions. On the other hand, conditionality ensures that adjustment is undertaken in ways that are conducive to national and international prosperity, providing guarantees to the IMF that it will be repaid and that the world's financial system will not suffer from disruptive systemic crises.

In order for the effects of IMF-supported programs to be fully realized, however, the policies they envisage must be implemented to the fullest possible extent. Many programs are in fact interrupted amid political or economic turmoil, in circumstances in which it is not possible to agree on conditionality to underpin new or revised programs. The implementation record of IMF-supported programs has been rather disappointing. About 44 percent of all programs approved between 1992 and 1998 were not completed, experiencing irreversible interruptions.

In this paper, the quality of implementation of IMF-supported programs is linked to three groups of factors: (a) the political characteristics of borrowing countries; (b) IMF conditionality and the human and financial effort the IMF invests in programs; and (c) internal economic conditions in countries implementing programs and the external conditions affecting them. Implementation, as we use the term, is to be contrasted with overall program success, defined as the achievement of its macroeconomic and structural objectives. Previous econometric studies (Bird, 2000, provides a review) commonly assessed the success of IMF-supported programs by examining macroeconomic indicators such as budget deficit, international reserves, inflation, and growth before and after the program. However, there is no reason to expect that a program will realize its macroeconomic and structural objectives if implementation consistently falls short of program intentions. Understanding the factors that affect program implementation is thus the first step in understanding the determinants of overall program success.

Our analysis focuses on program implementation for a sample of countries that made conscious decisions to enter into agreements with the IMF. We do not address the prior questions of what makes a country commit to an IMF-supported program and whether countries have a better chance of succeeding in their macroeconomic and structural adjustment by having an IMF program in place. To answer these questions would require an assessment of economic performance of countries whose adjustment programs were not supported by the IMF, and comparable information is not readily available.

The literature offers several clues indicating that the primary factors influencing the implementation of IMF-supported programs lie in the domestic political economy of borrowing countries. Interruptions of programs supported by the IMF's concessional

[1] This is a revised version of IMF Working Paper 03/08. For useful comments and discussion, we would like to thank the participants in the Second Annual IMF Research Conference, Washington, November 29–30, 2001. We are especially indebted to Patrick Conway, our rapporteur at the conference; Graham Bird; Jim Boughton; Peter Clark; Charles Engel; Judy Gold; Arthur Goldberger; Mohsin Khan; Tony Killick; and Sunil Sharma. Tim Lane encouraged us to undertake this project and made invaluable comments and suggestions on earlier drafts. We alone, however, are responsible for any remaining errors.

facilities—the Structural Adjustment Facility (SAF) and the Enhanced Structural Adjustment Facility (ESAF)—were primarily caused by domestic political economy factors, not poor program design (Mecagni, 1999). Similarly, the success of World Bank–supported adjustment programs is attributed to favorable domestic political conditions and institutions, including lack of ethnic and linguistic divisions, government stability, and democratic regimes (Dollar and Svensson, 2000). It is important to note that World Bank conditionality and resources allocated to program design and monitoring did not seem to matter at the margin. Finally, case study evidence suggests that in some countries, the ambivalence of the top political leaders and resistance by senior officials and special interests were key to the failures of IMF-supported programs.[2] When lack of political commitment resulted in stop-and-go program cycles, the imposition of large numbers of prior actions had limited success, pointing to the need for greater selectivity in lending. In other countries, participatory processes that actively involved the country's top leadership were instrumental in overcoming domestic divisions, building ownership for programs, and ensuring program success.

Our analysis of the determinants of program implementation is made possible by the availability of new datasets. First, political scientists have in recent years developed several quantitative indicators of political conditions in borrowing countries. Second, during the last decade, the IMF has improved its monitoring of programs and internal resource allocation. This allows us to develop indicators that capture program conditionality, the quality of its implementation, and the IMF's human and financial effort in program countries.

In ascertaining the impact on program implementation of variables under IMF control, a key empirical issue is the need to properly account for the endogenous nature of IMF decisions. A second key issue, based on the findings of recent theoretical work on conditionality and program ownership, is to test for the impact on program implementation of special interests resisting reforms.[3] We develop an index of the power of special interests in parliament and examine the impact on program implementation of parties representing religious, nationalistic, regional, and rural interests.

Our main results are easily summarized. On the one hand, the implementation of IMF-supported programs is strongly influenced by recipient countries' domestic political economy. Weak program implementation was strongly associated with strong special interests in parliament, lack of political cohesion, inefficient bureaucracies, and ethno-linguistic divisions. The strong association between program implementation and political economy variables is robust across different econometric specifications. On the other hand, initial economic conditions, IMF effort, and the breadth and depth of conditionality do not seem to materially influence program prospects when they are properly instrumented for. Other recent studies corroborate this finding. Program implementation is not related to the number of conditions or the number of prior actions[4] (IMF, 2001c; and Thomas, 2003). Structural conditionality does not influence medium-term fiscal developments (Bulíř and Moon, 2003).

The rest of the paper is organized as follows. The second section describes the sample and various implementation measures. The third section describes the econometric methodology and presents the main results. The fourth section is the conclusion.

Characteristics of IMF-Supported Programs

Measuring Program Implementation

We analyzed the implementation of 170 IMF-supported programs approved between 1992 and 1998 (Table 1). The choice of the time period was determined by the availability of information on conditionality in the MONA database[5] and the difficulty in assessing programs approved after 1998, some of which were still ongoing when the paper on which this chapter is based was prepared. The largest collection of programs (about 48 percent of the total) in the sample were Stand-By Arrangements (SBAs). The second-largest group of programs (38 percent) were programs under concessional facilities,[6] followed by programs under the Extended Fund Facility (EFF) (15 percent).

IMF-supported programs are complex in nature, making it difficult to arrive at a single metric of program success. In general, a program is considered to be successful if its principal macroeconomic and structural objectives are met. Lacking a single indicator of success for IMF-supported programs, such as the one produced by the World Bank's Operations Evaluation Department for Bank-supported programs, we focus on the narrower measures of successful program implementation, which is a prerequisite for overall program success.

Our strategy was to construct multiple measures of implementation for each program in our sample. These measures capture program performance from

[2] See IMF (2001a, 2001b), Bredenkamp and Schadler (1999), IMF (1998), and Boughton and Mourmouras (2004).

[3] See Mayer and Mourmouras (2002) and Drazen (2002).

[4] Prior actions are conditions that must be implemented before the IMF can approve or continue disbursements of its loans.

[5] The Monitoring of IMF Arrangements (MONA) database is maintained by the IMF's Policy Development and Review Department. MONA was started in 1992 and is missing 18 programs approved in that year.

[6] The ESAF was restructured and renamed the Poverty Reduction and Growth Facility (PRGF) in 1999.

Table 1
Program Implementation by Type of Arrangement

Type of Arrangement	Number of Programs[1]	Number of Programs Excluding Precautionary Arrangements and Cancelled and Ongoing Programs[1]	Share of Programs Having Interruptions[2,3]	Share of Programs Having Irreversible Interruptions[3,4]	Average Macro Implementation Index[3,5,6]	Average Structural Implementation Index[3,6,7]	Average Overall Implementation Index[3,6,8]	Average Share of Committed Funds Disbursed[1]
			(in percent)					
EFF	25	13	68	40	87.0	75.4	83.3	72.1
PRGF/ESAF	64	51	73.4	45.3	77.1	71.3	72.9	77.2
SBA	81	41	67.9	43.2	81.0	60.8	76.0	63.7
Total	170	105	70.0	43.5	80.3	67.4	75.8	71.3

Notes: EFF denotes Extended Fund Facility; PRGF denotes Poverty Reduction and Growth Facility; ESAF denoted Enhanced Structural Adjustment Facility; and SBA denotes Stand-By Arrangement.

[1] Multiyear arrangements are treated as one program. This is a sample of programs approved between 1992 and 1998 and available from the IMF's Monitoring of IMF Arrangements (MONA) database. (Our sample is missing 16 SBAs, one ESAF, and one EFF program approved in 1992.) The sample of EFF programs is quite small to use for drawing reliable conclusions regarding relative performance of EFF programs compared with ESAF and SBA programs. The average share of disbursed funds is computed across a sample of programs that excludes arrangements that were either precautionary upon approval or later became precautionary, as well as canceled and ongoing programs.

[2] An interruption occurs if an SBA program review was delayed by more than three months or not completed at all; if a program review for ESAF/PRGF programs was delayed by more than six months or not completed at all; if there was an interval of more than six months between two subsequent years of a multiyear arrangement; or if at least one of the annual arrangements was not approved (exceptions are programs that were canceled and replaced by another program, in which case noncompleted reviews and nonapproved annual arrangements are not counted as interruptions).

162

[3] The *macroeconomic and structural implementation indices* were computed from information available in MONA. Since MONA questionnaires are sent only for programs for which IMF Executive Board meetings are scheduled, implementation information is not available on many conditions for programs with noncompleted reviews. Since these were typically interrupted programs, the macroeconomic and structural indices overstate program implementation. Interruption indices were constructed using additional information from country documents and other sources.

[4] An irreversible interruption occurs if either (a) the last scheduled program review was not completed (all programs); or (b) all scheduled reviews were completed but the subsequent annual arrangement was not approved (ESAF/PRGF arrangements).

[5] The *macroeconomic implementation index* for a given macroeonomic performance criterion is equal to 100 percent if the said criterion was met or met after modification and it is equal to zero if the said criterion was not met, not met after modification, waived, or waived after modification. The *macroeconomic implementation index* for a program is the average of the *macroeconomic implementation indices* across all macroeconomic performance criteria for this program.

[6] The sample size for implementation indices was smaller (150 programs), which corresponds to the sample constructed for "Structural Conditionality in IMF-Supported Programs"; we simply extended the structural index used in this paper to macroeconomic and overall implementation indices.

[7] The *structural implementation index* for a given structural condition is equal to 100 percent if the structural condition was met or met with a small delay for structural benchmarks; it is equal to 50 percent if the structural condition was partially met or delayed for performance criteria; and it is equal to zero if the structural condition was not met. The *structural implementation index* for a program is the average of the *structural implementation indices* across all structural conditions for this program.

[8] The *average overall implementation index* for a given program is the average of *macroeconomic and structural implementation indices* over all conditions in this program.

different angles.[7] Viewed from this narrower perspective, implementation is measured by the extent to which the program was completed without undue delays, the extent to which macroeconomic and structural conditionality was met, and the extent to which funds committed by the IMF were disbursed.

Our first indicator of program implementation is a binary variable measuring program interruptions. This variable captures both major and minor interruptions and is motivated by Mecagni's work. We say that an *interruption* occurred if an SBA review was delayed by more than three months or not completed at all, if a program review for EFF/PRGFs was delayed by more than six months or not completed at all, if there was an interval of more than six months between two subsequent years of a multiyear

[7] An alternative to this approach is to construct a comprehensive indicator of implementation to reflect the extent to which programs reach their broad objectives. Dollar and Svensson (2000) used such a definition, based on the independent (but subjective) judgments of the World Bank's Operations Evaluation Department. No such measure was available to us—the IMF's Independent Evaluation Office (IEO) was set up only in 2001.

arrangement, or if at least one of the annual arrangements was not approved.[8]

The second indicator is a binary variable identifying irreversible program interruptions. This measure captures programs that went off track and were not revived subsequently (i.e., were either canceled or were allowed to lapse because of policy slippages). More precisely, we say that an *irreversible interruption* occurred if either the last scheduled program review was not completed (all programs) or all scheduled reviews were completed but the subsequent annual arrangement was not approved (ESAF/PRGF arrangements). Third, we constructed a quantitative indicator of implementation of IMF conditionality, the *overall implementation index*, which represents the average fraction of macroeconomic and structural conditionality implemented. This indicator is an extension of the structural conditionality index developed in the IMF's Policy Development and Review Department (PDR) during the 2000–2002 review of conditionality (IMF, 2001c). Finally, we also computed the *ratio of disbursements to commitments*. The last two indicators are continuous variables that take values between zero and 100.

Each of our indices captures an important dimension of program implementation. The macroeconomic and structural implementation indices provide quantitative information on implementation rates by type of condition. Their main drawback is that they overstate the degree of implementation because, as is well known, MONA fails to capture information on interrupted programs that were not subject to further Board reviews.[9] The interruption dummies, which are based on MONA data and additional information from program documents, complement the macroeconomic and structural implementation indices by capturing significant program stoppages. The share of disbursed funds provides useful information on the proportion of approved assistance actually delivered for non-precautionary arrangements and also on the actual versus scheduled duration of the program. The implementation indices and interruption dummies provide useful information about precautionary programs, canceled programs, and some unusual cases in which no drawings were made despite good results.

Descriptive Statistics

Table 1 summarizes program implementation by type of arrangement. About 44 percent of all programs experienced an irreversible interruption, while 70 percent of all programs experienced either a major or a minor interruption. Nonetheless, approximately 71 percent of committed funds were disbursed on average (excluding precautionary arrangements, and canceled and ongoing programs). The average implementation index for programs for which information is available in MONA is 76 percent. The macroeconomic implementation index is significantly higher than the structural implementation index (80 percent versus 67 percent). However, implementation indices most likely overstate program performance. MONA collects data only for program test dates subject to Board approval or review. Information on later stages of some programs experiencing major interruptions is, therefore, not available.

The four measures of program implementation are significantly correlated (Table 2).[10] However, the correlation coefficients are not very high in most cases, reflecting the fact that the various implementation measures capture quite different angles of program performance. The correlation coefficient between the macroeconomic and structural implementation index is only 0.2. This is consistent with the recent finding by Bulíř and Moon (2003) that the implementation of fiscal measures in IMF-supported programs was not strongly correlated with the implementation of structural measures.

Several differences stand out between successfully implemented and interrupted programs (Table 3). First, countries that implemented their IMF-supported reform programs were experiencing much higher inflation at the start of the program than countries whose programs were interrupted. Although the difference in inflation rates was not statistically significant in the year in which the program was approved, inflation was significantly higher in countries with successfully implemented programs one year before the program started. Countries that implemented their programs started with substantially smaller budget deficits (2½ percent of GDP on average) compared with countries in which programs were interrupted (4¾ percent of GDP on average). In countries with interrupted programs, terms of trade shocks were stronger, the strength of special interests was higher, and the degree of political cohesion was lower. Interestingly, the effort invested by the IMF and the extent and structure of conditionality are similar in interrupted and implemented programs.

Correlation of Implementation Measures with Macroeconomic Performance

IMF-supported programs aim to strengthen the borrowing countries' balance of payments and overall

[8] Exceptions are programs that were canceled and replaced by other programs, in which case noncompleted reviews and nonapproved annual arrangements are not counted as interruptions. The appendix explains in detail the definitions of program implementation and the political and other variables used in the econometric work.

[9] Changes in MONA submissions instituted in 2002 have corrected this weakness.

[10] The only exception was the reversible-interruption indicator, which is not significantly correlated with the structural implementation index. Since the reversible-interruption dummy captures "small" policy slippages that were subsequently corrected, we decided not to include this measure in our econometric analysis.

Table 2
Correlations of Implementation Indices
(excluding arrangements precautionary on approval)

Pearson Correlation	Average Macro-economic Imple-mentation Index[1,2]	Average Structural Imple-mentation Index[2,3]	Average Overall Imple-mentation Index[2,4]	Interruption Index[5]	Irreversible Interruption Index[6]	Average Share of Committed Funds Disbursed
Average macroeconomic implementation index[1,2]	1.000					
Average structural implementation index[2,4]	**0.211** (0.01)	1.000				
Average overall implementation index[3,4]	**0.782** (0.00)	**0.653** (0.00)	1.00			
Interruption index[5]	**−0.286** (0.00)	−0.050 (0.56)	**−0.30** (0.00)	1.00		
Irreversible interruption index[6]	**−0.263** (0.00)	**−0.279** (0.00)	**−0.39** (0.00)	**0.55** (0.00)	1.00	
Average share of committed funds disbursed	**0.211** (0.01)	**0.346** (0.00)	**0.38** (0.00)	**−0.42** (0.00)	**−0.75** (0.00)	1.00

Notes: The two-tailed significance level appears in parentheses. Figures significant at the 0.05 level are in boldface. Multiyear arrangements are treated as one program. These programs were approved between 1992 and 1998 and are taken from the IMF's Monitoring of IMF Arrangements (MONA) database.

[1] The *macroeconomic implementation index* is equal to 100 percent if macroeconomic performance criteria were met or were met after modification; and it is equal to zero if macroeconomic performance criteria were not met, not met after modification, waived, or waived after modification.

[2] The *macroeconomic and structural implementation indices* were computed from information available in MONA. Since MONA questionnaires are sent only for programs for which IMF Executive Board meetings are scheduled, implementation information is missing on many conditions for programs with noncompleted reviews. Since these were typically interrupted programs, the macroeconomic and structural indices overstate program implementation. Interruption indices were constructed using additional information from country documents and other sources.

[3] The *structural implementation index* is equal to 100 percent if structural criteria were met or met with a small delay for structural benchmarks; it is equal to 50 percent if structural criteria were partially met or delayed for performance criteria; and it is equal to zero if structural criteria were not met.

[4] The *average overall implementation index* is the average of macroeconomic and structural implementation indices over all conditions for a given program.

[5] An interruption occurs if a Stand-By Arrangement program review was delayed by more than three months or not completed at all; if a program review for Enhanced Structural Adjustment Facility (ESAF)/Poverty Reduction and Growth Facility (PRGF) programs was delayed by more than six months or not completed at all; if there was an interval of more than six months between two subsequent years of a multiyear arrangement; or if at least one of the annual arrangements was not approved. (Exceptions are programs that were cancelled and replaced by another program, in which case noncompleted reviews and nonapproved annual arrangements are not counted as interruptions.)

[6] An irreversible interruption occurs if either (a) the last scheduled program review was not completed (all programs); or (b) all scheduled reviews were completed but the subsequent annual arrangement was not approved (ESAF/PRGF arrangements).

Table 3

Features of Successfully Implemented and Interrupted IMF Programs

	Successfully Implemented		Interrupted		*t*-test for Equality of Means[1]	
	Average	Number of programs	Average	Number of programs	*t*-statistics	*p*-value
Political economy characteristics						
Ethnic fractionalization	46	58	51	50	−0.86	0.39
Political instability[2]	4.75	67	5.68	57	−1.16	0.25
Executive index of electoral competitiveness *(in percent)*[3]	62	86	56	66	0.69	0.49
Time in power *(years)*	5.73	86	4.52	66	1.00	0.32
Strength of special interests[4]	16	66	25	54	**−1.74**	0.04
Index of political cohesion[5]	2.36	85	2.06	66	**2.45**	0.01
Quality of bureaucracy[6]	1.72	67	1.81	57	−0.68	0.50
Change of chief executive[7]	18.18	99	28.38	74	−1.59	0.11
Variables under IMF control						
IMF effort per program year *(in millions of U.S. dollars)*[8]	1.01	[illegible]	1.03	68	0.13	0.90
Total number of conditions per program year	40	95	38	65	0.48	0.63
Share of quantitative program criteria (PCs) waived *(percent)*	8.33	99	7.22	73	0.60	0.55
Share of structural conditions *(percent)*	37	95	40	68	−0.74	0.46
Loan size *(agreed amount, in millions of SDRs)*	620	95	526	69	0.30	0.76
Macroeconomic characteristics						
Initial GDP per capita per year *(U.S. dollars)*	1,494	98	1,291	74	0.81	0.42
Initial debt to the IMF *(actual holdings as a percentage of quota)*	177	99	159	74	1.16	0.25
Initial central government balance *(percent of GDP)*	−2.50	88	−4.74	68	**3.70**	0.00
Reserve holdings *(as percent of imports)*[9]	36.72	81	32.98	68	0.85	0.40
Initial inflation *(percent per year)*	80	98	53	74	0.89[10]	0.37
Initial current account balance *(percent of GDP)*	−5.32	98	−5.87	74	0.42	0.67
Terms-of-trade shock *(growth rate during program period, in percent)*[11]	−90	98	−15	74	***−1.30***	0.10

Notes: Bold figures indicate significance at the 5 percent level; bold italic figures indicate significance at the 10 percent level. PCs denote performance criteria; SDRs denotes Special Drawing Rights.

[1] The null hypothesis is stated as follows: H_0: mean(implemented) − mean(interrupted) = 0. The alternative hypothesis was different for different cases. In cases in which the means were significantly different we report *t*-statistics for the relevant one-sided alternative hypothesis—for example, for the index of political cohesion we report *t*-statistics for the null hypothesis as specified above versus the alternative hypothesis (that the degree of political cohesion is higher for successfully implemented compared with interrupted programs), which in fact, cannot be rejected at the 5 percent significance level), otherwise we report *t*-statistics for the alternative hypothesis (that the difference in means is not equal to zero).

[2] This index is computed based on the index of internal conflict provided by the *International Country Risk Guide (ICRG)* on a scale from 0 to 12. Higher values of the index correspond to more internal political instability. We replaced the value of this variable by its maximum score (12) if there was a change of chief executive in the course of the IMF program.

[3] Dummy variable, which equals unity if the executive index of electoral competitiveness is equal to seven, and zero otherwise. The executive index of electoral competitiveness is from the Database of Political Institutions at the World Bank. It ranges from unity to seven, with higher values corresponding to more competitive elections.

[4] Computed as the maximum share of seats in the parliament held by parties representing special interests (Political Institutions Database, World Bank). Four special interest groups are identified: religious, nationalistic, regional, and rural.

[5] The index of political cohesion is defined as follows: in presidential systems, a high degree of political cohesion is said to exist if the same party is in control of the executive and legislature; in parliamentary systems, a high degree of political cohesion means a one-party majority government. See the appendix for a more detailed definition.

[6] Bureaucracy quality *(ICRG)* measures the quality of a country's bureaucracy on a four-point scale. See the appendix for a more detailed definition. This variable was interacted with the dummy indicating that there was a change of chief executive (Political Institutions Database and CIA *World Factbook* for most recent years).

[7] The variable, change of chief executive, is equal to 100 if the chief executive changed during the program period.

[8] IMF effort is the estimated dollar cost of IMF programs computed based on the IMF's Budget Reporting System (BRS) data on hours spent by the staff on program implementation (which includes both preparation and supervision of the program) and estimated average salaries of the staff by grade. We also made use of data provided by the IMF's Office of Personnel Management (OPM) on the dollar costs of resident representatives.

[9] Although the average inflation rate in the approval year was not significantly different for successfully implemented and interrupted programs in the year preceding the approval year, the average inflation rate for implemented programs was significantly higher than for interrupted ones.

[10] Reserves here do not include gold.

[11] Average growth rate of dollar export prices multiplied by the initial share of exports in GDP *minus* average growth rate of dollar import prices multiplied by the initial share of imports in GDP over the course of the program.

Figure 1
Inflation Dynamics for Successfully Implemented and Interrupted IMF Programs

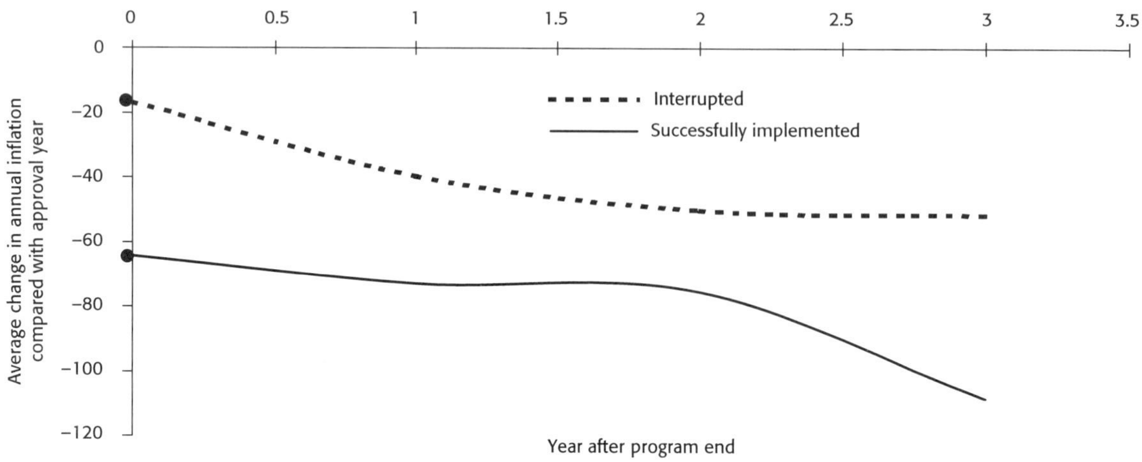

Figure 2
Reserves-to-Imports Dynamics for Successfully Implemented and Interrupted IMF Programs

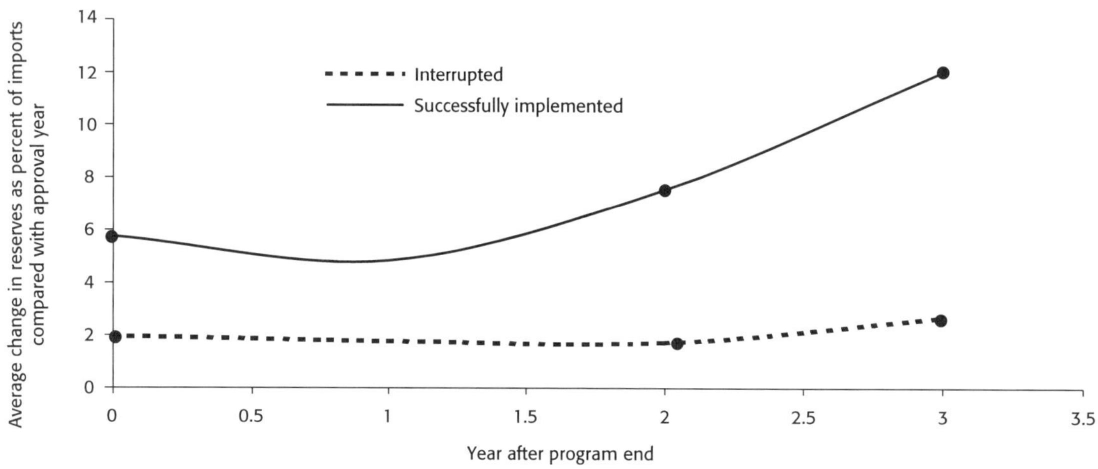

macroeconomic performance. This section presents a preliminary assessment of whether program implementation improves macroeconomic performance, both over the course of programs and after their expiration.

Figures 1–3 show how the main macroeconomic magnitudes evolved in uninterrupted and interrupted programs from the year in which the program was approved until three years after the program ended. The variables plotted are the average changes in inflation, the ratio of reserves to imports, and real GDP growth. The eyeball test (Figure 1) indicates that inflation for both implemented and interrupted programs continued to decline after the program ended, but the reduction in inflation (compared with the approval year) was greater for implemented than for interrupted programs.[11] However, this difference was significant only for the end year of the program, as indicated by solid dots on the graph. The average level of inflation itself in the end year was also significantly lower for uninterrupted than for interrupted programs but was not significantly different in later years. The high variability of inflation in the data contributed to the differences in the changes in inflation being indistinguishable between implemented and interrupted programs in later years. Completed programs were associated with better performance, at least as far as the evolution of the reserve coverage of imports

[11] Uninterrupted programs started with significantly higher inflation as measured one year before the approval year.

Figure 3
Real GDP Growth Dynamics for Successfully Implemented and Interrupted IMF Programs

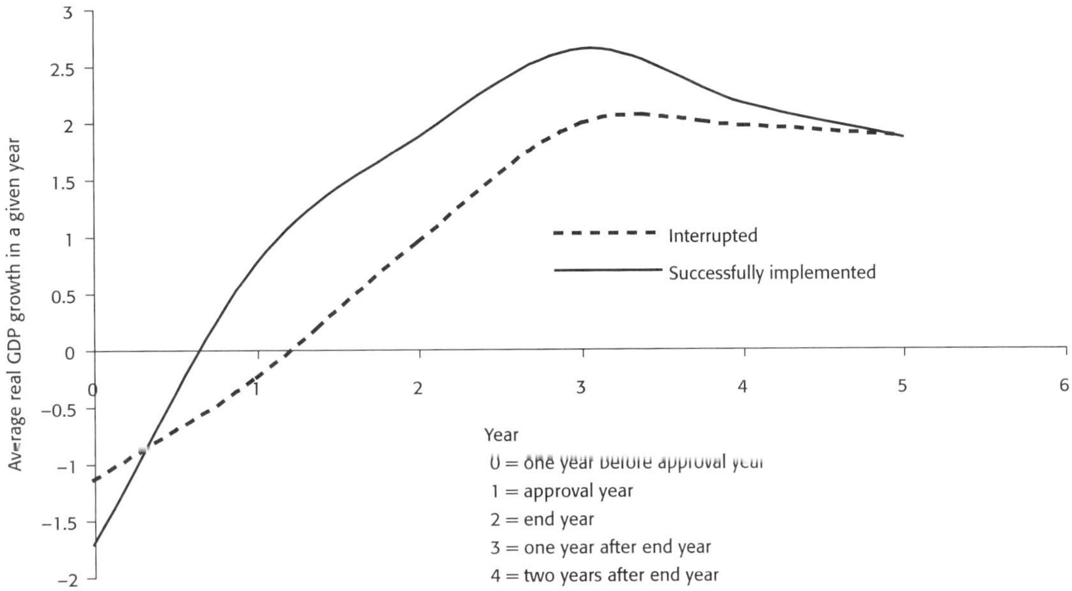

was concerned (Figure 2). Reserves in relation to imports experienced significantly higher growth, over the course of the program, in uninterrupted programs than in interrupted ones. Changes in the reserve cover of imports were also significantly and positively correlated with the share of disbursed funds and, in one case, with the no-interruption dummy. However, the correlation of the reserves-to-imports ratio with the overall implementation index took the "wrong" sign (it was negative), although it was insignificant in almost all cases.

Countries that completed their IMF-supported programs started with deeper recessions (more negative GDP growth rates) but grew faster than countries where programs were interrupted, both right after the programs expired and for a couple of years after that (Figure 3). However, these differences in growth rates were not statistically significant. Once initial GDP and inflation are controlled for, only the overall implementation index was significantly positively correlated with growth in the program's end year.

What, then, is the association between program implementation and macroeconomic performance? Although not especially strong in our sample, these results provide some evidence that countries that complete their IMF-supported programs also manage, on average, to reduce inflation, increase their relative reserve holdings, gain export competitiveness, and accelerate growth more than do countries where programs are interrupted. These results are generally consistent with those of the literature: program implementation helps countries strengthen their current account, external reserves, and balance of payments.[12] Economic growth, which is depressed in the short run as program reforms begin to "bite," also improves eventually. One noteworthy difference with previous studies concerns inflation performance. Whereas previous studies generally have been inconclusive regarding the impact of IMF-supported programs on inflation, inflation performance improves with program implementation in our sample.[13]

Econometric Analysis

Model Specification

We identify three major groups of factors that might affect the prospects of successful implementation of IMF-supported programs. These are political economy variables, variables describing IMF behavior, and initial and external conditions.

On the political economy side, we collected data from various sources, namely, the Political Institutions Database at the World Bank (Beck and others, 2001), the *International Country Risk Guide (ICRG)*,

[12] The authoritative survey of the empirical literature is Haque and Khan (1998). See also Schadler and others (1995a, 1995b); Conway (1994, 1998); and Joyce (2002).

[13] Studying fully the relationship between success in IMF programs and improvement in macroeconomic performance requires a more elaborate econometric framework. In particular, one needs to take into account the dynamic structure of participation in IMF programs. Conway (2000) presents such a framework.

the Polity IV dataset, and the CIA *World Factbook*. The main hypothesis that emerges from the theoretical model presented in a companion paper (Mayer and Mourmouras, 2002) is that the implementation of reforms is affected by the strength of special interest groups in countries using IMF resources. In practice, it is difficult to identify and measure the strength of organized lobbies. To develop a suitable measure of the strength of special interests, we relied on the observation that in many countries political parties represented in government or the legislature (or both) sometimes represent specific interests. Legislatures are crucial players in policymaking: legislative approval is required for successful implementation of almost all key reforms.[14] While many different organized interest groups can and do block reforms, special interest groups in parliament seem a natural candidate.

The Political Institutions Database (Beck and others, 2001) identifies four groups of parties in parliament that represent nationalistic, rural, regional, and religious special interests. Key components of the platforms of these parties are the creation or defense of a national or ethnic identity and of rural, regional, or religious issues. Sometimes nationalistic special interests have persecuted minorities (nationalist special interests), with disastrous consequences for economic development. In any event, special interests in parliament influence government policy choices through the exercise of their political power and, perhaps, through monetary exchanges.

An important question is whether the interests of the political parties representing these interest groups run counter to the reform objectives of IMF-supported programs. While the motives of each of these four types of parliamentary groups are different, each is clearly committed to promoting the interests of only a segment of the population. As such, these parties are likely to support policies favored by the groups they represent even if they harm aggregate welfare. In short, special interests in the parliament serve as our proxy for special interest groups in the theoretical model. To test whether the presence of influential lobbies lowers the probability of successful program implementation, we use the maximum share of seats in parliament held by parties that represent nationalistic, religious, rural, and regional interest groups as a measure of the strength of special interests.

Regarding the remaining political economy variables, we include political instability, ethnic fractionalization and ethnic fractionalization squared, political cohesion, and the interaction term of the quality of bureaucracy and the change of chief executive. (See the appendix for more details on the definitions of the political variables and their sources.) Program implementation might be jeopardized by political instability, which measures the degree of internal conflict and the extent of drastic political change, such as the installation of a new chief executive. Ethnic fractionalization may lead to tensions in society and is, therefore, a potential threat to reforms. Political cohesion emphasizes the heterogeneous nature of the government and the legislature. In countries with poor bureaucracies, changes in government tend to be traumatic as they are often accompanied by disruptions in policy formulation and day-to-day administrative functions, which can have a negative impact on program implementation. A high-quality bureaucracy has the strength and expertise to govern without drastic changes in policies and, therefore, can act as a shock absorber to reduce policy deviations from program goals when governments change. Since the importance of bureaucracy is more sharply felt in times of government change, we included only a term that interacts the strength of the bureaucracy with the dummy variable indicating a change of chief executive.[15]

To test how factors under IMF control affect program implementation, we included three major groups of factors in our regressions: measures of IMF effort, the extent of IMF financing, and measures of the extent and structure of conditionality.

To test the hypothesis that more IMF support improves the prospects of programs, we constructed three variables. The first is IMF effort, measured by the dollar cost of each program. This variable is based on (a) internal IMF data on staff hours allocated to Use of Fund Resources (UFR) work, which is program related, and staff hours devoted to technical assistance and support tasks in member countries; (b) information on average staff salaries by grade; and (c) the costs of running the IMF's resident representative offices in member countries with programs (data were provided by the IMF's Office of Budget and Planning (OBP) and Office of Personnel Management (OPM)). The second variable is the number of IMF staff missions, and the third is the number of mission days.[16]

It also has been argued that the size of IMF loans may not be large enough to induce substantial changes in domestic policies. To test how the extent of IMF financing influences program implementation, we included loan size as a percentage of quota in our regressions.

[14] Hence, this test is also related to the theory of veto players. See Drazen (2002) and Tsebelis (2001).

[15] When we included the quality of bureaucracy itself in the regression, the coefficient on that term was not statistically significant.

[16] For all IMF effort variables, we had to make a decision on how to attribute the data on hours/missions available by countries and months to specific programs. We used approval dates and actual end dates of programs. Recognizing that we might be losing a significant part of IMF effort invested in program preparation, we also constructed alternative measures of these variables, taking into account IMF effort in the country three and six months before program approval. Econometric results for alternative measures were essentially the same and are not reported here but are available from the authors upon request.

Box 1. List of Instrumental Variables

It is difficult to find instruments for all endogenous variables simultaneously. Out of all IMF variables, the share of structural conditions in the total number of conditions seems the least subject to later revisions in the course of the program, so we treat this variable as exogenous. For the remaining IMF variables, we use the following IVs (see Table 6 for first-stage regressions). F-statistics on the IV set for all endogenous variables were significant.

The average share of bilateral aid provided to the country by the Group of Seven (G-7) before the start of the program.[1] This variable is positively correlated with the loan size in relation to quota and with the share of quantitative performance criteria (PCs) waived, although these correlations are not significant even at the 10 percent significance level.

Approval year. Since the number of conditions per program year has been increasing over time, it is positively correlated with the approval year and we can use the latter as an IV.

Expected program duration. A program's expected duration is positively correlated with the loan size in relation to quota and negatively correlated with the share of quantitative PCs waived. The longer the program, the larger is the loan and the more time the IMF has to adjust its conditionality.

[1] Since G-7 members comprise 45 percent of the IMF's voting power, this variable could be related to the "weight" the IMF puts on particular borrowers. See Mayer and Mourmouras (2002) for details.

IMF quota (log). The quotas of members with IMF-supported programs are significantly positively correlated with IMF effort per program year and with the share of quantitative PCs waived. A higher quota is associated with greater IMF effort in a program and a higher share of quantitative PCs waived for two main reasons. First, the quota determines the size of the IMF loan to a member and the amount "at stake" for the IMF. Second, the quota also determines the member's voting power in the IMF.

GDP per capita (log). This variable is negatively correlated with IMF effort per program year. Richer countries require less IMF effort, get higher loans as a percentage of quota, receive fewer waivers, and get fewer conditions per program year. (This coefficient is significant at 10 percent significance level only.) This is the only initial condition included in the IV set.[2]

Regional dummies. IMF effort per program year is higher in Latin America and the Caribbean compared with Europe and the Middle East. Compared with the other regions, loan size in relation to quota is higher in Latin America and the Caribbean, sub-Saharan Africa, and East Asia. The share of quantitative PCs waived is higher in East Asia (significant at the 10 percent significance level only).

Population (log). This variable is negatively correlated with the share of quantitative PCs waived and positively correlated with the loan size as a percentage of quota.

[2] This variable was not significantly correlated with successful program implementation when we included it in the original regression.

To analyze the impact of conditionality on program implementation, we employed the following measures: (a) the number of conditions per program year, which measures the extent of overall conditionality; (b) the share of quantitative performance criteria waived, which measures the strength of enforcement and associated flexibility of conditionality; and (c) the share of structural conditions in the total number of conditions, which measures the weight that programs put on structural reforms. As an alternative to the last measure, we also included the number of structural conditions per program year in the regressions to capture the extent of structural conditionality. As the results were unaffected, they are not reported separately.

Variables under IMF control are endogenously determined. Hence, a list of appropriate instrumental variables (IVs) must be employed in order to glean the impact of IMF variables on the probability of successful implementation of IMF-supported programs. These instruments must be correlated with variables that are under IMF control, be uncorrelated with the shocks hitting programs, and not be direct determinants of program implementation. The choice of instruments is described in more detail in Box 1.

Another key issue is the impact of initial and external conditions and shocks on the implementation of IMF-supported programs. One possibility is that countries that start with unfavorable initial conditions or are hit by unfavorable shocks have a harder time meeting program targets. Alternatively, these countries could face stronger incentives to reform and might be more successful in implementing IMF-supported programs. A third possibility is that programs are designed and negotiated optimally, taking into consideration all the relevant factors, including initial conditions and the frequency, intensity, and nature of economic and other shocks. If programs are tailored to the circumstances of each member country, differences in initial or external conditions and in exposure to shocks may not play a big role in program implementation.[17] It turns out

[17] Tailoring programs to members' circumstances is a key principle underlying the IMF's 2002 conditionality guidelines (IMF, 2002). On flexibility in the design of IMF-supported programs, see also Mussa and Savastano (1999); and Boughton and Mourmouras (2004).

that it is not possible to distinguish empirically among these three possibilities. All we can say is that the data are consistent with the notion that initial and external conditions do not represent a major stumbling block for program implementation.

Variables included as initial conditions in our regressions were as follows: the central government fiscal balance in relation to GDP, the current account balance in relation to GDP, the level of gross reserves at the start of the program, initial inflation, initial GDP per capita, and initial debt to the IMF in relation to a member's IMF quota. To control for external conditions, we use the term "trade shock"—namely the difference between the growth rate of dollar export prices times the share of exports in GDP and the growth rate of dollar import prices times the share of imports in GDP.

Econometric Methodology

Our strategy is to relate the various indicators of implementation, either in isolation or in a pooled sample, to various right-hand-side variables. These "explanatory" variables include observable characteristics of borrowing countries, such as initial conditions and features of their domestic political economy, and variables under IMF control, as described in the previous section.

Our choice of econometric technique was guided by the need to make efficient use of the information
170 contained in our implementation indicators and by data availability. One complication is that one of our indicators is a binary variable while the other two vary continuously, which makes it difficult to combine all three in a single model. Limited availability of political economy data is an additional consideration. Even though implementation measures are available for 170 programs, political economy variables are available for only about 60 programs. Crucially, some of the political economy data are not available for all former centrally planned economies for the period under consideration.[18] The limited sample also forced us to set aside problems of prolonged use of IMF resources. As some of the countries in the complete sample had multiple programs with the IMF, there is strong cross-sectional correlation between observations in the entire sample. But since 56 percent of our working sample comprised countries with only one program, and only 8 percent of countries in the sample had three or more programs, we could not apply panel data techniques.

Owing to the small sample size, we estimate several specifications to check the robustness of our conclusions. Our approach is to first apply the Multiple Indicators and Multiple Causes (MIMIC)[19] model (see Joreskog and Goldberger, 1975), which combines three implementation measures in one econometric model. We then re-estimate models that feature each implementation measure separately using proper econometric techniques. Amemiya's IV probit method is employed to estimate regressions where the left-hand-side variable is a binary indicator. Amemiya's IV tobit is used in regressions of the share of disbursed funds and the overall implementation index.

Formally, our model can be described as follows. If y_i^* is the unobservable probability of successful program implementation, then

$$y_i^* = a_y + \gamma_y' P_i + \beta_y' F_i + \varepsilon_{yi}, \tag{1.1}$$

where P_i is a vector of country i political economy variables; F_i is a vector of variables under IMF control; a_y, γ_y, and β_y are vectors of coefficients; and ε_{yi} is a stochastic disturbance term. The variables controlled by the IMF are given by

$$F_i = \alpha_F + \gamma_F' P_i + \lambda_F' Z_i + \varepsilon_{Fi}, \tag{1.2}$$

where α_F, γ_F, and λ_F are vectors of coefficients; ε_{Fi} is another error term; and Z_i is a vector of exogenous variables that are correlated with donor behavior but do not systematically influence the probability of successful implementation. Since the IMF responds to shocks hitting programs by adjusting its effort and conditionality, ε_{yi} and ε_{Fi} are correlated. We use IV techniques to obtain consistent estimates of the coefficients in equation (1.1).

Since we do not observe y_i^*, we cannot estimate equation (1.1) directly. However, we have three indicators of implementation, which are correlated with y_i^*. We can relate our observed measures of implementation to the unobserved probability of successful implementation as follows:

$$y_{i1} = \delta_1 y_i^* + U_{i1} \tag{1.3}$$

$$y_{i2} = \delta_2 y_i^* + U_{i2} \tag{1.4}$$

$$y_{i3} = \delta_3 y_i^* + U_{i3}, \tag{1.5}$$

where y_{i1}, y_{i2}, and y_{i3} are our three implementation measures, and U_{i1}, U_{i2}, and U_{i3} are measurement errors that are possibly mutually correlated.

[18] This is unfortunate, as economies in transition are good "candidates" for testing the negative impact of special interest groups on the implementation of IMF-supported programs. Rent-seeking behavior and state capture in transition economies are well documented in the literature: see Hellman and Kaufmann (2001); Åslund (1999); Odling-Smee (2001); Havrylyshyn and Odling-Smee (2000); and the discussion in the conference version of this paper available at *http://www.imf.org/external/pubs/ft/staffp/2001/00-00/pdf/aiwmgaam.pdf*.

[19] The MIMIC model is a special case of covariance structure model (LISREL), which is a generalization of the factor analysis model.

Equations (1.1)–(1.5) represent a special case of the MIMIC model analyzed in Joreskog and Goldberger (1975). To estimate this model, we first substitute equation (1.2) into (1.1) and (1.1) into (1.3)–(1.5) to obtain a system of equations that can be treated as seemingly unrelated regressions. This system can be estimated to obtain reduced form coefficients that we can use to recover the parameters γ_y and β_y. To calculate the variance of γ_y and β_y we employ the delta method. This approach requires normalization of one of the coefficients δ to one. Since the model is overidentified, we also had to impose nonlinear constraints to obtain unique parameter estimates. Because of computational complexity, we estimate the general form of the MIMIC model (1.1)–(1.5) including only one variable under IMF control, namely the IMF effort.

A computationally convenient version of this model arises if the coefficients δ are all unity. In this case, substituting (1.1) into (1.3)–(1.5) and setting the δs to one, we have:

$$y_{i1} = \alpha_y + \gamma_y P_i + \beta_y' F_i + \varepsilon_{yi} + U_{i1} \qquad (1.6)$$

$$y_{i2} = \alpha_y + \gamma_y P_i + \beta_y' F_i + \varepsilon_{yi} + U_{i2} \qquad (1.7)$$

$$y_{i3} = \alpha_y + \gamma_y P_i + \beta_y' F_i + \varepsilon_{yi} + U_{i3}. \qquad (1.8)$$

The system (1.6)–(1.8) is a random-effects model with random effect ε_{yi}. If IMF effort were not simultaneously determined with the probability of successful implementation, then the random effect ε_{yi} would be uncorrelated with the set of regressors in F_i and be P_i. We could then obtain consistent estimates of this model by pooling the three implementation measures in one variable and regressing it on the same set of political economy and IMF effort variables for a particular program using the random-effects estimator. However, since IMF effort is simultaneously determined with the probability of successful implementation, we apply the random-effects IV estimator to obtain consistent estimates of the coefficients on political economy and IMF effort variables.[20]

To summarize, we proceed as follows: we first estimate linear-in-probability and tobit regressions that combine three implementation measures in one model employing the random-effects estimator—that is, equations (1.6)–(1.8). Two variants are examined, one that ignores the endogeneity of variables under the IMF's control (Table 4) and another dealing with this endogeneity through IV techniques (Table 5). The set of IVs employed is specified in Table 6. Table 5 also reports a third, more general, version of the MIMIC model. This is specification (1.1)–(1.5) with only one endogenous variable, namely, IMF effort per program year (Table 5, column 1).[21] We then re-estimate our chosen specification of political economy variables with each of the implementation indices in isolation, not taking into account endogeneity of the variables under IMF control (Table 7) and instrumenting for these variables (Tables 8–10).[22]

Results

Main Findings

Program prospects depend on the domestic political economy. In particular, strong vested interests in parliament, lack of political cohesion, poor quality of bureaucracy, and ethnic divisions significantly undermine program implementation. We first estimated random-effects regressions on a pooled sample, both for linear-in-probability and tobit specifications (Table 4, column 2). The coefficient on the strength of special interests is negative and significant at the 5 percent significance level. The strong empirical evidence of the adverse role of special interests on reforms is reassuring because it comes from a sample that excludes some transition economies. The coefficients on the index of political cohesion as well as on the interaction term of the quality of bureaucracy and the change of chief executive is positive and significant. Interestingly, once we added to the regression three more political economy variables,[23] which might affect the probability of successful implementation, the coefficients on ethnic fractionalization and ethnic fractionalization squared became significant.

The impact of ethnic fractionalization on program performance is nonlinear. Large and small ethnic divisions are both bad for program implementation.[24] The results remain essentially the same when we re-estimate the model using the more general MIMIC specification given by equations (1.1)–(1.5) (Table 5) and when each of the implementation measures are considered in isolation (Tables 7–10).[25]

[20] Note that since the question is narrowly focused on a set of countries that each had an IMF-supported program, there is no issue of selection bias.

[21] The reason for testing the hypothesis about the importance of IMF effort only in this model is that computing standard errors using the delta method with more than one endogenous variable in the MIMIC model is cumbersome.

[22] We estimate IV regressions on each of the implementation measures separately using Amemiya's generalized-least-squares (GLS) IV probit/tobit estimators.

[23] Table 5 (column 1) presents regressions of our implementation measures on the political economy variables used by Dollar and Svensson (2000). These coefficients are insignificant, both individually and jointly.

[24] The turning point varies between 44 and 55 on a 0–100 scale (Tables 5–7). This is close to the range estimate (44–49) obtained by Dollar and Svensson (2000) in their study of World Bank programs.

[25] In this model, $\delta = 1$ only in the equation relating the probability of successful implementation and irreversible interruption dummy while allowing the other two δs to vary.

Table 4
Random-Effects Model: Linear in Probability and Tobit Regressions

Regression Number	(1)		(2)		(3)		(4)	
Dependent variable: Program implementation indices	Linear in probability	Tobit	Linear in probability	Tobit	Linear in probability	Tobit	Linear in probability	Tobit
Number of observations	240	240	170	170	179	179	167	167
Political economy variables								
Ethnic fractionalization	0.12	0.31	**1.07**	**1.99**	**1.16**	**2.14**	**1.31**	**2.45**
	(0.25)	(0.34)	(2.07)	(2.34)	(2.46)	(2.64)	(2.70)	(2.94)
Ethnic fractionalization *(squared)*	0.00	0.00	−0.01	***−0.02***	**−0.01**	**−0.02**	**−0.01**	**−0.02**
	−(0.17)	−(0.39)	−(1.34)	−(1.76)	−(2.03)	−(2.30)	−(2.38)	−(2.59)
Political instability[1]	−0.39	−1.31	−1.49	−5.47	***−2.85***	**−5.87**	**−3.11**	**−5.54**
	−(0.41)	−(0.75)	−(0.69)	−(1.53)	−(1.87)	−(2.23)	−(2.03)	−(2.15)
Executive index of electoral competitiveness[2]	9.64	15.18	8.23	18.85	12.69	22.36	***13.25***	***23.33***
	(1.27)	(1.11)	(0.88)	(1.28)	(1.57)	(1.64)	(1.67)	(1.79)
Time in power	0.34	1.90	1.32	3.70	1.22	3.54	2.24	***4.88***
	(0.30)	(0.91)	(0.73)	(1.29)	(0.78)	(1.33)	(1.46)	(1.90)
Time in power *(squared)*	0.00	−0.04	−0.07	***−0.18***	−0.07	***−0.16***	***−0.10***	**−0.20**
	−(0.08)	−(0.80)	−(1.21)	−(1.92)	−(1.29)	−(1.84)	−(1.93)	−(2.35)
Strength of special interests[3]			**−31.72**	**−69.73**	**−34.46**	**−68.41**	**−36.39**	**−70.49**
			−(2.14)	−(2.87)	−(3.08)	−(3.53)	−(3.19)	−(3.62)
Index of political cohesion[4]			**9.66**	**19.52**	**11.49**	**20.58**	**13.22**	**22.85**
			(1.98)	(2.50)	(2.95)	(3.11)	(3.20)	(3.32)
Quality of bureaucracy interacted with change of chief executive[5]			12.82	***33.25***	***16.25***	**31.30**	**20.77**	**36.82**
			(1.19)	(1.85)	(1.92)	(2.13)	(2.52)	(2.63)
Initial and external conditions								
Central government balance *(percentage of GDP)*			0.93	0.98				
			(0.76)	(0.50)				
Level of reserves			0.00	0.00				
			(0.46)	(0.72)				
Inflation			0.00	−0.27				
			(0.01)	−(0.97)				
Current account balance *(percentage of GDP)*			−95	−123				
			−(1.26)	−(1.02)				
GDP per capita (log)			5.39	4.75				
			(0.81)	(0.44)				
Debt to the IMF *(percentage of IMF quota)*			4.62	13.21				
			(0.37)	(0.63)				
Terms-of-trade shock[6]			−0.01	−0.01				
			−(1.15)	−(0.34)				
Variables under IMF Control								
IMF effort per program year (log)[7]							3.81	11.91
							(0.78)	(1.48)
Loan size as percentage of quota (log)							7.01	11.45
							(1.63)	(1.55)
Number of conditions per program year (log)							−6.43	−13.80
							−(0.99)	−(1.29)

(Table continues on next page)

Table 4 *(concluded)*

Regression Number	(1)		(2)		(3)		(4)	
Dependent variable: Program implementation indices	Linear in probability	Tobit	Linear in probability	Tobit	Linear in probability	Tobit	Linear in probability	Tobit
Share of quantitative PCs waived *(percent)*							***−0.49***	**−1.05**
							−(1.98)	−(2.56)
Share of structural conditions *(percent)*							0.16	0.21
							(0.98)	(0.77)
Wald chi-square statistics	2.95	5.00	34.29	42.63	33.32	38.31	45.86	48.33
p-value	0.81	0.54	0.01	0.00	0.00	0.00	0.00	0.00

Notes: Bold figures indicate significance at the 5 percent level; bold italic figures indicate significance at the 10 percent level. PCs denote performance criteria.

The model was estimated on a pooled sample of three implementation measures as left-hand-side variables, ignoring the endogeneity of variables under IMF control. The measures of program implementation used are (a) a binary variable indicating no irreversible program interruption; (b) the share of funds committed by the IMF under an arrangement disbursed (we excluded the measure of committed funds disbursed for arrangements precautionary on approval; canceled programs that did not have irreversible interruption; and arrangements that turned precautionary were treated as fully disbursed (100 percent)); and (c) the average share of conditions implemented. Regression also included the constant term, which is omitted in the table.

[1] This index is computed based on the index of internal conflict provided by the *International Country Risk Guide (ICRG)* on a scale from zero to 12. Higher values of the index correspond to more internal political instability. We replaced the value of this variable by its maximum score (12) if there was a change of chief executive in the course of the IMF-supported program.

[2] Dummy variable equals one if the executive index of electoral competitiveness is equal to seven, and zero otherwise. The executive index of electoral competitiveness is from the Database of Political Institutions at the World Bank. It ranges from one to seven, with higher values corresponding to more competitive elections.

[3] Computed as the maximum share of seats in the parliament held by parties representing special interests (Political Institutions Database, World Bank). Four special interest groups are identified: religious, nationalistic, regional, and rural.

[4] The index of political cohesion is defined as follows: in presidential systems a high degree of political cohesion is said to exist if the same party is in control of the executive and legislature; in parliamentary systems a high degree of political cohesion means a one-party majority government. See the appendix for a more detailed definition.

[5] Bureaucracy quality *(ICRG)* measures the quality of a country's bureaucracy on a four-point scale. See the appendix for a more detailed definition. This variable is interacted with the dummy indicating that there was a change of chief executive (Political Institutions Database and CIA *World Factbook* for most recent years).

[6] Average growth rate of dollar export prices multiplied by the initial share of exports in GDP *minus* average growth rate of dollar import prices multiplied by the initial share of imports in GDP over the course of the program

[7] IMF effort is the estimated dollar cost of IMF-supported programs computed based on the IMF's Budget Reporting System (BRS) data on hours spent by the staff on program implementation (which includes both preparation and supervision of the program) and estimated average salaries of the staff by grade. We also made use of data provided by the IMF's Office of Personnel Management (OPM) on the dollar costs of resident representatives.

Table 5

Random-Effects (IV) and MIMIC Models: Linear-in-Probability Regressions

	Random Effects IV Regressions[1]					MIMIC Model[2]
Regression Number	(1)	(2)	(3)	(4)	(5)	(6)
Number of observations	165	165	165	165	165	165
Dollar and Svensson variables						
Ethnic fractionalization	**1.08**	***0.91***	***0.94***	***1.25***	***0.99***	**2.50**
	(2.09)	(1.70)	(1.75)	(2.44)	(2.05)	(3.55)
Ethnic fractionalization *(squared)*	***–0.01***	–0.01	–0.01	**–0.01**	***–0.01***	**–0.03**
	–(1.76)	–(1.42)	–(1.48)	–(2.07)	–(1.68)	–(3.53)
Political Instability[3]	**–3.91**	**–3.82**	**–3.93**	**–4.58**	**–4.48**	**–4.23**
	–(2.49)	–(2.43)	–(2.50)	–(2.90)	–(2.82)	–(2.20)
Other political economy variables						
Strength of special interests[4]	**–39.78**	**–33.86**	**–34.01**	**–45.47**	**–37.38**	**–38.69**
	–(3.57)	–(2.80)	–(2.81)	–(3.99)	–(3.24)	–(2.48)
Index of political cohesion[5]	**10.03**	**10.55**	**8.78**	**9.86**	**9.69**	**14.02**
	(2.74)	(2.87)	(2.17)	(2.43)	(2.39)	(2.86)
Bureaucracy quality interacted with change of chief executive[6]	**21.39**	**21.36**	**22.02**	**24.97**	**24.50**	**21.05**
	(2.68)	(2.68)	(2.75)	(3.11)	(3.02)	(2.16)
Variables under IMF control						
IMF effort per program year (log)[7,8]	1.54	–2.14	–0.49	7.06		–9.29
	(0.23)	–(0.29)	–(0.07)	(0.99)		–(1.06)
Loan size as a percentage of quota (log)[8]		6.89	7.35		6.58	
		(1.26)	(1.33)		(1.30)	
Number of conditions per program year (log)[8]			–9.87	–15.77	–13.70	
			–(1.05)	–(1.55)	–(1.43)	
Share of quantitative PCs waived *(percent)*[8]				–0.67	–0.47	
				–(1.59)	–(1.17)	
Share of structural conditions *(percent)*	0.14	0.11	0.06	0.16	0.14	
	(0.83)	(0.62)	(0.32)	(0.92)	(0.77)	
Wald chi-square statistics	26.92	28.50	29.57	31.62	31.93	
p-value	0.00	0.00	0.00	0.00	0.00	
Overidentifying restrictions test	12.67	10.42	8.83	8.04	6.91	
Degrees of freedom	9	8	7	7	7	
p-value	0.18	0.24	0.27	0.33	0.44	
Hausman *t*-test	0.38	0.92	1.04	0.84	0.83	
p-value	0.54	0.63	0.79	0.84	0.84	

Notes: Boldfaced figures indicate significance at the 5 percent level; bold italic figures indicate significance at the 10 percent level. PCs denote performance criteria.

[1] This model was estimated on a pooled sample of three implementation measures as left–hand-side variables, using a random-effects IV estimator with the set of instruments as specified in Table 6. The measures of program implementation used are (a) a binary variable indicating no irreversible program interruption; (b) the share of funds committed by the IMF under an arrangement actually disbursed. We excluded the measure of committed funds disbursed for arrangements precautionary on approval; canceled programs that did not have irreversible interruption; and arrangements that turned precautionary, which were treated as fully disbursed (100 percent); and (c) the average share of conditions implemented. The regression also included the constant term, which is omitted from the table.

[2] This model comprises equations (1.1)–(1.5) in the text. It is essentially a system of seemingly unrelated regressions which can be estimated to obtain reduced-form parameters. Since the model is overidentified, we had to impose nonlinear constraints to obtain unique estimates of coefficients. Then the structural parameters were computed using estimates of reduced-form parameters and their variance was estimated using the delta method. (More details are available from the authors upon request.)

[3] This index is computed based on the index of internal conflict provided by the *International Country Risk Guide (ICRG)* on a scale from 0 to 12. Higher values of the index correspond to more internal political instability. We replaced the value of this variable by its maximum score (12) if there was a change of chief executive in the course of the IMF-supported program.

[4] Computed as the maximum share of seats in the parliament held by parties representing special interests (Political Institutions Database, World Bank). Four special interest groups are identified: religious, nationalistic, regional, and rural.

[5] The index of political cohesion is defined as follows: in presidential systems a high degree of political cohesion is said to exist if the same party is in control of the executive and legislature; in parliamentary systems a high degree of political cohesion means a one-party majority government. See the appendix for a more detailed definition.

[6] Bureaucracy quality *(ICRG)* measures the quality of a country's bureaucracy on a four-point scale. See the Appendix for a more detailed definition. This variable is interacted with the dummy variable indicating that there was a change of chief executive (Political Institutions Database and CIA *World Factbook* for most recent years).

[7] IMF effort is the estimated dollar cost of IMF-supported programs computed based on the IMF's Budget Reporting System (BRS) data on hours spent by the staff on program implementation (which includes both preparation and supervision of the program) and estimated average salaries of the staff by grade. We also made use of data provided by the IMF's Office of Personnel Management (OPM) on the dollar costs of resident representatives.

[8] Treated as an endogenous variable in this regression.

Table 6
First-Stage Regressions

Dependent Variable	IMF Effort Per Program Year (log)[1]	Loan Size as Percentage of Quota (log)	Number of Conditions Per Program Year (log)	Share of Quantitative PCs Waived *(percent)*
Number of observations	57	57	57	57
Political economy variables				
Ethnic fractionalization	−0.021	0.006	0.008	0.031
	−(1.56)	(0.58)	(0.84)	(0.12)
Ethnic fractionalization *(squared)*	0.000	0.000	0.000	−0.002
	(1.39)	−(0.51)	(0.620)	−(0.57)
Political instability[2]	−0.034	0.008	−0.012	0.316
	−(0.66)	(0.20)	−(0.34)	(0.34)
Strength of special interests[3]	0.391	−0.05	−0.042	−9.424
	(1.15)	−(0.20)	−(0.18)	−(1.51)
Index of political cohesion[4]	−0.008	−0.092	−0.093	−0.060
	−(0.06)	−(0.86)	−(0.98)	−(0.02)
Bureaucracy quality interacted with change of chief executive[5]	0.007	0.009	0.055	0.391
	(0.02)	(0.04)	(0.29)	(0.08)
Variables under IMF control				
Share of structural conditions *(percent)*	−0.003	0.007	0.009	0.064
	−(0.30)	(1.11)	(1.59)	(0.42)
Instruments				
Average share of bilateral aid by Group of Seven (G-7) to the country before the program start	0.060	0.153	−0.038	3.009
	(0.49)	(1.60)	−(0.45)	(1.35)
Approval year	0.119	0.052	**0.110**	−0.199
	(1.55)	(0.86)	(2.04)	−(0.14)
Expected program duration	0.123	**0.251**	0.059	**−5.512**
	(0.93)	(2.40)	(0.63)	−(2.27)
IMF quota (log)	**0.469**	−0.128	0.219	**17.421**
	(2.01)	−(0.70)	(1.33)	(4.06)
Dummy for ESAF/PRGF	0.306	0.167	**−1.063**	**16.555**
	(0.80)	(0.56)	−(3.95)	(2.37)
GDP per capita (log)	**−0.442**	**0.418**	***−0.218***	**−8.443**
	−(2.45)	(2.93)	−(1.71)	−(2.55)
Latin America and Caribbean	**1.095**	**0.784**	0.313	0.303
	(2.29)	(2.08)	(0.93)	(0.03)
Sub-Saharan Africa	0.222	**0.968**	−0.046	13.041
	(0.40)	(2.24)	−(0.12)	(1.30)
East Asia	0.724	**1.609**	−0.005	***18.280***
	(1.31)	(3.70)	−(0.01)	(1.81)
Population (log)	−0.020	**0.291**	−0.121	**−10.740**
	−(0.11)	(2.02)	−(0.94)	−(3.21)
R^2	0.56	0.75	0.57	0.549
F-statistic on instruments	**3.37**	**9.48**	**3.55**	**2.94**
p-value	0.00	0.00	0.00	0.01

Notes: PCs denote performance criteria; ESAF denotes Enhanced Structural Adjustment Facility; and PRGF denotes Poverty Reduction and Growth Facility. Estimated by ordinary least squares (OLS) with robust standard errors. Regression also included the constant term, which is omitted in the table. Bold figures indicate significance at the 5 percent level; bold italic figures indicate significance at 10 percent level.

[1] IMF effort is the estimated dollar cost of IMF-supported programs computed based on the IMF's Budget Reporting System (BRS) data on hours spent by the staff on program implementation (which includes both preparation and supervision of the program) and estimated average salaries of the staff by grade. We also made use of data provided by the IMF's Office of Personnel Management (OPM) on the dollar costs of resident representatives.

[2] This index is computed based on the index of internal conflict provided by the *International Country Risk Guide (ICRG)* on a scale from zero to 12. Higher values of the index correspond to more internal political instability. We replaced the value of this variable by its maximum score (12) if there was a change of chief executive in the course of the IMF-supported program.

[3] Computed as the maximum share of seats in the parliament held by parties representing special interests (Political Institutions Database, World Bank). Four special interest groups are identified: religious, nationalistic, regional, and rural.

[4] The index of political cohesion is defined as follows: in presidential systems a high degree of political cohesion is said to exist if the same party is in control of the executive and legislature; in parliamentary systems a high degree of political cohesion means a one-party majority government. See the appendix for a more detailed definition.

[5] Bureaucracy quality *(ICRG)* measures the quality of a country's bureaucracy on a four-point scale. See the appendix for a more detailed definition. This variable is interacted with the dummy indicating that there was a change of chief executive (Political Institutions Database and CIA *World Factbook* for most recent years).

Table 7

Linear-in-Probability and Probit/Tobit Regressions on Three Implementation Measures Separately Ignoring Endogeneity of Variables Under IMF Control

	Our Specification of Political Economy Variables + Variables Under the IMF's Control					
Dependent Variable	Non-interruption dummy		Share of committed IMF disbursed[1]		Average overall implementation index	
Model	Linear in probability	Probit	Linear in probability	Tobit	Linear in probability	Tobit
Number of observations	57	57	53	53	55	55
Dollar and Svensson variables						
Ethnic fractionalization	1.50	0.05	**1.13**	**1.98**	**0.61**	**0.66**
	(1.58)	(1.43)	(2.28)	(2.24)	(2.47)	(2.91)
Ethnic fractionalization *(squared)*	−0.01	0.00	**−0.01**	**−0.02**	**−0.01**	**−0.01**
	−(1.18)	−(1.06)	−(2.05)	−(1.91)	−(2.34)	−(2.84)
Political instability[2]	**−8.13**	**−0.31**	**−3.79**	**−6.31**	−0.37	−0.30
	−(3.22)	−(2.52)	−(2.10)	−(2.51)	−(0.41)	−(0.44)
Other political economy variables						
Strength of special interests[3]	**−73.98**	**−2.83**	**−32.17**	**−60.48**	**−17.07**	**−17.25**
	−(3.92)	−(3.03)	−(2.92)	−(3.02)	−(2.96)	−(3.37)
Index of political cohesion[4]	**20.52**	**0.83**	**11.67**	**16.35**	−0.83	−1.17
	(3.26)	(2.50)	(3.00)	(2.70)	−(0.50)	−(0.65)
Bureaucracy quality interacted with change of chief executive[5]	**45.85**	**1.83**	**17.28**	**28.47**	4.36	4.28
	(4.16)	(2.51)	(2.29)	(2.20)	(0.97)	(1.21)
Variables under IMF control						
IMF effort per program year (log)[6]	***16.93***	***0.65***	−0.88	6.37	2.42	2.88
	(1.79)	(1.85)	−(0.17)	(0.77)	(1.29)	(1.30)
Loan size as percentage of quota (log)	4.92	0.15	3.29	3.10	2.28	2.34
	(0.54)	(0.56)	(0.64)	(0.42)	(1.63)	(1.19)
Number of conditions per program year (log)	−10.71	−0.49	−7.53	−13.18	**−11.44**	**−12.93**
	−(0.93)	−(0.97)	−(1.08)	−(1.28)	−(4.57)	−(4.14)
Share of quantitative PCs waived *(percent)*	−0.87	**−0.03**	0.09	−0.21	**−0.56**	**−0.58**
	−(1.45)	−(2.02)	(0.41)	−(0.48)	−(6.21)	−(5.12)
Share of structural conditions *(percent)*	0.22	0.01	0.15	0.28	−0.12	***−0.14***
	(0.73)	(0.86)	(0.98)	(1.00)	−(1.60)	−(1.78)
R^2	0.41		0.46		0.58	
Predictive ability of the model *(percent)*[7]		75.44				

Notes: Boldfaced figures indicate significance at the 5 percent level; bold italic figures indicate significance at the 10 percent level. PCs denote performance criteria.

[1] For the regression of the share of committed funds disbursed, we excluded arrangements precautionary on approval. Canceled programs that did not have irreversible interruption and arrangements that turned precautionary were treated as fully disbursed (100 percent).

[2] This index is computed based on the index of internal conflict provided by the *International Country Risk Guide (ICRG)* on a scale from zero to 12. Higher values of the index correspond to more internal political instability. We replaced the value of this variable by its maximum score (12) if there was a change of chief executive in the course of the IMF-supported program.

[3] Computed as the maximum share of seats in the parliament held by parties representing special interests (Political Institutions Database, World Bank). Four special interest groups are identified: religious, nationalistic, regional, and rural.

[4] The index of political cohesion is defined as follows: in presidential systems a high degree of political cohesion is said to exist if the same party is in control of the executive and legislature; in parliamentary systems a high degree of political cohesion means a one-party majority government. See the appendix for a more detailed definition.

[5] Bureaucracy quality *(ICRG)* measures the quality of a country's bureaucracy on a four-point scale. See the appendix for a more detailed definition. This variable is interacted with the dummy variable indicating that there was a change of chief executive (Political Institutions Database and CIA *World Factbook* for most recent years).

[6] IMF effort is the estimated dollar cost of IMF-supported programs computed based on the IMF's Budget Reporting System (BRS) data on hours spent by the staff on program implementation (including both preparation and supervision of the program) and estimated average salaries of the staff by grade. We also made use data provided by the IMF's Office of Personnel Management (OPM) on the dollar costs of resident representatives.

[7] The predictive ability of the model is computed as follows: if the predicted value from the probit regression was higher or equal to ½, we count this prediction as no interruption; otherwise, we count it as an interruption. We then compare the actual outcome with the predicted outcome and compute the share of correct predictions.

Table 8

IV Regressions for Non-Interruption Dummy Taking into Account Endogeneity of Variables Under IMF Control

Dependent Variable	Non-Interruption Dummy			
Regression number	(1)	(2)	(3)	(4)
Number of observations	61	61	61	61
Dollar and Svensson variables				
Ethnic fractionalization	0.042	***0.033***	0.027	0.037
	(1.32)	(1.09)	(0.86)	(1.17)
Ethnic fractionalization *(squared)*	0.000	0.000	0.000	0.000
	–(1.03)	–(0.70)	–(0.49)	–(0.72)
Political instability[1]	**–0.256**	**–0.251**	**–0.255**	**–0.318**
	–(2.40)	–(2.31)	–(2.31)	–(2.42)
Other political economy variables				
Strength of special interests[2]	**–2.329**	**–1.887**	**–1.974**	**–2.479**
	–(2.95)	–(2.51)	–(2.50)	–(2.97)
Index of political cohesion[3]	**0.636**	**0.632**	0.484	**0.856**
	(2.33)	(2.33)	(1.54)	(2.44)
Bureaucracy quality interacted with change of chief executive[4]	**1.355**	**1.435**	**1.345**	**1.656**
	(2.12)	(2.36)	(2.16)	(2.14)
Variables under IMF control				
IMF effort per program year (log)[5,6]	0.271			
	(0.57)			
Loan size as percentage of quota (log)[6]		0.464		
		(1.34)		
Number of conditions per program year (log)[6]			–0.356	
			–(0.52)	
Share of quantitative PCs waived *(percent)*[6]				–0.045
				–(1.34)
Predictive ability of model[7]	70.49	72.41	66.67	63.93

Notes: Boldfaced figures indicate significance at the 5 percent level. PCs denote performance criteria. ESAF denotes Enhanced Structural Adjustment Facility, and PRGF denotes Poverty Reduction and Growth Facility.

For IV estimation on each of the implementation measures separately, we use shorter sets of IVs:

For IMF effort per program year (log): expected program duration, quota (log), and GDP per capita (log);
For loan size as percentage of quota (log): expected program duration, GDP per capita (log), and population (log);
For number of conditions per program year (log): approval year, dummy for ESAF/PRGF, and GDP per capita (log); and
For share of quantitative PCs waived (percent): quota (log), GDP per capita (log), and population (log).

IV regression for non-interruption dummy was estimated using the two-stage Amemiya GLS procedure (IV probit).

[1] This index is computed based on the index of internal conflict provided by the *International Country Risk Guide (ICRG)* on a scale from 0 to 12. Higher values of the index correspond to more internal political instability. We replaced the value of this variable by its maximum score (12) if there was a change of chief executive in the course of the IMF-supported program.

[2] Computed as the maximum share of seats in the parliament held by parties representing special interests (Political Institutions Database, World Bank). Four special interest groups are identified: religious, nationalistic, regional, and rural.

[3] The index of political cohesion is defined as follows: in presidential systems a high degree of political cohesion is said to exist if the same party is in control of the executive and legislature; in parliamentary systems a high degree of political cohesion means a one-party majority government. See the appendix for a more detailed definition.

[4] Bureaucracy quality *(ICRG)* measures the quality of a country's bureaucracy on a four-point scale. See the appendix for a more detailed definition. This variable is interacted with the dummy variable indicating that there was a change of chief executive (Political Institutions Database and CIA *World Factbook* for most recent years).

[5] IMF effort is the estimated dollar cost of IMF-supported programs computed based on the IMF's Budget Reporting System (BRS) data on hours spent by the staff on program implementation (which includes both preparation and supervision of the program) and estimated average salaries of the staff by grade. We also made use of data provided by the IMF's Office of Personnel Management (OPM) on the dollar costs of resident representatives.

[6] Treated as an endogenous variable in this regression.

[7] The predictive ability of the model is computed as follows: if the predicted value from the probit regression is higher or equal to ½, we count this prediction as no interruption; otherwise, we count this prediction as an interruption. We then compare the actual outcome with the predicted outcome and compute the share of correct predictions.

Table 9

IV Regressions for the Average Share of Committed Funds Disbursed Taking into Account Endogeneity of Variables Under IMF Control

Dependent Variable	Share of Committed Funds Disbursed			
Regression number	(1)	(2)	(3)	(4)
Number of observations	55	55	55	55
Dollar and Svensson variables				
Ethnic fractionalization	1.234	***1.478***	***1.553***	1.165
	(1.38)	(1.88)	(1.95)	(1.45)
Ethnic fractionalization *(squared)*	–0.010	–0.012	–0.013	–0.008
	–(1.03)	–(1.46)	–(1.54)	–(0.97)
Political instability[1]	**–6.022**	**–5.351**	**–5.925**	**–6.289**
	–(2.42)	–(2.26)	–(2.45)	–(2.48)
Other political economy variables				
Strength of special interests[2]	**–49.287**	**–49.505**	**–51.833**	**–50.597**
	–(2.58)	–(2.80)	–(2.97)	–(2.77)
Index of political cohesion[3]	**16.820**	**17.807**	**13.194**	**18.703**
	(2.95)	(3.18)	(2.03)	(2.87)
Bureaucracy quality interacted with change of chief executive[4]	**26.162**	***23.426***	***25.209***	***27.253***
	(2.00)	(1.88)	(1.99)	(2.03)
Variables under IMF control				
IMF effort per program year (log)[5,6]	–1.311			
	–(0.10)			
Loan size as percentage of quota (log)[6]		4.349		
		(0.49)		
Number of conditions per program year (log)[6]			–22.011	
			–(1.30)	
Share of quantitative PCs waived *(percent)*[6]				–0.638
				–(0.78)

Notes: Boldfaced figures indicate significance at the 5 percent level. PCs denote performance criteria; ESAF denotes Enhanced Structural Adjustment Facility, and PRGF denotes Poverty Reduction and Growth Facility.

For IV estimation on each of the implementation measures separately, we use shorter sets of IVs:

For IMF effort per program year (log): expected program duration, quota (log), and GDP per capita (log);
For loan size as percentage of quota (log): expected program duration, GDP per capita (log), and population (log);
For number of conditions per program year (log): approval year, dummy for ESAF/PRGF, and GDP per capita (log); and
For share of quantitative PCs waived (percent): quota (log), GDP per capita (log), and population (log).

IV regression for the share of committed funds disbursed was estimated using two-stage Amemiya (1978) GLS procedure (IV tobit).

For the regression of the share of committed funds disbursed, we excluded arrangements precautionary on approval. Canceled programs that did not have irreversible interruptions and arrangements that turned precautionary were treated as fully disbursed (100 percent).

[1] This index is computed based on the index of internal conflict provided by the *International Country Risk Guide (ICRG)* on a scale from 0 to 12. Higher values of the index correspond to more internal political instability. We replaced the value of this variable by its maximum score (12) if there was a change of chief executive in the course of the IMF-supported program.

[2] Computed as the maximum share of seats in the parliament held by parties representing special interests (Political Institutions Database, World Bank). Four special interest groups are identified: religious, nationalistic, regional, and rural.

[3] The index of political cohesion is defined as follows: in presidential systems, a high degree of political cohesion is said to exist if the same party is in control of the executive and legislature; in parliamentary systems, a high degree of political cohesion means a one-party majority government. See the appendix for a more detailed definition.

[4] Bureaucracy quality *(ICRG)* measures the quality of a country's bureaucracy on a four-point scale. See the appendix for a more detailed definition. This variable is interacted with the dummy variable indicating that there was a change of chief executive (Political Institutions Database and CIA *World Factbook* for most recent years).

[5] IMF effort is the estimated dollar cost of IMF-supported programs computed based on the IMF's Budget Reporting System (BRS) data on hours spent by the staff on program implementation (which includes both preparation and supervision of the program) and estimated average salaries of the staff by grade. We also made use of data provided by the IMF's Office of Personnel Management (OPM) on the dollar costs of resident representatives.

[6] Treated as an endogenous variable in this regression.

Table 10

IV Regressions for Average Overall Implementation Index Taking into Account Endogeneity of Variables Under IMF Control

Dependent Variable	Average Overall Implementation Index			
Regression number	(1)	(2)	(3)	(4)
Number of observations	55	55	55	55
Dollar and Svensson variables				
Ethnic fractionalization	0.525	**0.695**	**0.697**	**0.668**
	(1.63)	(2.49)	(2.32)	(2.69)
Ethnic fractionalization *(squared)*	***–0.006***	**–0.008**	**–0.008**	**–0.007**
	–(1.74)	–(2.63)	–(2.40)	–(2.59)
Political instability[1]	–0.329	–0.076	–0.080	–0.417
	–(0.38)	–(0.09)	–(0.09)	–(0.56)
Other political economy variables				
Strength of special interests[2]	**–14.183**	**–15.304**	**–16.680**	**–18.900**
	–(2.12)	–(2.41)	–(2.52)	–(3.42)
Index of political cohesion[3]	–1.675	–0.747	–0.911	1.143
	–(0.77)	–(0.35)	–(0.34)	(0.55)
Bureaucracy quality interacted with change of chief executive[4]	3.457	3.375	3.069	4.369
	(0.77)	(0.77)	(0.64)	(1.11)
Variables under IMF control				
IMF effort per program year (log)[5,6]	–5.095			
	–(1.15)			
Loan size as percentage of quota (log)[6]		3.188		
		(1.01)		
Number of conditions per program year (log)[6]			2.126	
			(0.32)	
Share of quantitative PCs waived *(percent)*[6]				**–0.600**
				–(2.51)

Notes: Boldfaced figures indicate significance at the 5 percent level. PCs denote performance criteria; ESAF denotes Enhanced Structural Adjustment Facility, and PRGF denotes Poverty Reduction and Growth Facility.

For IV estimation on each of the implementation measures separately, we use shorter sets of IVs:

For IMF effort per program year (log): expected program duration, quota (log), and GDP per capita (log);
For loan size as percentage of quota (log): expected program duration, GDP per capita (log), and population (log);
For number of conditions per program year (log): approval year, dummy for ESAF/PRGF, and GDP per capita (log); and
For share of quantitative PCs waived (percent): quota (log), GDP per capita (log), and population (log).

IV regression for the average overall implementation index was estimated using the two-stage Amemiya GLS procedure (IV tobit).

[1] This index is computed based on the index of internal conflict provided by the *International Country Risk Guide (ICRG)* on a scale from 0 to 12. Higher values of the index correspond to more internal political instability. We replaced the value of this variable by its maximum score (12) if there was a change of chief executive in the course of the IMF-supported program.

[2] Computed as the maximum share of seats in the parliament held by parties representing special interests (Political Institutions Database, World Bank). Four special interest groups are identified: religious, nationalistic, regional, and rural.

[3] The index of political cohesion is defined as follows: in presidential systems a high degree of political cohesion is said to exist if the same party is in control of the executive and legislature; in parliamentary systems a high degree of political cohesion means a one-party majority government. See the appendix for a more detailed definition.

[4] Bureaucracy quality *(ICRG)* measures the quality of a country's bureaucracy on a four-point scale. See the appendix for a more detailed definition. This variable is interacted with the dummy variable indicating that there was a change of chief executive (Political Institutions Database and CIA *World Factbook* for most recent years).

[5] IMF effort is the estimated dollar cost of IMF-supported programs computed based on the IMF's Budget Reporting System (BRS) data on hours spent by the staff on program implementation (which includes both preparation and supervision of the program) and estimated average salaries of the staff by grade. We also made use of data provided by the IMF's Office of Personnel Management (OPM) on the dollar costs of resident representatives.

[6] Treated as an endogenous variable in this regression.

Neither incumbents' democratic credentials nor their newness in office is associated with better program implementation (Table 4).[26] The coefficients on democratic election of a leader (dummy variable) and time in power were insignificant in almost all specifications. Likelihood-ratio tests for the tobit specification confirmed that these exclusions did not substantially worsen model performance. The first result corroborates anecdotal evidence that the implementation of IMF-supported programs does not suffer in countries with authoritarian regimes.

The magnitude and even direction of impact of most reforms is ambiguous, especially at the outset, making them unpopular with policymakers and their public even as these reforms enhance welfare in the long run. This may lead to democratic administrations in developing or transition countries having a harder time than dictators marshaling the support they need to pursue successful reforms. The absence of significant correlation between a government's length of tenure and the probability of successful program implementation is also intriguing. It suggests that one should not expect too much of new, reform-minded governments implementing IMF-supported reforms in countries with adverse political economy characteristics. Perhaps the lack of correlation also reflects public sector characteristics we have not captured.

Initial and external economic conditions do not seem to influence program implementation much once political economy variables are taken into account. The coefficients on all initial and external conditions in the random-effects regressions came out individually and jointly insignificant (Table 4).[27] Initial conditions were insignificant in the IV regressions as well—to save space, we do not present these results here. The coefficients on the political economy variables do not change appreciably when the estimation excludes initial conditions (Table 4, column 3). As already mentioned, the fact that initial conditions do not affect the probability of program implementation does not necessarily imply that IMF-supported programs are optimally designed. It does, however, indicate that unfavorable initial or external conditions per se do not compromise programs' prospects of being successfully implemented.

Variables controlled by the IMF, including financial and human effort and the breadth and depth of conditionality, do not affect program implementation once domestic political economy variables are taken into account. IMF effort was measured by the dollar cost of staff hours spent on UFR and on technical assistance tasks per program year and the loan size in relation to a country's IMF quota. The extent of conditionality was captured by the total number of conditions per program year, the share of quantitative performance criteria waived, and the share of structural conditions in conditionality.[28,29] Once their endogeneity was accounted for, IMF-related variables did not significantly affect the probability of successful program implementation (Tables 6, 8–10).[30] The overidentifying restrictions test confirmed the validity of including additional IVs in the regressions. The Hausman test suggests that IV random-effects regressions were not much different from the simple random-effects model.

The coefficients on IMF-related variables were insignificant in many regressions when their endogeneity was ignored (Tables 4 and 7, column 4). We note two exceptions. First, the share of quantitative performance criteria waived was, in several cases, negatively correlated with the probability of successful program implementation. This partly reflects the nature of the implementation index, which is assigned a value of zero if the condition is waived. Second, IMF effort was positively correlated (at the 10 percent significance level) with the index of completion of IMF-supported programs (Table 7). This correlation vanished when the endogeneity of these two variables was taken into account.

Illustration

It is helpful to illustrate the estimated impacts of political economy variables on the probability of program implementation. Consider the marginal effects of improved political stability, political cohesion, and the quality of bureaucracy, based on the IV regression of the no-interruption dummy (Table 8,

[26] It will be recalled that Dollar and Svensson (2000) concluded that the implementation of Bank-supported programs improves in countries with democratically elected governments.

[27] The null hypothesis that the coefficients on all of these variables are jointly insignificant could not be rejected at the 5 percent significance level. Likelihood-ratio test statistics for this test going from the tobit regression in column 2 of Table 5 to the tobit regression in column 3 of Table 5 was 6.98 with p-value equal to 0.43.

[28] We also tried the number of structural conditions per program year as an alternative measure of the extent of structural conditionality. We do not report the results of this estimation, as the results were essentially the same. Interestingly, the coefficient on the number of structural conditions turned negative in many cases, although still insignificant.

[29] IMF-related variables are included in these regressions taking into account the limitations of our small sample size. See the notes to Tables 8 through 10 for the description of the shorter IV sets used in the regressions of the implementation measures separately.

[30] We also included the share of prior actions and conditions for completion of review in the total number of conditions in our work. We tried two regressions, one ignoring the endogeneity of prior actions and a second one in which we instrumented for this variable. In both cases, the coefficient on prior actions was insignificant and is not reported. It appears that more careful study on prior actions is needed in order to analyze their impact on program implementation. One consideration is the lack of information on programs that are not approved or of program reviews that are not completed as a result of failing to meet prior actions. (MONA does not provide this information.) In our view, it is unlikely that this result will change even if the selection bias is properly accounted for.

Figure 4
Probability of Successful Implementation, Strength of Special Interests and Political Instability

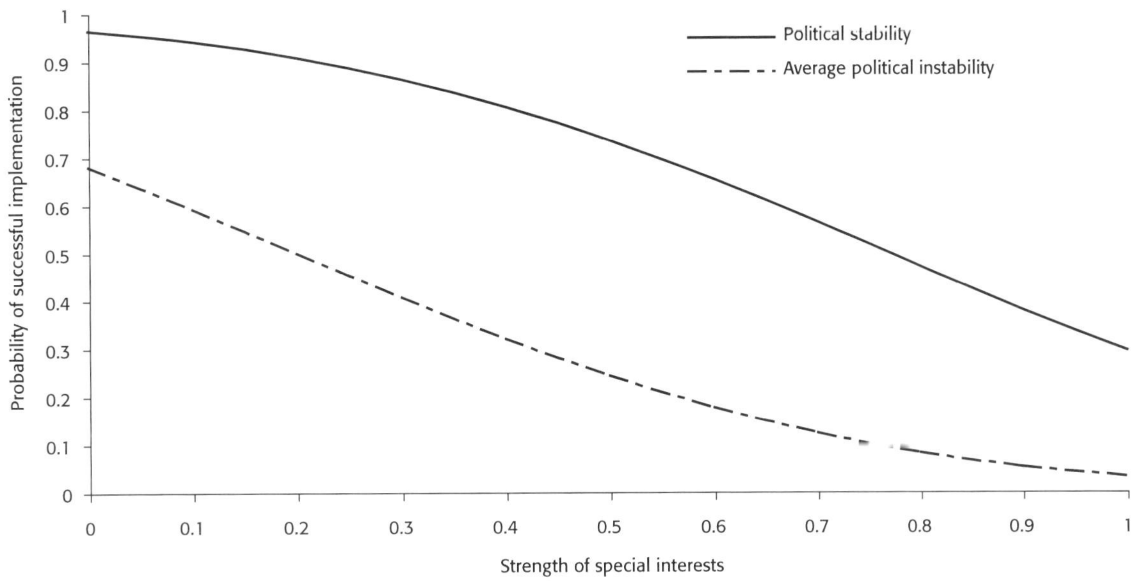

Note: Probabilities are evaluated at the means of other explanatory variables.

column 1). For a country that enjoys perfect political stability and no special interests in parliament, the probability of program implementation is very high (96 percent). If political stability is only average, the chances of successful program implementation decline to 70 percent (Figure 4). If parties representing special interests occupy 20 percent of the seats in parliament, a program only has a 50-50 chance of implementation.

Lack of political cohesion reduces the probability of program implementation by 50 percentage points (from 70 percent to 20 percent) when there are no special interests. If 20 percent of the seats in parliament are controlled by special interests, the probability of program implementation drops another 10 percentage points (Figure 5). The impact of a country's bureaucracy on program implementation is also substantial. On the one hand, in the absence of special interests, the probability of program implementation increases from 50 percent when the quality of the bureaucracy is low to 74 percent when the bureaucracy is of average quality (Figure 6). If, on the other hand, special interests control 20 percent of the seats in parliament, the probability of program implementation increases from 33 percent when the quality of the bureaucracy is low to 50 percent when the bureaucracy is of average quality.

Robustness Checks and Limitations

Although our relatively small sample size makes it difficult to reach definitive conclusions, our findings appear to be robust to the specification of regressions, the choice of left-hand-side variable, and the choice of the measure of IMF effort. As already demonstrated, our main conclusions regarding the effect of political economy and IMF-related variables on program implementation are robust to the precise specification of the econometric model. Estimating random-effects models on a pooled dataset and re-estimations using the appropriate probit and tobit technique for each of our three implementation measures separately lead to similar conclusions.

Our basic conclusions also are robust to alternative specifications of IMF effort. We tried various alternatives to our primary IMF effort variable (the dollar cost of IMF hours invested in country work between the approval and actual end dates of the program). Various other measures, such as the number of missions per program year and the number of mission days per program year, yield qualitatively similar results. Even though the number of missions and mission days are positively and strongly correlated with program implementation when their endogeneity is not accounted for, this association disappears in the proper IV regressions.[31] We also considered a measure of IMF effort scaled by the loan size, correcting for their strong correlation. While the IMF exerts greater effort in monitoring larger loans (as measured by staff hours per dollar

[31] It will be recalled that this linkage was not present when IMF effort was proxied by the estimated cost of IMF-supported programs.

Figure 5
Probability of Successful Implementation, Strength of Special Interests, and Political Cohesion

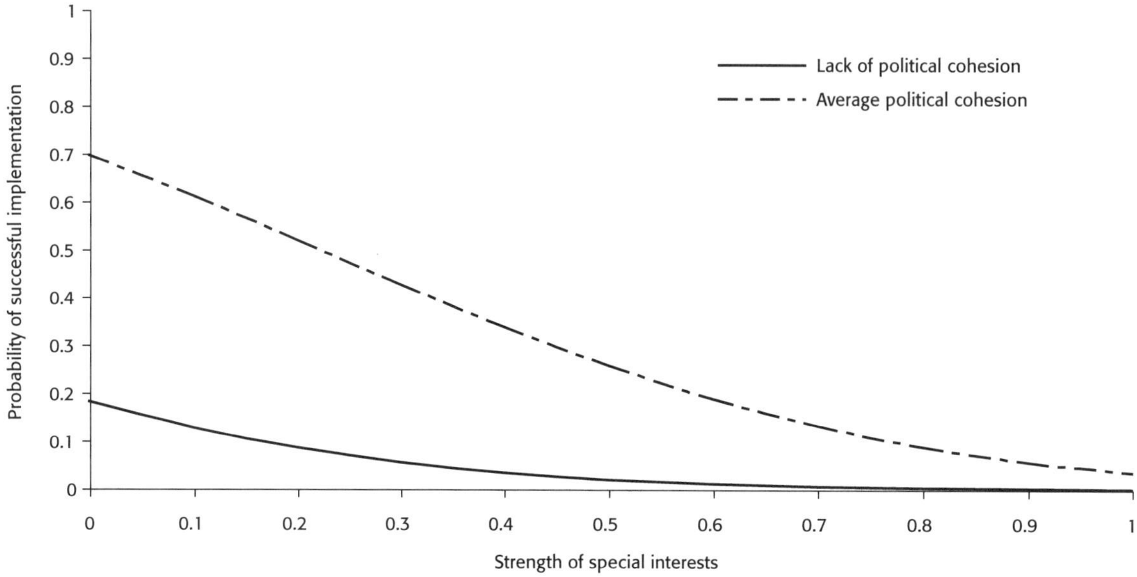

Note: Probabilities are evaluated at the means of other explanatory variables.

Figure 6
Probability of Successful Implementation, Strength of Special Interests, and Quality of Bureaucracy

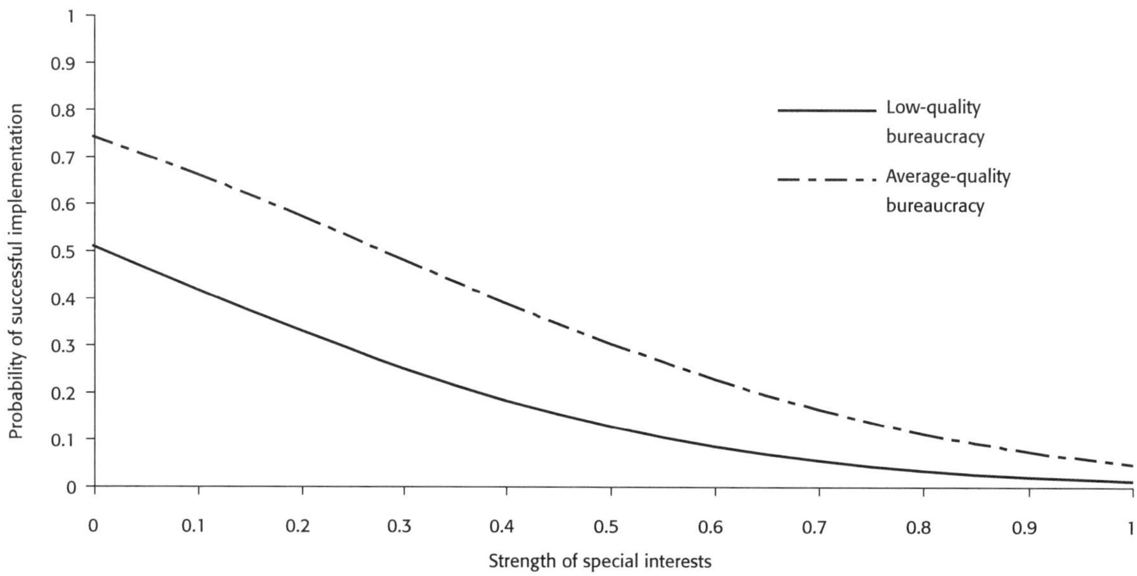

Note: Probabilities are evaluated at the means of other explanatory variables.

lent), this does not lead to better program implementation. Finally, investing more IMF effort into program preparation, as measured by the dollar cost of staff hours and the number of missions or mission days to a country three and six months before program approval, does not affect program implementation either.

While useful, our approach is not without limitations. To begin with, the linear-in-probability specification may not be an appropriate statistical model for the irreversible-interruptions indicator. Moreover, the assumption of constant variance needed to apply the random-effects model is hard to justify in the linear-in-probability model. We believe that these drawbacks are outweighed by the substantial informational advantages from pooling the implementation indicators in one econometric model (see, for example, Lubotsky and Wittenberg, 2001). As additional political economy data become available, it should be possible to extend our dataset and provide a more thorough check of the robustness of our results.

Concluding Remarks

This paper makes a start on providing an econometrically informed assessment of the factors influencing the implementation of IMF-supported programs. This approach fills a gap in a literature that, until recently, has evaluated the macroeconomic and structural impacts of these programs without making adequate distinctions between implemented and nonimplemented programs. The paper presents a variety of (new and old) statistical indicators of program implementation and the groups of factors that could affect it, including (a) quantitative measures of the political environment in borrowing countries, (b) the conditionality and financial and human resources invested by the IMF in programs, and (c) initial economic conditions and subsequent shocks in borrowing countries. The main findings are as follows:

- Failures in program implementation are associated with a small number of observable political indicators in borrowing countries, including the strength of special interests in parliament, lack of political cohesion in the government, ethnic fragmentation in the broader society, and the combination of political instability and an inefficient bureaucracy.
- Indicators of the IMF's investment of financial and human effort in programs and the depth and breadth of conditionality are not good predictors of program implementation. This is an uncomfortable conclusion, although it could be partly due to imprecise measurement of IMF inputs into programs.
- There is no association between initial and external conditions and the probability of program implementation, indicating that program targets may incorporate realistic goals and be related effectively to a member's initial "position." Interestingly, and despite previous evidence to the contrary (see Killick, 1998), a member's initial indebtedness does not affect the outcome of IMF-supported programs.

The strong empirical link between political variables in borrowing countries and the outcomes of IMF-supported programs documented in the paper suggests some changes in the way the IMF approaches the extension of its financial support. First, the IMF could take political information and constraints in borrowing countries into consideration systematically. With the adoption of new conditionality guidelines in 2002, the IMF has streamlined its conditionality and is more carefully tailoring programs to members' circumstances. The IMF also has committed itself to changing its interactions with borrowing countries to put them in the driver's seat in designing and implementing reforms. Second, to make systematically informed political judgments, the IMF could methodically collect the growing numbers of political indicators made available by research in quantitative political science. Such information could be used much like economic information, as one input in forward-looking quantitative assessments of program prospects and risks in individual countries. Third, the close connection between the strength of special interests and weak program implementation documented in the paper underscores the need for programs to take measures to inform and defuse resistance to reforms. These actions are described in detail elsewhere (see Boughton and Mourmouras, 2004). Related to this, the paper's results strongly suggest that programs need to take into account more systematically than in the past the way legislatures and other key domestic players affect the implementation of reforms. While this will undoubtedly make programs more complex to design and negotiate, the additional payoff in terms of improved implementation may be well worth the extra effort.

The paper's results are also relevant in addressing the issue of selectivity in IMF financing. How high should the IMF set the bar in approving (or continuing) programs if objective political indicators and other evidence (including prior IMF experience with failed programs) indicate that these programs would have a low probability of implementation, despite the IMF's anticipated best efforts? In some cases, the IMF may have no choice but to stay involved, if only because broader considerations are involved. This could be the case, for instance, in some low-income countries in which donor aid, including support under the debt initiative for Heavily Indebted Poor Countries (HIPCs), is predicated on the presence of an active IMF-supported program. In other cases, however, if the probability of implementation is judged to be below some acceptable threshold, the IMF and its membership might fare better if the IMF exercised greater selectivity in providing financing.

The combination of more selectivity, streamlined conditionality, and enhanced ownership would enable the IMF to counter criticisms that it grants too many waivers or is otherwise lax in its enforcement of conditionality. This combination would also improve the quality of IMF-supported programs as signals and catalysts of private investment. The IMF also could become a better catalyst for change in borrowing countries that do not meet the threshold required to receive its assistance. Even though the IMF would not be providing loans to these countries, it would continue being active through surveillance, economic education, and technical assistance, and encouraging open debate about policy options and trade-offs. Especially useful in this regard would be dialogue with reform-oriented groups in borrowing countries, both explaining the IMF's points of view and hearing their perspectives (see Birdsall, 2000).

Future work in this area will involve both a more systematic collection of information on IMF-supported programs and more careful econometric modeling of these programs' impacts. The top priority is establishing on a firmer basis the relation between program implementation and macroeconomic impact. Even though this paper presented some evidence that improved program implementation was associated with strengthened economic performance, econometric research on the connection between program implementation and macroeconomic success is at an early stage. A more definitive econometric study is needed to measure the impact of improved program implementation on fiscal and balance of payments outcomes, and inflation and growth. The connection between IMF efforts in borrowing countries and program outcomes needs to be reassessed as well. The indicators of IMF effort need to be refined by, among other things, examining in greater detail how missions and staff inputs are related to specific programs and their outcomes. One would hope that the IMF's Independent Evaluation Office would follow the example of the World Bank's Operation Evaluations Department in collecting and analyzing information on lender efforts at the program design, negotiation, and implementation stages. Such disaggregated information on IMF efforts would permit researchers analyzing IMF-supported programs to ascertain the effectiveness with which the IMF allocates its resources in addressing the needs of borrowing countries.

Appendix. Detailed Definitions and Data Sources

Program Implementation

An interruption occurs if an SBA program review was delayed by more than three months or not completed at all; if a program review for ESAF/PRGF programs was delayed by more than six months or not completed at all; if there was an interval of more than six months between two subsequent years of a multiyear arrangement; or if at least one of the annual arrangements was not approved. Exceptions are programs that were canceled and replaced by another program, in which case noncompleted reviews and nonapproved annual arrangements are not counted as interruptions.

An irreversible interruption occurs if either the last scheduled program review was not completed (all programs) or all scheduled reviews were completed but the subsequent annual arrangement was not approved (ESAF/PRGF arrangements).

The Macroeconomic Implementation Index for a given macroeconomic performance criterion is equal to 100 percent if the macroeconomic performance criterion was met or met after modification; it is equal to 0 if the macroeconomic performance criterion was not met, not met after modification, waived, or waived after modification. The Macroeconomic Implementation Index for a program then is computed as the average of Macroeconomic Implementation Indices across all macroeconomic performance criteria for this program.

The Structural Implementation Index for a given structural condition is equal to 100 percent if the structural condition was met or met with small delay for structural benchmarks; it is equal to 50 percent if the structural condition was partially met or delayed for performance criteria; and it is equal to 0 if the structural condition was not met. The Structural Implementation Index for a program then is computed as the average of Structural Implementation Indices across all structural conditions for this program.

The Average Overall Implementation Index for a given program is the average of Macroeconomic and Structural Implementation indices over all conditions in this program.

Political Indicators

Ethnic fractionalization measures the probability that two randomly selected people in a country belong to different ethno-linguistic groups. (In regressions, this variable was scaled to range between zero and 100.) (See Easterly and Levine, 1997.)

The *political instability index* is computed based on the index of internal conflict provided by the ICRG on a scale from zero to 12. Higher values of the index correspond to more internal political instability. We replaced the value of this variable by its maximum score (12) if there was a change of chief executive in the course of an IMF-supported program.

The *executive index of electoral competitiveness* is a dummy variable that is equal to one if the executive index of electoral competitiveness is equal to seven and 0 otherwise. The executive index of electoral competitiveness is from the Database of Political Institutions of the World Bank. It ranges from one to seven, with higher values corresponding to more competitive elections.

Time in power is the number of years a chief executive has been in power by the approval year of the program. We assigned zero to this variable if there was a change of chief executive in the course of the program (Database of Political Institutions and CIA *World Factbook* for the most recent years).

The strength of special interests is computed as the maximum share of seats in the parliament held by parties representing special interests (Database of Political Institutions, World Bank). Four special interest groups are identified: religious, nationalistic, regional, and rural.

The *index of political cohesion* is defined as follows: "For presidential systems, it is zero if different parties are in control of the executive and legislature (if multiple pro-presidential parties, they must not control the legislature); it is one if the same party is in control of the executive and legislature (if there are multiple pro-presidential parties, they must together control the legislature)."

For parliamentary systems, the index is zero for a minority government, one for a coalition government with three or more parties, two for a coalition government with two parties, and three for a one-party majority government (Database of Political Institutions, World Bank).

Bureaucracy quality (ICRG) measures the quality of a country's bureaucracy on a four-point scale. There was a change in scale for this variable, from a six-point to a four-point scale, in August 1997. We rescaled the older series to be measured on a four-point basis. We interact this variable with the dummy indicating that there was a change of chief executive (Database of Political Institutions and CIA *World Factbook* for the most recent years).

IMF-Related Variables

IMF effort is the dollar cost of IMF programs computed based on its Budget Reporting System (BRS) data on hours spent by staff on program implementation (it includes program preparation and supervision) and estimated average salaries of the staff by grade. Alternative measures of IMF effort were *dollar costs of resident representatives* (provided by the Office of Budget and Planning (OBP)), *number of missions*, and *number of mission days* (both were provided by the Policy Development and Review Department (PDR)).

Number of conditions per program year is the total number of conditions (structural and quantitative) divided by the actual duration of the program (the IMF's Monitoring of IMF Arrangements (MONA) database).

Share of quantitative PCs waived is the number of quantitative performance criteria waived over the course of the program divided by the total number of quantitative performance criteria for this program, in percentage points (MONA).

Share of structural conditions is the number of structural conditions divided by the total number of conditions, in percentage points (MONA).

Loan size as percentage of quota is the total committed amount including augmentations divided by the country's quota at the IMF (International Financial Statistics (IFS)).

Debt to the IMF as percentage of IMF quota is actual holdings as percentage of quota from IFS.

Program approval year from MONA.

Expected program duration is the number of years the program was scheduled to last (MONA).

IMF quota is from the IMF's International Financial Statistics database.

Economic Conditions and Policies

Terms of trade shock is the average growth rate of dollar export prices multiplied by the initial share of exports in GDP *minus* average growth rate of dollar import prices multiplied by the initial share of imports in GDP over the course of the program, from IFS.

The following variables are from IFS: *central government balance*, *GDP*, *reserves minus gold*, *CPI inflation*, and *imports*.

The following variables are from the IMF's World Economic Outlook (WEO) database: *current account balance*; *initial population*.

Finally, *GDP per capita* is from the World Bank's *World Development Indicators* (*WDI*).

Other

The average share of bilateral aid given by the Group of Seven (G-7) to the country before the program start was computed as the average of the shares of gross official transfers that each of the G-7 countries allocated to a particular country one year prior to the approval year of the IMF program for that country (Organization for Economic Cooperation and Development (OECD)).

References

Åslund, Anders, 1999, "Why Has Russia's Economic Transformation Been So Arduous?" paper prepared for the Annual World Bank Conference on Development Economics (Washington: Carnegie Endowment for International Peace), April 28–30.

Beck, Thorsten, George Clarke, Alberto Groff, Philip Keefer, and Patrick Walsh, 2001, "New Tools in Comparative Political Economy: The Database of Political Institutions," *World Bank Economic Review*, Vol. 15 (September), pp. 165–76.

Bird, Graham, 2002, "Conditionality and Ownership: How to Improve the Implementation of IMF Programmes," Working Paper (Guildford, Surrey, United Kingdom: Surrey Center for International Economic Studies, University of Surrey).

Birdsall, Nancy, 2000, "The World Bank of the Future: Victim, Villain, Global Credit Union?" remarks delivered at the conference "Promoting Dialogue: Global

Challenges and Global Institutions" (Washington: American University), April 13, available on the Web at *http://www.odc.org/commentary/bird-au.html.*

Boughton, James M., and Alex Mourmouras, 2002, "Whose Programme Is It? Policy Ownership With Conditional Lending," Chapter 9 in *The IMF and its Critics*, ed. by David Vines and Christopher L. Gilbert (Cambridge, United Kingdom: Cambridge University Press), pp. 225–53.

Bredenkamp, Hugh, and Susan Schadler, eds., 1999, *Economic Adjustment and Reform in Low-Income Countries* (Washington: International Monetary Fund).

Bulíř, Aleš, and Soojin Moon, 2003, "Do IMF-Supported Programs Help Make Fiscal Adjustment More Durable?" IMF Working Paper 03/38 (Washington: International Monetary Fund). This paper also appears, in somewhat different form, as Chapter 14 in this volume.

Conway, Patrick, 1994, "IMF Lending Programs: Participation and Impact," *Journal of Development Economics*, Vol. 45, pp. 365–91.

———, 1998a, "Evaluating Fund Programs: Methodology and Empirical Estimates" (unpublished working paper: University of North Carolina at Chapel Hill).

———, 1998b, "IMF Programs and External Balance: The Crisis-Participation Dynamic" (unpublished working paper: University of North Carolina at Chapel Hill).

Dollar, David, and Jakob Svensson, 2000, "What Explains the Success or Failure of Bank-Supported Adjustment Programs," *Economic Journal*, Vol. 110 (October), pp. 894–917.

Drazen, Allan, 2002, "Conditionality and Ownership in IMF Lending: A Political Economy Approach," *Staff Papers*, International Monetary Fund, Vol. 49, Special Issue, pp. 36–67.

Easterly, William, and Ross Levine, 1997, "Africa's Growth Tragedy: Policies and Ethnic Divisions," *Quarterly Journal of Economics*, Vol. 112, pp. 203–50.

Haque, Nadeem Ul, and Mohsin S. Khan, 1998, "Do IMF-Supported Programs Work? A Survey of the Cross-Country Empirical Evidence," IMF Working Paper 98/169 (Washington: International Monetary Fund).

Havrylyshyn, Oleh, and John Odling-Smee, 2000, "Political Economy of Stalled Reforms," *Finance & Development*, Vol. 37 (September), pp. 7–10.

Hellman, Joel, and Daniel Kaufmann, 2001, "Confronting the Challenge of State Capture in Transition Economies," *Finance & Development*, Vol. 38 (September), pp. 31–35.

International Monetary Fund (IMF), 1998, *External Evaluation of the ESAF: Report by a Group of Independent Experts* (Washington: International Monetary Fund).

———, 2001a, "Strengthening Country Ownership of Fund-Supported Programs" (Washington: International Monetary Fund), available on the Web at *http://www.imf.org/external/np/pdr/cond/2001/eng/strength/120501.pdf.*

———, 2001b, "Conditionality in IMF-Supported Programs—Policy Issues" (Washington: International Monetary Fund), March, available on the Web at *http://www.imf.org/external/np/pdr/cond/2001/eng/policy/021601.pdf.*

———, 2001c, "Structural Conditionality in IMF-Supported Programs" (Washington: International Monetary Fund), March, available on the Web at *http://www.imf.org/external/np/pdr/cond/2001/eng/struct/cond.pdf.*

———, 2002, "Guidelines on Conditionality" (Washington: International Monetary Fund), September, available on the Web at *http://www.imf.org/External/np/pdr/cond/2002/eng/guid/092302.htm.*

Joreskog, Karl G., and Arthur Goldberger, 1975, "Estimation of a Model with Multiple Indicators and Multiple Causes of a Single Latent Variable," *Journal of the American Statistical Association*, Vol. 70 (September), pp. 631–39.

Joyce, Joseph P., 2002, "Through a Glass Darkly: What We Know (and Don't Know) About IMF Programs," paper presented at the IMF Conference on Research on IMF-Supported Programs, Washington, June.

Killick, Tony, with Ramani Gunatilaka and Ana Marr, 1998, *Aid and the Political Economy of Policy Change* (London: Routledge).

Lubotsky, Darren, and Martin Wittenberg, 2001, "Interpretation of Regressions with Multiple Proxies," (unpublished working paper; Princeton, New Jersey: Princeton University).

Mayer, Wolfgang, and Alex Mourmouras, 2002, "Vested Interests in a Positive Theory of IFI Conditionality," IMF Working Paper 02/73 (Washington: International Monetary Fund).

Mecagni, Mauro, 1999, "The Causes of Program Interruptions," in *Economic Adjustment and Reform in Low-Income Countries*, ed. by Hugh Bredenkamp and Susan Schadler (Washington: International Monetary Fund).

Mussa, Michael, and Miguel Savastano, 1999, "The IMF Approach to Economic Stabilization," IMF Working Paper 99/104 (Washington: International Monetary Fund).

Odling-Smee, John, 2001, "Belarus: Recent Experience and Challenges Ahead," speech given at the Belarusian Academy of Management, Minsk, November 6, available on the Web at *http://www.imf.org/external/np/speeches/2001/110601.htm.*

Schadler, Susan, Adam Bennett, Maria Carkovic, Louis Dicks-Mireaux, Mauro Mecagni, James H. J. Morsink, and Miguel A. Savastano, 1995a, *IMF Conditionality: Experience Under Stand-By and Extended Arrangements, Part I: Key Issues and Findings*, IMF Occasional Paper No. 128 (Washington: International Monetary Fund).

———, 1995b, *IMF Conditionality: Experience Under Stand-By and Extended Arrangements, Part II: Background Papers*, IMF Occasional Paper No. 129 (Washington: International Monetary Fund).

Thomas, Alun, 2003, "Prior Actions—True Repentance? An Evaluation Based on IMF Programs over the 1992–1999 Period" (unpublished paper; Washington: Policy Development and Review Department, International Monetary Fund).

Tsebelis, George, 2001, *Veto Players: How Political Institutions Work* (Princeton, New Jersey: Princeton University Press and Russell Sage Foundation).

Part III. Effectiveness

CHAPTER

11 International Bailouts, Moral Hazard, and Conditionality

Olivier Jeanne and Jeromin Zettelmeyer[1]

The large international bailouts of the 1990s have been criticized for generating moral hazard at the expense of the global taxpayer. We argue that this criticism is misleading because international bailouts create either no or very few costs to the international community. Instead, the problem is that bailouts may be used to facilitate bad domestic policies, thus creating moral hazard at the expense of domestic taxpayers. Ensuring that this does not happen may require a shift toward ex ante conditionality, in the sense that the availability and size of official crisis lending need to be conditional on government policies before the crisis.

Introduction

The 1990s have seen international official crisis lending of unprecedented size (Table 1). Advocates justified these bailouts as a form of international financial safety net to deal with new risks arising from the international financial integration of emerging economies, most notably the rollover risk on foreign currency debt (Fischer, 1999; and Summers, 1999). At the same time, critics argued that international bailouts were instead a factor contributing to financial crises, because of the moral hazard that they create. There has been a lively debate on whether the practice of large international bailouts should be continued, discontinued, or reformed.[2]

That financial safety nets create moral hazard, and possibly *excessive* moral hazard, seems fairly uncontroversial.[3] However, much of the policy debate on how to reduce moral hazard seems to hinge on an erroneous view of how moral hazard is created by international bailouts, namely, the analogy between international bailouts and a standard insurance arrangement (for example, fire insurance or medical insurance). We dismiss this view on empirical grounds and offer an alternative interpretation of how moral hazard might be created by international crisis lending. We then draw the policy implications.[4]

In a standard insurance contract, the consequences of a bad outcome are mitigated by a state-contingent transfer. For example, if an insured person gets sick, medical insurance will cover part of her treatment costs. Moral hazard arises because the existence of this transfer makes her less anxious to avoid the bad state, at the expense of those who ultimately finance the transfer. One widespread view of international bailouts is based on the transposition of this argument to the international level: a country gets "sick" and receives a transfer, in the form of a subsidized loan from the international community. Moral hazard arises at the expense of those who supposedly pay for that transfer, namely, the global taxpayers. As noted in an April 23, 1998 *Wall Street Journal* editorial, "What really happens is that the U.S. ends up subsidizing the IMF's growing practice of making large loans at low interest rates to very risky economies ... and U.S. government money comes from taxpayers."

This view is inconsistent with the available evidence on the repayment record on international official lending. The IMF's large-scale crisis loans of the 1990s were made at a low interest rate, but in most cases they have been repaid or are in the process of being repaid, as Figure 1 shows. This is

[1] This paper was first published in *Economic Policy* in 2001 and has not subsequently been revised or updated. It appears here with the permission of Blackwell Publishing, the journal's publisher. An earlier version was presented at the 33rd Economic Policy Panel Meeting, which was held in Stockholm April 6–7, 2001. We are grateful to our two discussants at the Panel, Philippe Bacchetta and Andrew Scott, as well as the editor, Charles Wyplosz, for very useful comments and suggestions. We also thank Mark Allen, Reza Baqir, Eduardo Borensztein, Barry Eichengreen, Gaston Gelos, Ken Kletzer, Tim Lane, Paul Masson, Carlos Medeiros, Christian Mulder, Mike Mussa, Sanjaya Panth, Steve Phillips, Andrea Richter, Ken Rogoff, Nouriel Roubini, Alexander Swoboda, Tessa van der Willigen, Alexander Wolfson, and especially Daniel Cohen for discussions and/or comments on earlier drafts. Our thanks also go to several colleagues at the IMF—including Jim Boughton, Christina Daseking, Leyla Ecevit, Doris Ross, and Barry Yuen—for data and information on IMF financial operations. Any remaining errors, however, are our sole responsibility.

[2] See Shultz, Simon, and Wriston (1998); Schwartz (1998); Edwards (1998); Feldstein (1998); Eichengreen (1999, 2000); Council on Foreign Relations Task Force (1999); de Gregorio and others (2000); IFIAC (2000); Goldstein (2000b); and Calomiris (2001), among many others.

[3] The distinction between moral hazard and *excessive* moral hazard is emphasized by Mussa (1999). The relevant question from a policy perspective is not whether international bailouts generate moral hazard per se, but whether this moral hazard is excessive in view of the benefits of the international financial safety net.

[4] Note that we are not concerned with quantifying the extent to which international bailouts create moral hazard. This is the subject of a recent set of papers by Nunnenkamp (1999); Zhang (1999); Lane and Phillips (2000); Dell'Ariccia, Gödde, and Zettelmeyer (2000); and McBrady and Seasholes (2000).

Table 1

IMF-Supported Crisis Packages of the 1990s: Financing Commitments and Disbursements[1]

(in percentage of initial GDP)

	Date of Approval	Financing Commitments		Disbursements	
		Total	IMF	Total	IMF
Mexico	Feb. 1995	18.3	6.3	9.1	4.6
Thailand	Aug. 1997	11.5	2.7	9.6	2.3
Indonesia	Nov. 1997	19.6	5.2	9.3	4.8
Korea, Rep. of	Dec. 1997	12.3	4.4	6.5	4.1
Brazil	Dec. 1998	5.4	2.3	3.4	1.4
Memorandum item					
Russia	n.a.[2]	...	...	...	6.6[3]

[1] GDP in year of program approval (for Russia, we used 1995).
[2] Russia had several consecutive IMF programs during the 1990s. The first large-scale loan was a stand-by arrangement approved in April of 1995.
[3] Total disbursements in the 1990s.

Figure 1

Use of IMF Credit by Mexico, Thailand, Indonesia, the Republic of Korea, Brazil, and the Russian Federation, 1994–2001

(in billions of U.S. dollars)

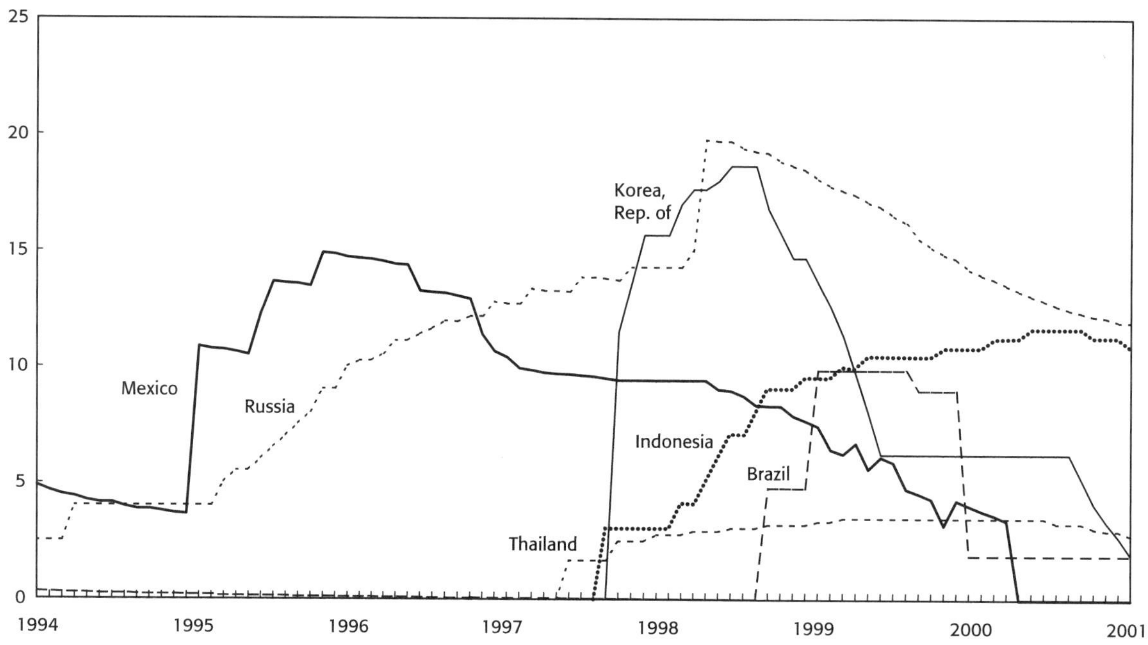

typical of the IMF repayment record with countries that have access to international financial markets. Thus, the international safety net does not involve any state-contingent transfers from the global taxpayer to crisis countries. Instead, it involves state-contingent loans, which do not embody any significant subsidy.

The fact that the simple insurance analogy is wrong and moral hazard does not arise at the expense of the international taxpayer does *not* imply that international bailouts cannot create excessive moral hazard. However, it does imply that one needs to think harder about the mechanisms that might be causing it. If official crisis lending comes at no cost to the rest of the world, and is voluntary on the side of the crisis countries—which are free to reject the offer of assistance, and sometimes do—where is the problem? The problem, in our view, lies in the interaction between international bailouts and domestic policies, as pointed out by Calomiris (1998).

The international financial safety net increases the scope for bad policies as well as good policies. International bailouts can help countries implement good policies, but they could also make the consequences of bad domestic policies much worse.

For example, consider the design of domestic financial safety nets in a financially integrated emerging market economy. A good policy, in this context, could be defined as a well-designed system of deposit insurance that would provide a limited guarantee on both domestic currency and foreign currency deposits in the domestic banking system. An example of bad policy could be an implicit government guarantee on the debt of the policymaker's friends and relatives. The international safety net could be used to back one or the other. The fact that its operation costs nothing to the global taxpayer does not imply that it is going to be used to back good policies. It simply implies that the consequences of domestic policies, good or bad, are going to be borne by the domestic taxpayer. Excessive moral hazard might arise not because international bailouts involve an international transfer, but because they facilitate a domestic transfer from the domestic taxpayer to the borrowers that benefit from implicit guarantees (Jeanne and Zettelmeyer, 2001a).

A similar story can be told about sovereign debt crises. The expectation of full repayment even in an economic crisis could make international investors more lenient in granting new loans or rolling over existing loans to a government ("investor moral hazard"). Official crisis lending can provide governments with liquidity to implement such a bailout. However, if it does not carry a subsidy, and if the government maximizes domestic welfare—with due weight given to the domestic taxpayers who will pay for the bailout in the event of a crisis—this cannot generate excessive moral hazard. For moral hazard to be excessive, there must be a discrepancy between the policymaker's objective and the domestic taxpayers' long-term interests (Jeanne and Zettelmeyer, 2001b).

If the problem is that the international community creates moral hazard by playing the role of accomplice in bad domestic policies, what is the appropriate policy response? Increasing the interest rate on international loans, or collateralizing IMF lending, will clearly not do—such proposals miss the point. Instead, our preferred answer is to make the international community an accomplice in the implementation of *good* domestic policies. We argue in this paper that this requires shifting the weight of conditionality from traditional conditionality ex post, as an accompanying element of official lending after the crisis, to conditionality ex ante, in the sense that the availability and size of official lending need to be conditional on government policies before the crisis. The international community's lending policies must create a link between domestic efforts at preventing crises ex ante and the extent of insurance ex post. In our conclusion, we discuss some problems involved in making further progress in this direction, as well as possible solutions.

The IMF Lending Record

In this section, we address a question involving a (hypothetical) emerging economy that must repay on its sovereign or private debt 10 percent of its GDP to foreign creditors—the rough order of magnitude of the large bailouts of the 1990s (see Table 1, or the average fiscal cost of banking crises in Frydl, 1999). The country could default, or, alternatively, it could repay its foreign creditors using a loan from the international community amounting to 10 percent of GDP. Based on the historical record, how much of this 10 percent could the country hope to transfer to the global taxpayer by not repaying the loan? The answer, we are going to argue, is "not very much"—at most a fraction of a percentage point of GDP.

Our answer is based on the historical lending record of the IMF. The justification for concentrating on the IMF is its role as the preeminent official crisis lender. While other multilaterals (in particular, the World Bank, the Asian Development Bank, and the Inter-American Development Bank) also have played a role, their financial involvement in a crisis context has been much more modest than that of the IMF (whose share in multilateral crisis lending has ranged from about 63 percent for Thailand to 100 percent for Mexico). Large-scale bilateral crisis lending has taken place in only three cases: Mexico (1995), Thailand (1997), and Brazil (1998). In two of these—Mexico and Brazil—bilateral lenders have by now been repaid in full. In Thailand's case, the bilaterals are being repaid in tandem with the IMF. The two most recent crisis packages, for Turkey and Argentina, were largely financed by the IMF on its own.

Ignoring bilateral lending might be misleading in one important sense. Conceivably, the repayment of IMF loans could be financed by bilateral loans—that is, the IMF could be bailed out by its own shareholders. Bulow, Rogoff, and Bevilaqua (1992) present evidence suggesting that the repayment of nonconcessional World Bank loans to a group of low- and middle-income countries during the 1980s was financed either by bilaterals or by the World Bank's own concessional lending. Thus, for these countries, the repayment record of international financial institutions (IFIs) could give an overly optimistic picture of the repayment record of the official sector as a whole. However, we think that this is unlikely to be a problem in the class of countries that are candidates for large international bailouts—relatively advanced emerging economies with access to international capital markets. In Appendix I, we present evidence indicating that repayments to the IMF are not financed by new bilateral debt to this group of countries, although the same analysis supports Bulow and others' (1992) results for the group of heavily indebted poor countries (HIPCs). Given that the focus of this paper is on IMF lending to the first group, we ignore bilateral financing in the remainder of the paper.

How do we measure the potential transfer entailed in IMF lending? We say that IMF loans involve a transfer if their interest rate is not high enough to offset the default risk faced by the IMF. In other words, we define the absence of transfer as a situation where the IMF makes zero profit on average. Conceivably, the IMF could charge a higher interest rate and make a strictly positive profit. Some would argue that the failure to do so—to exploit the IMF's monopoly rent in crisis lending—constitutes an implicit transfer, or a subsidy. This is not, however, what the IMF critics mean when they claim that its loans are subsidized.

The IMF's default risk is not necessarily the same as that faced by private lenders. The ability to impose conditionality ex post, which is typically justified by the need to ensure repayment, might imply that the IMF has a more direct influence on measures that improve country solvency than do private institutions. In addition, the IMF may be in a better position to deter default. It can deny further IMF lending and thus effectively bar access to the multilateral financial safety net in the future (this occurs automatically if a country accumulates arrears to the IMF). It can also exert pressure on a country through the actions of its major shareholders, which may link bilateral lending, or other bilateral policies, to a country's good standing with the IMF.

It follows that the question of whether IMF lending implies a transfer cannot be answered by simply comparing IMF interest rates to market interest rates prevailing during crises, as has been argued in, among other places, the *Wall Street Journal's* editorial dated April 23, 1998 (quoted in the previous section) and Calomiris (2001). Instead, the relevant comparison is between the interest rate charged by the IMF and the default risk it faces.

What Interest Rate Does the IMF Charge?

The relevant interest rate for the bulk of IMF lending is the "basic rate of charge on ordinary resources."[5] The rate of charge is set as low as possible while covering the IMF's financing costs, its administrative budget, and the accumulation of some "precautionary balances" (IMF, 1998). The IMF's financing costs, in turn, depend on the portion of member currency holdings that are remunerated, and the rate of remuneration that is applied. Prior to 1969, the IMF did not compensate its member countries for their currency holdings. The remuneration of member holdings was introduced after 1969 and was increased in various steps during the 1970s and 1980s (Boughton, 2001, Chapter 17, provides the details). Since 1987, the rate of remuneration has been equal to the SDR interest rate (a weighted average of three-month money market interest rates of the five major currencies). Since all but a small portion of member currency holdings are remunerated, this implies that since 1987, the basic rate of charge is effectively set as a markup over the SDR interest rate.

Figure 2 shows that prior to the mid-1980s, the IMF's basic rate of charge was lower than both the U.S. three-year government bond rate—which is a useful benchmark in view of the average maturity of IMF nonconcessional loans (of two to five years)—and the market-determined SDR interest rate. Thus, in this period, IMF interest rates generally implied a subsidy, in the sense that a borrowing country could have made a small, risk-free profit on IMF loans by maintaining reserves borrowed from the IMF in liquid money market instruments denominated in SDR currencies. Since the mid-1980s, the IMF's rate of charge has fluctuated around the U.S. three-year government bond rate. Moreover, since the introduction of the Supplemental Reserve Facility (SRF) in December 1997, the IMF has begun to impose surcharges for large-scale lending. Since November 2000, surcharges apply to most nonconcessional IMF lending that exceeds 200 percent of quota—see IMF (2000b) for details.

The IMF Repayment Record: Is the Past a Good Guide for the Future?

Does the interest rate charged by the IMF since 1987 reflect the default risk to which it is exposed? If so, the default risk facing the IMF would need to be very low, since the SDR and U.S. interest rates comparable with the IMF basic rate of charge are virtually risk free. Given that the IMF typically lends to crisis countries that appear very shaky—and are often cut off from private financing or face prohibitively high market interest rates precisely for that reason—this seems a tall order. However, it is exactly what the IMF's repayment record suggests, at least on first appearance. The recent HIPC Initiative is the first case of IMF claims reduction, and arrears cases to the IMF are few and far between. Most of them are settled eventually, and they generally involve countries that go through wars or violent internal conflicts.[6]

[5] This is the interest rate that applies to the standard (nonconcessional) IMF lending facilities. The interest rate charged by the IMF on its concessional facilities—the Enhanced Structural Adjustment Facility (ESAF) and its successor, the Poverty Reduction and Growth Facility (PRGF)—is much lower (currently 0.5 percent). Concessional lending targets very poor countries and has not been used to deal with the international financial crises that we focus on in this paper.

[6] Total arrears to the IMF in 2000 amounted to US$3 billion, about 4.5 percent of its total loans and credits outstanding. The following countries were in arrears: Afghanistan, the Democratic Republic of the Congo, Iraq, Liberia, Somalia, Sudan, and the Federal Republic of Yugoslavia. For a comprehensive documentation of IMF arrears cases, see Aylward and Thorne, 1998.

Figure 2
IMF Basic Rate of Charge and Market Interest Rates
(in percentage points)

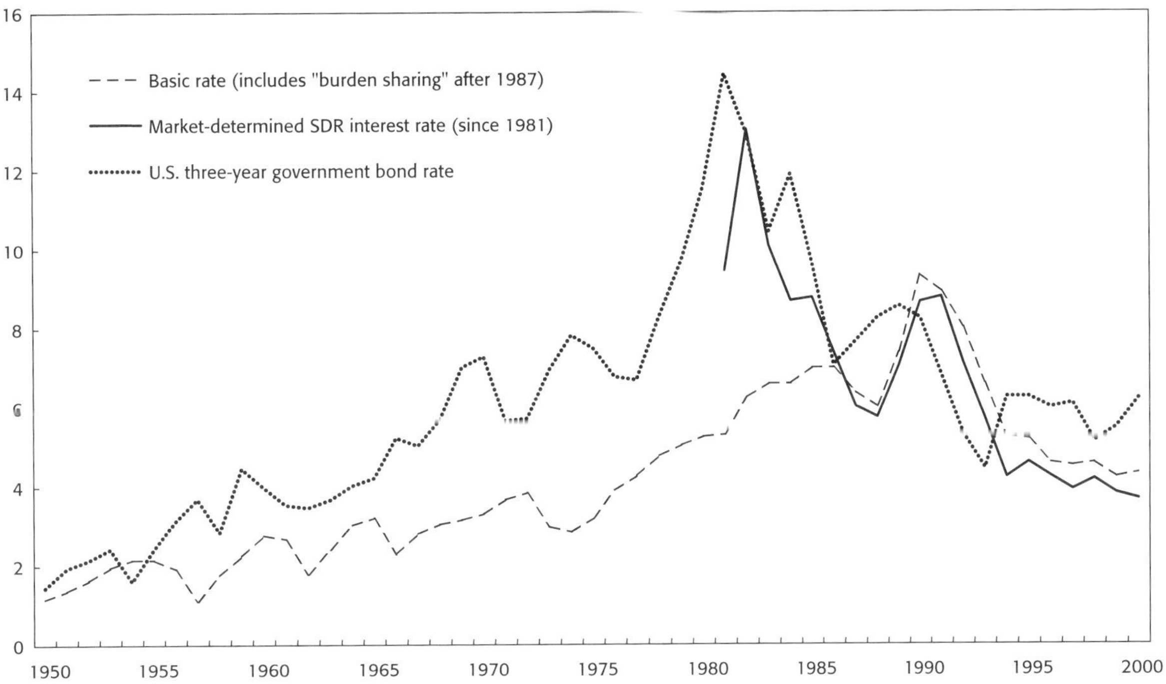

However, the relatively small number and volume of arrears cases are evidence of low default risk only if we assume that the IMF's repayment record over the last 50 years will continue to apply in the future. Some skeptics have expressed doubts about this. They argue that the IMF's past repayment record was made possible by the IMF's practice of refinancing its loans to countries that were unable to repay. If this is true, bad loans will increasingly tend to crowd out good ones in the IMF loan portfolio, and we eventually should observe either an increase in the rate of default on IMF lending, or debt reduction, as in the case of the HIPC initiative.

The fraction of IMF programs that end up in long-term lending relationships is examined in Table 2. We report the number of "complete" and "incomplete" lending cycles over IMF history. A lending cycle is defined as an uninterrupted period of strictly positive "Total Fund Credits and Loans Outstanding," as reported in *International Financial Statistics*. A lending cycle is "complete" if it ends prior to 2000. We refer to countries with outstanding debt in 2000 as being in an "incomplete" lending cycle.

Overall, and in most regions, the number of complete lending cycles exceeds that of incomplete ones. There are two main exceptions: Africa and non-OECD (Organization for Economic Cooperation and Development) Europe. The situation in the latter is due to a number of relatively recent lending cycles with transition economies that borrowed from the IMF for the first time in the 1990s. In contrast, the large proportion of incomplete lending cycles in Africa reflects the prevalence of successive borrowing arrangements from the IMF over many years.

Unsurprisingly, the occurrence of long incomplete cycles is especially high in HIPCs. Almost all of these countries (38 out of 42) have ongoing lending relationships with the IMF that started more than twenty years ago, on average, and incomplete lending cycles far outnumber completed cycles. The IMF experience with HIPCs illustrates the possibility that very long lending cycles might turn into "bad loans" that the international community will eventually have to forgive, at least in part. However, this experience concerns very poor countries that have little in common with the group of countries that are the main focus of this paper—the relatively advanced emerging economies that have benefited from the large international bailouts of the 1990s. The question is how widespread the long-term continuous lending relationships with the IMF are in the latter group.

To answer this question, we look at the length of lending cycles in the emerging market–country group tracked by J.P. Morgan's "EMBI Global" Index (EMBIG). This is a group of 27 relatively advanced emerging market countries—the most internationally financially integrated countries in the

Table 2
Completed and Incomplete Debt Cycles, 1947–2000[1]

	Number of Countries	Complete Debt Cycles	Incomplete Debt Cycles	Average Duration of Cycles (years)	
				Complete	Incomplete
All countries	186	165	88	7.1	17.9
Industrial countries	25	31	0	4.7	n.a.
Developing countries	161	134	88	7.6	17.9
Africa	52	28	38	6.1	22.7
Asia	29	23	13	9.0	21.2
Europe	28	12	21	10.2	7.9
Middle East	14	14	2	6.5	9.5
Western Hemisphere	37	57	14	7.6	18.1
HIPC countries[2]	42	25	38	6.1	23.5
Non-HIPC developing countries	119	109	50	8.0	13.6
EMBIG countries[3]	27	38	15	7.8	13.8
Non-EMBIG countries	134	96	73	7.6	18.8
Memorandum item (excluding cycles initiated after 1991)					
EMBIG countries[3]	27	37	8	7.9	20.6

[1] Number of countries with outstanding debt in 2000.
[2] HIPCs (see Appendix II for full list).
[3] Countries whose bond spreads are tracked by J.P. Morgan's "EMBI Global" Index (see Appendix II).

nonindustrial country group. Appendix II has a full list of these countries. All major capital account crises of the 1990s involved members of the EMBIG group. Table 2 shows that the number of incomplete lending cycles in the EMBIG group (15) is low relative to the number of completed cycles, and that the incomplete cycles' average length is substantially shorter than that of the non-EMBIG developing countries (13.8 versus 18.8). However, as the last line of the table shows, even in the EMBIG group, about half of the incomplete lending cycles in 2000 have been ongoing for, on average, more than 20 years. This is driven mainly by four long-term lending relationships: Côte d'Ivoire (since 1974), Panama (since 1974), Peru (since 1976), and the Philippines (since 1968). Thus, among the more advanced developing countries, which are the focus of this paper, long-term lending relationships with the IMF are not the rule, but neither are they nonexistent. On this basis, we proceed under the assumption that the IMF's repayment record so far need not necessarily reflect the steady state even in this group of countries.

Estimating an Upper Bound for the Transfer Element in IMF Lending

If one accepts that, in principle, the IMF's excellent repayment record need not continue indefinitely, estimating the subsidy element in IMF lending raises a fundamental difficulty. An estimate must be conditional on an assessment of the future repayment prospects of countries that are currently indebted to the IMF, and such an assessment is necessarily highly subjective. Rather than speculating about default probabilities for individual countries, we address these issues by computing a crude upper bound to the redistributive element implicit in IMF lending.

Our methodology relies on the notion of a hypothetical long-run IMF lending regime. This long-run regime involves two types of IMF lending cycles: those that are eventually repaid, and those that would go on forever unless the country either defaulted or received some multilateral debt relief. We refer to the first type as "finite," and to the second as "infinite," cycles. The latter are motivated by the long lending cycles observed in Table 2, and the worry that such cycles could reflect a process by which the IMF refinances its own obligations, leading to increasing country debt levels that need to be eventually recognized as unsustainable—as in the case of HIPCs. We estimate the fraction μ of "infinite" cycles, using the method presented in Box 1.

Table 3 summarizes our results. It presents point estimates and p-values for μ for the countries in Table 2, along with δ, the maximum amount that countries can borrow from the IMF based on their quotas (see Box 2). The maximum ex ante transfer for each subsample (assuming a zero recovery rate for infinite cycles) is then given by the product of the two ($\tau = \mu\delta$). Thus, τ is the maximum transfer

Box 1. Estimating the Fraction of "Infinite" Cycles

Suppose that a fraction μ of lending cycles is of the infinite type, and denote the average net present value of debt owed to the IMF at the time the lending cycles are recognized as unsustainable as δ. Then, given that the IMF lends at approximately the riskless interest rate, the average ex ante transfer is equal to the frequency of infinite lending cycles, times the country's indebtedness to the IMF, times the loss rate on infinite cycles:

$$\tau = \mu\delta(1 - \rho)$$

where ρ is the average IMF "recovery rate" for infinite lending cycles. The strategy is to estimate an upper bound for τ by assuming an upper bound for δ and a lower bound for ρ, while attempting to estimate μ from the data. The most pessimistic assumption one can make about the recovery rate is obviously that $\rho = 0$, i.e., that debt owed on infinite cycles is forgiven in full.

To set δ, we make the radical assumption that all countries on infinite lending cycles will be allowed to borrow up to the full amount of their cumulative debt ceilings prior to defaulting or receiving debt relief, namely, 300 percent of quota. This is about three times as high as the average actual indebtedness to the IMF in 2000. While the 300 percent cumulative debt ceiling can be waived in exceptional circumstances, this has occurred only in rare cases—which in the 1990s have mostly coincided with the large crisis packages we briefly discussed in the introduction.

We estimate μ using a simple parametric duration model (Greene, 1993). To do so, we need to assume a distribution for the duration of the finite lending cycles. We use a standard generalization of the constant hazard rate model, the Weibull model, which allows for increasing or decreasing the hazard rate as a function of duration.

Table 3

Maximum Average Ex Ante Subsidy

(in percentage of debtor country GDP in 2000)

	Total Number of Countries	μ[1]	*p*-Value (H_0: $\mu=0$)	Debt Limit[2]	Actual Debt in 2000[3]	Maximum Subsidy $\tau=\mu\delta$
All countries, average	186	0.25	0.00	11.2	4.4	2.81
Industrial countries, average	25	0.00	1.00	4.1	n.a.	0.00
Developing countries, average	161	0.28	0.00	12.3	4.4	3.46
Africa	52	0.58	0.00	17.1	5.7	9.88
Asia	29	0.28	0.00	8.9	2.2	2.48
Europe	28	0.12	0.28	11.5	4.7	1.32
Middle East	14	0.00	0.89	7.2	4.6	0.00
Western Hemisphere	37	0.09	0.16	10.5	2.5	0.99
HIPC countries[4]	42	0.59	0.00	18.4	5.6	10.84
Non-HIPC developing countries	119	0.11	0.00	9.0	1.3	0.96
EMBIG countries[5]	27	0.05	0.66	7.0	1.7	0.37
Non-EMBIG countries	134	0.29	0.00	12.5	2.6	3.58

[1] Maximum-likelihood estimate of fraction of "infinite" lending cycles for various subsamples.
[2] 300 percent of quota in 2000, as a percentage of 2000 GDP.
[3] In percentage of 2000 GDP.
[4] Heavily indebted poor countries (see Appendix II for full list).
[5] Countries whose bond spreads are tracked by J.P. Morgan's "EMBI Global" Index (see Appendix II).

that a country can expect ex ante, i.e., based on our best estimate of the fraction of infinite cycles and without knowing whether its lending cycle is of the infinite type or not. For purposes of comparison with δ, we also show the actual outstanding average debt to the IMF in 2000 for each subsample, in terms of that year's GDP.

For the whole sample, the estimated fraction of "infinite" cycles, μ is about 25 percent. However, this masks enormous disparities across regions and income groups. In the HIPC sample, the estimated fraction is almost 60 percent—which is perhaps not surprising given that we know that countries in these groups are eligible for multilateral debt relief. For the 119 non-HIPC developing countries, the estimated proportion of cycles that look like they could go on forever is only 11 percent. For the EMBIG countries, the fraction falls to just 5 percent,

Box 2. Quotas and IMF Credit Limits

A "quota" is a country's capital contribution to the IMF. It determines voting power within the institution as well as access to IMF financing. Quotas are set as a function of a country's GDP, openness, the volatility of exports (or current receipts), and the level of reserves (see IMF, 1998, Box 3). Large countries with diversified exports tend to have much smaller quotas, as a share of GDP, than do small countries whose exports are concentrated in a few sectors. For example, the median quota in 2000 was about 2.7 percent of GDP, but the United States' quota was only about 0.5 percent, and Zambia's was about 18 percent. Quotas are reviewed periodically (about once every five years).

Until 1963, a country's total borrowing limit was 100 percent of quota. This was gradually relaxed during the 1960s and 1970s, in step with the creation of new lending facilities, reaching about 300 percent by 1978 (see Boughton, 2001). Following the second oil shock, access limits were briefly raised much higher, and remained at approximately 450 percent until 1992, when the Ninth Review of Quotas increased quotas by 50 percent. Since then, the limit on total cumulative borrowing from the IMF has been 300 percent of quota, with the understanding that this could be exceeded in "exceptional circumstances." Recently, two new facilities have been created: the Supplemental Reserve Facility (SRF), for cases of "exceptional balance of payments difficulties," and the Contingent Credit Lines (CCL), as a defense against contagion. These facilities are exempted from the formal access limit, but are also subject to much shorter repayment periods and much higher rates of charge.

Since 1992, the 300 percent cumulative ceiling has so far been exceeded in six cases: Mexico (peak: 607 percent of quota in 1995), Thailand (400 percent in 1998), the Republic of Korea (1,500 percent in 1998), Indonesia (431 percent in 1998), Turkey (445 percent in early 2001), and briefly Russia, whose outstanding debt reached 318 percent of quota in 1998. The FY 1998/99 Brazil package stayed within the 300 percent cumulative limit, in spite of the use of the SRF.

At present (in mid-2001) two countries still have liabilities to the IMF that exceed the standard cumulative debt ceiling, namely Turkey and Indonesia. For most countries, actual levels of debt outstanding in 2000 are one-third to one-fourth, on average, of the theoretical debt ceilings (see Table 3).

and is insignificantly different from zero. The more restrictive the definition of the subsample in terms of income levels and access to capital markets, the lower the estimated fraction of "infinite cycles."

In the last column, we multiply cumulative debt limits with the estimated fraction of "infinite cycles." As one would expect, this results in a further magnification of the cross-regional variations that were noted earlier. For the HIPC group, the upper bound for the ex ante transfer is more than 10 percent of debtor country GDP. Of course, the actual transfer that these countries can expect from the IMF as a result of the HIPC initiative is far lower, both because the actual debt levels are much below the assumed debt ceilings, and because the HIPC Initiative does not envisage a complete debt write-down, as assumed in Table 3; see IMF (1998). For the group of emerging economies that are our main focus here, i.e., the EMBIG countries, the estimated upper bound is only 0.37 percent of GDP. This is driven by the fact that the estimated fraction of "infinite" cycles is very small in this group.

We can now answer the question that was asked at the beginning of this section. Based on the historical record, an EMBIG economy that borrows 10 percent of its GDP would fail to repay with a probability of at most 5 percent—the probability of an "infinite cycle" for this class of countries. The implicit transfer, which results because the interest rate charged by the IMF fails to reflect this default risk, is thus less than 0.5 percent of the country's GDP. If the country represents 1 percent of the world population and GDP (this corresponds to a large emerging economy, between Argentina and Brazil in size), the per capita cost of the bailout for the global taxpayer would amount to less than 0.0005 times that borne by the domestic taxpayer. It bears emphasizing that even these small numbers are based on an extreme assumption underpinning our hypothetical worst-case scenario, namely, that none of the outstanding debt on "infinite" lending cycles will be recovered. Thus, a reasonable estimate of the ex ante subsidy implicit in IMF lending is likely to be much smaller.

Policy Discussion

In light of the evidence presented in the previous section, we now return to the main question motivating this paper—namely, how the international community can best limit moral hazard. In addition to the papers and editorials cited in the introduction, a number of reports have been written on the reform of international financial institutions in the aftermath of the Asian crisis (see Williamson, 2000 for a review). One report that has been especially influential in the policy debate was prepared by the International Financial Institution Advisory Commission established by the U.S. Congress and chaired by Allan Meltzer (IFIAC, 2000, hereinafter referred to as the Meltzer report). We present a brief review of the different policy approaches in these reports, before presenting the case for ex ante conditionality and concluding with a discussion of some objections against it.

Policy Approaches

Proposals to reform IMF lending policies for the purposes of reducing moral hazard have varied along three main dimensions:

First, *increasing the price* (making it more costly for countries to borrow from the IMF). The Meltzer report argues that the IMF should charge a penalty rate (above the borrower's recent market rate) and secure its loan by a clear priority claim on the borrower's assets. As documented in the previous section, the IMF increased some of its lending rates in November 2000.

Second, *decreasing the quantity* (limiting the size of bailouts). The Council on Foreign Relations Task Force (1999) proposes that the IMF return to normal lending limits (100 percent to 300 percent of quota) for "country crises," that is, for crises that do not threaten the performance of the world economy. Larger loans could be made under a systemic facility, which would require a supermajority of creditors to be activated. Arguments that there should be more "private sector involvement" in financing crises (Haldane, 1999; and Roubini, 2000) are in the same vein. Eichengreen (1999, 2000) advocates improving crisis resolution mechanisms through changes in the law governing private debt contracts, or through officially sanctioned standstills as a way to resolve investor panics. These can be interpreted as proposals that seek to reduce the need to resort to large official bailouts as the main way of mitigating the consequences of an international financial crisis.

Third, *introducing ex ante conditionality* (sometimes also referred to as "selectivity" or "prequalification"). The idea is to make the generosity of international bailouts in a crisis conditional on the quality of domestic policies, particularly in the financial sector, before a crisis erupts. The Council on Foreign Relations Task Force suggests that the IMF should distinguish among three categories of countries on the basis of their compliance with a set of standards and good practices, and publish regular reports assessing countries' progress in meeting these standards. (The standards and practices include, among others, the IMF's Special Data Dissemination Standard and the Basel Committee's Core Principles of Effective Banking Supervision.) A country's class would then determine the availability of official assistance and the interest rate at which it would be charged in the event of a crisis. The Meltzer report takes a similar approach, but in a more extreme form. It recommends that IMF lending be restricted to a group of countries selected for the soundness of their banking policies, with other countries being altogether ineligible for official crisis lending. The idea of ex ante conditionality is also embodied in a new IMF facility, the Contingent Credit Lines (CCL), which provided for exceptional access to IMF resources for countries that qualified ex ante on the basis of sound policies and progress toward meeting internationally accepted standards. (For a precise statement of the conditions that were required to qualify for the CCL, see IMF, 2000a.)[7]

The Case for Ex Ante Conditionality

We do not think that there is much to be gained from measures that increase the price of official crisis lending—at least in terms of reducing moral hazard. It amounts to fixing a problem that does not exist. The welfare losses stemming from excessive moral hazard, if any, are in the countries receiving international financial assistance, not in the contributing countries. Nor will the proposals in this category work as an incentive mechanism: in countries with severe policy failures, governments are unlikely to be deterred by higher interest rates, since they ultimately do not bear the costs of such interest rates.

Institutional and legal changes that reduce the "demand" for big bailouts by making debt restructurings less costly are clearly desirable from the point of view of reducing moral hazard. Moreover, even if such changes are not successful in eliminating the need for an international financial safety net, systematically smaller bailouts would be optimal if one viewed domestic policy failures as pervasive. In other words, it would be optimal to systematically restrict the policy options of countries if one thought that they would systematically use them to implement bad policies. This is a possible view of the world, but we see it as overly pessimistic. There might be "good countries"—that is, those that put the international financial safety net to good use—and their welfare would be decreased by a one-size-fits-all reduction in bailouts.

Ideally, one would like to reserve the international financial safety net for countries with good policies and deny it to countries with bad ones. This, in essence, is what ex ante conditionality attempts to achieve. There are two benefits. First, this targets financial assistance to countries that are likely to make the best use of it. Second, it gives all countries an incentive to improve their policies (Jeanne and Zettelmeyer, 2001a).

The conclusion that crisis lending should be linked to policies *before* the crisis does not rely on a

[7] No country has applied for the CCL, in part because it was viewed as offering few advantages when compared with the Supplemental Reserve Facility (SRF), which has been used for large-scale lending without formal prequalification. In response, in November 2000, the IMF lowered the rate of charge on the CCL relative to the SRF, and made several other changes designed to enhance the CCL's attractiveness.

specific model of how policy failures arise. Rather, it follows from the general trade-off between incentives and insurance. The better the institutions and policies that prevail before the crisis, the more "insurance" can be provided, in the form of an international financial safety net, without destroying private sector incentives. Conversely, the worse institutions are, the greater the degree of market discipline required to offset their adverse incentive effects.

An additional benefit of linking crisis lending to ex ante policies is that they could reduce the extent and intrusiveness of ex post conditionality. After the Asian crisis, IMF structural conditionality was criticized for being excessive (Goldstein, 2000a). One reason why more conditions may have been imposed than were perhaps necessary to ensure repayment (the standard justification for IMF conditionality), is that the IMF sought to take advantage of the time window in which it had some leverage over the governments—that is, while the countries needed IMF support. Imposing some conditions for crisis lending ex ante rather than ex post would give the IMF more leverage in good times, allowing it to allocate conditionality over time in a more efficient and balanced way.

Problems with Ex Ante Conditionality

Greater reliance on ex ante conditionality raises a number of questions related to design and implementation. One issue is precisely what ex ante conditions should be imposed. This is beyond the scope of our paper, but the basic principle is clear: the maximum level of crisis assistance ex post (and possibly the interest rate at which it is provided) should depend on the sustainability of fiscal policies, public debt management, and the extent to which a country implements financial sector policies that mitigate excessive risk taking. The last factor includes policies for effective banking supervision along the lines described in the Basel Committee's "Core Principles" (Basel Committee on Banking Supervision, 1997), accounting standards, and public disclosure requirements.

One important problem with ex ante conditionality is that it may not be time-consistent (De Gregorio and others, 2000). The temptation to bail out all investors is typically greater ex post than ex ante. This is a real problem, but it is not specific to international bailouts; it arises, to some extent, with all financial safety nets (Rochet, 2000). The institutional design of these safety nets is aimed precisely at solving this problem. The solution, as is the case with time-consistency problems in monetary policy, involves rules, delegation, and reputation. Nor is the time-consistency problem specific to ex ante conditionality. Conventional IMF conditionally faces a similar problem, since it is often optimal ex post to release the next disbursement even if preceding performance criteria have been violated. In practice, this is dealt with through rules that determine in which circumstances program requirements can be waived.

A related issue concerns the room that should be left for "constructive ambiguity." The need to preserve a measure of constructive ambiguity is the most serious objection against ex ante conditionality. On the one hand, it is important that the link between the quality of domestic policies and the extent of crisis lending be governed by explicit rules—both to deal with the time-consistency problem and to ensure universality of treatment ex ante. On the other hand, there will need to be exceptions to these rules. For example, a crisis that is clearly triggered by a financial panic may call for a rescue package even when the policy record prior to the crisis was mixed, or the risk of international contagion may require intervention even when the country would not, in isolation, have qualified for a loan. Conversely, limited fund availability may prevent the IMF from fulfilling its commitments to prequalified countries if a large number of them are simultaneously hit by a crisis. These circumstances cannot always be incorporated into the rules because they are difficult to describe ex ante or to verify ex post.

However, the need for constructive ambiguity does not in itself invalidate the case in favor of some ex ante conditionality. Domestic attempts at reconciling the two are instructive in this regard. For example, the reform of the U.S. deposit insurance system that followed the saving and loan crisis attempted to mitigate the moral hazard resulting from constructive ambiguity by establishing a system of checks and balances that places stringent accountability conditions on economic officials when they decide to rescue a bank because it is "too large to fail" (Council on Foreign Relations Task Force, 1999; Tirole, 2001).[8] This approach is consistent with an important lesson from the theory of incomplete contracts: when contracts cannot fully specify the actions of the contracting parties, they should instead focus on the rules by which these actions will be decided—the allocation of "decision rights." Thus, behind the move toward ex ante conditionality in international bailouts looms the broader question of the governance structure—the rules and procedures by which the international community determines its response to international financial crises.

[8] The Federal Deposit Insurance Corporation Improvement Act (FDICIA) of 1991 makes it harder for regulators to bail out uninsured creditors. An extension of the guarantee to all bank creditors is possible in exceptional circumstances, but this requires the explicit consent of the secretary of the treasury in consultation with the president of the United States, two-thirds of the governors of the Federal Reserve System, and two-thirds of the directors of the FDIC.

Appendix I. IMF Lending and Bilateral Lending

This appendix deals with Bulow, Rogoff, and Bevilaqua's (1992) argument that "any ability IFIs [international financial institutions] have to extract repayments ahead of private creditors may come almost entirely at the expense of bilateral government creditors." We undertake a simple empirical exercise showing that the relationship between repayments to the IMF and bilateral lending by OECD members (both concessional and nonconcessional) looks quite different depending on the level of income and capital market integration of the creditor countries.

Consider a regression of changes in IMF debt stocks on contemporaneous and lagged changes in the stock of bilateral developing country debt held by OECD countries (these data, going back to 1975, are available from the OECD). In the extreme case, in which repayments to the IMF are entirely financed by new bilateral debt, the contemporaneous and recent lagged changes in OECD debt should have coefficients that add up to –1. In the less extreme case, in which new OECD debt contributes to, but does not fully finance, IMF repayments, the coefficients should be negative, and add up to less than unity in absolute value. Table A1 presents results from such a regression based on a panel of 161 developing countries, restricting attention to episodes of repayments to the IMF (i.e., conditioning on *negative* changes in the IMF debt stock).

The results indicate that the Bulow, Rogoff, and Bevilaqua (1992) hypothesis is not supported on the entire sample of developing countries, where we see small and insignificant coefficients on the contemporaneous OECD debt change and its first lag, and a significant positive coefficient on the second lag. But the picture is strikingly different if one considers only heavily indebted poor countries. Both the first and second lags are now negative and highly significant, and add up to about –0.25. If attention is restricted to all "non-emerging" developing countries, the negative effect is smaller (about –0.1), but still significant. In contrast, the relatively richer and "emerging" developing countries show a significant *positive* relationship between repayments to the IMF and to OECD members.

These findings may not be entirely surprising. As Bulow, Rogoff, and Bevilaqua point out, one would expect bilateral transfers to facilitate multilateral debt repayment if bilaterals cared about multilaterals being repaid, and the amounts involved were small. But crisis lending to middle-income countries is often large, and may be politically much more costly than lending through specialized multilateral institutions. This is suggested by the shrinking role of bilateral crisis lending after the Mexico crisis and its complete absence in the recent lending packages to Argentina and Turkey.

Appendix II. Countries in HIPC and EMBIG Groups: Definitions Used in Previous Section

Heavily Indebted Poor Countries (*HIPCs*): Angola, Benin, Bolivia, Burkina Faso, Burundi, Cameroon, the Central African Republic, Chad, Congo,

Table A1
Correlations Between IMF and Bilateral Debt Stock Changes, 1975–99

	Regression Sample				
Independent variable	All developing	HIPC[1]	Non-HIPC	Non-EMBIG	EMBIG[2]
OECD debt change	–0.001	0.001	–0.001	0.000	–0.098
	(–0.28)	(0.29)	(–0.22)	(–0.05)	(–1.21)
OECD debt change (–1)	–0.026	–0.016	–0.032	–0.098	0.027
	(–1.00)	(–3.73)	(–0.93)	(–5.27)	(0.39)
OECD debt change (–2)	0.128	–0.019	0.139	0.008	0.207
	(4.64)	(–4.41)	(3.79)	(0.39)	(2.84)
Regression constant	–153.6	–14.3	–235.8	–37.3	–577.6
	(–7.40)	(–12.7)	(–6.82)	(–3.58)	(–5.63)
Number of countries	117	40	77	93	24
Number of observations	954	370	584	771	183

Notes: Dependent variable is the change in total IMF credits and loans outstanding; panel regressions are estimated using fixed effects, with *t*-values in parentheses. OECD denotes the Organization for Economic Cooperation and Development.

[1] Group of heavily indebted poor countries.

[2] Group of emerging market countries whose sovereign bond spreads are tracked in J.P. Morgan's "Emerging Market Bond Index Global." (See Appendix II.)

Côte d'Ivoire, the Democratic Republic of the Congo, Equatorial Guinea, Ethiopia, The Gambia, Ghana, Guinea, Guinea-Bissau, Guyana, Honduras, Kenya, the Lao People's Democratic Republic, Liberia, Madagascar, Malawi, Mali, Mauritania, Mozambique, Myanmar, Nicaragua, Niger, Rwanda, São Tomé and Príncipe, Senegal, Sierra Leone, Somalia, Sudan, Tanzania, Togo, Uganda, Vietnam, the Republic of Yemen, and Zambia.

EMBI Global Index (EMBIG) countries: Algeria, Argentina, Brazil, Bulgaria, Chile, China, Colombia, Côte d'Ivoire, Croatia, Ecuador, Hungary, the Republic of Korea, Lebanon, Malaysia, Mexico, Morocco, Nigeria, Panama, Peru, the Philippines, Poland, Russia, South Africa, Thailand, Turkey, Ukraine, and República Bolivariana de Venezuela.

Bibliography

Andrews, David, Anthony R. Boote, Sitad Rizavi, and Sukhwinder Singh, 1999, *Debt Relief for Low-Income Countries. The Enhanced HIPC Initiative*, IMF Pamphlet No. 51 (Washington: International Monetary Fund). Also available on the Web at *http://www.imf.org/external/pubs/ft/pam/pam51/contents.htm*.

Aylward, Lynn, and Rupert Thorne, 1998, "An Econometric Analysis of Countries' Repayment Performance to the International Monetary Fund," IMF Working Paper 98/32 (Washington: International Monetary Fund).

200 Basel Committee on Banking Supervision, 1997, "Core Principles for Effective Banking Supervision," document available on the Web at *http://www.bis.org*.

Boughton, James M., 2001, *Silent Revolution: The International Monetary Fund, 1979–1989* (Washington: International Monetary Fund).

Bulow, Jeremy, Kenneth Rogoff, and Alfonso S. Bevilaqua, 1992, "Official Creditor Seniority and Burden-Sharing in the Former Soviet Bloc," *Brookings Papers on Economic Activity: 1*, Brookings Institution.

Calomiris, Charles W., 1998, "The IMF's Imprudent Role as Lender of Last Resort," *Cato Journal*, Vol. 17, No. 3.

________, 2001, "How New Is the 'New IMF?'" Testimony Before the Joint Economic Committee of the United States Congress (March 8).

Council on Foreign Relations Task Force, 1999, *Safeguarding Prosperity in a Global Financial System: The Future International Financial Architecture* (Washington: Institute for International Economics).

De Gregorio, José, Barry Eichengreen, Takatoshi Ito, and Charles Wyplosz, 2000, *An Independent and Accountable IMF*, Geneva Reports on the World Economy Report, Vol. 1 (September).

Dell'Ariccia, Giovanni, Isabel Gödde, and Jeromin Zettelmeyer, 2000, "Moral Hazard and International Crisis Lending: A Test" (unpublished; Washington: International Monetary Fund).

Edwards, Sebastian, 1998, "Abolish the IMF," *Financial Times*, November 13.

Eichengreen, Barry, 1999, *Toward a New International Financial Architecture. A Practical Post-Asia Agenda* (Washington: Institute for International Economics).

________, 2000, *Can the Moral Hazard Caused by IMF Bailouts be Reduced?* Geneva Reports on the World Economy, Special Report No. 1.

Feldstein, Martin, 1998, "Refocusing the IMF," *Foreign Affairs*, Vol. 77.

Fischer, Stanley, 1999, "On the Need for an International Lender of Last Resort," *Journal of Economic Perspectives*, Vol. 13 (Fall).

Frydl, Edward, 1999, "The Length and Cost of Banking Crises," IMF Working Paper 99/30 (Washington: International Monetary Fund).

Goldstein, Morris, 2000a, "IMF Structural Programs" (unpublished; Washington: Institute for International Economics).

______, 2000b, "Strengthening the International Financial Architecture: Where Do We Stand?" Institute for International Economics Working Paper No. 00-8 (Washington).

Greene, William H., 1993, *Econometric Analysis*, 2nd ed. (New York: Macmillan).

Haldane, Andy, 1999, "Private Sector Involvement in Financial Crisis: Analytics and Public Policy Approaches," *Bank of England Financial Stability Review* (November).

International Financial Institutions Advisory Commission (IFIAC), 2000, "Report of the International Financial Institution Advisory Commission," Allan H. Meltzer, Chairman (Washington) (also referred to as the Meltzer report).

International Monetary Fund (IMF), 1998, *Financial Organization and Operations of the IMF*, IMF Pamphlet No. 45 (Washington: International Monetary Fund). Also available on the Web at *http://www.imf.org/external/pubs/ft/pam/pam45/contents.htm*.

______, 2000a, "Summing Up by the Acting Chairman of the IMF Executive Board: Contingent Credit Lines," IMF Executive Board Meeting, November 17 (Washington: International Monetary Fund). Also available on the Web at *http://www.imf.org/external/np/pdr/fac/2000/02/111700.htm*.

______, 2000b, "*Review of Fund Facilities: Proposed Decisions and Implementation Guidelines*," prepared by the Legal, Policy Development and Review, and Treasurer's Departments, November 2. Available on the Web at *http://www.imf.org/external/np/pdr/fac/2000/02/index.htm*.

Jeanne, Olivier, and Jeromin Zettelmeyer, 2001a, "International Safety Nets, Private Debt Crises and Moral Hazard" (unpublished; Washington: International Monetary Fund), forthcoming as an IMF Working Paper.

______, 2001b, "International Bail-Outs, Domestic Policy Failures and Moral Hazard" (unpublished; Washington: International Monetary Fund), forthcoming as an IMF Working Paper.

Lane, Timothy, and Steven Phillips, 2000, "Moral Hazard in IMF Financing," IMF Working Paper 00/168 (Washington: International Monetary Fund).

McBrady, Matthew, and Mark S. Seasholes, 2000, "Bailing-In" (unpublished; University of California, Berkeley).

Meltzer report—*see* IFIAC.

Mussa, Michael, 1999, "Reforming the International Financial Architecture: Limiting Moral Hazard and Containing Real Hazard" (unpublished; Washington: International Monetary Fund).

Nunnenkamp, Peter, 1999, "The Moral of IMF Lending: Making a Fuss About a Minor Problem?" Kiel Discussion Paper No. 332 (Kiel, Germany: Kiel Institute of World Economics).

Rochet, Jean-Charles, 2000, "The Future of Banking Supervision: Market Discipline vs. Centralized Supervision" (unpublished; Toulouse, France: Institut d'Economie Industrielle, Université des Sciences Sociales).

Roubini, Nouriel, 2000, "Bail-In, Burden-Sharing, Private Sector Involvement (PSI) in Crisis Resolution and Constructive Engagement of the Private Sector" (unpublished; Department of Economics, New York University).

Schwartz, Anna J., 1998, "Time to Terminate the ESF and the IMF," Cato Institute Policy Briefing No. 48 (Washington: Cato Institute).

Shultz, George, William E. Simon, and Walter B. Wriston, 1998, "Who Needs the IMF?" *Wall Street Journal*, February 3.

Summers, Lawrence H., 1999, "The Right Kind of IMF for a Stable Global Financial System," remarks to the London School of Business, December 14.

Tirole, Jean, 2001, "Financial Crises, Liquidity Provision and the International Monetary System," manuscript prepared for the Paolo Baffi Lecture on Money and Finance.

Williamson, John, 2000, "The Role of the IMF: A Guide to the Reports," IIE Policy Brief No. 00-5 (Washington: Institute for International Economics).

Zhang, Xiaoming Alan, 1999, "Testing for 'Moral Hazard' in Emerging Markets Lending," IIF Research Paper No. 99-1 (Washington: Institute of International Finance).

CHAPTER

12 Bedfellows, Hostages, or Perfect Strangers? Global Capital Markets and the Catalytic Effect of IMF Crisis Lending

Carlo Cottarelli and Curzio Giannini[1]

During the 1990s, the concept of "catalytic official finance" (COF) gained prominence in policy debates. The concept revolves around the idea that the propensity of investors to lend to a country increases when the IMF provides its "seal of approval"—backed up by only limited official financing—on the country's economic program. COF aims at avoiding, on the one hand, the massive use of public money to bail out private investors and, on the other, the recourse to coercive bailing-in mechanisms. This paper concludes that COF, while possibly useful in other contexts, is less reliable when used to manage capital account crises.

Chi non può quel che vuol, quel che può voglia[2]
—Leonardo da Vinci

Introduction

Ever since Walter Bagehot's times, it has been recognized that emergency liquidity support, to be effective, must in principle be unlimited. Of course, the precept should not be taken too literally. What Bagehot meant, and central banks duly understood, was that the lender of last resort (LOLR) should provide money in amounts large enough to make good all the ailing bank's short-term (and therefore "liquid") liabilities, so as to reassure their holders that all claims would ultimately be met. In a panic, Bagehot reasoned, partial insurance is no insurance at all. To meet the precept, sometimes central banks have acted on their own, availing themselves of the capacity to create money out of nothing. In other instances, exploiting their authority as bank supervisors, they have managed to arrange "lifeboats," or concerted rescues, involving the participation of a group of private institutions with sufficient liquidity to soothe the markets (Freixas and others, 2000).

Generalizing Bagehot's precept to international liquidity support directed at countries undergoing a foreign exchange crisis has proved a daunting task. Some argue that this was only natural, given the lack of a truly supranational currency that could be supplied in unlimited amounts (Capie, 2002). But this explanation sounds unconvincing. Surely, the lack of a world currency notwithstanding, sufficient resources could be mustered to cope even with relatively large countries' foreign exchange crises, if the political will of a group of powerful nations could be harnessed? (Fischer, 2002). Thus, to explain the lack of a Bagehotian LOLR at the international level, one must look for something deeper.

More plausibly, attention could be directed at the fragmentation of the regulatory and political environment in a world of sovereign nations. As Charles Goodhart and Gerhard Illing have recently argued, at the international level,

> ...the whole process is far more complex than in the national case, with a multiplicity of participants (governments, central banks, creditors and debtors), of legal systems and infrastructures. So, besides the standard concerns about contagion on one side, and moral hazard on the other (which remain just as strong in the international as in the national contexts), questions about the design and conduct of an international LOLR are complicated by externalities due to coordination problems among many agents and the lack of enforcement mechanisms among sovereign states. (Goodhart and Illing, 2002, p. 21)

Operationally, this greater complexity is felt at various levels (Giannini, 1999): in the greater difficulty of reaching agreement within the official community as to when, how, and in what amount LOLR operations should be conducted; in the lack of regulatory (i.e., externally enforced) means to hold sovereign debtors true to their promise to reimburse the emergency finance they have received—hence the need to "safeguard" the resources of the international LOLR through conditionality; in the relative ineffectiveness of moral suasion, especially when the

[1] This paper has benefited from the comments of Michael Bell, James Boughton, Marco Committeri, Stanley Fischer, Rex Ghosh, Rakia Moalla-Fetini, Pier Carlo Padoan, Dani Rodrik, Alina Rubino, Massimo Russo, and the participants in seminars held at the European I Department of the IMF and at the Banca d'Italia. This is a slightly revised version of a paper presented at the conference on "The Lender of Last Resort—Experiments, Analyses, Controversies," held in Paris September 23–24, 2002 and first published in *Cahiers d'économie politique*, No. 45 (2003) (Paris: Editions L'Harmattan).

[2] Translation: "He who cannot get what he wants had better want what he can get."

bulk of a country's external debt takes the form of bond financing, since bondholders are hard to bind in the "mutual hostage" relationship that is the typical effect of moral suasion.

These impediments to the working of an international LOLR were less significant in the postwar world of pervasive capital controls and relatively underdeveloped international capital markets. It is because of this supportive institutional setup that at Bretton Woods the IMF could be assigned a limited LOLR role—that of providing short-term financing to overcome current account imbalances (Helleiner, 1994).

With the almost universal move toward financial liberalization in the 1980s, and the associated reprise in capital mobility, this "reductionist" strategy could no longer work. Hence, the task of adapting domestic LOLR practices to the international environment had to be faced squarely. Major overhauls of the Bretton Woods framework were ruled out by the political impracticality of reaching agreement on a new international treaty, which meant that adjustment had to take place at the margin. Under the pressure of events, there thus emerged a new kind of LOLR, in the form of catalytic official finance (COF). The underlying idea of COF is that the provision of official resources—typically the IMF's—to a country in the context of a full-fledged program might increase the propensity of private investors to hold financial assets in the country concerned. In other words, COF postulates that under appropriate conditions private capital flows may be expected to behave like dependable "bedfellows" of official finance, thanks to the various services provided by the IMF through its lending and other activities.

The notion of COF has been invoked in practically all the capital account crises of the period 1997–2002 (Ghosh and others, 2002), and as a consequence references to "catalytic" forces have also multiplied until recently in policy documents. However, after the difficulties encountered by IMF programs in Argentina and Turkey—where private and official financial flows have behaved more like perfect strangers than dependable bedfellows—attitudes toward COF have begun to change. Thus, no reference to "catalysis" can be found in the press communiqués issued by the International Monetary and Financial Committee (IMFC) at the 2002 and 2003 Annual Meetings of the IMF and the World Bank.

The time therefore seems ripe for a comprehensive assessment of COF, its potentialities, and its limitations. In this paper, we have set ourselves three tasks. The first is to trace the process through which (and the reasons why) the notion of COF has taken shape. The second is to survey the empirical evidence on the existence and magnitude of catalytic effects. And the third is to suggest possible ways to rationalize COF in theoretical terms, thereby also identifying the conditions that must be met in order for COF to work.

Three things ought to be stressed right at the outset to avoid misunderstandings. First, the notion of COF does not pertain only to the handling of confidence crises—the typical domain of domestic LOLRs. One may also find catalytic effects at work under more ordinary circumstances, such as in helping a country gain access to international capital markets under a prolonged period of financial isolation. Indeed, as we shall try to show in the section on the history of COF, the notion of COF originally had nothing to do with capital account crises. Second, under crisis conditions the notion of COF attempts to cover the gray area between the two extremes of *full bail-out* (the typical outcome of Bagehotian lending) and *full bail-in* (the immediate impact of either default or a temporary suspension of debt service) of the country's creditors. This gray area is the domain on which we focus. Our analysis therefore does not directly deal with the pros and cons of the two polar opposites that delimit the chosen turf, although of course much of what we will be saying might be seen as relevant for that purpose as well. Third, the catalytic effect is by no means the only channel through which IMF programs work (see Mussa and Savastano, 1999, for a comprehensive assessment of the economics of IMF programs). Conclusions regarding the strength—or weakness—of catalytic effects are directly relevant only for programs that can be expected to work only if catalytic forces are at play. Regarding other programs, the following analysis has very little to say.

Defining Catalytic Official Finance

Despite the frequency with which the notion is invoked, no precise definition of COF has ever been provided. This is hardly surprising. COF is built around a metaphor, much like the invisible hand or the inconsistent trinity. Like all such mental constructs, this too is hard to pin down into an operational concept. Looking for guidance, we have decided to take the metaphor at face value and consulted a Webster's dictionary, where a (chemical) catalyst is defined as "any substance that initiates a reaction and enables it to take place under milder conditions than in [its] absence."

Three features of this definition ought to be stressed. First, the reaction, though clearly intended by the chemist, is *spontaneous*. In our context, this means that COF should be distinguished from other potential ways of addressing unstable capital flows, ranging from direct intervention (suspension of payments or capital controls) to milder actions (moral suasion, concerted lending), which have also found application at the international level in recent times. Second, the purpose of catalysis is *to alleviate the burden* associated with the intended event. We take the "intended event" of IMF financial packages as being the restoration of the medium-term sustainability of the financial profile of a given country. The purpose of COF should therefore be construed as bringing about such an event at lower cost for the country (i.e., with less domestic adjustment) and for the international community (i.e., with less direct exposure and less moral hazard) than would otherwise be the case. Third, even if not explicit in Webster's definition, the amount of the catalyst substance *is supposed to be limited* with respect to the substance that reacts to it. For our purposes, this can only mean that the amount of IMF resources should be limited compared with the potential capital outflow a country is subject to.

Accordingly, the IMF's involvement in a country has a catalytic effect to the extent that the announcement of an economic program backed up by a limited amount of IMF resources (compared with the size of the potential capital outflow) increases the propensity of private investors to lend to the country concerned, thereby reducing the adjustment burden falling on the debtor country with respect to the no-catalysis scenario.

This definition is not yet operational, as it leaves unspecified the exact meaning of the expressions, "potential capital outflow" and "limited." As regards the former, a useful benchmark is the total amount of the country's external short-term liabilities. But it ought to be borne in mind that this is just a benchmark, more useful under ordinary conditions than
204 during a generalized confidence crisis. In fact, with full capital account convertibility, residents might at any time decide to convert the entire stock of short-term assets into foreign exchange. This would increase the "potential" capital outflow dramatically.

As to the meaning of "limited," it is clearly tied to the potential outflow, but the relationship is not mechanical, the more so in view of the inevitable ambiguity we have just pointed out in the benchmark. Zettelmeyer (2000), for example, considers "limited" any package that is not large enough to finance outflows assuming a zero rollover rate of the existing short-run external liabilities. But a "limited" package of, say, US$40 billion might have a stronger impact on the private sector's investment decisions than would a US$4 billion one, especially if the intervention is appropriately timed. That is, definitional ambiguities cannot simply be dispelled altogether, and we must live with them. All that can sensibly be said is that the smaller the amount of financing compared with the size of the potential capital outflow, the larger the reliance on catalytic forces. Conversely, a large package will more closely mimic an "unlimited" package.

IMF lending may have a catalytic effect regardless of whether the country is already facing a capital account crisis, but clearly under crisis conditions the concept assumes particular importance. It would be useful if one could have a precise definition of what should count as a "crisis." Alas, after decades of reflection on LOLR practices at the national level the subject is still a matter of great controversy, and we shy away from the task. Suffice it to say that we use a notion of crisis broad enough to encompass not only situations in which a country is experiencing a massive capital outflow but also precrisis situations, such as when the country's foreign exchange reserves no longer exceed scheduled amortization of external debt during the next year or so.[3] When COF is used for countries that find themselves in such circumstances, we refer to it as being used for crisis management purposes. This is to differentiate it from two other possible uses of COF, namely for a crisis prevention purpose (as in "precautionary" IMF programs) or for crisis resolution (as in the context of debt restructuring following default).

The History of COF: A Tale of Two Crises

Until the 1970s, the notion of catalytic lending had never been entertained, either at the domestic or at the international level. As already remarked, Bagehot's principle dictated that domestic emergency lending should be provided to whatever extent was needed to meet the demand for liquidity expressed by the market. As for international practices, the Bretton Woods architecture was conceived to rule out by construction *any* form of LOLR in excess of temporary current account financing. To make the restriction tighter, each member's access to IMF credit was bound by its quota. Moreover, the IMF's Articles of Agreement explicitly prohibited granting credit to finance a sustained capital outflow.

While domestic practices have not substantially changed to this date, international practices have evolved over time, especially since the late 1970s. The seeds of catalytic emergency lending were sown in the late 1970s in the context of the recycling of oil-surplus funds, but the notion came to full blossom only in the following decade, with the protracted attempt to find a way out of the developing country debt crisis. By the end of the decade, however, the effectiveness of catalytic lending was increasingly being questioned. A new change in attitudes occurred during the late 1990s, essentially on the initiative of the Group of Seven (G-7), which had grown concerned about the drawbacks of the large financial package assembled to overcome the Mexican crisis of 1994–95. Catalytic lending was then made a central pillar of the official strategy for crisis management at the IMF 2000 Annual Meeting in Prague. Ever since then, the pendulum seems to have swung backward, with the merits (and

[3] This is, for example, the benchmark proposed by the former Argentinean Deputy Treasury Minister, Pablo Guidotti, as a measure of prudent risk management on the part of domestic authorities. See Financial Stability Forum (2000).

effectiveness) of catalytic lending once again being increasingly called into question.

A New Notion Begins to Take Shape (Late 1970s to Early 1980s)

In the context of the limited capital mobility of the postwar period, the IMF recipe for addressing balance of payments difficulties was fairly straightforward. When a country faced current account pressures, the IMF would typically arrange a program featuring a combination of official financing and domestic policy adjustment, the latter including a currency depreciation in cases of "fundamental disequilibrium." Within this mechanism, quotas—that is, each country's contribution to IMF resources—played the dual role of a constraint on the capacity of each member to borrow and of a ceiling on the resources each member would have to contribute to the common pool.

The ability of the IMF to play its intended role came under stress during the 1970s, as a consequence of worldwide inflation, which reduced the real value of existing quotas, and larger current account imbalances in the aftermath of the oil crises. Faced with the prospect of being unable to meet the members' needs arising from the first oil shock, the IMF was forced to contemplate at least a partial transformation from a credit union into a financial intermediary. This essentially meant bringing borrowing into the panoply of funding means. The possibility of direct borrowing on financial markets was ruled out at the outset, because it would have fundamentally altered the intergovernmental nature of the institution. As a consequence, the IMF's financing needs would have to be satisfied by borrowing from member countries. To be sure, this transformation already had begun in 1963, with the creation of the General Arrangements to Borrow (GAB). But the departure from previous practice remained modest until the 1970s. In February 1977, IMF Managing Director H. Johannes Witteveen proposed a Supplementary Financing Facility that would link traditional lending based on quotas with funds obtained through borrowing from countries.

The transformation of the IMF into a financial intermediary, however, did not go unchallenged. First, this looked much more controversial in the late 1970s, after international financial markets had taken up the key role in "recycling" the current account surpluses of Organization of Petroleum Exporting Countries (OPEC) members. Second, and more important from our perspective, the notion that IMF lending could cause moral hazard and therefore that "taxpayers' money" should not be used to bail out private investors was increasingly attracting political attention.

It is in connection to this latter problem that the idea that IMF resources, rather than substituting for private capital, could be used to sustain financial markets' confidence and catalyze private capital flows began to take shape. This is most evident in the testimony given in 1977 by Anthony Solomon, Undersecretary of the Treasury for Monetary Affairs, before the Committee on Banking, Finance and Urban Affairs of the U.S. House of Representatives. To defend the proposed Witteveen facility, Solomon made the case that the new IMF window would not be used to bail out the private banks, as the latter typically *follow* the IMF in their lending decisions:

> The very fact that [countries] are meeting the IMF's performance criteria and thus continue to be eligible to draw from the IMF tends to represent a kind of Good Housekeeping seal of approval. Good performance under an IMF program tends to result in private capital inflows, private banks being willing to lend more to the country concerned. (U.S. House of Representatives, 1977, p.72).[4]

The notion that private capital may tend to "follow" IMF lending had also begun to gain currency within the IMF itself. Margaret Garritsen de Vries, for many years the IMF's historian, described the mechanism as follows:

> A close tie between the willingness of commercial banks to lend to a country and the country's having a stand-by arrangement with the IMF became almost standard after commercial banks encountered repayment problems with Zaïre in 1976 and 1977.... Commercial bank officials were beginning to be more familiar with IMF parlance and policy, and the test which they devised to judge the creditworthiness of a country was whether it could meet the conditions needed for a stand-by arrangement with the IMF in the upper credit tranches. This test induced private commercial banks to have prospective borrowing countries obtain the stamp of approval of the IMF by obtaining a stand-by arrangement in the upper credit tranches.[5]

De Vries might have overstated the importance attached to the mechanism in the "IMF parlance

[4] Solomon produced as supporting evidence a short empirical study, showing that between 1970 and 1975 a number of IMF programs had been followed by an increase in private lending (see the section on the history of COF). Interestingly, virtually the same wording is included in an oft-quoted remark made twenty years later during the debate on the role of the IMF that took place in the Treasury Committee of the U.K. House of Commons: "But is there not an all pervasive conventional wisdom that if you do sign up to an IMF programme you get the Good Housekeeping Seal of Approval and away you go!" (quoted by Bird and Rowlands, 1997).

[5] de Vries (1985), pp. 493–94. A reference to banks following the IMF seal of approval in this period, made by a private banker, is Guth (1979), member of the board of the Deutsche Bank and former Executive Director for Germany at the IMF.

and policy," however. Indeed, references to what we now call catalytic effects in the writings of IMF staff remained for a while episodic.[6] Moreover, it seems clear from reading such texts that at that time the seal-of-approval mechanism was not seen as having major implications for the way the IMF operated. Thus, Manuel Guitián, who would later become head of the Monetary and Exchange Affairs Department of the IMF, argues, in a paragraph remarkably entitled "The Fund as Catalyst," that "a critical side effect of the mix of adjustment and financing that is typically built into the programs supported by Fund resources has been to help members attract flows of capital from sources other than the Fund" (Guitián, 1982, p. 91).

This passage solicits two remarks. First, contrary to Dooley's (1994) suggestion that the notion of catalytic lending is to be attributed to the Baker Plan of 1985, one can see that not only the notion, but also the label, was known to IMF staff several years earlier. Second, Guitián does not argue that the effect lies at the core of the IMF's role. Rather, he is quite explicit that this is but a "side effect" (although a "critical" one) of IMF programs. The reason probably is that Guitián was still contemplating a world in which balance of payments crises were predominantly being determined by the behavior of the current account.

206

The Debt Crisis, 1982–93

Increased financial liberalization and capital mobility during the 1980s were making the latter assumption increasingly questionable. The capital account was rapidly becoming as important a source of balance of payments pressure as the current account. But capital account pressures are far more complicated to deal with. The problem arose for the first time in August 1982, when Mexico started having trouble in servicing its external debt, in the aftermath of a generalized increase in international interest rates. The problem soon spread to at least eight other countries in Europe, Africa, and Latin America. The IMF was called in to help solve the problem, but it soon became apparent that "the old approaches would not work, because new financing from the Fund would quickly be siphoned off as the indebted countries would have to repay other creditors" (Boughton, 2000a, p. 171).

In the old approach the IMF could work out the needed amount of "policy adjustment" and "financing" on the assumption that the overall financing gap the country faced was given and easy to measure. Now, the possibility of a drawdown in the foreign sector's holdings of domestic debt—as well as of an increase in residents' assets abroad—implied that the size of the overall financing gap depended on the credibility of the promised policy adjustment. Unless one found a way to convince investors not to liquidate their holdings, financing a country's balance of payments crisis might turn into trying to fill up a bottomless pit. Of course, the problem could have been obviated by providing a full bail-out of, at least, foreign creditors, but this option was never seriously contemplated in policy circles, on the grounds that it would conflict with both the credit union structure and the monetary nature of the IMF (Boughton, 2001), not to mention obvious political difficulties in raising sufficient funds.

With the "Bagehotian" solution ruled out, the official sector's strategy took at first the form of *concerted lending*.[7] The strategy was inaugurated in November 1982, when the IMF's then–Managing Director, Jacques de Larosière, informed a gathering of bankers in New York that the IMF would not approve a request by Mexico for a US$4 billion loan until private banks provided written assurances that they would as a group increase their Mexican exposure by US$5 billion.

With respect to domestic experiments with orchestrated rescues, all of which are ultimately based on the power of the central bank to hold private banks "hostage" through moral suasion, this international version's main novelty lay in its formalized character. Under the "financing assurances policy," as it came to be known, the IMF would suspend access to its own money if creditor banks refused to reschedule the country's debt (Boughton, 2001, p. 477). Such a high degree of formalization was required to make up for the IMF's lack of direct powers over commercial banks. It had a serious drawback, though, in that it virtually gave banks veto power over the approval and financing of adjustment programs. More bluntly, under the new practice it was unclear who was being made hostage to whom.[8]

Yet, the concerted lending strategy was applied with some success to a dozen cases between 1982 and 1986 (Boughton, 2000a, p. 172). By 1985, however, the strategy was no longer working, essentially because of commercial banks' growing unwillingness

[6] Bird and Orme (1981) argue that "the Fund itself clearly believes ... that borrowing from it, particularly on the basis of a stand-by agreement, acts as a catalyst for the generation of private capital inflows" and quote Sturc (1978), Gold (1979), and de Larosière (1980) as relevant references. However, only the lattermost includes an explicit reference to the fact that *the adoption and pursuit of suitable adjustment programs in cooperation with the Fund generally tends through enhancement of the creditworthiness of borrowing countries to facilitate the attraction of private capital*. Note also that the reference in de Vries (1985) quoted above covers less than one page in her 600-page history of the IMF in the 1970s.

[7] Hereinafter we refer to a Bagehotian solution in a rather loose sense, since, as already remarked, international rescue packages have always involved a measure of conditionality, something that Bagehot never contemplated.

[8] And, in fact, to encourage banks to take a cooperative stance, authorities in creditor countries made some concessions as to how the new loans would have to be treated for supervisory purposes. See Sgard (2002).

to be "concerted." Financial and macroeconomic developments converged to harden bankers. On the financial side, the time gained through the concerted packages had allowed banks to build up considerable provisions against sovereign credit risk. Feeling less exposed to the threat of outright default, banks gradually assumed a tougher negotiating position. On the macroeconomic side, the policy adjustment of the countries benefiting from concerted lending had been insufficient, particularly in the structural area, resulting in protracted stagnation. This made concerted lending increasingly unpopular, as banks feared they would end up throwing good money after bad. Indeed, net bank lending to developing countries declined dramatically in 1985, and turned negative the next year.

All this provided the setting for the U.S. Treasury Secretary James Baker's famous October 1985 speech laying out a "Program for Sustained Growth" later to be known as the Baker Plan. The plan's underlying idea was that to avert massive cuts in lending to developing countries, growth had to be revived. To this end, what was needed was a combination of structural reform in recipient countries and the mobilization of financial resources on a large scale. How to achieve the first was fairly straightforward: one needed only to extend the scope of IMF conditionality to structural aspects, something the IMF had already begun doing. The latter task was more complicated. It is here that the notion of "catalysis" came in handy.[9] The Baker Plan posited that the provision of sufficient amounts of official financing in the context of structural reform aiming at economic liberalization would catalyze private sector lending to the extent needed to fill whatever financing gap was created in the process of spurring economic growth. It was estimated that the money needed to finance the plan during 1986–88 was US$17–18 billion for official money and US$20 billion for private lending (Boughton, 2001, p. 428).

This first experiment with using COF in crisis management yielded mixed results. Actual official lending was very close to the planned figure, but the catalytic effect on private lending sought was hardly visible.[10]

Leaving figures aside, the experiment led to widespread frustration. As Paul Volcker puts it, barely a year after the launching of the plan "any sense of enthusiasm was very much gone" (Volcker and Gyohten, 1992, p. 215). Even the most ardent advocates of the plan had to recognize that "by 1988 there was no question that the banks' willingness to provide new financing was essentially finished" (Boughton, 2001, p. 428). The symbolic *coup de grâce* to the Baker Plan came when, in 1988, Citicorp provisioned US$3 billion against Citibank's exposure toward developing countries. While the price of Citicorp stock skyrocketed, the prices of developing countries' loans on secondary markets plummeted. Not surprisingly, new lending to developing countries nearly dried up over the next two years.

In this environment, proposals to deal with the developing countries' problems by resorting to some form of debt relief began to gain currency, first in Europe and Japan, then in the United States. The IMF itself began to show dissatisfaction with both concerted lending and catalytic financing by adopting a new operational framework called the "menu approach," which entailed dealing with individual crises by presenting creditors with a range of options, all of which implied replacing old loans with new instruments that more accurately reflected secondary market values.

There was a critical problem, however, before the new strategy could be translated into concrete actions. Under the "financing assurances" policy, the IMF was for all practical purposes unable to force debt relief onto recalcitrant creditors. This policy had to be modified. Thus, the plan concocted by U.S. Treasury Secretary Nicholas Brady in the late 1980s, envisaging a comprehensive scheme for debt reduction, also encouraged the IMF to reconsider its financing assurances policy to reduce the risk that some creditors might hold out for a protracted period, thereby undermining the success of the debt-reduction strategy in individual cases. The IMF Board endorsed the Brady Plan in May 1989. Under the new operational framework, an accumulation of arrears to banks could be tolerated even pending agreement between the country and its creditors, provided "negotiations continue and the country's financing situation does not allow (arrears) to be avoided." The new policy meant adapting COF to the needs of crisis resolution, as the IMF, through its lending into arrears, would now pressure creditors to reach agreement with the country's authorities on the appropriate amount of debt reduction.

The Brady Plan can be counted among the successes of international cooperation. By 1993, eight Latin American countries, through a variety of operations, reduced their external obligations by US$42 billion, out of an initial stock of obligations of about US$104 billion (Boughton, 2001, p. 552). Over the same period, rescheduling agreements with bilateral official creditors achieved through the

[9] It is indeed in the mid-1980s that use of the word "catalytic" becomes more frequent in the literature on international financial arrangements. See, for example, Kenen (1986); Buira (1987); and the empirical literature cited in this paper's section entitled "A Survey of the Empirical Evidence."

[10] On the basis of stock data, IMF staff estimated zero net private lending over 1986–88. Other analysts, such as Cline (1989), whose views appear to have been shared by the U.S. Treasury, estimated actual flows at some US$13 billion, still well below the planned US$20 billion. As Boughton (2001, p. 428) explains, the difference was to be attributed to some offsetting transactions (in the form of swaps, write-downs, and buybacks) that the major banks put in place to contain their overall exposure while increasing direct lending.

Paris Club totaled about US$35 billion. The developing country debt crisis was finally over.

The Emerging Market Crisis, 1994–2002

After the launch of the Brady Plan, discussions on international crisis lending stopped for several years—because of the lack of major *new* balance of payment crises, among other things. The idea that IMF lending could catalyze private financial inflows had not lost its appeal, however, particularly within the staff and management of the IMF (see, for example, IMF, 1992; and Guitián, 1992, p. 20).

As a matter of fact, the catalytic effect lay at the heart of "precautionary" programs aimed specifically at promoting financial markets' confidence through the IMF seal of approval, rather than providing member countries with official finance. "Precautionary" programs—programs in which the country authorities state their intention not to draw—became quite popular in the early 1990s, especially in those countries with a recent history of government intervention in the economy, and therefore with a structural credibility deficit (Dhonte, 1997). By the time of the outbreak of the Asian crises, such programs accounted for one-third of all Stand-By and Extended Fund Facility (EFF) Arrangements. Moreover, the ratio between actual and potential borrowing in all outstanding IMF arrangements—excluding those off track—
208 declined significantly between the early 1980s and the middle of the 1990s (Cottarelli and Giannini, 1997).

Interestingly, however, when Mexico was hit by a devastating capital account crisis in late 1994, the catalytic effect was not invoked. Indeed, as Kenen (2001, p. 22) remarks, the package that was mounted to cope with the crisis (totaling about US$50 billion, mostly from the IMF) had all the features of a Bagehot-style LOLR operation:

> The official financing for Mexico was unique in more than its unprecedented amount. Although other crisis-stricken countries obtained large-scale official financing in subsequent years, the amounts involved were not intended—nor were they sufficient—to pay off those countries' short-term foreign debts. The size of the Mexican package, by contrast, was meant to extinguish the whole stock of tesobonos, to help Mexico cope with large dollars withdrawals [sic] from its banking system, and to help it rebuild its reserves.

Of course, no one at either the IMF or the U.S. Treasury really thought that the package should be used to pay back the *tesobonos*. Only, the package was big enough to ensure holders of *tesobonos* that the Mexican authorities would have sufficient money to honor their short-term debt, *even if that implied redeeming it in full.*

But why was COF not tried out for Mexico?[11] An important chunk of the answer is probably political in nature (one could maliciously ask why a Bagehot-style operation of such a size proved so easy to arrange, after all). But this is hardly the whole story. One should add to it that until then no one had yet contemplated the idea of using COF as a crisis management tool *while financial markets stayed open.* As we have seen, the Baker Plan had been concocted in quite different circumstances, since all the crisis countries had already suspended external debt service long before.

But the Mexican full-rescue package raised a number of problems that would later generate the attempt to use catalytic lending as a tool for crisis management also for major emerging markets. First, the sheer size of the package was hard to replicate, should more than one country be hit by a crisis. Second, it generated moral hazard concerns. Third, and perhaps most important, the idea that taxpayers' money should be used to bail out private banks was hard to sell. Thus, it is not surprising that immediately after the announcement of the Mexican program, references to COF as a market-friendly crisis management tool became more frequent.

For example, in April 1995 the Interim Committee of the IMF already refers explicitly to the "catalytic role" that the IMF could play in assisting members in coping with sudden market disturbances. Later that year Michel Camdessus made it plain that the Mexican package was to be regarded as an exception:

> We have agreed on procedures through which the Fund can respond rapidly—as it did in Mexico—to help put appropriate adjustment measures in place and avoid spill-over effects. We have made clear, however, that the use of such procedures will be limited to truly exceptional circumstances. The extent of our support will depend, as always, on the strength of the country's own adjustment effort, and we will take appropriate steps to ensure that its support remains catalytic in nature. (Camdessus, 1995)

More extreme measures, reminiscent of the way the developing country debt crisis had been handled,

[11] The amount the IMF was willing to lend to Mexico was increased by US$10 billion in February 1995, after the initial forecasts on the behavior of private investors had proved overly optimistic. Was this yet another example of a failed catalytic effect? Our reading of the episode is that the problems initially encountered by the program had more to do with the uncertainty surrounding the amount of the U.S. contribution to the package (which turned out to be less than originally envisaged) than with the program itself. See Boughton (1997) and De Long and Eichengreen (2001) for detailed accounts of the Mexican packages.

were also contemplated. Thus, at the Halifax summit, in June 1995, the G-7 recommended an in-depth reflection on crisis management tools. The task was taken up by the Group of Ten (G-10), which set up a working group whose report (the so-called Rey report, named after the group's chairman) was published in May 1996. The report did accept the importance of catalytic lending.[12] But it also warned that, given the difficulty of arranging a concerted package when a large share of "lending" takes place through bonds held by a myriad of investors, a temporary suspension of debt payments (a standstill) might sometimes prove desirable, as a way to gain time and better assess the sources of market turbulence. The Rey report, however, met with fierce opposition from the private sector. A counter-report published by the Institute of International Finance in September 1996 called its approach "misguided," on the grounds that the approach would face enormous implementation problems and, if implemented, would fuel moral hazard on the debtor side. As a result, the report's recommendations never won enough consensus to be adopted.

With the concerted approach increasingly regarded as difficult to implement, and the standstill approach facing strong opposition, by default the catalytic approach saw its appeal as a crisis management tool unquestionably rise.[13] The Asian crises provided a first testing ground for the new technique.

Several excellent descriptions of the Asian crises are already available (see, for example, IMF, 2001a; and Kenen, 2001). Here, it will suffice to note that COF—with IMF resources provided in large amounts, yet falling short of Bagehot-style LOLR financing—featured in all the main Asian crises, notably in Thailand, Indonesia, and the Republic of Korea. Indeed, as noted by IMF staff, "most of the capital account crisis programs [of the late 1990s] were predicated on just such a catalytic effect of official financing" (Ghosh and others, 2002, p. 8). As it happens, the catalytic effect failed to materialize, leading to sharper domestic adjustment, further injection of IMF resources and, in some cases (such as the Republic of Korea) the recourse to stronger forms of concerted lending.

Russia's crisis, in the summer of 1998, although different in both causes and ending, confirmed that the effectiveness of COF in the new environment could not be taken for granted. There, too, the existence of an IMF-supported program failed to provide sufficient confidence to markets. Yet, for want of better alternatives, the official community continued to bet on the idea. Thus, the report on international financial crises published by the so-called Group of Twenty-Two (1998), reiterates that "in most cases when a country experiences payment difficulties, the combination of adjustment and financing of a typical IMF programme can be expected to restore market confidence and catalyze private capital flows."

While the new report was being published, a new crisis broke out, this time in Brazil. The financial package the official community mounted this time totaled about US$42 billion, almost half of which came from the IMF. The package was heavily front-loaded, as about 90 percent of the sum was to be made available within 13 months. Both the size of the package and its time profile were clearly unprecedented. Yet, the package remained, according to our definition, catalytic in nature, since Brazil's short-term debt exceeded US$100 billion at the time. After the announcement of the program, markets stabilized for a while, but then, in late December 1998, new pressures emerged in the foreign exchange market. This time, financial conditions improved only after the floating of the real, and the announcement of a rollover agreement between the Brazilian government and international banks. Such deals, contrary to the Republic of Korea's, had not been actively promoted through moral suasion at the international level, but this one proved successful. Brazil's external problems subsided. Eventually, only a fraction of the US$42 billion package was actually drawn. The whole episode was widely read as a success story for COF, although some commentators invited caution in drawing lessons from it.[14]

After Brazil, official thinking on crisis management proceeded along two parallel paths. A first path led to giving center stage to the notion of catalytic lending, which was in fact enshrined in repeated public statements. The other led to the notion of "private sector involvement" (or PSI, a general term encompassing a range of options, from concerted lending to mandatory solutions), which clearly underscored the belief that catalytic lending might not be sufficient in a number of cases. Indeed, some debt-restructuring operations were actively promoted, if somewhat implicitly, in a number of small countries with limited financial ramifications.

---

[12] For example, it noted that "the official community has several objectives, including … catalyzing finance in support of adjustment efforts, when the latter are credible" and that "the main instruments of the official sector are signaling confidence in the good faith of the debtor and the economic soundness of its adjustment programme and providing the prospects of limited finance, subject to conditionality, to foster the resumption of spontaneous inflows."

[13] At this juncture, references to catalytic lending can, once more, be found in the communiqués of the IMF Interim Committee. The one issued on September 21, 1997 states that "the Fund will continue to play a critical role in helping to mobilize financial support for members' adjustment programs. In such endeavors, the Fund will continue its central catalytic role while minimizing moral hazard."

[14] De Long and Eichengreen (2001, p. 55), for example, remark that "the very different aftermath of Brazil's crisis remains one of those late-20th centuries mysteries to be unraveled by future historians."

This two-pronged approach culminated in the "Prague Framework" issued at the 2000 IMF Annual Meeting, which hinged around three propositions. The first simply reiterated the belief that, in some cases, catalytic lending would be sufficient to overcome a crisis. The second pointed to the usefulness of voluntary PSI in many circumstances. The third announced that "in exceptional cases, countries might impose capital or exchange controls as part of payments suspensions or standstills, in conjunction with IMF support for their policies and programmes, to provide time for an orderly debt restructuring." In such a context, "IMF lending into arrears might be appropriate."

In practice, however, experimentation continued for only the first two propositions of the Prague Framework. Thus, COF was again invoked, this time coupled with PSI, in two prominent cases, Turkey and Argentina. Both countries had requested an IMF program in December of 1999, for precautionary purposes in Argentina, and to strengthen the credibility of disinflationary policies in Turkey. Both programs initially worked, but then for a number of reasons, including policy slippages, financial conditions deteriorated. In line with the Prague Framework, in the course of 2000 the programs were increased in size (in IMF technical jargon, they were "augmented") and expanded to include a PSI component. But this provided only a brief respite. Financial conditions stabilized in Turkey only after a further "augmentation," at the end of 2001, brought financial support up to Bagehotian levels, namely about 1,500 percent of Turkey's quota in the IMF. In Argentina, a third augmentation, in August 2001, proved unable to restore calmer financial conditions. The following December, the authorities then declared a moratorium on foreign debt to private creditors.

In light of these experiences, it is not surprising that the emphasis on COF as a crisis management tool has more recently been declining. As Eichengreen (2001) puts it:

> The main lesson of the Turkish and Argentine experiences is that the markets are likely to disappoint official hopes. In the climate of uncertainty that invariably surrounds a crisis, waiting has option value. Investors have an incentive to wait and see whether the commitment to reform is sustained instead of being first to provide new money.

A Survey of the Empirical Evidence

The narrative in the previous section casts doubts on the magnitude of catalytic effects, at least for capital account crises, but clearly more systematic evidence is needed to enable us to rule on this issue. We have surveyed 26 papers—to our knowledge the whole empirical literature on catalytic effects. They are here classified in three branches—case studies, statistical studies of capital inflows, and statistical studies of interest rate spreads in international capital markets—which will be reviewed in turn. One should be aware before proceeding that several methodological difficulties make the measurement of catalytic effects particularly troublesome. Here is a tentative list of empirical hurdles.

- First of all, one must allow for the so-called counterfactual problem. The IMF seal of approval may not raise capital inflows, but one could argue that, in its absence, capital inflows might have been even weaker. This argument is sometimes used to explain the absence of obvious catalytic effects. Case studies are liable to this criticism—much less so those studies that model the behavior of capital movements, which are able to control for a variety of factors before and after the crisis.
- Second, one should properly specify the relevant time horizon over which the catalytic effect is expected to take place. Some studies focus on the short term, which is more relevant for assessing the IMF role in stemming a sudden confidence crisis. In such a context, however, it is critical to use high-frequency data, so as to be able to distinguish preprogram from postprogram observations. Failure to do so would bias the results toward the rejection of the existence of catalytic effects.
- Third, it may be difficult to distinguish between demand-driven and supply-driven capital movements. In particular, under a floating exchange rate with no intervention (although not necessarily under fixed exchange rates or in the presence of intervention) a decline in the current account deficit—a frequent goal of IMF-supported programs—must be associated with a *decline* in net capital inflows (as the balance of payments is by definition in equilibrium). This again may create a bias against finding catalytic effects. The studies focusing on interest rate spreads, rather than on capital movements, are, however, not affected by this problem.
- Fourth, in assessing whether it is the IMF seal of approval that makes the difference, one should control for the adjustment in economic policies. A strengthening of investors' confidence may be due to a policy change, rather than to the IMF seal of approval on those policies. Thus, not controlling for policy changes creates a bias in favor of the existence of catalytic effects.
- Fifth, one should control for steps taken in support of catalytic programs. Some programs were supported by various forms of private sector involvement, in which the private sector was nudged into action through more or less

Figure 1
Current Account Adjustment in Selected Crisis Countries
(As percentages of GDP)

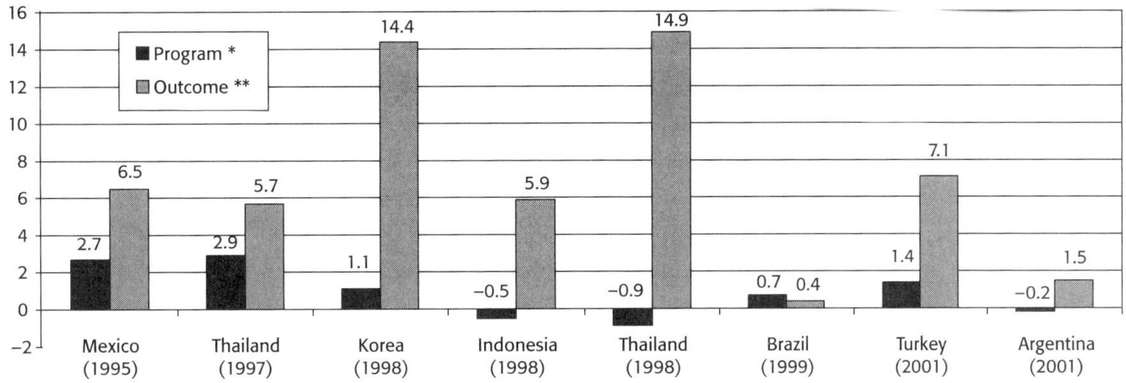

Sources: IMF, World Economic Outlook database; Ghosh and others (2002).

formalized regulatory means. Failure to control for these supporting steps also creates a bias in favor of catalytic effects.

- Sixth, one should control for the purpose COF is used for (whether for crisis prevention, management, or resolution), if truly operational implications are to be drawn from the analysis. But classifying programs according to purpose is clearly no straightforward matter.

These difficulties, as mentioned, affect to various degrees the three empirical methodologies that have been followed in the literature. Thus, by contrasting the results obtained on the basis of each of them, one should be able to arrive at a better picture of the actual extent of catalytic effects. This is what we will try to do in the rest of this section. Our reading of the evidence is that, while catalysis may be found at work in quite specific circumstances, such as in precautionary IMF programs or in the context of crisis resolution, overall its magnitude is small, and tends to become yet smaller as a country approaches the crisis stage.

Case Studies

Few papers have focused on case studies. An early example of the case study approach is Killick (1995), who discusses the experience with IMF-supported programs in 17 countries, concluding that there is no evidence of catalytic effects on private capital inflows.[15]

A comprehensive discussion of country experiences is also presented in Bird, Mori, and Rowlands (2000).[16] This paper looks at the experience of 17 countries during the 1980s and 1990s and draws four conclusions: (a) involvement by the multilaterals will not guarantee an inflow of capital from other sources; (b) what really matters is the perceived commitment by a government to a policy agenda that is seen as sound and internally consistent; (c) catalysis with the multilaterals is likely to be stronger and more positive in the case of bilateral aid flows; and (d) the nature and extent of catalysis may differ between the IMF and the World Bank, with the IMF having a stronger but *negative* effect.

A significant contribution to the case study approach has recently been given by the IMF staff in their study of IMF-supported programs in capital account crises (Ghosh and others, 2002). This paper looks at the experience of eight programs for large emerging markets during the 1990s and points mostly to the absence of strong catalytic effects:

> It is striking that, in *every* [emphasis in original] instance in our sample, the outcome [for private capital inflows] was worse than projected. Even in cases where the magnitude of the error was small, such as Argentina (1995), the program does not appear to have had a strong catalytic effect, at least in the very short run. (Ghosh and others, 2002, p. 11)

The resulting financing gap had to be filled with larger current account adjustment than originally envisaged. The amounts were not negligible, as Figure 1 testifies. The discrepancy reached a peak in 1998 (in the Republic of Korea and Thailand, where actual current account adjustment was 13–15 percentage points larger than planned), but remained

[15] Another early paper sometimes credited with reporting evidence of catalytic effects is de Vries (1986). It should be noted that in the de Vries paper the term catalytic is used with reference to "concerted lending," rather than to the meaning used in this paper.

[16] The same results are also reported in Bird and Rowlands (2000).

sizable also afterwards (in Turkey and Argentina). The only exception to this pattern is Brazil in 1999, where the outturn was about 1 percentage point below the planned figure.[17]

Effects on Capital Inflows

Several papers have focused on testing statistically how the existence of an IMF-supported program, or the size of IMF financing, has affected private capital inflows. Various methodologies have been used, with the predominant result being that catalytic effects, if any, are small. Three approaches have been followed (Table 1).

Analysis of the demand for IMF credit. Several papers have explored the issue of why countries need IMF credit. These papers do not typically focus on the existence of catalytic effects, but are often quoted in this context because the right-hand side of the econometric equations describing the demand for IMF credit usually include the amount of private capital inflows. The sign of the coefficient on this variable is seen as having a bearing on the catalytic issue: a positive sign would indicate complementarity between IMF credit and private credit (as one would expect when catalytic effects are in place); a negative sign would indicate substitution. The first of these papers (Bird and Orme, 1981) does find a positive and significant correlation for a cross section of 1976 programs, but no correlation for the 1977 cross section. A positive correlation, albeit a weak one, is found also in Bird (1994; published also in Bird, 1995). Other papers (Cornelius, 1987; Joyce, 1992) find negative (and typically nonsignificant) coefficients.[18]

Before-after tests. This approach focuses on whether the inception of an IMF-supported program involves a statistically significant increase of capital inflows (or of variables related to them, such as foreign exchange reserves) with respect to the preprogram period. The first of these studies is the short paper (see the section entitled "The History of COF: A Tale of Two Crises) prepared by the U.S. Treasury in 1977 as background for the discussion on the Witteveen facility (United States, Department of the Treasury, 1977). This analysis of 36 Stand-By Arrangements (SBAs) during 1970–75 finds that in most cases SBAs were followed by an increase in bank lending. Reichmann and Stillson (1978), although not directly aiming at measuring the existence of catalytic effects, also find that net foreign assets typically increase as a result of IMF-supported programs, but note that in only one-fourth of their sample is this increase statistically significant. Some evidence of catalytic effects in also found by McCauley (1986): in only one-third of the programs considered in his sample did bank lending decline in the year following the inception of a program. The relative frequency of outflows, however, increases to 50 percent by the end of his sample (the year 1981). A more negative assessment of the existence of catalytic effects can be found in Killick, Malik, and Manuel (1991).[19] They find that, on a two-year time horizon, the effect on private capital inflow is negative or small: the improvement in the overall balance of payments position, which they also observe, is thus generally due to the improvement of the current account.

They also note that the programs do not affect net inflows or gross flows much (there is no increase in gross disbursements). Another paper finding weak catalytic effects was prepared by IMF staff (Schadler and others, 1995). This paper, covering 45 IMF loans from mid-1988 to mid-1991, finds that there were large increases in capital inflows in only one-third of the cases. A more sophisticated variant of this approach is found in Conway (1998), who explores whether the probability of a foreign exchange crisis is reduced by the existence of an IMF-supported program. However, as the "crisis" is defined as foreign exchange reserves falling below a certain threshold, and as the behavior of foreign exchange reserves is modeled through a simple time-series model, this approach essentially focuses again on whether on average the reserve position increases after the inception of a program. The results show that reserves do increase when a program is in place, but that this is no longer true for countries under a program for an extended period.

Capital inflows models. The before-after approach does not address the "counterfactual" problem. A solution to this problem is to model directly the behavior of capital inflows, and evaluate whether this behavior was changed by the existence of an IMF-supported program (or by the amount of financing provided through them). Early results in this area were obtained by Hajivassiliou (1987), who, while not focusing directly on the existence of catalytic effects, does find a nonsignificant (and, indeed, negative) effect of the lagged presence of an IMF program on the supply of new private loans. In this paper, however, the dummy measuring the existence of a program also measures the existence of a previous rescheduling (being built to signal the existence of previous payment difficulties). A more direct attempt to assess the existence of catalytic effects on capital inflows is Rodrik (1996),[20] who finds that the effect of IMF lending on net private capital

[17] On the Brazilian crisis and its peculiarities, see the subsection entitled "The Emerging Market Crisis, 1994–2002."

[18] Faini and others (1995) compute, outside a regression approach, the correlation between capital inflows and the amount of IMF credit. They find a negative and significant correlation.

[19] The same results are also reported in Killick (1995).

[20] Rowlands (1994) is an earlier contribution, but we could not acquire a copy of this paper in time for the current draft. According to Bird and Rowlands (1997), this paper concludes for the absence of catalytic effects on private capital inflows.

Table 1
Private Capital Inflows and IMF Lending

	Methodology	Question	Sample	Main Findings
		I. Papers Estimating the Demand for IMF Credit		
Bird and Orme (1981)	Regression analysis	What determines the drawings by program countries?	31 developing countries that made drawings in 1976 and (an unspecified number of countries with drawings in) 1977 *(annual data)*	In 1976 significant positive correlation between drawings from the IMF and borrowing from euromarkets
Cornelius (1987)	Regression analysis	What determines the IMF drawings?	11 sub-Saharan countries, during 1975–77 and 1981–83	Negative and nonsignificant correlation between drawings and borrowing from foreign and international capital markets
Joyce (1992)	Regression analysis	What determines the decision of a country to enter an IMF-supported program?	45 countries, annual data for 1980–94	The commitment of new funds from private creditors relative to imports has a negative impact on requests for IMF assistance, but it is not significant.
Bird (1994); results also published in Bird (1995)	Regression analysis	What determines the drawings in program countries?	1980–85 for 27 countries	Positive but weak correlation between drawings and net disbursement of debt-creating private finance
		II. Papers Based on Before-After Tests		
U.S. Treasury (1977)	Inspection of changes in capital inflows	Does bank lending to program countries increase or decrease with the inception of a program?	36 program countries during 1970–75	In most cases, bank lending increased.
Reichmann and Stillson (1978)	Mann-Whitney test for difference in frequency distribution	Is the increase in net foreign assets observed statistically significant?	85 programs during 1963–72 *(quarterly data)*	Improvement observed in two-thirds of cases, but statistically significant only in less than one-fourth of cases
McCauley (1986)	Before-after analysis	Does a program affect bank lending to a country in the year following the inception of a program?	99 programs covering 56 countries during 1976–81	Generally supportive of the catalytic approach, with only one-third of countries showing a decline in private lending. The frequency of these cases, however, increases over time (to half by 1981).
Killick, Malik, and Manuel (1991); same results reported in Killick (1995)	Before-after analysis of differences from base (preprogram value); time horizon: four-year period	Is the size of private long-term capital inflows different from the preprogram period over a four-year horizon?	16 developing countries with IMF programs commenced during 1979–85	Small effects and negative on net capital accounts, with net repayment of foreign loans and no increase in disbursements
Hajivassiliou (1987)	Regression analysis	What determines the supply of new loans?	79 countries during 1970–82, annual data	There is a negative (although barely significant) correlation between the supply of new loans and the lagged presence of IMF support or request for a rescheduling.

(Table continues on next page)

Table 1 *(concluded)*

	Methodology	Question	Sample	Main Findings
		III. Papers Estimating Capital-Inflow Models		
Rodrik (1996)	Regression analysis	What determines net private capital inflows?	87 developing countries, averaging six-year periods (1970–93)	Effect of IMF lending not significantly different from zero, negative in some cases
Adji and others (1997)	Regression analysis	What determines foreign direct investment?	Annual data for 23 developing countries during 1970–81	No significant effect of the amount of IMF lending on foreign direct investment
Bird and Rowlands (1997)	Regression analysis	What determines new lending commitments (net of repayments)?	90 developing countries, annual data for 1974–89	The catalytic effect on private flows is either negative (and significant) or nonsignificant; there is some positive and significant effect on official inflows, not private.
Bird and Rowlands (2000)	Regression analysis and questionnaires	What affects private (portfolio, foreign direct investment, and other debt) and bilateral capital inflows?	96 developing countries during 1980–95, annual data; 15 interviews with financial market managers	No evidence of a positive catalytic effect and some evidence of a negative one for the private inflows; some (weak) effect on bilateral inflows; no evidence that the catalytic effect has strengthened over time
Edwards (2000)	Regression analysis	Do private inflows (commitments) and foreign direct investment react positively to IMF programs?	106 countries, annual data for 1979–95	No catalytic effect from the existence of an IMF program, even in countries with a good record of compliance with past programs; negative effects for countries with IMF programs that experienced compliance problems
Marchesi (2001)	Regression analysis	Does an IMF program facilitate debt rescheduling by commercial creditors?	93 developing countries, annual data during 1983–95	The presence of an IMF program increases the probability that a country benefits from debt restructuring.
Schadler and others (1995)	Inspection of capital inflows	What is the effect of a program on capital inflows?	45 IMF loans from mid-1988 to mid-1991	Large increases in capital inflows in only one-third of cases
Conway (1998)	Regression analysis	Is the probability of exiting a crisis (defined as a deviation of the reserve-to-import ratio from a certain threshold) affected by the existence of an IMF program?	84 countries, quarterly data for 1973–92	Countries participating in IMF programs are less likely to enter crisis, but this benefit is lost by countries whose IMF programs continue for extended periods.

inflows was not significantly different from zero and was negative in many cases. No effect of IMF lending on foreign direct investment is found by Adji and others (1997). Similar conclusions were reached by Bird and Rowlands (1997 and 2000), using a more sophisticated capital inflows model, although the authors do find some evidence of catalytic effects on bilateral official inflows. One should note that the dynamic specification of these papers is absent or very basic, and one wonders whether the use of longer lags, and perhaps higher-frequency data, would have helped. The fact that annual data do not reveal catalytic effects suggests, however, that if those effects are present, they do not show up very rapidly and are thus not very valuable for crisis management.[21] Edwards (2000) also fails to identify positive catalytic effects, after controlling for the record of past implementation of IMF programs. Indeed, he finds that while a program does not have catalytic effects even following a record of good program implementation, it does have negative catalytic effects if coupled with a recent history of nonperformance. The only paper that does find catalytic effects on private capital flows is Marchesi (2001). Marchesi focuses on a very specific form of such flows, however, namely the decision to reschedule existing external obligations: a program would raise the probability of a rescheduling. In principle, the decision to reschedule a loan can be seen as equivalent to granting a new loan—and therefore as providing a new capital inflow. However, the paper does not make allowance for rescheduling decisions that were part of concerted strategies as distinct from decisions that were due to genuine catalytic effects. And there is no doubt that the IMF did play a major role in several cases of concerted rescheduling (Milivojević, 1986). Moreover, the paper does not control for the effect of a change in policies on the decision to reschedule; the latter, rather than the IMF seal of approval, may be responsible for the increased probability of a rescheduling.[22]

[21] It would also be necessary to control for simultaneity issues: the IMF may step in to stem capital outflows, but the use of annual data (mixing pre- as well as post-IMF intervention periods) may preclude the identification of the catalytic effect. However, Bird and Rowlands (2000) also present results based on a questionnaire sent to financial managers. The sample would show that financial managers do find that signing an agreement with the IMF or the World Bank makes a country more attractive, but none of them regarded IMF or World Bank involvement as one of the five principal reasons for investing in a country. The sample of respondents was, however, quite small (15 managers). Bird (1995, p.175, n. 51), also reports mixed evidence on catalytic effect from interviews with bankers held during the 1980s.

[22] One paper that does try to distinguish between the effect of changes in policies and the seal-of-approval effect (or "credentialing," in the author's terminology) is Conway (1994). This paper focuses directly on the effect of programs on economic performance, concluding that there is no evidence of the IMF's seal of approval having improved performance, after controlling for policy changes.

Effects on Spreads

One obstacle in estimating capital inflows equations is that capital movements are typically very noisy. In addition, as noted, a decline in net capital inflows may merely reflect an improvement in the external current account. Thus, some papers have focused on how the interest rates charged on a country's debt are affected by a program (Table 2).

The first paper to include a dummy for the existence of an IMF-supported program is Özler (1993). She finds that programs are associated with an increase in spreads, a result that is interpreted as indicating that IMF-supported programs signal (or are associated with) payment difficulties. The effect is statistically significant, albeit less so in specifications including more variables. More recently a similar conclusion was reached by Haldane (1999) who focuses on the behavior of secondary market spreads on the bonds issued by large emerging economies. He finds that a large spread persists after the initiation of a program and that, indeed, the spread "typically widens further in the immediate aftermath of a program."

Haldane's paper, however, looks only at seven countries in a relatively short time frame, and does not test statistically his conclusions, reaching them from visual inspection of the spreads. A more systematic approach is followed in Eichengreen and Mody (2000). This paper has two advantages over others: it is based on a large sample and on high-frequency data (thus reducing the risk of averaging between before- and after-program data). The paper looks at the spread at launch on bond issues during the 1990s. The strongest catalytic effects are found for EFF loans (Extended Fund Facility, which provides the IMF's longer-term loans) and, to a lesser extent, SBA loans (the traditional shorter-term loans) in equations when the number of quarters under a program is also included with a positive coefficient. This means that a program lowers the spread but the effect declines over time.

The authors conclude that their results "will hearten official observers concerned to document the 'catalytic effect' of IMF programs," although they also suggest caution about the type of programs that exercise this effect.[23] Two qualifications should be made in interpreting these results. First, the regressions do not control for the change in economic policies that typically characterizes an IMF-supported program. This means that it is impossible to distinguish between the decline in the spread that is due to sounder policies, and that arising from the IMF seal of approval: as noted, catalytic effects

[23] Indeed, the authors find that Enhanced Structural Adjustment Facility (ESAF) loans (those addressed to poorer countries) do not have a significant effect on spreads (and the coefficient is positive). Moreover, they find that the effect is significant only for countries with an intermediate credit rating.

Table 2
Spreads and IMF Lending

	Methodology	Question	Sample	Main Findings
Özler (1993)	Regression analysis	Does the existence of an IMF-supported program affect the spread over LIBOR on commercial bank loans?	1,525 commercial bank loan contracts for 26 countries over 1968–81	The effect is positive (i.e., the existence of a program raises the spread). The effect is statistically significant, although less so in specifications with more variables.
Haldane (1999)	Inspection of spreads	Does a program affect spreads on secondary bond markets?	7 large emerging markets during 1996–99	A large spread persists after the program initiation. Indeed, the spread "typically widens further in the immediate aftermath of a program."
Eichengreen and Mody (2000)	Regression analysis	Does a program affect the spread at launch on international bonds?	All bond issues by emerging markets from 1991–I to 1999–IV	Negative effect of the existence of a program on the spread. The effect is statistically significant in some regressions, in particular for EFF programs and, to a lesser extent, SBAs, but only in equations including the duration of programs with a positive sign (i.e., the effect is negative, but declines over time). The size of the effect is small, however.
Mody and Saravia (2003)	Regression analysis	Does a program affect the spread at launch on international bonds?	All bond issues by emerging markets from 1991–I to 1999–IV	Broadly in line with the previous paper, but, in addition, the size of a program matters, with stronger effects for larger programs; precautionary programs are those where the effect is stronger (and, indeed, the catalytic effect does not matter for nonprecautionary programs).

Note: LIBOR denotes the London interbank offered rate.

should refer only to the latter.[24] Second, though significant, the effect of the programs remains small: the spread is lowered by some 9 percent, or 24 basis points in the sample average.

This is not much compared with the average volatility of spreads in international markets. Similar conclusions are reached in Mody and Saravia (2003), with the presence of a program lowering spreads on average by 8 percent. In addition, this paper shows that the size of a program does matter: an additional program size of 10 percent of a country's long-term debt lowers spreads by about 20 percent. While this effect remains fairly low, it underscores that what matters more than the seal of approval is the amount of financial support that the IMF makes available. A second interesting finding relates to precautionary programs (those for which either the authorities declared that there was no intention of actually borrowing, or those for which no borrowing took place): the paper shows that the whole negative effect on spreads comes from these programs. This, of course, may be tautological: if a program succeeds, this should be reflected in both a decline in spreads and the fact that the country does

[24] Of course, it could be argued that, without the IMF, those policies would not have been implemented, as policymakers needed, for internal political reasons, an outside "policy enforcer." However, this points to an entirely different channel through which the IMF might have a role, *even in the absence of catalytic effects*.

not need to borrow from the IMF. In any case, this result suggests that if catalytic effects are present, they do not arise under crises situations (when programs are not precautionary).

In Search of Theoretical Underpinnings

Where does all this leave us? None of the papers surveyed finds evidence of strong catalytic effects, although some of them do find the existence of moderate effects. Besides, this overall unfavorable outcome has been reached in spite of the failure to control for policy changes, which should have biased results in favor of COF. Moreover, there are indications that to the extent that catalytic effects do exist, they are diminishing over time, are weaker for countries that went through a series of IMF-supported programs, and are weaker in crisis situations.

Why are catalytic effects empirically weak? Is there anything that the IMF could do to enhance them? Has the trend toward increased capital mobility affected their magnitude? Are any developments in the international financial markets likely to make them stronger? Conversely, why should there be any catalytic effect at all? Answering these questions requires discussing the analytical bases of the very notion of COF.

If IMF support to a country boosts the confidence of private investors, it must be because the IMF is supplying something to the private sector, and something that, presumably, cannot be provided by market forces. An IMF program does indeed provide "services," and, based on these services, one can identify five channels through which the catalytic effect, in principle, operates. While these channels are not mutually exclusive, it is useful to discuss them separately, not only because their effectiveness depends on different conditions but also because there are cases in which they may conflict with one another, thus weakening potential catalytic forces.

For each channel or service, we first identify some key "requirements" (seven altogether) needed for its effectiveness. Then, we assess whether these requirements are likely to be met under ordinary and extraordinary circumstances, and point out a number of adverse interactions among the various conditions. Channels and requirements are summarized in Table 3.[25]

[25] It has been argued (see, for example, Bird, 1994; Killick, 1995; and Bird and Rowlands, 2001) that the catalytic effect fails to materialize because the record on IMF-supported programs in achieving their objectives is poor. Leaving aside the difficult issue of assessing the effectiveness of these programs, however, programs may not achieve their results precisely because the intended catalytic effects fail to materialize. Explaining this failure with the programs' alleged poor record thus involves a logical circularity.

Five Channels for the Catalytic Effect

Channel I: Policy Design

Bird and Rowlands (1997) note that "for the [international financial institutions] to have a possible catalytic effect there must be a presumption that economic policy will be better designed and more appropriate to a country's existing economic situation and needs."

The IMF—an agency specialized in macroeconomic adjustment policies—provides key advice in the design of programs, thus supplementing the human resources of the program country. Indeed, IMF-supported programs are often perceived as having been designed by the IMF. The catalytic effect would arise because the private sector would be reassured that, thanks to the "technical assistance" of the IMF, the best policy design has been adopted.

In principle, this service could be provided by private sector consultants. There are three reasons why the IMF may have a comparative advantage in this area. First, as a public agency that member countries commonly "own," the IMF is in a better position to guarantee the confidentiality of (at least some) of the information on which the process of policy design is based. Thus, it may be easier for the IMF to obtain the full collaboration of the government in disclosing all the relevant data. Second, it may also be politically more acceptable to receive advice from an international agency than from private agents. Third, as a lending institution that puts its own resources at risk and as administrator of conditionality, the IMF may have stronger incentives in delivering high-quality advice. That is, the unique combination of services it provides tends to give the IMF a competitive edge in the advisory business.

For this channel to operate effectively, two requirements must be met:[26]

- The IMF should have all necessary information available to optimize the policy design: there should be no information asymmetries between the program country and the IMF.
- The IMF should provide the best advice for the country, regardless of other considerations. This means that the program should be the "best"

[26] One additional condition, for this as well for other channels to operate, is that the IMF be endowed with sufficient resources and skills to perform its tasks. Rodrik (1996) makes this assumption explicitly. Other authors have challenged it, blaming the failure of some IMF-supported programs in restoring confidence on errors in policy design, possibly because of poor judgment (see, for example, Stiglitz, 2000). There has been no systematic analysis of whether the human resources available to the IMF are adequate to the task. Nevertheless, this line of criticism is not particularly relevant from an analytical standpoint, as it points to a problem that, at least in principle, could be easily handled by enhancing the IMF's human resources.

Table 3
Conditions for Existence of Catalytic Effects

	(1) Sufficient Information[1]	(2) No Constraint on Policy Design	(3) Transparency	(4) No Cost in Playing This Role Well	(5) Lending	(6) Conditionality Mechanism and Negotiation Process	(7) Reasonable and Predictable Costs for Slippages
Channel I *(provision of assistance in policy design)*	✓	✓					
Channel II *(provision of information)*	✓		✓	✓	✓		
Channel III *(provision of commitment technology)*	✓			✓	✓	✓	✓
Channel IV *(provision of a screening device)*	✓			✓		✓	
Channel V *(provision of liquidity insurance)*	✓				✓		

[1] This condition requires (a) for Channel II, that the IMF have better information than the market; and (b) for all other channels, that there be no information asymmetries between the IMF and the program country.

that can be designed under the circumstances for the specific country. It is important to stress that the focus here is on the absence of constraints that might arise from the fact that the IMF is a multicountry institution and may, as such, have to take into consideration costs that certain policies bring about for other countries. As we will see, problems of this type may arise.

Channel II: Information

Rodrik (1996) notes the following:

> Information about the broader investment environment and the quality of government policymaking is a public good: such information benefits all potential investors, regardless of specific projects.... [I]n view of the public nature of the benefit, individual investors have inadequate incentives to devote resources to information gathering of this particular kind and certainly little incentive to share with others the information they do gather.

Thus, it should be possible for the IMF to invest more resources on information gathering than the private sector and, consequently, to have an information edge over the private sector. Consequently, private investors should be willing to follow the IMF when the latter provides a positive assessment of macroeconomic conditions (a catalytic effect).[27]

Playing this monitoring role, however, requires a set of stringent requirements (Table 3):

- The IMF should, not only in theory but also in practice, have better information than do the markets.
- The monitoring should be transparent. The IMF could, of course, simply signal that the program is on track. However, a mere seal of approval not backed up by additional information is not equally effective. On this basis, Rodrik (1996) and other IMF watchers have argued that the IMF should play this role more transparently. And the IMF has responded to this call, increasing its transparency.[28]

[27] The critical role that the availability of adequate information to the IMF can play in enhancing catalytic forces is also highlighted in Corsetti, Guimarães, and Roubini (2003).

[28] Until the mid-1990s, the provision of information by the IMF was limited to statements that the program was on track, occasional public statements by IMF staff and management, and occasional contacts with the business community. The IMF is currently publishing virtually all letters of intent, as well as most staff reports for program countries.

- The IMF should not suffer major costs in providing information transparently, whether this information is "good news" or "bad news."
- The IMF should lend—monitoring can, of course, be decoupled from lending. But, as Rodrik (1996) notes, the word of the IMF acquires more weight if it "puts its money where its mouth is" (see also Masson and Mussa, 1995).[29]

Channel III: Commitment

This channel—perhaps the one that has attracted the most attention until recently—focuses on the mechanism of conditionality and its implications for the government's credibility in promising "good" policies. Conditionality in IMF-supported programs means that if these policies are not implemented the program country suffers an immediate cost.[30] In entering into a program that involves a clear and immediate penalty for noncompliance, a government ties its own hands, thus addressing the typical intertemporal consistency problem of economic policymaking (Sachs, 1989; Diwan and Rodrik, 1992; Masson and Mussa, 1995; Rodrik, 1996; Dhonte, 1997; Fischer, 1997; Cottarelli and Giannini, 1999; Dornbusch, 2001). A catalytic effect would in this case arise because the private sector would be reassured that policies will be implemented. The private sector could not play this conditionality-centered role, mainly because direct negotiation with the private sector is politically unacceptable: a public, multilateral institution such as the IMF is needed (Rodrik, 1996; Masson and Mussa, 1995).

Several requirements need to be met for this channel to operate smoothly. These can be more easily identified by interpreting the relation between the IMF and the program country as a principal-agent relationship (Killick, 1997). The IMF is the principal that wants to see certain policies implemented because this is good not only for the program country but also for the international community. The program country is the agent that receives a reward (IMF support) if the program is implemented. For a principal-agent relationship to work effectively, some key requirements must be met:

- The IMF and the program country should share the same information, so as to allow effective monitoring of the agent's policies.
- Lending (the reward for the agent) is needed as this channel is based on the program conditionality arising from lending.
- There should be a process for negotiations that allows the definition of the "contract" between the principal and the agent, as well as a process for renegotiation to take new information into account. This renegotiation is not a trivial aspect of an IMF-supported program, which involves essentially iterative processes, sometimes based on trial and error (Mussa and Savastano, 1999).
- The penalty for the program country in not delivering should be clear. It should also be "reasonable": it would not make sense to sever the principal-agent relation (i.e., stop the program) for minor deviations in implementation.
- There should be no large cost for the principal (the IMF) when the agent (the country) does not deliver: this is typically the situation in most principal-agent relationships in which the principal (say, the employer) has a large number of agents (employees).[31]

Channel IV: Screening

Marchesi and Thomas (2001) argue that only countries where the authorities' policies are fundamentally good can afford sustaining the costs arising from IMF policies. The authors do not say what the costs of entering into an IMF-supported program are, but one can make the case that countries suffer a short-run economic hardship under a program. Moreover, some measures are unpleasant to undertake, not least because they harm powerful political constituencies. Only countries with viable long-term plans are willing to face these costs. Thus, entering a program helps the private sector to single out (or to screen) the countries that (upon entering a program) will follow good policies, a point also made by Fischer (1997).

What is peculiar, and paradoxical, about this channel is that it does not require that the conditions "imposed" by the IMF be strictly necessary for the program's success (or even that they be

[29] Another requirement that is frequently mentioned is that the inception of an IMF program should not send a negative signal. The provision of information should not be distorted by the very fact that the country has entered an IMF-supported program. Many authors have noted that this may not be the case: the announcement of a program may be interpreted as signaling that the country is in trouble, which may weaken any catalytic effects (Killick, 1995; Eichengreen and Mody, 2000; and Bird and Rowlands, 2001). We do not find this argument convincing, as typically markets know already that a country is in trouble when it reaches the point of starting program discussions with the IMF.

[30] Note that the interruption of a program involves different types of costs for a country, ranging from the direct loss of IMF financial support, to political costs, to the loss of private sector support (assuming the existence of catalytic effects).

[31] It is worth noting that a principal-agent relationship will work less effectively, the stronger are the differences in the utility functions of principal and agent. With respect to IMF-supported programs, this means that a program works better if the program country owns the program. This has been long acknowledged. Some authors have raised the issue of whether the imposition of program conditionality does not in itself signal lack of ownership. We do not see this as a major issue: a policymaker that ties its own hands does not necessarily do it because the country does not own the program, but to reassure outsiders that the program will in any case be implemented.

economically useful): as long as they are not plainly inappropriate (which would signal only stupidity and thus reduce credibility), all that is required is that they involve costs—and thus are "difficult" to implement. While this is by no means the channel that is most frequently mentioned, it is not, at an analytical level, unreasonable, since it focuses on a form of signaling that is not uncommon in social behavior (acting "tough" is a signaling device; see, for example, Diamond, 1992). Critics of the IMF have also sometimes argued that certain measures (in particular those of a structural nature) are not clearly linked to program goals. One oft-heard rebuttal of this criticism is that, while not directly linked, these measures show the authorities' resolve to undertake difficult steps. This is the essence of the screening channel.

Although Marchesi and Thomas (2001) stress the difference between this channel and the more traditional commitment channel, the effectiveness of the screening mechanism is enhanced by many of the same factors required for Channel III to operate, namely those pertaining to the effectiveness of the "bargaining process" between the IMF and the country authorities, and to program monitoring: no information asymmetry, no costs to the IMF in enforcing the program conditions, and the existence of a negotiation/renegotiation process (see Table 3).

220 *Channel V: Insurance*

This is perhaps the trickiest channel of all, or at least the channel that has been most affected by the transition to capital account convertibility (and has thus attracted more attention recently). Knowledge that the IMF might step in should a country fall short of external finance might act as implicit insurance for investors that their claims will be honored. Indeed, such a mechanism lies at the root of the oft-heard criticism that the possibility that a country could rely on an IMF program to stem a capital account problem generates moral hazard—a typical by-product of any form of insurance. Leaving aside the issue of moral hazard, which need not concern us here, the gist of the argument is that the very existence of the IMF might reduce the probability of a self-fulfilling run caused purely by illiquidity problems (Haldane, 1999; Zettelmeyer, 2000; Miller and Zhang, 2000). The catalytic effect would arise from the provision to the private sector of the insurance service that is implicit in the LOLR function.

This service could in principle also be provided by the private sector: contingent credit lines could be made available by banks, against the payment of a fee. However, the cases in which this has happened so far are rare, and the results are hardly encouraging[32]—probably because it is hard to identify, or even define, cases of pure liquidity crises, in which the line of credit would become available. The traditional lending facilities of the IMF are not directly affected by this problem, because IMF programs always involve elements of conditionality.[33] It is thus somewhat academic to discuss the "insurance" channel as a separate one. Nevertheless, for the sake of completeness, it is worth pointing out the two requirements that are needed for this channel to operate:

- Once again, there should be no asymmetric information that would prevent the IMF from assessing whether the crisis is one of liquidity, or from requesting measures that would eliminate any solvency issues.
- Lending should be forthcoming in amounts sufficiently large to convince the private sector that the risk of being locked in is small.

Channel-Specific Problems

We now turn to the discussion of why some of the requirements summarized in Table 3 are unlikely to be realized in a number of practical cases, and especially under conditions prevailing in capital account crises. Four requirements may be particularly hard to meet in some circumstances.

Requirement 1: Sufficient Information

This requirement takes two forms. The information channel requires that the IMF have better information than the market. All other channels require that there be no major information asymmetries between the IMF and the program country. As to the first aspect, the process of financial consolidation and technical improvements in information technology have reduced the private sector's disadvantage in gathering and processing macroeconomic information. Consequently, the resources invested in these tasks by the private sector have increased and the information edge of the IMF may have declined in comparison with, say, the late 1970s. Note also that some information that becomes more critical in capital account crises (that is, that related to financial transactions and intermediaries) may be more easily accessible to financial analysts than to the IMF. And concerning the assumption of no major information asymmetries between the IMF and the program country, there are also some problems. The IMF does not control directly the information produced by the program country and has to rely on the data provided by country authorities. Nevertheless,

[32] See Kenen (2001) for an account of the experience with private contingent credit lines.

[33] This is not entirely true of the CCL, the facility established in 1999 to deal with "pure" liquidity problems, which, to some extent, worked on the basis of preselection. The CCL attracted no applicants, however, and was allowed to expire on its scheduled sunset date in November 2003. See Giannini (2002) for a criticism of the CCL.

while there have been cases of data misreporting, it is fair to say that, under ordinary conditions, countries do provide timely and accurate information for program design and monitoring. Problems may, however, arise under crisis conditions, when events develop rapidly and the timeliness of the policy response becomes as important as the nature of the response. In these circumstances, complete sharing of all relevant information between the IMF and country authorities obviously becomes more difficult and information asymmetries may arise.

Requirement 2: No Constraint on Policy Design

The policy design channel (Channel I) assumes that the IMF can identify and promote the best program for each country. Leaving aside the issue of possible errors in policy design, a more intrinsic problem arises from the very nature of the IMF as a multicountry agency. For lack of a better term, we will refer to this problem as "policy contagion." Suppose the best program that could be designed for a country requires a measure that markets fear may also be introduced in other countries. If the IMF had to deal only with one country, its unconstrained advice would be to introduce that measure. However, the IMF may not go ahead because of the implications that this may have for other countries. To make the case more concrete, the measure in question may be the introduction of some form of capital control or of debt restructuring. The fact that the IMF is supporting this measure in one country (where it could be implemented rapidly, thus minimizing disruptions) might be perceived by markets as indicating that the same approach would be followed for other program countries. The latter perception could trigger speculative attacks. Fearing this, the IMF would stop short of including in a program a measure that would be optimal for that country. This is an extreme case, involving a strong (and very contagion-prone) measure. But the point is more general (it affects, for example, advice regarding the choice of the exchange rate regime). IMF advice to a country does not take place in a vacuum, and this may constrain its policy advice, particularly in crisis management packages where more radical (and contagion-prone) measures may be needed.

Requirement 5: Lending

Lending, of course, takes place (at least potentially) in all IMF programs. The real question, however, is whether the "limited" lending that characterized catalytic programs is enough to raise the propensity of the private sector to invest in the program country, particularly in a capital account crisis. This issue is particularly problematic for the insurance channel (Channel V), as highlighted by Zettelmeyer (2000), Eichengreen and Mody (2000), and Ghosh and others (2002). In particular, the analytical model in Zettelmeyer (2000) demonstrates that limited financing does not eliminate the risk for creditors of being locked into pre-default situations; indeed, limited financing may *prompt* a speculative attack as investors take the opportunity of closing their positions.

Requirement 7: Reasonable and Predictable Costs for Policy Slippages

The costs of noncompliance in the execution of IMF-supported programs could be clearly defined in the "old days." Lack of implementation of critical measures would cause the interruption of a program and of IMF financial support. The latter could be resumed after the implementation of corrective measures. This is still the way things work in a number of countries—those less involved in international financial markets, mostly pure cases of "external current account crises." But in capital account crises, the penalty for noncompliance cannot be set a priori: it depends on the markets' reaction. The latter may be disproportionately large owing to bandwagon effects. Consequently, the magnitude of the penalty is also difficult to predict.[34] The unpredictability of the penalty can have severe effects on the IMF's willingness to promptly react to lack of compliance and, hence, on its credibility and the strength of catalytic effects. Fearing an excessive market response, the IMF may not respond in a timely way to inappropriate policies, thus undermining its role both as provider of information (Channel II), provider of credibility (Channel III), and provider of a screening device (Channel IV).

Channel Inconsistencies

It would be somewhat reassuring if the seven requirements for effectiveness we have identified could be shown to have no adverse interaction. However, this is not the case: some requirements, while making some channels stronger, tend to weaken the others. Thus, attempts to enhance one channel, for example through changes in the way the IMF operates, may yield ambiguous results overall. There appear to be three main "channel inconsistencies," respectively associated with "conflicts of interest in blowing the whistle," "transparency and

[34] On this issue, Ghosh and others (2002) note,

> There is no country that has not at some point of time experienced hesitations and lapses in policy implementation, mixed political signals, untimely release of bad news, and uncertainties in particular elements of financing. The difference is, in a capital account crisis, the country's entire macroeconomic prospects may be hostage to such events—and the markets are unforgiving of any lapses.

the conditionality process," and "conditionality and insurance services."[35]

Conflicts of Interest in Blowing the Whistle

The information channel (Channel II), the commitment channel (Channel (III), and the screening channel (Channel IV) all require that the IMF be an unbiased observer and that "blowing the whistle" not be costly for the IMF. However, when the IMF is involved in policy design (Channel I) and insurance (Channel V), blowing the whistle is costly.

Channels II, III, and IV require that the IMF play its role fairly: it should provide the relevant information to the market (Channel II) and enforce the implementation of the program policies, interrupting the program in case of noncompliance (Channels III and IV). However, the larger the cost that the IMF faces when it blows the whistle, the larger will be the disincentive in playing its role effectively.

Unfortunately, the IMF does face large costs in blowing the whistle. According to some IMF watchers, because of the IMF's political nature—the IMF is administered by a board of Executive Directors who are political appointees—these costs are primarily political. If this were the whole story, the solution would be to give the IMF more independence, as indeed is proposed in De Gregorio and others (1999). But there are costs that arise from the
222 very function the IMF is required to play:

- No matter how much stress is put on program ownership, IMF-supported programs are perceived as IMF programs. In a way, this is desirable, as the fact that IMF expertise is used to build the program should support the catalytic effect (Channel I). But this implies that the IMF suffers a cost in terms of reputation if the program does not work. Note that the cost is there even if the program fails because of lack of implementation: the IMF could in this case be accused of having supported a government that did not deserve credit, possibly because of a "bias toward lending."[36]
- As mentioned earlier, stopping a program can trigger a crisis, with major costs for the program country. A crisis involves costs for the IMF as well—not only because the program country is an IMF member but also because of possible contagion effects to other IMF members. Thus, from the perspective of an international agency, it may be preferable to wait to "blow the whistle" as this allows the agency to "buy time," giving financial markets time to differentiate and reducing, in this way, contagion effects. The cost of this for the IMF is a weakening of its credibility, and thus a weakening of catalytic effects. Needless to say, this cost grows as more countries are exposed to the risk of a capital account crisis.[37]

Note also that these costs exist not only when a program is already in place but also when the IMF has to decide whether to start a new program.

Transparency and the Conditionality Process

Channel II requires transparency, but transparency enhances problems in the process of conditionality and negotiation required by Channels III and IV.

As stressed by Mussa and Savastano (1999), the conditionality mechanism is not based on a "contract," but is rather a "process":

> A typical IMF-supported program is not set in stone at its inception, either proceeding subsequently in exact accord with the initial plan, or terminated because of some minor deviation. [D]isbursements proceed automatically if all the performance criteria are met as initially specified. This rarely happens all the way through an arrangement. Instead, if various conditions are not met, deviations may be accommodated with "waivers," projections may be revised, and numerical targets changed. Those who participate in the process of IMF-supported programs, from both sides, do so with full awareness of their fundamental iterative, open-loop character.

The "constructive imperfection" of this process is plain in these words. Economic policymaking is not an exact science. The process of steering an economy back on track is a continuous one and may require, for example, waiving some conditions that had been initially regarded as critical, or, instead, halting the program if a sufficient number of conditions initially regarded as not critical are not met, or, again, changing conditions. In virtually all of these cases, judgment and negotiation will play a critical role.

[35] Some of the problems highlighted in this section are also "channel specific," i.e., would arise even in the absence of inconsistencies. For example, this is true for some of the costs that the IMF suffers when it blows the whistle on a member country.

[36] The existence of a conflict between monitoring activities (the so-called *surveillance*), on one side, and program design and negotiation, on the other, is probably at the root of the proposal by Chancellor Gordon Brown (Brown, 2001) "to make the IMF's surveillance and monitoring functions independent of the intergovernmental decisions about financial support for crisis resolution."

[37] Rodrik (1996) points to the fact that the IMF can no longer be regarded as an unbiased observer merely because it lends (another form of channel inconsistency as, at the same time, lending is needed for the working of all of the above channels; see Table 3). It is not clear whether this is a severe problem, however, taking into account that IMF lending has seniority over private sector lending, so that the IMF should not be concerned about the effect that stopping a program would have on the likelihood of recovering its investment.

Transparency, in particular the publication of letters of intent, even though critical to enhancing the information channel, makes this process more difficult to manage. For example, failure to implement a certain measure may trigger a crisis, even when the IMF would have been willing to grant a waiver. Conversely, the granting of a waiver may be seen as a watering down of the program, which could be construed as being done for political reasons.

It may be argued that these problems could be solved through *increased* transparency. For example, the IMF could be more explicit or more prompt in clarifying what is critical and what is not, and under which circumstances it would be willing to support a change in policies. This is a naïve view. Not only is the range of events that a program can face too large to be subject to pre-specification, but, more fundamentally, pre-specification would be inconsistent with the negotiation aspects of an IMF-supported program. Suppose financial markets reacted negatively to the lack of implementation of a measure included in a published letter of intent. If the IMF immediately stated publicly its willingness to waive the condition, so as to stem a speculative attack at its inception, it would lose any leverage in negotiating remedial actions. Thus, in these circumstances, what the IMF might end up doing would be to provide some halfhearted support, which would not be fully convincing for the markets (it might indeed be even counterproductive).

The critical point here is that the process of negotiation and conditionality requires time, and transparency, coupled with high capital mobility, dramatically cuts the time available for the process to continue effectively and to lead to an optimal redesign of programs as they are implemented. In this environment, conditionality may become perverse: not only does it not provide credibility, it may end up being used as a coordinating device for speculative attacks, with program benchmarks and performance criteria inappropriately assuming the role of triggering devices.[38]

Conditionality and Insurance Services

The commitment and screening channels presuppose conditionality, and this creates uncertainty about the availability of IMF resources; but certainty that sufficient resources will be made available is key to the working of the insurance channel.

Channel IV requires that liquidity be available "with no strings attached." Ever since Bagehot (1873), it has been recognized that the attempt to tighten the type of "security" required for granting liquidity support during a panic would have disastrous results. But this is inconsistent with conditionality.[39] It could be argued that this inconsistency could be addressed by eliminating the conditionality in pure "liquidity" crises. This is the logic underlying the recommendations of the Meltzer Commission: liquidity support should be restricted to countries that have prequalified by meeting a (limited) number of performance criteria ahead of a crisis. There is a difficulty, though, in this logic, since countries, unlike the representative individual of most economic models, may be subject to sudden regime changes. No matter how good the historical record has been (and typically for most IMF borrowers, "historical" means a decade or so), the domestic political process may engender a coalition that is simply "unwilling" to accept the burden of past policies. It is not accidental, in our view, that in most cases capital account crises burst out in the vicinity of a major election, in the run-up to which one or more of the candidates has won large popular support precisely by promising a "regime change." A measure of conditionality, and of discretion by the crisis manager in assessing the credibility of the ruling coalition, is therefore inevitable. But the insurance service provided by an insurer that feels the need to insure itself against the adverse event is unlikely to meet with success in the eyes of private investors.

Conclusions

In this paper, we have reviewed the historical evolution, empirical record, and theoretical underpinnings of the notion of "catalytic official finance." Our reading of the history of COF has yielded three insights.

First, the idea that official lending might play a catalytic role was recognized and accepted by IMF staff before the generalized move toward capital account liberalization that took place during the 1980s. But in the era of capital account inconvertibility this was considered just a side effect of IMF programs, not the main hinge around which IMF activity revolved.

Second, with the opening up of the capital account, the emphasis on catalytic effects drastically changed. Attitudes toward COF appear to have followed a similar pattern in the course of the two major crisis episodes that have marked the last twenty years. In both the developing country debt crisis of the 1980s and the capital account crisis of the 1990s and early 2000s, COF emerged as the official community's preferred option out of dissatisfaction

[38] This is consistent with the empirical results in Edwards (2000) discussed earlier. The possibility of a negative catalytic effect (triggering a crisis) related to IMF discussions is also mentioned in IMF (1999, p. 35).

[39] As remarked in the IMF staff's account of the recent crises, "the IMF's own financing was phased and conditional on program implementation, implying that markets could not count on the availability of this financing" (Ghosh and others, 2002). The study mentions this as one of the main reasons why, in those cases, the IMF program failed.

with the alternatives. In the 1980s, it was the erosion of the concerted approach that prompted creation of the Baker Plan. In the 1990s, the proximate cause was the moral hazard concern generated by the "Bagehotian" Mexican package. In both cases, private flows and official finance were postulated to be dependable "bedfellows" only for want of a better alternative. However, since more recently it eventually became evident that private capital flows were reacting as "perfect strangers" to policy impulses, the focus on catalytic lending as a tool to address capital account crises has declined.

Third, the major difference between the developing country debt crisis and the emerging markets crisis, apart from the composition of external debt, is that in the former, crisis management took place in the context of a suspension of debt service, whereas in the latter the official packages' primary objective was precisely to avoid such a suspension. This difference is responsible both for the greater variety of recent packages (as they had to be fine-tuned to the circumstances of time and place) and for the greater size of IMF lending and ultimate exposure (since the crisis package had to be big enough to "impress" the market).

On the basis of this historical review, we then turned to a more systematic evaluation of the empirical record of COF. Here the evidence appears mixed, but consistent overall with the reading we have proposed. All in all, catalytic effects do not appear to be strong, which is all the more remarkable since most empirical studies fail to control for actual policy change, thereby biasing results *in favor of* COF. Slightly stronger results tend to be obtained when COF is used either in the context of precautionary programs (that is, for crisis prevention) or in association with debt rescheduling and/or restructuring (that is, for crisis resolution).

The theoretical review contained in the last part of the paper tried to make sense of this rather dismal record. It so happens that the conditions for having strong catalytic effects, always rather demanding, become yet more severe when COF is used as a crisis management tool. Reviewing theoretical rationales for COF, we have identified five channels through which the announcement of an IMF program might prop up the propensity of private investors to lend to a financially distressed country. We have labeled these channels "policy design," "information," "commitment," "screening," and "insurance." The dependability of each channel appears weaker under the conditions that typically accompany a capital account crisis, impending or actual. The main problems stem from (a) the costs that the IMF suffers when programs go off track (in terms of reputation, and of the risk of being accused of precipitating a crisis through the announcement that the program has derailed); (b) the uncertainty regarding the penalty for lack of compliance, which depends on the markets' reaction (an important precondition for the conditionality mechanism to work properly); (c) the inadequacy as an insurance mechanism of a form of lending that is limited (compared with the potential capital flight) and conditional; and (d) the asymmetric information between the IMF and country authorities.

On the basis of these considerations, we conclude that COF should be handled with great care. Its potential as a crisis management tool, in particular, appears at best limited. This by no means implies that, if and when catalysis fails, IMF programs will likely be ineffectual, because catalytic effects are not the only channel through which programs work. Our argument solely implies that one should not have crisis management programs that can be expected to work only if strong catalytic forces are at play.

Bibliography

Adji, S.S., Y.S. Ahn, C.M. Holsey, and T.D. Willett, 1997, "Political Capacity, Macroeconomic Factors, and Capital Flows," in *Political Capacity and Economic Behavior*, ed. by Marina Arbetman and Jacek Kugler (Boulder, Colorado: Westview Press).

Bagehot, Walter, 1873, *Lombard Street* (London: Murray).

Bird, Graham, 1994, "The Myths and Realities of IMF Lending," *World Economy*, Vol. 17 (September), pp. 759–78.

_______, 1995, *IMF Lending to Developing Countries: Issues and Evidence* (London: Routledge).

_______, Antonella Mori, and Dane Rowlands, 2000, "Do the Multilaterals Catalyze Other Capital Flows? A Case Study Analysis," *Third World Quarterly*, Vol. 21, No. 3, pp. 483–503.

Bird, Graham, and Timothy Orme, 1981, "An Analysis of Drawings on the International Monetary Fund by Developing Countries," *World Development*, Vol. 9, No. 6, pp. 563–68.

Bird, Graham, and Dane Rowlands, 1997, "The Catalytic Effect of Lending by the International Financial Institutions," *World Economy* (November), pp. 967–92.

_______, 2000, "The Catalyzing Role of Policy-Based Lending by the IMF and the World Bank: Fact or Fiction?" *Journal of International Development*, Vol. 12, pp. 951–73.

_______, 2001, "Catalysis or Direct Borrowing: The Role of the IMF in Mobilizing Private Capital," *World Economy* (January), pp. 81–98.

Boughton, James M., 1997, "From Suez to Tequila: The IMF as Crisis Manager," IMF Working Paper 97/90 (Washington: International Monetary Fund).

_______, 2000a, "Historical Perspectives on Financial Distress: A Comment," *Carnegie-Rochester Conference Series on Public Policy*, Vol. 53, pp. 169–77.

_______, 2000b, "Northwest of Suez: The 1956 Crisis and the IMF," IMF Working Paper 00/192 (Washington: International Monetary Fund).

_______, 2001, *Silent Revolution: The International Monetary Fund, 1979–1989* (Washington: International Monetary Fund).

Brown, Gordon, 2001, speech given at the Federal Reserve Bank of New York, November 16.

Buira, Ariel, 1987, "Adjustment with Growth and the Role of the IMF in the 1980s," in *The International Monetary System and Its Reform, Paper Prepared for the*

Group of Twenty-Four, ed. by Sidney Dell (Amsterdam: Elsevier Science).

Camdessus, Michel, 1995, "The International Monetary Fund and the Challenges of Globalization," address given at the Free University, Amsterdam, November 28.

_______, 1999a, "Camdessus Outlines Role for Private Sector in New Financial Architecture," *IMF Survey*, Vol. 28 (March 8), p. 76.

_______, 1999b, "Report of the Managing Director to the Interim Committee on Progress in Strengthening the Architecture of the International Financial System" (Washington: International Monetary Fund). Available on the Web at *http://www.imf.org/external/np/omd/1999/092499.htm*.

Capie, Forrest, 2002, "Can There Be an International Lender-of-Last-Resort?" in *Financial Crises, Contagion, and the Lender of Last Resort: A Reader*, ed. by Charles Goodhart and Gerhard Illing (Oxford University Press).

Cline, William R., 1989, "The Baker Plan and Brady Reformulation: An Evaluation," in *Dealing with the Debt Crisis*, ed. by Ishrat Husain and Ishac Diwan (Washington: World Bank).

Conway, Patrick, 1994, "IMF Lending Programs: Participation and Impact," *Journal of Development Economics*, Vol. 45, pp. 365–91.

_______, 1998, "IMF Programs and Economic Crisis: An Empirical Study of Transition" (unpublished; Washington: World Bank).

Cornelius, Peter, 1987, "The Demand for IMF Credits by Sub-Saharan African Countries," *Economics Letters*, Vol. 23, pp. 99–102.

Corsetti, Giancarlo, Bernardo Guimarães, and Nouriel Roubini, 2003, "The Tradeoff Between an International Lender of Last Resort to Deal with Liquidity Crisis and Moral Hazard Distortions. A Model of the IMF's Catalytic Finance Approach" (unpublished; New York University).

Cottarelli, Carlo, and Curzio Giannini, 1997, *Credibility Without Rules? Monetary Frameworks in the Post-Bretton Woods Era*, IMF Occasional Paper No. 154 (Washington: International Monetary Fund).

_______, 1999, "Inflation, Credibility, and the Role of the International Monetary Fund," *International Economic Policy Review*.

De Gregorio, José, Barry Eichengreen, Takatoshi Ito, and Charles Wyplosz, 1999, *An Independent and Accountable IMF* (Geneva: International Center for Monetary and Banking Studies).

de Larosière, Jacques, 1980, "Managing Director Tells ECOSOC He Foresees Sufficient Resources for Expanded Fund Recycling Role," *IMF Survey* (July), pp. 202–206.

De Long, J. Bradford, and Barry Eichengreen, 2001, *Between Meltdown and Moral Hazard: The International Monetary and Financial Policies of the Clinton Administration*, paper presented at the conference on "The Economic Policies of the Clinton Administration," Kennedy School of Government, held June 26–29 in Cambridge, Massachusetts.

de Vries, Margaret Garritsen, 1985, *The International Monetary Fund, 1972–1978: Cooperation on Trial*, Vol. I (Washington: International Monetary Fund).

_______, 1986, "The Role of the International Monetary Fund in the World Debt Problem," in *World Debt Crisis*, ed. by Michael P. Claudon (Cambridge, Massachusetts: Ballinger).

Dhonte, Pierre, 1997, *Conditionality as an Instrument of Borrowed Credibility*, IMF Paper on Policy Analysis and Assessment 97/2 (Washington: International Monetary Fund).

Diamond, Jared M., 1992, *The Third Chimpanzee: The Evolution and the Future of the Human Animal* (New York: Harper Collins).

Diwan, Ishac, and Dani Rodrik, 1992, *External Debt, Adjustment, and Burden Sharing: A Unified Framework*, Princeton Studies in International Finance No. 73 (Princeton, New Jersey: International Finance Section, Department of Economics, Princeton University).

Dooley, Michael P., 1994, "A Retrospective on the Debt Crisis," NBER Working Paper No. 4963 (Cambridge, Massachusetts: National Bureau of Economic Research).

Dornbusch, Rudi, 2001, *A Primer on Emerging Market Crises* (unpublished; Cambridge, Massachusetts: Massachusetts Institute of Technology, Economics Department).

Edwards, Martin S., 2000, "Reevaluating the Catalytic Effect of IMF Programs," paper for presentation at the annual meetings of the American Political Science Association held in Washington in September.

Eichengreen, Barry, 2001, "Crisis Prevention and Management: Any New Lessons from Argentina and Turkey?" (unpublished).

_______, and Ashoka Mody, 2000, "Bail-Ins, Bailouts, and Borrowing Costs," paper presented at the First IMF Annual Research Conference held November 9–10 in Washington.

Faini, Riccardo, Jaime de Melo, Abdel Senhadji-Semlali, and Julie Stanton, 1995, "Macro Performance Under Adjustment Lending," paper prepared for the World Bank symposium on "Adjustment Lending and Beyond," held in Washington in April.

Financial Stability Forum, 2000, *Report on Capital Flows* (Basel: Bank for International Settlements).

Fischer, Stanley, 1997, "Applied Economics in Action: IMF Programs," *American Economic Review, Papers and Proceedings*, Vol. 87 (May), pp. 23–27.

_______, 2000, *Strengthening Crisis Prevention: The Role of Contingent Credit Lines*, speech given at the Banco de México in Mexico City on November 15.

_______, 2002, "On the Need for an International Lender of Last Resort" in *Financial Crises, Contagion, and the Lender of Last Resort: A Reader*, ed. by Charles Goodhart and Gerhard Illing (Oxford, Oxford University Press).

Freixas, Xavier, Curzio Giannini, Glenn Hoggarth, and Farouk Soussa, 2000, "Lender of Last Resort: What Have We Learned Since Bagehot?" *Journal of Financial Services Research*, Vol. 18, No. 1.

Ghosh, Atish, Timothy Lane, Marianne Schulze-Ghattas, Aleš Bulíř, Javier Hamann, and Alex Mourmouras, 2002, *IMF-Supported Programs in Capital Account Crises*, IMF Occasional Paper No. 210 (Washington: International Monetary Fund).

Giannini, Curzio, 1999, "Enemy of None but a Common Friend of All?" An International Perspective on the Lender-of-Last-Resort Function," Princeton Essays in International Finance No. 214 (Princeton, New Jersey: International Finance Section, Department of Economics, Princeton University).

_______, 2002, "Pitfalls in International Crisis Lending," in *Financial Crises, Contagion, and the Lender of Last Resort: A Reader*, ed. by Charles Goodhart and Gerhard Illing (Oxford University Press).

Gold, Joseph, 1979, *Conditionality* (Washington: International Monetary Fund).

Goodhart, Charles, and Gerhard Illing, 2002, "Introduction," in *Financial Crises, Contagion, and the Lender of Last Resort: A Reader*, ed. by Charles Goodhart and Gerhard Illing (Oxford: Oxford University Press).

Group of Ten, 1996, *The Resolution of Sovereign Liquidity Crises* (the Rey report) (Basel).

Group of Twenty-Four, 2000, "Intergovernmental Group of Twenty-Four on International Monetary Affairs Communiqué (April 15)." Available on the Web at *http://esa.un.org/ffd/policydb/PolicyTests/G24-1.htm.*

Group of Twenty-Two, 1998, *International Financial Crises* (Washington).

Guitián, Manuel, 1982, "Economic Management and the International Monetary Fund Conditionality," in *Adjustment and Financing in the Developing World: The Role of the International Monetary Fund*, ed. by Tony Killick (Washington: International Monetary Fund).

_______, 1992, *The Unique Nature of the Responsibilities of the International Monetary Fund*, IMF Pamphlet Series No. 46 (Washington: International Monetary Fund).

Guth, Wilfried, 1979, "Sources of Finance for Development: The View of a Developed Country," paper presented at the 32nd International Banking Summer School, "The Financing of Long-Term Development," held in August at St. John's College, Cambridge, United Kingdom.

226 Hajivassiliou, Vassilis A., 1987, "The External Debt Repayments Problems of LDC's," *Journal of Econometrics*, Vol. 36, pp. 205–30.

Haldane, Andy, 1999, "Private Sector Involvement in Financial Crises: Analytics and Public Policy Approaches," *Financial Stability Review*, November.

Helleiner, Eric, 1994, *States and the Reemergence of Global Finance* (Ithaca, New York: Cornell University Press).

Institute of International Finance (IIF), 1996, *Resolving Sovereign Financial Arrears* (Washington: Institute of International Finance).

International Monetary and Financial Committee (IMFC), 2001, "Communiqué of the International Monetary and Financial Committee of the Board of Governors of the International Monetary Fund," IMF Press Release No. 01/20, April. Available on the Web at *http://www.imf.org/external/npsec/pr/2001/pr0120/htm.*

International Monetary Fund (IMF), 1992, Press Release No. 2/181, November 9.

_______, 1999, "Involving the Private Sector in Forestalling and Resolving Financial Crises" (unpublished; Washington: Policy Development and Review Department, International Monetary Fund).

_______, 2001a, "Assessing the Determinants and Prospects for the Pace of Market Access by Countries Emerging from Crises—Country Cases" (Washington: International Monetary Fund). Available on the Web at *http://www.imf.org/external/npsec/pr/2001/pr0120/htm.*

_______, 2001b, "The IMF and the Private Sector," available on the Web at *http://www.imf.org/external/np/exr/facts/privsec.htm.*

Joyce, Joseph P., 1992, "The Economic Characteristics of IMF Program Countries," *Economics Letters*, Vol. 38, pp. 237–42.

Kenen, Peter B., 1986, *Financing, Adjustment, and the International Monetary Fund* (Washington: Brookings Institution).

_______, 2001, *The International Financial Architecture. What's New? What's Missing?* (Washington: Institute for International Economics).

Killick, Tony, 1995, *IMF Programmes in Developing Countries—Design and Impact* (London: Routledge).

_______, 1997, "Principals, Agents, and the Failings of Conditionality," *Journal of International Development*, Vol. 9, No. 4, p. 483.

_______, Moazzam Malik, and Marcus Manuel, 1991, "What Can We Know About the Effects of IMF Programmes?" ODI Working Paper No. 47 (London: Regent's College, Overseas Development Institute).

Marchesi, Silvia, 2001, "Adoption of an IMF Programme and Debt Rescheduling: An Empirical Analysis," Development Studies Working Paper No. 152 (University of Oxford/Queen Elizabeth House).

_______, and Jonathan P. Thomas, 2001, "IMF Conditionality as a Screening Device," *Economic Journal*, Vol. 109 (March), pp. C111–C125.

Masson, Paul, R., and Michael Mussa, 1995, *The Role of the IMF: Financing and Its Interactions with Adjustment and Surveillance*, IMF Pamphlet Series, No. 50 (Washington: International Monetary Fund).

McCauley, R., 1986, "IMF: Managed Lending," in *World Debt Crisis: International Lending on Trial*, ed. by M. Claudon (Cambridge, Massachusetts: Ballinger).

Milivojević, Marko, 1986, *The Debt Rescheduling Process* (London: Frances Pinter).

Miller, Marcus, and Lei Zhang, 2000, "Sovereign Liquidity Crises: The Strategic Case for a Payment Standstill," *Economic Journal*, Vol. 110 (January), pp. 335–62.

Mody, Ashoka, and Diego Saravia, 2003, "Catalyzing Capital Flows: Do IMF-Supported Programs Work as Commitment Devices?" IMF Working Paper 03/100 (Washington: International Monetary Fund).

Mussa, Michael, and Miguel Savastano, 1999, "The IMF Approach to Economic Stabilization," IMF Working Paper 99/104 (Washington: International Monetary Fund).

Niinistö, M. Sauli, 1999, "Statement by M. Sauli Niinistö in His Capacity as Chairman of the EU Presidency to the IMF and World Bank Annual Meetings in September 1999," available on the Web at *http://www.imf.org/external/am/1999/icstate/eu.htm.*

Özler, Şule, 1993, "Have Commercial Banks Ignored History?" *American Economic Review*, Vol. 83 (June), pp. 608–20.

Reichmann, Thomas M., and Richard T. Stillson, 1978, "Experience with Programs of Balance of Payments Adjustment: Stand-By Arrangements in the Higher Tranches, 1963–72," *Staff Papers*, International Monetary Fund, Vol. 25 (June), pp. 49–79.

Rodrik, Dani, 1996, "Why Is There Multilateral Lending?" in *Annual World Bank Conference on Development Economics*, ed. by Michael Bruno and Boris Pleskovic (Washington: World Bank).

Rowlands, Dane, 1994, "The Response of New Lending to the IMF," Norman Paterson School of International Affairs Development Studies Working Paper No. 7 (Ottawa: Carleton University).

Sachs, Jeffrey D., 1989, "Conditionality, Debt Relief, and the Developing Country Debt Crisis," in *Developing Country Debt and Economic Performance*, Vol. I, ed. by Jeffrey Sachs (University of Chicago Press).

Schadler, Susan, Adam Bennett, Maria Carkovic, Louis Dicks-Mireaux, Mauro Mecagni, James H.J. Morsink, and Miguel A. Savastano, 1995, *IMF Conditionality: Experience Under Stand-By and Extended Arrangements*, IMF Occasional Paper No. 128 (Washington: International Monetary Fund).

Sgard, Jérôme, 2002, *L'Économie de la Panique. Faire Face aux Crises Financières* (Paris: Éditions La Découverte).

Stiglitz, Joseph, 2000, "The Insider," *New Republic*, April 17.

Sturc, Ernest, 1978, "The Role of the International Monetary Fund in International Development Financing," paper presented at the World Scientific Banking Meeting, "International Financing of Economic Development," held in Dubrovnik, Croatia, October–November 1977.

United States, Department of the Treasury, 1977, "Why the Witteveen Facility Is Not a 'Bail Out' for the Banks," in *U.S. Participation in the Supplementary Financing Facility of the International Monetary Fund*, in United States, House of Representatives (1977), pp. 80–84.

United States, House of Representatives, 1977, *U.S. Participation in the Supplementary Financing Facility of the International Monetary Fund*, Hearings Before the Subcommittee on International Trade, Investment, and Monetary Policy of the Committee on Banking, Finance and Urban Affairs, House of Representatives, Ninety-Fifth Congress, First Session, on H.R. 9214 (Washington: U.S. Government Printing Office).

Volcker, Paul A., and Toyoo Gyohten, 1992, *Changing Fortunes: The World's Money and the Threat to American Leadership* (New York: Times Books).

Zettelmeyer, Jeromin, 2000, "Can Official Crisis Lending Be Counterproductive in the Short-Run?" *Economic Notes*, Vol. 29, No.1.

CHAPTER

13 Keeping Capital Flowing: The Role of the IMF

Michael Bordo, Ashoka Mody, and Nienke Oomes[1]

In this chapter, we examine the IMF's role in maintaining the access of emerging market economies to international capital markets. We find evidence that both macroeconomic aggregates and capital flows improve following the adoption of an IMF program, although they may initially deteriorate somewhat. Consistent with theoretical predictions and earlier empirical findings, we find that IMF programs are most successful in improving capital flows to countries with bad, but not very bad fundamentals. In such countries, IMF programs are also associated with improvements in the fundamentals themselves.

Introduction

Recent research on the role of the International Monetary Fund can, broadly speaking, be divided into two strands. Studies focusing on the immediate response of the IMF to financial crises—the first strand of literature—have assessed whether IMF-supported programs stemmed the crises, prevented contagion, and helped countries regain access to international capital markets—without inducing the harmful side effect of imprudent lending by international creditors.[2] Others—constituting the second strand—have been concerned with the longer-term macroeconomic implications of IMF programs.[3]

Future research on the role of the IMF faces three challenges. First, the two separate strands of literature need to be brought closer together. In particular, the following question needs to be asked: do IMF programs serve primarily as a source of emergency finance or do they, by improving macroeconomic fundamentals, also help to ensure longer-term access to international capital markets? Second, a greater appreciation of differences in countries' initial economic conditions is necessary to understand the effects of IMF intervention. Initial conditions influence subsequent dynamics, as well as strategic behavior of the country authorities and international creditors. Third, the channels—or mechanisms—through which the IMF is able to influence economic outcomes need to be identified for the forward-looking design of IMF policy and the international financial architecture.

This paper presents an initial investigation of this ambitious agenda by focusing on the relationship between IMF programs and private international capital flows. This is a natural setup to address the first challenge—bringing the two strands of literature closer together—since, to the extent that IMF programs succeed in keeping capital flowing, they can help to both contain financial crises and stimulate longer-term investment and growth. To take on the second challenge, we examine the possibility of a nonlinear response of capital flows to initial conditions. Finally, we deal with the third challenge by identifying the main mechanisms that allow the IMF to maintain capital flows. We argue that a "good housekeeping seal of approval" may not be operative, leaving in contention the "delegated monitoring" and "catalytic lending" roles of the IMF.[4]

The IMF itself has increasingly viewed the stabilization and fostering of capital flows as crucial to its evolving role. In the 1990s, private capital flows to developing economies resumed after the hiatus following the debt crises of the 1980s. This resumption in capital flows represented both an opportunity to accelerate economic development and a threat in situations where a "sudden stop" of capital flows was associated with a sharp contraction in economic activity. As the fluctuations in countries' capital accounts acquired greater importance—and sometimes even dominated current account fluctuations—the IMF increasingly came to view the facilitation and maintenance of capital flows to developing countries as one of its essential functions. A clear indication of this was the formation of the IMF's International

---

[1] This paper was previously published in 2004 in *International Finance*, Vol. 7, No. 3, pp. 421–50 and appears here with the permission of Blackwell Publishing, the journal's publisher. It has also been issued as IMF Working Paper 04/197. The authors are grateful to Barry Eichengreen, Stephen Morris, two anonymous referees, and reviewers from the IMF's Policy Development and Review Department for very helpful comments on earlier drafts. They are also indebted to Tom Walter for excellent editorial comments and to Adrián de la Garza and Wellian Wiranto for valuable research assistance. The authors are, however, solely responsible for any remaining errors.

[2] See, for example, Boorman and Allen (2000), Bordo and Schwartz (2000), Meltzer (2002), and Ghosh and others (2002).

[3] An early survey of this literature was carried out by Haque and Khan (1998). More recent articles on this subject include Przeworski and Vreeland (2000), Hutchison (2001), Barro and Lee (2003), and Hajro and Joyce (2004).

[4] Cottarelli and Giannini (2002) discuss in greater detail the IMF's channels of influence.

Capital Markets Department in 2001, which was introduced by former Managing Director Horst Köhler as follows: "Because private capital flows are an indispensable source of financing for development, another crucial function of the IMF's new Capital Markets Department will be to strengthen our ability to help countries gain access to international capital markets" (Köhler, 2001, paragraph 13).

The main goal of this paper is to study whether IMF programs have indeed helped countries gain or regain access to international capital markets and, if so, through which channels. Since we focus on capital flows, we limit our empirical analysis to 29 emerging market economies.[5] We thus exclude IMF programs supported by the low-interest Poverty Reduction and Growth Facility (PRGF), which are targeted at low-income countries. We cover the period 1980–2002, during which these 29 countries contracted 119 programs with the IMF. The unit of analysis is a program-country pair. Since the number of observations declines considerably as we control for country conditions, we mainly present descriptive evidence on the effects of IMF programs on aggregate performance (growth, inflation, the current account, and capital flows).

A key issue in empirical analysis of IMF programs is the characterization of the appropriate counterfactual.[6] That is, in addition to studying how economic conditions changed after the adoption of an IMF program, it is necessary to benchmark those changes against the evolution that would have occurred in the absence of an IMF program.

We proceed in three steps. As a first step, we compare the average macroeconomic performance of emerging market countries before and after IMF program initiation. The results suggest that macroeconomic aggregates—GDP growth, inflation, and the current account—and capital flows improve following the adoption of an IMF program, albeit often with a lag. In particular, we find that GDP growth rates and capital flows display a "dip and recovery" pattern—that is, performance deteriorates somewhat in the first year of the program but improves significantly in the second year.

We are careful not to commit the *post hoc, ergo propter hoc* fallacy. That is, from the observation that performance improved *after* adoption of the IMF program, we cannot necessarily conclude that performance improved *because of* program adoption. In fact, one would expect a certain amount of selection bias, in that countries that adopt IMF programs are likely to have worse initial conditions than countries that do not adopt IMF programs (i.e., selection into IMF programs is not random). Given such selection bias, it would be quite natural to observe a recovery for the group of program countries, simply because of mean reversion, that is, an inbuilt tendency for improvement in performance following a setback. In order to reduce this selection bias, one should compare the performance of program and nonprogram countries with similar initial conditions.

Before doing that, we investigate, as a second step, the role of initial conditions. In particular, we examine whether the response of capital flows depends on the state of a country's external fundamentals just prior to the start of an IMF program. We show that the improvement in aggregate performance following program adoption reflects primarily success in maintaining capital flows to countries with intermediate initial external fundamentals. That is, in measuring fundamentals in terms of four states (very bad, bad, good, and very good), we find that IMF programs are more effective in countries with bad, but not very bad, fundamentals. Interestingly, this finding is consistent with the empirical results in Mody and Saravi (2003), as well as with the predictions of recent models of catalytic lending (Morris and Shin, 2003; and Corsetti, Guimarães, and Roubini, 2003) and of the IMF's delegated monitoring role (Tirole, 2002). The results are generally robust to using four different external fundamentals: the current account balance as a share of GDP, the reserves-to-imports ratio, the ratio of short-term debt to reserves, and the ratio of total external debt to GDP.

Finally, in our most ambitious attempt at providing a counterfactual, we compare the performances of countries that adopted IMF programs with those of countries that did not adopt IMF programs, but that had similar initial conditions. We do this by estimating the probabilities of transitioning between the four different states and by comparing the estimated transition probabilities of program countries with those of nonprogram countries. For most initial conditions, except very good ones, we are able to reject the null hypothesis that nonprogram countries perform similarly, given similar initial conditions. That is, we show that the observed increase in capital flows to program countries with intermediate initial fundamentals is accompanied by an improvement in the fundamentals themselves, an improvement that is not observed for nonprogram countries with similar intermediate initial fundamentals.[7]

[5] Our definition of "emerging market economies" is the definition used by the IMF's International Capital Markets Department for the purpose of producing "early warning signals," and includes the following 29 countries: Argentina, Bolivia, Brazil, Chile, Colombia, Cyprus, the Czech Republic, Egypt, Hungary, India, Indonesia, Israel, Jordan, the Republic of Korea, Lebanon, Malaysia, Mexico, Pakistan, Peru, the Philippines, Poland, the Slovak Republic, South Africa, Sri Lanka, Thailand, Turkey, Uruguay, República Bolivariana de Venezuela, and Zimbabwe.

[6] For early discussions of counterfactuals in the context of IMF programs, see Goldstein and Montiel (1986); and Khan (1990).

[7] Goldstein and Montiel (1986) propose simulating a policy response to a crisis without IMF presence and, further, an output response to policy to generate a counterfactual. Estimating such functions can be complicated and the results unreliable. An alternative is to run regressions while controlling for factors likely to explain macroeconomic performance and to include a dummy variable for an IMF program. For recent examples, see Barro and Lee (2003) for the analysis of growth; and Mody and Saravia (2003) for the analysis of bond spreads.

We conclude that countries in severe distress (i.e., in a very bad state) are unable to revive their capital flows under an IMF program. Countries with good initial conditions possibly benefit from IMF programs by maintaining relatively stable capital flows after being hit by temporary liquidity shocks. However, IMF programs play their most important role when countries are in an intermediate regime (with bad, but not very bad, initial conditions). In such economies, capital flows and external fundamentals improve over a two- or three-year time period following the start of the program.

The remainder of the paper is organized as follows. We begin with a discussion of the three channels through which the IMF can help maintain capital flows. Next, we describe the evolution of macroeconomic performance—GDP growth, inflation, the current account balance, and capital flows—following the commencement of an IMF program. We then disaggregate the response in capital flows by the state of a country's initial external fundamentals. Next, we examine whether IMF programs influence the transition probabilities across states. We synthesize the principal results in the concluding section.

The Role of the IMF in Facilitating Capital Flows

Under the Bretton Woods par value system, characterized by pervasive capital controls, the IMF was primarily concerned with surveillance of the exchange rate system and provision of temporary finance to manage current account deficits. Following the breakdown of the Bretton Woods system in 1973, the IMF has faced a new environment encompassing a significant increase in its membership (both developing countries and transition countries), a myriad of exchange rate arrangements, and, especially, new problems arising from open capital accounts and financial globalization. With the opening of international capital markets to advanced countries in the 1970s and to emerging markets in the 1980s, the focus of the IMF has shifted toward new market failures and the new public goods needed to maintain financial stability.[8]

How can the IMF add value in this new environment? We begin with the premise that maintaining the flow of international capital is valuable to the countries that receive those flows, as well as to the international financial system as a whole. Capital flows, as the evidence of the 1990s amply bears out, are subject to sudden stops and sharp reversals (Calvo, 1998). The IMF can be particularly important to the international financial and economic order if it can mitigate these stops and reversals and, thereby, maintain the flow of capital even when a country is vulnerable to a loss of confidence.

This section discusses three possible channels through which the IMF can help maintain capital flows (for a more extensive discussion, see Cottarelli and Giannini, 2002). First, if the IMF has information that the private sector does not have, it can provide a valuable signal that can act as a good housekeeping seal of approval. Second, when the IMF does not have an informational advantage but a country lacks credibility in being able to honor its external debt obligations, the IMF can act as a delegated monitor. Finally, catalytic lending by the IMF can induce lenders to roll over their credits and, hence, prevent an exodus of capital from the country. However, IMF lending could also encourage moral hazard, inducing private lenders to be less careful in their credit decisions in the expectation of being bailed out.

In the rest of this section, we examine in more detail these three channels through which the IMF can redirect capital flows to an emerging market economy at risk of losing access. We analyze the logic of each channel and highlight the likely observable implications of influence exercised through each channel.

Good Housekeeping Seal of Approval

A good housekeeping seal of approval from a respectable institution can facilitate market access for emerging country borrowers. It can act as a signal that members have sound financial institutions and follow sensible policies. The credibility of such a seal of approval depends, however, on an informational advantage (Rodrik, 1996). For the IMF to provide such a seal, it should possess superior information and be able to communicate its assessment in a transparent manner.

An earlier successful example of an international institution serving as a seal of approval was the classical gold standard in the pre-1914 era of financial globalization. Under the institution of the gold standard, adherence to gold convertibility served as a signal to international lenders that a country had healthy financial institutions and followed sound financial policies (Bordo and Rockoff, 1996). It also served as a credible commitment mechanism, in that gold adherence required that countries keep inflation low and budgets balanced (Bordo and Kydland, 1995 and 1996). Countries that successfully adhered to gold convertibility were able to borrow from London at rates significantly lower than those that did not (Bordo and Rockoff, 1996; and Obstfeld and Taylor, 2003).[9]

[8] Bordo and James (2000) refer to several such public goods, including short-to-medium-term capital for credit-constrained countries, coordination of lenders in debt crises, international liquidity in financial crises, and "early warning signals."

[9] Other institutional factors may have also served as a good housekeeping seal, such as being part of the British empire (Ferguson, 2002). However, Obstfeld and Taylor (2003) report evidence that the gold standard played a significantly more prominent role.

Does the gold standard have resonance for today? There are several key differences between the operation of the gold standard and of the IMF. The gold standard, unlike the IMF, was an informal institution that had evolved from centuries of market experience. As such, "membership" in the standard was at the initiative of the individual countries, and country policies would determine if a country was on or off the standard.

When international financial crises occurred under the gold standard, as they frequently did, domestic lenders of last resort, individually and cooperatively, provided emergency liquidity. At the same time, financial institutions adopted preventive measures, such as maintaining high capital and liquidity ratios (Bordo, 2003). Moreover, the advanced (core) countries could temporarily leave the gold standard during a crisis or a war to follow countercyclical policies—the belief that they were credible adherents of the gold standard allowed this departure from "the rules of the game."

Even at that time, the emerging countries faced a different environment. In the face of shocks (terms of trade and political instability), they often left the gold standard, devalued their currencies, and did not return except at a devalued parity. They also occasionally defaulted on their debt (Reinhart, Rogoff, and Savastano, 2003). Because of their inability to adhere consistently to the gold standard, they paid a significant currency risk premium and lost the seal of approval.

Thus, the seal of approval worked because a set of credible policies and institutions backed up the adherents of the gold standard. Where gold was merely a temporary prop, its seal was of little value.

It is unclear whether the seal of approval is an important mechanism through which the IMF helps maintain capital flows, because the IMF's informational advantage over the private sector appears to have declined. First, transparency has increased both at the IMF, which now makes most of its data and reports publicly available on its website, and in many emerging market countries, especially following the Asian crisis. Second, while in some instances IMF reports remain unpublished at the request of the member country, such "privileged information" tends to convey economic concerns and vulnerabilities that could scarcely constitute the basis for a positive signal. Third, there is no evidence that the IMF's economic forecasts are superior to those of other institutions. For example, Loungani (2001) finds that IMF forecasts of economic growth are no better—though typically no worse either—than those of the private sector. Finally, there may be some concern that IMF signals are influenced by political considerations and, hence, not reliable.

Nevertheless, there are some reasons to assume that the IMF still has an informational edge over the private sector. Disparate market actors may be better at assessing and synthesizing data than the IMF, but it is not obvious that they have better information than the IMF. For example, an investment bank research team typically has one analyst covering multiple small countries, while the IMF usually has multiple economists covering even small countries. In addition, one could argue that the IMF is better placed to verify data and to make judgments regarding the intentions of the authorities.

Even if IMF surveillance could constitute a seal of approval, it is difficult to develop an empirical strategy through which the importance of the IMF's informational advantage can be inferred. The IMF, in principle, monitors all countries and the world economy on an ongoing basis, and virtually all countries have been members of the IMF for a long time. As such, creating a counterfactual for inferring an IMF informational advantage is not straightforward. There exists a better possibility of identifying the effects of IMF programs, conditional on the information that the IMF surveillance process generates. We thus turn to the effects of IMF programs, through which the IMF plays the roles of delegated monitor and lender.

Delegated Monitor

While the IMF may not have an informational advantage over private creditors and investors, it can play the role of a monitor in situations where governments have more information about their economic condition and their intentions than the rest of the world. In such situations of asymmetric information, problems related to contract enforcement have impeded the free movement of financial capital, resulting in frequent financial crises characterized by sudden stops in foreign lending and, on occasion, debt defaults. The IMF can serve as a delegated monitor (Tirole, 2002), that is, it can complete contracts between international lenders and both sovereign and private borrowers in emerging market economies through its lending conditionality.

According to Tirole (2002), the market failure in international financial markets arises from two problems identified in the corporate finance literature: the dual and common agency problems. The *dual agency problem* occurs because emerging market governments are potential spoilers of international financial arrangements between foreign lenders and private domestic borrowers. A contract between an advanced country lender and an emerging country private borrower can be threatened ex post by government policies such as devaluation, capital levy, or opportunistic behavior in the political interest of the decision makers. These actions will reduce the ex post returns received by the lender, which, in turn, will discourage future lending. A delegated monitor, such as the IMF, can reduce this problem by constraining opportunistic behavior through conditionality imposed ex post.[10]

The *common agency problem* arises when an emerging country borrows from a myriad of lenders; when booking the loans, these lenders do not pay adequate attention to the loans already issued, which leads to overborrowing. In the face of a crisis, the lenders rush to the exits to avoid being caught by the default, and thus ensure its eventual occurrence. A delegated monitor can serve to coordinate lenders and prevent the overborrowing problem or, after a crisis has occurred, arrange an orderly workout. These actions can reduce the disruption in access to capital markets.

While the delegated monitoring role can follow from basic IMF membership (which serves as a commitment to follow certain rules of conduct)[11] and IMF surveillance (using the information gathered from members via Article IV consultations), it comes into play especially in the context of an IMF program. Mere membership and surveillance do not induce implementation of prudent policies and financial stability. In contrast, an IMF program, with the carrot of access to financial resources and the stick of conditionality, creates the conditions for country commitment that the IMF can then monitor. In particular, the fact that IMF programs provide credit in tranches, in accordance with specific policy commitments, helps the IMF limit the risk of opportunistic debtor behavior.

In turn, country commitment to good performance and, hence, ability to service external debt arises from three overlapping sources: policy design, conditionality, and the costs associated with these policies and conditionality. Private investors will be more likely to invest their capital when they believe that an IMF program will improve the country's economic policy (e.g., Rodrik, 1996; Masson and Mussa, 1995; and Bird and Rowlands, 1997) or that loans will be repaid (Tirole, 2002). Conditionality works if the country can, in fact, overcome political and other implementation barriers. Even if previous programs have not been fully implemented, investors may still view the adoption of a new program favorably if the borrowing government must enact policy changes to access new credit (Marchesi and Thomas, 1999).

In a recent paper, Mody and Saravia (2003) argue that the delegated monitor role, although important, is effective only under particular country conditions. If a country has apparently sound economic fundamentals, entering into an IMF program may actually signal a problem and, hence, make market access worse. At the other extreme, if country fundamentals already place it in a crisis mode, the commitment implied by an IMF program may not be credible and thus, once again, be of limited value. Indeed, Powell and Arozamena (2003) argue that when a country is in a crisis, "gambling for resurrection" may lead countries in IMF programs to behave in a manner contrary to that required for achieving stabilization and recovery. Mody and Saravia (2003) find empirical support for their proposition that the IMF's delegated monitor role is likely to work best when fundamentals are in an intermediate range.

Catalytic Lending

By providing liquidity to a country, the IMF can be a catalyst, in that it reduces the probability of default and can solve the coordination problem between private creditors (e.g., Miller and Zhang, 2000; Morris and Shin, 2003; and Corsetti, Guimarães, and Roubini, 2003). That is, even if the seal of approval and delegated monitor channels do not work, the mere provision of credit by the IMF can give private creditors an incentive to roll over their existing loans and possibly supply new loans. If IMF programs are catalytic, they should be expected to increase gross capital flows.

For this channel to work, the IMF should have sufficient information to determine whether the problem is mainly illiquidity, as opposed to insolvency, and it should be able to decide the optimal amount of lending—that is, the amount of lending that is large enough to convince private creditors to roll over their loans. Successfully performing this role requires balancing the benefits of the program against the costs of moral hazard.[12]

Morris and Shin (2003); and Corsetti, Guimarães, and Roubini (2003) present models that show that IMF lending lowers the threshold for preventing default (that is, it lowers the minimum rate of return necessary to prevent default and thereby lowers the probability of default).[13] Their main conclusions, summarized in Table 1, are as follows:

---

[10] However, as Ivanova (2003) shows, IMF conditionality may not be effective when there is opposition to reforms by domestic lobbies. If domestic lobbies are strong enough, the government may not be able to commit itself to "good" policies even in the presence of the IMF (and even more so if the IMF has imperfect information about government decisions).

[11] These rules of conduct are given in the IMF's Articles of Agreement, which are available on the Web at *http://www.imf.org/external/pubs/ft/aa*.

[12] Lerrick and Meltzer (2003) offer a specific proposal that would enable the IMF to preclude panic and contagion while limiting moral hazard. The IMF would perform its lender-of-last-resort role by making a cash support bid at a discount to a government's minimum offer for the restructured value of the debt. The IMF floor would guarantee liquidity and create a functioning market in the defaulted debt, while lenders would be forced to bear the risks they undertake, thereby reducing moral hazard and future instability. In this proposal, however, there is no guarantee that the IMF would not overbid.

[13] The model by Corsetti, Guimarães, and Roubini (2003) also suggests that the IMF's catalytic impact is greater if it is able to distinguish between an insolvent and an illiquid debtor, and that its lending serves as a signal to the market. This relates to the "seal of approval" discussed previously.

Table 1
Summary of Predictions by Morris and Shin (2003) and Corsetti, Guimarães, and Roubini (2003)

	Fundamentals			
	Very bad	Bad	Good	Very good
Effect of IMF lending on adjustment effort	None	Positive	Negative (moral hazard)	None
Effect of IMF lending on capital flows	None	Positive (catalysis)	None	None

- *For very bad fundamentals* (bad enough that, even with IMF support and a maximum adjustment effort, the country cannot prevent default), IMF programs have no effect. This is because the country's benefits from preventing default do not exceed the cost of the necessary adjustment effort needed to improve fundamentals.
- *For bad fundamentals* (bad enough that, without the IMF, it would not be worthwhile for the country to make the adjustment effort needed to prevent default), IMF programs can have a positive effect on both the country's adjustment effort and private creditors' willingness to roll over their loans. Absent the IMF, the country is "vulnerable." With IMF support, default is avoided, private capital flows are catalyzed, and fundamentals improve.
- *For good fundamentals* (good enough that, even without the IMF, the country would be willing to put in the adjustment effort needed to prevent default), IMF programs can have a negative effect on the country's adjustment effort, and fundamentals may actually worsen. At the same time, there is no effect on private capital flows (i.e., there is no catalysis).
- *For very good fundamentals* (good enough that, even without the IMF, the country can prevent default without any adjustment effort), IMF programs have no effect on the adjustment effort (since there would be no effort in either case) and no effect on capital flows (since creditors would have rolled over their loans in any case).

Aggregate Trends Before and After Program Adoption

In this section, we present descriptive evidence on aggregate performance following the start of an IMF program. Our main finding is that macroeconomic fundamentals (growth, inflation, and the current account) and capital flows all improve after a program has been adopted, albeit often with a lag. We observe a "dip and recovery" pattern for growth and capital flows, with an initial deterioration in first-year performance but a significant improvement in the second year and stabilization in the third year.

As noted in the introduction, our definition of emerging market economies is the one used by the IMF's International Capital Markets Department and comprises 29 countries. The period covered is 1980–2002.[14] Performance is measured in terms of real GDP growth, inflation, the current account balance (in percentage of GDP), and capital flows (also in percentage of GDP). Our measure of capital flows is the aggregate of gross bond, equity, and loan flows.[15] We use gross flows, rather than net flows, since we are interested in a measure of access to international capital markets. Net flows could be small either because a country has lost contact with international capital markets or because it is repaying old loans that are being rolled over.

Average Performance

We start by comparing the average performance in the 12 months prior to the start of a program ("Year Before IMF Program") with the average performance in the first 12 months ("First Year"), the second 12 months ("Second Year"), and the third 12 months ("Third Year") after the start of each program.[16] We are interested in studying a country's performance immediately following the start of an

[14] By merging data from the 1980s and the 1990s, we implicitly assume that the behavior of creditors has not changed over time. For future research, however, it may be useful to study the 1980s and 1990s separately, given the changes in the type of lending (from sovereign syndicated bank lending to a sovereign bond market and short-term cross-border bank lending), the growing trend of capital account liberalization in the 1990s, and the gradual decline in the IMF's role in explicitly coordinating creditor behavior.

[15] The source of our bond, equity, and loan data is Dealogic. All other data are from the IMF's International Financial Statistics and World Economic Outlook databases and other IMF sources.

[16] We are able to date the start of the IMF program precisely. For example, if a program were started in March 1998, but before March 15, then the first year of the program would include the months March 1998 through February 1999, while if a program were started after March 15, the first year would include the months April 1998 through March 1999. Using this definition of years, the data on capital flows and inflation, being available at a monthly frequency, can be timed quite precisely. For data that are not available at a monthly frequency (e.g., real GDP growth and the current account balance), we follow the convention of constructing monthly values by interpolation (i.e., assuming a constant growth rate during a quarter or year).

Figure 1
Average Performance of Emerging Market Economies with IMF Programs
(in percent)

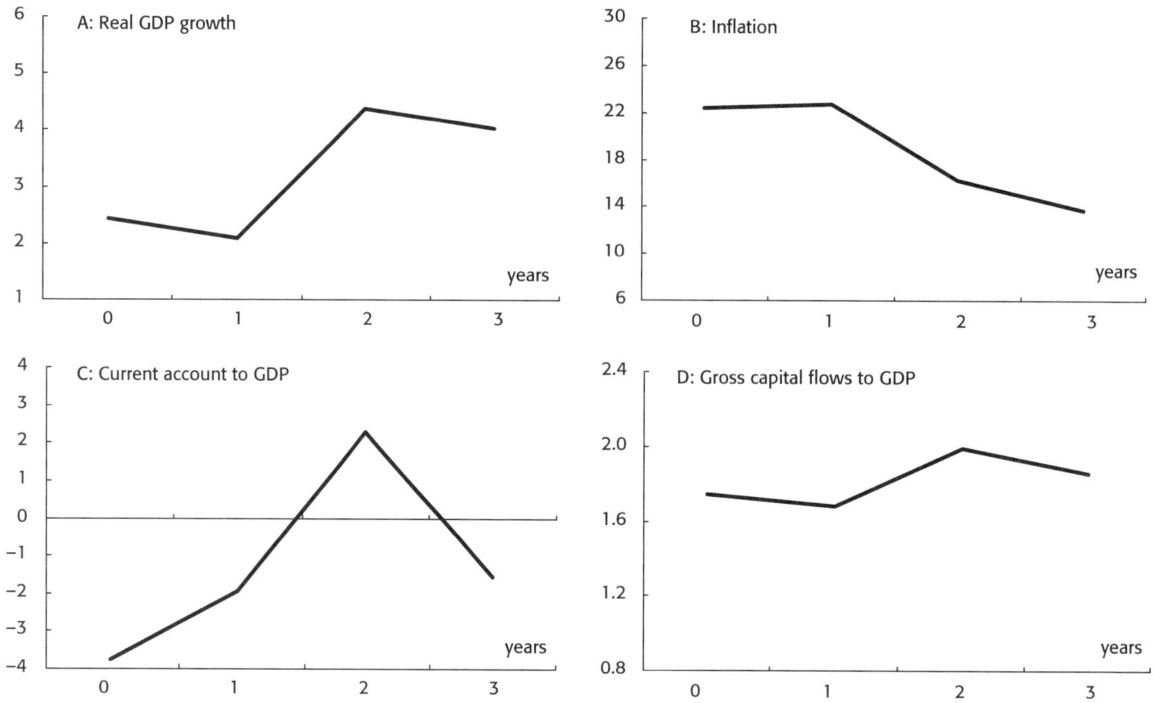

IMF program, since both the seal of approval and catalytic lending channels would suggest that the effect of IMF program adoption on performance is immediate, while the delegated monitoring channel becomes effective during the course of a program. Since it takes time for macroeconomic fundamentals to adjust, we study their evolution up to three years after the start of the program.

We treat each program as a separate observation and average across programs. To make the averages comparable across each year, we use a balanced sample, in which the set of programs over which we average is the same for all years. We thus exclude programs where no data are available for the year before or any of the three years following the program.[17]

Our main finding here is that both macroeconomic aggregates and capital flows improve following the adoption of an IMF program. This is consistent with Morris and Shin's (2003) hypothesis that the catalytic effect on capital flows and adjustment effort go hand in hand. For growth and capital flows, we observe a dip and recovery pattern: in the first year of the program, performance fails to improve and may even worsen; the second year tends to see a large improvement; and, in the third year, a weaker improvement or even a slight fallback may occur, possibly because of mean reversion. However, in spite of the possible fallback in the third year, the overall effect after three years for the different indicators is generally positive.

Panel A of Figure 1 illustrates the dip and recovery pattern for real GDP growth: growth dips in the first year of the program, recovers in the second year, and falls somewhat in the third year while remaining well above the low point and even above the level before the start of the program. Inflation performance (Panel B) fails to improve in the first year, but then exhibits a large improvement (i.e., a reduction in inflation) in both the second and third years following the start of the IMF program. Countries with IMF programs, not surprisingly, tend to start with a high current account deficit (Panel C); this deficit tends to be reduced immediately in the first year of the program and even turns into a surplus

[17] Data may not be available because the program started only recently or because a new program started within three years of the old program. Dropping programs followed by other programs within the balanced-sample period could lead to selection bias, because such programs are likely to have failed. However, even if we did not drop these programs, average performance would still be overestimated in situations where performance improved under the second programs, since this improved performance would then be considered a result of both the first and second programs. While we could have considered two consecutive programs simply as one program, we decided not to do so for the following reasons: (a) the new program may have a separate signaling effect; (b) the amount under the second program may be different from the first; and (c) the second program may be of a different type.

Table 2.
Average Performance of Emerging Market Economies with EFF and SBA Programs
(in percent)

A. Average Performance of Emerging Market Economies with EFF Programs

Fundamental	Year Before IMF Program	First Year	Second Year	Third Year
Current account to GDP	−3.8	−2.7	3.2	−3.2
Gross capital flows to GDP	1.1	1.0	1.7	1.5
Inflation	23.5	18.7	13.5	11.0
Real GDP growth	1.4	2.6	5.2	4.3

B. Average Performance of Emerging Market Economies with SBA Programs

Fundamental	Year Before IMF Program	First Year	Second Year	Third Year
Current account to GDP	−3.7	−1.5	1.7	−0.5
Gross capital flows to GDP	2.1	2.1	2.2	2.1
Inflation	21.8	25.4	18.0	15.3
Real GDP growth	3.0	1.8	3.9	3.9

Notes: EFF denotes Extended Fund Facility; SBA denotes Stand-By Arrangement.

in the second year (presumably, as import compression continues). However, as conditions become more normal in the third year, the current account returns to a lower (possibly, more sustainable) deficit than at the start.

The pattern for capital flows is similar to that of real GDP. As Panel D of Figure 1 shows, gross capital flows tend to fall somewhat in the first year of the program—especially for bonds and loans, which we do not show separately here. However, flows increase thereafter. By the second year of the program, the different components of capital flows tend to be higher than in the year preceding the program, and the bond component continues to increase in subsequent years (while equity flows "overshoot" in the second year and then decline).

Program Duration

We next compare performance across two different IMF programs: the Stand-By Arrangement (SBA) and the Extended Fund Facility (EFF). Although these programs share several common features, an important difference is that programs under the SBA are shorter than programs under the EFF. While SBAs are designed to address short-term balance of payments problems and typically last 12–18 months, EFFs are designed to address more structural balance of payments problems and last about 3 years. Also, repayment for SBAs is expected within 2¼ to 4 years, while repayment for EFFs is expected within 4½ to 7 years.

Interestingly, we find some evidence that EFFs are associated with better performance than are SBAs (Table 2). Given the small number of observations in each category (90 SBA programs versus 29 EFF programs), these results should be interpreted with caution. However, they do suggest that longer-term IMF lending for structural reform is more effective than short-term lending for balance of payments adjustment. A possible explanation for this result is that EFFs require a stronger—or at least longer—commitment by the IMF, implying a stronger seal of approval, a longer period of delegated monitoring, and often—but not always—more lending. An alternative explanation is that EFF programs work better because they give countries more time for repayment.[18]

Another interesting result is that EFF programs are associated with higher capital flows (again, with a slight dip in the first year), while the impact of SBA programs on capital flows is roughly nil on average. An explanation for this could be that countries that enter into an EFF program tend to start from a low base and have larger chances of being rewarded with high capital flows than do countries that enter an SBA program. The latter countries supposedly have fewer deep-seated structural problems and therefore are already able to borrow more, although they have to struggle to regain market confidence if they are experiencing temporary liquidity

[18] For example, in August 1998 Indonesia requested to replace its 1997 SBA program with an EFF program, with the explicit goal of lengthening the repayment period. In this case, the amount of credit available under the EFF and its duration were identical to those remaining under the SBA; hence, the EFF could not necessarily be regarded as reflecting a stronger IMF commitment than the SBA.

Table 3
Definitions of States in Terms of Fundamentals
(in percent)

Fundamentals	Current Account to GDP	Reserves to Imports	Short-Term Debt to Reserves	External Debt to GDP
1 (Very bad)	Deficit larger than 6	Between 0 and 1.25	Larger than 4	Larger than 0.6
2 (Bad)	Deficit between 3 and 6	Between 1.25 and 3	Between 2 and 4	Between 0.4 and 0.6
3 (Good)	Deficit between 0 and 3	Between 3 and 7	Between 1 and 2	Between 0.2 and 0.4
4 (Very good)	Surplus	More than 7	Between 0 and 1	Between 0 and 0.2

problems.[19] As Table 2 shows, countries with EFF programs start with an initially lower level of capital flows than do countries with SBA programs, but their recovery is subsequently stronger.

Impact of Initial Fundamentals and Lending Levels on Performance

In the previous section, we reported some preliminary evidence that IMF programs are associated with improvements in both macroeconomic performance and capital flows, typically exhibiting a dip and recovery pattern. However, we cannot exclude the possibility that these observed improvements simply reflect mean reversion. That is, to the extent that economic conditions may naturally improve after a crisis even without a program, the observed improvement cannot necessarily be attributed to the program alone.

Although it is the case that the initial conditions of countries that enter into an IMF program are likely to be worse than those of nonprogram countries, in practice we find considerable variation in the initial conditions of program countries themselves. To test whether initial conditions matter, this section disaggregates the response in capital flows by the state of a country's external fundamentals in the year prior to the adoption of an IMF program. The goal here is to examine whether there is a differential response to an IMF program depending on initial conditions: if there is mean reversion, is it the same irrespective of the starting point, or are there systematic differences? We also briefly discuss whether the level of IMF lending matters in helping to maintain capital flows.

Defining Initial Conditions

To operationalize the predictions by Morris and Shin (2003) and others in Table 2, we use four indicators to assess the state of those external fundamentals that can affect the probability of a country's default. We use two indicators of liquidity risk (ratios of short-term debt to reserves, and reserves to imports), one indicator of insolvency (total external debt to GDP), and one indicator that is a measure of both illiquidity and insolvency (current account deficit to GDP). The indicators of illiquidity measure the risk of running out of reserves, while the indicators of insolvency assess whether, with IMF lending and external adjustment, the country will be able to pay its overall debt. Although the four indicators are obviously related, the response of capital flows is expected to be different depending on whether the main problem is illiquidity or insolvency.

Next, we define the thresholds defining whether the state of fundamentals is very bad, bad, good, or very good. While the choice of thresholds is necessarily ad hoc, we base them, as far as possible, on commonly accepted thresholds used in the financial crises literature and in IMF surveillance.[20] Thus, for example, we consider a country to be in a very bad state during the 12 months preceding the start of an IMF program if the current account deficit is higher than 6 percent of GDP; if reserves are less than 1.25 months of imports; if short-term debt is more than four times reserves; or if total external debt exceeds 60 percent of GDP. In these cases, a country is generally not expected to be able to prevent default, even with IMF support and maximum adjustment effort. Table 3 summarizes this information, and also contains similar definitions of "bad," "good," and "very good" states.

Results

Table 4 summarizes the evolution of capital flows conditional on the four states defined in Table 3.

[19] For example, as Argentina's debt levels built up in the 1990s, it had to struggle just to attract the capital flows needed to refinance its external debt—particularly after Brazil's devaluation.

[20] As an alternative to predefining thresholds for each state, more sophisticated ways could be used to determine the thresholds. For example, using a Markov switching model, one could define the states by an unobserved composite state variable that depends in certain known ways on the observed fundamentals. Another possibility is to define, for example, the threshold for a very bad current account deficit as a deficit above two standard deviations from its mean. We leave these as suggestions for future research.

Table 4

Average Capital Flows to Emerging Market Economies Conditional on External Fundamentals

(in percent of GDP)

A. Conditional on Reserves to Imports

State	Year Before IMF Program	First Year	Second Year	Third Year	Number of Observations
Very bad	1.5	1.2	0.5	0.5	8
Bad	1.5	1.2	2.1	2.2	16
Good	2.2	2.4	2.5	2.0	11
Very good	2.3	2.4	2.8	2.8	6

B. Conditional on Short-Term Debt to Reserves

State	Year Before IMF Program	First Year	Second Year	Third Year	Number of Observations
Very bad	1.6	1.9	1.6	1.5	4
Bad	1.6	0.8	1.8	1.9	9
Good	2.0	2.6	2.3	1.9	9
Very good	2.2	2.2	2.7	2.6	12

C. Conditional on Current Account Deficit to GDP

State	Year Before IMF Program	First Year	Second Year	Third Year	Number of Observations
Very bad	2.4	2.3	1.8	2.2	10
Bad	2.1	1.9	2.7	2.2	13
Good	1.0	1.2	1.1	1.1	12
Very good	0.7	1.2	2.3	1.6	5

D. Conditional on External Debt to GDP

State	Year Before IMF Program	First Year	Second Year	Third Year	Number of Observations
Very bad	1.5	1.7	1.6	1.8	14
Bad	1.4	1.7	1.9	2.1	11
Good	1.9	1.7	2.7	1.9	13
Very good	0.0	1.1	0.0	0.5	2

Our general findings, explained below in more detail, are as follows. First, conditional on very bad initial external fundamentals, IMF programs are typically unable to reverse the slide in capital flows: capital flows either fail to increase or continue to fall. Second, IMF programs seem most successful in maintaining capital flows to countries with bad external fundamentals before the start of a program, when fundamentals are stronger than in the very bad case, but the country is still vulnerable to an external crisis. IMF programs in this state are typically followed by a dip and recovery pattern, suggesting that countries and the IMF are able to enter into a joint commitment to a policy effort that is credible to foreign investors, although the effort may take some time to bear fruit. Finally, as external fundamentals improve further (good and very good states), the role of the IMF diminishes, although it can help in situations where a temporary shock requires short-term external assistance.

As Table 4 shows, countries starting out in a very bad state generally experience a slide in capital flows despite the introduction of an IMF program. This is most clear for the reserves-to-imports measure: just before the program starts, a low reserves-to-imports ratio is already associated with relatively low capital inflows, and three years after the start of the program, the capital flows-to-GDP ratio has fallen even further, to only one-third of its initial level. When the ratio of short-term debt to reserves—the second measure—is in a very bad state, capital flows increase somewhat in the first year of a program but fall thereafter. When the problem is a very high current account deficit—the third measure—capital flows are substantial in the run-up to the program (presumably because the deficit was being financed by external flows), but once the program has started, capital flows decline for as long as two years before bumping back up. In countries starting out in a very bad state, only in the case of the external debt-to-GDP ratio—the fourth measure—is there some slight indication that capital flows increase after the start of a program. But this increase is unlikely to be statistically significant, given the small number of observations.[21]

Starting from a bad state before program adoption, a dip and recovery pattern for capital flows is observed for all external fundamentals, except for external debt, conditional on which capital flows increase steadily without a dip. For all other fundamentals, however, capital flows fall in the first year, suggesting that IMF programs are initiated at the moment when things are worsening. In the second and third years, capital flows for all four fundamentals recover and are above their level before the start of the program. It is as if IMF programs slow the deterioration and help these countries transit to a more benign state. The indicators that most clearly represent this dip and recovery pattern are the liquidity risk indicators: the ratios of reserves to imports and of short-term debt to reserves. The pattern also holds for the current account, where the second year sees a sharp recovery following a shallower dip.

For countries with good or very good fundamentals, the evidence is mixed. When countries start in a good state, IMF programs seem to make very little difference in the trend of capital flows, as predicted by Morris and Shin (2003). Surprisingly, however, when countries start in a very good state, there is some indication that capital flows actually improve following the start of an IMF program (except for very good external debt conditions, but this is based on only two observations). Most likely, these countries with very good external fundamentals had experienced temporary liquidity difficulties that led to an IMF program, but the sound fundamentals reasserted themselves soon thereafter.[22]

[21] Formal tests for statistical significance would require estimation of the distribution of the external fundamentals, which is beyond the scope of this paper.

[22] Another possibility is that, in such cases, liquidity problems were not the main reason for starting an IMF program. For example, prior to its July 1996 SBA program, República Bolivariana de Venezuela was in very good shape, judged by (a) its current account, which was in surplus because of a devaluation at the end of 1995; (b) its reserves, which amounted to over seven months of imports; and (c) its short-term debt, which was less than 50 percent of its reserves. However, an SBA was considered necessary because of banking sector problems, high inflation (about 70 percent in the year prior to the program), high unemployment (over 10 percent in 1995), and low growth in the non-oil sector. The program was successful at lowering inflation and improving confidence, which likely contributed to a rebound in capital flows, although in this case the rebound was also helped by high oil prices.

Finally, we consider the relationship between the amount of IMF lending and the evolution of capital flows. The evidence, presented in Table 5, is inconclusive. With a larger lending amount, capital flows increase over the course of the following three years; however, the initial level of capital flows is also low in cases where the IMF has made large loans, so that it is unclear whether the increase is a response to IMF lending or to the relatively low initial level of capital flows.[23]

Transition Probabilities

Our third step, and most ambitious attempt at a counterfactual, is the comparison of the evolution of external fundamentals for program and nonprogram countries, disaggregated by initial conditions. This allows us to test the null hypothesis that the observed improvements in performance following IMF program adoption, reported in the paper's third section, might be simply the result of mean reversion.

In the previous section, we studied whether and how the evolution of capital flows following a country's adoption of an IMF program depends on the state of the country's initial external fundamentals. Our results seem to confirm that IMF programs are most successful at keeping capital flowing to countries with bad, but not very bad fundamentals. However, the fact that countries with bad fundamentals appear to be better at escaping from near-crisis situations than countries with very bad fundamentals may be a general phenomenon and not necessarily the result of entering into an IMF program. To determine whether IMF programs were the main factor in keeping capital flowing, we would need to know what would have happened to these same countries if they had not adopted an IMF program. While it is impossible to answer this counterfactual question, we can approximate it quite closely by comparing the performance of program countries with the performance of countries that did not adopt an IMF program but had similar fundamentals.

Our methodology is as follows. First, we consider a country's initial state to improve if the probability of moving to a better state is raised, or if the probability of moving to a worse state is lowered. Next, to determine whether IMF programs are associated with an improvement in a country's initial state, we calculate a transition probability matrix for the four states, both for countries with IMF programs and for countries without IMF programs. We then test whether the transition probabilities for countries

[23] The results, in this case, are quite sensitive to the specification. When we consider two-year samples, the picture is less clear, suggesting that countries that start a new program within a three-year period do not obviously gain from larger amounts of IMF lending (results available from the authors upon request).

Table 5

Average Capital Flows to Emerging Market Economies Conditional on IMF Lending Amount

(in percent of GDP)

A. Amount to Reserves

State	Year Before IMF Program	First Year	Second Year	Third Year	Number of Observations
Low	1.8	2.6	1.3	2.4	6
Medium	2.1	1.9	2.4	1.9	22
High	1.1	0.9	1.5	1.6	13

B. Amount to Short-Term Debt

State	Year Before IMF Program	First Year	Second Year	Third Year	Number of Observations
Low	1.5	2.1	0.9	1.1	8
Medium	2.4	2.2	2.3	2.1	12
High	1.8	1.5	2.9	2.6	15

C. Amount to Imports

State	Year Before IMF Program	First Year	Second Year	Third Year	Number of Observations
Low	2.2	1.9	1.7	2.2	11
Medium	2.2	2.4	2.3	2.0	12
High	1.1	1.1	1.9	1.5	18

D. Composite Amount Index

State	Year Before IMF Program	First Year	Second Year	Third Year	Number of Observations
Low	2.2	2.6	1.6	2.1	11
Medium	1.8	1.4	2.1	1.8	27
High	1.1	1.2	2.2	1.7	10

with IMF programs are significantly different from those for countries without IMF programs.

To calculate these transition probabilities, we define a state variable S_T that specifies whether external fundamentals are very bad ($S_T = 1$); bad ($S_T = 2$); good ($S_T = 3$); or very good ($S_T = 4$) during period T. Since IMF programs take at least a year to have an effect, we are interested in comparing the fundamental states in the year before and in the second year after the start of a program. Thus, for each country-program pair, we calculate the following:

- S_T = average state of external fundamentals during the year before the start of a program (i.e., T encompasses the months $t-11$ through t, where t is the month in which the program starts); and
- $S_T + 2$ = average state of external fundamentals during the second year following the start of the program (i.e., $T+2$ encompasses the months $t+13$ through $t+24$).

For nonprogram countries, there is no natural starting point, t. Nevertheless, it would be misleading to calculate transition probabilities using pairs of S_T and S_{T+2} for every month in a given year, as this would generate a large amount of similar observations and, therefore, would lead to artificially low standard errors when testing for differences between the two transition probability matrices. Instead, we calculate only the states for one month (January) in a given year for each nonprogram country. In addition, for nonprogram countries, we use only the observations of S_T and S_{T+2} if no IMF program was in place during any of the months $t-11$ through $t+24$. This gives us around 250 nonprogram observations, compared with some 100 program observations.

The null hypothesis is that IMF programs have no effect even after two years, that is, $\Pr(S_T + 2 \mid S_T)$ is the same regardless of whether an IMF program was present in month t. The alternative hypothesis is that these transition probabilities are different for countries with and without IMF programs. To determine whether any observed differences are significant, we conduct a two-sided test and consider differences as "significant" when they are statistically significant at the 5 percent level. (For the calculation of *p*-values, see the appendix).

The main result (Table 6) is that IMF programs are generally associated with improvements in external fundamentals, except when these fundamentals are already in very good shape (State 4). As Table 6 shows, even for countries that start out in a very bad state (State 1), IMF programs significantly increase the probability of moving to a better state. For countries that start out in a bad state (State 2), the programs also significantly increase the probability of moving to a better state after two years, except for the indicator of short-term debt-to-reserves.[24] For countries that start out in a good state (State 3), fundamentals significantly improve following the start of an IMF program, that is, all external fundamentals are significantly more likely to have improved from State 3 to State 4 after two years.[25]

Synthesis and Conclusion

The IMF has evolving functions in the changing world economy. In this paper, we have put the spotlight on a set of emerging market economies and the IMF's role in maintaining their access to international capital markets. Our results reinforce theoretical predictions and earlier empirical findings on the value of IMF intervention for countries in vulnerable—as distinct from extreme distress—situations.

We identified three channels through which the IMF potentially helps emerging market economies maintain access to international capital markets: (a) by providing a good housekeeping seal of approval, (b) by means of delegated monitoring, and (c) through catalytic lending. We argued that, although the good housekeeping seal presupposes superiority of information held by the IMF, it is not evident that the IMF has significantly more comprehensive or more timely information on a sustained basis than, say, investment banks or credit rating agencies. The IMF does have an informational role to play, but this more likely occurs in the context of agency problems, where a country, as an "agent" of international investors, needs to be monitored by a credible external agency. In this context, the second and third channels are more important than the first. As a delegated monitor, the IMF can constrain opportunistic behavior through its program benchmarks and conditionality imposed ex post. As a lender, the IMF can reduce the probability of default and solve the coordination problem between private creditors, simply through its ability to provide financial resources.

We started by making a simple before-after comparison (in the third section) suggesting that, on average, both macroeconomic aggregates and capital flows improve following the adoption of an IMF program, albeit with lags. The first year of IMF programs is typically associated with some initial decline in performance, but by the second year growth is up and inflation is down. The current account is initially compressed but by the third year appears to return to a more sustainable deficit than at the start of the program. Capital flows follow a path similar to growth: an initial small dip followed by a modest recovery. These findings are, of course, based on averaging across programs.

We also found that three-year programs (EFFs) are associated with better performance than are shorter-term programs (SBAs), suggesting that the improvement in performance depends positively on the duration of the program. A possible explanation for this result is that EFFs imply a stronger seal of approval, a longer period of delegated monitoring, and often—but not always—more lending.

We next attempted to test whether the effect of IMF programs on capital flows was conditional on the state of a country's initial external fundamentals (in the fourth section), and whether these fundamentals themselves improved following program adoption. Table 7 summarizes our findings on capital flows and improvements in fundamentals, as assessed by changes in the probability of transitions across states.

Our results suggest that when a country starts out in a situation of economic distress (with very bad external fundamentals), an IMF program is at best associated with stemming the decline in capital flows and is at worst associated with the country's continued loss of access to international capital markets. External fundamentals, starting from this distressed situation, do improve, as the current account deficit declines and reserves rise. However, when these improvements do occur, they are possibly the consequence of significant import compression and, hence, are not necessarily sustainable. Thus, when initial fundamentals are extremely weak, IMF programs may be associated with some adjustment effort, but this is not sufficient to ensure a significant turnaround in capital flows.

In contrast, we found that when a country is vulnerable (with bad, but not very bad external fundamentals), an IMF program is associated with both better market access and improvements in the country's external fundamentals. It may well be possible that, in such vulnerable initial conditions, the country is itself able to engineer the recovery. It

[24] We also calculated the transition probabilities between S_T and S_{T+1} and found that IMF programs do not have a significant effect in one year (results available from the authors upon request).

[25] Even within one year, the reserves-to-imports and current account-to-GDP ratios are significantly more likely to improve from State 3 to State 4 under an IMF program. However, reserves may be increasing in some cases just because of IMF disbursements.

Table 6

Two-Year Transition Probabilities for Emerging Market Economies With and Without IMF Programs

(in percent)

A. Current Account Balance to GDP

		$S_{T+2} = 1$	$S_{T+2} = 2$	$S_{T+2} = 3$	$S_{T+2} = 4$
$S_T = 1$	Program	0.23	0.15	0.38	0.23
(Very bad)	Nonprogram	0.29	0.49	0.17	0.06
	P-value	0.35	0.01	0.05	0.03
$S_T = 2$	Program	0.14	0.14	0.48	0.24
(Bad)	Nonprogram	0.26	0.43	0.28	0.03
	P-value	0.12	0.01	0.04	0.00
$S_T = 3$	Program	0.10	0.10	0.55	0.25
(Good)	Nonprogram	0.08	0.27	0.55	0.10
	P-value	0.37	0.05	0.50	0.04
$S_T = 4$	Program	0.00	0.11	0.33	0.56
(Very good)	Nonprogram	0.10	0.13	0.36	0.41
	P-value	0.15	0.44	0.44	0.21

B. Reserves to Imports

		$S_{T+2} = 1$	$S_{T+2} = 2$	$S_{T+2} = 3$	$S_{T+2} = 4$
$S_T = 1$	Program	0.42	0.17	0.42	0.00
(Very bad)	Nonprogram	0.71	0.24	0.05	0.00
	P-value	0.04	0.30	0.00	n.a
$S_T = 2$	Program	0.13	0.35	0.52	0.00
(Bad)	Nonprogram	0.13	0.62	0.24	0.00
	P-value	0.49	0.01	0.01	n.a
$S_T = 3$	Program	0.06	0.06	0.39	0.50
(Good)	Nonprogram	0.00	0.14	0.78	0.07
	P-value	0.01	0.15	0.00	0.00
$S_T = 4$	Program	0.00	0.00	0.20	0.80
(Very good)	Nonprogram	0.00	0.05	0.16	0.80
	P-value	n.a	0.24	0.37	0.49

C. Short-Term Debt to Reserves

		$S_{T+2} = 1$	$S_{T+2} = 2$	$S_{T+2} = 3$	$S_{T+2} = 4$
$S_T = 1$	Program	0.20	0.50	0.30	0.00
(Very bad)	Nonprogram	0.63	0.32	0.05	0.00
	P-value	0.01	0.15	0.03	n.a
$S_T = 2$	Program	0.18	0.09	0.45	0.27
(Bad)	Nonprogram	0.04	0.33	0.38	0.25
	P-value	0.07	0.05	0.32	0.44
$S_T = 3$	Program	0.00	0.15	0.23	0.62
(Good)	Nonprogram	0.04	0.09	0.76	0.11
	P-value	0.22	0.24	0.00	0.00
$S_T = 4$	Program	0.00	0.00	0.17	0.83
(Very good)	Nonprogram	0.00	0.03	0.08	0.89
	P-value	n.a	0.24	0.12	0.23

Note: The abbreviation n.a indicates that the *p*-value could not be calculated.

Table 7
Summary of Main Results

Initial Fundamentals	Capital Flow Trends	Change in Fundamentals
Very bad (State 1)	Either continued decline after initiation of program or, at best, no improvement	Some improvement in external fundamentals, but related to domestic recessionary conditions
Bad (State 2)	Dip and recovery, as the decline in capital flows is stemmed and a rise is initiated	Strong evidence of improvement in external fundamentals
Good and very good (States 3 and 4)	Either no change or evidence consistent with stabilization of flows following a temporary shock	Ambiguous

may, however, also be the case that, although the effort is essentially undertaken by the country, the IMF is used as a commitment mechanism or delegated monitor. Either way, this is where we have the strongest evidence that IMF programs are associated with increased capital flows and improved fundamentals.

Finally, for countries with relatively strong initial conditions (good or very good external fundamentals), we found that IMF programs can sometimes help to stabilize capital flows following temporary shocks, while their effect on fundamentals is ambiguous. While Morris and Shin (2003) make a distinction between good and very good states, such a distinction is not clear in the data examined. Moreover, there is no clear evidence that in countries with good fundamentals, IMF lending may lead to moral hazard (that is, reduced adjustment effort by the country itself).

Our results are subject to several caveats. First, although we have attempted to construct the best counterfactual possible, by comparing the performance of program countries with that of nonprogram countries with similar initial conditions, there may be other important observed or unobserved initial conditions that we have not controlled for. While it would be useful to extend our analysis by widening our definition of initial conditions, the fact remains that we will never know what would have happened to program countries had they not adopted a program. Hence, one can never conclude with certainty that IMF programs necessarily had the determining influence in the observed improvement in performance. Second, since we limited ourselves to emerging market economies between 1980 and 2002, our results cannot necessarily be generalized to apply to all IMF programs. Finally, while we distinguished between EFF and SBA programs, we otherwise treated all programs as more or less uniform. In reality, however, IMF programs differ in both their design and their execution, and these differences may affect the private sector's response in terms of capital flows.

We have several suggestions for future research. First, the list of variables used to characterize a country's initial condition could be expanded to include real GDP growth, inflation, and even capital flows themselves. Second, more sophisticated econometric methods could be used to derive, rather than predefine, the thresholds for the states of external fundamentals. For example, one could use a Markov switching model to estimate an unobserved composite state variable that depends in certain assumed ways on the observed fundamentals. Third, rather than treating IMF programs as a "black box," one could further differentiate between IMF programs in terms of their design (e.g., precautionary versus nonprecautionary programs) and execution (e.g., canceled versus completed programs). Fourth, the determinants of capital flows could be better modeled. While this paper focused on the supply-side determinants of capital flows (i.e., decisions on the part of creditors as to whether to roll over their loans or issue new loans), it would be useful to capture demand-side determinants as well by, for example, scaling capital flows in terms of gross financing need. Similarly, it would be useful to try to distinguish between "pull" and "push" factors as determinants of capital flows.

Appendix. Calculation of *p*-Values for Differences in Transition Probabilities

Let p_1 denote the transition probability between two states for countries with an IMF program, and let p_0 denote the transition probability between the same two states for countries without an IMF program. Let $D = p_1 - p_0$ denote the difference between the two transition probabilities. The standard deviation of D is then given by

$$\sigma_D = \sqrt{\left(\frac{p_0(1-p_0)}{n_0} + \frac{p_1(1-p_1)}{n_1}\right)},$$

where n_0 and n_1 are the number of observations corresponding to each row in the transition probability matrix (e.g., for p_{11}, this is the number of cases where $S_T = 1$). Under the null hypothesis, we have H_0: $p_1 = p_0 = p$. Let $\hat{p}_0$, $\hat{p}_1$,and $\hat{p}$ denote the estimates of the respective transition probabilities, i.e., the sample proportions. We then have

$$\hat{p} = \frac{X_0 + X_1}{n_0 + n_1},$$

where X_0 and X_1 are the number of transitions without and with an IMF program, respectively. This gives the following estimate of σ_D under the null hypothesis:

$$SE_{Dp} = \sqrt{\hat{p}(1-\hat{p})\left(\frac{1}{n_0} + \frac{1}{n_1}\right)}.$$

If n_0 and n_1 are large, the standardized difference $z = (\hat{p}_1 - \hat{p}_0)/SE_{Dp}$ is approximately $N(0,1)$. The p-value for a test of the null hypothesis (H_0: $p_1 = p_0$) against the alternative hypothesis H_a: $p_1 \neq p_0$ is thus given by $Pr(Z \neq z)$, where Z is a standard normal random variable.

References

Barro, Robert J., and Jong-Wha Lee, 2003, "IMF Programs: Who Is Chosen and What Are the Effects?" Working Papers in Trade and Development No. 2003/09 (Canberra, Australia: Australian National University). Available on the Web at *http://post.economics.harvard.edu/faculty/barro/papers/IMF_Programs.pdf*.

Bird, Graham, and Dane Rowlands, 1997, "The Catalytic Effect of Lending by the International Financial Institutions," *World Economy*, Vol. 20, No. 7, pp. 967–91.

Boorman, Jack, and Mark Allen, 2000, "A New Framework for Private Sector Involvement in Crisis Prevention and Crisis Management," in *Reforming the International Financial System: Crisis Prevention and Response*, ed. by Jan Joost Teunissen (The Hague: Forum on Debt and Development), pp. 101–23.

Bordo, Michael D., 2003, "Market Discipline and Financial Crisis Policy: A Historical Perspective," in *Research in Financial Services: Private and Public Policy*, Vol. 15, ed. by George G. Kaufman (Greenwich, Connecticut: JAI Press), pp. 157–82.

———, and Harold James, 2000, "The International Monetary Fund: Its Present Role in Historical Perspective," NBER Working Paper No. 7724 (Cambridge, Massachusetts: National Bureau of Economic Research).

Bordo, Michael D., and Finn E. Kydland, 1995, "The Gold Standard as a Rule: An Essay in Exploration," *Explorations in Economic History*, Vol. 32, No. 4, pp. 423–64.

———, 1996, "The Gold Standard as a Commitment Mechanism," in *Modern Perspectives on the Gold Standard*, ed. by Tamim Bayoumi, Barry Eichengreen, and Mark P. Taylor (Cambridge, New York, and Melbourne: Cambridge University Press), pp. 55–100.

Bordo, Michael D., and Hugh Rockoff, 1996, "The Gold Standard as a 'Good Housekeeping Seal of Approval,'" *Journal of Economic History*, Vol. 56, No. 2, pp. 389–428.

Bordo, Michael D., and Anna J. Schwartz, 2000, "Measuring Real Economic Effects of Bailouts: Historical Perspectives on How Countries in Financial Distress Have Fared With and Without Bailouts," NBER Working Paper No. 7701 (Cambridge, Massachusetts: National Bureau of Economic Research).

Calvo, Guillermo A., 1998, "Capital Flows and Capital-Market Crises: The Simple Economics of Sudden Stops," *Journal of Applied Economics*, Vol. 1, No. 1, pp. 35–54.

Corsetti, Giancarlo, Bernardo Guimarães, and Nouriel Roubini, 2003, "International Lending of Last Resort and Moral Hazard: A Model of IMF's Catalytic Finance," NBER Working Paper No. 10125 (Cambridge, Massachusetts: National Bureau of Economic Research).

Cottarelli, Carlo, and Curzio Giannini, 2002, "Bedfellows, Hostages, or Perfect Strangers? Global Capital Markets and the Catalytic Effect of IMF Crisis Lending," IMF Working Paper 02/193 (Washington: International Monetary Fund). This paper also appears, in somewhat different form, as Chapter 12 in this volume.

Ferguson, Roger W., 2002, "Understanding Financial Consolidation," *Economic Policy Review*, Federal Reserve Bank of New York, Vol. 8 (May), pp. 209–13.

Ghosh, Atish, Timothy Lane, Marianne Schulze-Ghattas, Aleš Bulíř, Javier Hamann, and Alex Mourmouras, 2002, *IMF-Supported Programs in Capital Account Crises*, IMF Occasional Paper No. 210 (Washington: International Monetary Fund).

Goldstein, Morris, and Peter Montiel, 1986, "Evaluating Fund Stabilization Programs with Multicountry Data: Some Methodological Pitfalls," *Staff Papers*, International Monetary Fund, Vol. 33 (June), pp. 304–44.

Hajro, Zlata, and Joseph P. Joyce, 2004, "A True Test: Do IMF Programs Hurt the Poor?" Wellesley College Department of Economics Working Paper No. 04-01 (Wellesley, Massachusetts: Wellesley College).

Haque, Nadeem Ul, and Mohsin Khan, 1998, "Do IMF-Supported Programs Work? A Survey of the Cross-Country Empirical Evidence," IMF Working Paper 98/169 (Washington: International Monetary Fund).

Hutchison, M., 2001, "A Cure Worse Than the Disease? Currency Crises and the Output Costs of IMF-Supported Stabilization Programs," NBER Working Paper No. 8305 (Cambridge, Massachusetts: National Bureau of Economic Research).

Ivanova, Anna, 2003, "IMF Conditionality and Implementation of IMF-Supported Programs" (Ph.D. dissertation; Madison, Wisconsin: University of Wisconsin-Madison).

Khan, Mohsin, 1990, "The Macroeconomic Effects of Fund-Supported Adjustment Programs," *Staff Papers*, International Monetary Fund, Vol. 37 (June), pp. 195–231.

Köhler, Horst, 2001, "Promoting Stability and Prosperity in a Globalized World," remarks by IMF Managing Director, Council of the Americas, Washington, May 7. Available on the Web at *http://www.imf.org/external/np/speeches/2001/050701.htm*.

Lerrick, Adam, and Allan H. Meltzer, 2003, "Blueprint for an International Lender of Last Resort," *Journal of Monetary Economics*, Vol. 50 (January), pp. 289–303.

Loungani, Prakash, 2001, "How Accurate Are Private Forecasts? Cross-Country Evidence from Consensus Forecasts of Output Growth," *International Journal of Forecasting*, Vol. 17 (July–September), pp. 419–32.

Marchesi, Silvia, and Jonathan P. Thomas, 1999, "IMF Conditionality as a Screening Device," *Economic Journal*, Vol. 109 (March), pp. 111–25.

Masson, Paul R., and Michael Mussa, 1995, "Long-Term Tendencies in Budget Deficits and Debt," IMF Working Paper 95/128 (Washington: International Monetary Fund).

Meltzer, Allan H., 2002, "New International Financial Arrangements," *Monetary and Economic Studies*, Vol. 20 (Special Edition, December), pp. 11–22.

Miller, Marcus, and Lei Zhang, 2000, "Sovereign Liquidity Crises: The Strategic Case for a Payments Standstill," *Economic Journal*, Vol. 110 (January), pp. 335–62.

Mody, Ashoka, and Diego Saravia, 2003, "Catalyzing Capital Flows: Do IMF-Supported Programs Work as Commitment Devices?" IMF Working Paper 03/100 (Washington: International Monetary Fund).

Morris, Stephen Edward, and Hyun Song Shin, 2003, "Catalytic Finance: When Does It Work?" Cowles Foundation Discussion Paper No. 1400 (New Haven, Connecticut: Yale University). Available on the Web at *http://ssrn.com/abstract=383604*.

Obstfeld, Maurice, and Alan M. Taylor, 2003, "Sovereign Risk, Credibility and the Gold Standard: 1870–1913 versus 1925–31," *Economic Journal*, Vol. 113 (April), pp. 241–75.

Powell, Andrew, and Leandro Arozamena, 2003, "Liquidity Protection Versus Moral Hazard: The Role of the IMF," *Journal of International Money and Finance*, Vol. 22 (Special Issue, December), pp. 1041–63. Available on the Web at *http://www.utdt.edu/~apowell*.

Przeworski, Adam, and James Raymond Vreeland, 2000, "The Effect of IMF Programs on Economic Growth," *Journal of Development Economics*, Vol. 62 (August), pp. 385–421.

Reinhart, Carmen M., Kenneth Rogoff, and Miguel Savastano, 2003, "Debt Intolerance," *Brookings Papers on Economic Activity: 1*, Brookings Institution, pp. 1–74

Rodrik, Dani, 1996, "Why Is There Multilateral Lending?" in *Annual World Bank Conference on Development Economics, 1995*, ed. by Michael Bruno and Boris Pleskovic (Washington: World Bank), pp. 167–93.

Tirole, Jean, 2002, *Financial Crises, Liquidity, and the International Monetary System* (Princeton, New Jersey and Oxford: Princeton University Press).

CHAPTER

14 Long-Term Fiscal Developments and IMF Conditionality: Is There a Link?

Aleš Bulíř and Soojin Moon[1]

The paper investigates fiscal developments in 112 countries during the 1990s. It finds that although the overall fiscal balance improved in most of them, the composition of this improvement differed. In countries without IMF-supported programs, revenues increased modestly and expenditure declined sharply, while in program countries both postprogram revenue and expenditure declined. In countries with programs that included fiscal structural conditions, however, the adjustment was effected primarily through sharp expenditure compression. No evidence of a statistically significant impact of IMF conditionality was found. Moreover, fiscal developments were influenced by cyclical factors and by the general stance of macroeconomic policies.

Introduction

What determines the composition of fiscal adjustment, and does it differ between countries with IMF-supported programs and those without such arrangements? Moreover, how relevant is IMF structural conditionality for postprogram fiscal developments? This paper attempts to answer these questions by investigating the fiscal developments in 112 countries during the 1990s, some with and some without IMF-supported programs.

A central objective of IMF-supported programs has been to reduce external imbalances. This often requires bringing the budget under control: first, fiscal profligacy often causes current account deficits, and, second, even if the initial budgetary position is sustainable, additional fiscal tightening may be needed if the domestic currency comes under pressure. This adjustment has been part of broader medium-term macroeconomic programs that also encompass supply-side structural reforms relevant for external stability.

This paper examines postprogram fiscal developments in countries with and without an IMF-supported program. It finds significant differences in the composition of adjustment between program and nonprogram countries as well as large differences among program countries. In nonprogram countries, revenue increased modestly and expenditure declined sharply, while in program countries both revenue and expenditure declined during the postprogram period. Moreover, in IMF-supported programs that included structural conditions, the adjustment was effected primarily through expenditure compression in order to offset revenue declines. We did not find any evidence that fiscal structural conditions improved revenue performance after the end of the program. Fiscal developments were affected by the business cycle and general stance of macroeconomic policies.

The paper is organized as follows. First, we review the stylized facts and define the sample. Second, we describe the techniques used in our estimations. Third, we present and discuss our results. The final section offers concluding remarks.

IMF Programs and Fiscal Developments

How to Measure the Impact of IMF-Supported Programs

What is the impact of IMF-supported programs on fiscal adjustment? In the literature, three influences have been construed. One view is that those programs provide external resources beyond the financing provided by the IMF itself to the extent that they have a catalytic effect—thus adjustments take place at lower costs than in the absence of such an arrangement. Hence, IMF-supported programs can be associated with either smaller or larger fiscal deficits, depending on the nature of the shock and the design of the program (Bird and Rowlands, 2002). A second view is that those programs prescribe fast adjustment by uniformly requiring excessive monetary and fiscal tightening, hurting both the poor and businesses in the process. A third view is that IMF-supported programs delay fundamental reforms by merely treating the symptoms of

[1] This article was first published in Vol. 46 (2004) of *Comparative Economic Studies*. It appears here with the permission of Palgrave Macmillan, the journal's publisher. The authors are indebted to Tim Lane and Alex Mourmouras for discussions and to Chistina Daseking, Kamil Dybczak, Gervan Fearon, Rex Ghosh, Sanjeev Gupta, Javier Hamann, Eduardo Ley, Alun Thomas, and participants in the 2002 Atlantic Economic Society conference, the 2002 Czech Economic Society conference, the 2003 International Institute of Public Finance conference, and International Monetary Fund seminars for comments.

financing needs by repeated lending to crisis-prone and structurally unstable countries (Bird, 1996).

In assessing the impact of IMF-supported programs, we ask two questions. First, what are the factors that lead to IMF-supported programs? Economic variables, such as the current account balance, inflation, international reserves, debt service, GDP per capita, and so on, together with participation in previous programs, explain reasonably well the approval of an IMF-supported arrangement (Conway, 1994; and Knight and Santaella, 1997). Policy commitments made by recipient governments matter as well—if the authorities promise stronger adjustment, the IMF is more likely to approve a bigger loan. Barro and Lee (2002) found that "better connected" countries are likely to get more money with fewer strings attached. In contrast, the literature found no relationship between political economy variables (political institutions, quality of bureaucracy, and so on) and participation in an IMF-supported program.

Second—and this is the question we are primarily interested in—what are the macroeconomic effects of IMF-supported programs? This strand of the literature has a few well-established stylized facts as well. IMF-supported programs were found to be associated with an improved postprogram current account balance. Inflation slowed down and real growth recovered, however, typically by less than what was projected under the program (Conway, 1994; Schadler and others, 1995; and Ghosh and others, 2002). In contrast, Barro and Lee (2002) reported opposite results—participation in an IMF-supported program was found to lower growth and investment.

Macroeconomic effects of IMF-supported programs depended, on the one hand, on borrowing countries' domestic political economy (Ivanova and others, 2003; Khan and Sharma, 2001), and on the other hand, on the technical design of the program (conditionality) or the amount of money borrowed (Schadler and others, 1995). Regarding the former, strong special interests, political instability, inefficient bureaucracies, lack of political cohesion, and ethno-linguistic divisions weakened program implementation. Adjustment programs were more successful in countries where they augmented home-grown reforms than in countries where the donors tried to impose them on unwilling authorities. Regarding the latter, the impact of conditionality seems governed by a "Laffer-curve" relationship, whereby a few, well-targeted conditions had a positive impact on economic performance, but too many or too intrusive conditions hindered such performance (Collier and others, 1997; Goldstein, 2000; and Bird, 2001).

To this end, we will use the IMF's Monitoring of IMF Arrangements (MONA) database, which collects information on conditionality under IMF-supported programs and which was first utilized in IMF (2001). Surprisingly, assessments of structural conditionality have been rare, and this paper is one of a few empirical exercises to address this conditionality's role in macroeconomic adjustment.

What Is IMF Conditionality?

Conditionality is an explicit link between the approval (or continuation) of IMF financing and the implementation of certain aspects of the authorities' policy program (Guitián, 1981). The conditions may be either quantitative (say, a limit on reserve money growth) or structural (say, the introduction of a value-added tax). In general, conditionality is designed to encompass policy measures that are critical to program objectives or key internal data targets that sound warning bells if policies veer off track. Whereas in the mid-1980s structural conditionality in IMF-supported arrangements was rare, by the mid-1990s about half of all programs included structural conditions. The average number of structural conditions in a program year increased from 2 in 1987 to more than 16 in 1997 (IMF, 2001).

These developments were the result of several forces. First, the IMF gradually placed more emphasis on supply-side reforms compared with demand management. Second, the IMF's involvement in low-income and transition countries was focused on the alleviation of structural imbalances and rigidities prevalent in these economies. Finally, the experience with monetary and fiscal policies indicated that their success depends critically on structural conditions. Indeed, most structural conditions were in the core area of IMF expertise.

In this paper, we focus on three main types of structural conditions tabulated in the MONA database: *prior actions*, which are stipulated as preconditions to the approval of an IMF-supported program; *structural performance criteria*, fulfillment of which is a formal precondition for program continuation; and *structural benchmarks*, which are agreed with the authorities and monitored by IMF staff, but are not a formal precondition for program continuation. The majority of conditions were structural benchmarks, while structural performance criteria were the least numerous conditions. The extent of structural conditionality was in part determined endogenously—countries with a large reform agenda or history of poor reform performance tended to get more conditions, although no clear-cut answers as to why some countries have many more conditions than others are available (IMF, 2001). If anything, distribution of structural conditions was positively correlated with the length of the programs.

All but two IMF-supported programs with structural conditionality in our sample contained at least one fiscal condition.[2] Indeed, fiscal structural conditionality was the most common area of structural

[2] Throughout the paper, we used a sample of 112 countries, of which 48 countries did not have a program during the sample period, and 31 and 33 countries had programs without and with structural conditions, respectively.

Table 1

Frequency of Fiscal Structural Conditionality

	Total Number of Conditions[1]	Implementation Ratio[2]
All conditions	15.4	77.4
Revenue conditions[3]	4.7	78.5
Expenditure conditions[3]	1.8	81.3
Neutral conditions[4]	8.7	71.4

Sources: IMF, Monitoring of IMF Arrangements (MONA) database; and authors' calculations.
[1] Sample average, per program, not adjusted for program length.
[2] Sample average, implemented conditions/total conditions, in percent.
[3] Conditions with identified impact on the overall balance.
[4] Revenue and expenditure conditions without a clear impact on the overall balance.

Table 2

Change in Fiscal Outcomes Three Years After End of IMF-Supported Programs[1]

(in percent of GDP)

	Overall Balance		Revenue and Grants		Expenditure and Net Lending	
	Change	Initial balance	Change	Initial revenues	Change	Initial expenditures
All countries						
Average	1.8	–4.4	–0.3	25.2	–2.0	29.2
Median	1.5	–3.7	0.0	24.2	–2.0	28.9
Of which:						
Nonprogram countries[2]						
Average	3.2	–4.5	0.4	27.0	–2.8	31.5
Median	2.4	–3.7	0.3	27.2	–2.6	31.5
Program countries						
Average	0.4	–4.2	–1.0	23.4	–1.2	27.0
Median	0.5	–3.7	–0.5	20.6	–0.8	24.7
Of which:						
Without structural conditions						
Average	–1.9	–2.9	–0.3	24.0	1.6	26.9
Median	–0.8	–2.7	0.2	22.2	1.0	24.2
With structural conditions						
Average	3.7	–6.3	–2.1	22.6	–5.2	27.1
Median	2.6	–5.9	–1.5	19.3	–4.7	25.4

Sources: IMF, World Economic Outlook database; authors' calculations.
[1] Three years after the end of the IMF-supported program *minus* the preprogram observation.
[2] 1999 for nonprogram countries. The median initial observation is 1993 and the median end-period observation is 1999.

conditionality, comprising about 50 percent of all conditions. While most fiscal conditions were designed as neutral with regard to the overall fiscal balance, some conditions were geared toward either higher revenue or lower expenditure. We classify all of those measures according to their expected revenue or expenditure impact (Table 1). Based on IMF country team assessments, close to ⅘ of all fiscal conditions were met.

Some Stylized Facts About Fiscal Developments in 1990s

Fiscal developments—besides the immediate, short-term impact of IMF-supported programs—are affected by the business cycle, political economy, and debt-sustainability factors. First, the impact of cyclical conditions was strong in our sample—while real GDP grew on average by 1.5 percent during 1993–94, the rate more than doubled to almost 4 percent during 1997–99. Second, the components of the overall fiscal balance were public choice variables, and voters decided how much tax they wanted to contribute and how they wanted the proceeds to be spent (Drazen, 2000). Third, debt sustainability constrained the fiscal stance: the deficits preferred by the electorate may not be sustainable (Hansson and Stuart, 2003).

The fiscal balance improved in ⅔ of all countries by an average of 2 percentage points of GDP between the preprogram and postprogram periods or between 1993 and 1999 for the nonprogram countries (Figure 1 and Table 2). The magnitude of the

Figure 1
Change in Overall Fiscal Balance
(in percent of GDP, 112 countries)

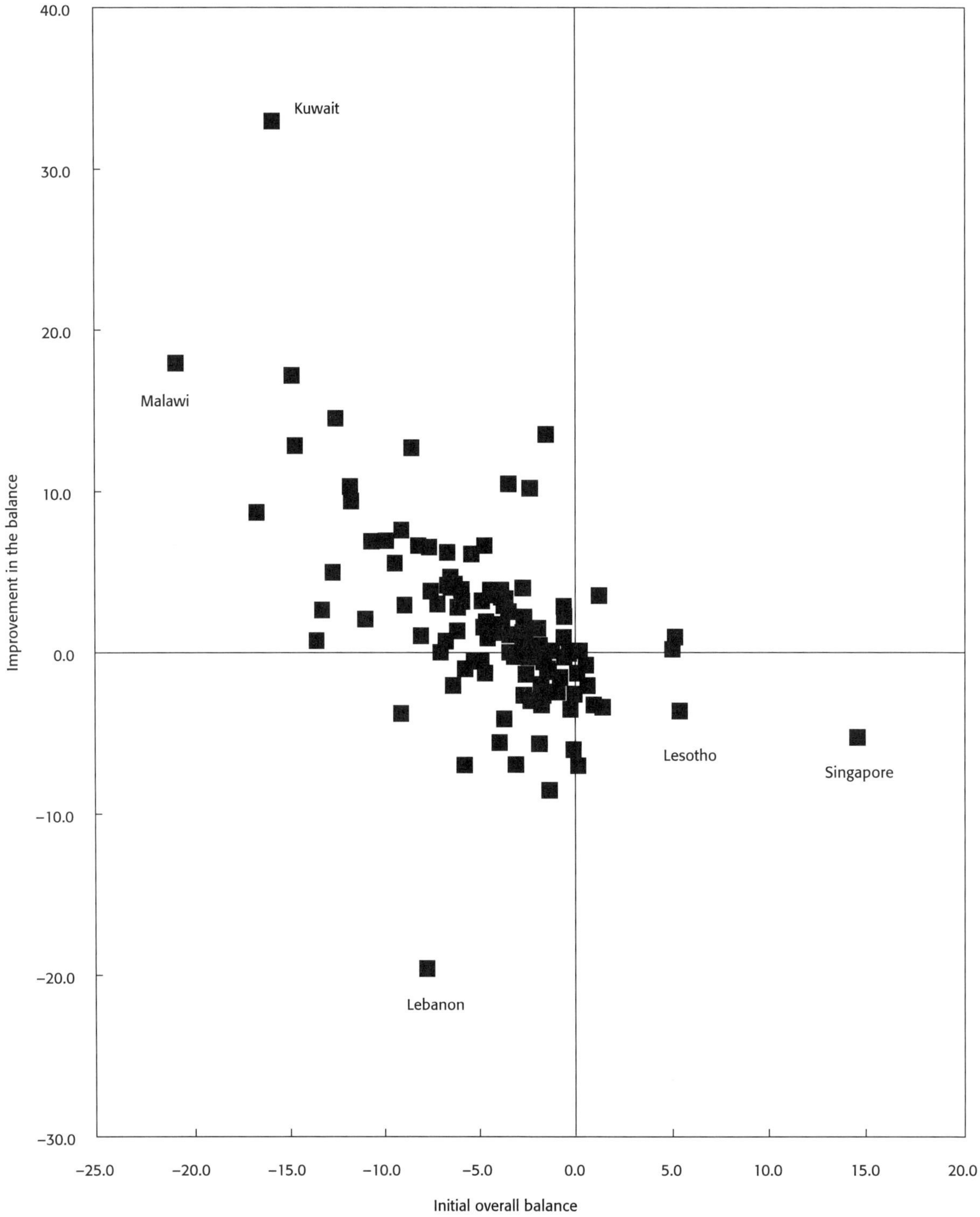

Sources: IMF, World Economic Outlook database; authors' calculations.

Note: The figure shows the change three years after the end of the IMF-supported program(s) or 1999 for nonprogram countries, compared with the initial observation. The median initial observation is 1993, and the median end-period observation is 1999.

Table 3
Selected Characteristics of Program and Nonprogram Countries

	Preprogram Developments						
	GDP per capita[1,2]	Current account[1,3]	Real GDP[1,4]	Terms of trade	Inflation[1,4]	Program Stoppage[5]	Postprogram Real GDP[4,6]
All countries							
Average	6,882	–4.4	1.5	0.8	229.0	n.a.	3.9
Median	1,954	–2.8	2.7	0.4	11.2	n.a.	3.5
Of which:							
Nonprogram countries							
Average	12,751	–2.3	3.9	0.9	6.1	n.a.	3.6
Median	12,772	–1.2	3.3	0.1	2.9	n.a.	3.1
Program countries							
Average	1,134	–6.6	–0.7	0.6	447.3	57.1	4.1
Median	774	–3.6	1.5	0.5	23.9	n.a.	3.7
Of which:							
Without structural conditions							
Average	1,511	–7.6	–1.5	2.0	610.2	40.3	3.5
Median	1,239	–3.2	1.2	0.5	28.1	n.a.	4.1
With structural conditions							
Average	587	–5.2	0.4	–1.5	211.1	70.0	5.0
Median	367	–3.9	2.8	1.0	19.9	n.a.	3.5

Sources: IMF, World Economic Outlook and Monitoring of IMF Arrangements (MONA) databases; authors' calculations.
Note: The abbreviation n.a. denotes not applicable.
[1] Average for 1993–94.
[2] In 1995 U.S. dollars.
[3] In percent of GDP.
[4] Percentage change.
[5] Program stoppage occurs if either (a) the scheduled program review was not completed, or (b) all scheduled reviews were completed but the subsequent annual arrangement was not approved. If a country had more than one program during this period, one stoppage overrides one or more successes.
[6] Average for 1997–99 for nonprogram countries.

postprogram fiscal improvement was not uniform, however, and nonprogram countries improved their fiscal balances more than program countries—by 3 percentage points versus ½ of a percentage point of cyclically nonadjusted GDP. Differences prevailed among program countries: while nonstructural program countries worsened their balances by some 2 percentage points of GDP, those with structural conditionality improved it by more than 3 percentage points of GDP. These findings are robust to the choice of the end-period observation: our results change little whether we assess them one, two, or three years after the end of the IMF-supported program.

How was the fiscal adjustment achieved? First, revenue adjustment was much weaker than expenditure adjustment. Revenue and grants declined in program countries and increased somewhat in nonprogram countries. The difference could not be accounted for by either the lowering of trade taxes or lower aid receipts. Regarding the former, we did not find any quantitative link between trade taxes and revenues. Regarding the latter, the contribution of grants is too small to account for the fall in the aggregate variable (Bulíř and Hamann, 2003). Second, the expenditure compression was strong in nonprogram and structural program countries (by 3 percentage points and 5 percentage points of GDP, respectively), while in nonstructural program countries postprogram expenditures expanded by 1½ percentage point of GDP.

The variability of program country results suggests that we control for exogenous and program-specific factors. First, the initial fiscal deficits in nonstructural program countries were smaller than those in structural program countries and did not pose such a threat to macroeconomic stability (Table 2). Second, the nature of the initial disequilibrium differed across countries: in nonstructural program countries, GDP declined more sharply prior to the program, and the countries' rates of inflation and GDP per capita were higher (Table 3). Third, structural conditionality programs had a higher incidence of program interruptions.[3] Finally, programs that did not include structural conditions were mostly short-term in nature, typically Stand-By Arrangements. In contrast, structural conditions were mostly applied in the context of the Enhanced Structural

[3] More conditions obviously increase the risk of missing some of them. However, missing one of the conditions does not stop a program—provided that the macroeconomic program has remained on track, the missed condition is typically waived.

Adjustment Facility (ESAF), which was succeeded by the Poverty Reduction and Growth Facility (PRGF), or the Extended Fund Facility (EFF).

Specification of Model

Fiscal developments are affected by various exogenous and country-specific effects and, therefore, we reexamine them in multivariate panel and cross-country regressions. The econometric investigation of the role of IMF-supported programs has traditionally been motivated by the following question: "Did the involvement of the IMF significantly improve the macroeconomic outcomes relative to what they would have been in the absence of an IMF-supported program?"[4] Macroeconomic outcomes, such as inflation or external balance, were described as a function of (a) policies that would have been observed in the absence of an IMF-supported program; (b) exogenous variables, such as terms-of-trade shocks or wars, and political economy variables, such as the stability of the government; and (c) the presence of an IMF-supported program.[5]

The simple model we have described has two drawbacks. First, "macroeconomic policies in the absence of an IMF-supported program" is an unobservable variable that has to be constructed in an ad hoc fashion. Second, the impact of IMF programs is ambiguous: an identical macroeconomic outcome can be achieved because of the confidence effect of a program, a cumulative impact of policies and IMF financing (the catalytic effect), or structural reforms.

The key empirical issue is the formulation of policies adopted in the absence of IMF involvement. These policies can be observed only for nonprogram countries and a counterfactual has to be estimated for program periods. Goldstein and Montiel (1986) suggested constructing a policy reaction function linking the changes in macroeconomic policies to the deviations of observed lagged outcomes from their preannounced target values, and lagged exogenous variables.

Our modification of the model is twofold. We attempted to separate the impact of the country's performance under the program, and structural conditionality. First, we checked compliance with program conditions. Successful programs were defined as those that either disbursed all committed resources without interruptions or those that were designed and executed as precautionary arrangements (see Ivanova and others, 2003). A statistically significant parameter would indicate that the IMF's emphasis on program implementation has some bearing on postprogram performance.

Second, we separated out the role of fiscal structural conditionality. We tested whether the presence and implementation of IMF fiscal structural conditionality led to fiscal outcomes that were statistically different from those without such conditionality. There was no need to establish counterfactual structural policies: similar fiscal structural reforms were introduced irrespective of the presence of an IMF-supported program.

Sample Selection and Estimation

We estimated the model in three steps. First, using data for nonprogram countries only, we estimated the policy reaction function for the relevant macroeconomic variables. Second, using the estimated parameters, we simulated macroeconomic policies in program countries to reflect what those policies would have been in the absence of an IMF-supported program. Hence, the vector of policies comprised actual observed policies in nonprogram countries and counterfactual policies in program countries. Third, we estimated the model for both program and nonprogram countries, capturing the impact of IMF-supported programs and structural conditionality residually.

We selected the 1993–96 period because of three considerations. First, this four-year period followed the IMF membership of transition economies in 1991–92, but preceded the "Asian" crisis of 1997–98. Second, during this period the IMF was deeply involved in structural reforms in developing economies. Third, we needed three years of after-program data for the General Evaluation Estimator (GEE) estimation, which made 1996 the latest permissible cutoff point in our sample.

Policy Reaction Function

The policy reaction function determined the stance of monetary, external, and incomes policies, respectively, as a function of the preannounced fiscal adjustment. The fiscal targets were derived from one-year-ahead World Economic Outlook (WEO) projections based on the annual policy discussions between the authorities and IMF staff, which reflect the authorities' policy stance for the period ahead.[6]

[4] Such a question can be answered using the General Evaluation Estimator (GEE), owing to Goldstein and Montiel (1988), who construct counterfactual economic policies first and then test the importance of IMF-supported programs. This approach was applied by, among others, Khan (1990); Conway (1994); and Dicks-Mireaux, Mecagni, and Schadler (2000).

[5] For a description of the model, see Bulíř and Moon (2004).

[6] The estimation was for the period 1992–97 with data for 48 countries that did not have an IMF-supported program during the 1991–97 period, or two years prior to 1991: Australia, Austria, The Bahamas, Bahrain, Belgium, Belize, Botswana, Canada, China, Colombia, Cyprus, Denmark, Fiji, Finland, France, Germany, Greece, Grenada, Hong Kong SAR, Ireland, Israel, Italy, Japan, Kuwait, Lebanon, Maldives, Malta, Mauritius, Myanmar, the Netherlands, New Zealand, Norway, Oman, Paraguay, Portugal, Qatar, Samoa, Singapore, the Solomon Islands, South Africa, Spain, St. Lucia, Swaziland, Sweden, Switzerland, the United Kingdom, the United States, and Vanuatu.

Table 4
Definitions of Variables

Variable	Description	Source[1]
Overall balance Revenue and grants Expenditure and net lending	Change from the preprogram year; in percentage of GDP	WEO
Real GDP growth	Gross domestic product at constant prices; year-on-year change, in percent	WEO
GDP per capita	Gross domestic product, in constant U.S. dollars	WEO
Aid-to-GDP ratio	External aid; change from the preprogram period	WDI
Inflation rate	Consumer price index (CPI); year-on-year change, in percent	WEO
Terms of trade	Terms of trade of goods and services; year-on-year change, in percent	WEO
Index of political cohesion	This variable measures the extent to which one party controls both the legislative and executive branches of the government.	DPI
Program stoppage	Program stoppage occurs if either (a) the scheduled program review was not completed; or (b) all scheduled reviews were completed but the subsequent annual arrangement was not approved.	IMMA
Current account balance	Estimated from the policy reaction function for program countries, actual data for nonprogram countries; in percentage of GDP	WEO
Nominal effective exchange rate	Estimated from the policy reaction function for program countries, actual data for nonprogram countries; change from the preprogram period, in percent	WEO
Real interest rate	Ex post real money market interest rate; deflated by the CPI; estimated from the policy reaction function for program countries, actual data for nonprogram countries; in percent	IFS
IMF program dummy	1 if the country had an IMF-supported program during 1993–96, 0 otherwise	MONA
Measures (count)	Number of fiscal measures (narrowly or broadly defined) adjusted for program duration	MONA
Measures (implementation)	Number of implemented fiscal measures (narrowly or broadly defined) adjusted for program duration	MONA

[1] The abbreviations stand for the following data sources: IMF, World Economic Outlook (WEO); World Bank, World Development Indicators (WDI); World Bank, 2001, Database of Political Institutions (DPI), Version 3.0; Ivanova and others (2003) (IMMA); IMF, International Financial Statistics (IFS) and Monitoring of IMF Arrangements (MONA) databases.

The difference between this projection and the current fiscal outcome then measured the fiscal disequilibrium to which the authorities reacted with changes in policy instruments in the coming year. Three policy variables were used: (a) the ex post real interest rate (the representative nominal interest rate *minus* the consumer price index, CPI); (b) the nominal effective exchange rate (NEER); and (c) the current account balance as a percentage of GDP (Table 4).

The set of potential endogenous policy variables was—using the general-to-specific approach—narrowed to five variables: (a) the change in the overall fiscal balance in percentage of GDP; (b) the terms-of-trade index; (c) the oil price (the international crude oil price in U.S. dollars); (d) the political cohesion index (a measure of political stability); and (e) an Organization for Economic Cooperation and Development (OECD) intercept dummy (Table 5). The estimated coefficients were statistically significant and corresponded to basic intuition: higher fiscal deficits were associated with higher current account deficits; improvements in the terms of trade were associated with narrower current account deficits; looser fiscal policy was associated with tighter monetary policy; developed countries tended to lower real interest rates; and so on. Only one political economy variable was significant: if one party controlled the government, the current account balance was more likely to improve and vice versa.

Table 5
Estimates of Policy Reaction Function
(heteroskedasticity-consistent, feasible GLS regression estimates, t-statistics in parentheses)

Dependent Variable	Current Account Balance	Nominal Effective Exchange Rate	Real Interest Rate
Overall fiscal balance ($y_t^* - y_{t-1}$)	0.21346***	4.56403***	−3.59938**
	(6.10)	(2.59)	(2.50)
Terms of trade	−0.00005**	−0.11601***	−0.01507*
	(2.05)	(3.50)	(1.64)
International oil prices		0.66082***	0.11747**
		(3.56)	(2.31)
Political cohesion	0.00170**		
	(2.30)		
Dummy for OECD membership			−1.12769***
			(5.34)
Wald test of joint parameter significance (χ^2)	43.08***	13.35**	61.96***
Log-likelihood	667.0774	−1,012.315	−630.634
Number of observations	288	288	288

Source: Authors' estimates.
Notes: All variables, except the Organization for Economic Cooperation and Development (OECD) dummy, are in first differences. The superscripts ***, **, and * denote the rejection of the null hypothesis that the estimated coefficient is zero at the 1 percent, 5 percent, and 10 percent significance levels, respectively. GLS denotes generalized least squares.

Generalized Evaluation Estimator

We consider three target variables measuring fiscal developments: (a) the overall central government balance; (b) central government revenue and grants; and (c) central government expenditure and net lending, all expressed as percentages of GDP, in 64 countries that operated under IMF-supported programs[7] and 48 nonprogram countries during 1993–96. While the first target variable is intuitively preferable to the other variables as a measure of the fiscal stance, revenue and expenditure regressions are useful checks of government policies. The endogenous policy variables stemmed from the policy reaction function and the exogenous variables were two-year averages, lagged one period: the terms of trade, GDP per capita in constant U.S. dollars, foreign aid in percentage of GDP, the rate of inflation, and real GDP growth. Given the inclusion of the preprogram fiscal observation, the model in levels can be rewritten into one with the dependent variables in first differences.

This paper is primarily interested in the long-term effects of IMF-supported programs, knowing that in the short run, fiscal developments could be affected by temporary budgetary adjustment in the context of an IMF-supported arrangement.[8] We want to measure the impact of IMF-supported programs beyond the initial, short-term impact; and, hence, we considered fiscal variables one, two, and three years after the initial program ended, with 112, 109, and 97 observations, respectively. For example, if a country had a three-year program from January 1993 to December 1995, our fiscal variables in the one-, two-, and three-year GEE estimation were dated 1997, 1998, and 1999, respectively, with a preprogram observation of 1992. Thus, we compared program periods of different lengths: the time span between the

[7] The following 31 countries' IMF-supported program did not contain any structural conditions: Azerbaijan, Belarus, the Republic of Congo, Costa Rica, Croatia, the Czech Republic, the Dominican Republic, Egypt, El Salvador, Estonia, Georgia, Haiti, Hungary, Jordan, Kazakhstan, Latvia, Lesotho, the former Yugoslav Republic of Macedonia, Mexico, Moldova, Nicaragua, Panama, Peru, the Philippines, Poland, Romania, Sierra Leone, the Slovak Republic, Turkey, Uganda, and Uzbekistan. Thirty-three countries with structural conditions were as follows (numbers of fiscal conditions are in parentheses): Albania (10), Algeria (3), Benin (8), Bolivia (8), Bulgaria (0), Burkina Faso (14), Cambodia (16), Cameroon (5), the Central African Republic (7), Chad (10), Côte d'Ivoire (8), Ecuador (1), Equatorial Guinea (4), Gabon (1), Ghana (8), Guinea-Bissau (11), Guyana (3), Kenya (4), the Kyrgyz Republic (9), the Lao People's Democratic Republic (10), Lithuania (0), Malawi (8), Mauritania (13), Mongolia (3), Niger (1), Pakistan (4), Papua New Guinea (5), the Russian Federation (2), Senegal (8), Togo (6), Ukraine (1), Vietnam (3), and Zambia (4).

[8] Gupta and others (2002) reported that the probability of a reversal in fiscal adjustment was as high as 70 percent at the end of the second postprogram year. Three possible explanations are available for this finding. First, poor fiscal discipline or a lack of ownership caused the reversal. Second, the initial fiscal tightening was excessively tight, necessitating a subsequent fiscal stimulus. Finally, the initial adjustment was a mirage: the fiscal authority ran arrears vis-à-vis its suppliers, improving the cash balance and worsening the accrual balance.

preprogram and first postprogram observations was as short as two years and as long as four years. For nonprogram countries, we used 1997–99 data and a two-year average for the "preprogram" period in 1991–92.

Results in Full Sample

In general, we find that cyclical variables drove the fiscal developments and that the impact of macroeconomic policy variables was comparatively small (Tables 6–8). In all cases, the robust estimators were the autoregressive terms, real GDP growth, and the real rate of interest, the stance of monetary policy being a good measure of the general tightness of macroeconomic policies. In some cases, we also found inflation and certain conditionality variables to be significant. The dummy measuring program participation was statistically insignificant, implying that past IMF-supported programs did not make the medium-term fiscal adjustment softer or stronger—on average, program countries adjusted as much as nonprogram countries. Countries in programs without interruptions adjusted somewhat more, but these results were statistically insignificant.

The lack of in-sample variability in the structural conditionality variables and their overall substitutability suggest that these variables operated more like a dummy variable. Unlike Ivanova and others (2003), who looked at performance during IMF-supported programs, we did not find any statistically significant postprogram impact of the political stability variables. Neither did we find any systematic impact of the type of IMF-supported program, its length, or the repeated use of IMF credit. The only statistically significant regional dummy was the sub-Saharan Africa dummy.

Overall Balance

The change in the postprogram overall balance was predicted reasonably well by the preprogram overall balance (a bigger initial deficit was associated with a bigger improvement), lagged GDP growth (faster growth improved the balance), and the level of development (countries with higher GDP per capita improved their overall balance more than did countries with low GDP per capita)—see Table 6. These variables accounted for almost all of the explained variance of the dependent variable (50–60 percent).

Several other variables were either marginally significant or significant only in some regressions. One of them was the aid-to-GDP ratio, indicating some stabilizing impact of foreign aid inflows.[9] Moderate inflation was associated with improvements in the overall balance, while countries with average annual inflation of more than 50 percent worsened their fiscal position. Countries with tighter monetary policies had a stronger improvement in their overall balances, presumably as a result of generally tighter macroeconomic policies. The IMF program performance variables were statistically insignificant for the postprogram period, although the signs of their parameters were intuitive. Countries with program stoppages did worse than the average, while those without interruptions did better. The conditionality variables were all statistically insignificant.

Revenue and Grants

Revenue regressions explained much less of the variance of the dependent variable (20–30 percent), even though the results were also dominated by the preprogram revenue levels and cyclical effects (Table 7). The revenue-to-GDP ratio worsened in countries with larger-than-average initial revenue and it was inversely related to real GDP growth. Both results were intuitive: on the one hand, the tax burden peaked in many countries in the late 1980s, and on the other hand, fast-growing economies did not need to increase their tax-to-GDP ratios.

The aid-to-GDP ratio was positive, but statistically insignificant in all but the one-year-after-the-program estimates. Inflation worsened revenue in most regressions—presumably through the Tanzi-Oliveira collection lag—and no nonlinearity in the inflationary impact was found. The real interest rate was significant and negative, indicating that tight macroeconomic conditions were not conducive to revenue collection.

We did not find any statistically significant impact of IMF-supported programs, although the parameter signs were consistently negative. Good performance under the program was linked to improved revenue collection by some 2 percent of GDP, but this marginally significant effect disappeared in the third year after the program. All but one of the variables describing the quantity of structural measures were statistically insignificant, although they all came with a negative sign. The latter results suggest that revenue-enhancing measures, and perhaps also technical assistance provided to program countries, failed to provide a sustainable increase in the revenue-to-GDP ratio.

Expenditure and Net Lending

The variance of the expenditure-to-GDP ratio was mostly explained by preprogram expenditure levels, the real rate of growth, and monetary policy (20–30 percent) (Table 8). Unlike in previous regressions, we found strong nonlinearity compared with past expenditure-to-GDP ratios: the expenditure-to-GDP ratio declined in countries with lower-than-average preprogram expenditure ratios, but increased in countries with higher-than-average levels thereof. The former group comprised mostly poorer

[9] The improvement in the overall balance was partly tautological, because total revenues included grants, a part of foreign aid.

Table 6

The Overall Balance After the End of the Program: Estimates of GEE

(heteroskedasticity-consistent OLS, t-statistics in parentheses)

	One Year After End of Program				Two Years After End of Program				Three Years After End of Program			
	(1)	(2)	(3)	(4)	(5)	(6)	(7)	(8)	(9)	(10)	(11)	(12)
Control variables												
Constant	−0.0274	−0.0264	−0.0203	−0.0372	−0.0296	−0.0332	−0.0308	−0.0297	−0.0356	−0.0433	−0.0429	−0.0487
	(2.09)	(2.47)	(1.95)	(3.99)	(1.86)	(2.48)	(2.23)	(4.52)	(2.92)	(4.41)	(4.04)	(6.78)
Initial value of the dependent variable	−0.7276	−0.7541	−0.7219	−0.7337	−0.9019	−0.9076	−0.8734	−0.9011	−1.0536	−1.0553	−1.0379	−1.0394
	(8.67)	(7.47)	(9.21)	(8.20)	(9.84)	(9.21)	(9.45)	(8.91)	(7.45)	(6.99)	(7.18)	(7.33)
Lagged real GDP growth	0.0039	0.0040	0.0039	0.0047	0.0016	0.0017	0.0019	0.0020	0.0025	0.0025	0.0025	0.0024
	(3.09)	(3.12)	(3.31)	(4.47)	(1.46)	(1.65)	(1.66)	(2.36)	(4.02)	(3.96)	(3.91)	(3.88)
GDP per capita	6.73E-7	5.87E-7	4.32E-7	9.79E-7	6.05E-7	7.13E-7	6.70E-7		9.47E-7	1.27E-6	1.27E-6	1.54E-6
	(1.68)	(1.67)	(1.07)	(3.52)	(1.02)	(1.32)	(1.18)		(1.46)	(2.15)	(2.04)	(4.61)
Aid-to-GDP ratio	0.0011	0.0011	0.0009		0.0010	0.0011	0.0011	0.0009	0.0006	0.0006	0.0007	
	(1.09)	(1.11)	(0.95)		(1.64)	(1.81)	(1.71)	(2.60)	(0.667	(0.63)	(0.70)	
Lagged inflation rate	0.0002	0.0001	0.0001	0.0002	−5.62E-5	9.22E-5	−1.74E-5		0.0001	0.0001	0.0001	0.0001
	(1.09)	(2.14)	(2.14)	(3.08)	(0.12)	(0.00)	(0.04)		(2.39)	(4.18)	(3.77)	(3.98)
High-inflation dummy[1]	−0.0474	−0.0366	−0.0386	−0.0441	−0.0015	−0.0024	−0.0027		−0.0043	−0.0097	−0.0111	
	(2.71)	(2.43)	(2.56)	(3.77)	(0.04)	(0.06)	(0.07)		(0.17)	(0.44)	(0.50)	
Lagged terms of trade	−0.0007	−0.0007	−0.0008		−0.0001	−0.0001	−0.0002		0.0002	0.0002	0.0001	0.0002
	(1.26)	(1.16)	(1.44)		(0.42)	(0.50)	(0.68)		(2.81)	(2.42)	(0.95)	(3.41)
Policy variables												
Real interest rate	1.68E-6	1.41E-6	1.48E-6		3.10E-6	2.24E-6	2.20E-6	3.09E-6	3.73E-6	3.15E-6	3.04E-6	2.92E-6
	(1.18)	(1.13)	(1.19)		(3.24)	(2.92)	(2.92)	(4.03)	(2.88)	(4.12)	(3.58)	(5.26)
Nominal exchange rate	2.20E-5	5.11E-6	2.13E-5		−6.75E-5	−7.25E-5	−6.23E-5		0.0002	0.0002	0.0002	0.0002
	(0.33)	(0.09)	(0.37)		(0.98)	(0.93)	(0.83)		(3.88)	(3.78)	(3.43)	(3.91)
Current account balance	0.1227	0.1234	0.1062		0.0636	0.0636	0.0506		0.0505	0.0456	0.0419	
	(1.18)	(1.20)	(1.13)		(0.92)	(0.90)	(0.78)		(0.60)	(0.53)	(0.53)	
IMF program performance												
IMF program dummy	0.0157				0.0132				0.0023			
	(0.89)				(0.82)				(0.14)			
Program stoppage	−0.0114				−0.0179				−0.0177			
	(0.85)				(1.62)				(1.07)			
"Successful IMF program" dummy[2]		0.0155				0.0145				0.0049		
		(1.01)				(1.35)				(0.42)		
Conditionality variables												
Fiscal measures (count)[3]			−0.0218				−0.0315				0.0301	
			(0.55)				(0.86)				(0.57)	
R^2	0.515	0.515	0.509	0.453	0.583	0.579	0.573	0.529	0.630	0.621	0.622	0.614
Log-likelihood	195.5	195.6	194.8	188.8	205.01	204.5	203.7	198.4	173.6	172.5	172.6	171.7
Number of observations	112	112	112	112	109	109	109	109	97	97	97	97
Normality test [$\chi^2(2,2)$]	64.25	64.72	75.90	131.68	9.73	12.57	11.98	26.66	32.55	32.94	34.24	48.06
Heteroskedasticity test (F)	1.70	1.89	2.10	0.81	0.95	0.97	0.69	0.66	0.50	0.46	0.54	0.67

Source: Authors' estimates.

Notes: GEE denotes Generalized Evaluation Estimator. OLS denotes ordinary least squares. Very small numbers are denoted as E-k, where E indicates the base of 10 and k indicates the position of the decimal point.

[1] The dummy takes the value of 1 if the lagged, two-year average inflation was higher than 50 percent a year; and 0 otherwise.

[2] The dummy is equal to 1 if either all committed resources were disbursed or if the program was precautionary; and 0 otherwise.

[3] Includes all structural measures with fiscal implications.

Table 7

Revenue and Grants After End of Program: Estimates of GEE

(heteroskedasticity-consistent OLS, t-statistics in parentheses)

	One Year After End of Program				Two Years After End of Program				Three Years After End of Program			
	(1)	(2)	(3)	(4)	(5)	(6)	(7)	(8)	(9)	(10)	(11)	(12)
Control variables												
Constant	0.0452	0.0395	0.0438	0.0321	0.0483	0.0462	0.0471	0.0425	0.0582	0.0420	0.0420	0.0514
	(2.95)	(2.98)	(3.16)	(2.74)	(4.31)	(3.85)	(3.96)	(3.99)	(4.14)	(3.65)	(3.71)	(4.35)
Initial value of the dependent variable	−0.1203	−0.1278	−0.1180	−0.1115	−0.1390	−0.1390	−0.1390	−0.1317	−0.1403	−0.1310	−0.1355	−0.1434
	(2.24)	(2.40)	(2.20)	(1.98)	(3.16)	(3.12)	(3.11)	(2.92)	(2.89)	(2.60)	(2.72)	(2.90)
Lagged real GDP growth	−0.0016	−0.0014	−0.0017		−0.0015	−0.0015	−0.0015	−0.0019	−0.0019	−0.0019	−0.0017	−0.0022
	(0.85)	(0.75)	(0.88)		(1.43)	(1.44)	(1.43)	(1.63)	(2.42)	(2.27)	(1.91)	(3.01)
GDP per capita	4.28E-8	2.97E-7	7.16E-8		3.38E-8	4.71E-8	6.36E-10		−3.85E-8	1.64E-7	1.77E-7	
	(0.09)	(0.70)	(0.18)		(0.07)	(0.09)	(0.00)		(0.75)	(0.34)	(0.40)	
Aid-to-GDP ratio	0.0018	0.0019	0.0016	0.0017	0.0006	0.0007	0.0006		0.0008	0.0007	0.0007	
	(3.21)	(3.60)	(2.90)	(3.71)	(0.91)	(0.99)	(0.80)		(1.41)	(1.09)	(1.04)	
Lagged inflation rate	−0.0002	−0.0002	−0.0002	−0.0002	−0.0006	−0.0006	−0.0006	−0.0006	−2.07E-5	−4.28E-5	−3.63E-5	
	(1.53)	(1.43)	(1.58)	(2.06)	(2.15)	(2.35)	(2.37)	(2.74)	(0.52)	(0.93)	(0.82)	
Lagged terms of trade	0.0002	0.0003	0.0001		−0.0003	−0.0003	−0.0002		3.51E-5	6.29E-6	8.17E-5	
	(0.34)	(0.61)	(0.14)		(1.95)	(2.10)	(1.53)		(0.33)	(0.05)	(0.55)	
Policy variables												
Real interest rate	−5.13E-6	−4.96E-6	−4.50E-6	−4.53E-6	−4.95E-6	−4.91E-6	−4.75E-6	−4.82E-6	−3.69E-6	−3.06E-6	−2.89E-6	−4.16E-6
	(2.36)	(2.36)	(2.34)	(2.52)	(4.20)	(3.86)	(3.87)	(3.61)	(3.54)	(3.69)	(3.72)	(3.87)
Nominal exchange rate	−4.14E-5	−6.31E-5	−4.76E-5		−7.75E-5	−7.89E-5	−8.14E-5		5.46E-5	7.40E-5	7.24E-5	
	(0.81)	(1.06)	(0.89)		(1.55)	(1.53)	(1.62)		(0.77)	(1.01)	(0.97)	
Current account balance	0.0303	0.0532	0.0246		0.0212	0.0253	0.0201		0.0328	0.0346	0.0391	
	(0.67)	(1.19)	(0.52)		(0.44)	(0.53)	(0.41)		(0.93)	(0.93)	(1.05)	
IMF program performance												
IMF program dummy	−0.0051				−0.0027				−0.0216			−0.0210
	(0.46)				(0.23)				(1.99)			(2.34)
"Successful IMF program" dummy[1]		0.0170				0.0020				−0.0053		
		(1.31)				(1.17)				(0.48)		
Conditionality variables												
Revenue measures (count)[2]			−0.0261				−0.0091				−0.0188	
			(1.46)				(0.73)				(0.81)	
R^2	0.214	0.228	0.239	0.189	0.235	0.234	0.238	0.195	0.266	0.239	0.242	0.240
Log-likelihood	191.8	192.8	193.6	190.0	197.9	197.9	198.1	195.2	175.1	173.3	173.5	173.4
Number of observations	112	112	112	112	109	109	109	109	97	97	97	97
Normality test [$\chi^2(2,2)$]	32.55	29.71	29.21	44.14	20.62	19.71	20.66	22.14	18.34	16.13	15.77	19.40
Heteroskedasticity test (*F*)	0.99	0.92	0.74	2.48	0.30	0.30	0.25	1.34	0.18	0.18	2.75	0.77

Source: Authors' estimates.

Notes: GEE denotes Generalized Evaluation Estimator; OLS denotes ordinary least squares. Very small numbers are denoted as E-k, where E indicates the base of 10 and k indicates the position of the decimal point.

[1] The dummy is equal to 1 if either all committed resources were disbursed or if the program was precautionary; and 0 otherwise.

[2] Includes all structural measures with revenue-improving implications.

Table 8

Expenditure and Net Lending After End of Program: Estimates of GEE

(heteroskedasticity-consistent OLS, t-statistics in parentheses)

	One Year After End of Program				Two Years After End of Program				Three Years After End of Program			
	(1)	(2)	(3)	(4)	(5)	(6)	(7)	(8)	(9)	(10)	(11)	(12)
Control variables												
Constant	−0.3782	−0.3864	−0.4089	−0.4362	−0.1969	−0.1958	−0.2240	−0.2897	−0.2080	−0.2133	−0.2382	−0.2695
	(3.66)	(3.88)	(4.06)	(4.09)	(1.67)	(1.72)	(1.80)	(2.45)	(1.81)	(1.90)	(2.07)	(2.69)
Initial value of dependent variable	−1.9127	−1.8570	−2.0240	−2.1711	−1.2162	−1.1908	−1.3675	−1.5827	−1.3773	−1.3504	−1.5737	−1.6354
	(4.26)	(4.60)	(4.82)	(4.84)	(2.90)	(2.86)	(3.07)	(3.71)	(3.32)	(3.34)	(3.90)	(4.79)
Initial value of dependent variable, squared	1.7620	1.7113	1.8882	2.0133	1.0374	1.0112	1.1944	1.4028	1.1697	1.1443	1.3550	1.4177
	(3.98)	(4.27)	(4.49)	(4.48)	(2.35)	(2.32)	(2.52)	(3.07)	(3.98)	(2.66)	(3.13)	(3.77)
Lagged real GDP growth	−0.0035	−0.0032	−0.0036	−0.0024	−0.0016	−0.0018	−0.0017		−0.0045	−0.0045	−0.0038	−0.0036
	(2.05)	(2.03)	(2.20)	(1.80)	(0.97)	(1.02)	(1.15)		(4.14)	(4.15)	(4.27)	(5.94)
GDP per capita	−9.88E-9	6.69E-7	−1.76E-7		−3.58E-7	−1.42E-7	−8.53E-7		−8.42E-7	−4.08E-7	−1.41E-7	
	(0.02)	(1.33)	(0.37)		(0.52)	(0.25)	(1.40)		(1.43)	(0.85)	(2.95)	
Lagged inflation rate	−0.0001	−0.0001	−0.0001		−0.0005	−0.0005	−0.0005		−0.0001	−0.0001	−1.16E-5	
	(1.31)	(1.33)	(1.70)		(1.31)	(1.30)	(1.51)		(1.58)	(1.73)	(0.22)	
Policy variables												
Real interest rate	−5.26E-6	−4.97E-6	−3.48E-6	−1.73E-6	−4.03E-6	−4.13E-6	−2.72E-6	−1.80E-6	−3.65E-6	−3.54E-6	−1.47E-6	−2.57E-6
	(2.78)	(2.90)	(2.74)	(1.70)	(2.65)	(2.57)	(2.50)	(1.72)	(2.59)	(2.65)	(1.65)	(2.47)
Nominal exchange rate	−1.58E-5	−2.94E-5	−1.97E-5		3.63E-5	2.95E-5	1.95E-5		−4.34E-5	−3.96E-5	−2.53E-5	
	(0.21)	(0.38)	(0.36)		(0.90)	(0.69)	(0.58)		(0.44)	(0.38)	(0.29)	
Current account balance	−0.1054	−0.0887	−0.0953		−0.0361	−0.0246	−0.0282		−0.0131	0.0098	−0.0165	
	(1.66)	(1.24)	(1.71)		(0.75)	(0.51)	(0.64)		(0.22)	(0.18)	(0.40)	
IMF program performance												
IMF program dummy	−0.0191				−0.0043				−0.0108			
	(1.00)				(0.25)				(0.54)			
"Successful IMF program" dummy[1]		0.0138				0.0107				0.0180		
		(0.88)				(0.67)				(0.85)		
Conditionality variables												
Structural conditionality (dummy)[2]			−0.0407	−0.0389			−0.0368	−0.0324			−0.0620	−0.0497
			(3.10)	(3.19)			(3.20)	(4.01)			(4.49)	(4.12)
R^2	0.454	0.449	0.505	0.470	0.319	0.322	0.371	0.337	0.448	0.452	0.534	0.503
Log-likelihood	176.8	176.3	182.3	178.4	166.7	166.9	171.1	168.2	144.1	144.6	152.5	149.3
Number of observations	112	112	112	112	109	109	109	109	97	97	97	97
Normality test [$\chi^2(2,2)$]	16.41	24.12	9.26	22.82	26.83	25.54	23.63	23.22	21.23	16.34	18.94	26.62
Heteroskedasticity test (*F*)	1.36	1.05	1.02	1.55	0.52	0.77	0.64	0.96	0.72	1.48	0.92	0.39

Source: Authors' estimates.

Notes: GEE denotes Generalized Evaluation Estimator; OLS denotes ordinary least squares. Very small numbers are denoted as E-k, where E indicates the base of 10 and k indicates the position of the decimal point.

[1] The dummy is equal to 1 if either all committed resources were disbursed or if the program was precautionary; and 0 otherwise.

[2] The dummy takes the value of 1 if the IMF-supported program included any structural conditions; and 0 otherwise.

Table 9

Fiscal Developments in Structural Conditionality Countries Relative to Nonstructural Conditionality Countries

(heteroskedasticity-consistent OLS regression estimates of structural conditionality and sub-Saharan Africa dummies, t-statistics in parentheses)

		Overall Balance	Revenue and Grants	Expenditure and Net Lending
One-year-after-program sample	SC dummy	−0.0018	−0.0106	−0.0192
		(0.17)	(0.72)	(1.15)
	Africa dummy	0.0327**	0.0258*	−0.0116
		(2.33)	(1.92)	(0.79)
Two-years-after-program sample	SC dummy	0.0163	−0.0224*	−0.0564***
		(1.28)	(1.73)	(2.94)
	Africa dummy	−0.0035	0.0203	0.0229
		(0.26)	(1.32)	(1.02)
Three-years-after-program sample	SC dummy	0.0325**	−0.0286***	−0.0810***
		(2.46)	(3.30)	(4.42)
	Africa dummy	−0.0126	0.0565***	0.0714***
		(0.54)	(4.27)	(3.33)

Source: Authors' estimates.

Notes: The superscripts ***, **, and * denote the rejection of the null hypothesis that the estimated coefficient is zero at the 1 percent, 5 percent, and 10 percent significance levels, respectively. OLS denotes ordinary least squares. SC denotes structural conditionality.

countries with structural conditionality programs, while the latter group comprised richer countries with nonstructural conditionality. Countries that grew faster and those with tight monetary policies also lowered their expenditure-to-GDP ratios.

We did not find any statistically significant impact of IMF-supported programs on expenditure developments. The structural conditionality variables were negative and significant, suggesting relative expenditure compression in countries with structural conditionality of 2 percentage points of GDP or more. It is problematic to distinguish whether expenditures that were cut were wasteful or whether the compression was excessive. We can only conjecture that the gradually increasing value of the structural conditionality parameter points to the former explanation, as expenditure compression accelerated after the end of the IMF arrangement. This observation is also consistent with a body of evidence that social and capital spending were protected during the program's existence (Abed and others, 1998).

Are Countries with Programs Containing Structural Conditionality "Different"?

The finding that conditionality variables were insignificant for all but the expenditure regressions is puzzling. We do not see a unique explanation for these findings, as they can be justified by alternative relationships. First, these results may imply that IMF-supported programs mechanically compensated with additional conditionality for historically poor performance, owing to deep-rooted structural weaknesses, or persistent shocks, or a lack of a reform drive, or a combination of all of those. Without addressing the causes of the past performance, additional conditions would not affect the fiscal performance. Second, IMF conditionality and donor technical assistance in the fiscal area may have failed to bring about sustained fiscal improvements, especially if the reforms were not supported by the public.

To understand better the developments in structural conditionality countries, we reestimated our regressions for the program countries only (Table 9).[10] While the size and signs of the individual coefficients were broadly unchanged compared to Tables 6–8, their statistical significance declined predictably with the loss of degrees of freedom. We found that the overall balance improvement was larger in countries with structural conditionality than in other program countries by about ½ and 3 percentage points of GDP. At the same time, revenue and grants declined by 2 additional percentage points of GDP in structural conditionality countries. Finally, the expenditure and net lending compression increased in structural conditionality countries over time—from about 2 percentage points of GDP one year after the program to 8 percentage points of

[10] The sample sizes for one-, two-, and three-year-after-the-program regressions were 64, 61, and 49 observations, respectively. The full set of results is available on request from the authors.

GDP three years after the program—and these results were statistically significant.

We also checked for the presence of fiscal reversals in low-income countries and found this effect to be at work only for the sub-Saharan Africa region. While African countries started with a better-than-average postprogram overall balance of more than 3 percent of GDP, this result disappeared in the second year after the end of the program period. On the expenditure side, the sub-Saharan average was statistically indistinguishable from the rest initially, but by the third year expenditures were higher than the average by 7 percentage points of GDP. Revenue performance in sub-Saharan Africa was better than average, although not sufficient to offset the expenditure increase.

These results seem to suggest that countries with structural conditionality were indeed different from the other program countries. First, they were subject to more pronounced shocks than were other program countries; for example, their terms of trade were twice as volatile. Second, the effort to address revenue weaknesses in those countries through structural conditionality failed, most likely because conditionality was a poor substitute for homegrown reform. Finally, postprogram fiscal performance in those countries was driven by accelerating expenditure compression, which may not be a bad thing, provided, for example, that the preprogram level of spending was wasteful or that a statist budget was replaced with a less intrusive one.

Concluding Remarks

This paper presents empirical tests of the relevance of IMF structural conditionality for postprogram fiscal performance in a large sample of countries during the 1990s. Although the overall balance improved in most countries, the impact of IMF-supported programs was not statistically significant, owing to the large variance in the sample of program countries. In structural conditionality countries, revenue declined slightly and expenditure declined significantly. In contrast, in countries that had nonstructural conditionality programs, revenue remained stable and expenditure increased somewhat. The postprogram statistical insignificance of IMF-supported programs indicates that program participation did not make the fiscal adjustment automatically softer—on average, program countries adjusted as much as nonprogram countries and fiscal adjustment continued in most countries even after the completion of the IMF-supported arrangement. The business cycle strongly influenced all fiscal variables, and an impact of the general macroeconomic stance was detectable as well.

Our results highlight the difficulty in identifying the impact of structural conditionality. Several effects seem to be in play. First, we found some evidence that programs with too many structural conditions had worse postprogram results than those with fewer program conditions. Second, we found no quantitative evidence that structural conditionality aimed at raising revenue was successful. Third, postprogram expenditure compression clearly was much stronger in countries with structural conditionality, but the risk of reversal was higher too, especially in sub-Saharan Africa.

The findings in this paper are not definitive and the possibilities for further research are extensive. First, more work is needed to examine the role of initial shocks, structural weaknesses, political economy, and regime-specific effects, such as the choice of the exchange rate regime. Second, the policy reaction function can be specified differently, reflecting, for example, policies that would stabilize the debt-to-GDP ratio or that would be based on "fiscal rules." Finally, some of the issues, such as the appropriateness of the initial revenue and expenditure levels, cannot be addressed adequately in a cross-country model and need to be investigated in case studies.

References

Abed, George T., Liam Ebrill, Sanjeev Gupta, Benedict Clements, Ronald McMorran, Anthony Pellechio, Jerald Schiff, and Marijn Verhoeven, 1998, *Fiscal Reforms in Low-Income Countries*, IMF Occasional Paper No. 160 (Washington: International Monetary Fund).

Barro, Robert J., and Jong-Wha Lee, 2002, "IMF Programs: Who Is Chosen and What Are the Effects?" NBER Working Paper No. 8951 (Cambridge, Massachusetts: National Bureau of Economic Research).

Bird, Graham, 1996, "Borrowing from the IMF: The Policy Implications of Recent Empirical Research," *World Development*, Vol. 24, No. 11, pp. 1753–60.

______, 2001, "IMF Programmes: Is There a Conditionality Laffer Curve?" *World Economics*, Vol. 2, No. 2, pp. 29–49.

______, and Dane Rowlands, 2002, "Do IMF Programmes Have a Catalytic Effect on Other Capital Flows?" *Oxford Development Studies*, Vol. 30, No. 3, pp. 229–49.

Bulíř, Aleš, and A. Javier Hamann, 2003, "Aid Volatility: An Empirical Assessment," *Staff Papers*, International Monetary Fund, Vol. 50, No. 1, pp. 64–89.

Bulíř, Aleš, and Soojin Moon, 2004, "Is Fiscal Adjustment More Durable When the IMF is Involved?" *Comparative Economic Studies*, Vol. 46 (September), pp. 373–99.

Collier, Paul, Patrick Guillaumont, Sylviane Guillaumont, and Jan W. Gunning, 1997, "Redesigning Conditionality," *World Development*, Vol. 25, No. 9, pp. 1399–1407.

Conway, Patrick, 1994, "IMF Lending Programs: Participation and Impact," *Journal of Development Economics*, Vol. 45 (December), pp. 365–91.

Dicks-Mireaux, Louis, Mauro Mecagni, and Susan Schadler, 2000, "Evaluating the Effect of IMF Lending to Low-Income Countries," *Journal of Development Economics*, Vol. 61 (April), pp. 495–525.

Drazen, Allen, 2000, *Political Economy in Macroeconomics* (Princeton, New Jersey: Princeton University Press).

Ghosh, Atish, Timothy Lane, Marianne Schulze-Ghattas, Aleš Bulíř, A. Javier Hamann, and Alex Mourmouras, 2002, *IMF-Supported Programs in Capital Account Crises*, IMF Occasional Paper No. 210 (Washington: International Monetary Fund).

Goldstein, Morris, 2000, "IMF Structural Programs," paper prepared for National Bureau of Economic Research Conference on "Economic and Financial Crises in Emerging Market Economies," held in Woodstock, Vermont in October.

________, and Peter J. Montiel, 1986, "Evaluating Fund Stabilization Programs with Multicountry Data: Some Methodological Pitfalls," *Staff Papers*, International Monetary Fund, Vol. 33 (June), pp. 304–44.

Guitián, Manuel, 1981, *Fund Conditionality: Evolution of Principles and Practices*, IMF Pamphlet Series, No. 38 (Washington: International Monetary Fund).

Gupta, Sanjeev, Benedict Clements, Emanuele Baldacci, and Carlos Mulas-Granados, 2002, "Expenditure Composition, Fiscal Adjustment, and Growth in Low-Income Countries, IMF Working Paper 02/77 (Washington: International Monetary Fund). This paper also appears, in somewhat different form, as Chapter 5 in this volume.

Hansson, Åsa, and Charles Stuart, 2003, "Peaking of Fiscal Sizes of Government," *European Journal of Political Economy*, Vol. 19 (November), pp. 669–84.

International Monetary Fund (IMF), 2001, *Conditionality in Fund-Supported Programs—Overview*. Available on the Web at *http://www.imf.org/external/np/pdr/cond/2001/eng/overview/index.htm*.

Ivanova, Anna, Wolfgang Mayer, Alex Mourmouras, and George Anayiotos, 2003, "What Determines the Success or Failure of Fund-Supported Programs?" IMF Working Paper 03/8 (Washington: International Monetary Fund). This paper also appears, in somewhat different form, as Chapter 10 in this volume.

Khan, Mohsin S., 1990, "The Macroeconomic Effects of Fund-Supported Adjustment Programs," *Staff Papers*, International Monetary Fund, Vol. 37 (June), pp. 195–231.

________, and Sunil Sharma, 2001, "IMF Conditionality and Country Ownership of Programs," IMF Working Paper 01/142 (Washington: International Monetary Fund). This paper also appears, in somewhat different form, as Chapter 7 in this volume.

Knight, Malcolm, and Julio A. Santaella, 1997, "Economic Determinants of IMF Financial Arrangements," *Journal of Development Economics*, Vol. 54 (December), pp. 405–36.

Schadler, Susan, Adam Bennett, Maria Carkovic, Louis Dicks-Mireaux, Mauro Mecagni, James H.J. Morsink, and Miguel A. Savastano, 1995, *IMF Conditionality: Experience Under Stand-By and Extended Arrangements*, IMF Occasional Paper No. 128 (Washington: International Monetary Fund).

World Bank, 2001, "Database of Political Institutions," Version 3.0 (Washington: World Bank).

CHAPTER

15 Evaluating IMF-Supported Programs in the 1990s: The Importance of Taking Explicit Account of Stoppages

Chuling Chen and Alun Thomas[1]

This paper contributes to the literature on evaluating the impact of IMF-supported programs on three key macroeconomic variables: inflation, the budget position, and growth. The paper documents the importance of distinguishing between completed programs and those that terminated prematurely, showing that they have significantly different impacts on these targets. While stopped programs are associated with higher inflation and budget deficits, and lower growth relative to periods without a program, completed programs are marginally associated with increased growth three years after the termination of the program.

Introduction

During the past two decades, a number of studies have explored whether IMF programs are effective in improving participating countries' current account, inflation, and growth outcomes. These studies developed different methodologies and used various datasets, and while coming to different conclusions on specific economic variables, the general thrust of the results is that IMF programs do not generally affect growth or inflation. This paper aims to provide some new insights on the effectiveness of IMF programs by using a new database for countries that did not participate in any IMF programs during the 1980s but were engaged in one or more programs in the 1990s. The sample characteristics of the data were chosen to better capture the independent effect of IMF programs on three target variables: inflation, budget conditions, and growth.

One of the major novelties of this approach is that it emphasizes the importance of implementing IMF programs by distinguishing between programs that were implemented successfully and those that were stopped prematurely. Surprisingly, this distinction has been largely absent from previous analyses of the effects of IMF programs. Indeed, stoppages are fairly prevalent in IMF programs, amounting to almost 40 percent of all programs during the 1992–2001 period. Distinguishing between IMF programs that were implemented successfully and those that broke down is essential in properly evaluating the effectiveness of IMF programs. The only study that previously addressed this issue was Killick (1995), which distinguished between these two groups by using the ratio of disbursements to committed amounts as controls.

The question of whether IMF-supported programs have significant independent effects on the macroeconomic outcomes of particular countries is difficult to answer because it requires the construction of a counterfactual indicating what policies and outcomes would have resulted in the absence of an IMF program. Since the mid-1980s, several papers have considered how to construct a counterfactual for such exercises through differentiating the effects of counterfactual policies from exogenous developments, initial conditions, and IMF support. The methodology that has been most widely applied, developed by Goldstein and Montiel (1986), uses policy reaction functions estimated for countries that did not have support from a particular international financial institution (IFI) to approximate the counterfactual for countries that did have IFI backing for their programs. Unfortunately, several recent studies have cast doubt on the appropriateness and reliability of this method. For instance, Dicks-Mireaux, Mecagni, and Schadler (2000) did diagnostic tests to show that the assumptions underlying the methodology may not hold.

Another method of evaluating the effects of IMF programs is the before-after approach, in which countries are evaluated for a number of years before and after the onset of an IMF program to identify whether IMF advice is able to improve the macroeconomic situation. The major problem with the simple before-after approach is that the economic condition of the country might have improved anyway without the presence of an IMF-supported program. Failure to take this into account leads to biased estimation of the coefficient associated with IMF programs.

This paper uses the two-step Heckman (1979) procedure to control for the bias caused by participation in an IMF program. In the first step, a probit

[1] The authors are grateful for helpful comments from the participants of various seminars held at the IMF and at the Western Economic Association International Annual Meetings held in Denver, Colorado in July 2003. Any errors that remain, however, are their sole responsibility.

model is used to capture the choice of participating in a program based on changes in initial economic and political conditions. A composite variable, the inverse Mill's ratio (IMR), summarizing this choice is then introduced into the second-stage least-squares regression of the determinants of the various macroeconomic targets. This variable gives an estimated probability of program participation and therefore controls for nonrandom selection into IMF programs by holding fixed an estimated probability for this selection. Similar treatment is also given to the stoppage variable to control for the possible endogeneity problem—that is, the possibility that a program might be terminated prematurely owing to unsatisfactory performance of the macroeconomic targets that are under examination. This distinction separates out the effects of IMF programs from the timing of a program, and provides insights on evaluating whether stopped programs are any different.

Since the sample splits between the 1980s and 1990s, it is possible that any improvement in the macroeconomic targets during the 1990s could be related to a more stable economic environment rather than to the availability of IMF advice. To control for this effect, time dummies are included in the specification so that any improvement associated with an IMF-supported program is independent of the strength of the world economic cycle.

Our findings demonstrate significant differences between successful and stopped programs, although the macro targets associated with successful programs are no different from their preprogram values. While stopped programs raise inflation and the budget deficit, and lower growth relative to periods without a program, completed programs are marginally associated with increased growth three years after the termination of the program.

Our paper is organized as follows: the second section reviews the related literature; the third section describes the data, model specification, and estimates; and the fourth section presents our conclusion.

Related Studies

Studies that have tried to identify the factors that induce countries to initiate IMF-supported programs have found that deteriorating external conditions such as the balance of payments, the debt position, and rapid exchange rate movements play an important role in the timing of programs. Conway (1994) used both probit and tobit models to analyze the participation of 74 countries in Stand-By Arrangements (SBAs) and Extended Fund Facilities (EFFs) during 1976–86 and found that past participation of IMF programs, real GDP growth, and external factors (terms of trade, current account, long-term external debt) were significant determinants of the timing of IMF involvement. Joyce (2002) used a panel dataset for 45 countries for 1980–84 and identified the ratio of government expenditures to GDP and the reserves-import ratio as significant factors. Edwards and Santaella (1992) used 48 devaluation periods in developing countries and identified GDP per capita and the ratio of net foreign assets to the money supply as the most important factors. Knight and Santaella (1997) employed a bivariate probit model to examine 91 non-oil countries for 1973–91. They concluded that the level of international reserves and GDP per capita were the most important factors in influencing a county's decision to negotiate programs while revenue and expenditure changes, domestic credit, and exchange rate movements were highlighted by the IMF.

In terms of the effects of IMF programs on key macroeconomic indicators, studies have found that IMF programs lead to immediate improvements in the current account and overall balance of payments, but do not have a consistent impact on inflation and economic growth. For example, Khan (1990), Schadler and others (1993), Conway (1994), Killick (1995), and Dicks-Mireaux, Mecagni, and Schadler (2000) all find a negative relationship between IMF programs and inflation, but the estimated effect is significant only in Killick's analysis. Some studies find a significant positive relationship with respect to growth in the short term (Killick, 1995; Bagci and Perraudin, 1997; and Dicks-Mireaux, Mecagni, and Schadler, 2000) and in the long term (i.e., three years after the program—see, for example, Conway, 1994) whereas others, in particular, Khan (1990) and Przeworski and Vreeland (2000), find significant negative growth effects both in the short and long term. Concerning budgetary conditions, Schadler and others (1993) find that fiscal deficits fall during IMF programs, while Bulíř and Moon (2002) are unable to identify significant effects. A summary of the findings can be found in Table 1.

Data and Empirical Results

Data

The data choice to highlight differences between stopped and completed programs was based on requiring a fairly long period to evaluate the effectiveness of programs. In the past, a number of studies have isolated specific years in which an IMF program did or did not take place. However, since the macroeconomic objectives of IMF programs generally have a much longer duration than one year, it seemed appropriate to ensure a fairly long period between engaging and not engaging in IMF programs. With these objectives in mind, the countries used in this paper are those that had IMF programs during the 1990s but did not have any type of IMF

Table 1

Summary of Recent Studies Analyzing the Impact of IMF Programs on Inflation, Budgetary Conditions, and Growth

Study	Sample	Inflation	Growth	Budget
Khan (1990)	1973–88, 259 programs	–	–*	
Schadler and others (1993)	1983–93, 55 programs	–	+	–
Conway (1994)	1976–86, 217 programs	–	–, +*	
Killick (1995)	1979–85	–*	+*	
Bagci and Perraudin (1997)	1973–92	-	+*	
Dicks-Mireaux, Mecagni, and Schadler (2000)	1986–91, 88 programs	-	+*	
Przeworski and Vreeland (2000)	1951–90, 226 programs		–*	
Bulíř and Moon (2002)	1993–96, 64 programs			+

Note: A single asterisk (*) indicates significance at the 10 percent level.

program between 1980 and 1988: Algeria, Benin, Bulgaria, Burkina Faso, Cambodia, Cape Verde, Colombia, Djibouti, Indonesia, Jordan, Mongolia, Nicaragua, Papua New Guinea, Poland, Rwanda, República Bolivariana de Venezuela, and the Republic of Yemen. Since Nicaragua and Cambodia were involved in civil wars during the 1980s, and the Republic of Yemen became a republic only in 1990, data points for these countries during the 1980s are excluded from the sample. Djibouti was also excluded because of lack of data during the 1980s. In the end, our sample covers 17 countries and 35 programs for the period from 1980 to 1999.[2]

Since the sample is restricted, it is important to determine whether it is representative of all IMF programs. To aid in this process, Table 2 provides various benchmarks for this sample as well as for all IMF programs negotiated between 1992 and 2000. The average per capita income levels in the two samples are close, at about $1,000–$1,100. Moreover, the type of conditions that were applied in the programs are comparable in terms of number and use of prior actions, with conditions in the restricted sample slightly more numerous. Interestingly, the percentage of stoppages is slightly lower in the restricted sample. In terms of the target variables, the initial conditions are also broadly similar, with inflation averaging about 30–40 percent and the general government budget deficit averaging 3½ percent of GDP. The initial current account and growth estimates differ more significantly between the two samples, with the current account deficit in the restricted sample at 3.1 percent of GDP and the corresponding deficit in the full sample at 5.7 percent of GDP. Moreover, growth in the initial period was considerably higher in the restricted sample at 1.7 percent, compared with 1.1 percent for the full sample.

[2] The appendix gives a list of program countries, years, and program types.

The behavior of the various target variables over time is also comparable between the two samples. The inflation rate declines through the program period and three years after the program to average about 11 percent in both samples, and the growth rate picks up to over 3 percent in both samples three years after the end of the program. In contrast, while the budgetary position improves in the reduced sample, the improvement shown in the full sample is temporary, since the budget deficit returns to its initial average value three years out. Similarly, while the current account position improves in the reduced sample, it initially deteriorates in the full sample and only returns to its initial value three years out.

First-Stage Probit Specification

As mentioned in the introduction it is necessary to correct for the timing of an IMF program so that this decision can be isolated from the effects of IMF policies. To this end, a probit model was estimated with the dependent variable representing the observed 0-1 dummy capturing whether a program was initiated or not. The independent variables fall into two categories: macroeconomic indicators at the beginning of the program (GDP per capita, inflation, government budget position, debt/GDP ratio, exchange rate depreciation) and political economy variables (the democracy index, a dummy for the change of government within three years of the commencement of the program, and time in power). The reason for including political variables is that recent studies have found that they are closely related to the success of programs (Dollar and Svensson, 2000; Ivanova and others, 2002; and Thomas, forthcoming) and they are therefore suitable instruments for identifying the timing of programs. Barro and Lee (2002) also emphasize the need for appropriate instruments in conducting this type of analysis but rely on political economy variables to achieve this objective,

Table 2
Comparing the Restricted and Full Sample Averages
(standard errors in parentheses)

	GDP Per Capita (In U.S. dollars)	Total Number of Conditions	Total Number of Prior Actions	Percentage of Stoppages
Restricted sample	1,010.41	25	9.9	36.4
	(733.2)	(21.7)	(12.9)	(48.9)
Full sample	1,091.52	22	6.6	41.8
	(1,315)	(23.2)	(12.8)	(49.5)

	Values at Specific Points in Program Cycle		
	At beginning of program	At end of program	3 years following program
		Inflation (*in percent*)	
Restricted sample	32.4	13.2	11.3
	(50.2)	(15.1)	(18.0)
Full sample	42.3	22.4	11.8
	(61.1)	(38.2)	(18.1)
		Government Budget Balance (*in percent of GDP*)	
Restricted sample	−3.3	−2.6	−2.3
	(3.6)	(4.1)	(5.0)
Full sample	−3.9	−3.5	−3.9
	(4.2)	(4.0)	(4.2)
		Current Account (*in percent of GDP*)	
Restricted sample	−3.1	−3.3	−2.5
	(9.7)	(8.6)	(11.1)
Full sample	−5.7	−5.9	−5.7
	(9.4)	(11.1)	(8.7)
		Growth (*in percent*)	
Restricted sample	1.7	3.8	3.3
	(6.1)	(3.8)	(3.8)
Full sample	1.1	2.7	3.9
	(7.2)	(6.2)	(5.8)

including each country's share of quotas and professional staff, as well as voting patterns in the United Nations.

The political economy variables used in this paper are constructed from the World Bank's Database of Political Institutions. The democratic index is coded from a democratic score on a 0–12 scale, with higher numbers associated with more democratic governments. For the democratic variable, the score was reclassified as a 1-0 dummy variable depending on whether the score was 9–12 or less; for the autocratic variable, the score was reclassified as a 1-0 dummy variable depending on whether the score was less than 3. The dummy variable for the change in government is 1 if there is a change in government within three years prior to the program and 0 otherwise. The variable, time in power, represents the log value of the years in power of the government at the time of program entry, assuming no change in the previous three years, and 0 otherwise. The dummy for the change in government is hypothesized to capture the raised likelihood of conditionality when a new government comes to power. In addition, separating out longer political regimes allows us to determine whether length of leadership influences the likelihood of having an IMF program. No dummy is included for past programs because the sample was identified on the basis that no program took place during the 1980s.

The results of the first-stage probit estimation can be found in Table 3. The overall performance of the various specifications is good in predicting the timing of an IMF program with at least 80 percent accuracy. Moreover, the accuracy of the predictions is

Table 3
Probit Model
(maximum-likelihood estimates)
Dependent Variable: *I* = 1 if there is an IMF program
I = 0 if there is no IMF program

Independent variables	(1)		(2)	
Constant	4.1509	1.0072	1.6528	0.3607
	(1.07)	(0.45)	(0.58)	(0.19)
Economic variables				
GDP per capita	−1.4485*	−0.6466**	−0.9085*	0.5697*
	(−2.03)	(−1.89)	(−2.18)	(−2.02)
Initial inflation	0.0519	−0.0164		
	(0.84)	(−0.46)		
Budget/GDP	0.0860	0.0930		
	(0.77)	(1.34)		
Debt/GDP	5.6267*	4.9920*	5.7400*	4.8957*
	(2.99)	(3.48)	(3.26)	(3.75)
Exchange rate depreciation	0.0630**	0.0771*	0.0741*	0.0636*
	(1.85)	(2.72)	(2.57)	(2.99)
Reserves/imports	0.3087	1.0624	0.1091	0.5228
	(0.17)	(0.86)	(0.07)	(0.48)
Political variables				
Democratic	−1.1778		−1.1849	
	(−1.25)		(−1.36)	
Autocratic	−1.3405		−0.8158	
	(−1.18)		(−0.87)	
Change of government 3 years before program	2.3233		1.2412	
	(1.44)		(1.13)	
Years in office (> 3 years)	0.9892		0.4009	
	(1.26)		(0.77)	
Observations	61	66	64	69
Pseudo *R*-square	0.6408	0.5478	0.6303	0.5382
Log-likelihood	−15.1833	−20.6884	−16.3871	−22.0553
Lr test of political variables		11.01***		11.34***

Notes: The *t*-statistics are in parentheses. One asterisk (*) denotes significance at 5 percent; two asterisks (**) denote significance at 10 percent. The *Lr* test is for the joint hypotheses that the coefficients of the four political variables are all zero; the chi-square (4) test statistic at 5 percent is 9.49. Therefore, the political variables are significant, which is denoted by three asterisks (***).

quite stable across the specifications (Table 4). The pseudo *R*-square[3] is also high compared with some studies, ranging from 53 percent to 65 percent.

Among the economic variables, we found that GDP per capita, the debt/GDP ratio, and the depreciation of the exchange rate were significant at the 5 percent level across all specifications, corroborating the results of previous studies. The higher the GDP per capita, the less likely that a country will enter a program, whereas higher debt/GDP ratios and exchange rate depreciations raise the likelihood that a country will come to the IMF for financial assistance. The initial inflation rate and the government budgetary position are insignificant in all cases.

The political economy variables also provide significant explanatory power. Indeed, including them raises the pseudo *R*-square by about 10 percentage points and a likelihood ratio test rejects the joint hypothesis that they are all equal to zero. Interestingly, highly democratic and autocratic countries

[3] Pseudo *R*-square is calculated as $1-[\log(Lur)-\log(Lr)]$, where *Lur* is the maximum-likelihood value of the unrestricted-likelihood function and *Lr* is the maximum-likelihood value of the restricted-likelihood function (constant only). Conway (1994) reports a 90 percent ratio whereas Dicks-Mireaux, Mecagni, and Schadler (2000) only records a 3.5 percent ratio for their best fitted probit model.

Table 4
Accuracy of Probit Predictions

	(1)		(2)	
Total predicted $I=1$	28	27	27	27
Total actual $I=1$	31	33	31	33
Accuracy *(percent)*	90.32	81.82	87.10	81.82
Total predicted $I=1$	27	26	28	30
Total actual $I=1$	30	33	33	36
Accuracy *(percent)*	90	78.78	84.85	83.33
Overall correct predictions	55	53	55	57
Overall actual programs	61	66	64	69
Overall accuracy *(percent)*	90.16	80.30	85.94	82.61

are less likely to enter IMF programs. A possible rationale for democratic countries not coming to the IMF is that considerable bargaining between political interest groups might be needed before an agreement is reached and this takes time. While this is not an issue for autocratic regimes, they may try to dissuade foreign institutions from closely scrutinizing their economic policies. Interestingly, Thomas (forthcoming) finds that once autocratic governments acquiesce to an IMF program, the program is much less likely to stop. New governments are more likely to enter an IMF program; and for those not changing office, longer incumbents are more likely to come to the IMF, although this effect tapers off after some time.

The stoppage variable is also an endogenous variable and therefore may require instruments. If a program is stopped because of unsatisfactory macroeconomic performance, it is inappropriate to use program stoppages as an exogenous variable when evaluating the effects of IMF programs on these same target variables.[4] Mecagni (1999) argues based on country report documentation that, in most cases, program interruptions were not associated with IMF conditionality that was too stringent. Rather, the interruptions were associated with domestic dissatisfaction with existing institutional and political arrangements or with preexisting problems. The robustness of this assumption is evaluated by comparing the estimates assuming that program stoppages are exogenous with those obtained from instrumenting for this variable.

Instruments for the stoppage variable comprise dummies for autocratic regimes and countries engaging in guerrilla warfare, a dummy representing a change in government within three years of the program, the total number of conditions, the real exchange rate depreciation during the year prior to the program, the initial inflation level, and the logarithm of GDP per capita. The estimation results can be found in Table 5. On the whole, we find that among the instruments used, the political variables have stronger effects on the likelihood of a stoppage than the economic variables. The hypothesis that the political variables are all equal to zero cannot be accepted at the 10 percent level by the likelihood ratio test. However, the hypothesis that the economic variables are all equal to zero can be accepted. In terms of the coefficients, the economic variables are all insignificant, while the democracy variable is consistently significant. The political variables suggest that the higher probability of stoppages is associated with less democracy and wars, but, perhaps surprisingly, not a change in government. The relatively weak effects of the economic variables mitigate somewhat concerns about the endogeneity of the stoppage variable. However, to make our analysis more robust, we experiment with both exogenous and endogenous stoppage variables.

Second-Stage Specification

One of the main subjects of interest in IMF programs is how they succeed in improving macroeconomic target variables during the duration of programs and following their termination. To analyze this issue effectively, the dependent variable is defined in two ways for each target variable. First, it is defined as the average change in the value of the target between the first year of the program and the final year of the program. Second, it is defined as the average change in the value of the target between the first year of the program and three years after the end of the program. For periods during which no

[4] The stoppage variable used in this paper represents programs that were abandoned because the authorities did not follow IMF policy recommendations. If IMF targets were not met because of exogenous shocks, this would not warrant a stoppage of the program but would be accommodated through the granting of a waiver.

Table 5
Probit Model for Stoppage

Dependent Variable: $I=1$ if there is an IMF program
$I=0$ if there is no IMF program

Independent Variables	(1)	(2)	(3)
Constant	−0.7245	0.3733	0.0034
	(−0.31)	(0.20)	(0.01)
GDP per capita	0.1637	−0.0349	
	(0.2671)	(−0.16)	
Initial inflation	−0.0099	−0.0008	
	(−0.94)	(−0.12)	
Exchange rate depreciation	0.0293	0.0169	
	(1.32)	(1.10)	
Total number of conditions	−0.1875	−0.3023	
	(−0.48)	(−0.82)	
Democratic	−1.2279		−1.0714
	(−2.05)		(−2.03)
Guerrilla wars	1.1445		0.6922
	(0.92)		(0.72)
Change of government 3 years before program	−0.3559		−0.1881
	(−0.61)		(−0.39)
Observations	35	35	35
Pseudo R-square	0.2177	0.0502	0.1404
Log-likelihood	−16.92	−20.54	−18.59
Restricted log-likelihood	−21.63	−21.63	−21.63
Lr test		7.25*	3.34

Note: For the joint test that all institution variables are zero, the chi(3) statistic at 10 percent is 6.25; for the joint test that all macroeconomic variables are zero, the corresponding chi(4) statistic is 7.78. Therefore, the institution variables are significant, which is denoted by an asterisk (*).

program was conducted (1980–92), three- and six-year intervals are used for the dependent variable. This time interval roughly corresponds to the average duration of IMF programs during the 1990s of 2½ years.

In many studies, the effects of IMF involvement in particular countries are identified through the inclusion of a dummy variable for the macroeconomic programs that were supported by the IMF. However, as indicated previously, it is also necessary to account for stoppages. In our sample of 35 programs, 12, or 36 percent, were stopped. Killick (1995) differentiates between countries that completed programs and those that terminated early by using a threshold value of 80 percent of the initial committed loan that was disbursed. He argues that this cutoff point is likely to be closely associated with successful completions based on a survey made of programs over the 1980–92 period. Consistent with his hypothesis, he finds that the inflation rate and the current account improved significantly for countries with completed programs relative to countries with noncompleted programs. This paper controls for the possible different impacts of completed programs and those that terminated early with a stoppage variable. Although as recorded most of the stoppages happened as a result of the program countries' failure to follow IMF recommendations, to account for the possible endogeneity problem, we consider both exogenous and endogenous stoppages.[5] Moreover, following Killick (1995), we construct the disbursement ratio as another proxy for stoppages. By doing so, the effectiveness of IMF programs on the target macroeconomic variables is evaluated more accurately, and the effects of stoppages are also analyzed. For the sample of observations in the 1980s when no program took place, the dummy variables are recorded as zero.

Since timing can make a large difference in the interpretation of results, annual time dummies were included in each specification to control for this factor. Owing to insufficient degrees of freedom, both

[5] In the endogenous version, the variable is instrumented by the predicted stoppage probability from the probit regression in Table 5.

Table 6
Inflation Equation During Program

Independent Variables	(1)	(2)	(3)	(4)	(5)
Initial inflation	0.3304*	0.3469*	0.3255*	0.3422*	0.3202*
	(5.92)	(5.89)	(5.48)	(5.51)	(5.40)
Change in exchange rate	0.6243*	0.6246*	0.6158*	0.6175*	0.6169*
	(6.59)	(6.67)	(6.03)	(6.15)	(6.08)
IMF program	−0.7319	−0.0217	−0.4574	0.1047	−1.9763
	(−0.48)	(−0.01)	(−0.21)	(0.04)	(−0.85)
Stoppage[1]	1.9962		2.2145		6.6876**
	(1.12)		(1.09)		(1.75)
Disbursement ratio		0.0407		0.3952	
		(0.02)		(0.19)	
Inverse Mill's ratio			−0.5546	−0.4308	−0.3682
			(−0.37)	(0.20)	(−0.24)
Number of observations	69	69	60	60	60
R-square	0.7569	0.7544	0.7485	0.7457	0.7525

Notes: The *t*-statistics appear in parentheses; one asterisk (*) denotes significance at the 5 percent level; two asterisks (**) denote significance at the 10 percent level.

[1] In column (5), the stoppage variable is instrumented using the following variables: dummies for autocracy, guerrilla warfare, changes in government, the total number of structural conditions, the change in the real exchange rate one year prior to the program, the initial inflation level, and the log of GDP per capita.

the dependent and time-varying independent variables were purged of the timing effect before being introduced into the second-stage equation.

For the inflation equation, the economic determinants include the level of inflation at the beginning of the period and the change in the local currency/U.S. dollar exchange rate. The variables representing IMF involvement include a dummy for IMF programs, a dummy for stoppages, and the IMR calculated from the first-stage probit estimation.

The first two columns of Table 6 present the results without correcting for the timing of IMF involvement. In this case, distinguishing between completed and stopped programs makes no difference because both coefficients are insignificant. Similar results hold when a dummy variable for programs with disbursed amounts over 80 percent of the committed total (comparable to Killick's definition) is substituted for the stoppage variable. Turning to the other variables, high-inflation countries have difficulty reducing inflation because the coefficient on the initial inflation level is significantly positive. Moreover, the change in the exchange rate is positive although significantly below unity. The inclusion of the IMR has little effect on the other variables in this specification (columns (3) and (4)). The major change in results occurs when the stoppage variable is instrumented, because the coefficient becomes significantly positive at the 10 percent level. The coefficient estimate implies that the inflation rate rises by 6½ percent a year during the program period in stopped programs.

In the regression of inflation changes over a longer horizon (Table 7), the coefficients on the program dummies are broadly similar to the previous specification, with the instrumented stoppage variable the only significant variable. The coefficient estimate of IMF programs is comparable in magnitude to that presented in the short-run equation, suggesting that the inflation rate keeps declining after the termination of the program. Both the initial inflation rate and the change in the exchange rate remain significant, with the exchange rate coefficient now insignificantly different from unity.

For the equation explaining the change in the budgetary position, the independent variables comprise the initial budget position, the change in inflation, and the change in the terms of trade. The change in the terms of trade proxies strong developments in GDP, which would likely lower the budget deficit. The change in the inflation rate is included to control for the Tanzi-Olivera effect, which postulates that as the inflation rate is lowered, the budgetary position would be expected to improve because the real value of conventional tax revenue rises on account of collection lags. The variables representing IMF involvement include the dummy for IMF programs, a dummy for IMF programs that terminated prematurely, and the IMR calculated from the first-stage probit estimation.

Table 7
Inflation Equation Three Years After Program

Independent Variables	(1)	(2)	(3)	(4)	(5)
Initial inflation	0.1717*	0.1789*	0.1209*	0.1354*	0.1245*
	(3.95)	(4.24)	(3.93)	(4.58)	(4.98)
Change in exchange rate	0.8509*	0.8503*	0.9124*	0.9119*	0.9037*
	(11.09)	(10.98)	(13.61)	(13.47)	(13.44)
IMF program	−0.4122	−0.1270	−0.0946	0.1684	−1.6231
	(−0.26)	(−0.08)	(−0.06)	(0.10)	(−0.95)
Stoppage[1]	1.0600		2.6809		5.8508**
	(0.61)		(1.55)		(1.76)
Disbursement ratio		0.2857		1.4460	
		(0.18)		(0.99)	
Inverse Mill's ratio			−1.7229	−1.5511	−1.5551
			(−1.45)	(−1.28)	(−1.34)
Number of observations	57	57	50	50	50
R-square	0.9144	0.9141	0.9390	0.9381	0.9397

Notes: The *t*-statistics appear in parentheses; one asterisk (*) denotes significance at the 5 percent level; two asterisks (**) denote significance at the 10 percent level.

[1] In column (5), the stoppage variable is instrumented using variables specified in footnote 1 to Table 6.

In the regression for the budgetary change during the program (Table 8), the initial budget level is consistently significantly negative, implying that the budgetary improvement is greater the larger the initial size of the deficit. But the budgetary position also weakens if the initial position is in surplus. The change in the inflation rate is significantly negative, suggesting that the Tanzi-Olivera effect holds. Indeed, a 10 percent decline in the inflation rate would raise the budget surplus by about ½ percent of GDP. In contrast, the change in the terms of trade does not play a significant role in budgetary developments. For the IMF dummies, while the coefficient on the completed IMF program is significantly positive in the specification without the inverse Mill's ratio, the coefficient is insignificant when the IMR is included. In contrast, the coefficient on the stoppage variable is significantly negative in each specification, with a particularly high value when instrumented.

Three years after the program has terminated (Table 9), initial conditions remain significant, although the impact is less strong. The dummy for completed IMF programs is insignificant in all specifications, so that the budgetary position is not affected by an IMF program. In contrast, for programs that stop, the budgetary position deteriorates relative to periods without an IMF program. Similar results hold when the dummy variable reflecting the disbursement ratio is used.

While improvements in the inflationary environment and in the budgetary position are important targets in themselves, they are not the ultimate goals of economic policy. The ultimate objective of a country's economic policy is to improve the welfare of its citizens, which is normally measured as the change in per capita income. There is a huge literature on the determinants of growth, and therefore this paper has chosen to be selective in deciding which controls to include in the specification. The paper takes as its point of departure the analysis of Doppelhofer, Miller, and Sala-i-Martin (2000), who has tried to detect the variables that are the most robust determinants of growth using the Bayesian updating technique. He finds that a dummy variable for sub-Saharan Africa, the initial level of GDP per capita (the convergence effect), and the primary school enrollment rate (measuring human capital) are robust to changes in specification. This paper includes the first two variables and substitutes the illiteracy rate for the primary school enrollment rate. We also include the change in the budget balance and the inflation rate to capture direct effects from the policy changes, and export market growth to capture exogenous effects.

In the regression for the change in growth during the program (Table 10), the initial convergence term is generally significant, indicating that each year poor countries make up 1 percent of the disparity in per capita GDP with the richest country, or that, holding all other factors constant, it would take them 100 years to fully catch up. Perhaps surprisingly, both policy variables represented by the change in the inflation rate and the budgetary

Table 8

Budgetary Positions During Program

Independent Variables	(1)	(2)	(3)	(4)	(5)
Initial budget level	−0.1782*	−0.1657*	−0.2242*	−0.2108*	−0.2220*
	(−3.02)	(−2.74)	(−4.85)	(−4.20)	(−4.58)
Change in inflation	−0.0429*	−0.0529*	−0.0471*	−0.0572*	−0.0495*
	(−3.12)	(−3.89)	(−3.61)	(−4.31)	(−3.74)
Change in terms of trade	0.0055	0.0096	0.0094	0.0137	0.0132
	(0.41)	(0.67)	(0.75)	(0.97)	(0.99)
IMF program	0.6094**	0.3872	0.3608	0.1858	0.6476
	(1.78)	(0.96)	(0.84)	(0.38)	(1.27)
Stoppage [1]	−1.1169*		−1.1380*		−2.0330*
	(−2.58)		(−2.25)		(−2.43)
Disbursement ratio		−0.3753		−0.4550	
		(−0.86)		(−0.92)	
Inverse Mill's ratio			−0.0779	−0.1371	−0.1389
			(−0.26)	(−0.49)	(−0.44)
Number of observations	65	65	57	57	57
R-square	0.4669	0.4324	0.6331	0.5994	0.6255

Notes: The *t*-statistics appear in parentheses; one asterisk (*) denotes significance at the 5 percent level; two asterisks (**) denote significance at the 10 percent level.

[1] In column (5), the stoppage variable is instrumented using variables specified in footnote 1 to Table 6.

Table 9

Budgetary Positions Three Years After Program

Independent Variables	(1)	(2)	(3)	(4)	(5)
Initial budget level	−0.1303*	−0.1264*	−0.1456*	−0.1400*	−0.1419*
	(−8.03)	(−7.26)	(−12.44)	(−9.43)	(−7.70)
Change in inflation	−0.0050	−0.0076	−0.0060	−0.0090	−0.0074
	(−0.82)	(−1.19)	(−0.98)	(−1.37)	(−1.09)
Change in terms of trade	0.0102	0.0091	0.0185	0.0185	0.0176
	(0.68)	(0.60)	(1.26)	(1.10)	(1.10)
IMF program	0.3831	0.3559	0.2819	0.2703	0.3330
	(1.56)	(1.26)	(1.05)	(0.87)	(0.99)
Stoppage [1]	−0.8651*		−0.9318*		−0.8644
	(−3.10)		(−3.03)		(−1.60)
Disbursement ratio		−0.6930*		−0.7108*	
		(−2.22)		(−2.07)	
Inverse Mill's ratio			−0.0988	−0.1308	−0.1440
			(−0.44)	(−0.62)	(−0.76)
Number of observations	53	53	47	47	47
R-square	0.5773	0.5607	0.6897	0.6668	0.6359

Notes: The *t*-statistics appear in parentheses; one asterisk (*) denotes significance at the 5 percent level; two asterisks (**) denote significance at the 10 percent level.

[1] In column (5), the stoppage variable is instrumented using variables specified in footnote 1 to Table 6.

Table 10
Growth Equation During Program

Independent Variables	(1)	(2)	(3)	(4)	(5)
Change in inflation	−0.0353	−0.0489	−0.0261	−0.0380	−0.0375
	(−0.77)	(−1.02)	(−0.51)	(−0.72)	(−0.70)
Change in budget position	0.0869	0.1247	0.1483	0.1786	0.1833
	(0.49)	(0.69)	(0.73)	(0.90)	(0.96)
GDP per capita	−0.6307**	−0.5604	−0.9826*	−1.0287*	−0.9078**
	(−1.65)	(−1.30)	(−2.03)	(−2.04)	(−1.76)
Export market GDP growth	0.2431	0.2582	0.1999	0.2273	0.1683
	(0.84)	(0.82)	(0.61)	(0.62)	(0.48)
Sub-Saharan region	−0.7704	−0.3896	−2.5127**	−2.4202*	−2.1550**
	(−0.74)	(−0.39)	(−1.94)	(−1.96)	(−1.84)
Illiteracy	−0.0070	−0.0137	0.0123	0.0068	0.0048
	(−0.30)	(−0.58)	(0.44)	(0.26)	(0.18)
IMF program	0.5904	0.2574	1.0676	0.8866	1.0665
	(0.92)	(0.29)	(1.46)	(0.88)	(1.22)
Stoppage[1]	−1.6959**		−1.7196**		−1.6672
	(−1.78)		(−1.66)		(−1.13)
Disbursement ratio		−0.4399		−0.8266	
		(−0.48)		(−0.86)	
Inverse Mill's ratio			−0.1578	−0.2179	−0.2613
			(−0.24)	(−0.33)	(−0.40)
Number of observations	65	65	57	57	57
R-square	0.1843	0.1484	0.2572	0.2246	0.2243

Notes: The *t*-statistics appear in parentheses; one asterisk (*) denotes significance at the 5 percent level; two asterisks (**) denote significance at the 10 percent level.

[1] In column (5), the stoppage variable is instrumented using variables specified in footnote 1 to Table 6.

position are insignificant, although the dummy variable for countries in sub-Saharan Africa is significantly negative in the specifications with the IMR. The other two macroeconomic variables, the export market growth and the illiteracy rate, are insignificant.

Turning to the direct effects of IMF programs, the dummy variable for completed programs is insignificant in all specifications whereas the stoppage variable is significantly negative in all specifications except the instrumented equation.

Over the longer run (Table 11), the effect of the change in inflation on growth is significantly negative, with a 10 percentage point decline in the inflation rate leading to a 0.5–0.6 percentage point improvement in the growth rate. This is comparable to the findings of Ghosh and Phillips (1998). GDP per capita is generally significantly negative, indicating that a lower growth rate is associated with a higher level of GDP per capita. The dummy for the sub-Saharan region is significantly negative at 5 percent when the inverse Mill's ratio is included, while the illiteracy rate is significantly negative when the IMR is excluded. It appears therefore that sub-Saharan countries and countries with high illiteracy rates have difficulty in raising their standard of living over the longer run.

In the long run, the IMF dummy for completed programs remains insignificant except in the specification including the IMR in which it yields positive effects on growth (Table 12). In contrast, the stoppage variable is significant except in the instrumented equation, and the coefficient implies negative effects on growth. The different results point to the possibility that a failure in macroeconomic performance could trigger a stoppage.

Conclusion

This paper has presented empirical evidence relevant to evaluating whether IMF programs have been effective in the 1990s in influencing three major macroeconomic variables: inflation, the budget position, and growth. To properly identify the effect of IMF policies on these aggregates, variables

Table 11

Growth Equation Three Years After Program

Independent Variables	(1)	(2)	(3)	(4)	(5)
Change in inflation	−0.0606*	−0.0668*	−0.0543*	−0.0603*	−0.0582*
	(−4.04)	(−4.17)	(−4.20)	(−4.50)	(−3.92)
Change in budget position	−0.0331	−0.0265	−0.0553	−0.0505	0.0307
	(−0.13)	(−0.10)	(−0.22)	(−0.20)	(0.13)
GDP per capita	−0.7701**	−0.7734**	−1.3182*	−1.3717*	−1.3237*
	(−1.93)	(−1.82)	(−2.73)	(−2.78)	(−2.64)
Export market GDP growth	0.3544	0.3678	0.3126	0.3213	0.2352
	(1.08)	(1.10)	(0.93)	(0.89)	(0.66)
Sub-Saharan region	−0.2987	−0.2148	−2.6695*	−2.5925*	−2.4166*
	(−0.34)	(−0.25)	(−2.57)	(−2.53)	(−2.28)
Illiteracy	−0.0347**	−0.0391*	−0.0083	−0.0136	−0.0136
	(−1.82)	(−2.07)	(−0.39)	(−0.66)	(−0.64)
IMF program	0.8097	0.7888	1.0505**	1.0283	1.1199
	(1.35)	(1.27)	(1.71)	(1.52)	(1.26)
Stoppage[1]	−1.7342*		−1.6221*		−1.4884
	(−2.57)		(−2.23)		(−1.03)
Disbursement ratio		−1.4352*		−1.2934*	
		(−2.23)		(−2.00)	
Inverse Mill's ratio			−0.3443	−0.3510	−0.4348
			(−0.72)	(−0.71)	(−0.93)
Number of observations	53	53	47	47	47
R–square	0.4078	0.3961	0.5160	0.5035	0.4852

Notes: The *t*–statistics appear in parentheses; one asterisk (*) denotes significance at the 5 percent level; two asterisks (**) denote significance at the 10 percent level.

[1] In column (5), the stoppage variable is instrumented using variables specified in footnote 1 to Table 6.

Table 12

IMF Dummy Only Versus Dummies Distinguishing Stoppage

	Inflation		Budget		Growth	
	During program	Three years later	During program	Three years later	During program	Three years later
Completed programs	–	–	+	+	+	+**
Stopped programs	+	+	–*	–*	–**	–*
Stopped programs (using instruments)	+**	+**	–*	–	–	–

Notes: One asterisk (*) denotes significance at the 5 percent level; two asterisks (**) denote significance at the 10 percent level.

were included to control for the timing of IMF programs. The paper finds that the timing of an IMF program can be represented well by the level of GDP per capita, the debt/GDP ratio, and the magnitude of the exchange rate depreciation, with over 90 percent of the timing decisions correctly identified. Although the inverse Mill's ratio is insignificant in all specifications, its inclusion does change the significance of the dummy for completed IMF programs in some cases, demonstrating the importance of its inclusion in the analysis.

The paper highlights the importance of distinguishing between completed and stopped programs because they are associated with significantly different macroeconomic outcomes. Since stoppages are likely endogenous, they were instrumented with both political and economic variables. Our analysis shows that political variables seem to have more impact than do economic variables on stoppages. On the whole, endogenizing the stoppage variable does not change our conclusion that stopped programs raise inflation, worsen the budgetary position, and impede growth, but it deepens the negative effects that a stopped program can have on inflation while it lessens the negative impact on budget conditions and growth. On IMF programs that end successfully, the only variable that appears to be affected in a positive way is growth, and the significance of this variable breaks down when instruments are found for stoppages.

One of the limitations of this analysis is the sample size. We avoid the problems with cross-country comparisons by making a clear split between program periods and nonprogram periods, but the trade-off is a relatively short sample that might make our results less convincing and less robust. We hope to tackle this problem in the future when more data become available. We also intend to dig deeper into whether IMF programs in the 1990s have succeeded in fostering growth by distinguishing among types of programs and between normal and prolonged users of IMF resources.

Appendix. List of Countries and Programs Considered in 1990s

Country	Type of Program	Start	End
Algeria	SBA	1994	1995
Algeria	EFF	1995	1998
Benin	ESAF	1993	1996
Benin	ESAF	1996	1999
Bulgaria	SBA	1992	1993
Bulgaria	SBA	1994	1995
Bulgaria	EFF	1996	1998
Bulgaria	SBA	1997	1998
Bulgaria	EFF	1998	2001
Burkina Faso	ESAF	1993	1996
Burkina Faso	ESAF	1996	1999
Burkina Faso	ESAF	1999	2002
Cambodia	ESAF	1994	1997
Cambodia	PRGF	1999	2002
Cape Verde	SBA	1998	1999
Colombia	EFF	1999	2002
Djibouti	ESAF	1996	1999
Djibouti	ESAF	1999	2002
Indonesia	SBA	1997	1998
Indonesia	EFF	1998	2000
Jordan	SBA	1992	1993
Jordan	EFF	1994	1996
Jordan	EFF	1996	1999
Jordan	EFF	1999	2002
Mongolia	ESAF	1993	1996
Mongolia	ESAF	1997	2000
Nicaragua	ESAF	1994	1997
Nicaragua	ESAF	1998	2001
Papua New Guinea	SBA	1995	1997
Poland	SBA	1993	1994
Poland	SBA	1994	1996
Rwanda	ESAF	1998	2001
Venezuela, República Bolivariana de	SBA	1996	1997
Yemen, Republic of	SBA	1996	1997
Yemen, Republic of	ESAF	1997	2000

Notes: SBA denotes a Stand-By Arrangement; EFF denotes the Extended Fund Facility; ESAF denotes the Enhanced Structural Adjustment Facility; and PRGF denotes the Poverty Reduction and Growth Facility.

References

Bagci, Pinar, and William Perraudin, 1997, "The Impact of IMF Programs," CEPR Working Paper No. 24 (London: Center for Economic Policy Research).

Barro, Robert, and J. W. Lee, 2002, "IMF Programs: Who Is Chosen and What Are the Effects?" NBER Working Paper No. 8951 (Cambridge, Massachusetts: National Bureau of Economic Research).

Bulíř, Aleš, and Soojin Moon, 2002, "The Composition of Fiscal Adjustment and Structural Conditionality Under IMF-Supported Programs," (unpublished; Washington: International Monetary Fund). This paper also appears, in somewhat different form, as Chapter 14 in this volume.

Conway, Patrick, 1994, "IMF Lending Programs: Participation and Impact," *Journal of Development Economics*, Vol. 45 (December), pp. 365–91.

Dicks-Mireaux, Louis, Mauro Mecagni, and Susan Schadler, 2000, "Evaluating the Effect of IMF Lending to Low-income Countries," *Journal of Development Economics*, Vol. 61 (April), pp. 495–526.

Dollar, David, and Jakob Svensson, 2000, "What Explains the Success or Failure of Structural Adjustment Programmes?" *Economic Journal*, Vol. 110 (October), pp. 894–917.

Doppelhofer, Gernot, Ronald I. Miller, and Xavier Sala-i-Martin, 2000, "Determinants of Long-Term Growth: A Bayesian Averaging of Classical Estimates (BACE) Approach," NBER Working Paper No. 7750 (Cambridge, Massachusetts: National Bureau of Economic Research).

Edwards, Sebastian, and Julio Santealla, 1992, "Devaluation Controversies in the Developing Countries: Lessons from the Bretton Woods Era," NBER Working Paper No. 4047 (Cambridge, Massachusetts: National Bureau of Economic Research).

Ghosh, Atish, and S. Phillips, 1998, "Inflation, Disinflation and Growth," *Staff Papers*, International Monetary Fund, Vol. 45 (December), pp. 672–710.

Goldstein, Morris, and Peter Montiel, 1986, "Evaluating Fund Stabilization Programs with Multi-Country Data: Some Methodological Pitfalls," *Staff Papers*, International Monetary Fund, Vol. 33 (June), pp. 304–44.

Haque, Nadeem Ul, and Mohsin Khan, 1998, "Do IMF-Supported Programs Work? A Survey of the Cross-Country Empirical Evidence," IMF Working Paper 98/169 (Washington: International Monetary Fund).

Heckman, James, 1979, "Sample Selection Bias as a Specification Error," *Econometrica*, Vol. 47 (January), pp. 153–62.

Ivanova, Anna, Wolfgang Mayer, Alex Mourmouras, and George Anayiotos, 2002, "What Determines the Success or Failure of Fund-Supported Programs?" (unpublished: Washington: International Monetary Fund). This paper also appears, in somewhat different form, as Chapter 10 in this volume.

Joyce, James, 2002, "Through a Glass Darkly: What We Know (and Don't Know) About IMF Programs," Wellesley College Working Paper No. 2002-04 (Wellesley, Massachusetts: Wellesley College).

Khan, Mohsin, 1990, "The Macroeconomic Effects of Fund-Supported Adjustment Programs," *Staff Papers*, International Monetary Fund, Vol. 37 (June), pp. 195–231.

Killick, Tony, 1995, IMF Programmes in Developing Countries: Design and Impact (London: Routledge).

Knight, Malcolm, and Julio A. Santaella, 1997, "Economic Determinants of IMF Financial Arrangements," *Journal of Development Economics*, Vol. 54 (December), pp. 405–36.

Mecagni, Mauro, 1999, "The Causes of Program Interruptions," in *Economic Adjustment and Reform in Low-Income Countries* (Washington: International Monetary Fund), pp. 215–76.

Przeworski, Adam, and James R. Vreeland, 2000, "The Effect of IMF Programs on Economic Growth," *Journal of Development Economics*, Vol. 62 (August), pp. 385–421.

Schadler, Susan, Franek Rozwadowski, Siddharth Tiwari, and David Robinson, 1993, *Economic Adjustment in Low-Income Countries: Experience Under the Enhanced Structural Adjustment Facility*, IMF Occasional Paper No. 106 (Washington: International Monetary Fund).

Thomas, Alun, forthcoming, "Prior Actions-True Repentance? An Evaluation Based on Active Programs over the 1992–99 Period," IMF Working Paper (Washington: International Monetary Fund).